The Encyclopedia of
the History of
American Management

THOEMMES CONTINUUM

THE ENCYCLOPEDIA OF
THE HISTORY OF
AMERICAN MANAGEMENT

GENERAL EDITOR

Morgen Witzel

First published in 2005 by

Thoemmes Continuum
11 Great George Street
Bristol BS1 5RR, England

http://www.thoemmes.com

The Encyclopedia of the History of American Management
1 Volume : ISBN 1 84371 131 1

© Thoemmes Continuum, 2005

British Library Cataloguing-in-Publication Data
A CIP record of this title is available from the British Library

Typeset in Sabon at Thoemmes Continuum.
Printed and bound in the UK by Antony Rowe Ltd.
This book is printed on acid-free paper, sewn, and
cased in a durable buckram.

CONTENTS

INTRODUCTION

Morgen Witzel's collection of some 260 biographies from his larger *Biographical Dictionary of Management* (Thoemmes, 2001) brings together into a single volume the major contributors to America's economic development, business ventures, academia, consulting, and the thinking of others whose ideas have influenced the theory and practice of management. Prepared by knowledgeable scholars who have a longer and broader perspective, these sketches follow in the grand tradition of using biography to understand the people behind the ideas that influence our everyday life. Lyndall Urwick and Edward F. L. Brech used biography to tell the story of *The Making of Scientific Management* (Management Publications Trust, 1945); followed by Urwick's *Golden Book of Management* (Newman Neame, 1956 and 1984) that sketched the lives of 70 pioneers in management in the U.S. and internationally. Urwick and Brech commented that to understand the ideas of people we had to know something about them. It is in this scholarly tradition that this series of biographies aim to explore and place in perspective the lives and ideas of a variety of individuals whose work created new industries and products and whose ideas shaped the way we think about the conduct of the business enterprise.

Occasionally we need to revisit the lives and contributions of these makers of history because we have a better perspective on the past and we can revitalize our thinking by looking backward with more confidence. The alphabetical organization of the biographies provides a useful ready reference to locate individuals, reducing the search time in finding the person or persons for study. The biographies provide insights into a subject's life, family, education, career, and some measure of that person's importance and place in history. History is a contextual subject, enabling us to place individuals in the times in which they lived and what 'historical moment' may have made a difference.

American business historians have held a long-time fascination with those who Alfred Chandler called the 'visible hand' of economic development (Harvard University Press, 1977). While the 'invisible hand' of Adam Smith explained the workings of factor markets, Chandler described the forces that shaped the modern corporate form of organization and how a managerial hierarchy developed to coordinate the tasks necessary for success. Daniel Wren and Ronald Greenwood presented a selection of these individuals as 'innovators' (Oxford University Press, 1998); Richard Tedlow wrote of the 'giants of enterprise' (Harper, 2001); and Edwin Locke used the term 'prime movers' (AMACOM, 2000) for certain leading individuals. In each of these histories of American business, a persistent theme is that of wealth creation—the story of persons who provided means for modern enterprise by inventing, innovating, forming, financing, and managing firms that became the source of jobs, products, services, and national income. The collection that Morgen Witzel has edited provides a much greater number of these wealth creators, enabling readers to be more selective in the historical periods, industries, or academic schools of thought in order to guide further study.

The versatility of Witzel's approach enables readers to study inventors, for example, such as Cyrus McCormick, whose reaper made America the world's breadbasket; Edwin Land, whose study of polarization of light enabled 'instant photography'; Thomas Edison, in whose laboratory an electrical age was cradled; George Eastman, another influential shaper of photographic imagery; Samuel Morse and his telegraph which triggered further advancements in applying principles of electromagnetism and created what some consider the first Internet in the nineteenth century; Alexander Graham Bell who kept us wired for over a century with his telephone; Robert Noyce, who discovered a reliable process for making semiconductors from silicon chips, created Fairchild Semiconductor Inc., and handed the reins to Andrew Grove (also in this collection) who took Noyce's Intel to new degrees of computing power; and this is only a sample of those who pioneered new products and processes, creating industries, and opening improved ways of doing our work and living our lives. There are also innovators who reshaped the way products were marketed, distributed, and/or advertised such as William Kellogg, Richard Sears and Alvah Roebuck, Sam Walton, James Cash (before 'credit') Penney, George Pullman, Frank Woolworth, and more.

It is also possible to follow a company through its rise, stagnation, and renewal in the story of the Ford family: Henry, Edsel, and Henry II. Henry the first was a master mechanic and innovator in manufacturing processes in an emerging industry whose firm dominated for a substantial number of years. Edsel, whose name is forever linked to the failure of an automobile named for him, was browbeaten in his young years by Henry I, his father, and was allegedly in charge when General Motors overtook Ford in the industry. Edsel's son, Henry Ford II, was a creative manager who established Ford Motor Company's international presence, hired brilliant staff people, and under his leadership Ford regained some of the ground it had lost.

Professional managers, non-owning and salaried as executives, also illustrate how firms handle succession problems to maintain, restore, or transform the success of the firm. For examples, see Alfred Sloan Jr. who built the M-form of organization at General Motors and enabled it to surpass Ford; Jack Welch, one of the celebrity managers of the twentieth century as CEO of General Electric; Robert Wood, who failed to convince Aaron Montgomery to add a retailing presence to Montgomery and Ward's catalogs, and then left that firm to strategically re-position Sears and Roebuck in opening retail outlets to supplement its catalog business; Charles Schwab the genius at Carnegie Steel and later at U.S. Steel; William Knudsen, who started with Henry Ford but left to gain acclaim at General Motors; and numerous others. These persons were in the right place at the right historical moment to make a difference.

If the reader is interested in some outstanding persons who were members of a minority group, there are a number of interesting examples: William Ellison, who was born a slave, but, through self-education bought his and his families freedom and became a successful manufacturer of cotton gins; Roberto Goizueta, Cuban born, who became chief executive of Coca-Cola and led it to international prominence; Berry Gordy, Jr, the founder of Motown Records; John H. Johnson began selling life insurance to African-Americans before branching out to found the magazine *Ebony*; and Annie Turnbo-Malone, the daughter of former slaves who became the world's first female African-American self-made millionaire with her hair-styling products.

Females who achieved acclaim represent another minority category included in the selections: for examples, Rosabeth Moss Kanter and Nancy Adler, well known to academicians; Katharine Graham of the *Washington Post*; Elizabeth Arden, cosmetics entrepreneur; Ayn

Rand, popular novelist and philosopher and a voice for rational capitalism; and more. America as the land of opportunity summoned many from other lands who would have distinguished careers: Fred Fiedler, born in Austria and an authority in leadership; Joseph Juran, Romanian by birth and world-wide authority on quality management; Joseph Schumpeter, born in Moravia (today part of the Czech Republic) noted economist and advocate of innovation as the market system's engine of change; Peter Drucker, also Austrian born and respected for his sage advice on management; Igor Ansoff, a noted figure in strategic management who was born in Russia; An Wang, Chinese by birth, computer scientist by occupation; Andrew Grove, Intel's genius for expanding computing power; and more. Without the efforts of these diverse groups of African-Americans, immigrants, and females, the American economic scene would not have been the same.

Academicians, those who teach, engage in research, and often serve as consultants, have not been neglected in this collection. When Arthur Bedeian and Daniel Wren asked Academy of Management (U.S.) Fellows to identify the 25 most influential books in management in the twentieth century, all but two (excluding four non-U.S. authors) are included in this biographical dictionary (*Organizational Dynamics*, 2001). These individuals come from the past and the present and can be studied in a variety of ways. For the 'learning organization,' one can read about Chris Argyris, Donald Schon, Peter Senge, and Andrew Pettigrew; for those whose work epitomizes product quality, see W. Edwards Deming, Joseph Juran, and Philip Crosby; on the subject of strategic management, there are Alfred Chandler, Jr., Paul Lawrence, Jay Lorsch, and Michael Porter; if decision making is your fancy, read Chester Barnard and Herbert Simon; or look for ideas on leadership and motivation in the work of Abraham Maslow, Warren Bennis; Douglas McGregor; and for one who writes on many topics, study Peter Drucker.

If the selections are sliced into historical periods, it is possible to sample the scientific management period in Frederick Taylor, Frank and Lillian Gilbreth, Carl Barth, and Harrington Emerson; for a progressive in the scientific management period, see Henry Dennison; and for human relations there are Fritz Roethlisberger, Elton Mayo, and Mary Follett. An evergreen issue such as corporate governance is a topic to be explored through John Davis, Adolf Berle, Gardiner Means, and James Burnham as individuals who were concerned with the separation of ownership and management and the behavior of those who, in Adam Smith's words, managed 'other people's money'.

Despite the mention of numerous persons, this is only the surface of the wealth of ideas that can be found in the pages that follow. All of these biographical entries were prepared by knowledgeable authors who enable readers to pursue a range of interests in the past and present, by practitioners or academicians, by topics, by industry, and/or by issues. These biographical entries provide the opportunity to examine the lives and works of the prime movers, the giants of enterprise, the inventors and innovators, and the writers who have, in some manner, influenced how we view and how we practice management today. We interpret the present in terms of the past and these biographies enable us to learn and grow in our understanding.

Daniel A. Wren
David Ross Boyd Professor of Management Emeritus
The University of Oklahoma

HOW TO USE THE *ENCYCLOPEDIA*

The *Encyclopedia* contains entries on approximately 270 important thinkers and practitioners in the history of management. The title of each entry gives the subject's name and dates of birth and death, where known. As far as possible, we have used the subjects' full given names. Further biographical details, again where known, are given in the opening paragraph or paragraphs of each entry. The remainder of each entry discusses the subject's work, writings, ideas and contribution to the history of management.

Bibliographies have been included with the great majority of entries. These should not be taken as full and complete bibliographies, which in some cases would take up many pages. Many of the subjects published very widely, often on many subjects apart from management, and many have also been the subjects of vast bodies of literature. We have tried to restrict bibliographies to the most important and relevant works to the subject at hand. Where possible, we have included the standard biography of each subject, and readers are referred to these for further bibliographical details.

Within the body of the entries there is a cross-referencing system referring to other entries. Names which appear in small capitals (e.g. DRUCKER) are themselves the subjects of entries in the *Encyclopedia*, and the reader may refer to these entries for more information.

GENERAL BIBLIOGRAPHY

The following were used in the preparation of this encyclopedia, and will contain further information on many of the subjects included.

Standard Reference Works

American National Biography (1999) ed. J.A. Garraty and M. Carnes, Chicago: Gale Research Incoporated.

Dictionary of National Biography (1885) ed. L. Stephen and S. Lee, first published London: Small, Elder and Co.; supplements cover the period up to 1980.

Who's Who 2000, London: A. & C. Black.

Who's Who in the USA 2000, New Providence, NJ: Marquis.

Who Was Who, London: A. & C. Black.

Who Was Who in the USA, New Providence, NJ: Marquis.

Works Specifically Concerning Management History

Brands, H.W. (1999) *Masters of Enterprise: Giants of American Business from John Jacob Astor and J.P. Morgan to Bill Gates and Oprah Winfrey*, New York: The Free Press.

Collins, J.C. and Porras, J.I. (1997) *Built to Last*, Berkeley, CA: University of California Press.

Crainer, S. (2000) *The Management Century*, San Francisco: Jossey-Bass.

Crainer, S. and Clutterbuck, D. (1990) *Makers of Management*, London: Macmillan.

Davis, W. (1987) *The Innovators: The Essential Guide to Business Thinkers*, London: Ebury Press.

Drury, H.B. (1915) *Scientific Management: A History and Criticism*, New York: Columbia University Press.

Duncan, W.J. (1989) *Great Ideas in Management*, San Francisco: Jossey-Bass.

Gabor, A. (1999) *The Capitalist Philosophers*, New York: Times Business.

George, C.S. (1968) *The History of Management Thought*, Englewood Cliffs, NJ: Prentice-Hall.

Gough, J.W. (1969) *The Rise of the Entrepreneur*, London: B.T. Batsford.

Ingham, John N. and Feldman, Lynne B. (1994) *African-American Business Leaders: A Biographical Dictionary*, Westport, CT: Greenwood Press.

Jeremy, D.J. (ed.) (1984–6) *Dictionary of Business Biography*, 5 vols, London: Butterworths.

Leavitt, J.A. (1985) *American Women Managers and Administrators: A Selective Biographical Dictionary of Twentieth-century Leaders*, Westport, CT: Greenwood Press.

Parkinson, C.N. (1977) *The Rise of Big Business*, London: Weidenfeld and Nicholson.

Piramal, G. (1996) *Business Maharajahs*, New Delhi: Viking.

Pollard, S. (1965) *The Genesis of Modern Management*, London: Edward Arnold.

Tsutsui, W.M. (1998) *Manufacturing Ideology: Scientific Management in Twentieth-century Japan*, Princeton, NJ: Princeton University Press.

Urwick, L.F. (ed.) (1956) *The Golden Book of Management: A Historical Record of the Life and Work of Seventy Pioneers*, London: Newman Neame.

Urwick, L.F. and Brech, E.F.L. (1947–9) *The Making of Scientific Management*, 3 vols, London: Management Publications Trust; vols 1–2, repr. Bristol: Thoemmes Press, 1994.

Warner, M. (ed.) (1998) *IEBM Handbook of Management Thinking*, London: International Thomson Business Press.

Wren, D. (1994) *The Evolution of Management Thought*, 4th edn, New York: John Wiley.

—— (ed.) (1997) *Early Management Thought*, Brookfield, VT: Dartmouth.

Wren, D. and Greenwood, R.G. (1998) *Management Innovators: The People and Ideas That Have Shaped Modern Business*, New York: Oxford University Press.

LIST OF CONTRIBUTORS

Editorial Board

Tim Ambler, Senior Research Fellow,
Department of Marketing, London Business
School

Greg Bamber, Graduate School of
Management, Griffith University

John Dunning, Professor Emeritus,
University of Reading

Kris Inwood, Department of Economics,
University of Guelph, Ontario

Anne Jenkins, University of Durham

David Charles Lewis, Los Angeles,
California

Liu Zenan, MTM Partnership, London and
Beijing

Karl Moore, Faculty of Management,
McGill University, Montreal and
Templeton College, Oxford

Sasaki Tsuneo, College of Economics,
Nihon University

Sawai Minoru, Graduate School of
Economics, Osaka University

Daniel Wren, Professor Emeritus,
University of Oklahoma

Malcolm Warner, Judge Institute of
Management Studies, University of
Cambridge

Contributors

MA   Mie Augier
Stanford University, California

GB   Greg Bamber
Professor, Graduate School of
Management
Griffith University, Australia

CB   Clayton Barrows
Associate Professor, School of
Hotel and Food Administration
University of Guelph, Ontario

BPB   Bob Batchelor
San Rafael, California

MB   Markus Becker
Assistant Professor, Department of
Marketing
University of Southern Denmark

PB   Philippe Bernoux
University of Lyons

REB   Richard E. Boyatzis
Professor, Department of
Organization Behaviour
Case Western Reserve University,
Cleveland, Ohio

BB   Brian Brennan
Calgary, Alberta

KB   Keith D. Brouthers
        University of East London Business
        School

JAEB   Jo Ann E. Brown
        The School of Business
        Administration
        University of Mississippi

CC   Charles M. Carson
        The School of Business
        Administration
        University of Mississippi

SC   Simon Coppock
        London

HC-H   Hunter Crowther-Heyck
        Assistant Professor, Department of
        the History of Science
        University of Oklahoma

WJD   W. Jack Duncan
        Professor, Graduate School of
        Management
        University of Alabama

DF   David S. Ferguson CSP
        Santa Rosa, California

TG   Timothy J. Gilfoyle
        Professor, Department of History
        Loyola University, Chicago

LG   Laurel D. Graham
        Associate Professor, Department of
        Sociology
        University of South Florida

RG   Regina Greenwood
        Department of Industrial and
        Manufacturing Engineering and
        Business
        Kettering University, Chicago

WJH   William J. Hausman
        Professor, Department of Economics
        College of William and Mary,
        Virginia

JCH   Jimmy C. Hinton
        The School of Business
        Administration
        University of Mississippi

JH   Jill Hough
        Assistant Professor of Management
        University of Tulsa, Oklahoma

AJ   Anne Jenkins
        University of Durham

MJ   Matthew Jones
        Judge Institute of Management
        Studies, University of Cambridge

PJ   Patrick Joynt
        Professor
        Henley Management College and
        Bodo Management School, Norway

EK   Eileen P. Kelly
        Professor
        Ithaca College School of Business,
        New York

KAK   K. Austin Kerr
        Professor, Department of History
        Ohio State University

TK   Thomas Kochan
        Professor of Work and Employment
        Research
        Sloan School of Management,
        Massachusetts Institute of
        Technology

SK   Stephen Koerner
        Victoria, British Columbia

FSL   Frederic S. Lee
Professor, Department of
Economics
University of Missouri–Kansas
City

DCL   David Charles Lewis
Los Angeles, USA

DM   David Mason
Professor, Department of History
Young Harris College, Georgia

PBP   Peter B. Petersen
Johns Hopkins University,
Maryland

AP   Anastasia Pseiridis
Judge Institute of Management
Studies, University of Cambridge

QY   Qu Yuxiu
School of Business Administration
University of Wisconsin at
Milwaukee

DR   Domagoj Racic
Trinity College, Cambridge

BR   Bradley R. Rice
Professor, Department of History
Clayton College and State University

MR   Martin Ricketts
Professor of Economics
University of Buckingham

KR   Khalil Rohani
Department of Consumer Studies
University of Guelph, Canada

CR   Chris Rowley
Department of Human Resource
Management and Organization
Behaviour
City University Business School,
London

STR   Stephen Todd Rudman
Judge Institute of Management
Studies, University of Cambridge

ST   Sasaki Tsuneo
Professor, College of Economics
Nihon University, Tokyo

DBS   David B. Sicilia
Professor, Department of History
University of Maryland, College
Park

HPS   Peter Starbuck
Open University Business School
Milton Keynes

TES   Timothy Sullivan
Professor, Department of Economics
Towson University, Maryland

DS   David G. Surdam
Adjunct Associate Professor of
Economics, Graduate School of
Business, University of Chicago

RT   Richard Trahair
School of Social Sciences
LaTrobe University, Australia

RV   Robert Vanderlan
Department of History
University of Rochester, New York

JW   John Wilcox
Yellowknife, Northwest
Territories, Canada

WTW   W. Thomas White
Curator
James J. Hill Library
St Paul, Minnesota

MLW   Morgen Witzel
Honorary Senior Fellow, School of
Business and Economics
University of Exeter

A

ACKOFF, Russell L. (1919–)

Russell Ackoff was born in Philadelphia on 12 February 1919. He graduated from the University of Pennsylvania in 1941 with a degree in architecture, but was inspired by the course in modern philosophy given by C. West CHURCHMAN, which sparked off a lifetime friendship and a productive collaboration between himself and Churchman. As an academic, Ackoff made a significant contribution to a number of fields in business and management, most notably operations research and interactive planning.

Ackoff began his academic career in 1941 when he joined the University of Pennsylvania as an assistant instructor in philosophy. During the Second World War he served in the US Army, but continued his correspondence with Churchman and completed his Ph.D. in 1947. He subsequently worked as assistant professor in philosophy and mathematics at Wayne University in Detroit, before moving to the Case Institute of Technology in 1951, where he became professor of operations research and director of the Operations Research Group, meanwhile taking up visiting professorships in the UK and Mexico. He returned to the University of Pennsylvania in 1964 and took a series of professorships and chairmanships in the departments of systems sciences and management science. Throughout his academic career he won significant acclaim and was awarded honorary doctorates (from the University of Lancaster, Washington University and the University of New Haven) and many prizes for his contribution to planning, and training and development.

Together with Churchman, he is acknowledged as the co-founder of the field of operations research. Their book *Introduction to Operations Research* (Churchman *et al.* 1957) was the first international textbook in the field. After the Second World War, when the growth in demand rose, operations research set out to address the problems of industry posed by this growth by applying a scientific method to improving production efficiency. The field of operations research grew in importance during that decade. It is characterized by a systems orientation and an interdisciplinary approach.

A practical person and practitioner-oriented academic, Ackoff has been driven by a commitment to participation. This comes out most clearly in his work on interactive planning and the circular organization, which is a form of democratic hierarchy.

As the problems of production capacity receded in the 1960s, Ackoff moved towards addressing new corporate problems of strategic planning. His approach concerned what he called the 'purposeful systems' of corporations, and the systems of interacting problems that they faced. He formulated his ideas as a participatory approach known as 'interactive planning'. This aims to encourage people to conceive unconstrained idealized designs for the future, and to invent ways of realizing

1

them. Ackoff believes that many obstructions to change reside in the minds of participants rather than in the problem context itself, and that many of these are unwitting assumptions. Interactive planning aims to free participants from these constraints by asking them to focus on an ideal future in which all constraints have been removed. When finding ways to achieve their desired future, participants are no longer plagued by obstructions. The ideas of interactive planning are set out in Ackoff's book *Creating the Corporate Future* (1981).

In interactive planning, Ackoff first advocates 'formulating the mess (or system of interacting problems)' by systems analysis, by clarifying obstructions and by making projections of plausible future performance should the current situation continue. This produces a reference scenario. Next comes a phase of 'ends planning' to design an ideal future, which must be both technologically feasible and lead to a learning organization. The 'means planning' phase closes the gap between the current reference scenario and the ideal future, and requires much creativity. The participation in the planning generates both motivation and commitment, and facilitates implementation of the plans. Interactive planning offers many benefits, although it has been criticized for its naive assumption that all participants are willing and able to engage in open debate, free of all power plays.

Ackoff later developed the concept of the circular organization, again to promote the cause of participation in the running of an organization. In *The Democratic Organization* he sets out the three main principles of participation through structure: (1) the absence of an ultimate authority; (2) the ability of each member to participate directly or through representation in all decisions that affect him or her directly; and (3) the ability of members to make and implement decisions that affect no one other than the decision maker(s). The circular organization enhances people's chances of participating and making rapid and meaningful contributions, and it increases flexibility in response to changing circumstances, although much depends on the rules governing the organization. Although it fails perhaps to take into account more fuzzy-edged boundaries between and within organizations, it offers a creative alternative to the dominant vertical hierarchy of many organizations, and it does so in a way that is complementary to their existing structure. As an adaptation rather than a revolution, it may be easier for firms to adopt.

Ackoff has constantly reiterated the need for involvement with his motto 'plan or be planned for'. He has shown himself to be future-oriented throughout his career, and committed to improving the future by establishing what can be done now to create the future rather than trying to ascertain what the future will be independently of our actions now.

Ackoff has devoted much time to applying his concepts to solving the problems and conflicts of numerous large public and private sector organizations. He has used his deep insights and experience, together with his irrepressible wit, to publish many astute fables on business and management. He will no doubt be remembered in management circles for this astuteness and charm, as well as his commitment to participation and creative problem solving in bringing about a better future.

BIBLIOGRAPHY

Ackoff, R.L. (1981) *Creating the Corporate Future*, New York: John Wiley.

——— (1991) *Ackoff's Fables*, New York: John Wiley.

——— (1994) *The Democratic Organization*, New York: Oxford University Press.

Ackoff, R.L. and Emery, F.E. (1972) *On Purposeful Systems*, London: Tavistock Institute.

Ackoff, R.L. and Sasieni, M. (1968) *Fundamentals of Operations Research*, New York: John Wiley.

Churchman, C.W. and Ackoff, R.L. (1950) *Methods of Inquiry*, St Louis, MO:

Educational Publishers.

Churchman, C.W., Ackoff, R.L. and Arnoff, E.L. (1957) *Introduction to Operations Research*, New York: John Wiley.

Flood, R.L. (1998) 'Ackoff, Russell L.', in M. Warner (ed.), *Handbook of Management Thinking*, London: International Thomson Business Press, 1–7.

AJ

ADLER, Nancy J. (1948–)

Nancy Adler was born in 1948 and educated at the University of California at Los Angeles (UCLA), where she received an AB in economics, and an MBA and Ph.D. in management. Since 1980 she has been a member of the faculty of management of McGill University in Montreal, where she is currently professor of organizational behaviour and cross-cultural management. She has been a visiting professor at leading universities, and a consultant to organizations and governments throughout the world. She is a fellow of both the Academy of Management and the Academy of International Business. In 1991 she was named the leading university professor in Canada in all disciplines. She is noted for her work on cross-cultural management, and also for her studies of the role of women in international management.

Adler's studies of cross-cultural management have produced a large quantity of research that is both academically rigorous and relevant to global managers. She defines cross-cultural management as 'the study of the behavior of people in organizations located in cultures and nations around the world' (1983: 231). Surveying articles on organizational behaviour published in leading American management journals in the period 1971–80, she found that less than 5 per cent

of these articles focused on cross-cultural issues, and the majority of these were single-culture studies. She concluded that 'growing internationalism demands that a narrow domestic paradigm be replaced with one that can encompass the diversity of a global perspective' (1983: 231).

Adler's research addresses questions that are of importance to international managers, yet have received comparatively little previous academic attention. An example is the question of whether North American firms can successfully assign women managers to work in Asian countries, nations where women traditionally have not held management positions. Her study of North American women managers working in Asian countries (Adler 1987) found that, contrary to what prevailing opinion would have predicted, the women surveyed were overwhelmingly successful. Adler's interviews with women managers working in Asia revealed the presence of what she identifies as the '*gaijin* syndrome' (*gaijin* being Japanese for 'foreigner'). North American women managers are, like their male colleagues, seen as and treated as foreigners, and are not expected to act like local women. Therefore, local cultural rules limiting access of local women to managerial positions do not apply to foreign women (Adler 1987: 186–7).

Adler has created a model for viewing the role of female managers within the changing business dynamics of transnational corporations engaged in global competition (Adler 1993). The impact of transnational corporations on women managers has been primarily positive, with transnational firms including and involving women managers in ways that domestic, multi-domestic or multinational firms do not (Adler 1993: 4). One of these positive impacts has been that trans-national corporations have begun to send women abroad as expatriate managers. The '*gaijin* syndrome' is not confined to Asia, and in most countries foreign women managers are viewed first and foremost as foreign managers and

3

only secondarily as women. Thus local clients and colleagues accord them the respect necessary for success (Adler 1993: 6).

Adler's strength as a scholar is exemplified by her willingness to recognize situations in which cross-cultural management researchers learn that, in her words 'we know that we don't know' (Adler *et al*. 1989: 73). The quotation is from a study by Adler and colleagues conducted in the People's Republic of China. This study attempted to investigate Chinese managerial behaviour using a survey instrument previously used in Europe and North America to assess managers' conceptions of management. The attempt failed, but investigating why it failed yielded important methodological insights regarding use of Western-based methodology in non-Western research sites (Adler *et al*. 1989: 61–2).

After recognizing that the methodology chosen was inappropriate, the article observed that the question now to be addressed is 'to discover a better way to learn' (Adler *et al*. 1989: 72). Nancy Adler's work in cross-cultural management has significantly contributed to that discovery process. Through her research, teaching and advocacy within academia, she has pioneered development of a globally relevant organizational science.

BIBLIOGRAPHY
Adler, N.J. (1983) 'Cross Cultural Management Research: The Ostrich and the Trend', *Academy of Management Review* 8(2): 226–32.
—— (1984) 'Understanding the Ways of Understanding: Cross-cultural Management Methodology Reviewed', in *Advances in International Comparative Management*, Greenwich, CT: JAI Press, 31–67.
—— (1987) 'Pacific Basin Managers: A *Gaijin*, Not a Woman', *Human Resources Management* 26(2): 169–91.
—— (1988) 'Women in Management Worldwide', *Interntional Studies of Management and Organization* 16(3–4): 3–32.
Adler, N.J. (1993) 'Competitive Frontiers: Women Managers in the Triad', *International Studies of Management and Organization* 23(2): 3–22.
—— (2000) *International Dimensions of Organizational Behavior*, 4th edn, Cincinnati, OH: South-Western College Publishing.
Adler, N.J. and Izraeli, N.D. (1994) *Competitive Frontiers: Women Managers in a Global Economy*, Cambridge: Blackwell.
Adler, N.J., Campbell, N. and Laurent, A. (1989) 'In Search of an Appropriate Methodology: From Outside the People's Republic Looking In', *Journal of International Business Studies* 20: 61–74.

SR

ANSOFF, H. Igor (1918–)

H. Igor Ansoff was born in Vladivostock, Russia on 12 December 1918 and immigrated to the United States with his parents in 1935. He pursued courses in higher education at the Stevens Institute of Technology (ME, MSc) and Brown University (Ph.D.). Initially, Ansoff worked for the RAND corporation (1948–56) in the project management office. Later he joined Lockheed Aircraft Corporation (1956–63), where he became a member of the Diversification Task Force. During this period Ansoff helped develop concepts of firm strategy and product/market diversification (Antoniou 1997).

Ansoff's academic career started in 1963 when he joined the faculty of Carnegie Mellon University. In 1968 he moved to Vanderbilt University as dean of a new graduate management School. Ansoff spent seven years (1976–83) in Europe with a joint appointment as professor at the European Institute for

4

Advanced Studies and the Stockholm School of Economics. He returned to the United States in 1983 to head the strategic management area at the United States International University in San Diego, California (Antoniou 1997).

Ansoff, one of the pioneers of strategic management, has often been referred to as the father of strategic management. His industrial experience appears to have been the catalyst to many of the strategic management concepts he was to write about in his later career. The product–market matrix, strategic contingency theory and strategic decision making all were initially developed based on his experiences working in industry. During his academic career, Ansoff concentrated on developing prescriptive strategic management solutions for managers, with little emphasis on empirical testing.

Unlike many fellow scholars, Ansoff's contributions to strategic management have been very broad and are difficult to summarize. Two early contributions have become foundations for strategy. First to be developed was Ansoff's product–market matrix (Ansoff 1957). Ansoff proposed that firms wishing to diversify had to make choices between product and market diversification (or a combination). His product–market matrix provided managers with four strategic diversification options. First, managers could choose to diversify their product line extension while maintaining their current market focus (i.e., sell new products/services to existing customers). Second, managers could maintain their current product line but expand their markets (i.e., sell current products to new customers, by expanding either geographically or a different customer set). Third, managers could choose to maintain both their current product and market mix. The final choice was to expand both the product line and markets. So popular has Ansoff's strategic product–market matrix become that today it is included in most textbooks on strategic management, international business and marketing.

Ansoff's second major contribution was to extend the work of Alfred CHANDLER (1962) and develop the contingency view of strategic management (Ansoff 1965, 1972, 1988). The contingency view, also called strategic alignment or strategic fit, suggests that firms can maximize their performance by aligning their strategy and organizational capabilities (including structure) with the turbulence (dynamism and volatility) of the environment. Ansoff continued to develop his contingency view, and in the 1990s, with the assistance of a group of Ph.D. students, provided empirical support for his model (Ansoff and Sullivan 1993).

Ansoff's (1988) view of strategic contingency theory differs from other scholars' in several important ways. First, Ansoff maintained that the environment is composed of four distinct, yet related factors: complexity, familiarity, rapidity of change and visibility of change. Complexity and familiarity are similar to more recent concepts of environmental dynamism. These two factors are concerned with the degree of change occurring in the environment and the ability of firm management to understand these changes. Rapidity and visibility of change are similar to recent concepts of environmental volatility. These factors are concerned with the frequency of change and the ability of firm managers to identify the changes before they impact the organization. Hence, Ansoff helps provide a better understanding of the dynamics of the business environment.

Second, Ansoff's (1988) contingency model is concerned with the aggressiveness of the strategies firms pursue. Unlike other strategy scholars, Ansoff does not offer a set of 'generic strategies' but suggests that strategies selected need to match the turbulence of the environment faced by the firm. Ansoff maintains that when firms are in low turbulent environments they need to use stable strategies (which he defines as procedure-oriented). As the level of environmental turbulence increases, he suggests the aggressiveness of the strategy also needs to increase. Hence, in highly turbulent environments firms should pursue aggressive innovative strategies.

The third part of Ansoff's (1988) contingency model is concerned not just with the structure of the organization but with firm-level capabilities. While Chandler (1962) found strong evidence that organizational structures need to change with changes in strategy, Ansoff took this thinking further and suggested that not only structures need to change but that other firm capabilities may also need to change as strategies change (Tavernier 1976). Further, he suggested that these capability changes were not driven by changes in strategy (as Chandler's work suggested) but that it was changes in the environment that triggered both the change in strategy and the change in capabilities. Ansoff's conceptualization of capabilities tends to be similar to what we now call resources (Barney 1991) or core competencies (Prahalad and Hamel 1990) (see HAMEL; Prahalad). Ansoff (1988, 1979, 1972; Ansoff et al. 1976) suggested that organizational capabilities include five different factors: organizational values, managerial competencies, organizational structure, processes and technology. Organizational values are concerned with the culture of the organization. These cultural beliefs influence the objectives and goals of the organization, and its norms and values, as well as the reward and penalty systems within the organization. Managerial competencies include the skill, aptitudes, knowledge, risk propensity and depth of experience of the management team. Organizational structure is concerned with the responsiveness of the structure to change, job definitions, informal power, information channels and capability for self-renewal. Processes include problem recognition and analysis, decision making, communication, motivation and follow-up processes. Finally, the technology component of organizational capabilities includes systems and procedures, environmental surveillance, planning, delegation, participation, control and computer systems. Ansoff suggests that these

five sets of factors, as well as the strategic aggressiveness of the firm, must align with the turbulence level of the environment to achieve superior performance.

Ansoff has also made major contributions in the area of strategic decision making. In his article in *Strategic Management Journal* (1987), he summarizes ideas initially explored in his 1979 book. In these works he provides a detailed discussion of the factors that impact strategic decisions. Among these factors are power, culture and leadership.

Ansoff suggested that strategic decisions might be impacted by the power structure of an organization. Power structures are conceptualized as autocratic, decentralized and distributed. These three structures attempt to describe the number and sources of power in an organization. Autocratic power structures usually are highly centralized with little influence by middle managers or external parties, while distributed power structures have numerous power-sharing groups both inside and outside the organization. Further, Ansoff describes three representative methods for exercising power: coercive, consensual and bargaining. He suggests that different groups attempt to influence organizational decision making by exercising their power in different ways.

Ansoff (1979) devotes one full chapter to discussing organizational culture and how culture may impact strategic decisions. He relates the type of culture required in differing environments, and details eight attributes of culture that may be important. Three types of leadership are discussed, and their impact on strategic decisions and internal politics is described. Ansoff also highlights the importance of different leadership types based on different strategic opportunities. Finally, he presents a detailed model of firm decision making which includes influences from internal and external stakeholders, political aspirations, power structures, perceptions of the environment, managerial aspirations, past performance, culture and capabilities.

Although first developed in 1979, Ansoff's decision model is as advanced as any model put forth today.

Ansoff closes the book with a few chapters on strategic change, how firms recognize change, and how and why they respond as they do to change. Ansoff relates change management to decision making because the ability of a firm to recognize and respond to change appears to be influenced by the same factors that influenced other strategic decisions.

As Mintzberg (1994) describes it, strategic planning was the initial direction to strategy, yet based on unsatisfactory results, and more was needed. By the mid-1970s Ansoff (Ansoff *et al.* 1976; Ansoff 1972; Tavernier 1976) had recognized the shortcomings of traditional strategic planning and had begun providing a solution through his work on strategic management and strategic adaptation. Although Ansoff's early work focused on strategic planning (1965), he quickly adjusted his theories, based on real-world observations, to focus on a more complete model of strategic management that included implementation of strategies as well as strategic planning (Ansoff *et al.* 1976; Tavernier 1976; Ansoff 1988). In his revised book *The New Corporate Strategy* (1988), he devotes the first half to strategic planning and devotes the second half to problems/solutions of implementation and adaptation. He was an enthusiastic proponent of expanding traditional strategic planning into a more comprehensive strategic management concept.

Ansoff (Ansoff 1971; Ansoff *et al.* 1976; Tavernier 1976) also detailed some of the problems of strategic planning including resistance to change and the need for strategic leadership. He spoke about the need to change organizational capabilities to take advantage of new opportunities provided by a rapidly changing environment. He discussed problems of organizational culture and how implementing new strategies often meant changing long-held cultural beliefs. As in his other

work, Ansoff continued to stress the driving force played by the environment and the need to maintain alignment between the environment, firm capabilities and firm strategy.

His work on change management (Ansoff 1979) was an attempt to provide a prescriptive dynamic technique for managers to expand strategic planning into the domain of strategic management. In this work he not only describes the sources of resistance to changes in organizational strategy and capabilities, but also describes four methods for overcoming resistance to change.

Because he recognized that strategic planning was static and that a more dynamic strategic management approach was needed, Ansoff (Ansoff *et al.* 1976) introduced the concept of planned learning as an alternative to either adaptive learning or planned change. He suggested that adaptive learning is most common and normally triggered by changes in the environment that the firm can no longer ignore. Adaptive response is normally to cut costs or increase marketing; however, the persistence of the environmental signals (poor results) continues. At this point adaptive learners attempt to find better strategies (product/markets) and make adjustments to structures (organizational capabilities). Ansoff contends that there are several problems with adaptive learning, including (1) the slow speed of recognizing the need to change which endangers the firm and results in poor performance, and (2) the additional losses accumulated during the strategy/structure search and implementation periods.

Planned change, Ansoff maintains, means that managers extrapolate the present environment into the future and then plan future changes in strategy and structure before they are needed. Hence, planned change suggests that firms will minimize any losses due to development of new strategies and structures when the time to change arrives. Yet again Ansoff finds fault with this theory suggesting that (1) changes in the environment may not be linear and, therefore, managers may not be in

7

a position to extrapolate them, and (2) managers may be unwilling/unable to conceptualize strategies/structure which differ significantly from historically/culturally held belief systems. Hence, managerial cognitive limitation may make planned change ineffective.

The alternative to these two strategic management methods is what Ansoff (Ansoff *et al.* 1976) calls planned learning. He states that 'excessive overplanning can be as unproductive as impulsive recourse to trial and error' (Ansoff *et al.* 1976: 72). He therefore suggests a technique that combines the benefits of both adaptive learning and planned change. Planned learning involves using organizational flexibility, testing of potential strategies/capabilities prior to implementation, and a pacing element which prioritizes potential changes.

The above discussion was intended as an introduction to Ansoff's major contributions to the field of strategic management. However, Ansoff was a prolific thinker and made numerous other valuable contributions, two of which are summarized below.

Ansoff was well aware that changes in the environment would drive changes in the products/services firms provided and the markets they served (Ansoff 1971). This, he knew, meant that managers would have to deal with change. Change would sometimes be rapid, other times slow. What was needed was a systematic method of determining how to respond to change. In an attempt to provide managers with prescriptive tools for identifying, planning for and managing changes in the environment, Ansoff developed both an issues management (Ansoff 1980) and a surprise management (Ansoff 1976) system. These systems, he suggested, can help managers systematically address changes in the environment by managing environmental scanning, strategy capabilities development, and implementation. These tools provide managers with a systematic set of decision rules, which provides a framework for evaluating the type, degree and intensity of strategic management adaptive behaviour required

in a firm. The issues management system is concerned with managing both strong and weak environmental signals, while the surprise management system address the importance of planning for major, potentially damaging, discontinuous shifts in the business environment.

Ansoff was also an early exponent of the use of technology in strategic management. In fact, one of the major internal capabilities in Ansoff's contingency model was technology, especially computer technology. Further, Ansoff (1986) has written about the role played by computers in aiding management during the strategic management process.

Much of Ansoff's writing is very technical, and therefore readers without background knowledge may find it difficult to understand. However, Ansoff and McDonnell (1990) provide a highly readable general overview of Ansoff's many ideas, concepts and models.

Ansoff's contributions to the field of strategic management were far ahead of his time and, perhaps because he was more interested in developing theory than in testing it, much of his work remains unexplored. Many of today's 'original' insights have their roots in Ansoff's work during thirty-five years as a strategic management scholar. Despite advances in the field, those interested in strategic management will still find it beneficial to look closely at Ansoff's work.

BIBLIOGRAPHY

Ansoff, H.I. (1957) 'Strategies for Diversification', *Harvard Business Review* (September–October): 113–24.

——— (1965) *Corporate Strategy*. New York: John Wiley and Sons.

——— (1971) 'Strategy as a Tool for Coping with Change', *Journal of Business Policy* 1(Summer): 3–7.

——— (1972) 'The Concept of Strategic Management', *Journal of Business Policy* 2(4): 2–7.

——— (1976) 'Managing Strategic Surprise by Response to Weak Signals', *California Management Review* (Winter): 21–33.

Ansoff, H.I. (1979) *Strategic Management*, New York: John Wiley and Sons.
—— (1980) 'Strategic Issues Management', *Strategic Management Journal* 1(2): 131–48.
—— (1986) 'Competitive Strategy Analysis on the Personal Computer', *Journal of Business Strategy* 6(3): 28–36.
—— (1987) 'The Emerging Paradigm of Strategic Behavior', *Strategic Management Journal* 8: 501–15.
—— (1988) *The New Corporate Strategy*, New York: John Wiley and Sons.
Ansoff, H.I. and McDonnell, E. (1990) *Implanting Strategic Management*, 2nd edn, New York: Prentice Hall.
Ansoff, H.I. and Sullivan, P.A. (1993) 'Empirical Proof of the Paradigmic Theory of Strategic Success Behaviors of Environmental Serving Organizations', in D.E. Hussey (ed.), *International Review of Strategic Management*, New York: John Wiley and Sons, vol. 4, 173–203.
Ansoff, H.I., Declerck, R.P. and Hayes, R.L. (1976) *From Strategic Planning to Strategic Management*, New York: John Wiley and Sons.
Antoniou, P. (1997) 'Ansoff, H. Igor', in M. Warner (ed.), *International Encyclopedia of Business and Management*, London: Routledge, vol. 1, 224–8.
Barney, J. (1991) 'Firm Resources and Sustained Competitive Advantage', *Journal of Management* 17(1): 99–120.
Chandler, A.D. (1962) *Strategy and Structure: Chapters in the History of the American Industrial Enterprise*, Cambridge, MA: MIT Press.
Mintzberg, H. (1994) *The Rise and Fall of Strategic Planning*, New York: Prentice Hall.
Prahalad, C.K. and Hamel, G. (1990) 'The Core Competence of the Corporation', *Harvard Business Review* (May–June): 79–91.
Tavernier, G. (1976) 'Shortcomings of Strategic Planning: An Interview with H.I. Ansoff', *International Management* (September): 45–7.

KB

ARDEN, Elizabeth (1878–1966)

Elizabeth Arden was born Florence Nightingale Graham in Woodbridge, Ontario on 31 December 1878, the daughter of William and Susan Graham. She died in New York City on 18 October 1966. She married Thomas Jenkins Lewis in 1915; after divorcing him in 1934 she married Prince Michael Evlanoff in 1944, but divorced him in 1946. After leaving school she trained as a nurse, moving to New York in 1907. In 1908 she took a clerical job in a beauty salon, learned about facial massage and cosmetics, and in 1909 opened a salon with a partner, Elizabeth Hubbard. In 1910 the partnership broke up and Graham opened her own salon, changing her name to Elizabeth Arden, a name she felt more appropriate for her profession (the surname came from the title of a Tennyson poem). By 1914 she was producing her own cosmetics, and opened a branch in Washington, DC; more branches followed, including one in Paris in 1922. By the 1930s she was selling a range of over 300 cosmetics, and had established salons across the United States and Europe.

As well as developing the mass production of cosmetics and adapting the chain store concept to beauty salons, Arden also pioneered the 'beauty farm' or 'health farm' in 1934, when she started up Main Chance Farm, a residential establishment which provided health and beauty care, including exercise routines, and advice on diet and nutrition. A second farm was established in Arizona in 1947, and the model for 'health tourism' has been widely copied.

Arden was exacting in her search for quality, and also understood the needs of her market, mainly wealthy women; her managerial ability lay in seeing the potential for adapting the beauty business to models worked out in other sectors. Much of her early success was due to her first husband, who acted as her general manager and organized the business on a sound footing. Arden herself was a harsh employer who reportedly gave more care to her racehorses than to her staff; in 1945 she was the leading racehorse owner in the United States in terms of prize money won, and her horses featured on the cover of *Time* magazine. Her later career featured a bitter personal feud with her competitor, Helena Rubenstein, a rivalry which both women exploited to considerable public relations advantage.

ARGYRIS, Chris (1923–)

Chris Argyris was born in Newark, New Jersey on 16 July 1923, the son of Stephan and Sophia Argyris. He grew up in Greece and New Jersey. According to Lundberg (1998), Argyris had in some respects a difficult childhood, particularly at school where he was a member of a minority group and had – initially – a limited command of English. This experience 'instilled in him two enduring characteristics: a propensity to examine himself carefully to discover his deficiencies, and a desire to work hard to change himself' (Lundberg 1998: 19). He served as an officer in the US Army Corps of Signals during the Second World War, and afterwards went to Clark University, from which he graduated with an AB in 1947. He completed his MA at Kansas University in 1949, and his Ph.D. at the School of Industrial and Labor Relations at Cornell University in 1951. He married Renee Brocoum in 1950; they have two children.

On completing his Ph.D., Argyris joined the faculty of Yale University. He served as director of research in labour from 1951 to 1954, associate professor from 1954 to 1959, and professor of business administration from 1960 to 1965; he was Beach Professor of Academic Services from 1965 to 1971. He then moved to Harvard University, where he has been James Bryant Conant Professor of Education and Organizational Behavior since 1971. He has held a number of other posts, including membership of the board of directors of National Training Laboratories and special consultant on human relations to the secretary of health, education and welfare, and has been associated with institutions as varied as the Ford Foundation, the National Institute of Mental Health, and the Air Force Personnel and Training Center.

The capacity for self-analysis which Argyris developed at an early age was soon extended to the study of others, both as individuals and groups. In his early work (Argyris 1957, 1960, 1962), he noticed what he termed a basic incongruence between the needs of individuals and the demands of organizations. Organizations, as they are usually structured, are hierarchical and control-centred. Communication is largely top-down. Managers, in guiding the efforts of those below them, impose strict limits on those efforts and on those people. Individuals, on the other hand, are independent, active, self-aware entities. In fact, as people grow more mature and wiser, these attributes tend to be enhanced. Experienced and knowledgeable people – who arguably make the best employees – are those most likely to be independent in thought and to find the internal climate of organizations restrictive. In other words, it is those employees with the greatest potential who are being most heavily restricted by the organization and its structure.

The result, in terms of organization culture, tends to be disbelief, distrust and inhibition. The trust and loyalty which the organization should be encouraging are not there. Instead, in frustration, people may even take negative steps towards the organization, reducing their work output, 'gold-bricking' or even leaving the organization altogether; high staff turnover can be read as one sign of an organization in which individual needs are being suppressed by organizational constraints.

One of the consequences of this incongruence can be the erection of barriers to organizational change. Argyris (1970, 1971, 1980, 1982) describes how what he calls 'defensive routines' inhibit change, retarding its progress or even blocking it altogether. These defensive routines are actions taken by employees or groups of employees for the specific purpose of warding off changes which they perceive to be dangerous or threatening. While some of these routines are obvious, others are much less so. The most problematic routines to deal with, says Argyris, are those undertaken for what are perceived as positive reasons. Defensive routines are not necessarily undertaken for selfish reasons: people may use them to 'support' the organization against changes which they believe would damage it, or to 'protect' other employees whom they believe to be vulnerable to unwanted change, or because they wish to be 'realistic' about the prospects for change. Many of these routines become so embedded in the organization that even the change strategies designed to overcome them begin to take on a defensive nature themselves.

How, then, to overcome these barriers and manage change? In the next phase of his work, Argyris turned to both his own background in psychology and to colleagues in sociology, most notably Donald SCHÖN, with whom Argyris had an extremely fruitful collaboration in the 1970s. Together, they developed the theory of 'action science'. Argyris and Schön decided to switch their attention from observed behaviour to the actual processes of reasoning, to get at the causes and sources of behaviour, specifically the knowledge and routines employed when planning and undertaking actions. The term 'action science' was developed as an alternative to the concept of 'normal science' as elaborated by T.S. KUHN. For Argyris, the static studies employed by conventional rigorous research are divorced from reality; science needs to be part of action, and vice versa. As he says: 'Action is how we give meaning to life ... Actionable knowledge is not only relevant to the world of practice, it is the knowledge that people use to create that world' (Argyris 1993: 1).

At the core of action science is learning and the circulation of knowledge. It is the circulation and use of knowledge, says Argyris, that leads to effective change; therefore the emphasis should be on the knowledge, not the change processes. He distinguishes between single-loop learning, in which feedback is used to alter actions, and double-loop learning, in which feedback is used to question the underlying assumptions on which action is based. Truly effective change, he says, must be based on double-loop learning. Here the problem of defensive routines becomes important once more: many people within the organization, through motives as various as pride in the status quo and fear of uncertainty, may resist double-loop learning as it threatens their own previously held beliefs and convictions. Time and effort must be spent breaking down these routines before double-loop learning can be put into place.

Action science is not a panacea, and the pitfalls for the researcher and change agent are many. But the concept has two important advantages: first, the research aspect of action science generates considerable quantities of new knowledge about the organization; second, the action this research calls for ensures a wide circulation of this knowledge. The breaking down of defensive routines calls for patience and persistence, but the new knowledge generated can itself be a powerful resource for doing this. Above all, perhaps, action science provides a clarity which other forms of research do not; as Lundberg comments, 'perhaps the most distinctive feature of action science is that is has the potential to uncover its own contradictions and alter its own learning processes accordingly' (Lundberg 1998: 22). This dynamism and flexibility means action science can be configured to a variety of organizational needs.

In the 1970s and again in more recent work (for example, Argyris 2000), Argyris has also paid attention to the role of the change agent. He is particularly critical of the forms of research which change agents use to gather information. He notes that research into the functioning of organizations tends to have some of the faults found in those organizations themselves. That is, it tends to be top-down and directive, with the researchers controlling the research programme and defining the tasks that subjects would undertake. This tends to distort the results. Argyris discovered that the results of studies of organizational behaviour seldom matched actual behaviour; there was a further incongruence, between what people actually *did* and what they *said* they did. This problem further fuels his belief in the need for action science, which, by shifting away from behaviour to knowledge and beliefs, has a capacity to get closer to the heart of the problem. The importance of a neutral, value-free change agent cannot be overstressed, but even these agents – such as consultants – can unwittingly reinforce or even create defensive routines. Ultimately, it is not so much the character of the agent that matters as the quality of the change created.

Argyris's work has not been universally accepted. His writing can be dense and impenetrable to the layman, and he has been accused of focusing too much on conceptual thinking and not enough on the practicalities of actually implementing action science. However, his conceptualizations of learning flows, knowledge in action and defensive routines are becoming increasingly relevant in modern knowledge-based businesses as we learn more about how knowledge functions and is controlled and distributed within organizations.

BIBLIOGRAPHY

Argyris, C. (1957) *Personality and Organization*, New York: Harper.
—— (1960) *Understanding Organizational Behaviour*, Chicago: Dorsey.
—— (1962) *Interpersonal Competence and Organizational Effectiveness*, Chicago: Dorsey.
—— (1964) *Integrating the Individual and the Organization*, New York: Wiley.
—— (1965) *Organization and Innovation*, Chicago: Irwin.
—— (1970) *Intervention Theory and Method*, Reading, MA: Addison-Wesley.
—— (1971) *Management and Organizational Development*, New York: McGraw-Hill.
—— (1972) *The Applicability of Organizational Sociology*, Cambridge: Cambridge University Press.
—— (1976) *Increasing Leadership Effectiveness*, New York: Wiley.
—— (1980) *Inner Contradictions of Rigorous Research*, New York: Academic Press.
—— (1982) *Reasoning, Learning and Action*, San Francisco: Jossey-Bass.
—— (1993a) *On Organizational Learning*, Oxford: Blackwell; 2nd edn 1999.
—— (1993b) *Knowledge for Action: A Guide to Overcoming Barriers to Organizational Change*, San Francisco: Jossey-Bass.
—— (2000) *Flawed Advice and the Management Trap: How Managers Can Know When They're Getting Good Advice and When They're Not*, Oxford: Oxford University Press.
Argyris, C. and Schön, D. (1974) *Theory in Practice*, San Francisco: Jossey-Bass.
—— (1978) *Organizational Learning*, Reading, MA: Addison-Wesley.
Argyris, C., Putnam, R. and Smith, D. (1985) *Action Science*, San Francisco: Jossey-Bass.

Lundberg, C. (1998) 'Argyris, Chris', in M. Warner (ed.), *IEBM Handbook of Management Thinking*, London: International Thomson Business Press, 18–23.

MLW

ARROW, Kenneth Joseph (1921–)

Kenneth Joseph Arrow was born in New York City on 23 August 1921. He was educated at the City College of New York, graduating with a degree in social science and mathematics, and then at Columbia University, where he gained an MA in mathematics in 1941. He served in the US Army from 1942 to 1946, reaching the rank of captain, and then returned to Columbia to study for his Ph.D., which he completed in 1951; at the same time he was research associate and assistant professor at the Cowles Commission for Research in Economics at the University of Chicago. He served as a consultant to the RAND Corporation for many years from 1948, and as an economic adviser on the US Council of Economic Advisors. In 1949 Arrow became acting assistant professor at Stanford University, where he rose rapidly through the academic ranks, becoming a professor in 1953. He moved to Harvard in 1968, and finally returned to Stanford in 1979 as professor of economics and operations research. He married Selma Schweitzer in 1947, and has two sons.

One of Arrow's first well-known works was his development of a general impossibility theorem (published in 1951 as *Social Choice and Individual Values*). Based on his doctoral thesis, this work set out to ascertain what conditions (if any) allowed group decisions to be· rationally and democratically derived from individual preferences. Arrow set out four conditions that had to be satisfied by any method of relating individual preferences to social choices. He proved that the four conditions are contradictory, and thus that it is impossible for any social welfare function to satisfy them all simultaneously. Arrow confirmed that democratic decision making as traditionally understood was, in principle, impossible. The impossibility theorem shows that there is not, and in principle cannot be, any perfect form of government. This led to the development of public choice economics. He later developed theories of social choice that allow decisions to be made in situations of multiple criteria, particularly in cases with conflicting and incommensurable criteria.

His work in developing the general equilibrium theory of economies and welfare economics was also of considerable importance. He used new mathematical techniques to provide better and more general proofs of the existence and uniqueness of general competitive equilibrium, proved that all competitive equilibria are optimal, and that all optimal states can be achieved through the competitive market process.

The economics of information, uncertainty, risk-bearing and insurance was the third of Arrow's three main fields of work (social choice theory and his work on general equilibrium theory being the other two). He was a pioneer in developing and applying the concepts of uncertainty and risk to economic analysis. He found that the efficient (Pareto's definition) use of resources in uncertainty depends partly on relationships or controls extraneous to the price mechanism, such as family ties, moral principles and so on. He argued that 'the uncertainties about economics are rooted in our need for a better understanding of the economics of uncertainty; our lack of economic knowledge is in good part our difficulty in modelling the ignorance of the economic agent' (Arrow and Raynaud 1986). A substantial amount of his work was directed towards this difficulty.

In addition to the considerable importance of each of Arrow's individual contributions, his contribution to economic thinking is significant for its breadth as well as for articulating new problems and promoting new paths for research. He was continually motivated to demonstrate that economic reasoning could be of real practical use to the problems of industrial decision makers of the time. Consequently, he worked on a diverse range of applied problems including the economics of medical care and health insurance (which broke new ground in the field, focusing particularly on the role of differential information), building theory and models of discrimination, impacts on urban economic development, social responsibility and economic efficiency, environmental preservation and irreversibility. Other significant papers by Arrow contributed to the stability analysis of market models, optimal inventory theory, mathematical programming and statistical decision theory.

Although highly technical, Arrow's work was concerned with basic economic issues and pressing social problems. He concerned himself with the most fundamental questions in economics, such as can the economic system achieve an equilibrium, and if so, how should it be evaluated in terms of social welfare? Can non-market choice rules be used instead of, or as an addition to, the market, and if so, how do these collective choice rules perform? Can the economic system function smoothly with uncertainty and imperfect information, and how might economic institutions be changed in the face of that uncertainty?

Arrow's career was long and outstandingly productive, and his many contributions to economic theory were well recognized by his colleagues, who acknowledged his unfailing genius and good humour. More publicly, he was recognized with the award of the Nobel Prize for Economics in 1972, in addition to many other awards and thirteen honorary doctorates. The Nobel Memorial prize was awarded (jointly with John Hicks) for his pioneering work to general economic equilibrium theory and welfare theory. Arrow was also cited by the Swedish Academy of Science for his contributions to growth theory and decision theory.

BIBLIOGRAPHY

Arrow, K.J. (1951) *Social Choice and Individual Values*, New York: Wiley.

——— (1971) *Essays in the Theory of Risk Bearing*, Amsterdam: North Holland.

——— (1974) *The Limits of Organization*, New York: W.W. Norton.

——— (1983–5) *The Collected Papers of Kenneth J. Arrow*, 6 vols, Cambridge, MA: Harvard University Press.

——— (1985) *Applied Economics*, Cambridge, MA: Belknap Press of Harvard University Press.

Arrow, K.J. and Raynaud, H. (1986) *Social Choice and Multicriterion Decision-making*, Cambridge, MA: MIT Press

Fisher, R.C. (1987) 'Kenneth J. Arrow', in R. Turner (ed.), *Thinkers of the Twentieth Century*, London: St James Press.

Oppenheimer, P.M. (1983) 'Arrow, Kenneth Joseph', in A. Bullock and R.B. Woodings (eds), *Fontana Biographical Companion to Modern Thought*, London: Collins.

Wasson, T. (ed.) (1987) 'Arrow, Kenneth J.', in *Nobel Prize Winners*, New York: H.W. Wilson Co.

AJ

ARTHUR, William Brian (1946–)

William Brian Arthur was born in Belfast on 21 July 1946, into a Catholic family living in a Protestant neighbourhood. He studied electrical engineering at Queen's University, Belfast, where he graduated with a first-class degree in 1966. He spent the following year studying for an MA in operations research at Lancaster University, and then moved to the University of Michigan to study mathematics, where he received his master's degree in 1969. He subsequently studied at the University of California at Berkeley, where he received an MA in economics and a Ph.D. in operations research in 1973. He then worked at the Population Council in New York, researching population and economic development in South Asia and the Middle East. In 1977 he was appointed a research scholar at the prestigious International Institute for Applied Systems Analysis in Austria, and conducted research on population economics and optimization theory.

From 1983 to 1996 Arthur was Morrison Professor of Population Studies and Economics, the youngest endowed-chair professor at Stanford University. He co-founded and chaired the Morrison Institute of Population Studies. In 1988 Arthur joined the Santa Fe Institute (SFI), an independent research institute in New Mexico, specializing in the development of the complexity sciences. He became the first director of the economics research programme at SFI, exploring the economy as an evolving complex system, and later joined the steering committee and board of trustees. At the time of writing he is Citibank Professor there, and is also a Coopers and Lybrand Fellow.

In his many papers Arthur pioneered the study of positive feedbacks or increasing returns in the economy, and in particular their role in magnifying small, random events. His interest in the history of technology and his study of the rise of Silicon Valley led Arthur to describe economics of the knowledge age as characterized by increasing returns, rather than the diminishing returns of traditional industrial economics, which are governed by the finite limits of physical resources, and hence lead to rising costs and decreasing returns. In contrast, in the world of information and the software industry, once the initial investment has been made, returns increase as each copy is sold.

Arthur developed a theoretical framework for economic allocation under increasing returns during the 1980s, which he published in his book *Increasing Returns and Path Dependence in the Economy* (1994). He asserts that high-technology industries operate under conditions of increasing returns, and that as modern economies have shifted towards high technology, the nature of competition, business culture and appropriate government policy are altered. Arthur's work highlights the importance of building up market share and the user base in developing corporate strategy in these markets. The once controversial concept of increasing returns is now widely accepted by economists as well as those working in technology industries.

Arthur identified three separate characteristics that contribute to increasing returns in high technology. The first is the high up-front costs of developing a product; the second are the so-called 'learning effects', which keep customers with the product they have learned to use. The third are 'network effects'. 'Network effects' occur as more and more people adopt a product, increasing the likelihood of others adopting it. This is due to the drive to minimize learning and maximize compatibility.

The combination of network effects and increasing returns means that companies or technologies that gain a dominant position early on tend to increase their domination. This he describes as resulting in 'lock-in' to a particular product or technology. Which product becomes locked in is dependent on the historical path of small events encountered along the way. These small events may be anything from chance meetings, sudden changes in regulations or clever strategizing, and are magnified by the force of increasing returns.

His 1990 article 'Positive Feedbacks in the Economy', published in *Scientific American*, brought his work to the attention of the lawyers in the anti-trust case brought against the software giant Microsoft. Arthur's theories helped legislators and lawyers make sense of economic activity in the new high-technology markets, and influenced the development of new precedents in anti-trust legislation.

Arthur himself notes that the concept of monopoly in high-technology industries is no bad thing, as it acts as a motivator for innovation. The many sources of increasing returns in this sector make monopolies almost inevitable; however, he notes that they are short-lived, temporary monopolies that exist only until the next wave of technology emerges. Problems arise when an extant monopoly suppresses innovation in the industry, and when the monopoly is unfairly used to gain advantage in a separate market.

Arthur continually challenged traditional economic thinking in his work, and is an outspoken critic of academic economists that focus too much on the formal neoclassical economic models developed in the first half of the twentieth century, and too little on how the world works. He emphasizes, however, that the theories of increasing returns are not in opposition to classical economic theories based on the assumption of diminishing returns, but complementary to them.

He met considerable opposition to his ideas on increasing returns at the outset. Many of these criticisms relate to ideologies of the 'rightness' of the market mechanism, which is challenged by Arthur's work on lock-in. However, Arthur is clear that he is an admirer of the free market mechanism. What he suggests, however, is that under the conditions of increasing returns, markets become unstable and can lock in to the dominance of one product, and occasionally lock in to less than optimal products, as illustrated by the widespread take up of the DOS operating system and the VHS video format. He emphasizes that the key point is not whether the product locked in is better or worse than others, but that these markets are unstable and tend to become temporarily dominated.

Arthur was awarded the Schumpeter Prize in Economics in 1990 and a Guggenheim fellowship in 1987, both for his work on increasing returns. Amongst his other research work, he has focused upon the role of cognition in the digital economy, in particular formulating economic theory to describe how human agents formulate problems in indeterminate situations. His pioneering contribution to economic theory has won much acclaim for explaining the dynamics of the emerging technology-dominated economy, and for shedding new light on strategy in such an economy.

BIBLIOGRAPHY
Arthur, W.B. (1990) 'Positive Feedbacks in the Economy', *Scientific American* (February): 92–9.
——— (1994) *Increasing Returns and Path Dependence in the Economy*, Ann Arbor, MI: University of Michigan Press.
——— (1994) 'Vita', http://www.santafe.edu/ arthur.htm, 15 March 2001.
Arthur, W.B., Lane, D. and Durlauf, S. (eds) (1997) *The Economy as an Evolving Complex System II*, Reading, MA: Addison-Wesley.
Gates, D, (1998) 'The PreText Interview', *PreText Magazine* May/June(6), http://www.pretext.com, 15 March 2001.
Kurtzman, J (1998) 'An Interview with W. Brian Arthur', *Strategy & Business*, Quarter 2, http://www.strategy-business.com/thoughtleaders/98209, 15 March 2001.

AJ

ASTOR, John Jacob (1763–1848)

John Jacob Astor was born in Waldorf, near Heidelberg, in the German state of Baden on 17 July 1763 and died in New York on 29

March 1848. His father, Jacob, a struggling butcher, raised John on his own after his wife Maria died in 1766. Apprenticing in the family shop, he later learned English while working for his brother in England between 1779 and 1783, and then sailed for America.

Astor settled in New York City, the ideal base for an aspiring fur trader. He married Sarah Todd in 1785. Brands (1999) relates how he journeyed up the Hudson, Mohawk and other inland waterways, buying otter and beaver pelts from the British colonies in Canada and the natives in western New York, and selling them to New Yorkers and Europeans. He then peddled imported goods to his native and Canadian suppliers. By 1800 Astor was America's leading fur trader, following the westward course of settlement to buy furs from the British in the territories of Ohio and Michigan. His operation also included Upper and Lower Canada.

Astor was the first American entrepreneur to think not only continentally but globally. Shortly after Lewis and Clark's overland journey to the Pacific (1808), he first tried to set up a trading post on the Columbia River, but this fell into the hands of his British competitors. But by 1809 Astor was selling American furs in China, Chinese goods in Europe, and European goods in America, all of which were carried in his own fleet. The war of 1812 helped the American Fur Company monopolize the American fur trade by securing preferential legislation from Congress. Between 1825 and 1830 it controlled the fur trade in the emerging American Midwest, then filling up with settlers.

Following the war, Astor's fleet of eight ships, led by the *Severn*, the *Magdalen* and the *Beaver*, resumed their global voyages. Leaving New York, they sailed to Latin America, the Pacific Coast, Hawaii, China, around to Europe and back to New York. He was America's first global trader, carefully watching the world market for every advantage. This global trade eventually yielded diminishing returns, and by 1827 Astor had sold his fleet, concentrating instead on fur trading in the Midwest.

Astor also served as a director of the New York branch of the Bank of the United States from 1816 to 1819, where he attempted to pursue fiscally conservative policies but was outvoted. He then settled in Europe, while attempting to manage the American Fur Company from abroad. By 1834, Astor realized that the age of the fur trader was passing. He had found in the meantime a new outlet for investment: real estate. Astor knew that the price of land in New York could only rise as the city's population swelled. As early as 1803 he had $180,000 invested in New York properties; by 1820, he had over $500,000, and by 1826 Astor owned 174 properties which provided him with $27,000 a year (Brands 1999). Following his retirement from the fur business, he invested a further $830,000 in real estate, becoming the largest property owner in the New York City. The quintessential manager of his day, John Jacob Astor died worth $10 million, the wealthiest tycoon in early nineteenth-century America.

BIBLIOGRAPHY
'John Jacob Astor' (1999) *McGraw-Hill Encyclopedia of World Biography*, Detroit, MI: Gale Research Inc., vol. 1, 351–2.
Williams, K.H. (1999) 'Astor, John Jacob', in J.A. Garraty and M. Carnes (eds), *American National Biography*, New York: Oxford University Press, vol. 1, 696–9.

DCL

B

BARBASH, Jack (1910–94)

Jack Barbash was born in New York City on 1 August 1910 and died on 21 May 1994 in Madison, Wisconsin. Barbash received his bachelor's and master's degrees in economics from New York University. His first professional job was with the New York State Department of Labor. In the late 1930s he and Kitty, his wife and research partner, moved to Washington DC, where they lived with international labour expert Morris Weisz and his family. Over the next two decades Barbash worked for, among other organizations, the National Labor Relations Board, the War Production Board, the Senate Labor Committee, the Department of Education, various individual trade unions and the Congress of Industrial Organizations (CIO). In 1955 he participated in the merger negotiations between the CIO and its rival union federation, the American Federation of Labor (AFL), which created the AFL-CIO. In 1957 he joined the faculty of the School for Workers at the University of Wisconsin, and subsequently was appointed the John E. Bascom Professor of Economics and Industrial Relations, a position he held until his retirement. He was elected president of the Industrial Relations Research Association in 1980 and of the Association of Evolutionary Economics in 1981.

Barbash was one of the great trade union intellectuals of the twentieth century. He was influenced by the ideological fervour and skills displayed by socialist and communist union organizers in the 1930s, and by the pragmatic trade union leaders who built the American labour movement during its years of rapid growth from the 1930s through the 1950s. His early books such as *Labor Unions in Action* (1948), *The Practice of Unionism* (1956), *Unions and Union Leadership* (1959) and *Labor's Grass Roots* (1961) drew on his first-hand acquaintance with the leading trade union figures of day such as John L. Lewis, Walter Reuther, David Dubinsky, George Meany and Arthur Goldberg. His writings displayed a keen understanding of how personal leadership and institutional and historical contexts interact to shape events.

Barbash is best known for providing a normative and intellectual framework for the field of industrial relations. His first sketch of this framework was published in a 1964 article, 'The Elements of Industrial Relations', and later expanded into a book of the same title (1985). To him, the field of industrial relations resolves around the search for institutional arrangements that can produce both equity and efficiency. His view was that employment relationships are characterized by a fundamental and enduring conflict between employers' efficiency interests and workers' security interests. Unlike Marx, however, he viewed these interests as a natural and enduring aspect of the structure of employment relationships. Conflicting interests would be present under any economic or political regime, not just under capitalism. But workers and employers also have some shared, common interests, and therefore the task of industrial relations institutions in general, and collective bargaining in particular, is to resolve these legitimate differences and search for solutions to shared problems. In this regard, Barbash was the leading third-generation spokesman for the Wisconsin School of Industrial Relations, founded on the ideas of Professor John R. COMMONS in the decades prior to the New Deal and carried on thereafter to the 1950s by Professor Selig Perlman.

Underlying all his work was an intellectual interest in what he often called 'the labor problem'. One of his favourite questions to students was: 'Do unions cause labour problems or do labour problems cause unions?' His answer was that both were true statements. Unions arose because employees needed collective strength to represent their interests at work, but, once created, the institutional needs of unions and the politics inside both union and employer bargaining organizations added additional issues and conflicts to the employment relationship.

While most of his writing focused on explaining or interpreting how labour and management structures and processes evolved, Barbash was most influential in laying out the normative premises for what industrial relations as an intellectual field of study and as a profession should strive to achieve. He chose, for example, to address the issue of 'values' in industrial relations in his 1980 presidential address to the Industrial Relations Research Association:

In a liberal society, the business of industrial relations is more than technique and know-how. It is also the values to which technique and know-how are directed. Equity, due process, fairness, rights, reasonableness, participation, incentive, alienation, privacy, democracy, self-determination, good faith, mutual survival, incrementalism, pragmatism, job satisfaction, order – these are some of the values that our field

has embedded into the practice of collective bargaining.

(Barbash 1980: 7)

His election to the presidency of the Association of Evolutionary Economics served to recognize Barbash's standing as one of the leading 'institutional' economists of his generation. Institutional economists seek to analyse the interplay of market forces with structural, political and legal factors, and use a blend of historical and empirical techniques to analyse economic events. Barbash was at his best when analysing and writing about how labour institutions fit with and evolved in democratic societies and capitalist economies.

Barbash was as well known for his considerable teaching and oratorical skills as for his writing. His courses on capitalism and socialism, trade unionism and industrial relations theory were sought out by generations of students at the University of Wisconsin, and have been replicated by faculty at other leading universities throughout the country. His educational impact, reaching far beyond Wisconsin, is perhaps his greatest and most lasting legacy.

BIBLIOGRAPHY

Barbash, Jack (1948) *Labor Unions in Action*, New York: Harper and Brothers.
——— (1956) *The Practice of Unionism*, New York: Harper and Row.
——— (ed.) (1959) *Unions and Union Leadership: Their Human Meaning*, New York: Harper and Row.
——— (1961) *Labor's Grass Roots*, New York: Harper and Row.
——— (1964) 'The Elements of Industrial Relations', *The British Journal of Industrial Relations* 2 (March): 66–78.
——— (1980) 'Values in Industrial Relations: The Case of the Adversary Principle', in B. Dennis (ed.), *Proceedings of the Thirty-second Annual Meeting of the Industrial Relations Research Association*, Madison, WI: Industrial

Relations Research Association, 1–9.
Barbash, Jack (1985) *The Elements of Industrial Relations*, Madison, WI: University of Wisconsin Press.

TK

BARNARD, Chester Irving (1886–1961)

Chester Irving Barnard was born in Malden, a provincial town in the vicinity of Boston, Massachusetts on 7 November 1886, the son of a mechanic. He died in New York on 7 June 1961. When he was five years old his mother, Mary Putnam Barnard, passed away, and Barnard was taken in by his maternal grandfather, a goldsmith. The family was poor but cultured and there was always a warm atmosphere full of music and philosophy. This environment exercised great influence over Barnard. His father remarried, and later a half-sister was born.

Since his father was unable to afford to send his son to higher education, Barnard worked for a piano factory in the neighbouring town of Lynn after he graduated from grammar school. While working in the factory, he mastered the skills of piano tuning. As well as working in the factory, he studied hard and was later admitted to Mount Hermon School on a scholarship thanks to his good marks. In 1906 Barnard went to Harvard University to study economics. While at university he also took on various part-time jobs including managing a dance band, piano tuning and translation. Although he had obtained almost all of the credits required for graduation before he became a senior, Barnard left Harvard University in 1909 without finishing his degree. He asked his uncle to introduce him to a family acquaintance, W.S. Gifford, then chief of statistics of AT&T. Through Gifford he got a job with the company's statistics department with a weekly salary of $11.50.

Barnard's first work was the translation of foreign documents concerning telephone charges. He soon became a commercial engineer, and came to be regarded as the most proficient expert in the Bell System owing to his study of telephone charges. He was then transferred to a managerial job. In 1922 he was appointed assistant to the vice-president and general manager of Pennsylvania Bell Telephone Company. In 1926 he was promoted to the post of vice-president in charge of sales. In 1927 he assumed the post of the first president of New Jersey Bell Telephone Company, and remained in this post for twenty-one years until retiring in 1948.

Barnard, who was highly public spirited, also engaged in many unpaid public activities. In the 1930s he was appointed head of the local public utility company in New Jersey. In October 1931, during the Great Depression, he organized New Jersey's Emergency Relief Administration at the request of the state's governor. During the Second World War, in 1941 he assumed the post of special adviser of the Secretary of Finance, and from 1942 to 1945 was chairman of the United Service Organization, which was organized by volunteers for the purpose of providing various services to the soldiers fighting at the front. In 1946 he was appointed adviser to the American delegation to the United Nations Atomic Power Committee, and he served as a member of the president's ad hoc committee concerning the unification of the governmental medical service. In 1948, after resigning from the presidency of New Jersey Bell Telephone, Barnard assumed the post of director-general of the Rockefeller Foundation.

While president of New Jersey Bell Telephone, Barnard was on friendly terms with many academic researchers. Taking up the sociology of Vilfredo Pareto as a common interest, he came to be friendly with the biochemist L.J.

Henderson. It was Henderson's influence that led Barnard to write his major book. The Lowell Institute at Harvard University held open classes every year, and Henderson recommended Barnard as a lecturer to the president, A. Lawrence Lowell, who was looking for a speaker for the year 1937. Barnard was invited to give a series of eight lectures in November–December 1937. The manuscripts for these lectures were arranged and published under the title *The Functions of the Executive* (1938).

Barnard felt that the research on organization and management which had been conducted up until that time was not in accord with his own business experiences. He made up his mind to construct a new theory as an action analysis of organizations based on a realistic human model. He denied the validity of conventional management theory, which held that humans are driven by economic motives to take actions rationally in order to achieve the maximum realization of benefit to themselves. Replacing this unrealistic understanding of humans, called the 'economic man model', Barnard placed instead at the basis of his theory a human figure who has his or her own intentions and psychological factors (i.e. a variety of motives), and makes decision and takes actions on his or her own responsibility even though he or she is subjected to many restraints.

To realize their goals, people often develop cooperative relationships with each other. An individual person requires that his or her own abilities be enhanced in order to realize his or her purpose and as a strategic decision, chooses cooperation with other people as a method of achieving that purpose. This is often seen throughout society. However, such cooperation can take different forms. Barnard defines cooperation generated in this manner as a system of physical, biological, personal and social components, which are in a specific systematic relationship by reason of the cooperation of two or more persons for at least one definite end.

The only factor common to the various kinds of concrete cooperative system we experience, says Barnard, is organization. That is to say, when all the concrete and specific elements possessed by a cooperative system are removed, the element which remains is a system of various kinds of force in concert with each other. In this sense, organization is a system of consciously coordinated activities or forces of two or more persons. It is a construct analogous to the field of gravity or electromagnetic field. This system is invisible, but it certainly exists.

An organization comes into existence when (1) there are persons able to communicate with each other; (2) those persons are willing to contribute action; and (3) they wish to accomplish a common purpose. These are necessary and sufficient conditions for the formation of the organization.

The problem as to whether the formed organization can remain continuously in existence depends on whether the double equilibrium of the organization as a system can be maintained. The organization, which is a system constituted by various kinds of forces, will come to a rupture unless, first, an equilibrium can be brought about *between* the system and its external environment, and, second, internal equilibrium can be maintained concurrently *within* the system. This internal equilibrium is the balance of the elements of organization; the communications which link the common purpose of the cooperative activity with the organization's members' willingness to make their personal contributions are particularly important. The external equilibrium of the organization, on the other hand, is the result of the effectiveness and efficiency of the organization. The *effectiveness* of the organization resides in the adequacy of organizational purpose, and therefore can be defined as the organization's ability to accomplish that purpose. Accordingly, effectiveness is founded in a technological sense on the rationality of the measures chosen for achieving that purpose. The *efficiency* of the organization, on the other hand, depends on the degree of satisfaction derived by the members of the organization from making their personal contribution and the incentives which they have to work. Even if organizational effectiveness is strong, organizational members' willingness to contribute cannot be maintained if the realization of the common purpose does not result simultaneously in the satisfaction of their own needs and the meeting of their own personal goals. If this does not happen, the organization as a cooperative system is unable to obtain the required level of contributive activity from its members, and thus begins to decline, finally becoming extinct. Therefore, if the organization is to continue in existence, it is necessary to maintain these two equilibria simultaneously.

The alignment of the various forces involved in cooperative activity so as to maintain dual equilibrium, and thus the organizational system as a whole, is the function of the executive. The work of the executive relates to the elements of the organization in its content, and is comprised of the following: (1) establishment and maintenance of a communication system; (2) promotion of incentives to all organizational members so that they work to achieve cooperation; and (3) the development and articulation of the organization's common purpose. Within the organization, a variety of desires, ideals, values and so on are held by its members. Unless these differing views can be aligned with a unified and settled set of overall organizational values, no effective organizational activity can be carried out; neither the effectiveness nor the efficiency of the organization can be realized. Leaders within the executive function must make decisions concerning the selection standards to which the organization's members must conform when they make organizational choices. Barnard insists that this is a moral aspect of leadership, and that the responsibility imposed on the executive is not to subject employees to reprimand, but gradually to establish an adequate criterion of value judgement for organizational behaviour.

Barnard's theory emphasizes the scientific analysis of organizational behaviour by placing importance on the choices that are involved in organizational activity and decision making. This new approach to the organization as a system made possible many new developments within the science of business administration. In this sense, Barnard can truly be said to be a giant who opened up the frontiers of the study of modern business organizations.

BIBLIOGRAPHY
Barnard, C.I. (1938) *The Functions of the Executive*, Cambridge, MA: Harvard University Press.
—— (1948) *Organization and Management: Selected Papers by Chester I. Barnard*, Cambridge, MA: Harvard University Press.
Iino H. (1978) *Barnard Kenkyu: Sono Soshiki to Kanri no Riron* (Study on Barnard: His Theory of Organization and Management), Tokyo: Bunshindo.
Katoh, K. (1996) *Barnard to Henderson: The Functions of the Executive no Keisei Katei* (Barnard and Henderson: The Formation Process of *The Functions of the Executive*), Tokyo: Bunshindo.
Wolf, W.B. (1972) *Conversation with Chester I. Barnard*, Ithaca, NY: Cornell University Press.
—— (1974) *The Basic Barnard: An Introduction to Chester I. Barnard and His Theories of Organization and Management*, Ithaca, NY: NYSSILR.
Wolf, W.B. and Iino H. (eds) (1986) *Philosophy for Managers: Selected Papers of C. I. Barnard*, Tokyo: Bunshindo.

ST

BARNUM, Phineas Taylor (1810–91)

Barnum was born in Bethel, Connecticut on 5 July 1810. He died on 7 April 1891 at his home in Bridgeport, Connecticut, following a stroke. After the death of his father, a local tavern-keeper, in 1825 Barnum worked as a store clerk to support his family and then went into business for himself, running a store, selling lottery tickets and editing a newspaper. He married Charity Hallett in 1829 and the couple settled permanently in New York, where they kept a boarding house.

In the 1830s Barnum made several attempts to break into show business, managing travelling shows and circuses. All the ventures failed, usually because they were poorly capitalized. His breakthrough came at the end of 1841 when he bought Scudder's American Museum, a fixed-site attraction on Broadway in New York. Barnum saw his opportunity: New York was growing rapidly, and its citizens lacked opportunities for entertainment. The Museum, a collection of stuffed animals and curios, was renamed Barnum's American Museum, and greatly expanded to include such attractions as ventriloquists, living statuary, educated dogs, music and dancing, jugglers, giants, dwarves, panoramas and dioramas of famous scenes such as Niagara Falls, and 'the first English Punch and Judy in this country' (Barnum 1889: 57).

Thanks to Barnum's flair for advertising, the attraction was immediately successful. He then moved into theatrical management, managing the Swedish singing star Jenny Lind and the midget entertainer General Tom Thumb. In 1865 he launched a new travelling circus, much larger and more successful than previous attempts. When his circus's success was challenged by a competitor, owned by James Bailey, Barnum's response was to suggest a merger; the result, Barnum and Bailey's Circus, married Barnum's marketing flair with Bailey's organizing abilities, and dominated the market into the twentieth century. Barnum continued to tour with the circus until well into his seventies; by this time his fame was such that he himself was one of the star attractions of the show.

As a marketer, Barnum did not conduct research into customer needs and then set out to meet them; instead, he designed products and then worked tirelessly to stimulate demand, using every available form of promotion. As he says, 'I often seized upon an opportunity by instinct, even before I had a very definite conception as to how it should be used, and it seemed, somehow, to mature itself and serve my purpose' (Barnum 1889: 57). His instincts told him that publicity was often cheaper and more effective than advertising, and he cultivated newspaper editors such as Horace Greeley in hopes of placing favourable stories; but he could turn even bad publicity to his benefit. His primary aim was volume business, and he frequently undercut competitors in order to gain a larger share of the market.

Barnum's showmanship, which often verged on self-parody, became in the end an attraction in itself, rather as some modern advertisements become as famous as the products they promote.

Barnum pioneered many of the techniques used in modern marketing, especially publicity and below-the-line promotions. He is often accused of cynicism – the phrase 'there's a sucker born every minute' is attributed to him – but he himself believed that he was neither more nor less dishonest than any business person: he once asked, 'In what business is there not humbug?' (Werner 1923: 274).

BIBLIOGRAPHY

Barnum, P.T. (1889) *Struggles and Triumphs, or, Sixty Years' Recollections of P.T. Barnum, Including His Golden Rules for Money-Making*, Buffalo, NY: The Courier Company.

Werner, M.R. (1923) *Barnum*, New York: Harcourt, Brace and Co.

MLW

BARTH, Carl George Lange (1860–1939)

Carl George Lange Barth was born in Christiana, Norway on 28 February 1860 and died in Philadelphia on 28 October 1939. After technical training at the Horten Technical School, an apprenticeship at the Navy Yard at Oslo and a period of teaching mathematics, he emigrated to the United States in 1881. From 1881 to 1895 he worked for the machine tool maker William Sellers and Company in Philadelphia, rising from draughtsman to chief designer. From 1895 to 1897 he worked as a draughtsman and designer in St Louis, and from 1897 to 1899 as an instructor in mathematics with the International Correspondence Schools and then the Ethical Culture School in New York. In 1899 he was invited by Frederick W. TAYLOR to join the latter's team at Bethlehem Steel Company, where his strong mathematical abilities helped Taylor solve a number of problems which had confronted his production system. His technical accomplishments there included the design of the Barth slide-rule and the formula of twelve variables which was incorporated into Taylor's *Shop Management* (1903).

Leaving Bethlehem in 1901, when Taylor and his followers were dismissed shortly before the takeover of the firm by Charles M. SCHWAB, Barth became a consulting engineer, working with Taylor and his team at several other factories, notably the Link-Belt Company in Philadelphia, and, with Horace HATHAWAY, at the Tabor Manufacturing Co. Within the team, Barth became known as the 'systems man' who would implement the systems Taylor designed, working out the technical bugs as he did so. He was noted for his attention to detail and strong technical abilities, and frequently designed the machinery to support Taylor's production systems.

Barth was an early supporter of Harvard Business School and its first dean, Edwin GAY; he was the first of the Taylor team to lecture there, and held a formal post as lecturer on scientific management from 1911 to 1916 and from 1919 to 1922. From 1914 to 1916 he also lectured on scientific management at the University of Chicago. He retired in 1923. Without Barth's technical genius, Taylor's system would have had much less impact and been less effective.

BIBLIOGRAPHY
Drury, H.B. (1915) *Scientific Management*, New York: Columbia University Press.
Urwick, L.F. (ed.) (1956) *The Golden Book of Management*, London: Newman Neame.

BEDAUX, Charles Eugéne (1886–1944)

Charles Eugéne Bedaux was born in Paris on 11 April 1886 into a lower middle-class family. He committed suicide in a US military prison on 18 February 1944 while awaiting trial on charges of treason. Details of his early career are patchy, and little is known about his education or early work; Ungar (1997) suggests he may have been involved in running a brothel in his late teens. At the age of twenty he emigrated to the United States, where his first job was as a construction worker digging tunnels for the New York City subway. He subsequently became a salesman, selling everything from life insurance to toothpaste.

In his late twenties, Bedaux moved to Grand Rapids, Michigan, where he took a job with a furniture manufacturer. Studying the movements of the workers, he hit upon a way of improving the accuracy of productivity and performance measurement in the workplace. His system was in essence an improvement on earlier systems of performance measurement developed by Frederick W. TAYLOR and Sanford THOMPSON. The latter's time study method involved breaking each job into its smallest components and then measuring the standard times required to achieve each component to create a total time required for the job. However, this system had been heavily criticized, not least for failing to take into account the effect of worker fatigue on performance (Kessler 1998).

Bedaux, like other observers, noticed that as workers became tired, their performance declined and standard tasks took longer. Giving workers rest breaks also tended to distort the picture, as it was not clear how much rest was needed to achieve optimal performance. Bedaux's solution was to factor the required time for rest into the task time. He developed what he called a 'relaxation curve', a tool for measuring the amount of rest employees required to achieve optimum task performance. With the rest period factored into the work, tasks could now be broken down into universal units or 'B units' (also sometimes known as 'work units' or 'allowed minutes') by which productivity could be measured and standards set. Bedaux also used the B-unit method to form a rating system for bonuses; workers who performed tasks faster than the minimum B-unit requirement had their speed of work measured and were then paid bonuses proportional to how far they exceeded this floor level.

Kessler (1998) notes that the Bedaux system had considerable advantages over earlier systems. One of the most important of these was that it could be applied across and between departments. By paying bonuses based on workers' ability to perform tasks rather than on the actual task (as in piecework systems), firms could apply the same system universally rather than having to develop new systems for each workshop or department. However, the system was highly complex and this, says Kessler, led to two disadvantages: first, the system was difficult to implement correctly, and second, workers found it difficult to understand the rationale behind the system and to know whether they were being treated fairly. Both these problems led to worker unrest in many plants where the Bedaux system was introduced.

Nonetheless, the promise of a standardized system which could be implemented across the board held great appeal for many companies, and Bedaux's persuasive salesmanship may have helped. He established his first consultancy firm in Cleveland, Ohio, advising firms on how to implement his system, and rapidly built up a network of consultancies across the United States and then in Europe. During the 1930s as many as 1,000 firms were using the Bedaux system around the world. Curiously, given earlier resistance to the scientific management movement, the system was particularly popular in Britain, where it was adopted by firms such as ICI and Lucas, which were already dominated by strong centralizing managements. Many of these firms suffered from severe labour disruption as a result, but it is difficult to assign blame for this entirely to Bedaux; his original idea seems to have been genuinely motivated by a desire to be fair to both workers and employers. He cannot be held solely to blame for the failures in execution of the system, although his consultants were usually involved in the initial application.

Although he had become an American citizen and had married an American, Bedaux returned to France in 1927, a wealthy man. He bought a sixteenth-century chateau, and became the darling of Parisian society. Among his friends was the Prince of Wales, who briefly became King Edward VIII and then abdicated to become Duke of Windsor; the Duke married Mrs Wallis Simpson at Bedaux's chateau. Among the more bizarre events of his life was the Charles E. Bedaux Sub-Arctic Expedition of 1934, when Bedaux attempted to pioneer an overland route through the wilderness from Edmonton, Alberta to Telegraph Creek, British Columbia and ultimately to Alaska. Expedition members included Bedaux himself, his wife, his mistress, several surveyors and a Hollywood cinematographer; supplies included large quantities of champagne, caviar and ball gowns for the ladies. Plagued by equipment failures, the 'Champagne Expedition' had to be abandoned before it reached its destination.

Bedaux's ideas on workplace efficiency had broadened into a more general technocratic philosophy, and he became an advocate of the application of scientific methods to social and political control. This led him into increasing involvement with right-wing politics. According to Kessler, 'he had a strong sense of mission, believing that poverty could be eradicated if production was organized on his methods and that an efficient society could be created if led by engineers and technocrats' (1998: 53). After the fall of France in 1940 he served as a technical adviser to the Vichy government and also to the occupying Nazi regime in northern France. In 1942 he went to North Africa where he began work on a project to lay a pipeline across the Sahara desert, and was captured by Allied forces at the end of the year. Still a US citizen, he was charged with treason and flown back to the United States, but took an overdose of barbiturates before he could be brought to trial. Conspiracy theorists continue to believe that he was murdered by the FBI, for motives unknown.

BIBLIOGRAPHY
Kessler, I. (1998) 'Bedaux, Charles E.', in M. Warner (ed.) *IEBM Handbook of Management Thinking*, London: International Thomson Business Press, 53–6.
Ungar, G. (1997) *The Champagne Expedition*, Ottawa: National Film Board.

MLW

BELL, Alexander Graham (1847–1922)

Alexander Graham Bell was born in Edinburgh on 3 March 1847, the son of Melville and Eliza Bell. He died in Baddek, Nova Scotia on 2 August 1922. He married Mabel Hubbard in 1877. Bell studied anatomy and physiology at the University of London, and became very much involved in the study if deafness; both his mother and wife were deaf (he met his wife while teaching at the Boston School for Deaf Mutes, where she was a pupil), and he was a friend of Helen Keller. His family moved to Boston in 1870 after the death of a brother and a sister from tuberculosis, and Bell became a professor of physiology at Boston University. He also began conducting experiments with sound apparatus, initially in hopes of developing a hearing aid. In this he was not successful, but he did discover a method of transmitting sound via electric signal over wires, and on 7 March 1876 was granted a patent for a telephone transmitter; the first successful transmission was made only a few days later, in Boston.

Bell continued to develop his telephones with experiments in Boston and Brantford, Ontario, where his parents had settled. The Bell Telephone Company was founded in 1877, although Bell himself took little part in running it; much of the work in bringing the telephone to a broader commercial market was done by Theodore VAIL and also by Bell's rival Thomas EDISON, who had also been working on a telephone and who now made a number of improvements to Bell's design. Bell himself went on to patent a number of other devices, including the photophone, a device for transmitting sound on a beam of light, and techniques for teaching speech to the deaf. In 1885 he settled on Cape Breton Island, Nova Scotia, and there took up an interest in designing aircraft; the *Silver Dart*, designed by Bell and Glenn H. Curtiss, and piloted by J.A.D. McCurdy, became the second successful powered aircraft design after the *Flyer* of Orville and Wilbur

Wright, and marked the beginning of Canadian aviation.

Bell was not a manager *per se*, although he appreciated the enormous commercial significance of telephones. His approach to the telephone, as to the aeroplane and his work with the deaf, centred around his belief in the value and importance of communication. The ability to communicate was essential in any sphere, personal, social or commercial, and his life's work was devoted to improving communication by whatever means.

BELL, Daniel (1919–)

Daniel Bell was born Daniel Bolotsky in Brooklyn, New York on 10 May 1919, of Eastern European Jewish parentage. His early years were harsh and painful: his father died when he was six months old, and his mother had to work in a factory and placed him in a day orphanage.

Like many in his community, during the 1930s Bell was attracted to socialism, having joined the Young People's Socialist League in 1932, at the precocious age of thirteen. Several years later he entered the City College of New York, graduating with a BSc degree in 1938. By this time he was a very articulate young spokesman for socialism in a country where the ideology had little appeal, particularly with the coming of Franklin Roosevelt's New Deal after the latter's election in 1933.

Bell continued writing for the socialist *New Leader*, serving as its editor between 1941 and 1945, and then writing for *Fortune* magazine between 1948 and 1956. Here he applied his knowledge of sociology to labour and business issues. After a brief sojourn in Paris with the Congress for Cultural Freedom, Bell entered the graduate programme in sociology at Columbia University in the autumn of 1957. Earning his doctorate in 1960, he then taught sociology at Columbia until 1969, when he moved to Harvard.

By the 1950s Bell had moved a long way from his youthful socialism. In 1960, he published his first noteworthy book, *The End of Ideology*. At a time when John F. Kennedy and Richard Nixon were running for the presidency of the United States on virtually identical platforms, Bell saw a Western world in which class war and class ideologies were things of the past and welfare capitalism worked in harmony with the public sector. Marxism, discredited by de-Stalinization and the Hungarian Revolution of 1956, was now irrelevant in the United States, where workers had company pensions, mowed their lawns in Levittown, and drove Chevrolets and Fords. However, Bell's 'end of ideology' argument was premature, for an anarchist and ecological left and a libertarian, populist right plunged the 1960s into turmoil. The 1972 US presidential campaign between Nixon and South Dakota Senator George McGovern was sharply polarized.

Bell was a noted futurist, and served on the Presidential Commission on the Year 2000, where he published his next major work. *The Coming of Post-industrial Society: A Venture in Social Forecasting* (1973) was a landmark. Bell defined a postindustrial society as one in which most of its work force operated in the tertiary or service sector. The concept began to germinate in Bell's mind as early as the 1950s, when his articles in *Fortune* dealt with the rise of service industries. Bell drew on the work of sociologist Colin Clark's *The Conditions of Economic Progress* (1940), which divided economies into primary (agricultural), secondary (industrial), and tertiary (service) sectors. Bell first used the term 'post-industrial' in a lecture in the summer of 1959 in Salzburg, and in 1962 he published a paper for the Boston Forum on 'The Post-industrial Society: A Speculative View of the United States in 1985 and Beyond'.

The Coming of Post-industrial Society opened with a discussion of some predictions of Bell's original mentor, Karl Marx. The Marx that Bell discussed, however, was not that of volume 1 of *Das Kapital* but that of the posthumous volume 3. Here Marx's writings, edited by Friedrich Engels, predicted the separation of ownership from control in the management of enterprises and the rise of a white-collar administrative class larger than the working class. Bell saw the prophecies of the late Marx as much more applicable than the earlier ones, given that the class war predicted in the *Communist Manifesto* of 1848 had not taken place. In the early 1970s, Africa and Asia still employed 70 per cent of their labour force in the primary sector, while Western Europe, the Soviet Union and Japan employed a majority in the secondary sector. Only in the United States had the postindustrial society arrived, with a majority (60 per cent) of the work force in the tertiary sector.

Postindustrial society was also characterized by the primacy of professionals, technocrats and theoretical knowledge. 'Industrial society', wrote Bell, 'is the coordination of machines and men for the production of goods. Post-industrial society is organized around knowledge ...' (Bell 1973: 20). He argued that economies in the twentieth century operated by trying to predict and plan the future. The First World War had inaugurated an era in which applied science and technology began to assume a major economic and social role. John Maynard Keynes provided a theory as to how government could fine tune the business cycle, and computers and statistics provided the tools and models as to how this could be done. Technological change in the nineteenth century was often unplanned, but that of the twenty-first century would be anticipated and even planned. Business productivity and profits became more dependent upon conscious theoretical knowledge. If United States Steel represented the ideal corporation of the 1920s, General Motors represented that of the 1950s, and International Business Machines (IBM) that of the 1970s.

In the remainder of the book, Bell elaborates upon the uniqueness of postindustrial society and the changes in occupations that characterize it. Focusing upon the importance of knowledge and technology, Bell predicted that the corporation would remain the dominant form of business organization through to the year 2000. In place of the old divisions between capitalism and socialism, he saw a tension between 'economizing' and 'sociologizing' modes in both systems. The former stressed short-term profits and efficiency while the latter looked at broader criteria. The main conflict in this new kind of society would be that between the new technocratic elite and the more populist masses: 'Now wealth, power, and status are not dimensions of class, but values sought or gained by classes' (Bell 1973: 43). The new leaders of society would be scientists, professors, programmers and engineers rather than steel-makers or manufacturers.

Bell looked at some of the cultural implications of the new economic order in his next major work, *The Cultural Contradictions of Capitalism* (1976). Here Bell reversed the Marxist idea that economics determines culture. Instead, Bell argued, there was now a radical tension between society and art. Society was ruled by economic efficiency and logic, while in the arts the self and what appealed to it were taken as the basis for value. *The Cultural Contradictions of Capitalism* drew its name from the paradox of a society grown wealthy from the virtues of hard work and self-denial, which then repudiated these virtues. The revolt against the Puritan work ethic, however, was not a recent development; it went back to the eve of the First World War. Nineteenth-century USA was a place of hardworking farmers and town merchants ruled by self-discipline and strong moral codes. By 1913, a new cultural elite, in a country grown prosperous from these very virtues, began to attack them. Walter Lippmann (1889–1974), John Reed (1887–1920) and Van Wyck Brooks (1886–1963) spearheaded this attack upon

Victorianism. Affluent young bohemians settled in Greenwich Village and San Francisco, reading Marx, Friedrich Wilhelm Nietzsche and Sigmund Freud, promoting birth control, free love, homosexuality and the rights of African-Americans and immigrants. Self-expression replaced self-discipline.

The unprecedented affluence of the 1920s, with its New Era capitalism based upon the automobile, encouraged the spread of this new ethic of hedonism, which was a consumption rather than a production ethic. According to Bell 'A consumption society was emerging, with its emphasis on spending and material possessions, and it was undermining the traditional value system, with its emphasis on thrift, frugality, self-control, and impulse renunciation' (Bell 1976: 64–5). The cinema provided new role models for youth, with new, more libertine and materialistic values; the automobile offered a private sanctum for sexual experimentation away from parents and local moralists.

The Great Depression and the Second World War slowed the trend to the consumption ethic, but it returned with a vengeance to dominate US culture in the affluent 1950s and 1960s. Nowhere was this more evident than in the individualistic lifestyle of southern California. A 'fun' morality, largely sexually oriented and an obsession with self-esteem, said Bell, had replaced virtue, but this had left capitalism with no restraining ethic. The US business ethic was no longer work and produce, but consume and enjoy. This was demonstrated by the growth of businesses in photography, travel, fashion and especially entertainment. Bell even saw the theory of Marshall McLuhan that 'the medium is the message', that form is more important than content, as another indicator of the temper of the age. For Bell, the 1960s counter-culture was far from a rebellion but merely an extension of the hedonism of the 1950s, an attack upon values that had faded decades before. Religion and morality were replaced by psychology.

All of this, Bell insisted, stemmed from the very contradictions of a capitalism that seemed to be digging its own grave not by any economic contradictions, as Marx had envisioned, but by the fact that it produced the very affluence that undermined its own work ethic:

On the one hand, the business corporation wants an individual to work hard, pursue a career, accept delayed gratification – to be, in the crude sense, an organization man. And yet, in its products and its advertisements, the corporation promotes pleasure, instant joy, relaxing, and letting go.

(Bell 1976: 71–2)

In 1999, Bell, now a Harvard professor emeritus, published a third edition of *The Coming of Post-industrial Society*, with a new foreword of over seventy pages. In it, he updated his tentative vision of a dawning postindustrial age. Bell observed that his term was now a part of the common language; political leaders now used it frequently. In 1973 the United States had been the only postindustrial country, but now Britain, Japan and most of Western Europe had joined the United States. Bell now saw the economy divided into *five* sectors: (1) primary: agriculture, (2) secondary: industry, (3) tertiary: transport and utilities, (4) quaternary: trade and finance, and (5) quinary: health and education. Postindustrial technology was being organized around microprocessors instead of motors. Economic geography had in the past determined where businesses located. With communication and knowledge becoming all-important, businesses would now cluster around universities and suburbs, not mines, rivers and cities. Considerations of time now overshadowed those of space. Markets 'are no longer places but networks', being everywhere at the same time when millions of pounds and dollars can move across borders with the click of a mouse (Bell 1999: xlvii). Bell found that in the postindustrial world, developing nations, such as those of Africa, which were living by exports of food and raw materials would be in serious trouble, for new technologies would eliminate demand in their markets. In the new global economy, each country was losing control over its currency and maybe even its culture as private global television networks such as the Cable News Network (CNN) rivalled state and national ones. Tastes and entertainment were becoming international. Postindustrial society, argued Bell, had also spawned a new knowledge class which was not conservative so much as libertarian, and a labour force in which women composed fully half of the managerial class.

Unlike Marx, Bell has abhorred violent revolution and radical socialist solutions. He has nevertheless sought to do for the late twentieth century what Karl Marx did for the nineteenth. He wished to present a comprehensive theory relating economic and social change. In this he succeeded, becoming the leading interpreter of the postindustrial age.

BIBLIOGRAPHY

Bell, D. (1973) *The Coming of Post-industrial Society, A Venture in Social Forecasting*, New York: Basic Books.
—— (1976) *The Cultural Contradictions of Capitalism*, New York: Basic Books.
—— (1999) 'The Axial Age of Technology, Foreword: 1999', in *The Coming of Post-industrial Society, A Venture in Social Forecasting*, 3rd edn, New York: Basic Books, ix–lxxxv.
'Bell, Daniel' (1999) *McGraw-Hill Encyclopedia of World Biography*, Detroit, MI: Gale Research Inc., vol. 2, 132–3.
Clark, C. (1940) *The Conditions of Economic Progress*, London: Macmillan.

DCL

BENIGER, James R. (1946–)

James Beniger was born in Sheboygan, Wiconsin on 16 December 1946. He graduated with a BA *magna cum laude* from Harvard University in 1969, then took his master's degree from the University of California at Berkeley in 1973 and his Ph.D. from the same institution in 1978. After completing his BA he worked as a journalist for several years, as a staff writer for the *Wall Street Journal* and later, briefly, with the *Minneapolis Star*. He has taught sociology at Princeton and Yale Universities, and is currently associate professor of communications and sociology at the University of Southern California. In 1989 he advised the then Soviet Academy of Sciences on the 'informatization' of the Russian economy. He married Kay Ferdinandsen in 1984; they have two children.

A sociologist who writes on issues such as communication and globalization, Beniger has also had an influence on modern management thinking, particularly relating to issues such as information and control. In his major work, *The Control Revolution* (1986), Beniger advances the view that modern society is dominated by institutions which aim to achieve control. These institutions include among them business corporations and other commercial organizations. One way in which control is exercised is through the control of the flow of information. By altering or stopping up information flows, one of the key components of modern society, institutions can achieve greater control over constituent groups such as customers, employees and society at large. As these large institutions are the only organizations with the power to affect information flows in this way, it is logical that they will achieve more control as time passes.

Beniger's work has echoes of earlier control theories, notably that advanced by James BURNHAM, although Beniger is more concerned with the means of control than the motives for it. It is notable, however, that in an age when many theorists argue that more information means more freedom and competitiveness in markets, Beniger is suggesting that it might actually mean less.

BIBLIOGRAPHY
Beniger, J.R. (1983) *Trafficking in Drug Users: Professional Exchange Networks in the Control of Deviance*, Cambridge: Cambridge University Press.
—— (1986) *The Control Revolution: Technological and Economic Origins of the Information Society*, Cambridge, MA: Harvard University Press.

BENNETT, James Gordon (1795–1872)

James Gordon Bennett was born in Keith, Scotland 1 September 1795. He died in New York City, following a stroke on 1 June 1872. After emigrating to New England, he spent some twenty years working as a journalist in Boston, Charleston and New York. In 1832 he started his own newspaper, the New York *Globe*, but this soon failed. In 1835 he tried again, with capital of $500 and an office in a basement on Wall Street, from where he launched the New York *Herald*. This paper survived and flourished, and ultimately made Bennett, its owner and editor for nearly four decades, a very wealthy man.

In New York in the 1830s there were many newspapers, mostly with small circulations and usually owned by competing business and/or political interests; their primary purpose was to serve as propaganda organs for their owners. Bennett's innovation was to see the news, and more particularly newspapers, as a commodity that could be sold like any other. The *Herald* formula had two ingredients. First, Bennett aimed to print news of events, rather than opinions of political elites, and his paper was therefore independent of the establishment of the day. Second, he printed the news that he thought ordinary people wanted to read: 'sin, science, and sensation' (Huntzicker 1999: 15). In 1836, the paper closely followed the police investigation into the murder of a prostitute, reporting the entire affair in graphic detail. Among the journalistic innovations were reports of interviews with police and detectives and eyewitness accounts of the murder scene. Circulation soared.

Bennett's press was dubbed 'yellow journalism', and in 1840 the other New York papers launched the so-called 'Moral War', attempting to drive Bennett out of business through pressure of public opinion. He defended himself so vigorously in print that circulation of his paper actually went up. Bennett had realized that the fierce struggle between the papers was actually expanding the market, as the furore over the Moral War led more and more people to buy papers.

More than any other editor of his generation, Bennett understood the power of the press. He once wrote: 'A newspaper can send more souls to Heaven, and save more from Hell, than all the churches or chapels in New York – and make money at the same time' (Mott 1941: 232). A curious mix of moral crusader, populist journalist and hard-headed businessman, Bennett knew that his paper's survival depended on its continually being able to report more and better news than its rivals. In 1862, during the American Civil War, the paper published a complete order of battle of the Confederate Army. This caused a sensation in New York, and Bennett was investigated as a possible Confederate spy; in fact, his reporters had pieced together the information from Southern newspapers smuggled into New York. Bennett was also the first to employ 'celebrity' writers such as Mark Twain, and was a great spotter of journalistic talent; it was Bennett who gave Henry Stanley his first break in journalism. By 1870 he had made the *Herald* the most successful newspaper in North America, through a combination of shrewd knowledge of his market, careful attention to detail in his product, and the ability to extract the best from those who worked for him. By doing so, he revolutionized journalism, and became the prototype of media barons such as William Randolph HEARST and Joseph PULITZER.

Bennett's son, also James Gordon Bennett (1841–1918), took over the management of the *Herald* in his father's later years. It was the younger Bennett who gave Stanley the cryptic order 'Go and find Livingstone!', which made Stanley's career and arguably changed the course of African history. He was an autocratic and domineering man who, unlike his father, would not delegate management; he once asked for a list of staff who were believed to be indispensable and, on receiving the list, summarily dismissed the lot, commenting that: 'On my newspaper, no one is indispensable.' He nevertheless ran the *Herald* competently until the early years of the twentieth century, when his own powers began to fail and he lost control of the paper, which soon after merged with the *Tribune*.

BIBLIOGRAPHY

Carlson, O. (1942) *The Man Who Made News*, New York: Duell, Sloan and Pearce.
Huntzicker, W. (1999) *The Popular Press, 1833–1865*, Westport, CT: Greenwood Press.
Mott, F.L. (1941) *American Journalism: A History of Newspapers in the United States through 250 Years*, New York: Macmillan.
Seitz, D.C. (1928) *The James Gordon Bennetts*, Indianapolis, IN: Bobbs-Merrill.

MLW

BENNIS, Warren (1925–)

Warren Bennis was born in New York City on 8 March 1925. After graduating from high school, Bennis served in the US Army from 1943–7. At the age of nineteen, he was one of the youngest infantry commanders to serve in the European theater during the Second World War, and was decorated with the Purple Heart and the Bronze Star. The lessons he learned in the army served him well, as it was the first organization that he was able to observe up close and in depth. Among these lessons were the effects of good and bad leadership upon morale, as well as the influence of command-and-control leadership and institutional bureaucracy.

After leaving the army, Bennis attended Antioch College from 1947 to 1951. Inspired by Antioch's progressive campus culture, Bennis wrote a series of satirical articles in the college literary magazine which were intended as challenges to the positions of more orthodox university figures. Douglas MCGREGOR, the president of Antioch College (1948–54), had a great influence on Bennis. McGregor came from Massachusetts Institute of Technology (MIT), where he had founded the industrial psychology department; in 1954 he returned to MIT, where he pioneered the study of human relations and organizational behavior.

In 1951 Bennis was admitted to MIT on the basis of his perfect academic record at Antioch and McGregor's letter of recommendation. After obtaining his Ph.D. in economics and social science, Bennis taught social psychology for a year (1955–6) as an assistant professor at MIT. Also in 1955, he was invited to Bethel, Maine, the summer headquarters of the National Training Laboratories (NTL). Founded by the psychologist Kurt LEWIN in 1947, NTL paved the way for intriguing research into a new social invention called T-groups (the T stood for training). Bennis learned much from leading empirical studies of the processes and outcomes emerging from T-groups. Later that year, he and Herbert

Shepard published two articles on 'natural groups' in *Human Relations*, in which they described the stages of group development (Bennis and Shepard 1956; Shepard and Bennis 1956).

Bennis left MIT in 1956 to take a position at Boston University for three years. He also conducted research and taught courses at Harvard University. He returned to MIT at Douglas McGregor's invitation in 1959. He served on the faculty of MIT's Sloan School of Management, and later succeeded McGregor as chairman of the Organizational Studies Department. With Ken Benne and Bob Chin, he produced his first book, a selection of readings entitled *The Planning of Change* (1961). He also published another book, *Interpersonal Dynamics: Essays and Readings on Human Interaction,* in collaboration with Edgar SCHEIN, Dave Berlew and Fritz Steele. From 1956 to 1967 his output was prodigious, including seventeen books and over 250 articles. He also consulted extensively as a leading organizational theorist and a pioneer in organization development.

In 1967 Bennis came to the State University of New York (SUNY) at Buffalo at the invitation and persuasive appeal of the incoming president, Martin Meyerson. He initially served as provost before assuming the roles of Vice President of Academic Development and Acting Executive Vice President of SUNY. During his tenure in these positions, Bennis learned a great deal, especially in regard to his thoughts about change. He learned that, to achieve and sustain change in an organization, the thoughts and beliefs of current members must be taken into account. He also realized that if a vision is not sustained by action, it is meaningless. In 1973, Bennis reflected on his experiences at SUNY-Buffalo in *The Leaning Ivory Tower*.

Bennis left Buffalo in 1971 to become president of the University of Cincinnati (1971–8). At the beginning of his tenure, he was disturbed by the tendency of routine work to divert his time and attention away from the more important non-routine work, such as creative planning and fundamental organizational change. He found that leaders of other institutions were bothered by the same problem. He resolved to be a president 'who led, not managed' (Bennis 1993: 31). In fact, Bennis was actively learning how to lead. From his experiences, he learned a number of important things about leaders and leadership, many of which were later captured in his book, *On Becoming a Leader* (1989). Thus, Bennis's experience as a real leader at both SUNY and Cincinnati helped him shape his thoughts about leadership. Witnessing at first hand the troubles that modern leaders encounter enabled him effectively to bridge the gap between leadership theory and practice in his subsequent writings.

Since 1979, Bennis has been a university professor and Distinguished Professor of Business Administration at the University of Southern California's (USC) Marshall School of Business. At USC, he has been able to consolidate what he learned 'about self-invention, about the importance of organization, about the nature of change, about the nature of leadership – and to find ways to communicate those lessons' (Bennis 1993: 35). In 1991 he became founding chairman of the Leadership Institute at USC. The institute has transformed the Marshall School into an intellectual centre for studying executive leadership. While the institute was the first of its kind in the United States, it has served as the prototype for some fifteen subsequent centres, including one at Harvard.

Bennis's influence has been profound. His contributions stem not from an analysis of what has already happened, but from his foresight into what may happen. In a landmark 1964 *Harvard Business Review* article, he and co-writer Philip Slater claimed that 'Democracy is Inevitable.' While this idea sounded outrageous at the time, it was supported in 1990 by the dramatic revolution of Eastern Europe and the demise of the Soviet Union. In 1966, Bennis published an article titled, 'The Coming Death of Bureaucracy', in which he argued that the old command-and-control, pyramidal organizational structures would be replaced by adaptive, rapidly changing temporary systems. His subsequent work – particularly *The Temporary Society* (1968), also co-authored with Phil Slater – explored new organizational forms. Bennis envisaged organizations as adhocracies – roughly the direct opposite of bureaucracies – freed from the shackles of hierarchy and meaningless paperwork.

In the 1980s, Bennis and others moved the study of leadership to a new stage. His book, *Leaders* (1985), co-authored with Burt Nanus, was a huge success. The authors argued that leadership is not a rare skill; leaders are made rather than born. Leaders are usually ordinary or apparently ordinary persons rather than charismatic individuals. Leadership is not solely the preserve of those at the top of the organization; it is relevant at all levels. Finally, leadership is not about control, direction and manipulation. *Leaders* and another best-seller, *On Becoming a Leader* (1989), were translated into twenty-one languages. His latest books, *Organizing Genius: The Secrets of Creative Collaboration* (1997) and *Co-Leaders: The Power of Great Partnerships* (1999), bring together the major themes of life's work: leadership, change, great groups and powerful partnerships.

Since he began his career over forty-five years ago, Bennis has authored or edited over twenty-six books, a number that continues to expand. He has also written over 1,500 articles in publications such as *Harvard Business Review*, *Wall Street Journal*, the *New York Times*, *Psychology Today*, *Esquire*, *Atlantic Monthly*, and many management publications. He was the founding editor of Addison-Wesley's Organization Development series. In 1998, Jossey-Bass Publishers introduced a new imprint for innovative books on change leadership – Warren Bennis Books.

Bennis has been an adviser to four US presidents, and currently serves on the boards of Antioch College, the Claremont University Center and Graduate School, Harvard's Center for Educational Leadership, the Salk Institute, and the Center for Professional and Executive Development at Hughes Aircraft. He is a founding director of the American Leadership Forum, and has served as director of Gemini Consulting, the Foothill Group and First Executive, and on the national boards of the US Chamber of Commerce and the American Management Association. In the international arena, he was the US Professor of Corporations and Society at the Centre d'Études Industrielles in Geneva, the Raoul de Vitry d'Avenecourt Professor at INSEAD in Fontainbleau, a professor at IMEDE in Lausanne, and a founding director of the Indian Institute of Management in Calcutta. Finally, Bennis has been a consultant for a wide variety of Fortune 500 firms, including Chase Manhattan Bank, Polaroid, Ford Motor Company, TRW, McKesson Equitable Life, Starbucks, Anderson Consulting, Linkage Inc. and Booz Allen.

Over the years, Warren Bennis has received numerous honours in recognition of his outstanding achievements and contributions. In addition to being the recipient of eleven honorary degrees, Bennis received the 1987 Dow Jones Award for 'outstanding contributions to the field of collegiate education for business'. He twice received the prestigious McKinsey Foundation Award for the best book on management: in 1967 for *The Temporary Society*, and in 1968 for *The Professional Manager*. In 1986, he received the First Annual Award from University Associates, and was presented with the Pericles Award from the Employment Management Association. Other honours include being admitted to *Training Magazine*'s Hall of Fame, the Distinguished Service Award from the American Board of Professional Psychology (its highest honour) and the Perry L. Roher Consulting Practice Award from the American Psychological Association.

Throughout his career, Bennis's ideas and research on leadership have always been cutting edge. He argues that the study of leadership, because of its practice-oriented nature, must link theory to the real world. From his experience as a leader, Bennis can serve as a model for connecting theory to practice. Although he has not held a formal leadership position since 1979, his studies remain firmly anchored in the real world. For example, he wrote *Leaders* after interviewing ninety US leaders. Such efforts have enabled him to have a far-reaching and sustained influence on the study and practice of leadership, an influence that continues in the twenty-first century.

BIBLIOGRAPHY

Bennis, W.G. (1966) 'The Coming Death of Bureaucracy', *THINK* 32(November–December): 32–3.

——— (1973) *The Leaning Ivory Tower*, San Francisco: Jossey-Bass.

——— (1989) *On Becoming a Leader*, Reading, MA: Addison-Wesley.

——— (1993) *An Invented Life: Reflections on Leadership and Change*, Reading, MA: Addison-Wesley.

——— (1997) *Managing People is Like Herding Cats*, Provo, UT: Executive Excellence Publishing.

Bennis, W.G. and Biederman, P.W. (1997) *Organizing Genius: The Secrets of Creative Collaboration*, Reading, MA: Addison-Wesley.

Bennis, W.G. and Nanus, B. (1985) *Leaders*, Reading, MA: Addison-Wesley.

Bennis, W.G. and Shepard, H.A. (1956) 'A Theory of Group Development', *Human Relations* 9: 415–37.

Bennis, W.G., and Slater, P.E. (1964) 'Democracy is Inevitable', *Harvard Business Review* (March–April): 51–9.

——— (1968) *The Temporary Society*, New York: Harper and Row.

Bennis, W.G., Benne K.D. and Chin R. (1961) *The Planning of Change: Readings in the Applied Behavioral Sciences*, New York: Holt, Rinehart and Winston.

Heenan, D.A. and Bennis, W.G. (1999) *Co-leaders: The Power of Great Partnerships*, New York: John Wiley.

Shepard, H.A. and Bennis, W.G. (1956) 'A Theory of Training by Group Methods', *Human Relations* 9: 403–14.

Who's Who In The World (1991–2), 10th edn, Chicago: Marquis Who's Who, Inc.

QY

BERLE, Adolf Augustus, Jr (1895–1971)

Adolf Augustus Berle was born in Boston Massachusetts on 29 January 1895 and died in New York City on 17 February 1971. He received his BA (1913) and MA (1914) from Harvard and his LLB in 1916 from Harvard Law School, and entered law practice in New York City. After service in the First World War, he returned to New York to practice corporate law. He went on to a career as a successful corporate lawyer, diplomat and close adviser to President Franklin D. Roosevelt.

The United States in the 1920s was undergoing the economic boom exemplified by the phrase 'the Roaring Twenties', and Berle's specialization in the emerging law of corporation finance gave him an excellent view of the operation of securities markets unencumbered by government regulation. Berle also earned a reputation as a legal scholar, writing many articles on his specialization. He taught at Harvard Business School, and joined the faculty of Columbia University Law School in New York. At Harvard he met Professor William Ripley, whom he later acknowledged as a major influence (see preface to Berle and Means 1932). Ripley's 1927 book *Main Street and Wall Street* was a description of the tumultuous world of contemporary corporation finance and securities trading, written for general audiences. The book, which cited or mentioned Berle's writings several times, argued that individual shareholders of large corporations were powerless against management.

Through Ripley, Berle obtained a foundation grant in 1927 for an interdisciplinary study of American corporations, and hired Gardiner MEANS, a graduate student in economics at Columbia, as research economist (Schwarz 1987: 51). The product of their research was *The Modern Corporation*, published in 1932. *The Modern Corporation*'s then revolutionary thesis, supported by Means's statistics, was that modern corporations represented unprecedented aggregations of economic power, subject not to the control of their shareholder-owners, but to that of professional managers. The 200 largest non-banking corporations in the United States possessed close to one-half of the non-banking wealth of the country, or almost one-quarter of the total national wealth (Berle and Means 1932: 19). Within these large corporations, control was separated from ownership. With so many shareholders, individual shareholders did not hold enough shares to be able to exercise control over management. Direction of the corporation passed from shareholders to professional, employed managers, who owned relatively few shares in the corporations employing them, and whose interests were in conflict with those of shareholders (1932, Book 2, chaps 5–6).

Because private owners no longer controlled corporations, and corporations possessed enormous and growing economic power, some arrangement had to be found to prevent possible abuse of that power. The historical significance of *The Modern Corporation* lies in Berle and Means's suggested solution. This was founded on the idea that 'neither the claims of ownership or those of control can stand against the paramount interests of the community' (1932: 312). *The Modern Corporation* did not offer a programme to protect the interests of the community versus

large corporations. Yet the book's successful intellectual challenge to *laissez-faire* property rights concepts was, in Berle's words, 'causative both in the development of legal and economic theory and in policies and measures of the United States government' (1932, preface to the revised edn: vii). *Time* Magazine may not have exaggerated when it called *The Modern Corporation* 'the economic Bible of the Roosevelt administration' (Hessen 1983: 279).

The Modern Corporation's continued importance rests not in economic history but in its recognition of the relationship between improved corporate governance through enhanced shareholder protection, increased shareholder value and efficient capital markets (Bratton 2001). In *The Modern Corporation*, Berle offered specific recommendations for protection of shareholders (Book 2, chaps 7–8; Book III, chaps 3–4). The recommendation that rules be imposed 'requiring general disclosure by the corporation of all material facts tending to change open [public securities] market appraisals' (Berle and Means 1932: 289) formed the basis of the US Securities Exchange Act of 1934. As Professor Bratton points out in his incisive article, improved corporate governance through enhanced fiduciary standards, and open public securities markets are issues that have a 'global venue'. In the future it is likely that *The Modern Corporation* will be 'causative in policies and measures' of governments throughout the world (Bratton 2001).

The Modern Corporation continues to justify the encomium: 'one of the most influential books of the twentieth century' (Moore 1982: 236). It provided intellectual support for the government intervention in the economy that was the centrepiece of Roosevelt's 'New Deal'. Yet its significance goes beyond economic history. Managers, investors, scholars and government officials are still wrestling with the problems stemming from the separation of ownership and control in large corporations described in the book. Later authors influenced by the book included figures as various as James BURNHAM, whose study of *The Modern Corporation* led him to conclude that ownership would follow control and ultimately pass to the managers, and Alfred CHANDLER, who not only accepted the thesis of the separation of ownership and control but saw it as the basis of an American style of 'managerial capitalism' which was in many ways superior to other forms.

BIBLIOGRAPHY
Berle, A.A., Jr and Means, G.C. (1932) *The Modern Corporation and Private Property*, New York: Harcourt, Brace and World, 1967.
Bratton, W.W. (2001) 'Berle and Means Reconsidered at the Century's Turn', *Journal of Corporation Law* 26.
Herman, E. (1981) *Corporate Control, Corporate Power*, Cambridge: Cambridge University Press.
Hessen, R. (1983) 'The Modern Corporation and Private Property: A Reappraisal', *Journal of Law and Economics* 26(2): 273–90.
Moore, T.G. (1982) 'Introduction to "CORPORATIONS AND PRIVATE PROPERTY", A Conference Sponsored by the Hoover Institution', *Journal of Law and Economics* 26(2): 235–6.
Ripley, W.Z. (1927) *Main Street and Wall Street*, Boston: Little, Brown.
Schwarz, J. (1987) *Liberal: Adolf A. Berle and the Vision of an American Era*, New York: Free Press.

SR

BERNERS-LEE, Tim (1955–)

Tim Berners-Lee was born in London on 8 June 1955. Raised in London in the 1960s, Berners-Lee was encouraged to think unconventionally by his parents, who met while working on the first commercially sold computer (the Ferranti Mark 1). He developed a love for electronics. He attended Emmanuel School in London from 1969 to 1973 and then Queen's College Oxford, graduating in 1976 with a BA in physics with first-class honours. He has since received a variety of honorary degrees, is an Honorary Fellow of the Institution of Electrical Engineers, and a Distinguished Fellow of the British Computer Society.

Upon graduation from Oxford, Berners-Lee was employed by Plessey Telecommunications, a major UK telecommunications equipment manufacturer, in Poole, Dorset. While employed there he worked on distributed transactions systems, message relay and bar code technologies. He joined D.G. Nash Ltd in Ferndown, Dorset in 1978, where he wrote software for intelligent printers and a multitask operating system until 1980. Following this, Berners-Lee spent a year and a half as an independent consultant. During a six-month stint at the European Particle Physics Laboratory (CERN) in Geneva, he developed a program for storing information (named Enquire, and never published) that formed the conceptual basis for the World Wide Web (WWW).

From 1981 to 1984 Berners-Lee worked on the technical design of graphics and communications software, and a generic macro language. In 1984 he took up a fellowship at CERN and worked on real-time systems for scientific data acquisition and system control. In 1989 he proposed a global hypertext project based on his earlier Enquire program, and work began in October 1990. This resulted in the development of three standards for weaving documents into the WWW: uniform resource locators (URLs), hypertext markup language (HTML) and hypertext transfer protocol (HTTP). This technology became available on the Internet in the summer of 1991. Berners-Lee continued to refine the design of the WWW through 1991–3 at CERN.

In 1994 he joined the Laboratory for Computer Science at the Massachusetts Institute of Technology (MIT) to direct the World Wide Web Consortium (W3C), which was designed to coordinate WWW development worldwide. He is presently director of W3C, and became the first holder of the 3Com Founders chair at MIT in 1999. His book, *Weaving the Web*, written with Mark Fischetti and published in the autumn of 1999, tells his story of the creation of the WWW and outlines his philosophy of an open-access, self-policing Web. It also deals with issues such as privacy, censorship, influence of software companies and his vision of where the Web is headed.

Unlike many of his contemporaries, Berners-Lee has not become wealthy from the new technology. He believes that proprietary control of the Web would have prevented its success. 'People only committed their time to it because they knew it was open, shared: that they could decide what happened to it next … and I wouldn't be raking off 10 per cent!', he said in a *Time* interview (1999) He has received numerous awards for his work from the scientific, communication, computer and technology communities, along with an OBE (2000).

Eric Schmidt, CEO of Novell, has called Berners-Lee 'the unsung hero of the Internet'. He continued, referring to computer networking, 'If this were a traditional science, Berners-Lee would win a Nobel Prize. What he's done is that significant' (quoted in Lohr 1995). In 1999 *Time* listed him as one of the 100 most influential minds of the twentieth century. Berners-Lee's achievement ranks as one of the great technological advances which have profoundly affected management, along with earlier achievements such as the computer, the telegraph, electricity, the factory system and printing. Although he is not himself a business manager as such, his influence on the modern shape of management – through both his technology and his philosophy of its use – has been profound.

BIBLIOGRAPHY
Anon. (2000) 'Longer Biography', http://www.w3.org/People/Berners-Lee/Longer.html, 5 March 2001.
Berners-Lee, T. and Fischetti, M. (1999) *Weaving the Web*, San Francisco: Harper San Francisco.
Lohr, S. (1995) 'His Goal: Keeping the Web Worldwide', *New York Times Business Day*, 18 December, http://www.w3.org/People/Berners-Lee/951217-NYT/951217-NYT-1.gif, 5 March 2001.
Time (1999) 'Interview with Tim-Berners Lee', 29 September, *Time Magazine Transcripts*, http://www.time.com/time/community/tran-scripts/1999/092999berners-lee.html, 5 March 2001.

JW

BOEING, William Edward (1881–1956)

William Edward Boeing was born in Detroit, Michigan on 1 October 1881 and died in Puget Sound on his yacht on 28 September 1956. His German immigrant father died in 1890, and Boeing was raised by his Austrian-born mother. After attending private schools in both the United States and Switzerland, he studied engineering at Yale University, from whence he graduated in 1904. Aviation was the furthest thing from Boeing's mind in 1903 and 1904 when Wilbur and Orville Wright were creating the first aeroplane. He wanted to be a lumber manager, and, relocating to the state of Washington in 1904, built up one of the most successful lumber businesses in the state.

Boeing's life and that of Seattle and the United States changed forever when, on 4 July 1914, he flew for the first time as a passenger in a Curtiss seaplane. He instantly fell in love with aircraft. By 1915 the thirty-four year old

Boeing was not only taking flying lessons but had set up a partnership with fellow engineer, Conrad Westervelt, to build his own seaplane. He set up a small hangar in Seattle, and in 1916 the B&W flying boat made its maiden voyage. Westervelt soon dissolved the partnership, but not before telling Boeing that the US Navy might be interested in his plane.

In November 1916 Boeing set up the Boeing Airplane Company, which during 1917 and 1918 laboured to fill an order for twenty-five Curtiss seaplanes. Military contracts would be the lifeblood of Boeing for many years, even though Boeing's real love was commercial aviation. In 1926 he lamented, 'Can't we build anything but warplanes?' (Ingells 1970: 28). The firm almost went bankrupt in 1919 but was saved by some new government contracts. One of the planes Boeing created was a large multi-engined triplane called the Ground Attack Experimental. Commercial aviation in the meantime was coming into its own, and Boeing was determined to help shape it. When the Post Office began airmail deliveries between Seattle and Vancouver, British Columbia on 27 December 1919, Boeing's B-1 seaplane, his first commercial aeroplane, made the deliveries.

In the early 1920s the United States led in neither military nor commercial aviation. American pilots in the First World War had flown French Spads. American aviation finally found an ally in President Calvin Coolidge (1923–9). Under Coolidge's administration the Army Air Corps was created, and the Air Mail and Air Commerce Acts were passed in 1925 and 1926. The Federal government's desire to stimulate commercial and military aviation created a windfall market for Boeing aircraft.

Boeing employed some 500 workers in 1926. Even then he had a vision of an airline and airmail industry that would rival both the railroads and the rising power of the automobile. The government in 1926 was beginning to privatize airmail services, and Boeing won the contract for the Illinois to California route. The Boeing 40 and the Boeing 40A were light and powerful enough to carry half a ton of mail and two passengers between Chicago and San Francisco for a cost lower than that of any competitor.

However, even before Charles A. Lindbergh's flight from New York to Paris in May 1927 created an aviation mania, Boeing was already facing stiff competition from Henry FORD (Ingells 1970). Ford Trimotors were already flying between Detroit, Chicago and Cleveland, and Ford had even built his own terminals. Boeing, in response, also began to internalize his operation. He formed, with his engine supplier Pratt and Whitney and Hamilton Propellor, the United Aircraft and Transportation Corporation. United bought the planes Boeing made. The new combined firm lasted for five years, and acquired routes from Seattle to Chicago and down the west coast to San Diego, as well as from Chicago to Fort Worth and to New York. Competition with Ford's airline, the ancestor of Trans World Airlines (TWA), which flew from New York to Los Angeles, spurred Boeing to develop even more advanced planes such as the Boeing 80A, which carried eighteen passengers.

Boeing's efforts to remain on the leading edge of aviation technology and to control commercial aviation allowed his company to weather the Great Depression. Boeing had a brand name, long experience and financial stability. There were few Boeing layoffs during the 1930s. In the meantime, competition from Ford and Martin drove Boeing into revolutionary designs that eventually helped make the United States second to none in both civilian and military aviation. The wooden biplanes of the 1920s were now replaced by steel monoplanes. Boeing's major coup in aviation was the Boeing 247. First flying in 1933, the sleek, twin-engine 247 was the forerunner of all modern bombers and airliners. It was all metal, had retractable landing gear and trim tab elevators, and obliterated all competition until Douglas Aircraft countered with the famous DC-3 (Ingells 1970).

Boeing's 247 was the prototype for even bigger planes such as the 299, which eventually became the famous B-17 Flying Fortress four-engine bomber. The Seattle firm began to expand once again in 1936 as Hitler's new Luftwaffe presented a formidable challenge. Boeing had almost 3,000 employees in 1938, and almost 29,000 on the eve of Pearl Harbor in 1941. The B-17 became Boeing's first principal contribution to victory. The aeroplane was mass produced by the thousands by Ford and other plants as well as by Boeing, and was deeply loved by the bomber pilots who flew it. It was sturdy and dependable: B-17s would return home from daylight bombing raids over Germany sometimes with a rudder or elevator missing, or three engines crippled, but still flying. The Flying Fortress was too short-range for the Pacific war, but by 1944 the faster and longer-range Boeing B-29 Superfortress was bombing the Japanese home islands from the Marianas, ultimately dropping the two atomic bombs.

After the war, Boeing had a much more difficult time than, for example, General Motors, in reconverting to a peace-time economy. It tried to diversify into consumer goods, but with little success. The intensification of the Cold War, however, sustained the firm. The B-47 Stratojet, produced in the hundreds, became the backbone of the American nuclear deterrent in the early 1950s. By 1956 the giant B-52 Stratofortress, still in service after forty years, had begun to replace the Stratojet.

Boeing had retired from active participation in his firm in 1933. He did not live to see the success of his greatest product, his airliners. The Boeing 707 went into service at the end of the decade, and the company sold hundreds not only to American carriers but to most international airlines as well. The same success was repeated later in 1970 with the giant 'jumbo' 747, which had a B-52's intercontinental range and could carry around 500 passengers. The 727, which could fly from smaller airports, opened even small cities to the global economy of jet travel. Since the 1970s Boeing's jets have dominated the market for global air travel, although by the 1990s European Airbus Industries, subsidized in part by European governments, was cutting into the Boeing market.

Boeing created an innovative, internalized enterprise that went on to dominate much of world aviation. He was the most successful aircraft-maker in history: his bombers helped to win the Second World War and wage the Cold War, and his company's airliners have helped create the global economy.

BIBLIOGRAPHY
Ingells, D.J. (1970) 747: Story of the Boeing Super Jet, Fallbrook, CA: Aero Publishing.

DCL

BOOZ, Edwin George (1887–1951)

Edwin George Booz was born in Reading, Pennsylvania on 2 September 1887, the son of Thomas and Sarah Booz. He died in Chicago on 14 October 1951. He married Helen Hootman in 1918, and they had two children. He attended Northwestern University, taking an AB in 1912 and an AM in 1914. In the latter year he also set up his own consultancy business, Edwin G. Booz Engineering Surveys. Like most of the early consultants, Booz called himself an 'efficiency expert' (the term 'management consultant' is of later origin), but the services he offered were wide-ranging. Like Arthur D. LITTLE, who had established his consultancy business in 1905, Booz was usually called in to solve specific technical problems, but often found that the demand for his services quickly widened as the solution to each problem uncovered other problems further along the line. Booz's firm offered advice on everything from plant location to marketing strategy. Not a functional expert himself (indeed, Booz, only twenty-seven when he went into the business, had little practical business experience), he based his advice on common sense and good judgement, qualities which he found lacking in many business leaders: famously, he once told one company president that the only thing wrong with his company was the man in charge.

Booz was a considerable success as a consultant, and his reputation grew. He served in the US Army 1917–18, finishing as a major on the staff of the Inspector General, with special responsibility for business organization. After the war his business grew rapidly. Booz hired technical experts in a variety of fields, many of them trained at Northwestern or the University of Chicago, which he used as his talent pool in much the same way that Little recruited from the Massachusetts Institute of Technology. The firm expanded to include offices in New York, Minneapolis and Los Angeles. Clients included Montgomery Ward, Western Union, RCA, Columbia Pictures and Sperry Corp. The Second World War also brought a great boost to the business, as companies involved in war work sought to increase production capacity rapidly; Booz and his team did much to ensure that such teams grew without sacrificing efficiency. The business survives today as Booz, Allen and Hamilton, one of the largest and most prestigious management consultancies in the world.

BOULDING, Elise (1920–)

Elise Boulding was born Elise Bjorn-Hansen in Oslo on 6 July 1920, daughter of Joseph Bjorn-Hansen, an engineer, and his wife Birgit. She received her BA in English from Douglass College in 1940 and married Kenneth Boulding, the noted economist, in the following year. She took an MS in sociology from Iowa State University in 1949, and a Ph.D. from the University of Michigan in 1969. She began her academic career in 1967, when she joined the sociology faculty of the University of Colorado at Boulder, where she became professor of sociology in 1971. She moved to become professor and chair at Dartmouth College, New Hampshire in 1978. Since 1985 she has been professor emerita of sociology at Dartmouth College.

Along with her husband Kenneth Boulding, she was among the founders of the field of peace and conflict research, and was a prolific author and activist on the subject. She further contributed to the development of the field through the many positions she held in influential organizations. Notable among these were the International Peace Research Association, where she served as secretary-general and foundation president; the Women's International League for Peace and Freedom, which she chaired from 1967 to 1970; and many others, including the Project on Conditions for a Just World Peace and the National Academy of Peace and Conflict Resolution. Boulding received many awards for her work towards a just peace, and continued to write well into her seventies. In 1990 she was nominated for the Nobel Peace Prize.

The breadth of Boulding's work is significant, and ranges from transnational and comparative cross-national studies on conflict and peace to social development, world order, women in society and futures studies. She did much pioneering work with the United Nations University on its Human and Social Development program and the Household, Gender and Age project (see Masini). The major themes of her work were the idea of the world as a dynamic, evolutionary, complex and diverse system, and the idea of how powerfully human visioning of the 'totally other' (radically different) can transform that system.

Boulding's work in futures studies began in 1961 when she translated Fred Polak's classic text *The Image of the Future* (1953) from the Dutch. She developed Polak's concept of images of the future and brought it into the mainstream of futures thinking, demonstrating how it could become the centrepiece of practical future-oriented action. She wrote a number of futures works including *The Social System of the Planet Earth* (1980), *The Future: Images and Processes* (1995), both with Kenneth Boulding, and *Building a Global Civic Culture* (1988). This last explores a number of important conceptual, organizational and human innovations for a more just and sustainable future. As Slaughter (1996) describes, the book also considers problems of knowledge in high-technology cultures, and how to recover a broader range of ways of knowing.

The mother of five children and with grandchildren, Boulding believed strongly in the value and role of the family in society, and she chaired the Parenting Center in Boulder, Colorado in the late 1980s. Her Quaker beliefs are evident throughout her writings, most obviously in *One Small Plot of Heaven: Reflections of a Quaker Sociologist on Family Life* (1989). These beliefs not only provided her with a strong foundational philosophy for her work in peace and conflict research, but were the basis for her pioneering contribution to the ethics of futures studies. She wrote a number of works addressing what she saw as neglected sectors of society, namely women and children. Amongst the most important of these are the *Handbook on International Data on Women* (1979b), *The Underside of History: A View of Women through Time* (1976) and *Women in the Twentieth Century World* (1977). She worked to bring women's issues to the fore in the work of various United Nations University programmes. She was engaged in work to establish the rights of children and the elderly, culminating in her book *Children's Rights and the Wheel of Life* (1979a), which reviews the lack of rights given to children until the age of twenty-one. In reviewing the age classifications and associated legal frameworks imposed in our society, she has been the forerunner of current societal debates about the age of responsibility and maturity with regard to serious crime, sexual consent and consent for medical treatment amongst children.

Boulding was concerned with increasing women's participation in policy and decision making. She notes that 'most female experience with participation in mixed settings is negative when it comes to agenda-setting, policy planning and decision making', and concluded that 'the distinctive contributions of women's culture cannot be made under such circumstances' and that there should be coexisting all-women's groups in which that culture can be nurtured, buttressed by strong separatist strategies of social innovation. She claims that the significance of these separatist strategies is that they provide working models of how things could be in the future. She sums up her view of the path forward for women's involvement thus:

The trip to the 'over-side' for women has to be a shuttling back and forth between women's and mixed spaces until women are socially strong enough and organisational structures have become open enough to sustain the feminist input into public life in its economic political and cultural dimensions.

She asserts that the sectors of society best equipped to replace hierarchy with decentralist structures, based on non-hierarchical communication are the women's movements.

Boulding has spent a productive lifetime working for peace, justice and the future. She continuously challenged the status quo in society, and tackled the development of a new social order from global, ethical and gender perspectives, with practical and valuable contributions. She is also recognized for her pioneering work in the ethics of futures studies and decision making.

BIBLIOGRAPHY
Boulding, E. (1977) *Women in the Twentieth Century World*, New York: John Wiley.
——— (1979a) *Children's Rights and the*

Wheel of Life, New Brunswick, NJ: Transaction Publishing.

Boulding, E. (1979b) *Handbook on International Data on Women*, London: Sage.

—— (1988) *Building a Global Civic Culture*, New York: Teachers College Press.

—— (1989) *One Small Plot of Heaven: Reflections of a Quaker Sociologist on Family Life*, Wallingford, PA: Pendle Hill Publications.

—— (1992) *The Underside of History: A View of Women through Time*, London: Sage.

Boulding, E. and Boulding, K.E. (1995) *The Future: Images and Processes*, London: Sage.

Boulding, K.E., Boulding, E. and Burgess, G.M. (1980) *The Social System of the Planet Earth*, Reading, MA: Addison-Wesley.

Slaughter, R.A. (1996) *The Foresight Principle*, Twickenham: Adamantine.

AJ

BRAVERMAN, Harry (1922–76)

Harry Braverman was born in Brooklyn, New York on 9 December 1922 to Polish-Jewish parents, and died there of lymphoma on 2 August 1976, at the age of just fifty-three. He attended City College, New York in 1937, but left after only one year in order to seek work. Braverman did eventually graduate some twenty-five years later, from the New School of Social Research in New York in 1963. His working life was bifurcated between several skilled manual jobs (1938–51) and white-collar employment (1951–76). He began his working life with a four-year apprenticeship (1938–42) as a coppersmith in Brooklyn naval shipyard, and he worked at this for a further three years, supervising up to twenty workers. He was then drafted into military service in 1945, when he repaired locomotives for the Union Pacific railway in Cheyenne, Wyoming. After demobilization Braverman moved to Youngstown, Ohio, where he spent seven years in steel fabrication at various trades, including pipe fitting, sheet metal work and layout, and also in two plants which fabricated heavy steel plate and structural steel into equipment for the basic steel industry, such as blast furnaces. Later he was a journalist and editor (1954–60) and entered publishing, becoming in turn editor, general manager and vice-president of Grove Press (1960–67) and director of Monthly Review Press (1967–76).

It was this working background, especially his observations on the rationalization and erosion of craft work, that created and polished the lens through which Braverman examined life and work, and forged the template for his analysis and writing. While he wrote an early book on the future of Russia and the Soviet Union and also pieces as a journalist and book reviewer, he remains best known throughout much of the world for *Labor and Monopoly Capital* (1974). This was a broad-ranging and seminal book on the labour process, which proved to be the anvil on which his reputation was forged, shaped and tempered.

A long-time Marxist and activist, Braverman joined the Socialist Workers' Party in the 1930s. He left with a group of others in 1954 and helped set up the magazine *The American Socialist*, which he also edited (1954–60). During the 1950s, in addition to his journalism, he wrote numerous book reviews and summaries for the Book Find Club. These high-quality pieces attracted the attention of the New York publisher, Grove Press, which recruited Braverman to work for it, where he displayed considerable business and management acumen. He subsequently moved to

Monthly Review Press as a return to socialist publishing, and it was here that he wrote his major work.

Braverman was never an academic as such. Indeed, he disliked what he saw as 'ivory tower' academics and those whom he labelled as not grounded in the world of work, although ironically, many academic careers were subsequently made on the bandwagon his book set in motion and the publications it engendered. Crucially, the views and themes in his famous book were driven by his particular approach, which was underpinned by his own experiences, observation and political outlook. Therefore, he theorized from his own work experience 'upwards', as he viewed the best methodology as being reflection on lived experience by the politically engaged. For Braverman, this was a far superior approach compared to what he saw as the inaccuracies of the academic and official descriptions of work. He believed that the literature on technical and management trends was based on little genuine information, and was too vague and general and full of 'egregious errors'.

Labor and Monopoly Capital was both highly influential and heavily criticized. In the wake of his book and thesis, Marxist analysis and work was revitalized and popularized (see Thompson 1989). Debate on the labour process developed, spread and lapped along many academic shores (Knights and Willmott 1990). These include the areas of history and labour economics (for example, Zimbalist 1979; Edwards 1979); industrial sociology (Littler 1982); industrial relations (Kelly 1982; Wood 1982, 1989; Edwards 1986); economics (Friedman 1977); organizational studies; economic history; and industrial geography, amongst others.

Braverman's book went on to gain an almost iconic status. It remains a classic, and for most people it is the main plank underpinning Braverman's reputation. He began the book in the late 1960s, working on it during the evenings while continuing with his 'day job'. The book's 450 pages are organized into an introduction and twenty chapters in five parts. The first part is 'Labor and Management', with chapters on labour and labour power, the origins of management, the division of labour, scientific management, the primary effects of scientific management, and the habituation of the worker to the capitalist mode of production. Second is 'Science and Mechanization', with chapters on the scientific-technical revolution, the scientific-technical revolution and the worker, machinery, and further effects of management and technology on the distribution of labour. Third is 'Monopoly Capital', with chapters on surplus value and surplus labour, the modern corporation, the universal market and the role of the state. Fourth is 'The Growing Working-class Occupations', with chapters on clerical workers, and on service occupations and retail trade. Fifth is 'The Working Class', with chapters on the structure of the working class and its reserve armies, the 'middle layers' of employment, productive and unproductive labour, and a final note on skill.

Braverman built on Marx's writings concerning the so-called labour process. This can be seen as involving the means by which 'raw materials' and 'objects' (in manufacturing and services) were transformed by human labour into 'products' for use, and 'commodities' to be exchanged. Therefore, the core of the labour process approach rests on the belief that the capacity to work was utilized as a means of producing value (Thompson 1989). The following points are important to this. First, the capital–labour relationship was essentially exploitative as the surplus value from work activities accrued to capital. Second, the 'logic of accumulation' required capital continually to develop the production process and cheapen the costs of production. Third, continued development of the production process required the establishment and maintenance of both general and specific 'structures of control'. Fourth, the resultant 'structured antagonism' relationship included systematic attempts by capital to obtain cooperation and consent, with a continuum of worker responses, from resistance to accommodation and compliance and consent. Thus, the problem of 'work' was about control and how managers ensured the maximum degree of effort for the minimum amount of reward. The solution was to extend the division of labour, separating the conception of work from its execution, and deskilling the work force. This would not only increase productivity and reduce labour costs, but also generate more compliant workers.

Braverman's thesis can be seen succinctly in the book's subtitle: *The Degradation of Work in the Twentieth Century*. In particular, Braverman analysed the effects of technology and scientific management on the nature of work. As we have noted, he disbelieved 'official' views in several areas, including the assertions that skills had been upgraded, that greater education time naturally meant more skilled or knowledgeable work, or that formal designations corresponded with actual skills. Rather, for Braverman, the drive for efficient production required managerial control of workers, excluding workers from control and ownership of knowledge and skills acquisition. This led to poorer quality and experience of labour. These processes applied to jobs across the employment spectrum, from manufacturing to services, and from design to clerical work. This degradation or 'deskilling' thesis suggested an underlying drive within capitalism to substitute less skilled or unskilled for skilled work.

Thus, the fundamental industrial relationship during the twentieth century was one of management exploitation and 'degradation' of labour by deskilling work, and this was through the use of Taylorism (see TAYLOR), scientific management techniques and work study to support the achievement of capital's objectives. Therefore there was the technical division of labour, involving the breaking down of tasks within former crafts at the initiative of employers in order to increase efficiency. The application of work study

techniques facilitated this disintegration of work into component tasks which could then be allocated to individuals (specialization). Management thereby cheapened the individual's input value to the production process (with tasks requiring less training, skill and responsibility), tied the individual more directly to the technical system (especially assembly lines) and made individuals or groups capable of being subjected to production output controls (such as bonus payments, quotas and so on). This thesis of Braverman's also presented management as a 'control' function. Management's basic task was to design, control and monitor work tasks and activities so as to ensure the effective extraction of surplus value from the labour activity of employees.

Further elements within the thesis concerned 'class'. There was a belief that there would develop a homogenization of socioeconomic classes; all workers would come increasingly to regard themselves as part of the 'working class' as they were subject to the same type of work controls and conditions as were manual workers. Braverman explored in depth the US class structure and its changes, which he saw as evolving from the self-employed to waged employees and a division into manufacturing and services and occupations engaged in jobs officially designated as skilled, but actually not so.

Braverman and his thesis can be attacked on several grounds (some of these are summarized in Noon and Blyton 1997). On the one hand, there is the antithesis and total opposition of the 'upskilling' camp. For the prophets of this group, technology actually increased skills, job satisfaction and so on. One strand of this concerns the ideas behind 'flexible specialization'. A wide range of more 'friendly fire' also rained down on Braverman. First, he was criticized for his broad brush universalism and limitations stemming from his US-centric bias. His ideas fitted less well in some societies, such as Japan and Germany. Capitalisms varied and were embedded in sociocultural and institutional contexts which imposed and impinged variously on trends and developments in work and the employment relationship.

Second, how skill was viewed and defined by Braverman was problematic. The implication was that skill was composed of technical components which could be objectively evaluated and observed. Yet his focus on 'objective' features of skill ignored 'tacit' skills and their importance, and the need for them in even formally 'unskilled' work, and those connected to gender or personality, such as services and emotions. Skill was also socially constructed, and a 'label' often negotiated and fought over irrespective of defined skill levels. He also exaggerated and romanticized the typicality and prior situation of skilled craft workers, and overlooked skill transfer possibilities. Indeed, management may well see it as advantageous in certain circumstances to upgrade rather than deskill employees.

Third, a major problem concerns Braverman's failure to explore and integrate ideas of 'social action' (although he may well have come to address this given time, of course). He oversimplified and homogenized both management and workers, ignoring alternative tactics, and strategies and control mechanisms. Organizations are viewed overrationally, as carefully, consciously and ruthlessly adopting policies. Yet, often decisions are made for a variety of reasons, with influences ranging from sectional interests to 'muddling through' and mistakes. Workers are heterogeneous, for example, by skill, gender and so on. Neither are they totally compliant, as they have resisted, challenged or modified deskilling to varying degrees, with some influence or control of their work situation via individual and collective action and organized labour. This is evidenced by the operation and power of so-called 'restrictive practices' at specific times and places. Indeed, managerial moves from 'simple' to 'technical' (mechanical assembly lines) and 'bureaucratic' (rules, procedures, regulations, internal labour

markets) control (Edwards 1979) can be seen as responses to this. Likewise, in the concept of segmented labour markets (and now in the fashionable guise of the 'flexible firm') organizations can divide workers. 'Core' and 'central' employees (whose role, skill and expertise are required for the viability of the organization) are distinguished from 'peripheral' or 'marginal' workers (with fewer links to an organization's success). This can lead to a fragmentation of interests and less effective resistance to control. Similarly, while 'direct control' was exercised through the application of scientific management, 'responsible autonomy' (Friedman 1977) can also be applied. This involves expanding or enhancing the employee's job situation so that it appears to allow some degree of self-control, but this is constrained and allowed only in areas and in a direction which supports management and organizational objectives. Thus, management has a variety of control methods. Furthermore, Braverman understates the degree of consent and accommodation by employees. This includes the view that work forces can consent to their own subordination (Burawoy 1979).

Fourth, there remains another major problem at the very heart of the Bravermanite thesis. It exaggerates and overstates management's unity, the coherence and consistency of strategy formulation, and the dominance and centrality of control, labour and work design in managerial thought and decisions. It underestimates the diversity, complexity (and competing nature) of management and broader business objectives. Control is not an end in itself, but rather is of interest only to the extent that it impacts on profits, dividends, share price and so on. All too often labour is a peripheral issue, or one that is dealt with in an ad hoc and 'fire-fighting' manner, not as a central issue, strategically or coherently.

Nevertheless, despite this plethora of criticisms and problems, the importance and continuing resonance of Braverman's views and thesis are apparent. This is indicated by such factors as the following. If, as argued by some (Armstrong 1988; Thompson 1989), a more subtle reading of Braverman is used, this weakens many of the criticisms. For example, work deskilling and degradation can be seen not as a universal 'iron law' operating in all cases, but as more of a 'tendency'. In addition, Braverman still provides a wealth of interesting description, cases and analysis of the evolution, development and roles of labour, management, capital and state. He usefully combines and links employee behaviour, industrial relations and questions of work design and organization, as well as management control to the political economy and wider, more macro issues and themes. Indeed, since its appearance, *Labor and Monopoly Capital* has not been out of print; it has sold over 120,000 copies in English, and still has an average of 2,000 annual sales; it has been translated into French, Italian, German, Dutch, German, Swedish, Norwegian, Spanish, Portuguese, Greek and Japanese, and remains the publisher's best-seller (Smith 1998). Braverman was also the catalyst for a huge volume of work by others, and his thesis remains an important perspective on a range of academic areas. Many courses in these fields contain coverage of his work as well as its followers and protagonists, while words related to his work have entered the lexicon of many academic fields.

Interestingly, Braverman's scepticism of official views on skills, the expansion of education equating to more skilled work and formal designations of skill also retain their importance, value and salience. His work serves as a counter and foil to much of the more banal posturing and platitudes propounded in this area, with talk of 'revolutionary' changes, such as the e-business phenomenon, and by those naively propounding technology's universalism and automatic utopia, with 'benefits' such as upskilling, job enrichment and so on. That technology may have a darker side can be seen in the grim panopticon-like employment conditions it has allowed in the increasingly numerous telephone 'call centres', with their close surveillance and control. As such, Braverman remains worth reading for those who have not done so and would repay rereading for those who need to refresh themselves.

Braverman became the main reference for many debates in diverse areas of management and business studies. He did much to put Marxist analysis back on the map, (re)launch and sustain many academic careers and fill the bookshelves of libraries and generations of academics and students. His ideas and views, while correctly criticized in some aspects, nevertheless still contain useful insights and analysis. As such, Braverman continues to resonate on into the twenty-first century.

BIBLIOGRAPHY

Armstrong, P. (1988) 'Labor and Monopoly Capital', in R. Hyman and W. Streeck (eds), *New Technology and Industrial Relations*, Oxford: Blackwell, 143–59.

Braverman, H. (1963) *The Future of Russia*, London: Collier Macmillan.

—— (1974) *Labor and Monopoly Capital: The Degradation of Work in the Twentieth Century*, New York: Monthly Review Press.

—— (1976) 'Two Comments', *Monthly Review* (June): 18–31.

Burawoy, M. (1979) *Manufacturing Consent: Changes in the Labor Process Under Monopoly Capitalism*, Chicago: University of Chicago Press.

Edwards, P. (1986) *Conflict at Work*, Oxford: Blackwell.

Edwards, R. (1979) *Contested Terrain: The Transformation of Work in the Twentieth Century*, London: Heinemann.

Friedman, A. (1977) *Industry and Labour: Class Struggle at Work and Monopoly Capitalism*, London: Macmillan.

Kelly, J. (1982) *Scientific Management, Job Design and Work Performance*, London: Academic Press.

Knights, D. and Willmott, H. (eds) (1990)

Labour Process Theory, London: Macmillan.

Littler, C. (1982) *The Development of the Labour Process in Capitalist Countries*, London: Hutchinson.

Noon, M. and Blyton, P. (1997) *The Realties of Work*, London: Macmillan.

Smith, C. (1998) 'Braverman, Harry', in M. Warner (ed.), *IEBM Handbook of Management Thinking*, London: International Thomson Business Press, 86–93.

Thompson, P. (1989) *The Nature of Work: An Introduction to Debates on the Labour Process*, London: Macmillan.

Wood, S. (ed.) (1982) *The Degradation of Work? Skill, Deskilling and the Labour Process*, London: Hutchinson.

—— (ed.) (1989) *The Transformation of Work? Skill, Flexibility and the Labour Process*, London: Unwin Hyman.

Zimbalist, A. (ed.) (1979) *Case Studies in the Labour Process*, New York: Monthly Review Press.

CR

BRONFMAN, Samuel (1889–1971)

Samuel Bronfman was born on 27 February 1889 either at Soroki, Bessarabia or en route to Canada from Russia (Newman, 1978, gives sources for both versions). He died of prostate cancer at Montreal, Quebec on 10 July 1971. The third son of a Jewish tobacco farmer who fled the pogroms in tsarist Russia, Bronfman spent his early life in Brandon, Manitoba. He left school at fifteen to join his father Ekiel and his brothers Abe and Harry, selling firewood in the summer and frozen whitefish in winter, and also selling half-broken wild horses to Manitoba farmers. The family enterprise flourished. In 1903, the Bronfmans were able to make a $5,000 Cdn down payment on the Anglo-American Hotel in Emerson, Manitoba. The hotel business boomed with construction of the Canadian Northern and Canadian Pacific railways, and within a few years the Bronfman family were running hotels in Winnipeg, Saskatchewan and Ontario. In his early twenties, Samuel Bronfman took charge of the family's largest investment, the $190,000 Cdn Bell Hotel in Winnipeg. Under his astute management, the hotel earned $30,000 Cdn profit a year. Bronfman made other investments, including a venture in muskrat furs that netted him $50,000 Cdn.

When prohibition came to Manitoba in 1916, the Bronfmans decided to quit the hotel business and turn their energies toward what became known in Canada as the inter-provincial package liquor trade – selling spirits through the mail. Samuel purchased the Bonaventure Liquor Store Company in Montreal, and stocked his warehouse with spirits produced by Canadian distilleries as he sought to satisfy a growing list of mail-order customers. He augmented his stock with imports of quality British brands. During the early 1920s the Bronfmans supplied much of the liquor exported from Canada, where it was largely legal, to the United States, where it was not. Prohibition drove US bootleggers and speakeasy operators towards Canada in search of liquor, and the Bronfmans served them from the French-owned islands of St Pierre and Miquelon, 24 kilometres (15 miles) off the Newfoundland coast.

In 1925 Samuel and his brothers Allan and Harry bought a distillery in Montreal and established a partnership with the Distillers Company of Edinburgh and London, manufacturer of such well-known Scotch brands as Haig, Black and White, Dewar's and Johnnie Walker. Three years later, Bronfman bought the Joseph E. Seagram and Sons distillery in Waterloo, Ontario. Deciding that prohibition could not last forever, he began to stockpile supplies. When US prohibition ended in 1933, Seagram was poised to serve the US hotel and liquor store market from one of the world's largest reserves of rye and bourbon whiskey.

Success in the United States made Seagram very profitable and led to the company's expansion throughout the world. Seven Crown and Seagram's VO became the world's largest-selling brands of whiskey. Under Bronfman's leadership, the company invested in wineries and distilleries, acquiring control of such brands as Chivas Regal scotch, Captain Morgan's rum, Mumm's champagne and Barton and Guestier wines.

In 1957, Bronfman, known to his family as 'Mr Sam', handed control to his son Edgar Miles Bronfman, who continued to increase Seagram's holdings in wine and spirits and also diversified into other industries including motion pictures and Broadway musicals. By 1965, Seagram's annual sales in 119 countries were estimated at more than one billion Canadian dollars. The company continued to grow and diversify after Bronfman's death; in 1995, Seagram became a major company in the entertainment field with its purchase of 80 per cent of the US entertainment conglomerate MCA. As of January 1995, Seagram had annual sales of $7.6 billion Cdn, assets of $18.2 billion Cdn and 15, 800 employees.

BIBLIOGRAPHY

Marrus, M.R. (1991) Mr. Sam, Toronto: Viking.
Newman, P.C. (1978) Bronfman Dynasty: The Rothschilds of the New World, Toronto: McClelland and Stewart.

BB

BURNHAM, James (1905–87)

James Burnham was born in Chicago on 22 November 1905, the son of Claude and Mary Burnham, and died at home in Kent, Connecticut on 28 July 1987. His family background was one of relative affluence, his father being a vice-president of the Burlington Railroad. Burnham was well educated, taking his BA in philosophy from Princeton University in 1927 and an MA in the same subject from Balliol College, Oxford in 1929. In 1930 he was appointed to teach philosophy at New York University, where he remained until 1953. He married Marcia Lightner in 1934; they had three children.

In the early 1930s, like many others of his background, Burnham was strongly drawn to communism, especially the brand espoused by Leon Trotsky. In 1935 he joined Trotsky's Fourth International Party, and wrote frequently for journals such as *New International* and *Partisan Review*. It is not known if he ever met Trotsky, who was then in exile in Mexico, but the two were frequent correspondents. Again like many others, Burnham became disillusioned with the Soviet state of Josef Stalin, and particularly by the alliance between the USSR and Nazi Germany on the eve of the Second World War. He quarrelled violently with Trotsky over the question of whether the USSR was in fact a socialist state (with Burnham maintaining that it was not). In March 1940 Burnham resigned from the party, continuing his polemic with Trotsky up until the latter's murder by Stalin's agents a few months later.

Although Burnham had rejected communism as a political ideology, he remained strongly influenced by Marxist thought, in particular the concept of the dialectic as a historical force. The next phase of his thought was characterized by a strong rejection of authoritarianism, in which category Burnham included not only fascism and Stalinism but also milder forms of state intervention such as Roosevelt's New Deal in the United States. His best and most influential books, *The Managerial Revolution* (1941) and *The Machiavellians* (1943), come from this period. In both works, his primary theme is power. Following the Marxist dialectic, he maintained that in any society there are two elite classes of people, those who have power and those who are attempting to take it. Both these groups are minorities, not representative of or working in the best interests of the masses.

From this position, Burnham moved almost inexorably towards libertarianism. In 1955, after leaving academia, Burnham took a post as a senior editor of the right-wing American journal the *National Review*, working closely with founder and owner William F. Buckley, Jr. Buckley and Burnham became close friends, and to Burnham is ascribed a role in toning down some of the journal's more radical right-wing views. He remained a bitter opponent of not only the USSR and its policies but of all those who advocated dealings with it; in *Suicide of the West* (1964), he accused Western liberals of opening up the Third World to Soviet domination through the withdrawal from empire. As well as Buckley, his admirers included Ronald Reagan, who, after becoming president of the United States, awarded Burnham the Presidential Medal of Freedom (1983). He had by then retired from the *National Review* after suffering a stroke in 1978.

In *The Managerial Revolution*, Burnham sets out an alternate view of social transformation from that espoused by MARX and his followers. In most types of society, says Burnham, the control of the means of production is in the hands of a small group. This group uses this power to give its members 'preferential treatment in the distribution of the products of those instruments' (1941: 56). Control alone, says Burnham, is never the ultimate end; elites use their control to determine both what is produced, and who receives the goods and services produced and in what quantity. Control of access and preferential treatment in distribution are thus closely related.

Marx hard argued that, just as the bourgeoisie had taken control of the means of production from the land-owning aristocracy, so in time the workers would take control from the bourgeoisie. Burnham, by 1941, believed Marx had been living in a fool's paradise. Rapid technological advance combined with the progressive de-skilling of workers through the division of labour meant that workers no longer had the capacity to take control; they lacked the skills to operate the means of production, even if they could manage to take *de facto* control.

Instead, said Burnham, a new class was rising to challenge the bourgeoisie, whom Burnham usually prefers to call the 'capitalists'. This was the 'new middle class': 'the salaried executives and engineers and managers and accountants and bureaucrats and the rest, who do not fit without distortion into either the "capitalist" or "worker" category' (1941: 48). Increasingly, these professional managers were removing control of instruments of production from the hands of the capitalists. He describes how this process happens, as the capitalists, who own those instruments, increasingly delegate their authority to others:

The big capitalists, legally the chief owners of the instruments of production, have in actual life been getting further and further away from those instruments, which are the final source and base of social dominance. This began some time ago, when most of the big capitalists withdrew from industrial production to finance ... the control necessarily became more indirect, exercised at second or third or fourth hand through financial devices. Direct supervision of the productive process was delegated to others, who, particularly with the parallel development of modern mass-production methods, had to assume more and more of the prerogatives of control – for example, the all-important prerogative of hiring and firing (the very heart of 'control over access to the instruments of production') as well as organization of the technical process of production.

(Burnham 1941: 95)

So far, this looks like nothing more than the separation of ownership and control thesis advanced by BERLE and MEANS in the previous decade. Burnham, however, believed that Berle and Means had not followed the concept through to its logical conclusion: that the managers, once they have achieved control, will then proceed to take ownership. In fact, says Burnham, the separation of ownership and control is largely an appearance: 'Ownership *means* control; if there is no control, then there is no ownership... If ownership and control are in reality separated, then ownership has changed hands, to the "control", and the separated ownership is a meaningless fiction' (1941: 87–8). And, by allowing managers control over the means of production, the capitalists had sown the seeds of their own doom:

> Control over access is decisive and ...will carry control over preferential treatment in distribution with it: that is, will shift ownership unambiguously to the new controlling, a new dominant, class. Here we see, from a new viewpoint, the mechanism of the managerial revolution.
>
> (Burnham 1941: 90)

The managerial revolution, says Burnham, is a struggle for power, in which the world is making the transition from a capitalist or bourgeois society into a managerial society. Moreover, the managers will be successful; the capitalists have neither the will nor the means to withstand them. From the perspective of the managers, they *must* take control in order to consolidate their own position. As long as they lack control, they can be hired and fired by the capitalist owners like any other employee, and their own privileged position – their own preferential access to distribution – will be lost. And in order to consolidate their control, they will take ownership as well.

Managerial control would not be exercised directly, however; on their own, managers were incapable of defeating the forces of capital. Burnham notes that there is little sense of a collective cause among managers, and it seems unlikely that they will unite to challenge the capitalists directly. Instead, he believes, they will take steps to exercise control over the state. It is the state which will be the managers' primary tool; state intervention and control will be the means by which they take over the means of production. 'Fusion with the economy of the state', he believed, offered managers their best chance of becoming the ruling class (Burnham 1941: 120).

That this revolution would be global in nature, Burnham did not doubt; forty years before globalization became a popular concept, he had already noted how 'the modern world is interlocked by myriad technological, economic, and cultural chains' (1941: 4). He predicted too the rise of economic superpowers dominating lesser states and, several decades before OHMAE's elucidation of the 'triad' theory, wrote that the United States, Japan and Europe would dominate the world between them (Burnham 1941: 167–8). George Orwell, who had read and critiqued *The Managerial Revolution* (Orwell 1946), borrowed elements of Burnham's theory for his novel *1984*.

What is particularly startling is Burnham's assumption that the managerial revolution would lead to totalitarianism. He saw German National Socialism and Soviet Marxist-Leninism as both being 'managerial ideologies'; in both states, wealth was concentrated in the hands of the upper classes, even more so than in the United States (this had been one of the causes of his argument with Trotsky). Although he does not say so explicitly, his argument implies that managers will develop a form of class consciousness, sufficient to allow them to recognize common interests and take concerted action using the state as a tool. At the time he was writing, this view would not have seemed far-fetched. Following the Wall Street crash of 1929, corporatism was in the air as corporations sought to defend their shrinking markets through alliances and combinations with government, trades unions and each other. Competition was seen by many as wasteful and ruinous; the free market was regarded by many even in high positions in industry with suspicion. As for managers themselves, they were being urged by writers such as Herbert CASSON to become more professional in their approach and to develop a stronger self-identity as managers.

In his subsequent work, *The Machiavellians*, Burnham looks once again at the question of power – who has it, and how they acquire it – in societies and organizations. His hero here is Niccolò Machiavelli, whom Burnham sees as a hero; Machiavelli, to him, is not a preacher of amoral political doctrines but a man who dares to tell the truth about how power is acquired and used. After him, Burnham lists a number of 'Machiavellians', scientists and writers who have explored the social foundations of power, including Gaetano Mosca, Georges Sorel, Roberto Michels and Vilifredo Pareto. Building on their work, Burnham sees all societies as characterized by a near-constant struggle between elites and non-elites; the rule of the former is based on a combination of force and fraud, constraining those groups who wish to overthrow the elites to use the same methods. The managers will triumph over the capitalists, he believes, because they have a greater will to win and because they believe their own survival as a class to be at stake.

The relationship between business and political control described here is an interesting one. Business stability requires political and economic stability; in the fifteenth century, Cosimo dei Medici had seized political power precisely to ensure such stability. In Aldous Huxley's novel *Brave New World*, of which Burnham certainly knew, a similar situation obtained. Burnham believed that if political control was threatened, the elites would move to secure their own position; thus the managers would take control of the state,

pushing the capitalists out of the dominant position.

Ultimately, however, this did not happen. Managers – like workers – remained more attached to their national, organizational and local identities and stayed largely loyal to the capital-owning classes. Burnham failed to foresee this, and he failed also to predict that managers would develop the ability to acquire ownership through the mechanisms of the market rather than turning to the state. By the 1990s, thanks to devices like executive share-ownership plans, mangers were well on their way to entering the owning classes, and the separation of owner and manager, like that of ownership and control, was beginning to blur. But if the managerial revolution did not turn out as Burnham predicted, his underlying thesis, that the growth of professional management was both part of and had a strong influence on the greater social changes of the twentieth century, remains a powerful one.

BIBLIOGRAPHY
Burnham, J. (1941) *The Managerial Revolution: Or, What is Happening in the World Now*, London: Putnam.
—— (1943) *The Machiavellians: Defenders of Freedom*, London: Putnam.
—— (1947) *The Struggle for the World*, London: Jonathan Cape.
—— (1964) *Suicide of the West: An Essay on the Meaning and Destiny of Liberalism*, London: Jonathan Cape.
Francis, S.T. (1984) *Power and History: The Political Thought of James Burnham*, New York: University Press of America.
Geiger, R. (1959) *Die Entwickzungstedenzen des Kapitalismus bei Keynes, Schumpeter and Burnham*, Winterthur.
Orwell, G. (1946) *James Burnham and the Managerial Revolution*, London: Socialist Book Centre.

MLW

BURRELL, Thomas J. (1939–)

Thomas J. Burrell was born in the Chicago suburb of Englewood on 18 March 1939, the son of a tavern-keeper and a beautician. Englewood was a black urban ghetto characterized by gang violence and race riots, in which Burrell grew up as something of an outsider. He did not do well at school, and was a failure in his first attempt to go to university; after dropping out he worked for a short time on an assembly line. Resolved to make a success of his career, and remembering a high-school aptitude test which showed he might make a good advertising copy-writer, he returned to Roosevelt University in 1957 and took a degree in English and advertising. In 1960 he took a job in the mailroom of Wade Advertising Agency in Chicago and began learning the business from the ground up, and on graduation the following year, Wade promoted him to copywriter; probably the only black advertising copywriter in Chicago, and one of the few in the country.

Through the 1960s Burrell worked with a succession of agencies, including Leo Burnett in Chicago and Foote, Cone and Belding in London. He proved to be a talented copywriter for television advertisements in particular, and was involved in a number of high-profile campaigns. Like other black members of creative teams in the industry, however, he was continually frustrated by the inability and/or lack of inclination of advertisers to appeal to the black market. Despite the rise of the civil liberties movement in the United States and consequent pressures on advertisers to recognize blacks in their advertising, the number of black subjects appearing in television advertisements was small and the ads themselves remained largely focused on the white market.

Believing he could break through in this sector of the market, Burrell and two colleagues established the Burrell McBain agency in Chicago in 1971 in a single-room office. Burrell believed that the best way to reach black viewers was not through promoting product features, but through 'lifestyle' advertising: 'to create and celebrate an image of black people that is positive and uplifting, which at the same time reflected positively upon the product' (Ingham and Feldman 1994: 124). He persuaded advertisers that this strategy would work, and quickly picked up high-profile clients such as Crest, Coca-Cola and McDonald's. In each case, he convinced the advertisers that their product-centred advertisements for the white market would not succeed with black consumers, and developed successful campaigns which centred on the core values of the black community. By 1980 Burrell's agency was by far and away the largest black-owned advertising agency in the country.

In the 1980s Burrell began moving out of advertising to purely black consumers and towards the general market. While product-oriented advertisements aimed at the white market would have limited appeal to black consumers, Burrell believed the reverse was not true: 'lifestyle' advertising would appeal to white consumers. His lifestyle advertisements for the general consumer market were widely imitated and won his agency several awards. His work has not only brought greater awareness of the needs and values of black consumers in the United States, it has also contributed greatly to general knowledge of consumer motivation and responsiveness to advertising. It has brought great success to his company, Burrell Communications, which had billings of $178 million in 1998 and was ranked the seventy-eighth largest advertising agency in the United States.

BIBLIOGRAPHY
Ingham, J.N. and Feldman, L.B. (1994) *African-American Business Leaders: A Biographical Dictionary*, Westport, CT: Greenwood Press.

MLW

C

CARNEGIE, Andrew (1835–1919)

Andrew Carnegie was born in Dunfermline, Scotland on 25 November 1835 and died in Lennox, Massachusetts on 11 August 1919. His father, Will Carnegie, and his mother Margaret were unemployed weavers, thrown out of work by the new industrial technology of the factory system. Impoverished by Britain's Industrial Revolution, the Carnegies took advantage of family ties to leave their home in Dunfermline and settle in Pittsburgh, Pennsylvania in 1848.

By 1853, Pittsburgh was a growing centre of about 50,000 people earning a living in coal and lumber. The city seemed sure to profit from the USA's dawning industrial age. The region where the tributaries of the Ohio river joined was rich in iron ore, bituminous coal and limestone. Already Pittsburgh boasted sixteen iron mills, and the nearby city of Connellsville was becoming the coke capital of the United States. When Carnegie arrived, a number of small plants and iron industries competed to service the local market.

Carnegie, then aged thirteen, had to enter the work force immediately. Like many immigrants, he was able to succeed not only by his dedication to hard work and learning on the job, but through the networking and support of his fellow Scottish immigrants. He began working as a bobbin boy in a textile factory owned by a fellow Scot, and from there graduated to another Scottish-owned factory where he managed the boiler room. The fact that his new boss could not write well enabled Carnegie to begin to help him with his books.

Carnegie was never one to neglect new ideas or methods of doing things, and this would be a paramount factor in his rise. He helped his boss during the day while studying accounting at night. His diligence soon led his boss to refer him to the Pittsburgh Telegraph Company. This new opportunity was the key to Andrew's future. Hired as a messenger, he was suddenly placed in contact with prominent Pennsylvania businessmen, whom he quickly impressed with his initiative. Seeing a future in new skills and technologies, he mastered Morse code.

By 1853, Andrew Carnegie was working as a telegraph operator, placed in one of the most strategic locations an entrepreneur could be. Western Pennsylvania boasted rich deposits of coal and oil, and had a lead in the railway and telegraph industries that, in the 1850s, were beginning to transform the United States. Carnegie was acquiring both networks and skills in a new economy that was poised on the verge of a take-off that would be accelerated by the Civil War. All his business dealings gave him expert market knowledge.

Carnegie took another major step at seventeen when he was hired to be the personal telegrapher of Thomas Scott, a prominent executive in the powerful Pennsylvania Railroad (the Penn). He worked for the Penn from 1853 to 1865, learning the skills of management, cost accounting, coordination of markets and personnel in an operation that extended from Philadelphia to Chicago. In his career at the Penn, Carnegie showed a remarkable initiative. When a derailment took place, he intervened, forging Scott's signature on an order to get the trains moving. In doing this he risked his entire career, but the risk paid off handsomely when he succeeded and Scott was impressed. By 1859, aged twenty-four, Carnegie was superintendent of the whole Penn Western Division.

In the meantime, he had become a successful investor due to dividends from some stocks he had acquired cheaply with Scott's help. When Scott entered into the partnership of the new Woodruff Sleeping Car Company, Carnegie was given 13 per cent of the shares, adding $5,000 a year to his income. Carnegie then proceeded to sink this new capital into the emerging oil industry. Less cautious than Ohio's John D. ROCKEFELLER, who would invest in refining, Carnegie, with capital to risk and spare, invested in the oil boom which swept Western Pennsylvania on the eve of the Civil War. He formed an oil partnership called Columbia Oil, and in the first year made a near 50 per cent profit on his investment.

The Civil War launched the fortunes of many of the USA's greatest tycoons, especially the giants Carnegie, Rockefeller and J.P. MORGAN. Columbia did so well that the one-time bobbin boy, making fifty dollars a year in 1848, earned almost $50,000 a year by 1863. He now managed a series of industries, including the Keystone Bridge Company, Union Iron Mills, the Superior Rail Mill and the Pittsburgh Locomotive Works. By 1868 he also had a share in Union Pacific, Western Union and the Pullman Palace Car Company. Carnegie, however, saw that his future and that of the United States lay in steel. Railroads, oil and steel formed a synergy in which growth in one stimulated growth in the others. As Americans fought to preserve the Union and poured westward into California, the Plains and the Rockies, forging a continental market linked by railways, Carnegie recognized that railroads

needed locomotives, rolling stock, rails and bridges.

Iron-making in the United States in the 1850s and even 1860s was still a slow business. Britain dominated the techniques and the market. British and early US foundries converted iron ore into pig iron by expelling the impurities. The more impurities one expelled from iron, such as oxygen, carbon or phosphorous, the stronger the iron would be. US iron-makers used charcoal and, at first, hard anthracite coal in their smelting process. As the railroads crossed the Alleghenies and joined the Northeast to the growing states of the Midwest, the demand for iron rails became insatiable. The coke ovens of Connellsville quickly became a major source of cheaper US pig iron, now smelted with the soft bituminous coal of Western Pennsylvania.

Carnegie set up the Cyclops Iron Works in 1864 and the following year he resigned from the Penn, never to work for a salary again. As the network of rail lines in the Northeast and Midwest turned into a thick web that thrust its strands into places such as Nebraska, Colorado, Texas and California, more trains ran on them and the trains were heavier. Iron rails wore out very quickly. Carnegie proposed to market sturdier and better rails. Telegraphy and railroads revolutionized the economy in the 1840s and 1850s, and Carnegie saw the potential of both. The same was true of steel, which was far sturdier than iron, but steel was too expensive to be profitably used at that time.

Carnegie, however, was aware that Henry Bessemer in 1856 had developed a cheap means of making steel by blowing compressed air through molten iron. The process, developed at the same time by William Kelly in the United States, was patented in 1866, opening the door for the commercial production of a metal that was far sturdier than even the purest wrought iron. Carnegie quickly decided that instead of diversifying in railroads, oil and iron, he would throw all his resources into the essential new technology of steel, and excel at it. Setting up

Carnegie, McCandless, and Company, he proceeded to hire the world's leading expert on Bessemer steel to design the state-of-the-art Edgar Thomson Steel Works, on the field where George Washington and General Braddock had been defeated by the French in 1754. The works, built by Carnegie engineer Alexander Holley (1832–82) between 1873 and 1875 were named after Pennsylvania Railroad President John Edgar THOMSON. Investing in a new plant in the depths of the 1873 depression seemed foolish to many, but Carnegie had the resources to do it, thanks to the careful and cautious management of his assets. The severe deflation, moreover, cut his costs and weeded out his potential competitors. Situated at the junction of the Allegheny, Monongehela and Ohio Rivers, and close to the Penn and B&O rail yards, the Thomson Works had easy access to coal, iron, oil and customers.

Rivers and rail lines gave the Thomson Works access to the newly discovered deposits of soft, easily-mined low-phosphorous iron ore found in Upper Michigan, and the soon to be uncovered beds of eastern Minnesota. By 1900 the Mesabi Range would provide one-third of all US iron and one-sixth of all the iron in the world. If Minnesota would provide the raw materials of US power, Carnegie would provide the means to turn it into the finished steel that guaranteed that power.

The new steel-maker's management skills allowed him, like Rockefeller, to outproduce and undercut any rivals. Carnegie possessed superior market intelligence and technology, and used both to his advantage. He applied his management experience learned on the railroad to control his costs systematically. For Carnegie, controlling costs was the key to profit, for costs were far more predictable than earnings. Unlike others, Carnegie knew well in advance whether a given year would show a profit or a loss. He could set his prices wherever he needed to keep his plants running at full capacity. He could threaten to undercut his competitors for, unlike them, he knew his steel cost fifty dollars a ton.

The millions Carnegie saved were ploughed into investments in new steel-making techniques. Quickly, the USA began to overtake Britain in steel production. In 1870, Britain produced 292,000 tons of steel to the USA's 69,000; by 1880 the USA, led by Carnegie, was catching up with 1,247,000 to Britain's 1,375,000. By 1890 Carnegie, and what was left of his competition, forged ahead: 4,217,000 to 3,679,000. By 1900 the giant Carnegie combine dominated a steel industry that produced twice as much steel as did Britain: 10,188,000 tons versus 5,050,000 tons in a world steel market of 28,273,000 tons.

Carnegie knew well that innovation cut costs and created profits, market shares and jobs. He was eventually able to make ever-larger steel production runs at no higher cost. He invested heavily in research to allow his firm to cut out any redundant steps in the process. Molten iron was poured directly into the steel converters, and steel ingots were loaded onto moving flatcars. Carnegie soon applied the new open-hearth process pioneered by Englishmen Sidney Thomas and Percy Gilchrist, which meant cheaper, faster and better steel production. By the 1890s this new steel was replacing Bessemer steel. Carnegie recognized what his British (and US) competitors did not: that investment in new plants and techniques might seem more risky and expensive at first, but that the productivity and market-share advantages would eventually even the score. Carnegie's cheaper, higher-quality steel captured the market from that produced by firms which still clung to the techniques of the 1860s in the 1880s and 1890s. From $200 per ton in 1810, the price of steel was reduced to $20 per ton by 1900. In 1860 iron-makers were shipping 100,000 tons of ore from Michigan; by 1900 Carnegie controlled the lion's share of over 10 million tons coming largely from the Mesabi.

Carnegie was a pioneer in mass production before Henry FORD. Machinery loaded his blast furnaces and dumped pig iron onto freight cars. Carnegie was now able to build blast furnaces that were 30 metres high, cutting his labour costs in half. Because of this and other innovations, Carnegie Steel prospered during the 1890s depression, expanding by 75 per cent while other firms were going under. Carnegie's strategy was to develop economies of scale, know the contours of the entire market, and gain as much market knowledge as possible to anticipate shifts ahead of time. According to his partner Charles SCHWAB, Carnegie's success was due to his ability to anticipate competitors in manufacturing better and cheaper than they did.

By the late 1880s Carnegie was riding a railway boom that saw the construction of many lines in the West and the South. He sensed that the market for steel rails would soon be saturated, while vast new markets for steel structures were opening up everywhere. The United States was fast becoming an urban nation as ranks of immigrants and displaced farmers flocked to the cities. A boom in construction of skyscrapers, steel-braced offices, elevated trains, trolleys, utility lines and bridges meant one thing for Carnegie: an enormous new market for all kinds of steel products.

Carnegie rose to the new challenge in the boldest manner possible, through vertical integration. He placed Henry Clay Frick in charge of rationalizing all Carnegie operations. The vast new mines of Minnesota were leased from the Rockefellers. Carnegie used Rockefeller's rolling stock and shipping, but soon bought his own ore ships and set up his own mining subsidiary, the $20 million Oliver Iron Mining Company. To further internalize his operations, Carnegie built his own rail line from Conneaut, Ohio, on the shores of Lake Erie, to Pittsburgh. Iron could now be mined, shipped and turned into steel without ever leaving Carnegie's control. The depression of the 1890s, the worst in US history at that time, only dented Carnegie's growth, with his annual profits still averaging $4 million a year between 1893 and 1896.

In spite of his enormous wealth, Andrew Carnegie remained socially progressive. He read widely, including the Bible, the classics, Shakespeare, Macaulay, Darwin and the works of the social Darwinist philosopher Herbert Spencer. Believing that all was well since all grew better, he, like J.P. Morgan and John D. Rockefeller, modified the freewheeling ideology of unrestrained market competition. Carnegie's own idea was that big firms like his own were actually good for competition because they would attract new enterprises and new money. Meanwhile, mass production and the application of technology and rational management would raise everyone's living standards.

Andrew Carnegie's philosophy, set forth in his 1889 *Gospel of Wealth* and his *Autobiography*, was a remarkable synthesis of social Darwinism and philanthropy in which the law of competition applied to firms more than individuals. *The Gospel of Wealth* contained in a single volume a defence of inequality linked to one of the strongest statements of *noblesse oblige* ever penned by a business leader. The revolution in productivity Carnegie had done so much to perfect now enabled the poor to 'enjoy what the rich could not before afford'. The only thing that made this possible was 'the concentration of business industrial and commercial, in the hands of a few; and the law of competition between these' as being beneficial and essential for the survival of the human race. Managers in this world must of necessity make as much profit as they could (Hacker 1968: 359).

Carnegie's defence of business concentration provoked a highly critical response, particularly in Britain, which linked the rise of firms such as Carnegie's to the growing disparity of rich and poor. In the British journal *Nineteenth Century*, Carnegie replied in 1891 by showing that the prosperity of the millionaire was inseparable from that of his fellow citizens: 'In a country where the millionaire exists there is little excuse for pauperism; the condition of the masses is satisfactory just in proportion as a country is blessed with millionaires' (Hacker 1968: 360). Large companies created wealth, not destroyed it. There were hardly any millionaires in all of Asia, more in Britain than in all of Europe, and even more in the United States, where a worker could make twice as much as in Britain and four times as much as in Europe. Millionaires created wealth for everyone, and would make no money by exploiting their workers. The higher the wages an employer paid, the higher would be his profits.

Andrew Carnegie was one of the most progressive employers of the Gilded Age. He paid his workers well, and acknowledged their right to form trade unions. He disdained the use of strike breakers. His reputation as a benevolent merchant prince was, however, to be forever tarnished by the bitter Homestead strike of 1892, for which he was not directly responsible. Carnegie had left the Homestead operation in the hands of Frick, whose philosophy of management was far more rigid than his own. When the steelworkers' contract came up for renewal, Frick rolled back their wages in a deepening recession. The workers, who mistrusted Frick, perceived an attempt on the part of management to destroy the union. Acting high-handedly, Frick sent a private army of Pinkertons (private detectives and security guards) to occupy the steel mills. One of the most ferocious industrial battles in US history then took place, with workers attacking the Pinkertons with a cannon and pouring oil into the Monongehela, which was then set on fire. Seven died and the Pennsylvania militia had to restore order. Frick himself was wounded by an anarchist agitator. The mills reopened, with non-union labour. Carnegie, in Scotland at the time, did nothing on behalf of the workers, but supported Frick. As a result, his progressive reputation received a blow from which it never fully recovered. According to the *St. Louis Post-Dispatch*: 'Three months ago Andrew Carnegie was a man to be envied. Today he is an object of mingled pity and contempt' (Smith 1984: 477). Homestead produced a great deal of soul-searching in Carnegie, which served to reinforce his philanthropic instincts.

Although he lived in a time in which the trust and the limited liability corporation were fast taking over US management, Carnegie still expressed a preference for the partnership form. In a corporation, bankers and promoters were too close to the seat of power to permit the best management decisions to be made. Carnegie felt that in his partnership of thirty-two executives, which resembled a giant replica of the ancient Roman publican partnership, the input and expertise of men like Frick and Schwab were indispensable to his success. In his huge operation, Carnegie saw himself merely as the first among equals and gave his partners due credit for their mutual success.

Nevertheless, Carnegie in 1900 defended the trust and corporate forms as essential in concentrating capital, accessing a national market and cheapening the cost of goods. In a piece entitled 'Popular Illusions about Trusts', he linked low prices to the scale of production: to 'make ten tons of steel a day would cost many times as much per ton as to make one-hundred tons ... the larger the scale of operation, the cheaper the product' (Hacker 1968: 361).

In spite of all his success, Carnegie by 1900 faced a challenge from one of the few powerful enough to challenge him. The banker J.P. Morgan was now branching into the steel industry and cutting into Carnegie's vast market. The new Morgan steel firms were no match for Carnegie, but it would take a decade to put them out of business, and Andrew Carnegie, at sixty-five, was not up to the struggle. Morgan had two assets: his money, and Charles Schwab. Schwab insisted that the steel industry now needed more, not less, specialization, as both Carnegie and his rivals sought to make the same kinds of steel. Schwab argued that plants should concentrate on rails, girders or pipes and relocate to the most cost-efficient locations, and envisioned an amalgamation of most (but not all) steel companies into one large firm. Morgan, dreading the prospect of a steel war with the Carnegie colossus, liked what he heard and offered $400 million for the Carnegie Company. Carnegie finally accepted $492 million in 1901.

Carnegie retired from the business world, leaving as his legacy the $1.4 billion United States Steel Corporation, a gargantuan trust made up of the Carnegie, National Steel, National Tube, American Steel and Wire, American Steel Hoop, American Tin Plate, American Sheet Steel, American Bridge, Shelby Steel Tube Companies and the Lake Superior Consolidated Iron Mines with all of its fleet, mines, and rail lines. Having never totally buried his egalitarian origins, he now devoted his life to donating some $350 million to libraries, parks, universities, trust funds and the cause of world peace, until his death in 1919.

After the American Civil War, steel became the key index of world power. The fact that the United States became the foremost steel-producing power in the world was due in part to its immense resources and huge domestic market, but the role of Andrew Carnegie and his prudent, innovative management was central. Carnegie's contributions to the advancement of US management were enormous in terms of both ideas and accomplishments. He created almost single-handedly the industry that made the United States the most powerful country in the world. Without him, Ford, General Motors, Boeing and Allied victory in both world wars would have been impossible. He pioneered the understanding that specialization and determined investment in new technologies was the key to both a firm's and a nation's competitiveness. Carnegie also led the way in systematic cost accounting which, coupled with a knowledge of past and present market conditions, gave him a great advantage over his rivals. Finally, his advanced views on labour relations and

corporate philanthropy, despite Homestead, foreshadowed the welfare capitalism of the 1950s.

BIBLIOGRAPHY
Hacker, L.M. (1968) *The World of Andrew Carnegie: 1865–1901*, New York: Lippincott and Co.
Smith, P. (1984) *The Rise of Industrial America: A People's History of the Post-Reconstruction Era*, vol. 6, New York: McGraw-Hill Book Company.
Wall, J.F. (1970) *Andrew Carnegie*, New York: Oxford University Press.

DCL

CARPENTER, Walter Samuel, Jr
(1888–1976)

Walter Samuel Carpenter was born in Wilkes-Barre, Pennsylvania on 8 January 1888 and died in Wilmington, Delaware on 2 February 1976. The son of an engineering contractor, also named Walter Samuel Carpenter, and his wife, Belle Carpenter née Morgan, Carpenter attended public schools in his hometown and graduated in 1906 from Wyoming Seminary, a prep school in nearby Kingston, Pennsylvania. He then entered Cornell University, where he planned to earn a degree in civil engineering. He never finished his degree. He worked at Du Pont every summer during his first three years at Cornell, and left university during his senior year to take a full-time job with the company in Chile's barren north coastal region. There he assumed responsibility for purchasing the vast tonnage of sodium nitrate needed for Du Pont's explosives operations.

The Chilean nitrate market was very competitive but Carpenter did well, obtaining the immense quantities Du Pont needed. After two years in Chile, in 1911 he was assigned to work in the development department at Du Pont's corporate headquarters in Wilmington, Delaware. In 1917, as the United States entered the First World War and the market for Du Pont explosives expanded, Carpenter was appointed director of the firm's development division. By 1919 he was a vice-president and, at the age of thirty-one, the firm's youngest director and executive committee member. The firm's three principals, the cousins Irénée, Lammot and Pierre DU PONT, were reshaping the family company at this time, and Carpenter was one of the key people they relied on as they moved forward.

Carpenter was involved in the early negotiations that were to carry Du Pont into such products as ammonia derivatives, rayon, celluloid and lacquers. Each became significant in the development of the new chemical and product divisions that fuelled the company's growth: Ammonia led to the manufacture of polychemicals. Rayon was a staple for developing the textile fibres division. Celluloid led to plastics, and lacquers became the foundation for Du Pont's paint manufacturing business.

In 1922 Carpenter was named treasurer of Du Pont, and successively served as a member of the finance committee, vice-chairman of the executive committee and chairman of the finance committee. In the latter role, he maintained Du Pont's investment in research and promoted the construction of new plants for new products. In 1927 he was one of a group of Du Pont executives elected to the board of General Motors after Du Pont made a major investment in the latter firm. He served on the General Motors board until 1959.

In May 1940 Carpenter succeeded Lammot du Pont to become the first president of Du Pont who was not a member of the du Pont family. With the United States poised to enter the Second World War, Carpenter spearheaded Du Pont's participation in a vast government production programme in which the firm designed, built and operated fifty defence plants, ranging from relatively small units to an engineering works in Hanford, Washington, where plutonium for the first atomic bomb was made.

After the war, Carpenter changed the business focus of the company to achieve production levels more suited to a peacetime economy, then stepped down as president in favour of Crawford Greenwalt. Carpenter became chairman of the board and served for fourteen years. In 1962 he accepted the rarely bestowed title of honorary chairman, which he held until 1975 when, at the age of eighty-seven, he chose not to stand for re-election. He thus ended a sixty-five-year career with Du Pont. At that point, the firm was manufacturing more than 1,600 chemical products, and had plants or offices in thirty-four states and several countries.

Carpenter died at his home in Wilmington at the age of eighty-eight. His peers remembered him as a thoughtful man who was able to grasp key points quickly, and who could see future needs and opportunities clearly. They also remembered him as a strong proponent of owner-management of large industrial firms, and how he saw this as one of the competitive advantages Du Pont wielded over the course of its long history. Carpenter was a firm believer in the philosophy that managers should have a stake in the company beyond their salaries by becoming major stockholders.

BIBLIOGRAPHY
Cheape, C.W. (1995) *Strictly Business: Walter Carpenter at Du Pont and General Motors*, Baltimore, MD: Johns Hopkins University Press.

BB

CASSON, Herbert Newton (1869–1951)

Herbert Newton Casson was born in Odessa, Ontario on 23 September 1869. He died at home in Norwood, Surrey on 4 September 1951. His father, the Reverend Wesley Casson, was a Methodist missionary from County Durham in northern England; his mother, Elizabeth Jackson, came from an immigrant family in Brantford, Ontario and had in her youth been known as 'the Belle of Brantford'. During Casson's youth the family moved around the remote bush towns of northern Ontario, as his father was posted to a new church every three years. The years 1877–80 were spent in the frontier province of Manitoba, whose population was still mostly nomadic Plains Indians and Métis (mixed race) peoples; years later, Casson recalled vividly the sight of armed Métis horsemen riding into the trading post where his father's church was located (Casson 1931). The family returned to Ontario in early 1880, shortly before the outbreak of the Métis rebellion led by Louis Riel.

Although he says he had no formal education until the age of seventeen, the years on the frontier taught Casson a great deal, including self-confidence and self-reliance. In his youth, he recalled, people turned their hands to everything necessary to make a living; if you did not know how to do something, then you learned. By the time Casson went to Victoria College (now part of the University of Toronto) in 1890 on a theology scholarship, he had acquired a hunger for knowledge, both theoretical and practical. The almost compulsive desire for learning is one of the constant features of his life:

I have found that knowledge is infinite. The longer I live, the more I realize that what I know is only a very small thing. On every road I have travelled, I have found there is no end to it. Every man who wishes to live a worth-while life must keep on learning as long as he has breath. I dare say that when my doctor tells me I have only three more days to live, I shall begin to study coffins.
(Casson 1931: 231–2)

Although Casson wished to study philosophy, the scholarship granted by the Methodist church would only allow him to study theology. Undeterred, he obtained permission to double up his courses and graduated with a joint degree from Victoria College in 1892. He was immediately offered a position by the church. He had not yet been ordained, but there was a shortage of ministers and Casson was given the church at Owen Sound, Ontario late in 1892, along with a small salary. Just twenty-three, he threw himself into his job, starting a temperance movement soon after his arrival. Quite what happened next, Casson does not relate, stating only that men flocked to his church, but women left it in large numbers. In the following year he was tried by the Methodist church council for heresy and found guilty. He resigned his position and went south to Boston, where he found work with a publishing company.

His brief career as a Methodist clergyman had given Casson a sense of social responsibility, and also seems to have encouraged a desire to rebel. In Boston in 1893 he visited the immigrant slums on the south side of the city and was shocked by the terrible poverty he found there. He became, almost overnight, a socialist; within a few months he was one of the USA's leading 'Red' agitators, leading mass demonstrations in Boston, drawing audiences of thousands to his lectures and rallies, and establishing links with socialist leaders elsewhere. Among the friends he made in this period – names he still mentions with affection forty years on – were the British socialist leader Keir Hardie, the American trade union boss Samuel Gompers, and Walter Vrooman, later co-founder of Ruskin College, Oxford. It was Hardie, Casson recalled in his memoirs, who first put into his head the idea of going to Britain (Casson 1931).

In 1898, following the destruction of the US battleship *Maine* in the port of Havana, Cuba, war fever swept the United States, fomented by newspaper owners like William Randolph HEARST and Joseph PULITZER. Casson, opposed to the war for both personal and ideological reasons, tried to organize a pacifist movement. Almost unanimously, his followers deserted him, clamouring in support of the war movement. Many years later, writing his autobiography, Casson's tone still betrays his bitterness: 'Everything that I had built up in six years was destroyed in a week' (Casson 1931: 57).

Seeking refuge from the crushing of his hopes, Casson joined what he thought would be a group of like-minded people, the Ruskin Colony, a socialist commune founded in Tennessee the previous year. He was bitterly disappointed. He found at Ruskin not the camaraderie of true socialists working together for a goal, but a group of quarrelling, factionalized, suspicious people living together in filth and abject misery on a diet of rice and beans. He stayed for six months, by the end of which the scales had fallen from his eyes. He wrote later:

> this strange adventure cured me of all sympathy with Socialism or Communism. It swept my mind clear of all the plausible theories of social democracy. It opened my eyes to the fact that there is no tyrant like the mob – that the most efficient thing in every nation is the leadership of the 'Efficient Few' ... As soon as I left Ruskin Colony, I became a defender of civilization.
> (Casson 1931: 60–61)

After some heart searching, he resolved on a complete change of course. As he puts it simply: 'I had seen the best the Communism could do. And now I wanted to see the best that could be done by private Capitalism' (Casson 1931: 65). He had heard something of the reputation of John PATTERSON at National Cash Register, and travelled north to visit the latter's factory in Dayton. The meeting with Patterson and his tour of the Dayton plant, clean and well-ventilated with comfortable dining and health facilities for the workers, made a deep impression; he described the passage from Ruskin to Dayton as one from squalor to opulence. Around this time too, Casson met and married Lydia Kingsmill Commander.

Casson had always had an ability to write, and he now went to New York, where he quickly found a job with Arthur Brisbane at the *New York Evening Journal*; here he spent six months learning the newspaper trade. He was then offered a job by Joseph Pulitzer on the *New York World*, and accepted (apparently ready to forgive Pulitzer's role in the war fever of 1898). The *World* at this point was abandoning its downmarket competition with the Hearst papers and was beginning to set new standards for quality journalism. Casson, after an interval, was made editor of the *World*'s Forum Page, where he made a speciality of interviewing people in positions of power. An early break came when he persuaded the notoriously taciturn President Grover Cleveland to grant him an interview. The two men became friendly, and Casson remained a confidante of Cleveland for many years. From politicians and leading academics Casson went on to interview inventors and scientists, including Marconi, Tesla, EDISON and BELL, and then businessmen such as Edward FILENE and John WANAMAKER. He became a leading member of the New York literary scene, friendly with Mark Twain and other leading writers. Among his coups was the first published interview with the brothers Orville and Wilbur Wright, shortly after their first powered flight at Kitty Hawk, North Carolina.

In 1905 the editor Frank Munsey offered Casson a job on *Munsey's Magazine*, with a brief to write a series of profiles of the steel barons. This later became Casson's first book, *The Romance of Steel: The Story of a Thousand Millionaires*, published in 1907. From this success he went on to write on the combine harvester industry and the development of the telephone; he also produced a biography of Cyrus Hall MCCORMACK at the request of the latter's widow. His pen portraits of American business leaders at the beginning of the century are still highly evocative: Andrew CARNEGIE he describes as 'one of the most original and sagacious men I have ever known'; Henry Clay Frick was 'a man of steel – keen, hard, competent'; Charles M. SCHWAB was 'always uncomfortable in the midst of his grandeur'; of J.P. MORGAN in a rage, 'the very look of him made my knees shake (Casson 1931: 107–15). Most moving of all, perhaps, is his decription of Joseph Pulitzer, blind, ill, gnawed by doubt, 'tearing his life into shreds and tatters' as he sat at the heart of his publishing empire (Casson 1931: 76).

Casson's research on the telephone industry had made him friends among the senior executives of Bell, and as a favour he did some publicity work and copy-writing for them. He later did the same for the cities of Buffalo and Denver. When Standard Oil found itself under public pressure following the publication of Ida M. TARBELL's *History of the Standard Oil Company* in 1904, the younger John D. Rockefeller, who knew Casson, recommended him to the company's executives; Casson helped manage Standard's public during the fight against the anti-trust suit filed by the US government, and became friendly with H.K. McCann, the company's advertising manager.

Casson was now working in the heart of American business, and his knowledge of varied business methods and far-flung network of contacts brought him to the attention of Harrington EMERSON, the efficiency expert and one of the country's leading business consultants. Emerson wrote to Casson in the spring of 1908:

He said: 'Perhaps you are not aware of it, but you have become an Efficiency Expert. Why not come and join my organization?' I went and became his partner. I may say that I was fascinated with him. I found that he knew clearly what I had discovered for myself vaguely.

(Casson 1931: 152)

Casson worked with Emerson for about a year, helping to publicize Emerson's work and becoming immersed in the details of this new movement. He perceived that the principles behind the efficiency movement, hitherto applied primarily to production techniques, could also be applied to marketing, especially to advertising and sales. He tried to persuade Emerson to develop business in this direction, but Emerson had doubts as to whether efficiency methods would work in marketing. Undaunted, Casson left Emerson and spent the following year researching and writing a book, *Advertisements and Sales* (1911). Shortly thereafter, Standard Oil was broken up at the successful conclusion of the government's anti-trust suit, and Casson's friend H.K. McCann found himself out of a job. Pooling their capital, Casson and McCann founded the H.K. McCann Advertising Company in 1911, based on the principles Casson had described in his book. Casson sold out his share of the partnership in early 1914, doubling his money. He later commented wryly that if he had kept his shares he would have become rich many times over; the H.K. McCann Company went on to become McCann-Erickson, one of the world's largest and richest advertising companies.

In 1914, however, Casson had decided that he wanted to retire, and revived his old dream of settling in England. In April 1914 he bought a house in Norwood, suburb of London, and settled his family there. A few months later the First World War broke out, and British industry went onto a war footing. Casson resolved to help his adopted country in any way that he could. Discovering – to his horror – that the efficiency movement was almost unknown in Britain, he set about publicizing it. He began programmes of lectures on efficiency and its merits for the managers of factories, most notable being the course of six lectures at the Manchester firm of Mather & Platt which the company itself later published (Casson 1917). He set up a publishing company and began writing a stream of books on efficiency and on management more generally; he also founded a journal, *Efficiency*, patterned partly on Arch SHAW's American journal *System*, which he published and also wrote in large part. Thus Casson embarked on his fifth and final career, as one of Britain's leading management consultants. He continued to write and publish through the 1920s and 1930s, and was in demand in Britain and around the world as a public speaker. In 1950 he embarked on a ten-month lecture tour of Australia, New Zealand and Fiji. He died shortly after his return.

Casson remains best known today as one of the first writers to introduce the work of Emerson and of Frederick W. TAYLOR to Britain, and as one of the most prominent early apostles of scientific management in that country. But there was much more to his work than that. His publications amount to some 170 books, and even if some of the later texts are repackaged versions of earlier works, the breadth of his interests was still great. He continued his emphasis on applying the principles of efficiency to marketing and sales; he also wrote a number of what would now be described as 'self-help books' for managers, encouraging them to improve their learning and reasoning abilities. Often these had catchy titles such as *Fifty-two Ways to Be Rich* or *Fourteen Ways to Increase Profits* and were little more than collections of aphorisms. But there is still a considerable body of work which focuses on the nature of management itself. Through much of his later writing, Casson is consciously trying to explain what management *is*, often to managers who had never considered the subject before.

One of the greatest failings in management, he found, was a reliance on tradition rather than reason and study:

Managers had never studied management. Employers had never studied employership.

Sales managers had never studied the art of influencing public opinion. There were even financiers who had never studied finance. On all hands I found guess-work and muddling ... A mass of incorrect operations was standardized into a routine. Stokers did not know how to stoke. Factory workers did not know how to operate their machines. Foremen did not know how to handle their men. Managing directors did not know ... the principles of organization... . Very few had LEARNED how to do what they were doing.

(Casson 1931: 222–3)

The result is confusion, error and myth: 'There are nearly as many myths and delusions in business as there were in ancient philosophies and religious. I have seen many an industrial process that was as absurd as a ceremonial in a temple in Thibet' (Casson 1931: 227).

To learn, Casson, concluded, it was necessary for a manager to swallow his pride and turn to the outside for help. One common objection to his work that he encountered throughout his consultancy career was from managers who believed that only they knew how their business worked. Casson believed this was impossible: no individual could know how the whole of a business worked, especially not a large business. As a result, managers mistook their own partial knowledge for knowledge of the whole. Following his lifelong credo, Casson says there is always room to learn, and expresses this in his usual robust fashion:

If a man says: 'I know all about my own business' he is ready to die; he is finished; he cannot go on amongst ordinary men any more; he knows to much. The only finished man is a dead man.

(Casson 1917: 3)

Bringing in outsiders cannot only provide new or missing knowledge, it can also shake up and alter ways of thinking. In his lectures at

Mather & Platt, Casson noted how many managers take their work for granted. They ask 'how' a thing is done, but they rarely ask the much more important question of 'why' it is done in a particular way. Outside consultants, by asking these kinds of questions, force managers to question and challenge their own beliefs and arrive at new ways of looking a things (Casson 1917). Although he also provided technical support, it was this challenging and analytical approach that lay at the core of Casson's business and consulting philosophy:

> When a man has studied many books and businesses, the secret of his success as an Efficiency Expert is not at all his cleverness. He may not be clever at all. He succeeds because of the magic of the SCIENTIFIC METHOD – because he notices, studies, leans and creates. He searches for facts. He doubts what he is told. He cares nothing for opinions. He looks at a business with sharp eyes, as a small boy looks at a circus. He follows up clues. He takes nothing for granted. He studies the business as a whole, and his purpose is to increase the percentage of the result.
>
> (Casson 1931: 226)

Casson, like Peter DRUCKER two decades later, believed that management is purposive action; in his philosophy, management is about getting things done. His approach is first to define action as 'the creation of causes that are likely to produce a certain desired effect'; the manager must 'first study the nature of the desired effect, then create the causes that are most likely to produce it' (Casson 1935: 13). He classes actions in two types: *routine*, doing what was done before, and *creative*, doing something new. Routine action is important and necessary, but creative action is what takes companies forward. Creative action includes staff training, finding customers, planning, employee relations, advertising and so on. He calls for an 'action habit of mind' to

be developed in managers, and comments that there is too much fear in the business world, especially fear of authority and fear of failure, and fear in turn inhibits action. He also argues for the importance of creativity (Casson 1928: 149), and is particularly admiring of the firm of Cadbury, which he regarded as being the best example in the world of a firm that had stimulated and harnessed the creativity of its employees (Casson 1928: 165). He argued that every firm should conduct research to generate new knowledge: there should be a nucleus of creative thinkers, which should be as large as possible (Casson 1928: 163).

Casson had a strong authoritarian streak, and he sometimes talked of progress being the result of the 'efficient few' pushing against the opposition of the many. He believed that leadership is essential to overcoming the barrier of inertia that he sees everywhere, in work as well as in society. Yet his model of organization was not simply command and control. Like Emerson, he pushed for the adoption of the line and staff model of organization, and believed discipline to be important. But authority alone cannot manage a successful company (Casson 1935: 20). Managers must also learn to motivate their employees, to make them feel respected and part of the organziation for which they work. Real authority, says Casson, derives from the respect rather than ranks or titles. He also takes a dynamic view of how businesses function, and advocates planning and process engineering: 'Work travels. Every job has a Cook's Tour through the factory; and it should not start until its journey has been planned and everything made ready for it' (Casson 1935: 25).

Casson developed an organic model of organization which used the human body as a metaphor; this was widely influential, being cited by early writers on organization such as Charles KNOEPPEL. He also became increasingly interested in psychology and the motivations for human action, in terms of both marketing and organizational study. *Human*

Nature (1918) is an attempt to explain some of the basics of motivational theory to managers, and makes a useful distinction between those motivating factors which relate to our individual needs and those which relate to our social needs; he classes these as *centrifugal* and *centripetal* needs, respectively:

> Each set of qualities needs to be offset by the other. If a man has centripetal qualities only, he is mere raw material. He is undeveloped. He has no personality. If he has centrifugal needs only, he is a crank, an outlaw, a genius or a lunatic.
>
> (Casson 1918: 191)

The need for balance, in organizations and in people, is constantly stressed. The same principles are considered in relation to marketing, notably in his earlier *The Axioms of Business* (1915), in which he argues that an understanding of consumer motivations and needs is the key to successful sales. Price, he says, is overrated as a factor; it does not matter so much as the nature of the proposition (Casson 1915: 64), and it is actually quite difficult to set prices too high:

> I once saw a millionaire Pittsburgher buy a painting of a cow for £11,000. He could have bought the cow herself for £15. But the painting had become famous. It was the only one of its kind. Everybody wanted it. And the Pittsburgher wanted it more than he wanted £11,000.
>
> (Casson 1915: 65)

How strong was Casson's influence? The question is difficult to answer. As noted, he was constantly in demand as a lecturer and speaker for the last forty years of his life, and his books between them sold at least half a million copies, possibly many more. Yet, as every management writer knows, it is one thing for an audience to receive a message, and quite another for them to act upon it. There is no indication that British industry as a whole responded on a wide scale to Casson's message; although as much of his consultancy work was with small and medium-sized firms, it may be that records simply do not survive.

Yet he was, and to some extent still is, a powerful influence. He brought the techniques of American scientific management and efficiency to Britain during the First World War, at a time when few others in the country were more than dimly aware of them. He paved the ground for the acceptance of these techniques in many quarters by arguing strenuously that they were not 'American methods' but universal principles: scientific management had been invented in the USA but was no more 'American' than electricity or the principles of astronomy.

His style of writing is terse and full of aphorisms, some of which can be quite abrasive, such as: 'Almost every works needs a bigger scrapheap. There are many obsolete machines inside that should be outside' (Melluish 1948: 133), and 'It would be far safer, sensible and more profitable to dismiss a do-nothing director and to put a bag of sand in his chair' (Melluish 1948: 134). His writing was determinedly populist, and would pass few tests of academic rigour: he repeats himself frequently, and some of his bases for argument, notably those resting on the physical sciences, are decidedly shaky. Yet against this, he had a powerful vision of what management could and should be, a strong philosophy based on some surprisingly modern concepts such as dynamic organization and, above all, the need for continuous learning. He deserves to be remembered as one of the twentieth century's great management writers.

BIBLIOGRAPHY

Casson, E.F. (1952) *The Life and Thoughts of Herbert N. Casson*, London: Efficiency Magazine.

Casson, H.N. (1907) *The Romance of Steel: The Story of a Thousand Millionaires*, New York: A.S. Barnes.

—— (1909) *Cyrus Hall McCormack: His*

Life and Work, Chicago: A.C. McLurg and Co.

Casson, H.N. (1911) *Advertisements and Sales: A Study of Advertising and Selling from the Standpoint of the New Principles of Scientific Management*, London: Pitman.

——— (1913) *Advertisements and Sales*, London: Pitman.

——— (1915) *The Axioms of Business*, London: Efficiency Exchange.

——— (1917) *Lectures on Efficiency*, Manchester: Mather and Platt.

——— (1918) *Human Nature*, London: Efficiency Magazine.

——— (1927) *Men at the Top: Twelve Tips on Leadership*, London: Efficiency Magazine.

——— (1928) *Creative Thinkers: The Efficient Few Who Cause Progress and Prosperity*, London: Efficiency Magazine.

——— (1929) *The Twelve Worst Mistakes in Business*, London: Efficiency Magazine.

——— (1931) *The Story of My Life*, London: Efficiency Magazine.

——— (1935) *How to Get Things Done*, London: Efficiency Magazine.

——— (1937) *What Makes Value?*, London: Efficiency Magazine.

——— (1939) *Making People Want to Buy*, London: Efficiency Magazine.

——— (1941) *Efficient Management*, London: Efficiency Magazine.

——— (1949) *The Business Omnibus*, London: Efficiency Magazine.

Kauffmann, K. and Kruse, U.J. (1928) *The Brain-workers' Handbook*, trans. F.H. Burgess and H.N. Casson, London: Efficiency Magazine.

Melluish, W. (ed.) (1948) *Effiency for All*, Kingswood: The World's Work Ltd.

Wirz, A. (1986) *Efficiency: Herbert Cassons Philosophie des Erfolgs*, Zurich: O. Füssli.

MLW

CHANDLER, Alfred Dupont, Jr (1918–)

Alfred Dupont Chandler was born in Guyencourt, Delaware on 15 September 1918, one of five children of Alfred Dupont Chandler and his wife, Caroline Johnston Ramsay. His great-grandfather was the business journalist Henry Varnum POOR, one of the founders of Standard and Poors, and there were also family connections with the du Ponts. After schooling he attended Harvard University, graduating in history in 1940. Among his classmates at Harvard was future US president John F. Kennedy; both men were members of the Harvard sailing team, and both joined the US Navy in the Second World War. Chandler finished the war with the rank of lieutenant-commander in the US Navy Reserves. Demobilized in 1945, he began graduate studies at the University of North Carolina, but in 1946 returned to Harvard to take his Ph.D. writing his thesis on Henry Poor (later published in 1956). In 1950 he was appointed to a teaching post at the Massachusetts Institute of Technology, where he taught history until 1963; from 1963–71 he was professor of history at Johns Hopkins University, where he was also editor of the presidential papers of Dwight D. Eisenhower. In 1971 he became professor of business history at Harvard; he is currently professor emeritus.

Unusually for a modern business school, Harvard has a long tradition of the teaching and researching of business history, which can be traced back to its founding dean, Edwin GAY, and which continued through later scholars such as N.S.B. Gras and Henrietta Larson. Chandler's achievement has been to make business history a part of the core curriculum at Harvard, and to instil in students a respect for and understanding of historical processes in business. Although his own historical work is open to criticism, he has set a benchmark for business historians in terms of both breadth of thinking and relevance to the practical problems of business.

It is Chandler's writing, however, rather than this teaching which has had the greatest impact. He has produced three seminal books – *Strategy and Structure* (1962), *The Visible Hand* (1977) and *Scale and Scope* (1990) – all of which have had great impact and all of which have been bestsellers. *The Visible Hand*, indeed, became the first business book to win a Pulitzer prize. A historian rather than a business academic, Chandler's writing has demonstrated how historical thinking can be applied to the problems of business. He achieved this first in his work on Henry Poor, which focused on Poor himself and his influence and impact on the growth of the American railways; and second, and perhaps most successfully, in *Strategy and Structure*, when he looked at corporate responses to the problems of diversification in the first half of the twentieth century. In these first two works, the scope of his enquiry was limited to a few organizations or businesses. In the later works, *The Visible Hand* and *Scale and Scope*, Chandler broadens his focus and becomes more general, looking for common patterns across and between national business cultures.

In *Strategy and Structure*, Chandler observes the growth of the large diversified corporation in the United States. He particularly notes the appearance of the multidivisional form (M-form), in which diversification proceeds by the establishment of a number of semi-independent operating divisions, focused either geographically or on a particular group of products, the whole being subject to the managerial oversight of corporate headquarters. The net effect is the partial devolution of power and control from headquarters to the heads of the divisions. Chandler notes that many of the successful firms in the United States between 1920 and 1960 had adopted the M-form. The core of the book is taken up with four case studies of such successful firms: Du Pont, General Motors, Standard Oil (New Jersey) and Sears Roebuck. Each of the four approached diversification and adaptation to the M-form in a different way and for different reasons; indeed, some were more successful than others in their implementation of it. Interestingly, much of the book then focuses on the organizational dynamics of each case, as Chandler follows the decision to adapt and the processes of adaptation through to their conclusion. In each case, the reorgnization had a champion: Pierre DU PONT at Du Pont and later at General Motors, Alfred SLOAN at General Motors, Walter TEAGLE at Standard Oil and General Robert WOOD at Sears Roebuck. It was the relationships between these men and their executives and employees that to a large extent determined the shape and success of the reorganization in each case, and one often overlooked aspect of this work is the way in which it highlights the close links between leadership and corporate reorganization or rejuvenation.

What do these case studies tell us? For Chandler, of primary importance is the link between corporate strategy and corporate structure. He defines strategy as 'the determination of the basic long-term goals and objectives of an enterprise, and the adoption of courses of action and the allocation of resources necessary for carrying out these goals' (Chandler 1962: 13). Structure, in turn, is

> the design of organization through which the enterprise is administered ... It includes, first, the lines of authority and communication between the different administrative offices and officers, and, second, the information and data that flow through these lines of communication and authority.
>
> (Chandler 1962: 14)

In Chandler's view, the choice of structure is an organizational decision which is dependent on the choice of strategy: 'The thesis ... is then that structure follows strategy and that the most complex type of structure is the result of the concatenation of several basic strategies' (Chandler 1962: 14).

'Structure follows strategy' is both the theme of this work and its fundamental lesson.

In the four case studies given, the companies in question were faced with the need to make a fundamental shift in strategy, resulting from changes in population, income, technology, etc. in their core markets. The strategy chosen by the executive was one of diversification; the M-form structure was the organizational response to this strategy. It must be emphasized that this is a historical account. In *Strategy and Structure*, Chandler is describing how and why the M-form, which appears to be the most powerful – though by no means the only – organizational model adopted by large American firms, came to be. He is *not* saying, at least not overtly, that this is the one best model of organization. While he remains firm in his conviction that structure follows strategy, he concedes that different strategies require different structures. However, as Whittington (1998) notes, this did not stop McKinsey and Company consultants from selling the M-form as the ideal organizational structure around the world in the 1960s.

In *The Visible Hand: The Managerial Revolution in American Business*, Chandler both expands on the themes of *Strategy and Structure* and develops new ones. It was clear in the earlier work that one of the key elements in the successful reorganization and transition to the new form was the quality of a firm's management. In *The Visible Hand*, then, Chandler looks at a parallel phenomenon to the rise of the M-form and one that may be connected to it: the rise of professional management. His basic thesis is that the rise of large-scale business was accompanied by the growth of a professional managerial class, and that there was a basic separation of ownership and control. (Interestingly, Chandler makes only passing reference to the earlier thesis on this subject by BERLE and MEANS; likewise, despite the subtitle of his own work, BURNHAM's *The Managerial Revolution* is referred to only in a footnote.)

In *The Visible Hand*, Chandler sets out to chart this process. Prior to the American Civil War, businesses in the United States were usually small, localized, and family owned and controlled. Larger, multi-unit enterprises began to emerge 'when administrative coordination permitted greater productivity, lower costs, and higher profits than coordinated by market mechanisms' (Chandler 1977: 6). Business activities which had been carried out between firms could not be internalized within a firm, with corresponding advantages in terms of control and economy of scale. The 'visible hand' of the title is a direct reference to Adam Smith, who postulated an 'invisible hand' of market forces which guided and regulated activity; the 'visible hand' is that of professional management, which can also provide guidance and control of business activity.

The advantages of internalization, says Chandler, could not be achieved until a managerial hierarchy had been put in place. Growth is thus a self-perpetuating process; firms need to grow in order to be able to put in place the management structure that allows them to achieve internalization of activity, which in turn permits further growth. Eventually, says Chandler, once a hierarchy has been established it becomes 'a source of permanence, power, and continued growth' (Chandler 1977: 13). As the business grows, the salaried managers within its upper ranks become more highly skilled and their work becomes more technical and complex. As this process of growth in size and complexity continues, the owners of the business find that they can no longer directly control the business, and increasingly delegate that control to the managers, leading to the aforementioned separation of ownership and control. This in turn leads to a changing strategic emphasis; professional managers, says Chandler, are more likely to emphasize long-term growth and stability than short-term profits. Finally, the size, economic power and strategic direction of these large business units changes and alters the economy itself, especially the industry sectors in which these firms operate. The final picture is a transition to what Chandler calls 'managerial capitalism', in which the chief decisions that determine the present and future trajectory of the business enterprise are made by its professional managers.

Tracing the historical origins of this shift in power, Chandler goes back to the mid-nineteenth century. Describing a picture which has become widely accepted by business historians, he says:

> The first modern enterprises were those created to administer the operation of the new railroad and telegraph companies. Administrative coordination of the movement of trains and the flow of traffic was essential for the safety of passengers and the efficient movement of a wide variety of freight across the nation's rails. Such coordination was also necessary to transmit thousands of messages across its telegraph wires. In other forms of transportation and communication, where the volume of traffic was varied or moved at slower speeds, coordination was less necessary.
>
> (Chandler 1977: 485)

He goes on to point out that when other industries began to grow, companies within them often borrowed the techniques already developed in the railway and telegraph industries; and indeed, it can be observed that many of the most prominent business managers of the late nineteenth century had at least some background in either industry. So, the railways and the telegraph had a dual function: they developed techniques for coordinated management of large organizations over large geographical space, and they provided marketing and distribution opportunities which made physical growth possible. He uses the example of the meat-packing industry, firms such as Armour and Swift, which was enabled by the railways to develop large vertically integrated organizations based on the large-scale rearing of livestock in the West and Midwest and selling meat in the urban centres of the East.

Other industries, such as steel, coal and oil, were also enabled to grow in this fashion. And, as firms and sectors grew, they developed management hierarchies and underwent their strategic transformations each in turn, thus creating the managerial revolution.

The growth described above gave US companies enormous advantages in terms of both economies of scale and economies of scope. Further, the internalization of management activity created advantages in terms of transaction costs. The costs of transactions conducted through a market were usually higher than those conducted within the firm through an efficient management hierarchy; thus vertical integration, for example, could make firms more effective competitors. For Chandler, this was the secret of US global success in the period 1930–70. To demonstrate his thesis, in his third major work, *Scale and Scope*, he compared and contrasted US 'competitive managerial capitalism' with the models he saw as dominating the economies of two of the USA's chief rivals, Britain and Germany. Germany, said Chandler, was dominated by what he calls 'cooperative managerial capitalism'. That is, German firms adopted a model of business much like that of the United States, characterized by hierarchies of professional managers, but for a variety of social and cultural reasons they preferred to conduct networks of inter-firm alliances rather than engage in full-scale competition. This professionalism, in his view, did much to explain Germany's economic resurgence after the Second World War. The British economy, on the other hand, comes in for severe criticism. Britain clung for far too long (in Chandler's view) to a model which he describes as 'personal capitalism', whereby the owners of businesses continued to exercise control and failed to hand over to professional managers. This lack of evolution stifled the growth and competitiveness of British industry and was a major factor in its postwar decline.

Scale and Scope has been roundly criticized, especially outside the United States. Of

Chandler's major works, it is probably the least successful, in that it does not fully demonstrate its thesis: that the transition to 'competitive managerial capitalism' enabled the United States to achieve economic power over and above that of its main rivals. Arguments can be advanced against this thesis on many levels. It is not at all clear that US economic dominance is due *solely* to any particular managerial form or structure. Chandler may also have been guilty of selecting his data to fit his thesis; neither the Far East nor southern Europe, especially Italy, where there have been and continue to be many examples of successful firms based on personal/family models of capitalism, figure in his analysis. His analysis of the British case also has flaws: professional management had advanced rather more rapidly in Britain than he allows, and there is a tendency to discount successful British firms that were managed personally by their owners, such as Imperial Chemical Industries in the 1920s (see Mond). Even in the United States, the dominance of managerial capitalism seems questionable, and in some cases participation by the owner's descendants and family in day-to-day management continues to this day. Chandler, it seems, does not seem to recognize that the owner of a business can also be at one and the same time a highly professional and efficient manager.

Other criticisms have been levelled at his work more generally. Whittington (1998: 99) suggests that Chandler has a 'rosy view of the historical origins of modern US capitalism' occasioned by his own family and personal connections to some of its leaders. David Teece has suggested that Chandler's emphasis on the M-form is itself becoming out of date, as the new business era now beginning will emphasize flexibility and speed of response over economies of scope and scale (Teece 1993); if Teece is correct, the business of the future will be prepared to put up with higher transaction costs in order to concentrate on core capabilities and innovation.

Despite these criticisms, Chandler's work has undeniable strengths. Although there are occasional flaws, his description of the evolution of large-scale US businesses and the simultaneous development of new techniques of professional management is clear and logically sound. He notes how changes in one sector, such as transportation, can have knock-on effects for many other sectors; a revolution in one business can lead to much more widespread change. His work on the relationship between strategy and structure remains pivotal to modern strategic thinking. Above all, perhaps, he has created an awareness that management is a historical concept, one that has developed over time and will continue to do so. His style of historical analysis, if not necessarily his conclusions, provides a sound platform for the consideration of future trends, and brings the role of historical understanding squarely to the centre of management thinking.

BIBLIOGRAPHY

Chandler, A.D. (1956) *Henry Varnum Poor: Business Editor, Analyst, and Reformer*, Cambridge, MA: Harvard University Press.
—— (1962) *Strategy and Structure: Chapters in the History of the American Industrial Enterprise*, Cambridge, MA: MIT Press.
—— (1977) *The Visible Hand: The Managerial Revolution in American Business*, Cambridge, MA: Harvard University Press.
—— (1990) *Scale and Scope: The Dynamics of Industrial Capitalism*, Cambridge, MA: Harvard University Press.
Chandler, A.D. *et al.* (eds) (1997) *Big Business and the Wealth of Nations*, Cambridge: Cambridge University Press.
McGraw, T.K. (1988) *The Essential Alfred Chandler: Essays Towards a Historical Theory of Big Business*, Boston, MA: Harvard Business School Press.

Teece, D.J. (1993) 'The Dynamics of Industrial Capitalism: Perspectives on Alfred Chandler's *Scale and Scope*', *Journal of Economic Literature* 31: 199–225.

Whittington, R. (1998) 'Chandler, Alfred Dupont, Jr', in M. Warner (ed.) *IEBM Handbook of Management Thinking*, London: International Thomson Business Press, 99–104.

MLW

CHERINGTON, Paul Terry (1876–1943)

Paul Terry Cherington was born in Ottawa, Kansas on 31 October 1876, the son of Fletcher and Caroline Cherington, and died in New York on 9 April 1943. Cherington received his bachelor's degree from Ohio Wesleyan University, then took a masters degree at the University of Pennsylvania in 1902. From 1897 to 1902 he was assistant editor of *The Manufacturer*, a journal published by the Philadelphia Commercial Museum; he went on to become the museum's director of publications from 1902 to 1908. In 1908 he was recruited to the faculty of Harvard University, and was one of the founder members of the new Harvard Business School, established that same year. Cherington worked closely with Dean Edwin GAY, and was responsible for the development of courses on marketing and advertising; he was regarded as a very gifted teacher, and his courses, always oversubscribed by students, helped shape future generations of teaching and research. He was also co-founder of Harvard's Bureau of Business Research, which he directed until 1919. He conducted the bureau's first major investigation, into the state of the shoe industry; the impression this survey made on him can be judged by the frequent references to shoemaking and shoe marketing in his later books. Melvin COPELAND, long-serving professor of marketing at Harvard and himself a major figure in marketing's development, regarded Cherington as something of a mentor. Also while at Harvard, in 1911 Cherington married Marie Richards; the couple had two sons.

Cherington was appointed assistant professor at Harvard in 1913, and professor of marketing in 1918. He left Harvard in the following year, taking up a post as secretary of the National Association of Wool Manufacturers from 1919 to 1922, and then was director of research for J. Walter Thompson from 1922 to 1931. He continued to hold academic posts: he was professor of marketing at Stanford University from 1928 to 1929, and taught at New York University from 1932 to 1935. From 1933 to 1938 he was a partner in the market research firm Cherington, Roper and Wood, working with one of the pioneers of opinion polling in the United States, Elmo Roper. Roper and Cherington predicted the results of the 1936 presidential election with great accuracy, and this helped to raise the profile of opinion polling very significantly, so that it became an important tool in both business and political management. In 1939 Cherington became a partner in McKinsey and Company. He also held a number of posts on government and university committees. He retired in the late 1930s.

He was a gifted teacher and highly original thinker and writer; among marketing academics, Cherington stands second only to Philip KOTLER in terms of importance and influence. Although Cherington's major influence was through his teaching and work, his writings were and remain important. He was one of the pioneers of the academic discipline of marketing, and his works not only show the problems which the early marketers were anxious to solve, but betray the influences and ideas they used to solve them. His two major works are *The Elements of Marketing*

(1920), which was highly influential and had many imitators, and *The Consumer Looks at Advertising* (1928), which reflects back on almost two decades of observation and practice. *Advertising as a Business Force* (1913) is an early casebook, written as an instruction aid while Cherington was still at Harvard. Of his remaining works, the most important is *People's Wants and How to Satisfy Them* (1935) which draws heavily on sociology and political science.

Cherington begins by considering why marketing suddenly became important in the first two decades of the twentieth century. The perceived wisdom at the time – as indeed it is today amongst some business historians – is that marketing emerged as a result of overproduction; large-scale production meant that, for the first time in history, manufacturers could make goods faster than they could sell them. It was therefore necessary to adopt marketing techniques to stimulate demand. Cherington does not fully accept this. Overproduction was indeed a factor, and he remarks that the ready availability of capital and labour in the United States meant there was more stimulus to overproduction than before (Cherington 1920: 5). However, the real consequence of large-scale production, he feels, is the breaking of the direct link between producer and consumer (1920: 1–2, 11).

Small, jobbing producers (such as shoemakers) can and often do sell directly to their end consumers, even making goods to order. They know their customers well, often personally, and can measure accurately their needs, wants and demands. The assemblage of capital, labour and raw materials required for large-scale production, however, means that this is no longer possible: goods are produced not for sale or consumption now, but at some point in the future. This leaves producers with the tasks of trying to anticipate demand of an unknown nature at an unknown future point, and of then trying to ensure that their goods are actually sold at a price which recoups the

cost of production, transport and distribution (Cherington 1928: 14–15).

Nor is it just the production factor that has changed: 'the conditions surrounding consumption have had quite as distinct an influence upon these problems and the mechanism which has been developed for their solution' (Cherington 1920: 3). Better education, greater mobility and increasing urbanization are just some of the factors that are causing consumer demand to change and evolve. Both changes in production and in consumption have resulted in 'maladjustments' between producer and consumer (1920: 3). It is the task of marketing to correct these.

The Elements of Marketing is, unsurprisingly, focused to a great extent on distribution. This was, after all, the key marketing problem that manufacturers had to solve at the time; product and price were important but less pressing than the fundamental issue of getting the product from the factory gate to the customer in an era when large-scale, long-distance transportation and communication were still in the throes of development. Cherington even debates whether 'marketing' is the correct term to use; he feels 'merchandise distribution' would be more accurate than 'marketing', which has connotations of 'provisioning a household', but concedes that the former term is awkward to use (1920: 1).

Setting this problem aside, he goes on to define the fundamental task of marketing: 'to effect a transfer of ownership of goods in exchange for what is considered to be an equivalent' (1920: 6). This is the *task*; the fundamental *activity* is 'to bring a buyer and a seller together in a trading mood' (1920: 9). This 'trading mood' assumes a predisposition by both parties to make the transaction; that predisposition can be assumed on the part of the seller, and later in the book Cherington describes how it may be stimulated in the buyer through branding and advertising.

In this definition, Cherington says, the essence of marketing has not really changed; the basic task of effecting a change of ownership in goods is faced by all businesses, no matter what their size.

> The increased complexity of modern marketing is not due to any change in the inherent nature of the elemental task of marketing, namely, effecting a change in the ownership of merchandise. It apparently arises partly from the addition of other supplementary tasks not necessary until recently; and partly from the development of more indirect forms for this task itself.
>
> (Cherington 1920: 5)

He classifies these tasks in three groups: (1) merchandise functions, (2) auxiliary functions and (3) sales functions.

The greatest amount of space is given to the first group. Merchandise functions are intended specifically to correct the 'maladjustments' in the market process between producer and consumer. These, says Cherington, come in four different types:

> (1) those between the quantity of merchandise produced and that sought for consumption; (2) those between the quality of merchandise produced and the various grades sought for consumption; (3) those between the time of production and the time of consumption; and (4) those between the place of production and the place of production.
>
> (Cherington 1920: 14)

Each of these can be dealt with by the corresponding merchandise function, namely (1) assembling, (2) grading and classing, (3) storage and (4) transporting. *Assembling* in this context means delivering the appropriate quantity of the appropriate goods to the customer; *grading and classing* involves ensuring that the goods are of the appropriate quality; *storage* involves the holding of goods already produced until the consumer is ready to purchase them; and *transporting* ensures that the goods are delivered to a geographical point where the consumer is willing to make a purchase.

Auxiliary functions are twofold: (1) financing and (2) the assumption of risk. Cherington and his contemporaries considered both of these to be of great importance. Firms at the time tended to think of distribution as a cost-free activity, a belief which Cherington strongly corrects: large-scale distribution is very costly and requires capital, from either inside or outside the producing firm. The assumption of risk usually requires two strategies: insurance to protect the actual goods from damage during distribution, and hedging activities in case market forecasts turn out to be wrong and goods remain unsold.

Sales functions relate to the actual exchange, and also to the stimulation of demand on the part of the consumer. Cherington was an early believer in the power and efficacy of advertising, in an era when large-scale advertising was widely criticized for being inefficient and wasteful. Acknowledging that advertising and distribution costs could make up more than half the sale price of some goods, Cherington believes these costs are justified if consumers are ready to pay them. Advertising and selling he sees as a service to the consumer. The role of advertising in particular is to provide information to the consumer. Advertising does not make the buying decision; it allows the consumer to make that decision in better informed manner (Cherington 1928: 74).

Cherington argues that consumers must become better informed and more educated, for their own good and that of the economy. When consumers have better information on which to base their choices, he says, inefficient and unfit producers will be eliminated, making the whole economy stronger (1928: xi). In *The Consumer Looks at Advertising*, Cherington moves the emphasis away from distribution and more towards understanding the consumer. The key principle here is the consumer's 'will to buy' (1928: 38). This demand factor, he says, 'is not a spineless effect, but a restless and irresistible cause' (1928: 38) and is the starting point for the consideration of all business problems. He spends some time breaking down the will to buy into separate motives, making distinctions between needs (the demand for necessities) and wants (the demand for non-necessities).

In *People's Wants and How to Satisfy Them* (1935) Cherington moves away from a consideration of purely marketing problems and looks at some of the social issues surrounding demand. Most people, he says, will aim to have a 'good life' in both spiritual and material terms. There are two ways of attempting to provide such a good life: the planned economy, which attempts to design the good life, and the free market, which allows the good life to evolve through the mechanisms of individual choice. The first society is rigid, the second is mobile and flexible. In this context, Cherington argues against measures undertaken to ensure business stability. The last thing businesses need is stability, as this usually means stagnation; instead, they should be constantly challenged by changing market conditions and consumer wants (1935: 161).

BIBLIOGRAPHY

Cattell, J.M., Cattell, J. and Ross, E.E. (1941) *Leaders in Education*, 2nd edn, Lancaster, PA: The Science Press.
Cherington, P.T. (1913) *Advertising as a Business Force*, New York and London: Pitman.
—— (1920) *The Elements of Marketing*, New York: Macmillan.
—— (1928) *The Consumer Looks at Advertising*, New York: Harper and Brothers.
—— (1935) *People's Wants and How to Satisfy Them*, New York: Harper and Brothers.
Cruikshank, J.L. (1987) *A Delicate Experiment: The Harvard Business School 1908–45*, Boston: Harvard Business School Press.

MLW

CHRYSLER, Walter Percy (1875–1940)

Walter Percy Chrysler was born in Wamego, Kansas on 2 April 1875 and died at his estate on Long Island, New York on 18 August 1940. The third of four children of a train engineer, Henry Chrysler, and his wife, Anna Breyman, Chrysler grew up in a neighbourhood which he described as tough ('if you were soft, all the other kids would beat the daylights of out of you', Chrysler 1973), and in response he developed an aggressive, quick-tempered personality. Chrysler played the drum, clarinet and tuba in the Ellis Band, having learned to read music at piano lessons. He left Ellis High School in 1892 and refused to go to college, wanting to work with machines instead. When his father refused to sponsor him as an apprentice, he took a job as a sweeper in the local Union Pacific railroad shop. His father relented and he took up his apprenticeship a few months later.

Chrysler was driven by a passion to learn about machines and engineering, and stayed up all night learning practical mechanics as he repaired locomotives. He described this as an exciting time: 'Not books, but the things themselves were teaching me what I wished to know' (Chrysler 1973). He also took correspondence courses on engineering from Salt Lake City Business School. In 1897 he finished his apprenticeship, a competent and spirited young mechanic. Years later he said, 'even now I can lie in bed at night and tell, from the sound of a distant locomotive as it labours with a heavy train whether its valves are rightly set' (Chrysler 1973).

His impatience with incompetence and his authoritarian manner meant that he moved frequently as a journeyman, six times in the three years to 1900. He then moved to the Denver and Rio Grande Western Railroad in Salt Lake City, and in the following year he married his childhood sweetheart Della Forker, the daughter of an Ellis shopkeeper. He was quickly promoted through the management ranks, and constantly sought new challenging positions, rising to be superintendent in charge of design of locomotives and the production process. His reputation grew when he turned an unprofitable plant into a money-maker.

In 1912 he was invited to manage the world's second largest car plant, the Buick Motor Company in Michigan, owned by General Motors. He had been fascinated by cars ever since he had bought a Locomobile in 1908, which he had completely disassembled and reassembled before putting it on the road. He was given the freedom to reorganize Buick's production, and more than doubled Buick's output while reducing the plant's payroll by a quarter. His innovations included comprehensive piecework schedules, cost-accounting methods and redesigned production processes. He conducted daily inspection tours in the vast plant, looking for ways to improve efficiency. He directed innovation, including the invention of special-purpose machines and assembly-line methods that amounted to true mass production. By 1915 he demanded and got a substantial pay rise that allowed him to buy General Motors stock; in the following year he was offered $500,000 a year to remain as president of Buick and vice-president of General Motors. He drew most of his salary as stock and quickly amassed a significant fortune. Three years later he resigned from the firm and the industry, having opposed General Motors' strategy of acquisitions, led by William C. DURANT.

Chrysler was persuaded to step in to rescue Willys Overland in 1920, the car-maker founded by John North WILLYS, with a salary of $1 million a year. However, the huge debt burden dragged the company down and it went into receivership. But Chrysler had recruited a team of the Willys engineers to design a radically new high-performance, moderately priced car. He had become chairman of the reorganizing committee of Maxwell Motors, and was duly made president of the restructured firm. The design team developed the new car, the Chrysler Six, and unveiled it in January 1924. It was low slung, had a short wheel base (which facilitated manoeuvrability), a high-compression engine and four-wheel hydraulic brakes. The car was an immediate sensation, and Chrysler was able to capitalize on its publicity to obtain the capital he needed to mass produce the Chrysler Six. It sold well and the company made a $4 million profit in 1925. The company was renamed Chrysler Corporation that year.

Three years later, in 1928, Chrysler had earned $46 million in profit and was the country's third largest car manufacturer. To break into the low-priced market dominated by Ford and General Motors, Chrysler acquired Dodge Motor Company. This allowed Chrysler to sell the popular Dodge car and simultaneously double the number of dealers for its own models. The acquisition also lowered the cost of basic components, preparing the way for the Plymouth, the 1928 entry into the low-priced market.

Although a great technological innovator, Chrysler was markedly less innovative when it came to the management of the work force. During the early years of growth Chrysler's workers faced virtually unlimited management control; Chrysler combined paternalism with support for strict plant discipline by the foremen. Conditions were poor, although conditions improved slightly following the acquisition of Dodge; improvements included group life insurance, free dances for employees and a welfare department. However, as the Great Depression of 1929–33 took hold, no jobs were safe and even skilled workers were laid off.

During the Depression, Chrysler directed the company's retrenchment, running his factories at less than 40 per cent capacity in 1932–3, but all the while continuing to fund fully his research and development capability. As the economy began to recover in 1933, the company introduced new body styling and improved suspension to enhance passenger comfort. Its strong sales enabled the company to surge ahead of Ford to become America's second largest car maker after General Motors.

Chrysler's last great project was the construction of the seventy-seven storey Chrysler building in new York City. Inspired by the Eiffel Tower, and fuelled by a desire by Chrysler to invest his fortune in something solid, it was for a short time in 1930 the tallest structure in the city. His wife died in 1938, and her death contributed to Chrysler's decline and death in 1940.

Chrysler was a major player in the US automotive industrial revolution. He is credited with personally bringing technological and managerial knowledge from the railroad industry into the automotive industry. Building on that knowledge, he developed modern mass-production methods at Buick, which paralleled the more famous developments by FORD.

BIBLIOGRAPHY
Chrysler, W.P. (1937) *Life of an American Workman*, New York: Dodd, Mead and Co.

AJ

CHURCHMAN, C. West (1913–)

C. West Churchman was born in Mount Airy, Pennsylvania in 1913. He was brought up in a Quaker background which undoubtedly contributed to his enduring moral and ethical stance. He studied philosophy and logic at university, and obtained his Ph.D. from the University of Pennsylvania in 1936. Shortly after, he joined the faculty there as an assistant professor. One of the first courses Churchman offered was 'Modern Philosophy' in 1939, which was attended by Russell ACKOFF. The two quickly established what became a lifelong friendship. They worked closely together for twenty years, and established the field of operations research (OR).

During the Second World War Churchman became head of the statistical section of the Frankford Arsenal. He was made a professor at the University of Pennsylvania when he returned in 1946. In 1947 he moved to Wayne University in Detroit, where he and Ackoff published *Methods of Inquiry* (1950). Churchman was concerned to apply his philosophy to industrial and government problems and moved, with Ackoff, to the Case Institute of Technology in 1951, where they set up the Operations Research Group with this aim. Churchman and Ackoff also produced, in collaboration with E.L. Arnoff, the first international textbook on OR, *Introduction to Operations Research* (1957). The book set out the philosophical aspects of an interdisciplinary approach to real-world problems, as well as setting out the techniques of OR such as linear programming, inventory control and production scheduling. This and their subsequent work was well received. Churchman was editor-in-chief of *Philosophy of Science* from 1949 to 1959 and of *Management Science* from 1956–61, and was made president of the Institute of Management Sciences in 1962.

However, Churchman became frustrated with the developments in OR during the 1960s as the techniques were increasingly used without reference to whole systems. He moved away from the field of OR to concentrate upon systems thinking. He similarly resigned as editor of *Management Science* because he felt that the journal's increasingly mathematical contributions were science for its own sake and were of little practical benefit to humankind. Churchman called relentlessly for a critically reflective and moral practice of science. This position included the awareness of and concern for future generations, again showing his naturally ethical and systemic tendencies, and the basis of many futurists' beliefs.

Churchman moved to the business school at University of California at Berkeley in 1958 to direct a Centre for Research in Management Sciences. The work he did there explored management as a philosophical challenge, testing people's capacity to appreciate the ethics of whole systems. He developed his systems thinking in the production of his next four books, *The Systems Approach* (1968), *Challenge to Reason* (1968), *The Design of Inquiring Systems* (1971) and *The Systems Approach and Its Enemies* (1979). The questions he raised in these books are still being addressed today. He remained at Berkeley, finally becoming professor emeritus of the business school there in 1981.

The two main strands of Churchman's thinking that endured throughout his long career were his systems perspective, and his concern and strong commitment for ethical alertness. He also believed that the two were entwined, that ethical alertness came from thinking systemically. His work was concerned always with humanity in scientific research. Churchman believed that an ethical and moral stance should be integrated into management practice and thinking, rather than being addressed as an afterthought.

Churchman can be described as a founder of the modern systems approach. Systems, to Churchman, are not existing identifiable entities, but 'whole systems judgements', that is judgements made in the knowledge of the totality of relevant conditions. His contributions to systems thinking were to define a systems teleology setting out the conditions under which a system could demonstrate purposefulness; and establishing ways of bounding problem contexts using concepts such as 'sweep in' (developing knowledge of the totality of relevant conditions), 'unfolding' (giving structure to problem contexts) to make explicitly 'boundary setting'. He gave emphasis to the notion that boundary setting is a matter of choice and can only ever result in partial boundaries. His systems approach was the forerunner to work on soft systems

thinking, developed by Peter CHECKLAND, and critical systems thinking, developed at the University of Hull in the 1980s.

Churchman is a philosopher who strove to apply philosophy, and science generally, to the betterment of humankind, in the field of management. He is renowned for his contribution to systems thinking, the establishment of OR and his contribution to the debate on the ethics of science. He also made contributions to research methodology, logic, modelling complex problems, and the world *problematique* of futures studies. He was an all-round thinker and an excellent writer with a knack for bringing his thinking into clear relief with the use of poetry, stories and example problems. His work continuously called for the recognition of the importance of wisdom and hope in management science. The importance of Churchman's contribution was recognized with his nomination for the Nobel Prize for Social Sciences in 1984.

BIBLIOGRAPHY

Churchman, C.W. (1948) *Theory of Experimental Inference*, New York: Macmillan.

—— (1968) *Challenge to Reason*, New York: McGraw-Hill.

—— (1968) *The Systems Approach*, New York: Delta.

—— (1971) *The Design of Inquiring Systems*, New York: Basic Books.

—— (1979) *The Systems Approach and Its Enemies*, New York: Basic Books.

Churchman, C.W. and Mason, R.O. (1976) *World Modelling: A Dialogue*, Amsterdam: North Holland.

Churchman, C.W., Ackoff, R.L. and Arnoff, E.L. (1957) *Introduction to Operations Research*, New York: Wiley.

Churchman, C.W., Auerbach, L. and Sadan, S. (1975) *Thinking for Decisions: Deductive Quantitative Methods*, Chicago: Science Research Associates.

Flood, R.L. (1998) 'Churchman, C. West', in M. Warner (ed.), *Handbook of*

Management Thinking, London: International Thomson Business Press, 122–7.

AJ

CLARK, Edward (1811–82)

Edward Clark was born in Athens, New York on 19 December 1811, the son of Nathan and Julia Clark. He died of typhoid at his home near Cooperstown, New York on 14 October 1882. He was educated at the Lenox Academy and at Williams College in New York, and was admitted to the bar in New York in 1834. He married Caroline Jordan in 1836. In 1838 he and his father-in-law, Ambrose Jordan, established a law practice in New York City. In 1848 Clark represented an impoverished inventor, Isaac SINGER, in a patent suit; unable to pay his legal bills, Singer instead gave Clark a one-third share in his patents. This apparent piece of charity work paid off when in 1850 Singer developed and marketed the first sewing machine. Clark bought out another partner and became an equal partner in the firm with Singer. During the period 1853–6 Clark represented the firm through a series of patent suits initiated by Singer's rival Elias Howe, and negotiated the patent pool arrangement that ultimately settled the issue.

This issue resolved, Clark took over the management of the firm's sales efforts. He tried selling territorial rights, in effect a franchise to sell Singer machines within a given region, and using commission sales agents, both with little success. Clark then decided to recruit his own sales force, beginning by recruiting workers from the Singer factory who showed some aptitude for sales; these men, who knew the machines well, were better able to describe the product features to customers. The sales force were trained to give demonstrations of the machine and instruct housewives in how to use it (for its time, the sewing machine was a very high-technology piece of equipment) and also to provide repairs. Clark extended credit to purchasers through a form of hire-purchase agreement. By the mid-1860s the firm had expanded its sales operation to include agencies in Britain and Germany; in 1882 the first European factory was opened in Glasgow. In the 1870s Clark devoted himself to rationalizing the company's marketing operations, among other things installing a formal reporting structure which allowed data and information from salesmen in the field to be passed quickly back to headquarters and analysed. Clark also undertook reforms in the firm's operations and management structure. Although Singer's was the mechanical and design genius that enabled the firm to produce a high-quality product, Clark's was the management expertise which allowed it to grow and become the world leader in its field.

BIBLIOGRAPHY
Davies, R.B. (1976) *Peacefully Working to Conquer the World: Singer Sewing Machines in Foreign Markets, 1854–1920*, New York: Arno.

CLARK, Fred Emerson (1890–1948)

Fred Emerson Clark was born in Parma, Michigan on 26 August 1890 and died at Evanston, Illinois on 26 November 1948. The son of Guy and Ida Clark, he was educated at Albion College and the University of Illinois, where he took his Ph.D. in 1916. He married Carrie Patton in 1915, and they had one son. Clark held a variety of short-term posts including instructor in commerce and industry at the University of Michigan (1916–17), professor of business administration at the University of

Delaware (1917–18), and assistant professor of economics at Michigan (1918–19). In 1919 he moved to Northwestern University, where he remained for the rest of his career, first as assistant professor of economics and marketing and then, from 1923, as professor of marketing. He also served as director of the Graduate School of Commerce at Northwestern from 1937 to 1947.

Clark was one of the group of academics, also including Homer Vanderblue and Walter Dill SCOTT, who established Northwestern University as a leading centre for marketing study and research, a tradition which has continued at Northwestern down to the present day under Philip KOTLER. He was by all accounts a highly effective teacher. The early marketing courses at Northwestern were modelled on those developed at Harvard Business School by CHERINGTON and COPELAND, but Clark and his colleagues made alterations and improvements. They put a stronger emphasis on consumer psychology, gradually shifting the emphasis away from distribution and price issues and towards greater consideration of product and promotion. They also expressed concern that the Harvard system was too 'functional', and both Clark and Vanderblue called for a more integrated approach to marketing.

Clark's basic conceptualization of marketing is outlined in his *Principles of Marketing* (1924). He defines marketing as 'those efforts which effect transfers in the ownership of goods, and care for their physical distribution' (1924: 1). The need for marketing, he says, stems from the division of labour, 'particularly as manifested in large scale production and in the localization of industry' (1924: 1).

This division of labor, in turn, is due to the diversity of human wants – a diversity which arises not merely from the demand for the prime necessities of life, but from that far greater number of acquired wants which result from the seemingly limitless possibilities for human beings to expand and develop their desires.

(Clark 1924: 1).

At the heart of marketing are two processes, concentration and dispersion. Goods are first collected by a marketing organization from producers and gathered at a central point. They are then dispersed to individual customers. The marketing organization rests on this focal point, where concentration ends and dispersion begins. Clark was much preoccupied with problems of marketing efficiency, and argued that both processes needed to become simpler and cheaper, or else the cost of the marketing system would outweigh its value. The vagaries of consumer demand, coupled with slowness of response by marketing organizations, meant that technical inefficiencies were a constant problem. Consumers demanded both a greater range of products and higher levels of service, and these could not be provided without an increase in cost to the system. These inefficiencies are, he says, an inevitable consequence of the free market, and cannot be escaped unless the entire competitive system is scrapped.

Recognizing this to be impossible, Clark calls instead for greater integration within the marketing system. In particular, he believes that there needs to be greater cooperation between consumers and producers, allowing for the pooling of information that would help producers predict demand more accurately, improve their physical distribution systems and eliminate unnecessary middlemen. Clark's ideas on the need to link consumers and producers more directly within the context of a free market were in advance of their time.

BIBLIOGRAPHY
Cattell, J.M., Cattell, J. and Ross, E.E. (1941) *Leaders in Education*, 2nd edn, Lancaster, PA: The Science Press.
Clark, F.E. (1921) 'Criteria of Marketing

Efficiency', *American Economic Review* 11: 214–20.

—— (1924) *Princples of Marketing*, New York: Macmillan.

—— (ed.) (1924) *Readings in Marketing*, New York: Macmillan.

Clark, F.E. and Weld, L.D.H. (1932) *Marketing Agricultural Products in the United States*, New York: Macmillan.

MLW

CLARK, Jim (1944–)

Jim Clark grew up, impoverished, in the Texas panhandle town of Plainview. The product of a broken home, Clark was suspended from high school at the age of sixteen and never returned. Eager to escape the confines of Plainview, at the age of seventeen he joined the navy and, after nine months at sea, surprised his instructors by getting the highest score of his class in a maths test. This resulted in his going to night school to earn his high school equivalency. In 1970 he graduated from the University of New Orleans with a BS in physics, and received his MA in physics from the same institution in 1971. He went from there to the University of Utah and graduated with a Ph.D. in computer science in 1974.

After university, Clark landed a job with the University of Santa Cruz as an assistant professor, and was already thinking of bringing 3-D computing to engineers. From 1979 to 1982, while working as an associate professor at Stanford University, he further developed his 3-D graphics work, and designed a computer chip which would later allow engineers to model designs on relatively inexpensive computers, saving them months of work and thousands of dollars. He dubbed his invention the 'Geometry Engine', and with the help of a $25,000 start-up loan from a friend and a handful of his students, whom he hired in 1982, Silicon Graphics Inc. (SGI) was born.

Silicon Graphics is probably most famous for the workstations it produced to create special effects for films such as *Jurassic Park* and *Forrest Gump*. Clark served as chief technical officer and chairman of the board until his departure from the firm in 1994. In order to finance the operation, Clark was forced to sell off much of his stock holdings to venture capitalists, and his frustration grew as his influence waned. A falling out with CEO Ed McCracken convinced Clark to move on. He later observed, 'I felt that someone had taken away one of the passions of my life' (*Business Week* 1998). Although the company had become a billion-dollar operation, the selling off of Clark's stocks whittled his share to $16 million.

In 1994 Clark, along with Marc Andreesen, a 22-year-old genius who had helped to create the Mosaic Web browser at the University of Illinois, founded Netscape Communications. Clark recruited James Barksdale to be CEO, and Andreesen rounded up the rest of Mosaic's core engineering team to develop and launch the Internet browser. The company thrived and in August of 1995 Netscape made headlines as the most successful initial placement offering (IPO) in the history of the United States. A $5-million investment by Clark in 1994 brought him 19 per cent of the company, and would ultimately make him the first Internet paper billionaire.

In 1995 Clark, who had been frustrated in his dealings with the health care system following a motorcycle accident in the early 1990s, founded Healtheon. His aim through Healtheon (later named Healtheon/Web MD Corp. in November 1999, and shortened in September 2000 to Web/MD Corp.) was to create a system that would slash red tape and create centralized information services to connect doctors, insurers, pharmacies and patients. The company had a rocky start in the first year, but the hiring of Mike Long as CEO and the willingness of investors to back Internet companies propelled the company into a billion-dollar operation. Clark is a major shareholder, and was chairman until his resignation in October 2000. Clark has also invested and served on the boards of My CFO, a personal finance site for the ultra-rich, and Shutterfly.com, an online photo-processing and delivery service. He is also very involved with a project to computerize totally the operation of his 150-foot, $30-million sailboat, *Hyperion*.

As the only person to have been involved in three start-up companies which each grew to over a billion dollars in value, Clark presents an interesting case study for both entrepreneurship and the management of innovation. Like other techno-entrepreneurs such as Mitch KAPOR and Robert NOYCE, he seems to derive more satisfaction from the start-up process; although he places less of a premium on personal control, he still sometimes appears to find growth to be an inhibiting rather than an enabling factor.

BIBLIOGRAPHY

Business Week (1998) 'Jim Clark is Off and Running Again', http://www.business-week. com/1998/41/b3599112.htm, 5 March 2001.

Clark, J. (1999) *Netscape Time*, New York: St Martin's Press.

Lewis, M. (1999) *The New New Thing: A Silicon Valley Story*, New York: W.W. Norton.

JW

COASE, Ronald (1910–)

Ronald Coase was born in Willesden, near London on 29 December 1910. He attended the London School of Economics, where he took a degree in commerce; among his influences there was Arnold Plant. In 1931 he visited the United States on a scholarship, where he conducted a study of variations in the structure of firms across industries. Returning to Britain, he joined the faculty of the London School of Economics, where he taught until 1951. During the Second World War he was engaged in government work at the offices of the War Cabinet. In 1951 he emigrated to the United States, teaching variously at the State University of New York at Buffalo, Stanford University and the University of Virginia before settling at the University of Chicago Law School, where he remained from 1964 to 1981. He was editor of the highly influential *Journal of Law and Economics*. He received the Nobel Prize for Economics in 1991.

Coase is one of the most influential economic thinkers of the twentieth century. Unlike most other well-known economists of the era, who tended to concern themselves with the great macroeconomic issues of their times – Maynard Keynes with unemployment, Milton FRIEDMAN with inflation and monetary theory – Coase focused on fundamental microeconomic questions. The result was a set of contributions which lay dormant for years before their implications became widely recognized. In the last quarter of the twentieth century, papers by Coase written in the 1930s and early 1960s became the foundation for whole new subdisciplines in economics.

For management theorists and students of business structure, Coase's work is of central importance. Indeed, as memories of the mass unemployment of the interwar years faded and the inflationary pressures of the 1960s and 1970s began to die away, long neglected issues of economic organization came once more to the fore. The collapse of the planned economies of Eastern Europe; the growth of multinational enterprise and the rise of globalization; the privatization of industries in the mixed economies of the West; the establishment of new regulatory agencies at both national and international levels; the advance of new technologies especially in the field of electronic communications: all this upsurge of organizational experiment and change reflected the urgency of the basic question at the heart of Coase's work. What determines the best organizational structure for the conduct of business?

In 1937 Coase had asked this question in a paper entitled 'The Nature of the Firm'. Why are some firms large and others small? Why are some vertically integrated while others specialize in a particular stage of production and trade with upstream and downstream firms across markets? Why do some firms control production activities in overseas countries while others simply purchase inputs from independent foreign suppliers? Coase's answer was simple. Firms will often find it profitable to undertake the supply of inputs themselves because 'there is a cost of using the price mechanism'. Transacting with other economic agents across markets is costly. If it were not costly to transact, the very existence of the 'firm' would be impossible to explain. Finding a suitable supplier, bargaining over the price, assessing reliability, explaining what is required, renegotiating at contract renewal, enforcing the contract terms; all these activities are costly. In the firm, some of these costs are reduced. When a supplier joins a 'firm', Coase argued that 'authority' replaces bargaining. Contracts within the firm are durable and non-specific. They permit the 'employer' to give (within limits) instructions to 'employees' or within firm 'suppliers' and to avoid the costs of frequent renegotiation.

On the other hand, there are also costs of organizing transactions within a firm. If decision making becomes too centralized and the firm becomes too 'bureaucratic', its administrative costs will rise. If this were not so, it would be efficient to organize the entire economy as one giant firm – as was indeed disastrously attempted in the planned economies. For Coase, the optimal scope of the firm is determined by the equality of marginal 'transactions cost' in the market and marginal 'organization cost' within the firm. As the firm grows and extends its activities, a point will come where the cost of organizing an additional transaction within the firm will rise to the level at which it can be transacted across the market. This will mark the 'boundary' of the firm.

The study of transactions costs is the core of Coase's contribution to economics. Before Coase, students of economic organization had been well aware of many of the factors to which Coase drew attention. But until Coase's brilliant identification of a class of costs labelled transactions costs, it was difficult for the study of economic organization to progress further than a form of applied common sense. Hitting on the right conceptual framework can be crucial to all forms of scientific advance. For several centuries, the costs of labour and capital had been familiar ideas. The startling organizational innovations of the first Industrial Revolution with the channelling of flows of labour, raw materials and capital resources through the factory system may have so overwhelmed the senses that the very din drew the attention towards technology and physical processes and away from the problem of transacting. Perhaps it is no accident that the communications revolution of the late twentieth century and the relative decline of manufacturing has tugged the attention back towards a more subtle type of cost – transactions cost – though one which is recognized as a powerful reality by every practical business person.

Modern work on business enterprise is heavily indebted to Coase's framework. Some explanations of multinational expansion, for example, rely on the costs of transacting in certain types of knowledge. A well-defined and protected patent right, for example, would permit a firm to license technology worldwide and thus to avoid multinational expansion. Other types of knowledge, however, may be vulnerable to theft, or may be impossible to codify and thus to trade. The 'core competence' of a firm or its 'competitive advantage' will often be made up of skills or reputational advantages which can be exploited only by means of internal expansion. Modern management thinking along these lines is thus profoundly 'Coasian' in its emphasis.

Public policy has also increasingly had to wrestle with Coase's problem of firm versus market. Privatized utilities, for example, have been broken into vertically disintegrated structures in order to encourage competition at those stages which are not naturally monopolistic. Transactions costs have thereby been incurred. Contracts now link electricity generation, transmission, distribution and retailing where once there was simply internal administration. The costs of contracting are thrown into sharp relief when 'qualitative' aspects of an industry's output such as its safety or reliability are involved. Sometimes competition between suppliers can be expected to improve service standards which are difficult to measure. Where consumers cannot 'observe' these qualitative factors at low cost, however, and where they are unable to switch to alternative suppliers, contracting can give rise to great problems. As Britain found in the early twenty-first century, the supply of 'safety' on the rail system is costly to produce by means of a set of contracts between track provider and train operating companies.

Coase's work forms the basis not only for modern work in the structure of business organization but also for the whole subdiscipline of 'law and economics'. In 'The Problem of Social Cost' (1960), Coase noted that if one person's activities adversely affected others (there were external costs) a solution could be found either through government intervention or through contract and agreement. Once more the choice would depend upon the costs of internal administration versus the costs of transacting. If transactions costs were negligible, all the law would need to do would be to define property rights clearly. If people have a property right to clean water in a river, for example, a firm wishing to pollute the river would have to purchase the right to do so from the people affected.

Presumably the firm would only go ahead if it were more than able to pay compensation to the people who would suffer. Conversely, if the firm had the right to pollute the river, those expecting to lose from the pollution could bribe the firm to reduce its emissions into the watercourse. Either way, bargaining would proceed until all the gains from trade were exhausted and social efficiency was achieved.

By using some celebrated legal cases from English common law, Coase illustrates the reciprocal nature of external harm. He does not pass judgement on who 'ought' to have the property rights – the complainant protesting about grinding noises or the apothecary wishing to pursue his trade – but merely observes that bargaining between the two litigants will, however the rights are assigned, be mutually advantageous. Transactions costs are once more central to the argument, however. In the face of very great bargaining and other transactions costs, it will obviously matter to whom property rights are assigned. This has led to the idea that the courts should 'mimic the market' and assign property rights to the party that values them most highly, and thus to the party that would be expected (in the absence of transactions costs) to purchase them (see Posner 1973). A further conclusion was that reducing transactions costs and encouraging private bargains was an important aspect of policy towards social cost. Establishing property rights in environmental resources and permitting trade in such rights has been an important addition to environmental policy because it supplements what would otherwise be complete reliance on administrative solutions. The imposition and policing of centrally set standards, instructing firms to operate in particular ways using specified technology, or the introduction of taxes on particular activities all rely on the centralized evaluation of costs and benefits rather than decentralized private agreement.

It is sometimes mistakenly thought that Coase is an advocate of market transacting over other solutions to organizational problems. As can easily be seen from the above, this is a misconception. For Coase, efficient economic organization is about economizing on all costs including the costs of 'market contract' and the costs of 'internal' administration. There is no single 'best' form of organization suitable for all circumstances. His reputation for supporting market processes probably derives from the fact that, in the context of the time at which his ideas were first developed, the claims of central administration were rather widely endorsed by many economic thinkers. In the 1930s and 1940s, for example, the advantages of central planning over the market were urged by theorists who greatly underestimated the information and control problems that would be encountered. Similarly, in the 1960s it was somewhat uncritically assumed, even by relatively free market economists, that the problem of social cost could only be solved by central government action and that this represented one of the 'classic' justifications for the existence of the state.

Given prevailing opinion, therefore, Coase's ideas tended to lend support for experiments with market transacting. Hence his support for creating private property rights in the broadcasting spectrum (Coase 1959) and allocating these by means of a competitive auction rather than by administrative fiat. Hence his interest in historical examples of people overcoming apparently high transactions costs in order to achieve a social goal. Even the lighthouse, that archetypal 'public good' mentioned in every public finance textbook, was introduced in England without recourse to government finance (Coase 1974). Nothing in Coase's view of the world, however, establishes the universal supremacy of contract. Indeed, the very notion of 'transaction cost' is in one sense subversive of markets and was introduced by Coase initially as an explanation of non-market forms of organization.

Coase's initial conception of transactions cost has been greatly refined by other theorists.

His distinction between 'market' and 'firm' as involving a simple contrast between voluntary contract and the exercise of 'authority' has been subject to much criticism. Firms can monitor outside 'independent' suppliers just as they may offer incentive contracts and a large measure of independent initiative to those within. Modern 'property rights theorists' have developed new ways of explaining why it is sometimes advantageous to 'own' a supplier and sometimes not (for example, Hart 1995). The 'New Institutional Economists' have analysed 'transactions' with greater sophistication than Coase's original framework provided (for example, WILLIAMSON 1985). However, all these scholars openly acknowledge the debt that they owe to the remarkable contributions of Ronald Coase.

BIBLIOGRAPHY
Coase, R.H. (1937) 'The Nature of the Firm', *Economica*, new series, 4(16): 386–405.
——— (1959) 'The Federal Communications Commission', *Journal of Law and Economics* 2: 1–40.
——— (1960) 'The Problem of Social Cost', *Journal of Law and Economics* 3: 1–44.
——— (1974) 'The Lighthouse in Economics', *Journal of Law and Economics* 17(2): 357–76.
Hart, O. (1995) *Firms, Contracts and Financial Structure*, Oxford: Clarendon Press.
Posner R.A. (1973) *Economic Analysis of Law*, Boston: Little, Brown.
Williamson, O.E. (1985) *The Economic Institutions of Capitalism: Firms, Markets, Relational Contracting*, New York: The Free Press.

MR

COLT, Samuel (1814–62)

Samuel Colt was born in Hartford, Connecticut on 19 July 1814, the son of Christopher and Sarah Colt. He died in Hartford on 10 January 1862. In 1856 he married Elizabeth Jarvis; the couple had four children. Colt's father was a textile merchant, whose business failed when Colt was still a boy. Working as indentured labourer from the age of ten, Colt developed an interest in firearms and explosives. He attended Amherst Academy, where at the age of sixteen he designed a fireworks display for the Fourth of July celebrations; this misfired literally as well as figuratively, and the school building was burned to the ground. Anticipating expulsion, Colt left the school and took a job as a merchant seaman. According to legend, it was while on a voyage to Calcutta that he first developed the idea of the revolver. In fact, his was not the first such design; patents for revolvers had been issued in the United States as early as 1913, and it is likely that Colt knew of these (Hosley 1996: 47).)

Returning home, Colt took a job in a textile factory, and then at the age of eighteen found work as a travelling salesman, touring New England selling nitrous oxide (laughing gas). He proved himself an adept salesman; he called himself Dr Colt, and quickly mastered the techniques of promotion. He used his earnings from this job to build prototypes of his revolver, and in 1835–6 took out US, British and French patents. In 1836, having found financial backing, he established his first factory in Paterson, New Jersey. Although Colt's revolvers proved effective, the US Army showed no interest and there was at this point little civilian demand; the company failed in 1842.

The turning point in Colt's fortunes came when Captain Samuel Walker of the Texas Rangers wrote to Colt with an enthusiastic endorsement of his revolvers, explaining how the quick-fire weapons effectively evened the odds when fighting against superior numbers.

Realizing that here was a valuable source of publicity, Colt returned to Connecticut. The Connecticut River valley was already a centre of arms-making, on its way to becoming what Hosley (1996) calls America's first centre of machine-based manufacturing. He first contracted with the arms-maker Eli Whitney Jr to make revolvers according to Colt's designs, while Colt himself promoted and sold the weapons.

It was at this point that Colt began deliberately to create the image of his revolvers, an image that was to become their single most important selling point. Rugged and durable though his guns were, they were not as good as some other designs, notably the English-made Adams revolver. What Colt was selling, however, was not so much the gun itself as its image. Hosley notes that the 1850s were the time of the beginning of the opening of the American West, when the pioneer and frontiersman became role models of great stature; this was the gun used by the Texas Rangers, by pioneers in their desperate battles with Indians, and the romance of the frontier began to cling to the product. This was also the beginning of the USA's gun culture, when it became popular and fashionable to own and use firearms. Colt certainly capitalized on the first, and probably contributed in no small way to the second (Hosley 1996: 72).

Colt developed his own image as well: in the 1850s he began calling himself 'Colonel Colt' (a title to which he had no more claim than the Dr Colt of his days selling laughing gas) and embarked on an assiduous campaign of self-promotion. Like his contemporary P.T. BARNUM, he deliberately cultivated myths about himself, which added to the stature of his products. In the meantime, he was a ruthless salesman who had few scruples about his clients. One of his first major contracts was to the army of Ottoman Turkey; during the Crimean War he sold arms to both Russia and England, and the Irish Fenians and Garibaldi's Redshirts were among his other customers.

But there was more to Colt than shrewd marketing. He knew that, given that his guns were often used in life-and-death situations, quality was essential; even a few stories of guns jamming in action could ruin the product's reputation. Further, like Richard Arkwright in England eighty years before, he realized that there was sufficient demand to make large-scale machine production possible. Accordingly, two years after teaming up with Whitney he resolved to build his own factory and run it on mass-production lines. Skilled workers were recruited from all over New England and Europe to build and run the factory machinery, and the talented engineer Elihu Root was hired as factory superintendent. High-speed automated production was the centre of Colt's concept of the factory; he later calculated that 80 per cent of his production costs were machine costs, while only 20 per cent were human labour costs, an astounding ratio for the time. Machine production ensured that quality could be engineered in, while maintaining a level of production high enough to meet demand.

Colt has sometimes been compared to Arkwright, not only for his appreciation of the importance of the factory system, but for his role in spreading that system and introducing it broadly into US industry. Colt's success inspired many emulators. Former Colt employee Christopher Spencer set up his own factory in 1860, making tube-fed magazine rifles of his own design, the famous Spencer rifle which was widely adopted by the Union army in the American Civil War; later, Oliver WINCHESTER adopted many of Colt's methods in making and selling his rifles. As in Arkwright's England, skilled artisans trained in the firearms factories helped spread factory techniques and methods into other industries as well. Colt is seen as an important anticipator of the systems of mass production based on division of labour, analysed in detail by F.W. TAYLOR and put into effective practice by Henry FORD. Hosley sums up Colt's contribution and abilities:

Indeed, Colt's greatest invention was not repeating firearms – he had plenty of competition – but the system he built to manufacture these and the apparatus of sales, image management and marketing that made his guns ... the most popular, prolific and storied handgun in American history. Colt was the Lee Iacocca of his generation, a man whose name and personality became so widely associated with the product that ownership provided access to the celebrity, glamour and dreams of its namesake. What Colt *invented* was a system of myths, symbols, stagecraft and distribution that has been mimicked by generations of industrial mass marketers and has rarely been improved upon.

(Hosley 1996: 73–4)

Colt had been suffering from rheumatism in 1858, and a combination of disease and overwork brought about his death at the age of forty-eight. His wife Elizabeth Colt took over the firm and guided it through its greatest period of prosperity, from 1870 to 1890, when famous designs such as the Colt .45 Peacemaker dominated the market. She sold the firm in 1901.

BIBLIOGRAPHY
Hosley, W. (1996) Colt: The Making of an American Legend, Amherst, MA: University of Massachusetts Press.
Rohan, J. (1935) Yankee Arms Maker, New York: Harper and Row.

MLW

COMMONS, John Rogers (1862–1945)

John Rogers Commons was born in Hollansburg, Ohio on 13 October 1862 and died in Raleigh, North Carolina on 11 May

1945. His early life provides important guidance to understanding his work. He was born in the midst of the American Civil War, to parents who were both staunch anti-slavery advocates. Ohio was part of the Union, but the area in which Commons was born and raised was known for sympathy with slavery, and Commons probably acquired experience in the upholding of unpopular causes very early in life. Commons's father was an unsuccessful businessman. One of his failed ventures was newspaper publishing, through which John learned the printer's craft. This provided him with a means of support as well as first-hand experience in working at a trade – experience unique to economists of that era.

Commons began his education in Ohio at Oberlin College in 1882, where he supported himself by working as a printer. After an education interrupted by emotional problems, Commons obtained an AB degree in 1888 and entered graduate school at Johns Hopkins University in Baltimore, Maryland. He did not receive his doctorate, either for financial or for academic reasons, and left Johns Hopkins in 1890. In the nine years that followed he taught at Wesleyan University, Oberlin, Indiana University and finally Syracuse University. The rapid succession of academic posts reflected the views of university administrations that Commons was a 'radical'. This reputation resulted from Commons's interest in several American reform movements of the era, including temperance, socialism and the 'Single Tax' movement of Henry George.

In 1904 Commons obtained an appointment in the department of political economy at the University of Wisconsin through Richard Ely, under whom he had studied at Johns Hopkins. He remained at Wisconsin until retirement in 1932, and it was here that he pioneered academic research into the history of labour in America. At the same time he became involved with the administration of Wisconsin governor Robert LaFollette, one of the leaders of the American 'Progressive' political movement. In response to America's rapid industrialization the Progressives advocated incremental changes to American laws and political institutions. Their goal was to enable American democracy to cope with dislocations caused by the new industrial society, without abandoning capitalism. Commons played an active role in the Progressive legislative programme, and was instrumental in drafting Wisconsin's civil service law (1905), the law regulating companies providing public utility services (1907) and the law creating the Wisconsin Industrial Commission (1911).

At the same time, Commons investigated the new industrial economy through detailed studies of the history of American industry and labour, including contemporary field research. He took over from Ely the directorship of a project to complete 'a history of industrial democracy in the United States'. With the aid of graduate students, he published the eleven-volume A Documentary History of Industrial Society (1910–11) and the first two volumes of the History of Labor in the United States (1918). Two more volumes of this work were published in 1935.

The literature concerning Commons is voluminous, and now includes at least 71,000 citations on the World Wide Web. However, Commons's economic theory is best summarized in his own words. The following summary is taken from his article 'Institutional Economics', published in the American Economic Review in 1931. Commons defines an 'institution' as 'collective action in control, liberation and expansion of individual action'. Collective action ranges from unorganized custom to what Commons calls 'organized going concerns', which include the family, corporations, trade unions and the state. This control of one individual is intended to, and does, lead to gain or loss to another individual. Control leads to duty, that is, conformity to collective action. It also leads to credit, that is security created by the expectation of individual conformity. Commons calls this 'incorporeal property'. Collective control can also take the form of prohibition of certain behaviour. This can create liberty in a person immunized against such behaviour, but a corresponding loss of liberty to a correlative person. As example, Commons cites the goodwill of a business, which he identifies as 'intangible property'.

The state, a cartel, a cooperative association or a trade union lays down and enforces rules determining for individuals this bundle of correlative and reciprocal economic relationships. These rules indicate what individuals can, must or may do or not do, enforced by collective sanctions. Analysis of these sanctions forms the correlation of economics, jurisprudence and ethics that is the prerequisite to the theory of institutional economics. Institutional economics goes back to David Hume, who, according to Commons, found the unity of economics, jurisprudence and ethics in the principle of scarcity, and the conflicts of interest that scarcity produced. According to Commons, Adam Smith isolated economics from the other two social sciences on assumptions of divine providence, earthly abundance and the resulting harmony of interest. Ethics consists of rules of conduct arising from the conflict of interests in turn arising from scarcity, and enforced by moral sanctions. Economics deals with the same rules of conduct enforced by the collective sanctions of profit and loss in case of obedience or disobedience; jurisprudence deals with the same rules enforced by the organized sanction of violence.

For Commons, collective action is more than control or liberation of individual action; it is the expansion of the will of the individual 'far beyond what he can do by his own puny acts. The head of a great corporation gives orders, whose obedience, enforced by collective action, executes his will at the ends of the earth' (Commons 1931: 519). To Commons, individual actions are really transactions, instead of either individual behaviour or the exchange of commodities. It is this shift in emphasis away from individual actors and commodities, to transactions and rules governing collective action, that marks the transition from what Commons calls the classical and hedonic schools of economics to institutional economics. Classical and hedonic economists founded their theories on the relation between individual and nature, but, in Commons's view, institutionalism is a relation between individual and individual.

> The smallest unit of the classical economists was a commodity produced by labour; the smallest unit for hedonic economists was the same or similar commodity enjoyed by ultimate consumers. In contrast, for institutional economists the smallest unit is a 'unit of activity', a transaction with its participants. Transactions intervene between the labor of the classic economists and the pleasures of the hedonic economists, simply because it is society that controls access to the forces of nature, and transactions are not the 'exchange of commodities' but the alienation and acquisition, between individuals, of the rights of property and liberty created by society.
>
> (Commons 1931: 519–20)

Transactions are the means, under operation of law and custom, of acquiring and alienating legal control of commodities, or legal control of the labour and management that will produce and deliver or exchange the commodities and services, forward to the ultimate consumer (Commons 1931: 525).

Based on studies of economic theory and of judicial decisions, Commons identified three types of transactions: *bargaining*, *managerial* and *rationing*. Bargaining transactions derive from the market, representing the best two buyers and the best two sellers in that market. Bargaining transactions rest on the assumption of equality of willing buyers and sellers. There are four types of conflict of interest in bargaining transactions: competition, discrimination, economic power and due process.

To govern them, the courts have fashioned four types of working rules.

Where both the two buyers and the two sellers are competitors, the courts, guided by custom, have created a long line of rules on fair and unfair competition. One of the buyers will buy from one of the sellers, and one of the sellers will sell to one of the buyers. Out of this type of transaction, custom and judicial decisions have created rules of reasonable and unreasonable discrimination. At the close of the transaction one seller, by operation of law, transfers title to one of the buyers and one of the buyers transfers title to money or a credit instrument to one of the sellers. Out of this purchase and sale arise the issues of equality and inequality of bargaining power, and rules of reasonable and unreasonable value. Finally, in the American system of jurisprudence, custom and judicial rules governing all of these transactions are subject to the ultimate review of the United States Supreme Court, on grounds that the custom or decision involves a taking of property or liberty without due process of law.

Unlike the assumption of equality of the parties in bargaining transactions, the assumption in managerial transactions, by which actual wealth is produced, is inequality. One party is the manager, executive or foreman, and gives orders. The workman or other subordinate must obey. Yet here also, custom and courts decisions develop rules as to what are reasonable and unreasonable commands, and what obedience is required.

Rationing transactions differ from managerial transactions in that the superior is a collective superior, while the inferiors are individuals. These transactions involve rationing of wealth or purchasing power to subordinates without bargaining, but with negotiation. Commons gives the example of the budget established by a company's board of directors, or the negotiations leading up to enactment of legislation favoured by economically powerful interests.

Commons's economic theory of transactions did not meet a favourable reception during his lifetime, or for some time thereafter. Even economists who respected his contributions to labour economics and social legislation were critical of this aspect of his work. Part of the criticism resulted from what some saw as Commons's 'fixation' and 'infatuation' with the legal basis of economic activity (Chamberlain 1964: 92–3). With time that view has changed, and Commons is rightfully credited as anticipating the work of the Nobel laureate Ronald COASE and developments in transaction costs theory led by WILLIAMSON (Van de Ven 1993: 150–51).

By contrast, Commons's contributions to labour economics and social legislation were immediately acknowledged. In Commons's view the employment relationship, like other transactions, was subject to institutional modification through court decisions and legislation. His emphasis on collective action as a means of expanding the power of the individual, along with his own work experience and field research, made him an important advocate of trades unions and their right to bargain collectively on behalf of members. Commons's influence was apparent in the National Labor Relations Act, which codified trades unions' right to legal recognition and to bargain collectively. This law has served as a model for labour legislation in several countries, including the 1979 legislation in the UK. The law was drafted by Senator Robert Wagner, a member of the American Association for Labor Legislation, whose executive secretary was a former Commons student. Another former student drafted the Social Security Act (Chasse 1997: 941).

Despite early flirtations with socialism, Commons was not a foe of capitalism. He was a friend of Samuel Gompers, one of the founders of the modern American trades union movement. They held a common view that the American labour movement should concentrate on economic gains, and avoid political involvement in efforts to eliminate capitalism (Oser and Blanchfield 1975: 399).

In 1919 Commons and some of his students conducted field research at thirty American businesses, 'looking for successful experiments in labor management' (Commons 1921: 281). Commons reported that: 'What we find that labor wants, as a class, is wages, hours and security, without financial [managerial] responsibility, but with power enough to command respect' (1921: 282). Capitalism 'is not the blind force that socialists supposed, and not the helpless plaything of demand and supply, but it is Management' (1921: 286). Commons foresaw that workers' focus on security in a well-paying job with fair treatment would confer opportunity and responsibility on management. Modern industrial relations and organizational behaviour are the study of the exercise of that responsibility, and Commons is also rightfully recognized as one of its founders (Van de Ven 1993: 139).

Commons also influenced the work of another Nobel laureate, Herbert SIMON. Commons's concept that transactions within institutions are governed by 'working rules' developed in part through bargaining influenced Simon in his creation of a 'new institutional economics for managers that studied bargaining inside bureaucracies' (Waring 1991: 52–3). Finally, Commons made another enduring contribution to the study of organizations through his emphasis on and skill in doing field research. Commons could never be confused with economists such the ones that Barbara Bergmann was referring to when she asked 'Why do most economists know so little about the economy?' (Bergmann 1986). In the words of Joseph Dorfman: 'few economists were as aware as he of the need to come to grips with the facts of the economic scene if society was to progress' (Dorfman 1949: 193). This is a fitting legacy.

Commons's life spanned a period of dramatic change in the United States, as an agrarian economy was displaced by industrialization. His detailed empirical studies of American society and the economy played a pivotal role in the enactment of social legislation during the first third of the twentieth century. As important as these activities were, his work retains equal contemporary significance. His theoretical work on institutional economics stressed the importance of the institutions of capitalism, especially the legal system. His emphasis on economic transactions provided the theoretical foundation for the later work of many others. Commons rejected the classical economists' view of labour as a commodity. His analysis of employer–employee relations in transactional terms recognized the conflicts inherent in the employment relationship. He emphasized the roles of bargaining and of institutional change in ameliorating these conflicts. He advocated legislation legitimizing trade unions and regulating working conditions and employment security.

BIBLIOGRAPHY
Bergmann, B. (1986) 'Why Do Most Economists Know So Little about the Economy', in B. Bowles et al. (eds), *Unconventional Wisdom: Essays in Economics in Honor of John Kenneth Galbraith*, Boston: Houghton Mifflin, 31–7.

Chamberlain, N.W. (1964) 'The Institutional Economics of John R. Commons', in C.E. Ayres, N.W. Chamberlain, J. Dorfman, R.A. Gordon and S. Kuznets, *Institutional Economics: Veblen, Commons and Mitchell Reconsidered*, Berkeley, CA: University of California Press, 61–94.

Chasse, J.D. (1997) 'John R. Commons and the Special Interest Issue: Not Really Out of Date', *Journal of Economic Issues* 31(4): 933–49.

Commons, J.R. (1921) 'Industrial Government', *International Labour Review* 1(1); repr. in *International Labour Review* 3(4): 281–6, 1996.

—— (1924) *Legal Foundations of Capitalism*, Madison, WI: University of Wisconsin Press, 1959.

—— (1931) 'Institutional Economics', *American Economic Review* 26: 648–57; repr. in

Gherity, J.A. (ed.) (1964) *Economic Thought: A Historical Anthology*, New York, Random House, 515–26.

—— (1934a) *Institutional Economics: Its Place in Political Economy*, Madison, WI: University of Wisconsin Press, 1959.

—— (1934b) *Myself, An Autobiography*, Madison, WI: University of Wisconsin Press, 1963.

—— (1950) *The Economics of Collective Action*, ed. K. Parsons, Madison, WI: University of Wisconsin Press, 1970.

Commons, J.R., Phillips, U.B., Gilmore, E.A., Sumner, H.L. and Andrews, J.B. (eds) (1910) *A Documentary History of American Industrial Society*, 10 vols, New York: Russell and Russell, 1958.

Commons, J.R. *et al.* (1935) *History of Labor in the United States*, vols 3–4, New York: Macmillan.

—— (1966) *History of Labor in the United States*, New York: A.M. Kelley, reprint of the 1918 edition, vols 1–2.

Dorfman, J. (1949) *The Economic Mind in American Civilization*, New York: Viking, 277–94.

Oser, J. and Blanchfield, W. (1975) *The Evolution of Economic Thought*, 3rd edn, New York, Harcourt, Brace, 383–400.

Van de Ven, A. (1993) 'The Institutional Theory of John R. Commons: A Review and Commentary', *Academy of Management Review* 18(1): 139–51.

Waring, S.P. (1991) *Taylorism Transformed*, Durham, NC: University of North Carolina Press, 52–3.

Wisconsin Lawyer (n.d.) 'Wisconsin's Legal History: John R. Commons', http://www.wisbar.org/wislawmag/archive/history/commons.html, 1 November 2000

SR

COPELAND, Melvin Thomas (1884–1975)

Melvin Thomas Copeland was born in Brewer, Maine on 17 July 1884, the son of Salem and Livonia Copeland. He died in Boston on 27 March 1975. He was educated at Bowdoin College and Harvard University, taking his Ph.D. from Harvard in 1910. He married Else Helbling in 1912; they had two daughters. After teaching at New York University from 1911 to 1912, he returned to Harvard, where he taught for the remainder of his career. He was appointed assistant professor of marketing in 1915 and professor of marketing in 1919, one of the first academics ever to hold those titles. He directed Harvard's Bureau of Business Research from 1916 to 1926.

Copeland played an important role in the early years of Harvard Business School, where he was brought in by the founding dean, Edwin GAY, to introduce new teaching methods such as the case study and classroom discussion. He also wrote a valuable history of the school's first forty years of operation, which is a useful source not only on the school itself but on the history of the development of management education generally. It is as a writer and theorist on marketing, however, that Copeland is best known. His work, notably *Problems in Marketing* (Copeland 1917a), a collection of 175 case studies, by far the richest teaching resource available at the time, and *Principles of Merchandising* (1924), show strongly the influence of earlier work by his Harvard colleague and mentor Paul CHERINGTON, with a continuing strong influence on distribution and management of producer–wholesaler–retailer relations. However, Copeland also shows the influence of emerging psychological theories of consumer demand, as espoused most notably by Walter SCOTT at Northwestern University, the other major centre for marketing study at the time.

Some of Copeland's ideas of marketing were quite advanced for their day. He was one of the first to note that the sales and production functions of an organization do not stand in splendid isolation, but are in fact dependent on each other to a large degree. He also noted that successful marketing can expand the overall demand for a product (Copeland 1924: 8). His work on consumer motivation is very well developed. He warns marketers that whereas the motives of sellers in any given market are usually simple, those of buyers are highly variable and usually complex. He goes on to distinguish between two classes of buyer motive: *emotional* motives and *rational* motives. The former may consists of factors such as emulaton, satisfaction of appetites, pride of personal appearance, securing home comfort, and so on; the latter include such factors as dependability, durability and economy in purchase (Copeland 1924: 162). Copeland's rational motives are based on the features of the product itself, while his emotional motives centre around the use and value of the product to the consumer. He stresses that any given buyer's motives are likely to be a set of multiple motives, including some rational and some emotional motives; he thus conceptualizes what later came to be known as the 'bundle of benefits' which accrue to a consumer when buying a product.

Copeland was also one of the first to make explicit the distinction between marketing to consumers and marketing to businesses, or industrial marketing. Although earlier writers had touched on the differences, Copeland devoted considerable time to the problems of industrial marketing. His *Cases in Industrial Marketing* (1930), providing more valuable case study material, contains a useful introduction which sums up many of the issues involved, including the motivation and buying characteristics of industrial purchasers.

In his later work (Copeland 1951; Copeland and Towl 1947), Copeland turned from the problems of marketing to the nature of management more generally. Managers, he says, are put into positions of authority over others, but that authority is not something that can be assumed as a perquisite of managerial rank:

Real authority is not a power attained by the bestowal of a title or by an entry on an organization chart, by the issuance of a directive or by the laying on of hands. Real authority must be won by the action of the executive himself.

(Copeland 1951: 5)

An appointment to office, he says, is no more than a chance to win authority. He notes the importance of information, and says it is essential for a manager to be well informed if correct decisions are to be reached. For Copeland in the years following the Second World War, the crucial challenge facing managers was the ability to manage change, to keep themselves and their organizations flexible and adaptible, while at the same time maintaining a unity of purpose and a focus on goals. Copeland and Towl (1947) also examine the nature of the relationship between managers in an executive function and the board of directors, and conclude that it is the function of the board to provide leadership and vision, delegating authority as far as possible to the executives beneath them to ensure that vision is met.

In both his writings on marketing and in his views on management in a world of change, Copeland was often ahead of his time; although much of his work is undeniably a product of its own era, many of his ideas sound remarkably modern. His influence on marketing thought and on management pedagogy remains strong to this day.

BIBLIOGRAPHY

Cattell, J.M., Cattell, J. and Ross, E.E. (1941) *Leaders in Education*, 2nd edn, Lancaster, PA: The Science Press.

Copeland, M.T. (1912) *The Cotton Manufacturing Industry of the United States*, Cambridge, MA: Harvard University Press.

Copeland, M.T. (1917a) *Problems in Marketing*, Chicago: A.W. Shaw.
—— (1917b) *Business Statistics*, Cambridge, MA: Harvard University Press.
—— (1924) *Principles of Merchandising*, Chicago: A.W. Shaw.
—— (1930) *Cases in Industrial Marketing*, New York: McGraw-Hill.
—— (1951) *The Executive at Work*, Cambridge, MA: Harvard University Press.
—— (1958) *And Mark the Era: The Story of Harvard Business School*, Boston: Little, Brown.
Copeland, M.T. and Towl, A.R. (1947) *The Board of Directors and Business Management*, Boston: Division of Research, Graduate School of Business Administration, Harvard University.

MLW

CORNING, Erastus (1794–1872)

Erastus Corning was born in Norwich, Connecticut on 14 December 1794, to Bliss and Lucinda Corning, and died on 9 April 1872. He played a key role in the coming of railroads, nineteenth-century America's take-off industry. Corning moved to Albany, New York in 1814, where he married Harriet Weld in 1819. He distinguished himself as an entrepreneur in several areas, owning an ironworks by 1826 and becoming president of the Albany City Bank and Mutual Insurance Company in the 1830s. He also became a powerful Democratic politician, and was mayor of Albany from 1833 to 1836.

Corning's greatest achievement was the realization of his vision of a railway along the route of the Hudson, the Mohawk and the Erie Canal, linking New York City with the Great Lakes. In 1827, he chartered the Mohawk and Hudson Railway linking Albany with nearby Schenectady. In the years that followed, seven other entrepreneurs built pieces of line to the west along the Mohawk and Erie Canal. Corning, always the innovator, profited through the sale of his iron and steel to these lines, and quickly saw the vision of a single line from New York to Buffalo. Settlers and merchants could go west by rail in one-tenth of the time taken by the slow mule-driven barges of the Erie Canal. Before 1851, the New York state legislature had granted the canal a monopoly. When this was revoked, Corning, using his powerful connections in the Democratic party, quickly secured the passage of a bill allowing him to consolidate all the rail lines under his ownership. By 1853 he had accomplished his goal, merging fourteen railway lines to create the New York Central: 'For many years it remained the largest corporate merger in American financial history' (Martin 1992: 247).

Corning was the founder and first president of the New York Central, which was destined, along with the Pennsylvania, to be the most powerful and profitable railroad in pre-Civil War America. 'Corning's entrepreneurial vision had started the avalanche that was railroad expansion ... and he was well paid for his efforts, especially those in behalf of what became the Central in 1853' (Martin 1992: 248). Corning died, secure in the knowledge that he would always be remembered as a builder of the state of New York, and of the federal Union.

BIBLIOGRAPHY
'Erastus Corning' (1999) *McGraw-Hill Encyclopedia of World Biography*, Detroit, MI: Gale Research, Inc., vol. 4, 238–9.
Larkin, F.D. (1999) 'Corning, Erastus', *American National Biography*, ed. J.A. Garraty and M. Carnes, New York: Oxford University Press, vol. 5, 525–7.
Martin, A. (1992) *Railroads Triumphant:*

The Growth, Rejection, and Rebirth of a Vital American Force, New York: Oxford University Press.

DCL

COUZENS, James Joseph, Jr (1872–1936)

James Joseph Couzens was born in Chatham, Ontario on 26 August 1872 and died in Detroit, Michigan on 22 October 1936. One of the original investors in the Ford Motor Company (1903), Couzens rose to the position of vice-president and treasurer of the company before eventually breaking with Henry FORD in 1915. In 1919 he sold his interests to Ford for roughly $30 million and that same year was elected mayor of Detroit. He was appointed to the US Senate in 1922 and was elected to the position two years later, where he served until his death.

Couzens' father migrated from England to Ontario, where he became a soap manufacturer. In an early declaration of independence from his father, the young Couzens insisted that he be known only as James Couzens. In 1890 he moved 80 kilometres (50 miles) across the border to Detroit. He became a car checker for the Michigan Central Railway, then, five years later, left to become a clerk for one of its customers, the Detroit coal dealer Alex Y. Malcomson. This alliance was to prove propitious. Malcomson formed a partnership with the young and struggling Henry Ford in 1902, and assigned his chief clerk to keep track of Ford's expenditures. Couzens, impressed with the operation, within a year scraped together $2,500 to invest in twenty-five shares of stock in the newly formed company, and effectively became its business manager.

Many have argued that Couzens, second only to Henry Ford himself, was responsible for the policies that led to the spectacular early success of the Ford Motor Company. Although Henry Ford conceived and helped design the Model T, Couzens put in place the structures that helped produce and sell it. He developed the decentralized system of geographically dispersed assembly plants and branch offices, in which branch managers recruited dealers and supervised dealerships that were not owned by Ford but that operated as franchised agencies, thus saving on investment costs. This network of dealers (over 7,000 in 1913) sold the Model T in prodigious numbers.

Couzens also had a strong hand in devising the famous wage offer of five dollars per day, announced in January 1914. The offer, approximately twice the going wage rate at the time, was contrived in part to stave off a growing unionization movement and in part to stop the extraordinarily high labour turnover rate at the Highland Park factory. Thousands – perhaps as many as 10,000 – job applicants converged on the Ford plant as the major financial newspapers of the nation castigated the policy as foolish utopianism or worse. But the immediate result of the policy was not the destruction of the company, or of capitalism, but of continued profits as other costs continued to decline and productivity increased.

Despite his success, Couzens was growing tired of the business, and he and Ford were beginning to have divergent views of where the company was headed. However, the final break with Ford came in 1915 over a political issue: pacifism, which Ford insisted on promoting in pamphlets directed at customers. Couzens objected and offered his resignation on 14 October. Ford accepted on the spot, thus ending Couzens' brilliant managerial career at Ford Motor Company.

Couzens had always had an active interest in Detroit politics, serving as commissioner of street railways (1913–15) even before his resignation from Ford. After his resignation he became commissioner of police (1916–18) and was elected mayor. In a twist of fate, he was appointed in 1922 to the Senate seat that Henry Ford had lost in 1918. Couzens was subsequently elected to the seat. He was considered a Progressive Republican and was a supporter of Franklin D. Roosevelt's New Deal. Couzens was defeated in the Republican primary in 1936, but died before his term expired.

BIBLIOGRAPHY

Barnard, H. (1958) *Independent Man: The Life of Senator James Couzens*, New York: Charles Scribner's Sons.

O'Brien, A.P. (1997) 'The Importance of Adjusting Production to Sales in the Early Automobile Industry', *Explorations in Economic History* 34: 195–219.

Rae, J.B. (1965) *The American Automobile*, Chicago: University of Chicago Press.

Sward, K. (1972) *The Legend of Henry Ford*, New York: Atheneum.

WJH

CROSBY, Philip B. (1926–)

Philip Crosby was born in Wheeling, West Virginia on 18 June 1926. He received a degree in podiatry (his father's profession), but decided not to pursue this career. Leaving the US Navy in 1952, he worked initially on an assembly line. Eventually he became a reliability engineer for the Crosley Corporation in Richmond, Indiana. At the time, Crosby realized 'that the way things worked assumed that nothing would ever be done right, so most of the effort was placed on checking initial results and then correcting them' (Crosby 1996a: xv). This approach to quality was accomplished very formally: papers were written about calculated risk and everyone accepted that there would be mistakes. 'This did not compute with the medical background

I had accumulated in the past few years' (Crosby 1996a: xv). Consequently, Crosby attempted (with little success) to change the corporate outlook that accepted defects. Eventually, he sensed that to advance in his career he needed to move from the Crosley Corporation to a more progressive firm, and found a position as a reliability engineer at the Bendix Corporation in Mishawaka, Indiana, where the company was building the Navy's TALOS missile. Results from Crosby's work at Bendix and the valuable experience he gained there helped him to advance to his next career move.

In May 1957 Crosby and his family moved to Orlando, Florida, where he joined the Martin Company as a senior quality engineer. A few years later he became a department manager at Martin and was in charge of the quality programme for the Pershing missile project. It was here that he developed the concept of 'zero defects' (Crosby 1996a: 80). The idea in this case was not to spot defects in finished products, but to prevent defects from occurring in the first place. Unlike in the Crosley Corporation, defects could not be accepted at any rate in missile construction. Unfortunately, Crosby's approach for zero defects 'was taken by the government and much of the aerospace industry as a motivation program rather than a management performance standard' (Crosby 1996a: 80). However, he took advantage of the opportunities for learning at Martin. During his eight years there, the company grew to approximately 10,000 employees. Crosby considered that the most important thing he learned at Martin was about relationships with people. While some thought that hiring subordinates with a lack of experience was a problem, Crosby considered it an advantage. People with no experience were easier to teach 'the correct way than for them to unlearn their bad habits' (Crosby 1996a: 81).

In 1963, when Crosby became responsible for the quality of the outputs of Martin's suppliers, he attempted to eliminate the need for inspecting and testing incoming materials from suppliers. While this was not completely accomplished, rejections were reduced to a small number and supplier quality improved substantially in just a year: 'This came about when the concept of Zero Defects became an actual working policy for the Purchasing and Quality Management [Department]' (Crosby 1996a: 86).

In 1965 Crosby assessed his future at Martin. He had been on a quick promotion track, 'however, all that was coming to a close. Since I was not an engineer there was no probability that I would go to corporate headquarters' (Crosby 1996a: 86). In May he accepted a position as quality director for ITT, then headed by Harold GENEEN. 'The company [ITT] was not quite $2 billion in revenue when I joined in 1965, but was $20 billion when I left 14 years later' (Crosby 1996a: 86). Reflecting on his prior experience as he started at ITT, Crosby realized that at the Crosley Corporation, acceptable quality levels meant a commitment to doing things wrong. Further, he learned while working at Bendix that he could set a new management standard with zero defects. Then, at Martin, he learned that to be taken seriously the quality outcome of zero defects had to be measured in terms of money. These experiences had helped to formulate his quality philosophy by the time he joined ITT.

As corporate vice-president of ITT for fourteen years from 1965 to 1979, Crosby applied this pragmatic philosophy in real-world settings. The nature of his job meant that he worked with many industrial and service companies around the world. As a result, he found that his approach to the management of quality worked in many types of situations. When, in 1965, top management at ITT decided to focus on quality throughout the corporation, Crosby established four objectives that continue to be part of his overall approach to quality management:

1. Establish a competent quality management program in every operation, both manufacturing and service.

2. Eliminate surprise nonconformance problems.

3. Reduce the cost of quality.

4. Make ITT the standard for quality worldwide

(Crosby 1979: 7)

Another aspect of Crosby's philosophy that also transcends much of his career is his belief that quality is free. In making this point, Crosby uses his 'cost-of-quality concept to demonstrate that quality is free' (Teboul 1991: 112). That is, Crosby believes that 'not achieving quality costs money. He argues that the real cost of quality is the cost of doing things *wrong*' (Thomas 1992: 32). The cost of quality represents expenses that could have been avoided by doing things right the first time. These overall costs, according to Crosby, can be attributed to four specific types of costs.

• Prevention costs: project reviews, design reviews, validation, training, maintenance, improvement projects, design of experiments, operating procedures, guidelines, etc.

• Appraisal costs: tests, inspection, audits, surveys, gathering and processing control data, reports, evaluation of suppliers, certification, etc.

• Internal failure costs: scrap, rework, lost time, reruns, unused capacity, engineering changes, etc.

• External failure costs: returns, recalls, complaints, replacements, compensation, field service, repairs under guarantee, product liabilities, etc.

(Teboul 1991: 112)

Not everyone agrees that quality is free. In considering both short-run and long-run performance goals, Cole considers that 'Philip

Crosby is wrong. Except in some trivial cases, "Quality is *not* free." It pays eventually but the investment – particularly of management time and effort – is substantial' (Cole 1995: 209). Nevertheless, both zero defects and cost of quality are solid parts of Crosby's philosophy. These ideas originated early in his career and continue as major underpinnings of his work today. In 1979, as his work with ITT drew to a close (he went on to set up his own private quality consultancy practice), Crosby stressed that: 'Used as a management tool for the purpose of focusing attention on quality management the COQ [cost of quality] is a positive blessing and serves a unique purpose' (Crosby 1979: 126).

Another articulation of Crosby's philosophy is embraced in his absolutes of quality management. Evans and Lindsay present a good summary of these absolutes.

• The definition of quality is conformance to requirements. Requirements setting is the responsibility of management. Requirements are communication devices and are ironclad.

• The system for causing quality is prevention. The first step toward prevention is to understand the production process. Once this is done, the objective is to discover and eliminate all opportunities for error. Statistical methods are useful in this regard.

• The performance standard is zero defects. Crosby feels that this is widely misunderstood and resisted. He claims that most people accept zero defects as a standard in many aspects of their personal lives and need only be taught and convinced that zero defects is a reasonable and essential standard in their work lives.

• The measurement of quality is the price of nonconformance. Quality cost data are useful to call problems to management's attention, to select opportunities for corrective action, and to track quality improvement over time.

(Evans and Lindsay 1989: 24)

Crosby believes that organizations can learn, and that management should adopt quality management because it is free and beneficial for the 'bottom line'. He also considers that 'the problem organization will benefit most from his quality management program' (Hunt 1992: 51). In his 1984 book *Quality Without Tears*, Crosby relates the symptoms of such a problem organization: (1) the outgoing product or service normally contains deviations from the published, announced, or agreed-upon requirements; (2) the company has an extensive field service or dealer network skilled in rework and resourceful corrective action to keep the customers satisfied; (3) management does not provide a clear performance standard or definition of quality, so the employees each develop their own; (4) management does not know the price of nonconformance. Product companies spend 20 percent or more of their sales dollars doing things wrong and doing them over. Service companies spend 35 percent or more of their operating costs doing things wrong and doing them over; and (5) management denies that it is the cause of the problem (Crosby 1984: 1–5).

In defining what he means by quality, Crosby emphasizes that 'quality has to be defined as conformance to requirements, not as goodness' (Crosby 1984: 64). That is, quality is conformance to requirements, and non-quality is non-conformance. When Crosby spoke about quality as conformance to requirements, he believed that any product that conformed to its design specifications was high quality. It followed then that 'a Pinto that met Pinto requirements was as much a quality product as a Cadillac that conformed to Cadillac requirements' (Costin 1994: 149). In addition, Crosby emphasizes that quality is not:

• Goodness, or luxury, or shininess.

• Intangible, therefore non measurable.

• Unaffordable.

• Originated by the workers.

• Something that originates in the quality department.

(Hunt 1992: 52)

Crosby considers that an organization's first step in moving toward a major improvement in its quality is to determine its current level of 'management maturity'. In this case, Crosby uses his Quality Management Maturity Grid. Consisting of five stages, the grid evaluates the organization's status in terms of measurement categories such as management understanding and attitude. The five stages of quality management maturity are: (I) Uncertainty; (II) Awakening; (III) Enlightenment; (IV) Wisdom; and (V) Certainty (Crosby 1996a: 32–3). Then, when a firm has determined its present maturity stage on the Quality Management Maturity Grid, it can implement a quality management programme based on Crosby's fourteen steps of quality improvement. These are:

1. Management commitment

2. Quality improvement team

3. Measurement

4. Cost of quality

5. Quality awareness

6. Corrective action

7. Zero Defects planning

8. Employee education

9. Zero Defects day

10. Goal setting

11. Error-cause removal

12. Recognition

13. Quality councils

14. Do it over again

(Crosby 1984: 99)

Each step is designed to move the organization's management style ultimately towards Stage V. At this stage 'conformance to the firms stated quality requirements [is] assured. A Zero-Defects culture is established and the cost of quality is reduced to its lowest possible level' (Hunt 1992: 54).

Crosby is closely associated with the concept of zero defects, which he created at the Martin Company in 1961. He defines quality as conforming to requirements, and measures quality by the cost of non-conformance. Subsequently, the Crosby approach focuses attention on developing processes and conditions that prevent defects. Consequently, inspection and other non-preventive approaches are not used. Further, he considers that 'statistical levels of compliance program people for failure' (Brocka and Brocka 1997: 61). Although zero defects were used as a motivational tool during the 1960s in the United States, the Japanese, by contrast, 'properly applied zero defects, using it as an engineering tool, with responsibility of proper implementation left to management' (Brocka and Brocka 1997: 62). Unfortunately, zero defects failed in the United States, where responsibility for the implementation was left to the individual worker. Crosby also urged that companies should develop a quality 'vaccine' to prevent non-conformance (defects) (Crosby 1984: 7).

In 1979, when Crosby reviewed his quality management strategy, he considered that concepts instead of techniques were important. That is, popular technique-based programmes were not major concepts. These included, for example, statistical process control and quality circles: 'They were just tools, and properly applied, could be useful' (Crosby 1996a: 136). Instead, Crosby built his Quality College on four absolutes of quality management that had evolved in his own thinking over the years:

1. Quality means conformance to requirements, not goodness.

2. Quality comes from prevention, not detection.

3. Quality performance standard is Zero Defects, not Acceptable Quality Levels.

4. Quality is measured by the Price of Nonconformance, not by indexes.

(Crosby 1996a: 136)

Crosby also found that a major need in terms of improving quality was to change the thinking of top management. If top executives expected defects it would get them, and workers would have similar expectations. However, 'if management established a higher standard of performance and communicated it thoroughly to all levels of the company, Zero Defects was possible' (Costin 1994: 149). Therefore, zero defects must be a management standard instead of a motivational slogan for workers.

In some accounts of quality management the major contributors to the field are identified as W. Edwards DEMING, Joseph JURAN and Crosby. 'In many versions Deming is the protagonist and Juran is a secondary character. In one article, Deming and Juran were portrayed as rivals. A close relative of W. Edwards Deming was quick to point out that this was not the case' (Petersen 1998: 35). While Deming disagreed about the extent of Juran's influence in Japan, he valued Juran as a colleague: 'Members of the Juran Institute are quick to point out that Juran and Deming respected each other, were colleagues, and were not rivals' (Petersen 1998: 35). Crosby, in commenting on Deming and Juran writes, 'If you do what they teach you will do very well. They are dedicated people and worthy of respect' (Bank 1992: 76). However, Crosby does not think that his relationship with Juran is one of mutual respect: 'Dr. Juran seems to think I am a charlatan and hasn't missed many opportunities to say that over the years' (Crosby 1989: 79).

It should also be noted that Crosby gives a good account of himself when compared with the other two gurus, Deming and Juran. Unlike them, Crosby was an excellent speaker and was able to charm corporate executives.

If style and manner of presentation are important, Crosby was the best of them all; but others will argue about the depth of Crosby's substance. It is also argued that Crosby's strong projection was overdone. In this regard, Wren and Greenwood claim that 'the most flamboyant of the leading U.S. quality experts is Philip B. Crosby' (Wren and Greenwood 1998: 217). In contrast, Lee IACOCCA considers Crosby to be the best: 'For my money nobody talks quality better than Phil Crosby. We thought enough of it [Crosby's quality college] that we established our own Chrysler Quality Institute in Michigan, modelled after his operation' (Iacocca 1988: 256–7).

In retrospect, Philip Crosby made a major contribution to the quality movement in the United States during the 1980s and 1990s. Having solid corporate experience, Crosby developed and taught a significant and far-reaching 'quality [management] process that is the basis for many quality improvement programs' (Schmidt and Finnigan 1993: 173). In 1994 he retired from his own consultancy firm, Philip Crosby Associates, in order to write and speak about quality, and also founded Career IV, a consultancy to help grow executives. He reports 'it is wonderful to be able to sit down in the morning and write for several hours without interruption' (Crosby 1994: ix). In his many reflections on his life's work, he adds this parting advice: 'make the customer successful, and that will make the company (and you) shine' (Crosby 1994: 210).

BIBLIOGRAPHY

Bank, J. (1992) *The Essence of Total Quality Management*, New York: Prentice Hall.

Brocka, B. and Brocka, M.S. (1992) *Quality Management: Implementing the Best Ideas of the Masters*, Homewood, IL: Business One Irwin.

Cole, R.E. (ed.) (1995) *The Death and Life of the American Quality Movement*, New York: Oxford University Press.

Costin, H.I. (1994) *Readings in Total Quality Management*, Fort Worth, TX: Harcourt Brace and Co.

Crosby, P.B. (1979) *Quality is Free: The Art of Making Quality Certain*, New York: McGraw-Hill.

———— (1984) *Quality Without Tears: The Art of Hassle-free Management*, New York: McGraw-Hill.

———— (1986) *Running Things: The Art of Making Things Happen*, Mentor Books.

———— (1988) *The Eternally Successful Organization: The Art of Corporate Wellness*, New York: McGraw-Hill.

———— (1989) *Let's Talk Quality: 96 Questions You Always Wanted to Ask Phil Crosby*, New York: McGraw-Hill.

———— (1990a) *Cutting the Cost of Quality*, New York: McGraw-Hill.

———— (1990b) *Leading: The Art of Becoming an Executive*, New York: McGraw-Hill.

———— (1994) *Completeness: Quality for the 21st Century*, New York: Plume.

———— (1995) *Reflections on Quality*, New York: McGraw-Hill.

———— (1996a) *Quality is Still Free: Making Quality Certain in Uncertain Times*, New York: McGraw-Hill.

———— (1996b) *The Absolutes of Leadership*, San Francisco: Jossey-Bass.

———— (1999) *Quality and Me: Lessons From an Evolving Life*, San Francisco: Jossey-Bass.

———— (2000) 'Phil's Page', Philip Crosby Associates, II Inc., http://www.philipcrosby.com, 15 March 2001.

Evans, J.R. and Lindsay, W.M. (1989) *The Management and Control of Quality*, St Paul, MN: West Publishing Company.

Hunt, V.D. (1992) *Quality in America: How to Implement a Competitive Quality Program*, Homewood, IL: Business One Irwin.

Iacocca, L. (1988) *Talking Straight*, London: Sidgwick and Jackson.

Main, J. (1986) 'Under the Spell of the Quality Gurus', *Fortune* 114(4): 30–34.

Petersen, P.B. (1998) 'Reflections about a Most Unforgettable Person: W. Edwards Dening (1900–1993)', in J.W. Cortada and J.A. Woods (eds), *The Quality Yearbook 1998 Edition*, New York: McGraw-Hill, 31–9.

Schmidt, W.H. and Finnigan, J.P. (1992) *The Race Without a Finish Line: America's Quest for Total Quality*, San Francisco: Jossey-Bass.

———— (1993) *TQ Manager: A Practical Guide for Managing in a Total Quality Organization*, San Francisco: Jossey-Bass.

Teboul, J. (1991) *Managing Quality Dynamics*, New York: Prentice-Hall.

Thomas, B. (1992) *Total Quality Training: The Quality Culture and Quality Trainer*, New York: McGraw-Hill.

Wren, D.A. and Greenwood, R.G. (1998) *Management Innovators: The People and Ideas that Have Shaped Modern Business*, New York: Oxford University Press.

PBP

CYERT, Richard Michael (1921–98)

Richard Cyert was born in Winona, Michigan on 22 July 1921 and died in Pittsburgh, Pennsylvania on 7 October 1998. He was educated at the University of Minnesota and graduated in economics in 1943. After serving as officer in the US navy for three years during the Second World War, Cyert entered graduate school at Columbia University, New York in 1946. He completed his degree in 1951. He received many rewards and honorary memberships for his work, and was until his death President Emeritus, and R.M. and M.S. Cyert Professor of Economics and Management at Carnegie Mellon University.

He is well known for his contribution to behavioural economics (in particular the behavioural theory of the firm), business administration and Bayesian economics, and for his leadership of Carnegie Mellon University.

Cyert has worked extensively within the fields of behavioural economics, economics in general, decision theory and management. Some of his most important books are *A Behavioral Theory of the Firm*, written with James G. MARCH (Cyert and March 1963) and *Bayesian Analysis and Uncertainty in Economic Theory* with Morris DeGroot (Cyert and Degroot 1987). Professor Cyert came to Carnegie Mellon University (then Carnegie Institute of Technology) in 1948 as instructor of economics, and was successively assistant professor of economics and industrial administration, associate professor and head of the department of industrial management, and finally professor; he was dean of the Graduate School of Industrial Administration (GSIA) (1962–72) and president of the university (1972–90). Even when taking on leadership duties as dean and president, he remained very active in publishing and research. Throughout his career he initiated, contributed to and maintained a keen interest in behavioural economics.

Cyert belonged to that small but select group of economists/political scientists/organization theorists who helped launch and develop the behavioural economic programme in the United States in the 1950s and 1960s, and he was one of the three 'founding fathers' (along with James G. March and Herbert A. SIMON) of behavioural economics, established at Carnegie Mellon during this period. His own interest in behavioural economics started with his doctoral thesis on price-setting in oligopolistic markets. Cyert found that neoclassical theory gave him very little support as a prescription for description of managerial and firm behaviour. As a result, Cyert and his colleagues at Carnegie Mellon University laid the research foundations for a series of contributions to organizational and behavioural approaches to economics and management (Augier and March 2001).

It was during his years as a doctoral student that Cyert realized that for economics to go anywhere it had to begin collaborating with other disciplines, such as organization theory, sociology, management and psychology. This interdisciplinary view was stimulated, encouraged and developed at Carnegie Mellon during his interaction and collaboration with Herbert Simon and James March. This is demonstrated in his attempts to go inside the 'black box' of neoclassical theory of the firm and understand the internal decision-making processes of the firm, especially in his work with James G. March. Their first co-authored paper, 'Organizational Behavior and Pricing Behavior in an Oligopolistic Market', was published in *American Economic Review* in 1955. Eight years later, they published *A Behavioral Theory of the Firm*. In this book, Cyert and March outlined a theory that was built around a political conception of organizational goals, a bounded rationality conception of expectations, and adaptive conception of rules and aspirations, and a set of ideas about how the interactions among these factors affect decision making in firms (Augier and March 2001). They emphasized the idea of problemistic search; the idea that search within a firm is stimulated mostly by problems and directed to solving those problems, and the idea of organizational learning. In *A Behavioral Theory of the Firm*, organizations learn from their own experiences and the experiences of others.

When *A Behavioral Theory of the Firm* was published, Cyert became the dean of GSIA, but he continued (as did March and Simon) working within behavioural economics, sometimes with other collaborators. With Robert Trueblood, he worked on statistical sampling methods and statistical decision theory (Trueblood and Cyert 1957). In the late 1960s, Cyert began working with Morris DeGroot, who was trained in Bayesian statistics. They published their first paper in 1970, and their book was published in 1987 (Cyert and DeGroot 1987). Most people would probably not be inclined to equate 'Bayesian' economics with 'behavioural' or 'managerial' economics, but, importantly, Cyert's approach to Bayesian economics was both a natural outgrowth of his work with March on behavioural economics and a contribution to behavioural economics itself (Day and Sunder 1996; Augier and March 2001). The argument that Cyert's work on Bayesian economics can be seen as a contribution to behavioural economics is twofold. First, in doing this kind of work, Cyert was interested in building a theory of *real economic behaviour* by taking uncertainty into account (Cyert 1970). This is consonant with modern behavioural emphasis on uncertainty and behavioural aspects of economics. Second, he built on his work with March and the idea of *organizational learning*. An important example of how learning can contribute to the development of Bayesian economics is found in Cyert's work on adaptive utility. Noticing the observable difference between the assumed fixed utility of decision making and the observed choices, Cyert wanted to apply the concept of learning to the concept of utility in such a way that changes in utility functions over time (as a result of learning) could be accounted for. This intertemporal aspect of learning is clearly a behavioural idea.

During his ten years as the dean of the GSIA and eighteen years as the president of Carnegie Mellon University, Cyert applied economics, particularly economics and strategy, to the management of organizations of higher education. Under Cyert's direction, the GSIA became a model institution for other schools in the United States and in Europe. Cyert believed in a close relationship between university and industry, and among his goals as a university president was to improve the quality of the university, and to develop a strategy for doing so within a balanced budget. This was not an easy task, but due to his knowledge of organization theory of management practice, he managed to achieve his goals and to bring Carnegie Mellon University onto the research map as a cutting-edge research institution.

In 1990 Cyert edited a book on university management, *The Management of Nonprofit Organizations*. The book includes several essays by Cyert in which he summarizes his approach to managing universities, drawing from both his training as an economist and his experience as a dean and a university president. A central basis for his writings on management is the distinction between the role of economics as an instrument for improving economic behaviour and its role as a description of that behaviour (Augier and March 2001). Cyert tried to keep the two aspects of economics separate. To him, economic theory represents the ideal-typical behaviour, but it is a poor description of real behaviour. Cyert maintained that economics needs to be behavioural in order to describe behaviour, but as a contributor to management thought, Cyert was a relatively traditional economist. He described his goals as an academic administrator as being to improve the quality of the university and to develop a strategy for doing so with a balanced budget. He advocated the application of economic analysis and decision theory to problems of firms and universities; and he recommended the application of conventional economic notions of marginal analysis, comparative advantage and the monitoring of behaviour and performance measures.

Although Cyert was an economist and thus, as a manager, departed somewhat from the principles he discussed in his work on the behavioural theory of the firm, he did not deviate from these in his understanding of how organizations work. Cyert believed that people make mistakes, and that these are important parts of the description of actual human behaviour. He saw universities and other organizations as deviating from the economic idea of efficient organizations, and portrayed them as being filled with conflict of interest and uncertainty about goals. As a manager, however, he saw these features of organizations as defects to be overcome or minimized.

BIBLIOGRAPHY

Augier, M. and March, J.G. (2001) 'Richard M. Cyert: The Work and the Legacy', in M. Augier and J.G. March (eds), *The Economics of Choice, Change and Organization: Essays in Memory of Richard M. Cyert*, Cheltenham: Edward Elgar.

Cyert, R.M. (1970) 'Implications for Economic Theory of a Behavioral Approach to the Firm', in W. Goldberg (ed.), *Behavioral Approaches to Modern Management*, Goteborg: Foretags- ekonomiske institutionen vid Handelshogshkolan I Goteborg.

—— (ed.) (1990) *The Management of Nonprofit Organizations*, Lexington, MA: D.C. Heath and Co.

Cyert, R.M. and DeGroot, M.H. (1970) 'Bayesian Analysis and Duopoly Theory', *Journal of Political Economy* 78: 1168–84.

Cyert, R.M. and DeGroot, M.H. (1987) *Bayesian Analysis and Uncertainty in Economic Theory*, Totowa, NJ: Rowman and Littlefield.

Cyert, R.M. and March, J.G. (1955) 'Organizational Structure and Pricing Behavior in an Oligopolistic Market', *American Economic Review* 45: 125–39.

Cyert, R.M, Dill, W.R. and March, J.G. (1958) 'The Role of Expectations in Business Decision Making', *Administrative Science Quarterly* 3: 309–40.

Day, R. and Sunder, S. (1996) 'Ideas and Work of Richard M. Cyert', *Journal of Economic Behavior and Organization* 31: 139–48.

Cyert, R.M. and March, J.G. and (1963) *A Behavioral Theory of the Firm*, Englewood Cliffs, NJ: Prentice Hall.

Trueblood, R.M. and Cyert, R.M. (1957) *Sampling Techniques in Accounting*, Englewood Cliffs, NJ: Prentice Hall.

MA

D

DANIELS, Jasper Newton (1846–1911)

Jasper Newton 'Jack' Daniels was born near Lynchburg, Tennessee on 5 September 1846 and died there on 10 October 1911. Jack Daniels was born the tenth and youngest child of a Tennessee family in a region already noted for whisky production. After a dispute with his stepmother, he left home at the age of seven and went to work at a whisky distillery at nearby Louse Creek. The owner, Dan Call, was also a Lutheran preacher. Daniels was well suited to the work and quickly learnt the skills of distilling. By the age of fifteen he was Call's business partner, and two years later he bought Call out and became sole proprietor. Call had been forced to give up his distillery business due to pressure exerted by his largely teetotal congregation ('Rare Jack Daniels' 1951: 103).

Daniels purchased a new site closer to Lynchburg, still the present-day location of his distillery. It is placed near to an iron-free spring, essential for the successful distilling of whisky, in a valley known locally as 'The Hollow'. The distillery produces a so-called 'Tennessee' whisky, which is essentially a variation of bourbon. It comes from a 'sour mash' composed primarily of corn, with some rye and malt added. What distinguishes Jack Daniels and other Tennessee whiskies from 'Kentucky' bourbon whisky is the fact that they are also filtered through charcoal (made from hard sugar maple) and then placed in new charred oak barrels for ageing.

In 1866 Daniels registered his distillery with the United States government, the basis of the company's ongoing boast that it is the oldest registered distillery in the country. For many years thereafter, Jack Daniels whisky was a regional beverage, rarely seen outside of Tennessee and neighbouring states. However, at the turn of the century, this began to change. In 1904 a case of Jack Daniels whisky was sent to the St Louis Exposition and won a Gold Medal. This success was followed by international recognition at the Anglo-American Exposition held in London during 1914. These awards did much to publicize Daniels' whisky, and sales increased accordingly in new markets. Jack Daniels is one of the very few brands of American whisky which sells in any quantity abroad.

Unfortunately, the new markets did little to protect either Jack Daniels or other American distillers and brewers from the growing prohibitionist movement. In 1909, Moore County, which includes Lynchburg, went 'dry,' although the distillery was allowed to sell its products elsewhere. In 1911 this too was prohibited, and the distillery faced a crisis. Daniels himself was by this time out of the picture; in 1905, during a characteristic display of temper, he had kicked his office safe when it failed to open. The incident created a blood clot which led in turn to gangrene and finally to amputation of his leg. He suffered from declining health thereafter, and in 1907 he handed over the distillery to his nephew, Lem Motlow. In 1911, the year

Daniels died, the distillery was mothballed and Motlow took up farming. The distillery reopened in 1937, several years after the repeal of nationwide prohibition, although Moore Country remains 'dry' to this day. One of the best-known brand names in the country, the Jack Daniels distillery premises have been added to the National Register of Historic Places.

Despite, or perhaps because of his humble origins, Daniels became something of a dandy and cultivated the image of an American country squire. He always wore a knee-length frock coat, a fawn coloured vest and a planter's hat, and grew an elaborate moustache and goatee, the image that continues to adorn the brand's label. A statue of Jack Daniels dressed in full regalia, erected by the man himself before he died, stands outside on the distillery grounds. Although a 'ladies' man', he never married.

BIBLIOGRAPHY
Green, B.A. (1967) *Jack Daniels's Legacy*, Nashville, TN: Rich Printing Company.
'Rare Jack Daniels' (1951) *Fortune* (July): 103–6.

SK

DAVIS, John Patterson (1862–1903)

John Patterson Davis was born in Niles, Michigan on 27 May 1862. He died in Asheville, North Carolina in early December 1903. He graduated from the University of Michigan with an AM degree in 1885 and trained as a lawyer, being called to the bar in Michigan in 1887 and then practising in Omaha, Nebraska from 1888 to 1892. Returning to the University of Michigan, he took a Ph.D. in 1894, and then taught history and economics at Michigan from 1894 to 1895. By this time his health had begun to deteriorate; he retired to Idaho in search of a better climate, devoting himself to writing and to the practice of law on a part-time basis until his final illness began.

Davis's major work, published posthumously, was *Corporations* (1905), a 600-page study of the evolution of the modern model of the corporation. His starting point was that the corporation was, at the most basic level, a social form. As such, corporations had a tendency to evolve and adapt over time: 'Like all other social forms, corporations are subject to modification: (1) internally, by the influence of their content, the social activity exercised by them, and (2) externally, by the influence of other social forms and social activity' (Davis 1905: 10–11). Social forms have a close relationship with their environment and, like species in the biological world, can undergo changes through contact with other forms.

Davis also makes explicit the link between form and function, the shape an organization takes and its purpose:

Social forms and social functions are intimately interdependent. Lack of adaptation of either to the other must result in modifications in one or the other or both ... If the form, whether originally or as the result of a subsequent more or less arbitrary modification, is unsuitable for a particular function, it must be altered to conform to the character of the function, or perish – unless it be adapted or adaptable to some other social function to which it may be readily transferred.

(Davis 1905: 11)

This adaptation, Davis says, is a historical process:

Corporate forms and functions and the environment by which they are influenced are all products of time. They are all meaningless except as they register past experience or predict future social growth, stagnation or decay. They must therefore be subjected to historical treatment.

(Davis 1905: 11).

He holds that the only way to understand both *how* and *why* corporations have evolved into their present form is to deal with them historically.

This, then, is the lens through which Davis looks at corporations. He believes that each historical era develops the corporations which suit its particular needs for social forms; remarkably for a modern economic writer, he makes no judgements about the past, believing that an evolutionary process ensures that each era has the most suitable form given its social and cultural characteristics. He traces the development of the corporation through ecclesiastical corporations (church and monasteries), the feudal system, which he sees as a corporation of sorts, municipalities, gilds, and education corporations such as the first universities. In volume 2 he goes on to more purely commercial enterprises such as regulated companies, joint-stock companies and colonial companies, coming finally to the many varieties of modern corporation which he sees as including both profit-making enterprises and non-profit bodies such as universities, charities, fraternities and lodges.

This is an important book: its second chapter remains one of the best and most succinct examinations of the corporation from a social point of view yet written, showing why we associate and how. Only now, a century later, are writers like Moore and Lewis (2001) returning to this theme and exploring the many forms that corporate organization has taken and can take.

BIBLIOGRAPHY

Davis, J.P. (1894) *The Union Pacific Railway: A Study of Political and Economic History*, Chicago: S. Griggs and Co.
—— (1897) 'The Nature of Corporations', *Political Science Quarterly* 12: 273–94.
Davis, J.P. (1905) *Corporations*, 2 vols, New York: G.P. Putnam's Sons.
Moore, K. and Lewis, D. (2001) *Foundations of Corporate Empire*, London: FT Prentice-Hall.

MLW

DELL, Michael (1965–)

Michael Dell was born in Houston, Texas on 23 February 1965. He was raised in an upper middle-class neighbourhood in West Houston; his father worked as an orthodontist, while his mother was a stockbroker. As he grew up he listened intently as his parents discussed interest rates and stocks around the family dinner table, which gave him insights into issues involving money. At the age of eight, he applied for a high school equivalency diploma from the back of a magazine, hoping to shortcut the system by eliminating the middleman – the school. By the age of twelve, he had earned $2,000 running a mail-order stamp-trading business.

The success with stamps and other money-making ventures gave Dell a strong sense of entrepreneurship. By the age of sixteen he had figured out a way to turn his summer job selling subscriptions to the *Houston Post* into a highly profitable venture, which netted him $18,000. He realized that targeting newly-weds and new homeowners with personalized letters led to a greater percentage of successful subscriptions. When one of Dell's high school teachers assigned the class the task of filling out a tax return, she was chagrined to find out her student made more money than she did that year.

Although Dell demonstrated a keen understanding of money, his worldview really changed when his parents let him buy his first computer, an Apple II, when he was fifteen years old. The computer was a natural progression for Dell. He had been fascinated with computing and maths since the age of seven, when he bought his first calculator. The first thing he did when he got his computer home was to take it apart to figure out exactly how it worked. As with stamps, Dell realized that his hobby could also be a business opportunity.

Quickly learning about both computers and the nascent computer industry, Dell believed that he could provide better customer service at a competitive price in relation to the computer stores popping up around Houston. Actually, from his perspective, the people working in the computer stores knew relatively little about computers, which they considered simply another big ticket item with a large sales mark-up. Dell began buying upgrade parts, such as memory chips, disk drives and faster modems, and installing them himself in IBM computers. He then sold the computers to people he knew for a tidy profit – all this while still a high school student.

Dell continued to rebuild computers while attending the University of Texas at Austin. While his parents hoped he would follow in his older brother's footsteps and study medicine, he remained focused on the idea of upgrading and selling computers. He recalled the day he left for school: 'I drove off in the white BMW that I had bought with my earnings from selling newspaper subscriptions, with three computers in the backseat of the car. My mother should have been very suspicious' (Dell 1999: 9).

Dell set up shop at the University of Texas and word spread quickly about his computer services. Businesspeople from Austin would trek up to his dorm room on the twenty-seventh floor and drop off or pick up computers. Dell even applied for a vendor's licence to take advantage of the open government bidding process in the state of Texas. Since Dell had no overheads, he won many bids and dramatically increased revenues. Soon the computer business took up more of Dell's time than his classes. After getting word that his grades were dropping, Dell's parents showed up in Austin for a surprise visit. They called him from the airport to let him know they were in town, which barely gave Dell enough time to hide all the excess computer parts behind the shower curtain in his roommate's bathroom.

In January 1984 Dell returned to Austin and formally set up a company called PCs Limited. Through word of mouth and an advertisement in the classified section of the local newspaper, Dell sold between $50,000 and $80,000 a month of upgraded computers, kits and components to customers in the Austin area. He left the dorm room and rented a two-bedroom apartment that could accommodate the thriving business. Several months later, Dell incorporated the company as 'Dell Computer Corporation', doing business as PC Limited. The fee to capitalize a company in Texas was $1,000; this was the total amount invested in the fledgling company, and a figure now part of Dell corporate lore.

Soon the business outgrew both the apartment and his parent's wishes for Dell to become a doctor. He dropped out of school after his freshman year and moved his company to a 1,000-square-foot office space in North Austin. Spurred on by the success of Apple and IBM, the personal computer industry exploded in the mid-1980s. Demand far outstripped the available supply. Dell refurbished IBM models, but realized that truly to revolutionize the industry his company would have to produce its own computers. He paid a local engineer $2,000 to build Dell's first 286 model. The company continued to grow at a startling rate, and in 1985 moved into a 30,000-square-foot building, but stayed there only two years before outgrowing that facility as well.

From his earliest days in business, Dell followed the 'direct model', which meant that the company built the types of computer people wanted and sold them directly to the public, also referred to as 'built to order'. The beauty of the direct model was that it eliminated resellers who marked up the cost of systems and added no value to the selling process beyond serving as a middleman in the system. This model of business allowed Dell to set the prices it charged for computers, and also made the entire production process more efficient. The cost of selling products in the computer industry averaged approximately 12 per cent of revenue, but Dell cut this figure down to 4–6 per cent. Internally, Dell also carried little extra inventory, usually eleven days of product, which eliminated the high costs associated with carrying excessive overheads; a marked difference from other manufacturers, who were forced to add additional cost to the overall price to pay for the overhead. 'While other companies had to guess which products their customers wanted, because they built them in advance of taking an order', Dell explained, 'we knew because our customers told us before we built the product' (Dell 1999: 22). Added together, the combination of high profit margins and low costs fuelled Dell's early success and solidified the advantage of the direct model.

In Dell's first eight years the company grew at an astonishing 80 per cent annually, then slowed slightly to 55 per cent. By the end of 1986, Dell's sales had hit $60 million. In comparison, by 2000 revenues had reached $32 billion. Initially Dell was viewed as a quirky upstart in the computer manufacturing industry, but the giants started to take notice of the band of rogues down in Austin. Companies such as Compaq, Hewlett-Packard and Gateway all tried to mimic Dell's built-to-order philosophy, but faced the problem of eliminating middleman who were firmly in place. This was never a problem which Dell had to worry about. His company delivered on the promises it made to customers, which fuelled greater customer loyalty, brand strength and a lower customer acquisition cost. Dell's success is built on relationships with both customers and suppliers. Taking the lead in adopting new technological innovations,

Dell set itself apart by moving to the Web and doing so profitably.

While it has become apparent that many companies have not been able to figure out how to use the Internet to their advantage, especially after the Nasdaq meltdown in 2000, Dell has been an e-commerce success story. In 1994 Dell launched its Web site with functionality that allowed users to calculate the cost of various configurations. Dell said:

> As I saw it, the Internet offered a logical extension of the direct model, creating even stronger relationships with our customers. The Internet would augment conventional telephone, fax, and face-to-face encounters, and give our customers the information they wanted faster, cheaper, and more efficiently.
> (Dell 1999: 91).

Internally, Dell utilized the Web to create efficient logistics and distribution systems. The company used the Internet and information technology to reduce obstacles to the flow of information, and to simplify various critical business processes. They allowed customers and suppliers inside the company through Internet browsers to share information and build a virtually integrated organization, linked by information. Since customers could order computers to their exact specifications via the site, it made the entire process more cost-effective. 'The Internet for us is a dream come true,' Dell explained. 'It's like zero-variable-cost transaction. The only thing better would be mental telepathy' (Dearlove and Coomber 2001: 54–5). By December 1996, the first year the company sold via the Internet, Dell's on-line sales had reached $1 million a day. Two years later, the company boasted Web sales of more than $12 million a day.

Dell himself began an internal Internet evangelism programme, going so far as to dress up like the famous Second World War Uncle Sam recruitment poster with the caption, 'Michael wants YOU to know the Net' (Dell 1999: 95).

He took the lead on the internal campaign so that every Dell employee would understand how the Internet could transform business, especially as it related to the Dell direct model. Today, roughly 50 per cent of Dell's sales are Web-enabled.

One of Michael Dell's strengths is the ability to interpret new trends and find ways to turn them into business advantages. Understanding the pervasive nature of the Internet led Dell to branch out beyond PCs and begin building Web-related products such as servers and storage devices. Dell has also nearly perfected the just-in-time process, so that 84 per cent of orders are built, customized and shipped within eight hours.

Over the last couple of years, Dell's stock has been hit by a worldwide slowdown in PC sales, and uncertainty regarding the American economy, especially after the Nasdaq downturn in early 2000. Dell set the bar so high in terms of growth that otherwise phenomenal growth rates look paltry compared to earlier statistics. In fiscal 2001 Dell grew at 25 per cent, a remarkable figure for most companies, but not for one that grew 59 per cent only three years earlier. Suddenly analysts wondered if the Dell rose had lost its bloom. However, Dell is still the market leader in desktop sales, laptops and workstations.

Critics claim that Dell cannot keep up the pace the company set in the 1990s. But Dell himself fights back. According to business writer Betsy Morris, 'Michael Dell portrays his company as the good guy, the Robin Hood going into battle on behalf of its customers against the bad guys: price gougers with fancy offices and corporate perks and silly old ways of doing things' (Morris 2000: 95). There have been missteps in the history of Dell, such as miscalculating the importance of laptops, but each challenge has brought out new skills in Dell and proven his leadership all over again.

Perhaps Dell's strongest management trait is developing a corporate culture that places the company in continuous growth mode, like a living organism. Under Dell, the company constantly adapts and changes to meet customer needs. Flexibility, speed and information are ingrained components of the Dell corporate DNA.

BIBLIOGRAPHY
Dearlove, D. and Coomber, S. (2001) *Architects of the Business Revolution*, Milford, CT: Capstone.

Dell, M. (1999) *Direct from Dell: Strategies that Revolutionized an Industry*, New York: HarperBusiness.

Morris, B. (2000) Can Michael Dell Escape the Box?, *Fortune* (October): 93–110.

Serwer, A. (1998) Michael Dell Rocks, *Fortune* (May): 58.

BPB

DEMING, William Edwards (1900–93)

W. Edwards Deming was born in Sioux City Iowa on 14 October 1900 and died at his home in Washington, DC on 20 December 1993. His early life was hard. The family farm in Wyoming was unsuccessful, and Deming began working at odd jobs while still a young child to help his family. He received an engineering degree in 1921 from the University of Wyoming and continued his education at the University of Colorado, where he obtained a master's degree in mathematics and physics in 1924. Deming went on to receive a Ph.D. in mathematical physics from Yale University in 1928. However, it was two summers of employment between Yale academic terms that provided what his leading biographer described as one of the most formative experiences of Deming's early career (Gabor 1990: 41). Deming worked as a student intern at the Hawthorne factory of Western Electric Company, a subsidiary of American

Telephone and Telegraph (later AT&T) in Chicago. The plant employed 46,000 people, who assembled telephones.

Deming's stay at Hawthorne coincided with the beginning of research there on worker motivation by Elton Mayo and Fritz Rothlisberger that became known as the Hawthorne Investigations (although Deming later insisted that he was unaware of the research while there: Gabor 1990: 42). Deming's experiences at Hawthorne were generally unpleasant. The reality of factory work was evidently a shock. According to Gabor, because of his frontier upbringing, 'Deming had no frame of reference for the demeaning drudgery the workers at the Hawthorne plant had to endure' (Gabor 1990: 42). Hawthorne probably helped shape Deming's dislike of American management and sympathy for American workers. But Hawthorne was also important to Deming in a positive way: it marked his exposure to the work of Walter Shewhart, of American Telephone and Telegraph Laboratories in statistical quality control (SQC).

SQC originated from agricultural research done by Britain's Sir Ronald Fisher. Research into better crop-growing methods was hampered because of the limited number of observations that could be done, due to the length of the growing season. Fisher developed statistical sampling techniques that enabled identification of interactions between multiple variables in crop growing, using a small number of observations. Fisher's work captured the attention of Shewhart, who was working on industrial quality control problems for Western Electric. Shewhart developed statistical sampling methods that identified variations in the quality of manufactured products. Prior to Shewhart, quality control depended upon inspection after manufacture, based on the Taylor's theories (Main 1994: 58–9).

The actual tools of SQC are fairly simple. They begin with the statistical control chart, developed by Shewhart, which measures variations in a process through sampling.

Shewhart, and later Juran, distinguished between 'random' and 'assignable' causes for variation; Deming used the phrases 'common' and 'special' causes for the same concepts (Deming 1986: chap. 11). For Deming, faults (variations) inherent in the system, are 'common'; faults (variations) from transient events are 'special' (Deming 1986: 314). Common or random causes are part of the production process, while transient or assignable causes are identifiable. It is important to be able to distinguish between the two because special causes can be removed through SQC while common causes can only be removed through improving the process itself. This insight was the foundation of Deming's theory of management. The central problem of management was to understand variation. Deming believed that 94 per cent of variation was common (systemic), and thus the responsibility of management, and 6 per cent was special. Thus, management bore the greatest responsibility, and 'the production worker [should be held] responsible only for what he can govern' (Deming 1986: 315).

After receiving his Ph.D. Deming went to work first for the US Agriculture Department, and then the Census Bureau in Washington, DC. Shewhart became both a friend and a mentor, and while in government service, Deming also spent a year in London studying statistical theory under Sir Ronald Fisher. During the 1930s Deming established himself as an authority in statistical sampling theory.

Deming first came to national attention in the United States during the Second World War. He played an important role in teaching SQC to some 2,000 engineers and industrialists involved in military production. In turn, this group went on to teach more than 30,000 others (Boardman 1994: 184). Despite the impact of SQC on American military production, Deming was dissatisfied with what he felt was a serious misapplication of what he and others were teaching. As he put it, 'brilliant applications attracted much attention, but the flare of statistical methods by themselves, in an atmosphere in which management did not know their responsibilities, burned, sputtered, fizzled and died out' (Deming 1986: 487). Following the war Deming joined the faculty of the school of business at New York University. Although angered by what he perceived as disinterest on the part of American management in SQC, he maintained an active consulting practice in statistics with a steady stream of US clients. In 1946 he became a founding member of the American Society for Quality Control. He also consulted for foreign governments regarding applications of statistical sampling to census taking. It was one such assignment that first brought him to Japan.

According to Professor William Tsutsui's incisive study of Deming and the quality movement in Japan (Tsutsui 1996), which draws extensively upon Japanese language sources, Japanese concern for industrial quality predated Deming's arrival. SQC became known in Japan in the 1930s, although it was not systematically applied by Japanese industry prior to 1945, when it was brought to Japan by the American military occupation authorities, the Supreme Commander, Allied Powers (SCAP). American telecommunications engineers assigned to SCAP were detailed to train Japanese engineers so that radios and telecommunications equipment could be mass produced in Japan, to assist in rebuilding the national communications infrastructure. During 1949–50 the engineers conducted training courses and wrote a textbook on production management. Some of the students in these courses later became leaders of companies such as Matsushita, Fujitsu and Sony (Wren and Greenwood 1998: 207–8). At the same time, the Union of Japanese Scientists and Engineers (JUSE), through its Quality Control Research Group, began offering training seminars in quality techniques (Tsutsui 1996: 305–307).

Deming himself first visited Japan in 1947, at SCAP's invitation, as part of a team of statisticians involved in preparing for the 1951 Japanese census. He travelled throughout Japan and developed an admiration for the country and its people. Through the work of the SCAP production management experts, Japanese engineers and industrialists had become familiar with Shewhart's work, including a book of lectures by Shewhart that Deming had edited. When the SCAP experts returned to the United States, Deming was invited to return to Japan by JUSE to lecture on quality control.

Contrary to legend, Deming's 1950 lectures to Japanese executives and engineers did not involve exposition of what Deming called the 'fourteen points' that formed the basis of his management philosophy (Tsutsui 1996: 309–10; Noguchi 1995: 42). Rather, the lectures to engineers, given as eight-day courses, explained basic SQC principles, including sampling, statistical control charts and Shewhart's 'Plan, Do, Check, Act' cycle, later known in Japan as the 'Deming cycle'. Deming's lectures to top management emphasized the importance of product quality as the key to developing export markets for Japanese products. Deming also stressed to management that quality is meaningless except in reference to whether a product meets customers' needs, and the importance of listening to the customer to ascertain those needs.

Deming's lectures were well attended and well received by both engineers and leading executives. JUSE published a Japanese translation and an English edition of the lectures. Deming generously donated the royalties to JUSE, which established the Deming prize in his honour in 1951. Within a decade this prize had become, in Tsutsui's words, 'the premier corporate accolade in Japan' (Tsutsui 1996: 309), and a valuable source of publicity for JUSE and the quality movement. Deming returned to Japan in 1951 and 1952 to conduct courses in SQC and market research. Although he travelled to Japan many times thereafter, particularly in connection with Deming prize events, the 1952 courses were the last that he taught there. The Emperor of Japan decorated Deming in 1960.

Although the legend propagated by the American media tells a different story, Deming was neither the only nor the most important American influence on Japan's postwar industrial resurgence. Noguchi Junji, who was a senior member of JUSE and an admirer of Deming, wrote that 'Deming's great legacy was that he opened the way for quality control by statistical methods in Japan' (Noguchi 1995: 36). However, Noguchi and other observers credited Joseph Juran with having a greater influence on Japanese quality management (Tsutsui 1996: 317–9; Green 1992: 17). At the same time, Tsutsui is correct in crediting Deming with an important role as symbolizing, for Japan's fledgling quality movement, the ideal of quality and the imperative for management reform (Tsutsui 1996: 324–5).

The 24 June 1980 NBC television documentary, *If Japan Can, Why Can't We?* presented a different version of events, however. America had faced many shocks during the 1970s, but perhaps none more serious to US business confidence than the capture of American markets by Japanese imported products, especially automobiles and home electronics. The television programme was the first attempt to explain Japanese industrial success to the American public. However, many American multinational companies were already very familiar with their Japanese counterparts through US–Japanese joint ventures operating in Japan, such as Xerox/Fuji Xerox and Hewlett-Packard/Yokogawa, as well as through the more painful experience of having to compete in the US against Japanese products that American consumers regarded as being superior in quality. Delegations from Ford and General Motors, among other companies, had visited Japan in the 1970s in search of answers. *If Japan Can, Why Can't We?* offered a simple explanation, one which met a favourable reception in America.

Deming had returned to teaching at NYU, and maintained a consulting practice that, at the time of the NBC programme had one US business client, Nashua Corporation. The producers of the documentary somehow learned of Deming, and first interviewed him at his Washington, DC home. Deming was then featured during the final portion of the actual broadcast. While Gabor's 1990 biography simply states that the program 'touted Deming's role in the revival of Japanese industry' (Gabor 1990: 223), Deming's rival Juran (who, according to his biographer, was also invited to appear on the programme, but declined; Butman 1997: 164) was more specific. In Juran's words:

In 1980 there emerged a widely viewed videocast, 'If Japan Can, Why Can't We?' It concluded that Japanese quality was due to their use of statistical methods taught to them by Deming. This conclusion had little relation to reality; however the program was cleverly presented and was persuasive to many viewers.

(Juran quoted in Tsutsui 1996: 323)

Tsutsui concludes that there is ample historical justification for Juran's contention, even though business rivalry may have been involved, since Deming and Juran were consulting competitors. Regardless, the television programme offered an appealing explanation to Americans troubled by Japan's business prowess: the Japanese were so effective because Deming, an American, had taught them to be. By extension, American companies could do what the Japanese had done by listening to Deming.

Deming's message of commitment to quality was delivered to an American corporate audience that was prepared to be receptive. The basic precept of total quality management (TQM), that quality is the responsibility of everyone in an organization, had been articulated by Dr Armand Feigenbaum of US General Electric in his 1950 book, *Total*

Quality Control. Philip CROSBY's book *Quality is Free* (1979), published a year prior to the NBC programme, had been a bestseller. Following the broadcast, demand for Deming's consulting services exploded. Major US corporations, first Ford, then General Motors, Dow Chemical, Florida Power and Light (later, the first American company to win the Deming prize) and others became clients. Deming also began offering four-day seminars, sponsored by a variety of organizations, at which he expounded his philosophy of management. He would continue offering these seminars until a few days before his death.

Deming's philosophy of management is encapsulated in his 'fourteen points for management', set forth in Deming (1986: 23–4). They are:

1. Create constancy of purpose toward improvement of product and service, with the aim to be competitive and to stay in business and to provide jobs.

2. Adopt the new philosophy. We are in a new economic age. Western management must awaken to the challenge, must learn their responsibilities, and take on leadership for change.

3. Cease dependence on inspection to achieve quality. Eliminate the need for inspection on a mass basis by building quality into the product in the first place.

4. End the practice of awarding business on the basis of price tag. Instead, minimize total cost. Move toward a single supplier for any one item, on a long-term relationship of loyalty and trust.

5. Improve constantly and forever the system of production and service, to improve quality and productivity, and thus constantly decrease cost.

6. Institute training on the job.

7. Institute leadership. The aim of supervision should be to help people and machines and gadgets to do a better job. Supervision of management is in need of overhaul, as well as supervision of production workers.

8. Drive out fear, so that everyone may work effectively for the company.

9. Break down barriers between departments. People in research, design, sales and production must work as a team, to foresee problems of production and in use that may be encountered with the product or service.

10. Eliminate slogans, exhortations and targets for the work force, asking for zero defects and new levels of productivity. Such exhortations only create adversarial relationships, as the bulk of the causes of low quality and low productivity belong to the system and thus lie beyond the power of the work force.

11. a. eliminate work standards (quotas) on the factory floor. Substitute leadership.

b. eliminate management by objective. Eliminate management by numbers, numerical goals. Substitute leadership.

12. a. remove barriers that rob the hourly worker of his right to pride of workmanship. The responsibility of supervisors must be changed from sheer numbers to quality.

b. remove barriers that rob people in management and in engineering of their right to pride of workmanship. This means, *inter alia*, abolishment of the annual or merit rating and of management by objective.

13. Institute a vigorous program of education and self improvement.

14. Put everybody in the company to work to accomplish the transformation. The transformation is everybody's job.

The fourteen points express familiar ideas and concepts. Deming disciples would argue that this is because Deming's management philosophy has been widely accepted, but Duncan and Van Matre (1990) and Vastag (2000), among others, have noted that little in

Deming's philosophy is really new. Gabor relates that Ishikawa Kaoru, a leader in the Japanese total quality control (TQC) movement, asserted that Deming had borrowed many of the ideas for his fourteen points from Japanese TQC and from Juran (Gabor 1990: 98). Duncan and Van Matre (1990: 5) point out that the only one of the fourteen points that is at odds with traditional management prescriptions is Deming's hostility to quantitative goal-setting. This is ironic, because an important difference between Deming's management philosophy and Japanese TQC is that in Japanese TQC managers set all manner of numeric targets, including targets that serve a motivational function only (Gitlow 1994: 202).

Whether or not Deming's philosophy was original, what impact did it have on contemporary American management? Extensive descriptions of Deming's work with American companies may be found in Gabor (1990, 2000a). She has characterized Deming's legacy at Ford as 'complicated' (Gabor 2000a: 195). This characterization is appropriate in describing the difficulty in specifying Deming's influence at companies where he worked. At Ford, he is credited with helping direct the company's focus towards customer satisfaction, and in influencing changes in Ford's goals and values, but he was unsuccessful in getting the company to abandon pay-for-performance reward systems (Gabor 2000a: 195-6). Nashua Corporation subsequently suffered serious financial problems through unsuccessful diversification, and chose not to replace the executive in charge of quality, a Deming disciple, when he retired. Florida Power and Light, the first American company to win the Deming Prize, thereafter changed its emphasis on quality when it changed CEOs (Main 1994: 198-209). An intensive survey of TQM deployment at forty-four leading US companies, including Ford and General Motors, disclosed that Crosby was more influential than either Deming or Juran, and that those companies that claimed to be following Deming's teachings adopted an approach to quality that emphasized SQC (Easton and Jarrell 2000: 102-107). Another study found Crosby, Deming and Juran to have largely similar approaches, and that companies often combined elements of all three to meet company-specific needs (Snyder *et al.* 1994: 46-7). But if Deming's impact on management practice was limited, this would appear to have been, at least partially, a self-imposed limitation. As Gabor observed, Deming created a personality cult, demanding absolute loyalty from his followers and taking on as clients only those companies in which top management showed itself willing to adopt his philosophy; a philosophy that required unquestioned acceptance of all of its tenets (Gabor 1990: 14, 186-7).

By the time of his death, Deming had attained a public status that transcended celebrity. He was lionized by the American media; an American magazine article that listed nine people or events that had changed the world began with the Apostle Paul and ended with Deming (Crainer 2000). One element of the Deming legend credited him with Japan's extraordinary industrial resurgence following the Second World War. The title of his biography hailed him as 'the man who discovered quality' (Gabor 1990). His accomplishments in research, teaching and popularization of SQC are significant. He wrote several major books and hundreds of articles on statistical theory and practice. His influence in raising awareness of the importance of quality in business was considerable; an estimated 50,000 people attended his four-day seminars on quality (Boardman 1994: 181). However, his actual accomplishments have become overshadowed by others' versions of those accomplishments. Despite his claim to have developed a profound system of knowledge that would remain useful for 100 years, his original contributions to management theory and practice remain difficult to identify.

In an article published on the hundredth anniversary of Deming's birth, Gabor observed that Deming's name has been all but forgotten in management but that the quality movement he helped inspire is very much alive. This is both a fitting and accurate epitaph (Gabor 2000b).

BIBLIOGRAPHY

Boardman, T.J. (1994) 'W. Edwards Deming, 1990–93', *The American Statistician* 48(3): 179–87.

Butman, J. (1997) *Juran, A Lifetime of Influence*, New York: John Wiley.

Crainer, S. (2000) *The Management Century*, San Francisco: Jossey-Bass.

Crosby, P. (1979) *Quality is Free*, New York: McGraw-Hill.

Deming, W.E. (1986) *Out of the Crisis*, Cambridge, MA: MIT Center for Advanced Engineering Study.

—— (1993) *The New Economics for Industry, Government, Education*, Cambridge, MA: MIT Center for Advanced Engineering Study.

Duncan, W.J. and Van Matre, J.G. (1990) 'The Gospel According to Deming: Is It Really New?', *Business Horizons* (July–August): 3–9.

Easton, G.S. and Jarrell, S.L. (2000) 'Patterns in the Deployment of Total Quality Management', in R.E. Cole and W.R. Scott (eds), *The Quality Movement and Organization Theory*, Thousand Oaks, CA: Sage, 89–130.

Feigenbaum, A. (1950) *Total Quality Control*, 3rd edn, New York: McGraw-Hill, 1991.

Gabor, A. (1990) *The Man Who Discovered Quality*, New York: Times Books.

—— (2000a) *The Capitalist Philosophers*, New York: Times Books.

—— (2000b) 'He Made America Think About Quality', *Fortune* (30 October): 292–3.

Gitlow, H.S. (1994) 'A Comparison of Japanese Total Quality Control and Deming's Theory of Management', *The American Statistician* 48(3): 197–203.

Green, C. (1992) *The Quality Imperative: A Business Week Guide*, New York: McGraw-Hill.

Kilian, C.S. (1994) *The World of W. Edwards Deming*, 2nd edn, Knoxville, TN: SPC Press.

Main, J. (1994) *Quality Wars: A Juran Institute Report*, New York: The Free Press.

Noguchi J. (1995) 'The Legacy of W. Edwards Deming', *Quality Progress* 28(12): 35–43.

Snyder, N.H., Dowd, J.J, Jr and Houghton, D.M. (1994) *Vision, Values and Courage: Leadership for Quality Management*, New York: The Free Press.

Tsutsui, W.M. (1996) 'W. Edwards Deming and the Origins of Quality Control in Japan', *Journal of Japanese Studies* 22(2): 295–325.

Vastag, G. (2000) 'W. Edwards Deming', in M.M. Helms (ed.), *The Encyclopedia of Management*, 4th edn, Detroit: Gale, 191–6.

Wren, D.A. and Greenwood, R.G. (1998) *Management Innovators*, New York: Oxford University Press.

STR

DENNISON, Henry Sturgis (1877–1952)

Henry Sturgis Dennison was born on 4 March 1877 in Boston, Massachusetts, the son of Henry Beals Dennison and Emma Stanley Dennison. He died in Framingham, Massachusetts on 29 February 1952. Henry Beals Dennison was president of the Dennison Manufacturing Company, founded in 1844 by his own father, Andrew Dennison, when the competition in the New England shoe industry forced Andrew to seek new business opportunities. Andrew's eldest son was a Boston jeweller, and suggested that his father transfer his skill from cutting leather to cutting paper, and that his two sisters then take the paper and cover jewellery boxes that could be sold in the jewellery store (Hayes 1929). This modest cottage industry eventually grew and diversified into a company selling a complete line of stationary items including labels, tickets, adhesives, paper decorations and shipping tags.

Henry Dennison attended the Roxbury Latin School and graduated from Harvard College in 1899. He was an accomplished violinist at the age of nine, and tuned his own piano. He was a naturalist and inventor, and was curious about psychiatry and public affairs (Galbraith 1981). Upon graduation from college he joined the family business and married Mary Tyler Thurber in 1901. The couple had four children. His first wife died in 1936, and in 1944 he married Gertrude B. Petri. Dennison worked in various positions with the family company before being elected a director in 1909.

John Kenneth GALBRAITH met Dennison in 1936 and stated that he was 'arguably the most interesting businessman in the United States at the time' (Galbraith 1981: 61). According to Galbraith, Dennison was a small man with a bald head whose 'need to attend to numerous interests caused him to dart rather than walk and to begin all sentences in the middle. It was only after considerable practice that it was possible to make sense out of what he was saying' (Galbraith 1981: 61). Feldman (1922) described him in terms routinely ascribed to modern leaders. He was certainly more than a manager. He was a man of broad vision who did not need to dominate because he could win by time and reason. He was a person of good cheer, poise and patience. To him, nothing was ever a failure if it served as an experiment. He did, however, hold many of his business associates in disdain, and a few of them reciprocated by boycotting Dennison products because of his radical tendencies (Galbraith 1981).

In 1917 Dennison succeeded his grandfather and father as president of the Dennison Manufacturing Company and built a reputation as author, industrialist, social reformer and public servant (Nelson 1999). Under Dennison's leadership, the company remained a *de facto* family business for more than a hundred years. In 1967 the Dennison Manufacturing Company merged with the National Blank Book Company, and in 1990 it became a subsidiary of Avery-Dennison Incorporated.

As an author, Dennison's most important contribution was *Organization Engineering* (1931), a pioneering work on the human factor in business. In this book, Dennison discussed a broad range of topics of contemporary interest including teamwork, leadership and the need for continuous reorganization in light of an ever-changing business environment. Other writings as a sole author and with other industrialists covered a variety of topics including monetary and fiscal policy, international trade, taxation and education (Leeds *et al.* 1938).

As an industrialist, Dennison implemented revolutionary reforms for workers. He made the Dennison Manufacturing Company his private laboratory for testing theories of social reform. The company had a clinic, library, cafeteria and savings bank. In 1913 he created a personnel department, and in 1916 he boldly introduced unemployment insurance for his employees. Dennison believed that unemployment could be prevented by good management, and considered benefit payments the penalty a company had to pay for failing to prevent unemployment. He was convinced that careful planning could buffer business organizations from the inevitable ups and downs of the business cycle. (Unfortunately, his company like many others suffered greatly during the Great Depression.) As President of the Taylor Society, he openly welcomed innovative executives and made the society a forum for industrial reform issues. He supported the International Management Institute, the National Bureau of

Economic Research and the Social Science Research Council (Earl 1955).

In the early 1920s, the Dennison Manufacturing Company, along with other major United States corporations such as Standard Oil of New Jersey, Goodyear, Westinghouse, International Harvester and American Telephone and Telegraph, implemented employee representation plans to provide avenues for employees to make suggestions for improved practices and for handling grievances (Gullett and Duncan 1976). The Dennison plan, however, was unique in the manner in which it allowed employee involvement in its design and implementation. The works committee at the company was instrumental in improving physical working conditions, facilitating two-way vertical communication, instituting an employee profit-sharing plan and establishing a housing fund from which employees could borrow at lower than market interest rates (Meine 1924).

As a social reformer, Dennison devoted a great deal of attention to his distrust of the corporate form of organization. His concern was more practical than academic, as demonstrated by the changes he made in his own company. His most ambitious and innovative undertaking was a plan to transfer the control of the company from outside stockholders to managers and employees.

In 1878 the Dennison Manufacturing Company incorporated and distributed voting stock to its owner-managers. However, by 1910 substantial blocks of the company's stock were held by outsiders. Henry Dennison, who was works manager at the time, and Charles Dennison, the president of the company, worried that outsiders would exercise too much control over operations (Vollmers 1997). With the aid of Mrs James Peter Warbasse, the company's largest stockholder, Dennison was able to accomplish an innovative reorganization that provided safeguards against excessive external control (Nelson 1999).

The impetus for Dennison's plan was the dysfunctional affects caused by absentee stockholders. In the typical corporation then, as today, most owners did not work for or manage the organization. The stockholder's concern was for the return they could make on their investment and little more. If they could make a higher return by selling their interest in one corporation and purchasing shares in another, the transfer costs were minimal. While absentee investors made a one-time contribution in the form of their investment, managers and workers had an ongoing personal stake in the success of the company.

Dennison believed that a new concept of corporate control was needed. His new concept was based on two principles of efficiency engineering and common sense: (1) responsibility must be closely related to ability, and (2) reward must be closely related to service. This required that businesses assure that voting control was retained by individuals familiar with and directly involved in the success of the firm, and that profits were shared with those who directly influenced productivity (Duncan and Gullett 1974). According to Dennison, once wages increased to the point of providing for essential needs, the distribution of profits became an important determinant of the energy expended towards greater production. It was his contention that the normal human being, in spite of the possibility of increasing his or her own earnings would reduce effort if it was known that increasing productivity would increase the returns of absentee stockholders (Dennison 1920: 159).

To prevent such a reduction in effort, Dennison devised a corporate structure whereby investors received a priority return for their act of investment and managers and workers received returns based on the company's performance. Prior to 1924, managers and employees of the Dennison Manufacturing Company were made partners in the business and participated in sharing the profits of the firm. This structure was developed in such a way that investors held either first or second preferred stock. First and second preferred paid fixed returns and were cumulative: all present and past earnings on preferred stock had to be paid in full before any payments could be made to holders of common stock.

The company directors declared a dividend on partnership stocks each year, and any amount remaining after the preferred stockholders were paid went to managers and employees. The management partners received two-thirds of the residual, and the employee partners received one-third. Payments to the management and employee partners were made in the form of stock, which was non-transferable. If a manager or employee left the firm, the stock was converted to second preferred. If the Company failed to produce the full amount of preferred dividends, control reverted to the holders of first preferred stock (Gorton 1926).

Dennison, although a reformer, was realistic about the likelihood of corporations willingly following his lead in the transfer of industrial control from investors to managers and workers (McQuaid 1977). In a book written with John Kenneth Galbraith (Dennison and Galbraith 1938), he therefore endorsed a number of reforms resulting from the Securities Exchange Act of 1934. The authors argued for the simplification of the corporate form of organization, separation of stockholder ownership and control of corporations, board of director responsibility and restriction on the number of board memberships, and government supervision of securities markets.

As a public servant, Dennison held numerous appointed positions. To illustrate only a few of the more important, he was adviser to the chairman of the War Industries Board and Assistant Director of the Central Bureau of Planning and Statistics from 1917 to 1918, a member of President Wilson's Industrial Conference in 1919 and a member of President Harding's Unemployment Conference in 1921. He was a director of the US Post Office Department's Service Relations Division 1922–8, chaired the Industrial Advisory Board of the US Department of Commerce in 1934, and was a director of the Federal Reserve Bank of Boston 1937–45.

BIBLIOGRAPHY

Dennison, H.S. (1920) 'Production and Profits', *Annals of the American Academy of Political and Social Sciences* 66(3): 159–61.

——— (1931) *Organization Engineering*, New York: McGraw-Hill.

Dennison, H.S. and Galbraith, J.K. (1938) *Modern Competition and Business Policy*, New York: Oxford University Press.

Duncan, W.J. and Gullett, C.R. (1974) 'Henry Sturgis Dennison: The Manager and the Social Critic', *Journal of Business Research* 2(2): 133–46.

Earl, P.A. (1955) 'Henry Sturgis Dennison', in J.A. Garraty (ed.), *Directory of American Biography*, New York: Charles Scribner's Sons, suppl. 5 (1951–5), 164–5.

Feldman, H. (1922) 'The Outstanding Features of the Dennison Management', *Industrial Management* 65(2): 67–73.

Galbraith, J.K. (1981) *A Life in Our Times: Memoirs*, Boston: Houghton Mifflin.

Gorton, J. (1926) *Profit Sharing and Stock Ownership for Employees,* New York: Harper and Brothers (see chapter on Dennison Manufacturing Company, 259–68).

Gullett, C.R. and Duncan, W.J. (1976) 'Employee Representation Reappraised', *Conference Board Record* 13(6): 32–6.

Hayes, E.P. (1929) 'History of the Dennison Manufacturing Company', *Journal of Economic and Business History* 1(4): 467–502.

Health, C. (1929) 'History of the Dennison Manufacturing Company II', *Journal of Economic and Business History* 2(1): 163–202.

Leeds, M.E., Flanders, R.E., Filene, L. and

Dennison, H.S. (1938) *Toward Full Employment*, New York: McGraw-Hill.

McQuaid, K. (1977) 'Henry S. Dennison and the Science of Industrial Reform 1900–1950', *American Journal of Ethics and Sociology* 36(4): 79–98.

Meine, F.J. (1924) 'The Introduction and Development of the Works Committee in the Dennison Manufacturing Company', *Journal of Personnel Research* 3(8): 130–41.

Nelson, D. (1999) 'Henry Sturgis Dennison', in J.A. Garraty and M.C. Carnes (eds), *American National Biography*, New York: Oxford University Press, 445–6.

Vollmers, G. (1997) 'Industrial Home Work of the Dennison Manufacturing Company of Framingham, Massachusetts, 1912–1935', *Business History Review* 71(3): 444–70.

WJD

DISNEY, Walter Elias (1901–66)

Walt Disney was born in Chicago on 5 December 1901 to Elias and Flora Disney, and died in Tulsa, Oklahoma on 15 December 1966. He was a product of the American Midwest. His childhood was spent on a farm in rural Missouri among dogs, ducks, cattle, pigs, cats and other animals, creatures that would one day inspire and populate his feature films and cartoons. From a very early age he had a love of drawing. Following service in the First World War, the largely self-educated Disney worked as a commercial artist in Kansas City and then ventured into the new realm of animation. The 1920s were a time of struggle for the start-up animator. His first business in Missouri failed, and in 1923, he moved to California and went into business with his brother Roy, whose business acumen meshed well with his own imagination.

Disney's first character, Oswald the Rabbit, was misappropriated by his distributor, who also enticed away most of his staff. Disney was determined never again to lose control of any of his characters and went about creating a new one, inspired by the mice that used to crawl through his Kansas City studio. His wife Lillian Bounds, whom he had married in 1925, suggested the name Mickey Mouse. Mickey's first feature, *Steamboat Willie*, premiered in November 1928 and he immediately won the hearts of millions, becoming a superstar of the 1920s. His antics and mannerisms were supposedly based on those of Charlie Chaplin.

Disney combined creative eccentricity and marketing genius, and knew cinema goers wanted escape in place of heavy social commentary. However, the Disney pictures unintentionally offered a form of social commentary all the same. Disney expressed a kind of populism, in which the mistreated underdog turned the tables on the villain trying to eat or defraud him. *The Three Little Pigs* (1933) was taken by many as a parable of the times, with the wolf symbolizing the Great Depression. Throughout the 1930s the Disney enterprise grew enormously. By the early 1940s Disney was creating animated feature films such as *Snow White, Pinocchio, Dumbo* and *Bambi*. The *New York Times* praised him as the 'Horatio Alger of the cinema', and many saw him as an entrepreneurial hero in the new field of entertainment.

Disney's business philosophy involved finding his niche, which was animation, and pursuing it with single-minded determination: 'Invent your own job; take such an interest in it that you eat, sleep, dream, walk, talk, and live nothing but your work until you succeed' (Brands 1999: 188). During the 1930s Disney films netted some $20,000 per picture.

Disney was also a marketing genius. He gave Disney a brand name. Mickey Mouse toys, lunchboxes, caps, shirts, watches and a multitude of other products with the Disney brand earned him millions. Disney also knew how to be on the leading edge of entertainment technology. He was a pioneer in sound and in Technicolor animation, and leaped quickly into the new media of television. The weekly *Disneyland* television show (1954) and the *Mickey Mouse Club* (1955) attracted 19 million viewers for each show. Also in 1955 Disneyland opened in Anaheim, California, where it became one of the biggest tourist attractions in the world. The tremendous synergy between the television, movie, theme park and other promotions created a marketing revolution, as each element in turn promoted the other.

By the late 1950s and early 1960s Disney's enormous enterprise was earning over $100 million a year and defined not only American marketing but American culture. Disney had set an example for other media producers to follow. His ideology remained a populist one, but one that had shifted more to the right. Once a New Dealer, Disney in 1964 supported the Republican candidacy of conservative Arizona senator, Barry Goldwater (1909–98). His entertainment was middlebrow and not targeted at elites. He promoted American heroes such as Davy Crockett and Francis Marion, and ridiculed big government and big business when they trampled upon the average American. There was a subtle pro-nature message and a belief that Americans could do anything they set their minds to.

By the time of his death in 1966, Disney had not only shaped the American and world entertainment of the twentieth century, but both reflected and defined much of what was quintessential in American popular culture. The inability of his successors to copy his genius and a changing cultural environment almost marginalized the Disney enterprise until Michael EISNER reinvented the Disney tradition in the mid-1980s.

BIBLIOGRAPHY

Brands, H.W. (1999) *Masters of Enterprise: Giants of American Business from John Jacob Astor and J.P. Morgan to Bill Gates and Oprah Winfrey*, New York: Free Press.

'Walter Elias Disney' (1999) *McGraw-Hill Encyclopedia of World Biography*, Detroit, MI: Gale Research, Inc., vol. 5, 26–7.

Watts, S. (1997) *The Magic Kingdom: Walt Disney and the American Way of Life*, Boston: Houghton Mifflin.

DCL

DREW, Daniel (1797–1879)

Daniel Drew was born on his family's farm near Carmel, New York, on 29 July 1797 and died in New York on 18 September 1879. Raised on a small farm in New York state, Drew was forced to quit school at an early age to help run the struggling enterprise. In his late teens he held a number of jobs as a cattle drover. An incurable schemer, he developed a technique of feeding his herd salt and allowing them to drink large quantities of water the night before a sale, thereby adding some fifty pounds to each head of cattle. He sold such 'watered stock' to Henry Astor, a prosperous New York City butcher and brother of fur and real estate tycoon John Jacob ASTOR, who subsequently and inexplicably had partnerships with Drew in other business dealings.

Later Drew entered the steamboat business, challenging Cornelius 'Commodore' VANDERBILT for control of the Hudson River traffic between Albany and New York City. As his empire expanded, Drew founded the Wall Street brokerage firm of Drew, Robinson and Company to finance his ventures. It quickly became his base of operations, as

Drew discovered he could make more money through speculation than operating steamboat companies.

Consequently, in the 1850s he followed his long-time rival and sometime partner Vanderbilt into the burgeoning railroad industry. Drew then devoted nearly all his energy to stock manipulations, particularly on shares of the Erie Railroad. During that phase of his career he continued to tilt with Vanderbilt, who had forged the powerful New York Central railroad system; this originally stretched from New York City to Albany and, after the Civil War, to the fast growing metropolis of Chicago. As president of the Erie, 'Uncle Daniel', as Drew was often called, infuriated Vanderbilt by launching a rate war, whereupon the 'Commodore' launched a campaign to obtain control of the Erie. Drew retaliated, enlisting new and powerful allies Jay GOULD and 'Jubilee' Jim Fisk. The trio moved the line's headquarters to New Jersey and, in a complex series of manoeuvres that included the issue of phoney common stock and the bribery of various public officials, fended off the Vanderbilt challenge. Their unethical business practices gave rise to the term 'watered stock'.

In the end, however, the allies fell out, and Drew resigned from the presidency, leaving Gould in control. His losses during the battle combined with further setbacks in the Panic of 1873 to ruin Drew. In 1876 he filed for bankruptcy and was forced to live on the charity of his family. He died three years later.

BIBLIOGRAPHY
Adams, C.F., Jr, and Adams, H. (1886) *Chapters of Erie and Other Essays*, New York: Henry Holt.
Browder, C. (1986) *The Money Game in Old New York: Daniel Drew and His Times*, Lexington, KY: University Press of Kentucky.
Klein, M. (1986) *The Life and Legend of Jay Gould*, Baltimore: Johns Hopkins University Press.
Mott, E.H. (1899) *Between the Ocean and the Lakes: The Story of Erie*, New York: John S. Collins.
White, B. (1910) *The Book of Daniel Drew*, New York: Doubleday, Page.

WTW

DRUCKER, Peter Ferdinand (1909–)

Peter Drucker was born on 19 November 1909 in Vienna. His father, Adolph Drucker, was a prominent lawyer and senior civil servant. His mother, Caroline Bond, had an English father, who had been a banker; she was one of the first women in Austria to study medicine, and attended lectures by Sigmund Freud. Both parents were high achievers. The household is described as being Lutheran and comfortable middle class, with a flow of visitors who were politicians, academics or from the arts.

By the middle of 1917, however, life in Austria was changing for all, as the effects of being on the losing side of the First World War took hold. Rampant inflation gripped the country, with the Austrian krone falling to one 75,000th of its value in the four years after 1917. It was in this rapidly changing world that Drucker grew up. Influences outside home also had an effect. His two junior schoolteachers set the basic template for his learning: one taught him to concentrate upon his strengths, and the other to learn by objective examination. After junior school Drucker was educated at the classics-based Vienna Gymnasium, but his interest in learning was also stimulated outside school at several Viennese intellectual salons, where he was treated as an adult, and where he had to learn to research and then have his work critically examined.

A week short of his fourteenth birthday Drucker, as the youngest and newest 'comrade', was honoured by being appointed a banner carrier at a Young Socialist rally. Partway through the walk he abandoned the march and the banner. He later said: 'I only found out I didn't belong. But of course I only found out that I was a bystander on that cold and blustery November day. Bystanders are born rather than made' (Drucker 1979: 4).

At seventeen, Drucker left school and Vienna and became an apprentice clerk in a small business in Hamburg that exported hardware to India. Despite his full-time job he enrolled as a part-time student in the law faculty at Hamburg University. Weekday evenings were spent in the library: 'I read and read and read everything in German, English and French' (Beatty 1998: 12). He learned that Verdi wrote his most difficult opera, *Falstaff*, when he was eighty, and this made an indelible impression on him: he resolved that he would use Verdi's principles as a life model in trying for perfection and not giving up in advanced age (Beatty 1998: 12).

While still in Hamburg Drucker had an experience, which would rank among the most fundamental of his life. Reading Søren Kierkegaard's *Fear and Trembling* reinforced his Christian beliefs and his commitment to the Protestant work ethic, emphasizing morality and integrity, and adding a spiritual need to the secular nature of his work and teaching. After fifteen months Drucker transferred to Frankfurt University, adding statistics to his subjects. Part of the general syllabus was admiralty law, which Drucker told Beatty was 'a microcosm of Western History, society, technology, legal thought and economy' (Beatty 1998: 14), which Drucker would later use as a template to teach management.

His fluency in English enabled his appointment as a securities analyst at an old merchant bank that had been taken over by a Wall Street brokerage business. One of his first published works celebrated the health of the stock market. The forecast proved wrong, as his job ended with the crash of the New York Stock Exchange in the autumn of 1929, but not before he had started to write articles for a learned econometric journal. Now twenty years of age, he was appointed a financial writer on Frankfurt's leading newspaper, *Frankfurt General Anzeiger*. Within two years he had become senior editor of foreign and economic news. By 1931, at the age of twenty-two, Drucker had obtained his doctorate in public and international law, adding lecturing at the university to his activities. With the completion of his doctorate and what was forecast to be a promising career, he became eligible to be appointed *dozent*, a university lecturer post which was conditional on his becoming a German national.

Drucker's rejection of this condition, and of the Nazis, came in the publication of a small monograph, *Fr J Stahl: Konservative Staatslehre & Geschichtliche Entwiclung Motrtueringan* (Fr J Stahl: Conservative Philosophy and Historical Continuity). Stahl was an obscure and difficult German philosopher from the first half of the nineteenth century, who believed that even in periods of political and economic change, conservatism based upon Protestant principles could continue, with a place for a constitutional monarch. Shortly before this work's publication in 1933, Drucker left Germany for Vienna. The work was recognized by the Nazis, as intended, as a rejection of their ideas. This, coupled with the Christian convert Stahl's Jewish blood, was sufficient for the work to be banned and burnt. Stahl's significance to Drucker was related to Drucker's acceptance that the old Cartesian world of everything having its place was over; but that order was still possible, with Stahl's philosophy, in what Drucker perceived to be a world of discontinuities. Berthold Freyberg, who claimed to be Drucker's oldest friend, having met him while they were clerk colleagues in Hamburg, wrote of Stahl: 'the work ... foreshadowed his entire subsequent development' (Freyberg 1970: 18).

After a short stay in Vienna, Drucker left for England to find work. His first job was as a trainee securities analyst in an insurance organization, and lasted a few months. Next he worked with a small London merchant bank, Freedberg and Company, as economic report writer and executive secretary to the partners. Subsequently he became a partner, learning about mergers and acquisitions, and how his clients' businesses worked. He stayed with the company until he moved to New York in 1937. While in England he continued his education by attending John Maynard Keynes's lectures at Cambridge University. Drucker said that while he could have been an economist, he realized that economists were only interested in inanimate items such as commodities, trade and finance, whereas his interest was in people. He also contributed to a book that disputed the Nazi version of the German economy, *Germany, The Last Four Years* (Germanicus 1937) By 1935 he had recommended his work in journalism, writing for American magazines and newspapers.

Before leaving for New York, Drucker married Doris Schmitz, a physicist and writer from Mainz, Germany on 16 January 1937. They have four children and six grandchildren. Drucker felt on arriving in America in 1937 that he had escaped the Old World. It was this promise to escape that he had made to himself at the youth rally as a teenager.

Drucker arrived in New York with commissions to write for two London newspapers including the *Financial News*, forerunner to the *Financial Times*, and other newspapers in Glasgow and Sheffield. He was also retained as a financial adviser and economist to a group of British investors for his previous merchant bank, Freedberg and Company. Drucker quickly added to his journalist commissions *The Virginian Quarterly Review*, *The Washington Post*, *Harpers Magazine*, *Asia*, *New Republic* and *Philadelphia Saturday Evening Post*. *Reader's Digest* and *The Review of Politics* were later added, as his range of topics extended from European history, economics, politics and foreign affairs to philosophy, education, religion and the arts.

Drucker's first book, *The End of Economic Man* (1939), a study of the new totalitarianism, was conceived in Europe but published in America. The first sentence, 'This book is a political book', sets out his purpose. The book tracks the breakdown of the events that caused the break-up of European society between the world wars. With the political, economic and spiritual world bankrupt, people had lost the will for freedom and had capitulated. The totalitarianism of Italy, Germany, Austria and Russia had filled the gap. Drucker suggested an alternative which would give freedom, status and function, one that was influenced by Stahl's discontinuities, Kierkegaard's existentialism and RATHENAU's social and industrial order. Although this is not a management book, Drucker describes Hitler's denationalization of the German banks; this would later develop into Drucker's concept of reprivatization, which the Thatcher government in the UK credited as the inspiration for its privatization policy. The book had a considerable impact; notably, communists attacked the suggestion that Hitler and Stalin would agree on a pact, but subsequent events proved this forecast correct. Others praised it, including Winston Churchill, who instructed that it should be essential reading for British military officer candidates.

In 1940 Drucker set up an independent consultancy as an adviser on the German economy and politics. His clients included the American government. His return to teaching began at Sarah Lawrence College in Bronxville, New York in 1941, teaching economics and statistics one day a week. In late 1941 he moved to Bennington College, Vermont on a weekly basis and also lectured to small colleges throughout America, having visited over fifty by the time the United States went to war in 1941. By the summer of 1942 Drucker had taken up a full-time appointment at Bennington, which was described as a highly visible woman's college because of its progressive teaching formats. During his stay there he became a US citizen. He remained at

Bennington until 1949, as professor of politics and philosophy. Drucker said that he knew that he wanted to keep on teaching, and was given the freedom to teach whatever subject needed teaching. He taught philosophy, political theory, economic history, American government, American history, literature and religion.

The End of Economic Man signalled the end of the Old World order. His next book, *The Future of Industrial Man* (1942), started to look forward to the new. The book has just one topic: 'How can an industrial society be built on a free society' (Drucker 1942: 7). The first task was to make the power of the management of business legitimate. After examination, Drucker agreed with BERLE and MEANS that the divorce of ownership of business from control by independent management is not legitimate power, as in practice it is power without responsibility. For Drucker, authority and responsibility are partners that should be indivisible. Power without responsibility is corruption. While accepting that the basis for business was legal, he could not agree that it was constitutionally legitimate. Management's first responsibility was to produce economic results as profits; the second responsibility was to work in a manner that is for the good of society while never attempting to take over the work of society. He warned that lack of responsible behaviour would result in hostility from society at large and interference from the government in particular. The major idea of the book was that the corporation, the big industrial business, should encourage a self-governing plant community, in which the worker would find his place in changing society. The influence was that of Rathenau, but Drucker's ideas were that people must have status and freedom of choice with responsibility, whereas Rathenau's ideas were more prescriptive. Both, however, agreed that the 'demon' was 'unemployment' and advocated social benefits such as economic support and training to provide opportunities. Drucker regards what

was to become his 'autonomous' self-governing plant community as one of his best ideas. But it was never fulfilled, as workers became more affluent and thus more independent of the workplace. Drucker's interest in management also emerges further in this work, which makes reference to FORD and TAYLOR, and also SCHUMPETER, to whom he attributed the most consistent and effective contemporary theory of capitalism.

Drucker had concluded while in Nazi Germany that totalitarianism was not the way for the world. His identification of American free market capitalism as an alternative was now emerging. What he had discovered was a dynamic force that drives capitalism. That force is management, which had received considerable attention from writers during the late nineteenth century and the preceding part of the twentieth century. By 1943 Drucker had decided that he wanted to make a study of contemporary management practices. He received an invitation from General Motors, then the largest corporation in the world with 500,000 employees, to conduct a study 'on the governance of the big organization, its structure and constitution, on the place of big business in society, and on the principle of industrial order' (Drucker 1979: 258). The results of this study were published as his first management book, *Concept of the Corporation* (1946), published in the UK as *Big Business* (1947), as the publishers believed that the American title would be meaningless in Britain. The book was the first ever about an industrial enterprise as a social organization. It put people at the centre of management activities. It reflects and acknowledges Mooney and Reiley's *Onward Industry!* (1931), which identified the organization as a social entity (later Drucker credited Rathenau with an earlier expression of this) and also that the life-giving element of an organization is management as the 'vital spark'.

Drucker describes Alfred P. SLOAN's structure of organization, federal decentralization and its components. The list is comprehensive, missing only Sloan's obsession with safety at work. What Drucker displayed is an ability to identify the essentials. All of the activities described would receive full treatment by Drucker in his later work. The needs of society, the worker and the enterprise are discussed, along with the essentiality of balancing their mutual interests. The job of top management is identified as being the setting of objectives (policies), the agreeing of targets and the measurement of the results. In addition, top management must plan for succession and obtain sufficient profit for the enterprise to continue and succeed in the future. This is the start of Drucker's thorough examination of the meaning of profit. Identified is General Motors' policy of making character loans to dealers who do not have normal asset collateral, this being today's 'venture capital'. Drucker commends its invention and advocates it as a general commercial policy. The power of the market is recognized, along with the essential need to satisfy the customer's wants, which may be 'economically irrational' (Drucker 1946: 248). The book is a mixture of advice, understanding, encouragement, criticism and required discoveries. What is emerging is a workable world, never perfect but dependent on everybody taking responsibility and performing their tasks. The manager, who must manage, will only be judged by results, which must always be obtained by acting ethically. Criticized are the labour unions, which have still to find a contributory role but never do. Also criticized is personnel management for failing to manage people by motivation, which is the key to people management. Personnel management, despite name changes to human relations and human resources, never escapes Drucker's criticism because in his view it concentrates on what people cannot do rather than what they can do. This is also at the root of his criticism of psychological tests as a human resources gadget. In later work, Drucker concludes that only a third of appointments succeed: a third fail from the employer's point of view, and the remaining third from the employee's point of view. Drucker later advised people to assess where they fitted in the new era of the knowledge worker, and to make quality decisions about their lives and families. He recommends proven psychological tests as a tool for individuals to determine their aptitude for their career.

The third area for criticism is traditional accounting methods, which are designed for an age of trading commerce rather than a processing one. General Motors, at the time of Drucker's research, had evolved what was the most appropriate cost accounts system. It replaced previous systems of control only, with control and measurement. What Drucker realized was that the method needed developing. Drucker's contribution in pioneering work on transactional analysis as a building block of activity accounting was acknowledged by specialists such as Robert Kaplan and N. Thomas Johnson. His view was that few, if any, systems are ever complete; they need refinement and complementing with alternative methodology.

Concept of the Corporation was an enormous success, and like many of Drucker's books has been in continual print since its launch. However, General Motors thought the book critical of the corporation and sympathetic to the unions, as the book's publication coincided with the unions calling a damaging 113-day strike. Sloan thought that Drucker was wrong, but was entitled to his opinion. The book launched Drucker's career as a management writer, but it also posed questions, not about his academic ability *per se*, but about his academic judgement in mixing economic and social sciences. He was not invited to continue his membership of the American Political Science Association.

Drucker's next book, *The New Society* (1949), was a development and tidying of his previous ideas. Its publication preceded his moving back to New York in 1950 as professor of management at the graduate business school of New York University, where he remained until 1971. His management consulting business was now becoming well established, with clients including Sears Roebuck, General Motors, ITT and major railroads. He was now further developing and refining his management ideas by practising with top corporations while researching and considering the work of others.

The Practice of Management (1954) is regarded by many as Drucker's seminal work. Together with his four preceding books, it is the foundation of his philosophy. *The Practice of Management* was written as a handbook for consultancy clients. Drucker accepted that management was older than the pyramids, but a book was needed to enable people to be able to learn it. The book is a guide rather than an orthodox textbook. While containing some checklists, it offers a more flexible approach than other management writings, and contains a mixture of the definitive and the exploratory. Managers, he says, must learn to think. In a world that is rapidly and unpredictably changing, the manager must be adaptable. He must shape the future to create opportunities rather than wait for the problems. The manager of the future will have to learn to look beyond his own speciality, even beyond his own organization and its industry. What is happening beyond will affect the future for the manager. The book introduced to the world 'Management by Objectives and Self-control' (MBO), which can be regarded as a 'philosophy of management' (Drucker 1954: 134). This enabled managers to help or set objectives, take responsibility and measure their own performance. It makes delegation a meaningful practice. It also makes possible a move away from command and control management.

The book has some very clear messages, some of which are drawn from his previous works. The first duty of a business is to survive: 'The guiding principles of business economics ... [are] the avoidance of loss' (Drucker 1954: 44). Drucker describes what objectives are and how the managers will set them. Central to the manager's role is the treatment of workers: they are not a commodity but a unique resource which, when properly motivated by being given opportunities and training, will contribute to and develop managerial vision, and take responsibility. The book recognizes that federal decentralization is the preferred organizational structure, but there are others as well. The first task is not to choose the structure but to ask, 'what is our business' and 'what should it be'? (Drucker 1954, chap. 6) Once these questions have been answered, then the structure can be chosen.

Drucker is fully aware that the organization has to perform economically, and confirms profit as an essential feature. However, his view is that its traditional definition is too narrow. The profit of the enterprise must provide, as its social responsibility, for yesterday's costs, today's and the future's needs, and pay taxes to fund government services. Very clearly described is how managers manage by objectives; what the objectives are; and how they must be set. The management function of the board of directors is defined as being policies, performance and results. The operations managers' function is to perform within the policies and produce their part of the results by applying Drucker's development of Henri FAYOL's five basic functions – setting objectives, organizing, motivation, measuring and communicating – not in a 'top-down' or 'bottom-up' sense, but in a multi-directional fashion. Drucker then adds a sixth basic function: the development of people; including oneself.

Drucker attributes Henry Ford's near failure at the end of the Second World War, after his incredibly successful empire-building in earlier decades, to his having not managers but only assistants. He feels that the way that work is carried out is changing. The growth of manual workers has peaked. The growing sector is now that of the knowledge worker and the professional. Most of these are not managers, but they make a managerial contribution. Drucker points out that Taylor's theories about productivity and the separation of work and planning are not applicable to knowledge workers, who must take responsibility for planning their own work, as they cannot be controlled as a manual worker might be. The problem of Taylor's separation of work and planning exercised Drucker's mind for several decades. He ultimately resolved this by arguing that Taylor did not say that work and planning had to be performed by different people. Once it was accepted that the same person could perform both tasks, then Taylor was appropriate for knowledge work. In fact, the only practical way that the new breed of worker, the knowledge technologist, could work was in this manner.

A working example of the integration of work and planning, albeit for manual workers, is Drucker's description of what Thomas J. WATSON's IBM had been practising since the 1930s. The workers' tasks are engineered to be as simple as possible. Then, with training, other skills are developed. The workers are then encouraged to contribute to the policy of continual improvements, resulting in increased productivity. The improvements are reflected in product improvement, which creates more sales, securing jobs and establishing attitudes of acceptance of the necessity to change. IBM managers are seen as assistants to their workers. What Drucker identified here is what would be later termed 're-engineering'; he gives credit to IBM executives, Charles R. Walker and E.L.W. Richardson for developing the method (Drucker 1954: 252). Influence from this book can also be found in McGREGOR's 'Theory Y' and HERZBERG's concept of 'hygiene factors'.

But arguably the most permanent impact of the book was encapsulated in the Drucker epigram: 'There is only one valid definition of business purpose: *to create a customer*' (Drucker 1954: 35; he later added, 'and get paid'). Because its purpose is to create a customer, any business enterprise has two and only these two basic functions: marketing and innovation. These are what Drucker calls the 'entrepreneurial functions'. As he goes on to say, 'The economic revolution of the American economy since 1900 has in large part been a marketing revolution ...' (Drucker 1954: 35–6). Theodore LEVITT later highlighted Drucker's contribution to this field: 'Peter Drucker created and publicised the marketing concept and nobody had ever really acknowledged it' (Levitt 1970: 8). A similar comment comes from George S. Day: 'Compelling visions are best nourished in market-driven organizations. While there are many views on what this means, all start with Drucker's original formulation' (Day 1999: 18).

Drucker went on to develop these ideas in *Managing for Results* (1964), a book that he claims was the first written on strategy but that is also very much a marketing book. He divides an enterprise's products into eleven groups, including 'yesterday's breadwinners', 'management's egos' and 'failures', all of which need to be disposed of. Today's and yesterday's breadwinners give large volumes and low margins. Tomorrow's breadwinners are 'what everybody hopes all products are', but are 'not as common as company press releases ... assume'; 'a company had better have at least one of them around' (Drucker 1964: 48–50). Drucker poses the question of whether Prince Charming will come before Cinderella gets old. The marketing concept was still further refined and developed in Drucker's later work. After initially identifying marketing and innovation as the two basic functions of the entrepreneurial function, by 1985 Drucker had developed a working discipline of innovation, 'the specific tool of the entrepreneur', 'which was capable of being learned, capable of being practised' (Drucker 1985: 17). The inspiration here was the Austrian economist Joseph SCHUMPETER, who had developed a theory of economics that incorporated the entrepreneurial function, and the French economist J.B. Say, who had identified the entrepreneur's function in the early nineteenth century. Drucker now added the entrepreneurial function to the practice of management.

In *The Practice of Management*, Drucker identifies the need for more leaders, as the few natural geniuses available will not meet the demand. In later work, he decided that leadership is a skill that can be learnt but not taught. Learning is made possible by developing and applying managerial skills. Drucker rejected the vogue of participation management of the 1980s as nonsense, because someone always had to make the final and often painful decision. Among leadership skills was the ability to be prepared for trouble, as it always arrives in all organizations sooner or later.

The Practice of Management was not only an immediate success but also, in common with many of his books, became a permanent classic, being awarded the 1998 Financial Times/Booz Allen Global Business Books award as a book which had stood the test of time as an important contribution to business thinking. The impact of the publication of *The Practice of Management* on management was considerable. Management by objective became the best-known practice in management for at least the next two decades. Although it is now considered by many a concept of the past, it is still practised today under various names. The book gave Drucker international recognition and made him perhaps the most sought-after practising management consultant in the world. He began his long association with Japan and was among the first Westerners to write knowledgeably and extensively about Japanese management and the influences upon it of Japanese culture. In addition, he continued to write books and articles, and to teach and undertake research. With an established readership for his articles and books, he was able to introduce managers to many new ideas. For example, he introduced demographics as a forecasting tool. He

once commented that 'The major events that determine the future have already happened – irrevocably' (Drucker 1957: 2), showing how the manager must operate simultaneously in two time scales, the present and the future.

Drucker was also one of the first writers to recognize that the impact of computers would be in data processing rather than in decision making. While others were forecasting redundancies, he was forecasting that computers would create work for thousands of clerks. However, the demands of business for knowledge workers would absorb the potential for increased leisure time by expanding the need for education. Knowledge was likened to electricity at the turn of the nineteenth and twentieth centuries, as the new 'energy'. Increased leisure time would do little to help the manager who spends most of his time attending to non-managerial priorities, resulting in a constant shortage of time. The solution for the manager was to recognize the difference between efficiency and effectiveness. Efficiency was getting things done right; but this poses a problem, as it may not be the right task. Effectiveness is 'to get the right things done' (Drucker 1966: 1).

The Age of Discontinuity: Guidelines to our Changing Society was published in 1969. In this work, Drucker wrote that 'we are disenchanted with government because it ... does not perform' (Drucker 1969: 226), and recommended for the first time that government required 'reprivatization' to shed some of its activities (Drucker 1969: 218). Drucker also forecast that the world was becoming 'the global shopping centre' (Drucker 1969: 71).

In 1970 Drucker moved to the Claremont Graduate School in California, where he was appointed Clarke Professor of Social Science and Management at the Graduate Management Centre (this was renamed after him in 1987, the first public management school to be named after a serving professor). His landmark book *Management: Tasks, Responsibilities, Practices* (1974), along with *The Practice of Management*, is considered a seminal work. It collects Drucker's ideas to date, with some additions. Whereas *The Practice of Management* was centred on management by objectives as part of a decentralized structure, *Management* identifies that while MBO is the practice, the structures of organizations are having to become more adaptable in a world that has changed (and is changing) since decentralization was the ideal. Various team structures are becoming appropriate. However, this is not the same as empowerment, which Drucker rejects as merely moving responsibility from the top of the organization to the bottom; which is still power. The total responsibility of every individual in MBO has been tempered. Drucker has accepted that Abraham MASLOW is correct and that he and Douglas McGregor are wrong. Maslow, while a supporter of Theory Y, that people want satisfaction from work, could not accept that all must and can take responsibility, or even that all will work: 'The world is not, Maslow concluded, peopled by adults. It has its full share of permanently immature' (Drucker 1974: 233).

It is the new knowledge industries that have changed the world. Managers who have never done the job themselves are supervising workers for the first time; layers of management are being stripped away as organizations become 'lean'. Structures are now compared to 'jazz combos', where each players knows what to do without being told, or to 'a symphony orchestra', where the conductor understands the score but expects players to perform their tasks. Regardless of the structure, the organization will have to produce results. This will still be the object of the structure, as it was and is with all other forms. Eventually, as knowledge work gathers momentum in all organizations, all will be both workers and managers, as all will have to manage their own contribution. Management has now become established as multi-organizational; it has extended its confines from business management to include organizations in the non-profit sector.

However, the warning that the latter will have to be managed differently from organizations that have profit as their goal is notably absent.

Drucker followed *Management* with *The Unseen Revolution* (1976), which he regarded as one of his best books. Its thesis was that American pensions and mutual funds were increasingly the major shareholders in big business, and that the workers were the investors in the funds. It followed that the funds, although not nationalized, were being socialized. Although the change is fundamental, it still does not make management power constitutional.

Since *The Unseen Revolution*, Drucker's books have continued in a regular pattern. He has continued to give advice, highlight problems and set new tasks for managers. In the 1980s he warned that management had moved from being non-controversial to being attacked. He also condemned the grey (black) economy as destructive. By the 1990s the future of the corporation was in doubt; the future seemed to lie with smaller entrepreneurial businesses. While organizations were collecting more and more information about their existing customers, Drucker warned that few knew much about their potential customers. He cited the mighty Wal-Mart, which while having 14 per cent of the American consumer market, needed to know about the 86 per cent who were not customers (Drucker 1995: 30). Despite Wal-Mart not knowing about their non-customers, however, they were obviously satisfying their customers. Not so Drucker's long-admired British firm, Marks and Spencer. He wrote about them first in *Managing for Results*, and continued to do so for the next three decades. The firm's recent failures suggest that they have forgotten advice from one of Drucker's many unique practical guides. Referring to an old retailer known as 'Uncle Henry', Drucker records his criticism of the new owners of what had been his 'retail chain'. 'I listened to a dozen buyers for the chain. They're very bright. But they're not buying bargains for the customers; they're buying bargains for the store. That's the wrong thing to do.' 'Uncle Henry' sold his shares. Within two years his forecast came true and the business began to decline (Drucker 1979: 201).

Drucker continues to desribe himself as a writer, teacher and consultant. He has published thirty-five books, which have sold millions of copies and which have been translated into over thirty languages. His works cover aspects of management, society, economics and politics, and also include 102 essays, some of which have been individually published, spread over three decades. Subjects of essays include Alfred P. Sloan, John Maynard Keynes, Joseph Schumpeter, Søren Kierkegaard, the need for lifestyle planning and extensive writings on Japan, including its art. He has written an autobiography and two novels, which also have management content. Many of his books have been continuously in print since their publication and have been prize-winners. Arrangements have been made with Harvard University Books to keep in print all of his books for seventeen years after his death. He has written for *Harvard Business Review* since 1950, the longest ever contributor. He has written for the *Wall Street Journal*, *Forbes*, *The Economist*, *Atlantic Monthly* and many other quality publications. Assessments of his written output confirm that his books contain three and a half million words and his other writing a similar amount.

While living in London Drucker became interested in Japanese painting of the fourteenth to nineteenth centuries, and has since become an expert, advising collectors and museums, including some in Japan. He is co-author of an exhibition catalogue, *Adventures of the Brush*, and from 1979 to 1985 was a professorial lecturer in Oriental history. The development of a network theory in higher mathematics is a further addition to his achievements.

Drucker's consultancy work has specialized in strategy and policy for businesses and non-profit organizations. His clients include many of the world's largest corporations as well as small and entrepreneurial companies; non-profit clients include universities, hospitals and community services together with international agencies and governments. He has numerous honorary doctorates and other awards reflecting his national and international standing. To mark his ninetieth birthday, his native Austria awarded him the Cross of Honour for Science and Art.

Drucker sees himself as an intellectual rather than an academic. His method is that of 1890s 'Gestalt psychology (German word for structure or configuration) in which we don't see lines and points but we see configurations as a whole' (Drucker 1970: 61). From this flows his holistic approach, which gives his work its unique character by joining together activities, disciplines and events that previously had not identified relationships with each other. As regards his view of the future, he told the guests at his ninetieth birthday party in Los Angeles in 1999 that big corporations did not seem to be able to survive for more than thirty years. The corporation, the unique invention of the twentieth century, is not going to be able to survive into the twenty-first century. Much of this is to do with management having lost its challenge, because we know much more about management, we know the routine. People will still work for a living, but the opportunities for the twenty-first century are going to be in the non-profit area, the social sector, as they were in business during the twentieth century. In anticipation of this change, Drucker has been spending more of his time in the non-profit sector. He is involved with charity work, and is the chairman of the Peter F. Drucker Foundation for Non Profit Management, the mission of which is to help the social sectors achieve excellence in performance and build responsible citizenship. There is also a Peter F Drucker Canadian Foundation.

A few days before Joseph Schumpeter died in 1950, he told Drucker's father: 'you know, Adolphe, I have now reached the age where I know its not enough to be remembered for books or theories. One does not make a difference unless it is a difference to people's lives'. Drucker says he has never forgotten that conversation; it gave him the measure of his achievement (Beatty 1998: 187–8). Drucker also wrote of a further Schumpeterian influence: for Schumpeter, what was important was not the answer but the right question.

Drucker is today the most quoted writer on management. He has been the subject of four full biographies and one guide. In compilations on management writers, it is almost impossible to find one that excludes him. Regularly in these compilations, his work is used to explain the ideas of others. He has more books in print than any other management writer. It is fair to mention, however, that he also has his critics. Some academics have criticized his writings for lacking academic rigour, as his collections of essays contain much journalistic work. Yet, none of Drucker's critics have sold a fraction of the numbers of books that he has, nor have any had his extensive influence. When Drucker writes that 'the purpose of a business is to create a customer', his book sales confirm that he is capable of practising his own philosophy. He writes for the market of businessmen and responsibly intelligent people. When asked who had directly influenced them, Bill GATES of Microsoft and Jack WELCH of General Electric, America's top businessmen, said: 'Drucker'. Among many other achievements in Drucker's career is the total adulation of one Korean businessman, who changed his name to Peter Drucker.

BIBLIOGRAPHY

Beatty, J. (1998) *The World According to Drucker*, London: Orion Business Books.

Day, G.S. (1999) *Market Driven Strategy*, New York and London: Free Press.

Drucker, P.F. (1939) *The End of Economic Man*, London: William Heinemann.

Drucker, P.F. (1942) *The Future of Industrial Man*, New York: The John Day Co.

—— (1946) *Concept of the Corporation*, New York: The John Day Co.

—— (1949) *The New Society*, London: William Heinemann.

—— (1954) *The Practice of Management*, London: Heron Books.

—— (1957) *America's Next Twenty Years*, New York: Harper and Brothers.

—— (1964) *Managing for Results*, London: William Heinemann.

—— (1966) *The Effective Executive*, New York: Harper and Row.

—— (1969) *The Age of Discontinuity*, London: William Heinemann.

—— (1970) *Technology Management and Society*, London: William Heinemann.

—— (1974) *Management: Tasks, Responsibilities, Practices*, London: William Heinemann.

—— (1976) *The Unseen Revolution*, London: William Heinemann.

—— (1979) *Adventures of a Bystander*, New York: Harper and Row.

—— (1985) *Innovation and Entrepreneurship*, London: William Heinemann.

—— (1995) *Managing in a Time of Great Change*, Oxford: Butterworth-Heinemann.

—— (1999) *Management Challenges for the 21st Century*, Oxford: Butterworth-Heinemann.

Freyberg, B. (1970) 'The Genesis of Peter Drucker's Thought', in T.H. Bonaparte and J.E. Flaherty (eds), *Peter Drucker: Contributions to Business Enterprise*, New York: New York University Press, 17–22.

'Germanicus' (1937) *Germany: The Last Four Years*, London: Eyre and Spottiswoode.

Kantrow, A. (1980) 'Why Read Peter Drucker?', *Harvard Business Review*, January–February.

Kennedy, C. (1991) *Guide to the Management Gurus*, London: Century Business Books.

Levitt, T. (1970) 'The Living Legacy of Peter Drucker', in T.H. Bonaparte and J.E. Flaherty (eds), *Peter Drucker: Contributions to Business Enterprise*, New York: New York University Press, 5–16.

Wren, D.A. (1994) *The Evolution of Management Thought*, New York: John Wiley and Sons.

HPS

DU PONT, Pierre Samuel (1870–1954)

Pierre Samuel du Pont was born in Wilmington, Delaware on 15 January 1870, to Lammot and Mary du Pont, and died there on 5 April 1954. His father was president of the old established firm of Du Pont, which is almost as old as the United States itself (Perrett 1989). In 1802 Robert Fulton, inventor of the steamboat, had persuaded Eleuthère Irénée du Pont de Nemours, a French chemist and gunpowder-maker, to come to America. Du Pont, who had been taught by the great French chemist Antoine Lavoisier, set up the first Du Pont factory in Wilmington, Delaware. Du Pont's gunpowder was both cheap and reliable, and it helped the US Army, his chief customer, to fight Britain to a draw in the war of 1812.

Du Pont became the quintessential American family enterprise. In 1837 Eleuthère du Pont passed the firm to his son Alfred, and in 1850 to Alfred's younger brother Henry. Henry and his nephew Lammot presided over the firm during the Civil War, earning over $1 million in profits. In 1872 Lammot was elected president of the Du Pont firm. He died in 1884, as did Henry du Pont in 1889, allowing a younger generation of the family to rise to power.

Pierre du Pont, along with his ten brothers and sisters, grew up in Philadelphia away from the family firm in Delaware. His father's death, however, made him the head of the family. In spite of this he was able to attend the Massachusetts Institute of Technology (MIT), whence he graduated with a degree in chemistry in 1890. Returning to the family firm in Delaware, he soon discovered that the Du Pont enterprise was hopelessly outdated in both its management and its technical expertise. At this time he was experimenting with smokeless gunpowder, but found little encouragement from the more conservative members of his family who still ran Du Pont.

Between 1899 and 1902 du Pont obtained valuable experience managing the Johnson Company in Lorain, Ohio, where he worked with his cousin, T. Coleman du Pont. He would also become acquainted with another manager, John J. Raskob. The Johnson Company was eventually liquidated, with its assets sold to J.P. MORGAN's Federal Steel Company. Pierre, Coleman, and Raskob then used the proceeds to invest in the streetcar system of Dallas, Texas. From managing these operations, du Pont emerged with both considerable management expertise and the nucleus of a management team.

In 1902 a quiet generational coup took place at Du Pont. In February, following the death of senior partner Eugene du Pont, the other partners planned to sell Du Pont to a competitor, Laflin and Rand. One of the youngest of the partners, Alfred du Pont, together with Pierre and Coleman, saved the firm, buying it outright for $12 million. Coleman was installed as president, Alfred as general manager and Pierre as treasurer. Pierre du Pont was now able to set about his plan for modernizing Du Pont. The E.I. du Pont de Nemours Powder Company was incorporated in May 1903. With Pierre negotiating the contracts, the new company expanded rapidly, buying Laflin and Rand and other competitors so that by 1904 it controlled 70 per cent of the gunpowder industry.

In the early 1900s Pierre and Coleman du Pont created the management structure of the twentieth-century corporation, described by Chandler and Salsbury (1971). Du Pont production was decentralized and organized into divisions for black powder, smokeless powder and dynamite. A central sales department and a purchasing organization were set up. The latter had its own nitrate mines and railway in Chile, as well as laboratories for research and development. Department managers, the most important of which served on the executive committee of the board of directors, were directly accountable to Coleman du Pont.

One of Pierre du Pont's most important contributions lay in the revolution in managerial accounting created by himself and Raskob. Du Pont was now a huge, vertically integrated multinational company, which needed to keep track of the profit and loss of all its divisions and subsidiaries. Pierre needed to know which was making money – and which was not – at any given time. He explored new methods of asset accounting and financial forecasting to determine what the rate of return on every investment would be. His accountants, using the new techniques of control accounting, were able to estimate income and expenditures for future years, making possible long-term planning.

In 1909 Pierre du Pont became acting president of the corporation. Like Standard Oil, Du Pont became a prime target of the anti-trust policies of both the Theodore Roosevelt and William Howard Taft administrations. In response, Pierre du Pont set up the Atlas and the Hercules companies to circumvent the anti-trust legislation.

No other American company stood to be more directly affected by the coming of the First World War than Du Pont. While the United States was not formally involved until 1917, from 1914 Du Pont struggled to fill huge contracts for both Britain and France. Du Pont knew he had to expand. In 1913 the

corporation made 8,400,000 tons of smokeless powder; by 1916 it was producing 200 million tons, rising to 455 million tons by the time the United States entered the war in 1917. Du Pont's accounting enabled him to project the potential losses if the war ended suddenly, so in the early stages he charged his customers high prices so as to pay for the building of new factories to expand production.

During the war du Pont married his first cousin, Alice Belin, in 1915. He also antagonized Alfred and much of his family during a dispute over some stock sold by Coleman du Pont, who was now personally investing in insurance and hotels. After the war Pierre du Pont resigned as chairman of the board. By the end of 1920, however, he was serving as president of the General Motors Corporation. The fortunes of General Motors (GM) and Du Pont had been linked since 1915.When William C. DURANT temporarily lost control of GM to a consortium of bankers, du Pont served as the temporary chairman of GM's board. Durant recaptured his company and asked du Pont to remain. Due to the war and unwise postwar expansion, Durant became heavily indebted to Pierre du Pont and the Du Pont company. When GM's stock collapsed in the autumn of 1920, a consortium of Du Pont and Morgan partners saved the auto-maker, but at the cost of Durant's resignation. Du Pont now owned 36 per cent of GM, and Pierre du Pont now ran it.

Pierre du Pont's brief reign at GM, described by SLOAN in his memoirs (1990), laid the groundwork for the auto-maker's future triumph over Henry FORD. More importantly, the Du Pont methods of control accounting and decentralization spread from GM to many large American corporations in the 1930s and 1940s, a process described by Alfred CHANDLER in his *Strategy and Structure* (1962). Du Pont did not reorganize GM alone, but worked with parts and accessories manager Alfred P. Sloan, Jr. He brought in experienced Du Pont managers who placed GM on the same systematic accounting basis they had implemented in Delaware. The operations of

Chevrolet, Cadillac and other divisions were decentralized, while a central office maintained overall direction and control just as it did in Delaware. In 1923 du Pont turned the company over to Sloan, remaining as chairman of the board until 1929.

Du Pont was active in civic society as well as the business world. Most notable was his interest in furthering public education. In 1918 he had helped form and fund the Service Citizens of Delaware. The following year he co-authored a report documenting the serious deficiencies in Delaware education. Becoming president of the Delaware school board, he worked to promote teacher training, school sanitation and improved attendance. By 1925 Delaware school attendance had doubled. Du Pont then served as school tax commissioner, securing funding for more schools and even contributing his own money to the cause. He helped fund the entire African-American educational system in Delaware. He also served as Delaware Tax Commissioner from 1929 to 1937 and from 1944 to 1949.

Du Pont's main political cause, besides education, was the repeal of the Eighteenth Amendment mandating prohibition of alcoholic beverages. Pierre saw prohibition as an unenforceable interference against personal rights, a major incentive to organized crime, and costly in terms of lost revenues and higher taxes. Traditionally a Republican, he supported the Democrats in 1928 when Raskob became Governor Alfred E. Smith's campaign manager. When the Great Depression came, Pierre served on a local unemployment relief commission, and supported Franklin Roosevelt for President in 1932. At first he took part in the New Deal, serving as an adviser to both the federal Commerce Department and the Industrial Advisory Committee of the National Recovery Administration (NRA), as well as the National Labor Board. By 1934, however, Pierre had broken with the New Deal and had returned his support to the Republican Party. He contributed financially to the conservative Liberty League, which opposed Roosevelt and his policies as 'socialist' and anti-business.

In the last twenty years of his life du Pont largely withdrew from business and public life. His legacy was the creation of the giant firms of Du Pont and GM, which served as the model for much of American management from the 1940s through to the 1960s. He was nothing less than the architect of the twentieth-century corporation:

> During that generation, the coming of the modern corporation was one of the most important developments in the American economy. And of that generation few men were more involved than Pierre du Pont in the shaping of this powerful economic institution.
>
> (Chandler and Salsbury 1971: 592)

BIBLIOGRAPHY

Chandler, A.D., Jr (1962) *Strategy and Structure: Chapters in the History of American Industrial Enterprise*, Cambridge, MA: MIT Press.

—— (1999) 'du Pont, Pierre Samuel', in J.A. Garraty and M.C. Carnes (eds), *American National Biography*, Oxford: Oxford University Press, vol. 7, 127–9.

Chandler, A.D. Jr and Salsbury, S. (1971) *Pierre S. du Pont and the Making of the Modern Corporation*, New York: Harper and Row.

Perrett, G. (1989) *A Country Made by War: From the Revolution to Vietnam – The Story of America's Rise to Power*, New York, Random House.

Sloan, A.P., Jr (1990) *My Years with General Motors*, ed. J.D. McDonald and C. Stevens, New York: Currency Doubleday.

Zilg, G.C. (1971) *Du Pont: Behind the Nylon Curtain*, Englewood Cliffs, NJ: Prentice-Hall.

DCL

DURANT, William Crapo (1861–1947)

William Crapo Durant was born on 8 December 1861 in Boston to William Clark Durant, a businessman, and his wife Rebecca Crapo Durant. He died in New York City on 18 March 1947. His father soon deserted the family, but the Durants were spared the ordeal of poverty by an inheritance from Rebecca's father, a successful investor and former governor of Michigan. In 1872 Durant moved with his family to Flint, Michigan. His numerous relatives were fairly well off. After attending high school and working in a family sawmill, he decided to become an entrepreneur on his own. He was a born salesman, and started with medicine, cigars and insurance. In 1885 he married Clara Pitt and eventually fathered two children. He and Clara divorced in 1908, and Durant then married Catherine Lederer; there were no children from this marriage.

Together with a friend, Durant bought a small cartage company in 1886, which they rechristened the Flint Road Cart Company. In the following fifteen years he turned this small firm into the Durant-Dort Carriage Company, the biggest carriage-maker in the United States. According to historian Richard Crabb, 'The Durant-Dort Carriage Company, with its coast-to-coast business and its component and assembly plants across the country, was the General Motors of the buggy industry' (Crabb 1969: 235). The company made wagons, carriages, buggies and carts. Durant-Dort had its local showrooms and service centres, and it purchased subsidiaries to make its wheels, axles and other parts. Durant became a millionaire and in the process laid the pattern that all future car manufacturers would follow.

In 1904 Durant made the leap from carriages to cars. Flint was also the home of the Buick Motor Company, one of a number of fledgling companies making 'horseless carriages' run by internal combustion engines, and these companies were already beginning to feel the pressure of a saturated market. The car in 1904 was still a luxury item which few could afford. There were few paved roads to drive it on. Durant, however, quickly saw the potential of the motor car, and acquired Buick. He began to run it like his carriage firm. He acquired supply companies, internalized his operations and set up his sales and service divisions. By 1907 Buick had the biggest car factory in the world and was marketing several models. Competition in this new world was already ruinous and Durant, like John D. ROCKEFELLER in petroleum, Andrew CARNEGIE in steel and John Pierpoint MORGAN in regards to railways, wanted to 'rationalize' the young auto market. He offered to merge with Ford, Oldsmobile and others, but they refused.

Henry FORD was by now mass producing the immensely popular Model T. Durant set out to become his chief rival, and on 28 September 1908 incorporated the General Motors Company in New Jersey. General Motors (GM) was in the beginning a holding company designed to allow Buick to circumvent anti-trust laws. This was but the first step in an expansion by which Durant acquired Oldsmobile, Cadillac and a score of other companies. According to Crabb, for Durant, 'building General Motors was simply an extension of his earlier career in horse-drawn vehicles' (Crabb 1969: 235). The acquisition of the highly profitable Cadillac Motor Car Company in 1909 for $4,500,000 'served notice on everyone that General Motors was a new force with which to reckon in the motorcar business of the United States' (Crabb 1969: 239).

Durant's philosophy of car-making was very different from that of Ford. While 'Ford was completely dedicated to the concept of building a single car capable of meeting a wide range of needs so that high volume could reduce production costs and, ultimately, the price of the car', Durant 'believed that the future would belong to the organization that produced a line of motorcars ranging from light, inexpensive vehicles to large, expensive automobiles' (Crabb 1969: 235).

Durant was a bold visionary, but hardly a systematic administrator, according to Lee Dunlap, his Oakland-Pontiac manager:

When Mr. Durant visited one of his plants it was like a visitation of a cyclone. He would lead his staff in, take off his coat, begin issuing orders, dictating letters and calling the ends of the continent on the telephone: talking in his easy way to New York, Chicago, San Francisco ... Only a phenomenal memory could keep his deals straight; he worked so fast that the records were always behind.

(Crabb 1969: 244)

GM made a profit of $9 million in 1908 and over $10 million in 1909. Few investors in 1910, however, believed that the car would actually replace the buggy. Durant meanwhile acquired the unprofitable Heany Lamp Company in 1910, paying for it with huge amounts of GM stock. This expansion took up so much capital that GM went heavily into debt in 1910 and had to be rescued by a consortium of bankers. Durant lost control of GM for the next five years, remaining a stockholder and director.

The low-priced Chevrolet was Durant's child not by birth but by adoption (Edsforth 1999). The real father was Louis Chevrolet, a Buick racing-car driver. Durant financed the car as well as two other smaller Flint companies that were buying up the dying carriage companies and converting them to making cars. In 1913 Durant had folded these firms into Chevrolet's Flint operation. Chevrolet continued buying up other small companies as the car market further began to shake out. Chevrolet was rechartered in Delaware, and Durant set up Chevrolet plants near New York, in St Louis, inFort Worth and in the San Francisco Bay area, and a Canadian subsidiary in Oshawa, Ontario. By 1915 only the Model T was selling more units than Chevrolet.

The growing success of the Chevrolet helped Durant regain control of GM. Under the bankers, GM had paid off its debts but had little to show in profits. Durant bought up GM stock in exchange for Chevrolet stock, permitting him to become president of the company once more in June 1916. He then reincorporated GM as a Delaware company including Chevrolet and the parts conglomerate United Motors; he went on to acquire Fisher Body and Frigidaire. In this new attempt to expand, Durant was dependent upon the capital of Pierre DU PONT. Durant and Du Pont, however, had a severe temperamental clash; du Pont was a systematic, procedure-driven manager who perfected the art of control accounting, while Durant was an entrepreneur who often went with his feelings, juggled his options and took risks, often in secret. Durant's dependency upon the du Ponts and weaknesses in his management once gain cost him ownership of GM, this time for good. Only Buick and Chevrolet were really making money; the rest of the group was far less profitable. The company was too disorganized and overcommitted in the stock market. In the downturn of 1920, the price of GM shares plummeted and du Pont took over the company.

For the remainder of his life, Durant went from one failed venture to another. He first tried to start his own car company, which struggled on through the 1920s and then was wiped out during the Great Depression. Other ventures met with even less success. Durant died in 1947. He lived long enough, nonetheless, to see GM transformed by his successor Alfred P. SLOAN into the most successful company in the world. Much of the solid GM edifice would be built by managers upon the foundation laid by Durant the entrepreneur.

BIBLIOGRAPHY

Crabb, R. (1969) *Birth of a Giant: The Men and Incidents that Gave America the Motorcar*, Philadelphia, PA: Chilton Book Company.

Edsforth, R. (1999) 'Durant, William Crapo', in J.A. Garraty and M. Carnes (eds), *American National Biography*, New York: Oxford University Press, vol. 27, 148–51.

Langworth, R.M. and Norbye, J.P. (1986) *The Complete History of General Motors, 1908–1986*, New York: Beekman House.

'William Crapo Durant' (1999) *The McGraw-Hill Encyclopedia of World Biography*, Detroit, MI: Gale Research, Inc., vol. 5, 158.

DCL

E

EASTMAN, George (1854–1932)

George Eastman was born in Waterville, New York on 12 July 1854 and died by his own hand at Rochester, New York on 14 March 1932. Eastman's father, a teacher of penmanship, founded Rochester's first commercial college. Eastman started work at the age of thirteen, working in an insurance office for three dollars a week. He later moved to the Rochester Savings Bank, where he advanced rapidly, earning $1,400 a year by the age of twenty-two. At this time he began experimenting with photography, first as a hobby and later with the idea of commercially manufacturing photographic plates. He was attracted to the possibility of developing a 'dry-plate' emulsion as an alternative to the cumbersome and difficult coating and developing of wet plates. He hoped his dry-plate emulsion would drastically reduce the size and weight of photographic equipment. By 1879 he was ready to patent his dry-plate process, and in 1880 he entered into a partnership with Henry A. Strong, quit his bank job, and devoted himself full-time to his small photographic business.

In 1884 he began searching for a transparent and flexible film and achieved his first breakthrough, preparing a paper-backed film. By 1888 he had expanded from dry plates and film to cameras, marketing the first Kodak. The Kodak (the name was invented by Eastman and chosen for its unique nature) was priced at twenty-five dollars and held film containing 100 exposures. The camera had to be mailed back to the factory, where the exposures were developed and the camera reloaded and returned to the customer. Despite this cumbersome process, it was a huge success. By 1889, largely due to the work of his chemist Henry M. Reichenbach, Eastman had patented a transparent film. This film proved crucial in the advancement of motion pictures.

By the end of the 1880s Eastman had emerged as a major figure in the plate, film, camera and motion picture industries. By the end of the 1890s, he dominated each of these fields. The company increased rapidly in size and capitalization, and continued to offer important innovations and improvements in its products. In short order Eastman introduced daylight loading film, a pocket Kodak, a five-dollar camera and stronger motion picture film. To manage the necessary production and expansion Eastman adhered to four key principles, all relatively new to American business: mass production, low unit cost, extensive advertising, and international distribution. In 1891 Eastman opened his Kodak Park plant. Sitting on 230 acres, with over 7,000 employees, Kodak was, in the words of historian Sanford Jacoby, a 'behemoth of capital-intensive mass production' (Jacoby 1997: 59). At Kodak Park, Eastman perfected the techniques of mass production long before Henry FORD brought them to the automobile industry. The resulting low costs were a necessary step in reaching Eastman's goal of bringing photography within the reach of most Americans.

With production increasing, Eastman's early and innovative use of advertising played an important role in helping to stimulate the necessary demand. The name Kodak joined the small list of brand names which came to be identified as their product, and Kodak's early slogan, 'You press the button. We do the rest,' was so successful Gilbert and Sullivan wrote it into the lyrics for their 1893 operetta *Utopia, Limited*. Kodak's targeted advertising especially sought to reach women, moving the camera from a predominantly male hobby to a family necessity. Finally, Kodak's early expansion overseas allowed it to rapidly consolidate control of the international market for film.

In addition, Eastman recognized the importance of scientific research and was a pioneer in the creation of corporate research and development facilities. He actively recruited scientists of international reputation and devoted a substantial sum to building research laboratories in Rochester. Utilizing its strong vertical, horizontal and spatial integration, and adhering to its core principles of low-cost production, effective advertising, international sales, and continual technical improvement and innovation enabled Eastman Kodak to dominate the film and camera markets.

Control of between 75 and 80 per cent of the American film market combined with massive profits at a time of heightened anti-trust concern, however, brought the attention of the Justice Department. Anti-trust investigations were begun in 1911. A prospective amicable settlement was abandoned by the government after the election of Woodrow Wilson in 1912, and in 1915 the Eastman Kodak Company of New Jersey (organized in 1901 to take advantage of the state's notoriously lax tax laws) was found to be in violation of the Sherman Anti-trust Act. The case was ultimately dismissed on appeal after Eastman signed a consent decree agreeing to sell some subsidiaries and change certain business practices. Thereafter, Eastman continued to fear government involvement in his business. This fear led him to cooperate with the government whenever possible to forestall scrutiny. During the First World War Kodak produced photographic materials for the army and navy, trained the US signal corps in photography, and manufactured numerous synthetic chemicals in an attempt to make the USA more economically independent. After the war Eastman made a point of cancelling government bills and refusing what he decided were excessive profits on war work.

As suggested by his war work, Eastman shared with many progressive-era industrialists the belief that corporations had a responsibility to serve the public good. Eastman was a pioneer in employee welfare programmes whose complicated origins can partially be explained by his paternalist belief that corporations could and should take over many of the functions that families and local communities seemed unable to discharge. But Eastman was aware of the resentment such paternalism could cause (he changed the name of the governing department from the Welfare Fund to the Kodak Employees' Association) and designed his programmes to provide more tangible benefits. As Eastman said, 'You can talk about cooperation and good feeling and friendliness from morn to midnight, but the thing the worker appreciates is the same thing the man at the helm appreciates – dollars and cents' (Jacoby 1997: 64).

To that end, Kodak's employee benefits were heavily economic. Kodak offered a share in the profits for executives, accident and sickness insurance for all employees, a building and loan association, a pension system and a stock purchase programme, along with the more common and less substantial corporate culture building events such as company picnics, dances, sports leagues and amateur theatricals. On three occasions Eastman distributed substantial amounts of his personal wealth to employees, either directly or by endowing various welfare programmes. Perhaps most unusual among the list of Kodak benefits was the wage dividend, instituted in

1912. As originally constituted, it paid employees a 2 per cent bonus on their wages for the previous five years. Kodak's pension, established in 1929, was also an important innovation. In an era when the few existing company pensions were discretionary and unfunded, the Kodak pension fund was the first in the nation, among major employers, to be contractual, non-discretionary and fully insured.

These programmes also originated in less idealistic and more practical concerns. Prominent among these was the desire to prevent the spread of unionization, something the deeply conservative and staunchly Republican Eastman adamantly opposed. Eastman was also continually concerned with the public reputation of his company, fearing more anti-monopoly proceedings and greater government regulation. All of Eastman's large stock gifts were bestowed during periods when Eastman perceived unionization as a threat, and his announcement of the wage dividend came the same year as the government's anti-trust case. A related motivation for corporate welfare work was Eastman's recognition that employee loyalty was a crucial component of his company's success and must be assiduously cultivated. Eastman recognized that his plants were unusually dependent on the disposition of their labour forces; sabotage was easy in a work environment where direct supervision was almost impossible, and the extreme spatial concentration of Kodak plants meant a strike could prove disastrous. Whatever the precise nature of their origins, Eastman Kodak provided one of the most expansive of benefit and welfare programmes during the heyday of welfare capitalism, and unlike many of the programmes founded concurrently, most of Kodak's programmes survived the Depression intact. Kodak's particular brand of welfare capitalism, with its emphasis on financial benefits and retaining its workers, was distinctive in its ability to last into the 1960s, long after most of industrial America had moved to collective bargaining as the basis for labour relations.

By the 1920s, with his company's dominant position consolidated and his edifice of welfare programmes constructed, Eastman decreased his involvement in Eastman Kodak and began to expand his philanthropic activities. His charitable giving had begun with a gift of $200,000 to the Rochester Mechanics Institute in 1899 and a later smaller gift to the University of Rochester. As he expanded the scale of his gifts, the majority were to institutions in his local community and to universities and colleges. Here again his motivation was both civic and practical. As he said, 'From the Kodak point of view I consider it a very highly desirable thing to have a good college here, not only to help train good men but also to make Rochester an attractive place for Kodak men to live and bring up their families' (Jacoby 1997: 60).

Eastman had a lifelong dislike of publicity and attention, and his early gifts to a favourite institution, the Massachusetts Institute of Technology (MIT), were presented on the behalf of 'Mr. Smith'. It was not until 1920, when Eastman, seeking to break up his large holdings of Kodak stock, gave MIT a large stock gift, that his identity was revealed. By then he had donated $20 million to the university. All told, he also donated more than $35 million to the University of Rochester, $2.5 million to create and fund a Rochester dental dispensary, $5 million to international dental clinics, and more than $2 million each to the Hampton (Virginia) and Tuskegee (Alabama) Negro Institutes.

Eastman had no wife or children. Living alone in the mammoth house he built in Rochester, he cultivated his interests in big game hunting, flowers and music. By nature an ascetic, taciturn and reticent man, he had never become much involved in the civic life of Rochester, despite his many donations. Most of his social life was with the people with whom he worked. By the early 1930s he was no longer directly involved either at the plant or at the office and rarely visited either. His health was deteriorating. On 14 March 1932, immediately after the signing of his last will, Eastman shot himself in the heart, leaving the note 'To my friends; my work is done. Why wait?' His work had included pioneering photographic innovations, the creation of a modern industrial giant built on principles of industrial organization and management that would be widely emulated, the innovative use of industrial research laboratories staffed by scientists of international repute, a humane and generous system of employee relations, and a key financial role in the development of educational institutions such as the University of Rochester. Eastman was a model of what the progressive businessmen could accomplish during an era when businessmen enjoyed both enormous prestige and power.

BIBLIOGRAPHY

Ackerman, C.W. (1930) *George Eastman*, Boston and New York: Houghton Mifflin.

Brayer, E. (1996) *George Eastman: A Biography*, Baltimore and London: The Johns Hopkins University Press.

Butterfield, R. (1954) 'The Prodigious Life of George Eastman', *Life*, 26 April.

Jacoby, S.M. (1997) *Modern Manors: Welfare Capitalism Since the New Deal*, Princeton, NJ: Princeton University Press.

RV

EDISON, Thomas Alva (1847–1931)

Thomas Alva Edison was born in Milan, Ohio on 11 February 1847, the son of Samuel and Nancy Edison. He died at home in Orange, New Jersey on 18 October 1931, a few days after collapsing at a celebration dinner marking the fiftieth anniversary of his invention of the light bulb. His father, a storekeeper, was one of the followers of the Canadian rebel William Lyon Mackenzie, and fled to the United States after the abortive revolt of 1837. Edison himself was educated largely at home, in a household that Israel (1998) describes as radical and free-thinking; Thomas Paine was one of Samuel Edison's favourite authors. His upbringing explains much of Edison's attitude to life and to science: challenging, innovative and unwilling to accept limits.

An entrepreneurial spirit was also revealed at an early age. By the age of twelve, Edison was selling newspapers and food to passengers on the local railway, and while in his middle teens he edited and published a local newspaper. He was fascinated by news of the invention of the telegraph, and received free tuition as a telegraph operator after he saved the life of the operator's son. From the age of sixteen he was working as a telegraph operator by day and experimenting with improvements to the apparatus by night. Despite a serious hearing problem, he worked his way to the top of his profession and was hired as a wire service operator by the Western Union. In 1867 he patented his first major invention, an improved duplex telegraph. In 1868 he moved to Boston, and then in 1869 to New York, where he became a full-time inventor. In 1870 he moved to New Jersey, finally settling at Menlo Park in 1876, the site of his most famous work.

The story of Edison's inventions is too complex to tell in a short space, and has been well described by Israel (1998) and Clark (1997). Edison took out 1,093 patents, more than any other person; the first was granted when he was twenty, the last was taken out a few days before his death. His attitude to invention was pragmatic, and he always sought a practical use, usually in business, for his inventions; if this failed to materialize, he quickly moved on to the next idea. The perfect research and development executive, Edison was a never-failing fund of ideas on which business could draw. The electric light bulb and the phonograph are his most famous work, but his experimentation in the field of electricity seemingly knew no bounds; he was even involved in early designs for an electric chair, and was involved in an actual execution in an attempt to prove the superiority of his direct current (DC) system over that of the rival alternating current (AC) developed by George WESTINGHOUSE.

Edison's influence on management is debatable. Many of his inventions, particularly in the communications field, such as improvements to the telegraph and the telephone (the latter invented by Alexander Graham BELL just ahead of Edison), were important in increasing the scale and scope of managerial work; faster communications meant improved coordination over distance. At a time when American companies were moving towards large-scale operations, this was very important. Personally, he is usually described as an inventor rather than a businessman; Herbert CASSON, who knew him well, dismissed his managerial abilities on the grounds that Edison seldom exploited his own inventions. Yet as Davis (1987) points out, Edison did exploit the electric light very successfully, raising funds from backers such as J.P. MORGAN to set up the Edison Electric Illuminating Company in New York.

Testimony to his greatest influence, though, comes from Henry FORD, who knew Edison well (the two used to go on camping trips together, along with Harvey FIRESTONE). Edison, says Ford, changed Americans' attitudes to science and how it could be used to solve basic problems, including in management; Edison's true achievement was in 'linking science with our everyday life and demonstrating that, through patient, unremitting testing and trying, any problem may eventually be solved' (Ford and Crowther 1930: 26). Edison, says Ford, showed how scientific methods could be used in industry in a wide variety of ways, not just in technology and machinery. Ford's final tribute is worth quoting:

he is the founder of modern industry in this country. He has formed for us a new kind of declaration of independence ... in the nature of a kit of tools, by the use of which each and every person among us has gained a larger measure of economic liberty than had ever previously been thought possible.
(Ford and Crowther 1930: 25)

BIBLIOGRAPHY

Clark, R.W. (1997) *Edison: The Man Who Made the Future*, London: Macdonald and Jane's.

Davis, W. (1987) *The Innovators: The Essential Guide to Business Thinkers*, London: Ebury Press.

Ford, H. and Crowther, S. (1930) *My Friend Mr Edison*, London: Ernest Benn.

Israel, P. (1998) *Edison: A Life of Invention*, New York: John Wiley and Sons.

Wachhorst, W. (1981) *Thomas Alva Edison: An American Myth*, Cambridge, MA: MIT Press.

MLW

EISNER, Michael Dammann (1942–)

Michael Eisner, current chairman and CEO of the Walt Disney Company, was born in Mount Kisco, New York on 7 March 1942, to J. Lester and Margaret Eisner. He was educated at prep school in Lawrenceville, New Jersey before going to Denison University in Granville, Ohio in 1961. He realized that a country's most lasting legacy is not political but artistic. Majoring in theatre, he began writing plays. Eisner soon displayed his lifelong talent for imagination and creativity, as well as his people and business skills. From 1963–7 he worked in entry level jobs at the National Broadcasting Corporation (NBC) and later at the Columbia Broadcasting Corporation (CBS).

In 1967 Eisner began a nine-year sojourn with the American Broadcasting Corporation

(ABC). ABC, fascinated with his 'simplicity, charm, enthusiasm, and lack of corporate polish', put him in charge of programme development (Flower 1991: 43). Soon, his popular shows such as *Happy Days*, a nostalgic romantic comedy set in an idealized 1950s, showed his intuition for what Americans wanted to watch. His flair at promoting the 'Fonz' and other loveable, eccentric characters helped the struggling ABC to overtake both NBC and CBS. In 1976 Eisner became President of Paramount film studios, where his popular films, including *Saturday Night Fever, Grease, Heaven Can Wait, Raiders of the Lost Ark, Airplane!*, the *Star Trek* series and *Flashdance*, helped Paramount's profits triple from $39 million in 1973 to $140 million in 1983.

In 1984 Eisner took over the troubled Walt Disney Productions. Once the giant of Hollywood family entertainment, the studio had produced only two successful films from 1969 to 1984. The studio was $900 million in debt, and desperately trying to fend off attacks by corporate raiders who wanted to dismantle it.

Eisner worked a managerial and marketing revolution. Walt Disney Productions became the Walt Disney Company. Working eighteen-hour days, he and his staff brought about one of the most remarkable turnarounds in business history. To do so, he had to transform Disney's culture without destroying it. Eisner had to deal with the question of, in his own words, 'whether or not we can evolve into a giant company without losing that family feeling' (Flower 1991: 197). That culture, however, was so entrenched that Eisner felt it could only be changed from the top down. Eisner brought in sixty new executives and let go 1,000 employees. He also set up a strategic planning department. While promoting classic Disney features such as *Pinocchio* on video, he began to rework Disney's image by making more adult films such as *Down and Out in Beverly Hills, Ruthless People* and *Good Morning, Vietnam* on the Touchstone label.

Eisner was not interested in short-term profits alone. The essence of Disney culture was safeguarding the reputation of a Disney brand name that was the key to far greater long-term profits. According to Disney executive Frank Wells, 'you really do have a larger responsibility when you carry that name around' (Flower 1991: 181).

Eisner reinvented Disney in a world being remade by globalization, high technology and demographics. The world of the 1980s craved American entertainment, and many could now afford to enjoy it on video recorders and cable television. People demanded more sophisticated films than those of the 1950s. Through aggressive marketing of the old and the new, Eisner transformed Disney from a faltering firm servicing a dwindling market to a formidable global competitor. Revenues grew from $98 million to almost $3 billion between 1984 and 1987 (Flower 1991). By 1990 Eisner had tripled Disney's assets and increased its stock value twelvefold. In the early twenty-first century, however, Disney ran into problems with sales and revenue declining, and Eisner came under increasing pressure from shareholders, including the Disney family.

BIBILOGRAPHY
Flower, J. (1991) *Prince of the Magic Kingdom: Michael Eisner and the Re-Making of Disney*, New York: John Wiley and Sons.

DCL

ELLISON, Lawrence Joseph (1944–)

Lawrence Joseph Ellison was born in New York on 17 August 1944. His mother was unmarried, and Ellison was adopted while still a baby by his aunt and uncle in Chicago. He has married three times, to Adda Quinn in 1967, Nancy Wheeler in 1977 and Barbara Boothe in 1983; all three marriages have ended in divorce. Ellison graduated from South Shore High School in Chicago in 1962 and entered the University of Illinois, but left after two years without taking a degree. He moved to California in 1966, apparently with the idea of studying medicine at the University of California, but he was already becoming fascinated with computers and had developed his skills as a programmer. From 1967 to 1971 he worked as a programmer and systems architect with Amdahl Corporation, a high-tech start-up near Santa Clara, California. He became particularly interested in relational databases, a new type of software program that began development around 1970.

In 1972, seeing only limited prospects, Ellison left Amdahl and joined Precision Instrument Company (later Omex) as vice-president in charge of systems development. In 1977 he and two partners, Bob Miner and Ed Oates founded the Oracle Company in Redwood, California, initially as a maker and supplier of relational databases. Ellison was chairman and chief executive officer of the new firm and, as rapidly became clear, the business brains behind it.

Ellison's strategy was simple: to grow the firm as quickly as possible. He believed that there would ultimately be a shake-out in the computer and software industries, as too many firms were chasing too small a market and many of these firms were not ultimately sound; when the crash came, only the strong would survive. To this end he pushed his product engineers and his sales staff relentlessly. His strategy has, to date, paid off: Oracle has climbed into the ranks of the world's most powerful high-tech firms along-side the likes of IBM, Microsoft, Sun Microsystems and Netscape.

Ellison achieved his goal by creating an atmosphere of relentless pressure within the firm (Wilson 1997). His sales force became notorious for their aggression. One member of the sales management team once suggested a simple strategy for dealing with competition: 'Cut off the oxygen' (Wilson 1997: 158). In a highly controversial move, which appears to have shocked even Ellison, the company sales director authorized sales staff to be paid, quite literally, in bags of gold.

Wilson, in his biography of Ellison, takes a highly critical view of his subject, but even this critique cannot obscure a picture of what is obviously a considerable managerial talent. Ellison's sense of strategic vision, of the necessity of growth in order to create bulwarks against future downturns, stands head and shoulders above the hit-and-miss approach of many of his competitors. Of all the high-tech entrepreneurs of the late twentieth century, only Andrew GROVE is his match in terms of management skill and perceptiveness. In the coming century, it is leaders such as Grove and Ellison who are likely to be the most reliable role models for managers in newly evolved business sectors.

BIBLIOGRAPHY
Wilson, M. (1997) *The Difference Between God and Larry Ellison*, New York: Morrow.

MLW

ELLISON, William (1790–1861)

William Ellison was born in 1790 (exact date unknown) on a plantation near Winnsboro, South Carolina. He died at his home near Stateburg, South Carolina on 5 December 1861. Originally christened April Ellison, he was born a slave, the son of a black slave woman and a white man; Johnson and Roark (1984) believe his father was the plantation's owner, himself called William Ellison. Most such children were sent to work as field slaves on the plantations, but Ellison received special treatment. At age eight he was apprenticed to a cotton gin maker in Winnsboro, learning the trade and also learning to read and write and some elementary accounting skills. In January 1811 he had a daughter by a slave woman named Matilda. He was emancipated in 1816; Johnson and Roark (1984) suggest that April Ellison purchased his freedom from his former master. He later purchased the freedom of Matilda and his daughter, and the couple married; they went on to have three sons. April Ellison changed his given name to William in 1820, on the grounds that 'April' was a slave's name, unsuitable for a man of business.

Following emancipation, Ellison set up his own business as a cotton gin maker in the town of Stateburg. This was a shrewd business move, as the cotton industry was growing rapidly and demand for gins was increasing. Ellison's industry and skill was such that he not only won an important share of the market in South Carolina but began exporting to other cotton-growing states. In order to expand, Ellison needed labour, and to acquire labour he did what any white businessman in the area would have done: he bought slaves. He purchased his first two slaves in 1820, and by 1840 he owned thirty adult slaves. Ellison's business boomed and he branched out into carpentry and blacksmithing, and by 1835 had begun to invest in land. He bought the former estate of the governor of South Carolina near Stateburg, and eventually acquired over 300 acres of cotton-growing land. By 1850 he was a very rich man, the value of his land and slaves putting him in the top 5 per cent of South Carolina's population in terms of wealth.

Ingham and Feldman (1994) note that because of his wealth and status, Ellison came to be held in high regard by the white elite in South Carolina. Close study of his career, however, suggests that the acquisition of wealth and status was itself a key element in Ellison's continued success. He had to tread a very fine line: too little ostentation would mark him down as nothing more than an ex-slave, while too much would arouse the envy of his white neighbours. Ellison chose an approach which ensured that the white planters could feel comfortable dealing with him, and allowed him to build close relationships with customers in the white community.

Ellison's career was remarkable in many ways. A highly able manager, he was entirely self-taught as a businessman and learned his way into management. His near-unique status as a wealthy black businessman in the white-dominated society of pre-Civil War South Carolina offers undoubted lessons for cross-cultural management. Modern historians have condemned Ellison for his part in enslaving his own people, but his management abilities continue to command respect. Those abilities not only made him wealthy, but they also allowed him to transcend his status and move across cultures.

BIBLIOGRAPHY

Ingham, J.N. and Feldman, L.B. (1994) *African-American Business Leaders: A Biographical Dictionary*, Westport, CT: Greenwood Press.
Johnson, M.P. and Roark, J.L. (1984) *Black Masters: A Free Family of Color in the Old South*, New York: W.W. Norton

MLW

EMERSON, Harrington (1853–1931)

Harrington Emerson was born at Trenton, New Jersey on 2 August 1853, the son of Edwin and Mary Louise Emerson. He died in New York on 23 May 1931. Emerson's father was a professor of political economy who taught at several European universities, and Emerson himself was educated at a variety of schools in Paris, Munich, Siena and Athens.

While in his late teens he saw at first hand the Franco-Prussian War of 1870–71, an event which made a deep impression on him. He was subsequently to say that a combination of French character and German military efficiency helped form his later ideas on management. Among other influences, he cited studies under a European music teacher, observing the results obtained by breeders of racehorses, and ideas passed on by a leading railway surveyor, A.B. Smith (Drury 1915: 113).

Emerson took a degree in engineering from the Royal Polytechnic in Munich. Returning to the United States, he took up a post as professor of modern languages at the State University of Nebraska, where he remained from 1876 to 1882. He married Florence Brooks in 1879, and the couple had three children; after her death he married again, to Mary Suplee in 1895, and they had three or four children (sources disagree on the number). Emerson left academia in 1883 and embarked on an entrepreneurial career, investing in finance and real estate but also returning to engineering. As a contractor for the US government he undertook a number of important surveys, notably of submarine cable routes to Alaska and Asia for the War Department, and later of West Coast coalfields. There are also references to his involvement in prospecting for gold in the Yukon, although this presumably was before the Klondike gold rush of 1898.

In the 1890s Emerson began a series of private consultancies with railway firms, particularly 'in the field of systematizing management in railway shops' (Drury 1915: 113). How he became involved in this field is not clear, but it seems that a combination of this practical experience with his engineering training and earlier exposure to European culture and science began to come together at this point. In 1895, Emerson told Drury, he began a series of surveys of American industrial plants, comparing their actual production costs with optimum costs. In 1900 he established his consulting firm, the Emerson Company, and began advising a variety of clients, primarily mining and railway firms; at this point he was still specializing in cost reduction, primarily through the elimination of wastes. However, Emerson's ideas were evolving all the time, and in 1902 he undertook his first full-scale reorganization of a factory. What Emerson was doing here was effectively process engineering; he worked his way through the processes of planning, scheduling and production, aiming to treat the firm as a harmonious whole, not a series of independent functions.

In 1904 Emerson took on the job that would make his reputation, the reorganization of the maintenance shops of the Santa Fe Railroad (as described in more detail in Emerson 1911; Drury 1915: 126–9). His task was to reorganize the motive power department, which handled the repair and maintenance of locomotives and which had been plagued with labour problems. The job took Emerson some three years, during which he employed thirty-one expert assistants to go through the department from top to bottom. The programme of improvements, known as 'betterment works', had two goals: (1) to restore labour peace, and (2) to improve workplace efficiency. Emerson saw these two goals as being linked; indeed, the first goal was contingent on the second. Reforms to the system of supervision and labour management could not proceed until the workers' own tasks and tools had been standardized. Emerson's team focused on the routing and scheduling of work, ensuring that jobs were carried out according to standard procedures: 'All the work in the machine shop was arranged so that it could be controlled from dispatch-boards located in a central office; likewise on a bulletin-board was indicated the progress of repair of each locomotive' (Drury 1915: 127). Once tasks and duties were standardized, everyone in the shop, workers, foremen and supervisors alike, knew what was expected of them and according to what schedule, and a major source of workplace friction was removed. The second half of Emerson's task was the introduction of a bonus system which rewarded those workers who performed efficiently and well. This system was not simply imposed on the workers; although Emerson insisted that the standardized times which formed the basis of work schedules were ones which any worker could achieve, nonetheless 'the schedule is a moral contract or agreement with the men as to a particular machine operation, rate of wages and time'. Gaining the informed consent of the workers to the new system was vital, and 'extreme emphasis was laid on the individual character of the relations of men and management' (Drury 1915: 127).

By 1906, says Drury (1915: 128), the Santa Fe had achieved cost savings on the order of $1.25 million. (During successive reorganizations part of Emerson's system was dismantled, but Drury concludes that the main part of the system remained intact even under new ownership and management.) The work attracted enormous interest, and Emerson became one of the most sought after consultants in the country. By 1915 he had introduced his efficiency methods into more than 200 firms, including many railways and mining firms but also a number of manufacturers. He continued to develop his system, producing his famous twelve principles of efficiency (Emerson 1913). In 1908 he approached Herbert CASSON, then enjoying considerable fame as a writer and speaker on business methods, and offered him a partnership. A year with the mercurial Casson seems to have been enough for both men; Casson departed to apply the techniques of efficiency to advertising and public relations, while Emerson continued to devote himself to production and labour issues. In 1921 he served as a member of Herbert Hoover's Commission on the Elimination of Waste in Industry, and published his final book, *The Science of Human Engineering*, a home-study course for managers that combined the features of efficiency with those of psychology. Little is heard of him after this, and he seems to have retired in the mid-1920s.

Following his success with the Santa Fe, Emerson published a series of articles in *The Engineering Magazine* in 1908–1909. Those articles were collected in one volume, *Efficiency as a Basis for Operations and Wages*, originally published by John Dunlap in 1909 and later republished by *The Engineering Magazine*. Publication of the articles together seems to have slightly dissatisfied Emerson, and he resolved to develop his system into a fuller scheme. The result was *The Twelve Principles of Efficiency*, which first appeared in 1911, appeared in revised form in 1913 and then went through several editions, remaining in print until after Emerson's death.

Emerson was one of the leading figures of the scientific management movement. A contemporary, H.B. Drury, noted that 'Emerson has done more than any other single man to popularize the subject of scientific management' (1915: 117). Herbert Casson, his friend, admirer and sometime business partner, also described him as the leading exponent of scientific management. Emerson himself, however, rarely used the term 'scientific management' in connection with his own work, preferring instead 'efficiency'.

Although his work has much in common with that of the gurus of scientific management such as Frederick W. TAYLOR, Henry GANTT and Frank and Lillian GILBRETH, there are also significant divergences. Notably, Emerson rejected the functional system of organization espoused by Taylor and Gantt, preferring instead the line and staff system. Credit for the adaptation of this system from military thinking and its subsequent dissemination in management thinking and practice belongs largely to Emerson, whose ideas were later taken up by writers as varied as Casson, Lyndall Urwick, Luther GULICK, Joseph JURAN and Philip Sargant Florence.

Emerson was largely responsible for introducing the word 'efficiency' into the language of business; today, it is a concept to which common reference is made. However, its meaning has evolved somewhat since

Emerson's day. In particular, Emerson saw efficiency as based on natural principles; nature, he believed, was ultimately efficient, and there were plenty of examples in the natural world to prove this. Achieving efficiency, then, was not so much about *imposing* an efficiency system as it was about structuring an organization so that efficiency would be achieved naturally – the best way to achieve efficiency is to eliminate inefficiency. This theme is returned to several times in the course of *Efficiency as a Basis for Operations and Wages*, which, as noted, was closely based on his work with the Santa Fe railway.

Inefficiencies, says Emerson, come in two forms: there are inefficiencies in processes and materials, and there are inefficiencies in people, societies and nations. Of the two, the first type of inefficiency is in many ways least harmful. If inefficient materials are used, they simply give way; if inefficient processes are in place, when the limits of their efficiency are reached they simply stop working. The second is much more serious in that 'to the inefficiency of an individual or a nation there is no predeterminable limitation' (Emerson 1909: 23). Human inefficiency is constant, especially when it is embedded in a society or culture. Yet, despite the importance of human inefficiency, Emerson notes that the attention of science is largely focused elsewhere: 'In the passion for modern scientific accuracy it has proved more interesting, and more has been done to solve the lesser problem of efficiency in process or material, almost wholly ignoring the larger problem of individual or national efficiency' (1909: 23).

Two conditions are necessary, says Emerson, for achieving human efficiency: (1) the right standards, and (2) the right organization. Of these, it is clear that the organization must come first. In *Efficiency as a Basis for Operations and Wages*, he devotes three full chapters to the line and staff method of organization. The line and staff model is in practice made up of a blend of two organizational sub-models, the line organization and the staff organization. The line organization is hierarchical

and functional; each member knows his or her place and carries out allotted tasks on a procedural basis. The staff organization is organic and interdependent, with members relying on each other to carry out their work. A crucial distinction between the two is the role of knowledge. In the line organization, 'one man knows much more than any other' (1909: 55) and that person guides the organization; so, if the leader loses direction, the organization is lost as well. All the other members of the organization depend on the leader, not on each other. In the staff organization, knowledge is held in common: 'The strength of the staff organization lies in its ability to multiply many-fold the effectiveness of other staff members, all co-operating to make possible such a wonderful thing as a man, a humming-bird, a midge, or a yellow-fever microbe' (1909: 56).

In fact, many organizations combine the line and staff principles, creating a mix of organism and construct. At a simple level, Emerson uses the example of a baseball team (1909: 58–9). The batting side uses the line principle: each player comes to the plate in turn in pre-arranged order and bats without any dependence on his team-mates. The fielding side use the staff principle: pitcher, catcher and fielders work together as a unit, all depending on each other to some degree. The two sides alternate these functions as the game progresses from innings to innings.

The greatest exponent of the line and staff principle in management, says Emerson, was not a businessman at all but a military commander, the Prussian Field-Marshal Helmuth von Moltke. As a young man, Emerson had witnessed at first hand Moltke's astonishing victory over the French army in the Franco-Prussian War. He says he saw the course of the war from both sides (intriguingly, he does not say how he managed this), and his conclusion was that the critical factor in the Prussian victory was the line and staff organization. The well-drilled line performed on the battlefield exactly as it ought, guided by the seemingly omnipresent and omniscient staff. The

French, relying almost exclusively on the line principle, could not respond effectively and were defeated. Moltke's great achievement, Emerson concludes (1913: 14–18), was to make rapid, decisive and relatively bloodless wars possible; long, bloody and inefficient conflicts such as the American Civil War were now a thing of the past.

There is irony here, in that Emerson was writing on the eve of one of the most bloody and inefficient conflicts of all time, the First World War – a conflict, moreover, in which most of the combatants had adopted the line and staff principle. With hindsight, the weakness in Emerson's proposition shows through. Moltke's victory was in large part due to his own brilliant leadership and planning, qualities conspicuously absent from most of the high commands in the First World War. The same defects must from time to time occur in business, and Emerson notes this when he describes the staff as being present to assist and support the leader. Ultimately, it would seem, no matter how good the staff work, if leadership is lacking, the enterprise will fail (1913: 401–403).

Emerson links the need for standards to the adoption of the staff principle. Line organization, he says dismissively, 'needs few standards, usually crude and often fictitious. Seniority or precedence is one of its standards, and closely interwoven is the fundamental standard of immediate and unquestioning obedience almost as automatic as the obedience of sheep to the leader' (1909: 96). Staff, on the other hand, has 'an unlimited multiplicity of scientific standards, higher than all personality ... The staff expert receives from his chief principles which are higher than the chief, since they are part of the eternal laws of the universe' (1909: 97). It is here that Emerson has most in common with the other proponents of scientific management: he believes that adherence to standards of measurement and process that are based on science will eliminate inefficiencies, and thus lead perforce to efficiency. He also believes in a process of continuous improvement, with standards constantly being revised in the light of new knowledge: 'Staff standards are based on specific human authority only until new facts substitute better authority' (1909: 98). Likewise, Emerson is clear that standards do not exist for their own sake:

Staff standards are not theoretical abstractions but scientific approximations, and are evolved for the use of the line, the sole justification of standards being that they will make line work more efficient. Staff standards, being for the benefit of the line and often entrusted to line officials, must be put in the form of permanent instructions so that all may understand what is being aimed at, and deviations by the line be noted and reprimanded

(Emerson 1909: 98)

Chapter 6 of *Efficiency as a Basis for Operations and Wages* offers the most detailed account of how standards are actually achieved in practice. The first stage consists of five detailed surveys of (1) methods of materials handling; (2) condition of machines and tools; (3) labour audits, noting discrepancies between what workers were supposed to be doing and what they were actually doing; (4) relationships between current costs and standard costs; and (5) the speed of movement of work through the shop (1909: 125). Each of these five lines of investigation is then developed as a field of measurement and control, in the charge of experts; the building up of this pool of experts in effect creates the staff. The experts devise and institute standardized systems for materials handling to eliminate wastage; maintenance to keep machines in good repair; wages to ensure workers are motivated and rewarded; costings to ensure that profit and loss can be measured accurately; and task and process times to ensure that work moves through the plant or shop at a natural rate, unencumbered by delays.

Working on and developing these concepts still further led Emerson to his famous twelve principles of efficiency (Emerson 1913). These are, in summary form:

1. Clearly defined ideals: the organization must know what its goals are, what it stands for, and its relationship with society.

2. Common sense: the organization must be practical in its methods and outlook.

3. Competent counsel: the organization should seek wise advice, turning to external experts if it lacks the necessary staff expertise.

4. Discipline: not so much top-down discipline as internal discipline and self-discipline, with workers conforming willingly and readily to the systems in place.

5. The fair deal: workers should be treated fairly at all times, to encourage their participation in the efficiency movement.

6. Reliable, immediate and adequate records: measurement over time is important in determining if efficiency has been achieved.

7. Despatching: workflow must be scheduled in such a way that processes move smoothly.

8. Standards and schedules: the establishment of these is, as discussed above, fundamental to the achievement of efficiency.

9. Standardized conditions: workplace conditions should be standardized according to natural scientific precepts, and should evolve as new knowledge becomes available.

10. Standardized operations: likewise, operations should follow scientific principles, particularly in terms of planning and work methods.

11. Written instructions: all standards should be recorded in the form of written instructions to workers and foremen, which detail not only the standards themselves but the methods of compliance.

12. Efficiency reward: if workers achieve efficiency, then they should be duly rewarded.

One of the truly modern aspects of Emerson's views is that he sees organizational efficiency as being achieved from the bottom up. The staff is there to serve the line, not the other way around; even if the staff have controlling positions, with powers of reprimand and discipline over the line, these functions are ultimately about moving the line to greater efficiency. The worker is there to assist his machine to run efficiently, not to exercise dominion over it; the foreman is there to help his workers achieve their targets, not to control them on behalf of the superintendent; and so on up the line to the chief executive who is ultimately the servant of the organization, not its master. Thus Emerson believes in basic principles such as full reward for efficient workers (he favours Taylor and Gantt's bonus system, and argues at one point in favour of a minimum wage).

Emerson also extends these principles beyond the organization, seeing businesses in the context of broader society and arguing that more efficient businesses will make for more efficient societies. He is highly critical of American society at the beginning of the twentieth century, which he sees as riddled with inefficiencies and ill-equipped to compete with either the established powers of Europe or the rising power of Japan. In part he blames this situation on the European heritage; an admirer of European culture, he feels nonetheless that this culture has been adapted too uncritically in the United States, without proper regard for the actual pragmatic needs of the new American society. By adopting efficiency methods such as the line and staff principle (itself, of course, a product of Europe), he believes the USA can eliminate waste and become efficient and competitive:

We have not put our trust in kings; let us not put it in natural resources, but grasp the truth that exhaustless wealth lies in the latent and as yet undeveloped capacities of individuals, of corporations, of states. Instead of oppression from the top, engendering antagonisms and strife, ambitious pressure should come from the bottom, guidance and assistance from the top.

(Emerson 1909: 242)

These two books mark out Emerson as an original thinker of some note. His relationship to the other figures of the scientific management movement is difficult to assess. He knew of Taylor's work, and Drury says he was among the audience when Taylor read his famous paper on shop management before the American Society of Mechanical Engineers in 1903. Drury says further that Emerson sometimes referred to Taylor as the source of his ideas (Drury 1915: 116). On the other hand, Emerson also believed that many of Taylor's ideas were overambitious and unlikely to succeed. The two men were never close; they met first in 1900 and seldom thereafter. Indeed, it is hard to imagine two men more unalike than Emerson, well-travelled and brought up in an academic milieu, erudite, cultured and cultivated, and Taylor, the exshop foreman, an engineer's engineer, pragmatic and somewhat puritanical. Whereas Taylor's ideas stemmed from intensive study and practice, Emerson's influences were more eclectic.

Emerson's influence on others is equally difficult to determine. He is credited as the great popularizer of scientific management, but there is little hard evidence to show how far Emerson was personally responsible for the take-up of scientific management by firms; in terms of method, it is the techniques pioneered by Taylor, Gantt and the Gilbreths that are more frequently observable. Emerson's influence was more general. He did not so much provide a toolkit – although he did try to provide concrete examples of how standardization could be achieved – as create the awareness that change was necessary and stimulate

managers and industrialists to look at new ways of thinking and practice. For such a highly successful communicator, he seems to have been unable – or perhaps unwilling – to explain in detail his equally successful consultancy techniques.

In part, this lack may be due to the fact that Emerson did not use or recommend standardized systems, only standard tools; he tended rather to argue for organizational flexibility. In the words of Drury, 'Emerson's methods are flexible, rather than stereotyped; his time studies and standards are approximate rather than exhaustively exact; and he relies much on the self-direction of his subordinates' (Drury 1915: 116). This is apparent in his espousal of the line and staff principle, his one undeniably influential concept; it is much more important to get the organization right than it is to set exact measurements. Efficiency, in the final analysis, is about eliminating waste, not creating systems.

Though he is called a prophet of scientific management, Emerson's work is closer to a philosophy than a science. In the final analysis, for all his devotion to New-World-style organization and principle, Emerson was at least as much a product of Europe as of America, and science and art would always be co-equal; management was not only about results, but about higher things as well. He rejects the idea that business is about 'supernal men working through principles to realize supernal ideals' (Emerson 1913: 423), but he believes that what is good for business is also good for society. As he concludes in *The Twelve Principles of Efficiency*: 'It is impossible that righteousness married to wisdom should rule without immensely benefitting humanity' (Emerson 1913: 423).

BIBLIOGRAPHY

Casson, H.N. (1931) *The Story of My Life*, London: Efficiency Magazine.

Drury, H.B. (1915) *Scientific Management: A History and Criticism*, New York: Columbia University Press.

Emerson, H. (1909) *Efficiency as a Basis for Operations and Wages*, New York: John R. Dunlap.
—— (1911) 'How Railroad Efficiency Can Be Managed', *Engineering Magazine* 42(October): 10–16.
—— (1913) *The Twelve Principles of Efficiency*, New York: The Engineering Magazine Company.
—— (1921) *The Science of Human Engineering*, New York: The Man Message Corporation.

MLW

ETZIONI, Amitai (1929–)

Amitai Etzioni was born in Cologne, Germany on 4 January 1929 to the German Jewish family of Willi and Gertrude Falk. Fleeing Hitler, the family settled in Palestine in 1938, where they changed their name to Etzioni. Etzioni took part in Israel's war of independence in 1948, and then earned his bachelor's degree in 1954 and his masters in 1956, both from Jerusalem's Hebrew University.

Etzioni entered the University of California at Berkeley in 1957, studying under the distinguished sociologist Seymour Martin Lipset. After earning his Ph.D., Etzioni began teaching at Columbia University in 1958. His major works centred around the realms of community and society. In 1961 he wrote *A Comparative Analysis of Complex Organizations*, in which he developed a common framework for comparing the organization of institutions such as a corporation or church with those of an army, a firm or a government.

In 1964 Etzioni went on to publish *Modern Organizations*. The first part of this work examined the goals of organizations, which he saw as serving many functions. A goal could often depict a future state of affairs or set down guidelines for activity, or become a source of legitimacy and standards. Organizations, however, could often acquire their own needs. A charitable fundraiser might begin spending more on its own buildings and staff than those it was set up to help.

Etzioni next looked at organizational structures. The classical scientific management approach pioneered by the disciples of Frederick W. TAYLOR saw workers as motivated by economic rewards. The system it recommended was hierarchical, tightly controlled and procedure-driven, and it divided labour into specific tasks. A second approach, based on human relations theory, arose in reaction to Taylorism. Founded on a series of experiments undertaken at the Western Electric plant in Hawthorne, Illinois between 1927 and 1932, human relations theory assumed workers had other goals besides money and preferred to labour in an environment that was less structured and based upon informal, emotional relationships (see MAYO and ROETHLISBERGER). Such a model might be found in Latin or Asian cultures.

Etzioni, drawing upon the work of Max Weber, argued for a third model of organization that he saw as more accurate than the other two. The scientific model assumed no conflict between the interests of labour and management in an organization. That workers might find repetitively turning the same screws on an assembly line mind-numbing or alienating was often ignored. The human relations model assumed that everyone in an organization operated like part of a harmonious family rather than an efficient machine. There were, however, tensions – group versus personal needs, discipline versus autonomy, rank versus division – that belied these neat models.

Looking at hospitals, prisons, churches, schools, social-work agencies and other organizations, Etzioni formulated a structural approach to organization theory. Organizations were large complex social units in which all kinds of groups interacted. Some might share an interest in making profits but not in how they were distributed. Frustration and tensions on the job were real, and there were limits to how far these could be reduced, for they were built into the very nature of the organization. The human relations approach argued that most labour/management problems might be solved through better communications. A rumour of mass layoffs demoralizes work on the shop floor until it is dispelled. What, asked Etzioni, happens if the rumour is true? Conflicting interests in the workplace were a reality, and recognizing them was the key to resolving them, or at least mitigating their effects. These themes also appear in *The Active Society*, published in 1968, which called for studying society as an organic whole, instead of a mere collection of groups or individuals.

While Etzioni was becoming conscious of the importance of community during the 1960s, he was and remains a strong believer in both the individual and democracy. He aligned himself with the left wing of the Democratic Party, championed arms control, and opposed both the Moon race and US participation in the Vietnam War. He also married Minerva Morales in 1965; the couple had five sons.

In the early 1970s, Etzioni focused upon the moral and social implications of genetic engineering and the new biotechnologies, expressing his concern over their effects on human liberty and morality. How would society be affected, he asked, if parents could choose the sex of their children? Throughout the remainder of the decade, he continued to teach sociology at Columbia and wrote numerous articles on social issues. From 1978 to 1979 Etzioni worked at the Brookings Institution, and he served as an adviser to Richard Harden, Special Assistant to US President Jimmy Carter from 1979 to 1980.

As Etzioni established his reputation as one of the United States' brightest sociologists, he was also becoming aware of the impact of the upheavals of the 1960s and early 1970s upon the nation's culture and society. Vietnam and Watergate undermined faith in government; the research of Ralph NADER undermined faith

in business; inflation and recession undermined faith in prosperity. Under Presidents Lyndon B. Johnson and even Richard Nixon, welfare programmes had expanded enormously and were seen by many as entitlements. The success of the African-American Civil Rights Movement inspired feminists and other groups to assert their rights, while many former activists turned inward to pursue personal fulfilment. The new climate of cynicism, when combined with the slowing of economic growth in the later 1970s, spurred the popularity of individualistic and libertarian thought which helped secure the election of Ronald Reagan in 1980.

By the early 1980s, Etzioni saw that something was terribly wrong, and in 1983 attempted to offer a diagnosis in the form of *An Immodest Agenda: Rebuilding America before the 21st Century*. This was a landmark work, setting the agenda for his later works and growing out of Etzioni's earlier concerns with viewing society as a community. That community, he argued, was now in grave danger, from the new pandemic of individualism. 'Many Americans', he lamented, '… are no longer willing or able to take care of themselves and each other' (Etzioni 1983: 3). While himself a Democrat, Etzioni blamed both 'ego-centered individualism' and big government for undermining the families, schools and neighbourhoods upon which communities depended. In this 'hollowing of America', family responsibilities declined at the same time that more was demanded of government in taking care of the children of working mothers and the elderly. People demanded more police while being less willing to help the victims of crime, and demanded more enforcement of ethical conduct while being less willing to practice it themselves. Admitting that bigger government 'lessens the individual and diminished individuals foster more government', Etzioni rejected the Reagan administration's belief that dismantling big government would automatically restore a moral society: 'Reducing the government does not by itself secure reconstruction of individuals. And without such reconstruction a vacuum will be created, leaving a viable community and a strong economy unprovided for' (Etzioni 1983: 4). The result would be either a backlash return to statism or a society so polarized that it would undergo a social catastrophe.

Etzioni sharply criticized the ideology of the individualist Reagan/Thatcher conservatives as it was represented by their chief economists, Milton FRIEDMAN and Friedrich von Hayek. Friedman contrasted market freedom with government coercion. In response to this debate between market individualism and state collectivism, Etzioni offered a communitarian alternative: 'People do not relate to one another only as participants in economic transactions or as subjects of a government' (Etzioni 1983: 9), but as parents, children, brothers, sisters, neighbours, friends and citizens. Such relationships of mutual respect, duty and concern pointed 'to the existence and significance of a third realm between government and market, the realm of community' (Etzioni 1983: 9).

To Etzioni, the authoritarianism of many religious fundamentalists, whom he called New Tories, was as repellent as libertarianism. Here the government was given the role of legislating morality, banning abortion and mandating the teaching of creationism in schools. According to Etzioni, this would do little good. Outlawing abortion would not save families; making children pray in school would not make them more righteous; imposing the death penalty would, he felt, deter few crimes. Community had to come from within, through the consent of free and committed individuals.

An Immodest Agenda symbolized the first important systematic attack by a major social philosopher upon the libertarianism of Friedman, Hayek and others, including Ayn RAND and David Stockman. To Etzioni, the libertarian creed was now far more influential than the handful of votes garnered by the US Libertarian Party. Market libertarians saw, he said, only the state versus the individual. Libertarians felt consumers could always tell a good product from a bad. People, they argued,

deserved the right to smoke, kill themselves, use harmful drugs, not use helmets or seat belts. Libertarians also believed that accidents and sickness were the fault of individuals who made wrong choices, not manufacturers who made unsafe products and polluted the environment, or health organizations that provided inadequate care. To this, Etzioni replied that personal lifestyles are shaped by communities. A careful driver can be killed in a community that tolerates drunken drivers.

Etzioni criticized libertarians, whom he dubbed the New Whigs, be they academic like Gary S. Becker, or popular, like Robert Ringer, for picturing 'the whole social world was dominated by the market, or the society itself as a market of sorts' (Etzioni 1983: 13). This led, he felt, to very destructive thinking. Marriage became a transaction in which benefits had to exceed costs, as did respect for the law. People were assumed to be cool and calculating instead of being emotionally tied to one another. People married for status, and performed acts of kindness on a value-for-value basis, expecting compensation in the marketplace of life.

Etzioni continued to develop this theme during the administrations of Ronald Reagan (1981–9), George Bush (1989–93) and Bill Clinton (1993–2001). As market-oriented thinking became more and more the prevailing orthodoxy, Etzioni intensified his intellectual counterattack. In 1991 he founded a quarterly journal, The Responsive Community, with the slogan 'Rights and Responsibilities'. The Responsive Community has served for a decade as the major intellectual organ for a growing communitarian movement which attracted both Democrats such as Senator Bill Bradley and Republicans such as Jack Kemp and William Bennett. By 1993 Etzioni had organized a citizen lobby known as the Communitarian Network. The organization's goals revolved around the rebuilding of family and local communities.

In 1993 Etzioni published The Spirit of Community, which defined the goals of the communitarian movement and reiterated his themes of 1983. In an age of a surging bull market, in which shareholder capitalism began to sweep all before it, he decried the practices of insider trading, churning accounts and cornering the market. The fruits of the new seemingly amoral business culture of downsizing and globalization were not good: 'Too many businesspeople', he said, 'no longer accept the responsibility of stewardship' or the duty 'to reach beyond furthering self or corporate advancement or to serve as trustees of a special undertaking'. Airlines and health care were less safe as:

> Speculation, cronyism, bribery, and raiding corporate coffers have left numerous savings and loans, banks, insurance companies, and pension funds teetering on the brink of insolvency and have shattered public confidence, which in turn damages the country's economic performance
> (Etzioni 1993: 28–9)

In the later 1990s, as the stock market rose ever higher, Etzioni published two more books, *The New Golden Rule: Community and Morality in a Democratic Society* (1997) and *The Limits of Privacy* (1999). In the latter book, Etzioni upheld his commitment to individual personal freedom and privacy while insisting that sometimes it would have to be subordinated, like all personal rights, to the public good.

Etzioni continues to be a prolific writer and a vocal critic of both libertarianism and conservative authoritarianism. No lover of big government, disliking the sense of rights without responsibilities he felt it bred, he nevertheless revived the old notion of the Greek city-state in which community and citizenship balanced the need for market freedom. Just as there could be no personal freedom without personal responsibility, there could be no market freedom without business ethics or responsibility.

BIBLIOGRAPHY

Etzioni, A. (1961) *A Comparative Analysis of Complex Organizations*, Glencoe, IL: The Free Press.

—— (1964) *Modern Organizations*, Englewood Cliffs, NJ: Prentice-Hall.

—— (1983) *An Immodest Agenda: Rebuilding America Before the 21st Century*, New York: McGraw-Hill.

—— (1988) *The Moral Dimension: Towards a New Economics*, New York: The Free Press.

—— (1993) *The Spirit of Community, The Reinvention of American Society*, New York: Simon and Schuster.

—— (1997) *The New Golden Rule: Community and Morality in a Democratic Society*, New York: Basic Books.

—— (1999) *The Limits of Privacy*, New York: Basic Books.

'Etzioni, Amitai [Werner]' (1980) in C. Moritz (ed.), *Current Biography Yearbook*, New York: The H.W. Wilson Company, 101–4.

DCL

F

FIEDLER, Fred Edward (1922–)

Fred Edward Fiedler was born in Vienna, Austria on 13 July 1922. His parents, Victor and Helga Schallinger Fiedler, owned a textile and tailoring supply store prior to 1938. Fred was their only child. After completing secondary school, he served a brief apprenticeship in his father's textile business before emigrating to the United States in 1938 and settling in South Bend, Indiana. After his high school graduation in 1940, Fiedler held a variety of low-level jobs in Indiana, Michigan and California, before returning to Indiana and a job at the Indiana and Michigan Electric Company. Following the German invasion of Austria, meanwhile, Fiedler's parents moved first to Shanghai and then to the United States in 1946.

In the summer of 1942, Fiedler enrolled in engineering courses at Western Michigan College of Education (now Western Michigan University, in Kalamazoo), but quickly decided engineering was not his field. He also applied to and was accepted by the University of Chicago. He served in the US Army from 1942 to 1945. Following basic training and a brief assignment in a medical battalion, he was sent to Indiana University for training in the Turkish Area and Language Studies programme. Later he served in an infantry battalion, military civilian affairs and the military government. During tours of duty in England and Germany, Fiedler was involved in training, interpreting, telephone communica-

tions and public safety. Fiedler had met Judith M. Joseph at the University of Chicago before entering the army, and they married shortly after his discharge on 14 April 1946. They have collaborated on research and writing over the years, and have four children.

Fiedler developed an interest in psychology in his early teens from reading his father's books on the topic. He took several extension courses in psychology while serving in the army. After his discharge from the army in November 1945, Fiedler was readmitted to the University of Chicago and resumed his study of psychology in January 1946. He received a master's degree in industrial and organizational psychology in 1947 and his Ph.D. in clinical psychology in 1949.

During his years at the University of Chicago, Fiedler was actively involved in research under some of the most prominent names in the field, such as Lee Cronbach and Donald Campbell. Among the university's professors were L.L. Thurstone and Thelma G. Thurstone, Donald Fiske, Carl Rogers and William Foote Whyte. Fiedler's master's thesis was on 'The Efficacy of Preventive Psychotherapy for Alleviating Examination Anxiety', and his dissertation, entitled 'A Comparative Investigation of the Therapeutic Relationships Created by Experts and Non-experts of the Psychoanalytic, Non-directive, and Adlerian Schools', is one of his most frequently cited works.

While at the University of Chicago he was a trainee and then a research assistant with the

Veterans Administration (VA), and continued working for a year after his graduation as a research associate and instructor for the VA in Chicago. Following a summer in the Combat Crew Research Laboratory at Randolph Field, he became associate director on a naval research contract at the University of Illinois' College of Education. His work during this period with Donald Fiske and Lee Cronbach sparked his lifelong interest in leadership.

From 1950 until 1969, Fiedler was on the faculty of the University of Illinois, where he initiated and directed the Group Effectiveness Research Laboratory (GERL). Harry Triandis and Joseph McGrath were associate directors. Research associates included Martin Chemers, Peter Dachler, David DeVries, Jack Feldman, Richard Hackman, J.G. Hunt, Edwin Hutchins, Daniel Ilgen and Terence Mitchell. While at the University of Illinois, Fiedler was appointed head of the social, differential, personality and industrial psychology divisions. His wife worked as a research sociologist in the university's Survey Research Center.

In 1969 Fiedler moved to the University of Washington where he remained on the faculty until his retirement in 1993. There he established the Organizational Research Group and directed the Group Effectiveness Research Laboratory. His wife became assistant director of the University of Washington's Educational Assessment Center. Among his associates were Gary Latham, Terence Mitchell, Lee Beach, Martin Chemers, James G. Hunt, Richard Hackman and Daniel Ilgen.

In the late 1940s the emphasis in leadership research shifted from traits and the personal characteristics of leaders to leadership styles and behaviours. From the late 1960s through the 1980s, leadership interests turned to contingency models of leadership. One of the earliest and best known is Fiedler's contingency model of leadership effectiveness. Published in 1967 as A Theory of Leadership Effectiveness, the model immediately drew attention as the first leadership theory operationally to measure the interaction between leadership personality and the leader's situational control in predicting leadership performance.

While many scholars assumed that there was one best style of leadership, Fiedler's contingency model postulates that the leader's effectiveness is based on 'situational contingency', or a match between the leader's style and situational favourableness, later called situational control. More than 400 studies have since investigated this relationship.

A key component in Fiedler's contingency theory is the least preferred co-worker (LPC) scale, an instrument for measuring an individual's leadership orientation using eighteen to twenty-five pairs of adjectives and an eight-point bipolar scale between each pair. Respondents are asked to consider the person they liked working with the least, either presently or in the past, and rate that co-worker on each pair of adjectives. High-LPC or relationship-motivated leaders describe their least preferred co-worker in more positive terms and are concerned with maintaining good interpersonal relations. Low-LPC or task-motivated leaders describe their least preferred co-worker in rejecting and negative terms, and give higher priority to the task than to interpersonal relations.

According to Fiedler, there is no ideal leader. Both low-LPC (task-oriented) and high-LPC (relationship-oriented) leaders can be effective, if their leadership orientation fits the situation. The contingency theory allows for predicting the characteristics of the appropriate situations for effectiveness. Three situational components determine the favourableness or situational control: leader–member relations, task structure and position power. Fiedler found that low-LPC leaders are more effective in extremely favourable or unfavourable situations, whereas high-LPC leaders perform best in situations with intermediate favourability.

Since personality is relatively stable, the contingency model suggests that improving effectiveness requires changing the situation to fit the leader. The organization or the leader may increase or decrease task structure and position power, and training and group development may improve leader–member relations. Leader-Match is a self paced leadership training programme designed to help leaders alter the favourableness of the situation, or situational control. The 1976 book describing Leader-Match was co-authored by Martin Chemers and Linda Mahar.

Fiedler's contingency theory has drawn criticism because it implies that the only alternative for an unalterable mismatch between leader orientation and an unfavourable situation is changing the leader. The model's validity has also been disputed, despite many supportive tests (Bass 1990). Other criticisms concern the methodology of measuring leadership style through the LPC inventory and the nature of the supporting evidence (Ashour 1973; Schriesheim and Kerr 1977a, 1977b; Vecchio 1977, 1983). Fiedler and his associates have provided decades of research to support and refine the contingency theory. Cognitive resource theory (CRT) modifies Fiedler's basic contingency model by adding traits of the leader (Fiedler and Garcia 1987). CRT tries to identify the conditions under which leaders and group members will use their intellectual resources, skills and knowledge effectively. While it has been generally assumed that more intelligent and more experienced leaders will perform better than those with less intelligence and experience, this assumption is not supported by Fiedler's research.

To Fiedler, stress is a key determinant of leader effectiveness (Fiedler and Garcia 1987; Fiedler et al. 1993), and a distinction is made between stress related to the leader's superior, and stress related to subordinates or the situation itself. In stressful situations, leaders dwell on the stressful relations with others and cannot focus their intellectual abilities on the job. Thus, intelligence is more effective and used more often in stress-free situations. Fiedler has found that experience impairs performance in low-stress conditions

but contributes to performance under high-stress conditions. As with other situational factors, for stressful situations Fiedler recommends altering or engineering the leadership situation to capitalize on the leader's strengths.

Fiedler is known around the world for his writing, lectures and consulting work. Throughout his career, Fiedler has received research grants and contracts from many government agencies and private foundations. He held research fellowships at the University of Amsterdam from 1957 to 1958, at the University of Louvain in Belgium from 1963 to 1964, and at Templeton College, Oxford from 1986 to 1987. He has served as a consultant for various federal and local government agencies and private industries in the United States and abroad.

Fiedler was recognized by the American Psychological Association for counselling research in 1971 and for his contributions to military psychology in 1979. He received the Stogdill Award for Distinguished Contributions to Leadership in 1978. The American Academy of Management honoured Fiedler as a Distinguished Educator in Management in 1993, and the Society for Industrial and Organizational Psychology recognized his outstanding scientific contributions in 1996. In 1999 the American Psychological Society presented Fiedler with its James McKeen Cattell Award. Fiedler is a member of the International Association of Applied Psychology and a past president of that organization's Division of Organizational Psychology. He is a fellow of the American Psychological Association and a member of the Society for Experimental Social Psychology and the Midwestern Psychological Association. He has authored or co-authored more than 200 scientific papers and several books. His articles are frequently cited by others and have been published by the most respected journals in the fields of psychology, leadership and management.

Fiedler's career spans more than fifty years. Even in retirement, he continues to inspire and encourage research on leadership and other related topics. He proposed the contingency theory of leadership very early in his career, and has spent years since then testing its assumptions and making revisions. He has willingly debated his critics, offering additional research and alternative explanations based on his own investigations and the growing body of knowledge in the field. Fiedler and his contingency theory of leadership deserve a prominent place in the history of management thought. He was one of the first to recognize and produce a leadership model that combines personality traits and contextual factors. The more recent cognitive resource theory promises to extend his influence many years into the future.

BIBLIOGRAPHY

Ashour, A.S. (1973) 'The Contingency Model of Leadership Effectiveness: An Evaluation', *Organizational Behavior and Human Decision Processes*, 9(3): 339–55.

Bass, B.M. (1990) 'Leader March', in *Handbook of Leadership*, New York: The Free Press, 494–510, 651–2, 840–41.

Fiedler, F.E. (1958) *Leader Attitudes and Group Effectiveness*, Urbana, IL: University of Illinois Press.

—— (1967) *A Theory of Leadership Effectiveness*, New York: McGraw-Hill.

—— (1971) *Leadership*, New York: General Learning Press.

—— (1981) *Leader Attitudes and Group Effectiveness*, Westport, CT: Greenwood Publishing Group.

—— (1992) 'Life in a Pretzel-shaped Universe', in A.G. Bedeian (ed.), *Management Laureates: A Collection of Autobiographical Essays*, Greenwich, CT: JAI Press, vol. 1, 301–34.

—— (1994) *Leadership Experience and Leadership Performance*, Alexandria, VA: US Army Research Institute for the Behavioral and Social Sciences.

Fiedler, F.E. (1997) *Directory of the American Psychological Association*, Chicago: St James Press, 419.

Fiedler, F.E. and Chemers, M.M. (1974) *Leadership and Effective Management*, Glenview, IL: Scott, Foresman and Co.

Fiedler, F.E. and Garcia, J.E. (1987) *New Approaches to Leadership, Cognitive Resources and Organizational Performance*, New York: John Wiley and Sons.

Fiedler, F.E., Chemers, M.M. and Mahar, L. (1976) *Improving Leadership Effectiveness: The Leader Match Concept*, New York: John Wiley and Sons.

Fiedler, F.E., Garcia, J.E. and Lewis, C.T. (1986) *People Management, and Productivity*, Boston: Allyn and Bacon.

Fiedler, F.E., Gibson, F.W. and Barrett, K.M. (1993) 'Stress, Babble, and the Utilization of the Leader's Intellectual Abilities', *Leadership Quarterly* 4(2): 189–208.

Fiedler, F.E., Godfrey, E.P. and Hall, D.M. (1959) *Boards, Management and Company Success*, Danville, IL: Interstate Publishers.

Hooijberg, R. and Choi, J. (1999) 'From Austria to the United States and from Evaluating Therapists to Developing Cognitive Resources Theory: An Interview with Fred Fiedler', *Leadership Quarterly* 10(4): 653–66.

King, B., Streufert, S. and Fiedler, F.E. (1978) *Managerial Control and Organizational Democracy*, Washington, DC: V.H. Winston and Sons.

Schriesheim, C.A. and Kerr, S. (1977a) 'Theories and Measures of Leadership', in J.G. Hunt, and L.L. Larson (eds), *Leadership: The Cutting Edge*, Carbondale, IL: Southern Illinois University Press, 9–45.

—— (1977b) 'R.I.P LPC: A Response to Fiedler', in J.G. Hunt, and L.L. Larson (eds), *Leadership: The Cutting Edge*, Carbondale, IL: Southern Illinois University Press, 51–6.

Vecchio, R.P. (1977) 'An Empirical Examination of the Validity of Fiedler's Model of Leadership Effectiveness', *Organizational Behavior and Human Performance* 19: 180–206.

Fiedler, F.E. (1983) 'Assessing the Validity of Fiedler's Contingency Model of Leadership Effectiveness: A Closer look at Strube and Garcia', *Psychological Bulletin* 93: 404–8.

JAEB

FILENE, Edward Albert (1860–1937)

Edward Albert Filene was born in Salem, Massachusetts on 3 September 1860 and died in Paris on 26 September 1937. His father, William Filene, was an immigrant from Eastern Europe who had settled in Boston and built up a small but prosperous retail business. After finishing high school, Filene had planned to attend Harvard University, but his father's ill health required that he take over the family business instead; he became president of William Filene's Sons in 1879, at the age of nineteen. Over the next thirty years he built up Filene's business, establishing one of the largest and most successful department stores in the country. He became a noted philanthropist and had some importance as a social commentator. Never married, he was reportedly a man of difficult temper who made few close friends, and his abrasive personality may have prevented his ideas from becoming more widely disseminated (Urwick 1956).

Filene's principles of marketing for retail operations were publicized in several books, notably *More Profits from Merchandizing* (1925) and *The Model Stock Plan* (1930), and were of considerable influence in the development of retailing in the United States.

He believed that the primary purpose of marketing is not to make a profit, but to satisfy customer needs; if this is done successfully, then profits will follow. He was one of the first to use the slogan, 'The customer is always right'. He competed successfully with his rivals on cost, aiming for low margins and rapid turnover of stock, the ancestor of the 'pile it high and sell it cheap' philosophy used by later retailers such as Sam WALTON. This philosophy was backed up with detailed accounting and inventory control systems. Urwick (1956) credits him with being the first to apply the principles of scientific management to retailing in the United States.

Filene was also noted for maintaining good relations with this staff, and was an early proponent of industrial democracy; major decisions affecting the running of the store were sometimes put to a vote. He paid well and reduced working hours. In the wider community, he was one of the early organizers of the credit union movement in the United States, and in 1920 used some of his wealth to found the Twentieth Century Fund, an institution conducting research into economic and social issues. In 1927, through the fund, he established the International Management Institute in Geneva, a permanent international body coordinating research and development in management.

In *Successful Living in this Machine Age* (1932), Filene pondered on the social changes that mass production and the rise of large corporations had wrought on America. He linked the rise of mass production to the rise of what VEBLEN had called 'the leisure classes', pointing out that many of the goods being produced and sold *en masse* were being purchased by those who had time and money to spare; thus mass production both led to greater consumer demand and was itself a product of greater consumer affluence. He believed that business owners and managers had a twofold responsibility to society: first, to provide employment which made affluence possible, and second, to provide goods which satisfied the needs of the newly affluent.

BIBLIOGRAPHY

Filene, E.A. (1925) *More Profits from Merchandizing*, Chicago: A.W. Shaw.
—— (1930) *The Model Stock Plan*, New York: McGraw-Hill.
—— (1932) *Successful Living in this Machine Age*, London: Jonathan Cape.
Urwick, L.F. (1956) *The Golden Book of Management*, London: Newman Neame.

MLW

FIRESTONE, Harvey (1868–1938)

Harvey Firestone was born in Columbiana County, Ohio on 20 December 1868 and died in Miami Beach, Florida on 7 February 1938. He was the founder and chief executive of the Firestone Tire and Rubber Company, which he led to become the second largest company in its industry. Firestone entered the tyre business through the buggy industry, which used solid rubber tyres. By 1900 he was based in Akron, Ohio, a centre of rubber manufacturing, with his own Firestone Tire and Rubber Company. The goal of the new firm was to produce tyres at lower prices, which it succeeded in doing in part by avoiding established patents and royalty charges. The future business strategy of the Firestone Tire and Rubber Company was set: the aim was to be a low-cost producer, with aggressive pricing and growth policies. Firestone refused to enter into agreements designed to maintain prices. He entered the tyre-manufacturing (as opposed to tyre-mounting) business in 1902. His firm was, however, rooted in the older solid tyre technology of the buggy business, not the newer pneumatic technology used by the rapidly growing automobile industry. Thus Firestone faced the major challenge of a declining market for solid tyres, although he continued to earn profits from solid tyres; pneumatic technology was too new and unreliable for fire engines, a tyre market that Firestone dominated.

Firestone met the automobile tyre challenge with characteristic aggressiveness, again with regard to patents. Pneumatic tyres were at the time attached to wheels using patents for a clincher system, by which the hard rubber bead on a tyre was forced inside the narrower rim of a wheel. The association controlling the patents for the clincher tyre, seeking to restrict entry into the field and thereby maintain high prices, refused Firestone a licence to use the technology. Firestone's response was to devise a cheaper means of mounting pneumatic tyres while avoiding the clincher tyre patents, and to reinvest the profits from the solid tyre business in the new pneumatic field. When Henry FORD, then a small automobile manufacturer near Detroit, asked for bids on a contract for his new Model N car, Firestone substantially undercut the price of a clincher tyre and won the business.

This deal began a lifelong personal friendship and business relationship, which lasted for the rest of the century, between Ford, Firestone and their firms. Eventually, the two entrepreneurs were able to break patent associations that restricted growth in their respective industries. Within a few years Ford had become the world's largest automobile manufacturer, and Ford favoured Firestone in tyre purchases.

Important as supplying tyres for new vehicles was to Firestone and his competitors, the more lucrative business was in replacement tyres. Firestone succeeded in this market by maintaining low prices and by using innovative and aggressive marketing techniques. Firestone practised vertical integration, complete with investments in a rubber plantation in Liberia and a chain of retail and repair shops.

By the 1930s Firestone was withdrawing from the day-to-day affairs of his firm. Firestone Tire nevertheless retained the strategy of its founder. After the Second World War the firm expanded aggressively and continued its reputation in the industry of being a low-cost and able manufacturer. In 1988, after the firm had suffered serious losses from the sales of defective radial tyres a decade earlier, it was purchased by the Japanese Bridgestone Company. This merger was part of a worldwide trend of consolidation in the tyre manufacturing business.

BIBLIOGRAPHY
Firestone, H. with Crowther, S. (1926) *Men and Rubber: The Story of Business*, Garden City, NY: Doubleday, Page.
French, M.J. (1991) *The U.S. Tire Industry*, Boston: Twayne.
Lief, A. (1951) *Harvey Firestone: Free Man of Enterprise*, New York: McGraw-Hill.

KAK

FLAGLER, Henry Morrison (1830–1913)

Henry Morrison Flagler was born in Hopewell, New York on 2 January 1830, the son of a Presbyterian minister. He died in Palm Beach, Florida on 20 May 1913. After leaving home at the age of fourteen Flagler worked at a variety of jobs, eventually becoming a grain merchant in the area around Sandusky, Ohio in 1850. Among his contacts was John D. ROCKEFELLER, then in the grain business in Cleveland. In the 1860s he relocated to Michigan, dealing in grain and also in salt; he prospered during the American Civil War, but went into debt in the postwar slump. Moving to Cleveland in 1865, he set up a general merchandise firm, and also renewed his contact with Rockefeller.

Rockefeller was at this point just entering the oil business, and in 1866 he invited Flagler to join him in the partnership Rockefeller, Andrews and Flagler. Energetic and decisive, Flagler used his experience and contacts as a merchant to organize the efficient shipment of oil by rail. He became second only to Rockefeller in the hierarchy of the rapidly growing organiztion, and in 1870 was named secretary and treasurer of the newly founded Standard Oil. Having moved to New York in 1877, in 1882 he became president of Standard Oil Company of New Jersey, remaining as a vice-president until 1908, and as a director until 1911.

Flagler had married Mary Harkness in 1853, and they had three children. After her death in 1881, Flagler married her nurse, Ida Shourds, in 1883. While honeymooning on the then undeveloped east coast of Florida, Flagler was captivated by the beauty of the area's natural surroundings. He wondered if rich Americans who habitually wintered on the French Riviera could be attracted here instead, and set out to answer his own question. Neither his own career nor Florida would ever be quite the same.

Florida at that point was rural and undeveloped, with less than 800 kilometres (500 miles) of railroad and virtually no infrastructure. Undeterred, Flagler built the $1 million luxury Ponce de Leon hotel in St Augustine in 1885–8, at the same time upgrading the railways so tourists could travel in comfort. When the venture proved to be an almost immediate success, more hotels followed. The railway began not only carrying tourists in but also hauling fruit out, bringing a boom to the Florida citrus fruit industry. When the severe winter of 1894–5 killed many fruit trees, Flagler gave the farmers free seed and made personal loans to those who were destitute.

In 1896 Flagler extended his Florida East Coast Railway south to Miami, where he built not only more hotels but all the infrastructure needed to support the town, including a power plant, street lights, sewerage works and even churches. Like Henry HUNTINGTON in California, Flagler found that to reach his own goals he had not only to manage his core business but also to serve in effect as planner and developer of the entire region. This activity he carried out with great skill. His final achievement was the bridging of the Florida Keys, linking Key West to Miami by rail in 1912.

In 1899 Ida Flagler was declared insane. Flagler was finally able to divorce her in 1901 and was married for the third time, to Mary Kenan, with whom he lived in the Miami suburb of Palm Beach, the object of some cynosure for having more or less abandoned his previous wife. Opinions of Flagler were generally mixed: some believed he exploited and ruined Florida for his own profit, but others hailed him as the builder and even saviour of the state.

BIBLIOGRAPHY

Akin, E.N. (1988) *Flagler: Rockefeller Partner and Florida Baron*, Kent, OH: Kent State University Press.

MLW

FLORENCE, Philip Sargant (1890–1982)

Philip Sargant Florence was born in London on 25 June 1890, the son of the musician Henry Smythe Florence and the artist and writer Mary Sargant Florence. He died on 29 January 1982 in Birmingham. After education at Rugby School and Caius College, Cambridge, where he took an MA, he went to New York to study for his Ph.D. at Columbia University. From 1917 to 1921 he was lecturer at the Bureau of Industrial Research and Bureau of Personnel Administration in New York. He married Lella Faye Secor in 1917, and the couple had two sons.

Returning to Britain, Florence held a variety of posts at Cambridge, mainly at Magdalene College and in the department of economics. He then moved to the University of Birmingham, where he remained for the rest of his career; he was professor of commerce from 1929 to 1955, and dean of faculty from 1947 to 1950. Florence was awarded the CBE in 1952.

Florence is best known as an industrial economist, focusing on theories of the firm and the impacts of human behaviour on economics and organizations. His early work on fatigue and industrial unrest (Florence 1918, 1924) convinced him that many of the problems faced by industry were not economic at all, but rather human in origin. That conviction comes through strongly in his principal work, *The Logic of Industrial Organization* (1933) and its two follow-up studies, *Investment, Location, and Size of Plant* (1948) and *The Logic of British and American Industry* (1953). Political science and psychology, he says, are at least as important in the study of organization as is economics, and he is highly critical of the growing trend towards abstract analysis which leaves the human factor out of the equation (Florence 1953: 1–2).

Florence begins with an apparent paradox. The logic of organizations, he says, seems to suggest that big is best. 'Big' here means both large-scale production and large-scale organization (he makes the valuable point that many large organizations actually undertake production on a fairly small scale) (Florence 1933: 1–2). Combining both would make for optimum efficiency, which he defines as 'maximum return physical, pecuniary or psychological at minimum physical, pecuniary or psychological cost' (1933: 260). Throughout his work, Florence is careful to stress that efficiency is not solely about profit and cost; other human factors are at play as well, and the most efficient factory is not necessarily the one with the best cost ratios.

Yet, despite this supposed logic, and despite numerous individual examples to the contrary, industry as a whole has not moved towards large-scale production and organization. In both Britain and the United States, small firms continue to outnumber large ones, and continue to account for the majority of production and employment. Whence, then, is the source of this 'illogic'? Florence identifies three principal factors: (1) the individual and 'illogical' nature of human demand; (2) the burdens which large-scale organization places on management in terms of control; and (3) the tendency of people to feel less involved in and committed to larger organizations than smaller ones. All three of these are social and psychological factors which are often omitted by analysts who see the firm, and particularly its management, as primarily rational in national: 'men engaged in business as administrators and investors are, no less than the labourers they employ, human beings, not, as is often assumed, hundred per cent efficiency experts' (1933: 263). Large-scale operation, then, does not necessarily result in efficiency.

As marketing writers such as CHERINGTON had been pointing out for at least a decade before Florence, there is a fundamental mismatch between consumer buying patterns and large-scale production, in that consumers tend to buy on a small scale, at uncertain times and places. This poses a problem for distribution and production planning. Consumers also vary not only their rate of consumption, but also the type of consumption, by demanding new or seasonal products; Florence points to the Christmas gift market as the prime example of this (1933: 60–64). Competitors complicate the picture by introducing their own new products and stimulating demand in different ways, so that the market as a whole is constantly evolving.

The question of the span of control is still more difficult. There is, Florence says, 'great difficulty in adjustment of employment, investment and management relations into the frame of large-scale organization' (1933: 263). The problems are both technical and human. Large-scale organization perforce

means specialization and localization, with concentration of different types or stages of production in different places; this leads to problems of coordination, and also in knowledge dissemination. Further to this, managers themselves, being human, tend not to come in standard forms, which efficiency would seem to require; they have different motivations, different needs, and different styles and habits of working. To illustrate this, Florence uses a series of management archetypes – the head of a family business, the entrepreneur, the ex-professional man, the ex-foreman, the ex-technician and so on – all of whom react to issues and solve problems in different ways (1933: 204–20, 265–6). This can be a source of great creativity, but it can also be a barrier to efficiency.

The question of human relations in large organizations is the most important of all: 'there is a specific loss of stimulus to the human factor psychologically connected with large-scale organization, and since scale of operation is partly dependent on scale of organizations, this offsets the physical advantages of large-scale operation' (1933: 264). Paradoxically, large-scale organization creates individual inefficiency; workers identify less with the firm and more with their own interests. Again, this is a human problem, not an economic one.

These three factors, then, tend to limit the size of firms, which grow to the limits imposed by their ability to meet customer demand, the ability of top management to exercise control, and by labour's apparent law of diminishing returns. The theoretical efficiencies of large-scale organization are thwarted by the practical inefficiencies or 'illogicalities' which occur during growth.

All three problems, Florence believes, are capable of partial solution. Firms need to give attention to forecasting and analysis of market demand, in order to reduce risk and uncertainty where consumers and competitors are concerned. The fluid, constantly changing nature of consumer demand means that these risks can never be entirely eliminated, but they can be minimized (1933: 260). The question of the span of control requires attention to organizational principles. Florence is critical of old-fashioned hierarchical management, based largely on military organization, which he sees as placing too much responsibility on those at the top of the pyramid; only an exceptionally gifted manager can govern a large firm directly (1933: 119–22). He also sees the functional system, based on Taylorism (see TAYLOR), as inefficient as it involves unnecessary duplication and organization (1933: 127ff.). In common with other British writers of the period such as Urwick, he believes that the best principle for organizing large-scale businesses is the line and staff principle, with line management functions delegated down to the lowest possible level, and staff functions concentrated at headquarters. He believes too that this principle, by allowing for maximum decentralization, helps solve the problem of labour inefficiency; workers will be more committed to their own unit than they will to the larger firm. The firm, he says, can be compared to the church, while the individual plant can be compared to the congregation; people feel themselves members of the first, but the truly important social relationships which lead to efficiency are constructed within the second. Florence mentions in this context the methods of the Czech entrepreneur Tomas BAT'A, who broke his large operation up into semi-autonomous subunits of no more than 200 workers, and believes that this may be a model to follow (1933: 163–4).

Yet although these measures can break down some of the barriers to large-scale organization, they cannot remove them all. What, then, is the optimum scale for organizations in order to achieve maximum efficiency? Florence is undecided on this, and even doubts whether it is possible to reach such a measure; the conditions for optimum efficiency vary greatly from industry to industry, and the constantly evolving nature of competition and consumer demand mean that even the very

measures of optimality tend to change. This, he points out, is the key problem with planned economies. It is not possible to plan production for optimum efficiency unless one can also plan *consumption*; and this, given the illogicality and irrationality of consumer demand, cannot be done (1933: 8). Far better to let the free market have its way, and ensure that companies are flexible and able to change and adapt their own organizations to meet the challenges of the market.

Florence does not develop a 'system' as such, and flexibility is not a word he uses frequently, but the thrust of his arguments is that firms need to develop flexible systems, especially human systems. He calls for firms to be viewed as political entities, and his discussions of political relations within the firm may be influenced by Machiavelli (1933: 118–9). More commonly, he speaks of the need to examine the firm's social systems; the powerful metaphor of the firm as church is used repeatedly. In *Investment, Location, and Size of Plant* (1948) he seems to move away from any idea of optimality at all, and instead argues that investment decisions need to be made on the basis of specific conditions at the time and place of operation.

Florence made a number of other useful contributions as well. His work on labour inefficiency was very important in its day, as he showed for the first time how it was possible to measure the impacts of factors such as fatigue, illness, accidents and labour turnover on efficiency and profitability; he may have been the first writer to work out the actual financial costs of labour turnover (his methods of measurement remain broadly accurate) (Florence 1924). His later work on labour looks at labour as a process, with various inputs – the workplace (including type and hours of work, physical conditions and social relationships), the wage (including amount and method of payment) and the worker (his or her personality, skills and training) – combining to produce what he calls the 'human factor'. The human factor is defined as a combination of the worker's *capacity* to work (how much he or she can do) and the worker's *willingness* to work (how much he or she will do). Inefficiencies in labour nearly always stem from a deficiency in one or the other aspect of the human factor. Such inefficiencies can be measured, Florence says, not only in the form of the quantity and quality of output, but also in areas such as accidents, absenteeism, strikes and industrial disputes, and labour turnover (Florence 1949).

Florence sums up the nature of management as 'the ability and will to control large organizations', combined with the older but still vitally important requisite for entrepreneurship. The two together represent the powers of coordination and the powers of initiative, a blend of which is required in every successful manager (Florence 1933: 241). Along with many writers of the 1930s and 1950s, he calls for the recognition of management as a profession, and for more and better education for managers.

Florence's work is now largely obscure, and he is not frequently cited even by industrial economists. He nonetheless made an important contribution with his views on the importance of the human factor, and these views, unfashionable in the 1960s and 1970s, are very much in line with the mainstream of thinking today.

BIBLIOGRAPHY
Florence, P.S. (1918) *Use of Factory Statistics in the Investigation of Industrial Fatigue*, New York: Columbia University Press.
—— (1924) *Economics of Fatigue and Unrest*, London: George Allen and Unwin.
—— (1933) *The Logic of Industrial Organization*, London: Kegan, Paul, Trench, Trubner.
—— (1948) *Investment, Location, and Size of Plant*, Cambridge: Cambridge University Press.
—— (1949) *Labour*, London: Hutchinson.
Florence, P.S. (1953) *The Logic of British and American Industry*, London: Routledge and Kegan Paul.
—— (1957) *Industry and the State*, London: Hutchinson.
—— (1964) *Economics and Sociology of Industry*, London: C.A. Watts.

MLW

FOLLETT, Mary Parker (1868–1933)

Mary Parker Follett was born in Quincy, Massachusetts on 3 September 1868, into an old New England family, and died in Boston on 18 December 1933. She was educated at the Thayer Academy in Boston, and then attended Radcliffe College, where she took a mixed degree in philosophy, law, history and political science. She spent a year studying at Newnham College, Cambridge and also spent some time in Paris before returning to finish her degree, graduating *summa cum laude* in 1898. Settling in Boston with her friend Isobel Briggs, Follett became involved in social work in the city, organizing centres to provide educational and social services in working-class districts; these centres later developed into placement bureaux and vocational training establishments.

Although the main focus of her education had been on politics (she had published her first book, *The Speaker of the House of Representatives*, in 1896 while still at Radcliffe), her experiences in Boston opened her up to a broader perspective in which political, social and economic issues were intertwined. Her next book, *The New State–Group Organization* (1918), was a consideration of the relationship between the individual and society, and on the role that relationship plays in the maintenance of democracy. By now

Follett was also beginning to consider the workings of the human mind, looking at the role that personal desires, needs and wants play in the individual's relations with society; psychology and the role of knowledge were added to the mix. The result of her deliberations on these themes was *Creative Experience* (1924), Follett's best book and the one which has had the most impact.

Creative Experience was widely read and reviewed on publication. In particular, the book was taken up by academics studying business administration, and even by many managers. Henry Metcalf, director of the Bureau of Personnel Administration in New York, saw the potential of Follett's work for management, and invited her to give a course of lectures. Across the Atlantic, Benjamin Seebohm ROWNTREE read the book and asked Follett to lecture at one of his annual conferences in Oxford; she went on to become a fixture at these events. At one conference she met Lyndall Urwick, who became a great supporter of her work and arranged for her to give further lectures in Britain, notably at the London School of Economics. In 1928, after the death of Isobel Briggs, Follett decided to settle in Britain and moved to London, where she lived in Chelsea with another friend, Dame Katherine Furze. In 1933 she returned briefly to Boston to settle some financial affairs, but fell ill and died there.

The popularity of *Creative Experience* should perhaps be understood against its background. By the mid-1920s, the scientific management movement dominated management thinking in both the United States and many parts of Europe. However, scientific management was not regarded with universal enthusiasm. In its extreme forms, such as that advocated with great success by Charles BEDAUX, scientific management could be technocratic and bureaucratic – it emphasized the role of the technical expert, and appeared (and in many cases actually did) downgrade the roles not only of the worker on the shop floor but also of senior managers, who often felt that the technical and efficiency experts were taking control of the business out of their hands (this situation had arisen at least in part because top managers themselves rarely had much technical training). The time was ripe for a theory of administration which would provide a more humanistic approach to the subject, and Follett's *Creative Experience* fit the bill.

That is not to deny the power of the book itself, which is justly seen as one of the most influential management texts of the twentieth century; but the book most certainly arrived at the right moment. Follett opens the book by questioning the whole concept of what she calls 'vicarious experience', that is relying on the experience and skills of others rather than acquiring knowledge for ourselves. She questions whether experts can be regarded as custodians of truth, in the same way that it is questionable whether the law is really the guardian of truth. She does not dismiss experts out of hand, and acknowledges that their own experience and knowledge means that they *do* have access to truth, or at least part of it; what is dangerous, she feels, is the way in which others rely unquestioningly on experts to do their thinking for them.

Follett's view of society, and of organizations is one where people at all levels are motivated to work and participate. They should gather their own information, make their own decisions, define their own roles and shape their own lives. She also rejects empiricism: experience should not be used to create theories and concepts, but to inform the mind and liberate the spirit in a process which she calls 'evocation'. In this way, experience can become truly creative, a powerful force that creates advancement and progress. As she sums up:

> We seek reality in experience. Let us reject the realm of the compensatory; it is fair, but a prison. Experience may be hard but we claim its gifts because they are real, even though our feet bleed on its stones. We seek

progressive advancement through the transformation of daily experience. Into what, conceptual pictures? No, daily experience must be translated not into conceptual pictures but into spiritual conviction. Experience can both guide and guard us. Foolish indeed are those who do not bring oil to its burning.

(Follett 1924: 302)

The importance of psychological theory is evident throughout *Creative Experience*, and Follett makes reference to concepts such as Gestalt. Ultimately, however, this is not a book about psychology any more than it is about any other branch of knowledge. Follett believed in the unity of knowledge, and she draws on political, social, economic and legal theory as well as psychology and biology to construct a holistic picture of how we think, feel and experience, not only as individuals but as individuals-in-groups. Urwick and Brech (1949) argued what Follett was aiming for was nothing less than an overarching philosophy of groups and organizations. *Creative Experience* did not provide a complete philosophy, but it set Follett and others – notably Metcalf, Urwick and the Australian psychologist Elton MAYO – down the road towards one.

The interest in Follett's work coming from the field of management and administration studies may have taken Follett somewhat by surprise; she had never written on this area before. But if so, she took this in her stride. As Urwick and Brech (1949) comment, she did not so much change direction to study business and management as incorporate these fields into her already broad area of interest. Her collected lectures at the Bureau of Public Administration, the Rowntree conferences and the London School of Economics (Metcalf and Urwick 1941; Urwick 1949) show how she applied a wide range of theory from many disciplines to the problems of management. She spoke constantly of the need for personal growth and development as a key to management success; the gathering of experience and knowledge broadened the person and made the manager more effective and better able to maintain and coordinate relationships, which she saw as all-important to both business and social effectiveness.

This emphasis on relationships and coordination is at the heart of what may be her best-known later work, her lectures on managerial control. One of these lectures, 'The Process of Control', delivered at the London School of Economics and reprinted after her death by Urwick and Luther GULICK in their landmark *Papers on the Science of Administration* (1937), sums up her thinking on this subject.

The purpose of control, says Follett at the start of the lecture, is not to control people but to control *facts*; in other words, the real control that matters is the control of information. Second, effective control of this sort cannot stem from one source; to be effective, control has to be 'the correlation of many controls rather than a superimposed control' (Follett 1937: 161). She goes on:

The ramifications of modern industry are too wide-spread, its organization too complex, its problems too intricate for it to be possible for industry to be managed by commands from the top alone. This being so, we find that when central control is spoken of, that does not mean a point of radiation, but the gathering of many controls existing throughout the enterprise.

(Follett 1937: 161)

What we mean by 'control', then, is really 'coordination'. In a famous and often cited passage, she goes on to offer four fundamental principles of coordination (Follett 1937: 161):

1. Coordination as the reciprocal relating of all the factors in a situation.

2. Coordination by direct contact of the responsible people concerned.

3. Coordination in the early stages.

4. Coordination as a continuing process.

The first of these is the most complex, and it takes us back to the heart of Follett's philosophy as spelled out in *Creative Experience*. When two or more people work together, she says, they combine their thinking through a process she calls 'adjustment'. In a game of doubles tennis, for example, each player has to adjust their thinking to take account of the movements and actions of their partner. In a large business organization the heads of each department constantly 'adjust' their thinking to reflect the actions and activities of their colleagues and their departments; this adjustment is reflected in the way in which each head controls their own department. At the same time, of course, they are *also* adjusting their thinking to a whole host of other factors going on in the environment around them. All these different sets of thinking interpenetrate each other, and the activities of any one department reflect this combined thinking set which governs its coordination. Thus no department exists in isolation, nor is the organization merely a set of departments set side by side; rather, it is a unified whole bound together by this set of thinking relationships. This affects everything the organization does. Follett gives an example: merchandising (or marketing) 'is not merely a bringing together of designing, engineering, manufacturing and sales departments, it is these in their total relativity' (Follett 1937: 162).

It is not enough to be able to view and see all the factors in a situation; we have also to be able to understand how each factor affects every other factor in that situation, and then view the outcome as a single yet complex and dynamic situation. Here Follett is influenced by biological science, and she may be the first management writer to speak of an 'environmental complex' in which a business exists and both affects and is affected by its environment (though very similar ideas had been advocated twenty years earlier by Thorstein VEBLEN). The principle of reciprocal relationship, which can be roughly summed up as everything in a given environment both affects and is affected by everything else in that environment is a core principle of Follett's work; it was a major influence on the development of human relations theory by the likes of Mayo, ROETHLISBERGER and WHITEHEAD, and its influence can be seen in a variety of versions of interdependence theory in the 1950s through to the 1970s, and wherever holistic thinking about management is found.

The remaining three principles are less complex. Follett advocates that coordination should be handled directly by the responsible managers, not from unseen figures on high; where spans of control are insufficiently large, lateral coordination between heads of department is preferable to vertical coordination from the top down. Generally, however, it is preferable that coordination should be undertaken by managers who are in direct contact with the workers.

By coordination at the early stages Follett means that coordination should be built into a system from its inception. Policy formulation should be coordinated from the outset, as in this way the interplay of ideas, the reciprocal relationship described above, makes itself felt early on and both smoothes coordination and adds value to the thinking and planning processes. By contrast, in systems where policy is developed in isolation and different elements are brought in afterwards to coordinate the execution of that policy, relationships are rougher, and coordinated thinking has less of a chance to make an impact. Finally, Follett views coordination as a continuous process, one which must happen as a natural part of the management of the business organization. She advocates continuous coordination on the grounds that it leads both to easier problem solving and to the generation of knowledge which can improve working methods in the future. In a prefiguring of later work on strategy and planning, she also argues that continuous coordination creates what later became known as feedback loops, whereby plans and policies can be easily adjusted in the light of fresh information.

In all this it is clear that Follett rejects the mechanistic view of the organization, and opts instead for a social and biological one. This is most clear when she discusses the nature of control. She argues that 'organization *is* control' – organizations in effect have no other purpose – but goes on to state that the real nature of control is about coordinating the parts:

Biologists tell us that the organizing activity of the organism is the directing activity, that the organism gets its power of self-direction through being an organism, that is, through the functional relating of the parts.

On the physiological level, controls means co-ordination. I can't get up in the morning, I can't walk downstairs without that co-ordination of muscles which is control. The athlete has more of that co-ordination than I have and therefore has more control ...

This is just what we have found in business.
(Follett 1937: 166–7)

Control by attempting to force one element to perform an action alone, says Follett, is not control at all. In the reality of business life, even the most autocratic of board of directors does not have sole control; as soon as lower layers of management are added, responsibility is delegated and control is shared, and from that moment on coordination becomes a necessity.

The most important control of all, Follett concludes, is self-control. In a passage which is a direct appeal to greater democracy in industrial organizations, she argues that a form of collective control which coordinates the actions of all members of the organization by allowing them participation in the control process is the right way forward for industry:

If you accept my definition of control as a self-generating process, as the interweaving experience of all those who are performing a functional part of the activity under consideration, does not that constitute an imperative? Are we not every one of us bound to take some part consciously in this process? Today we are slaves to chaos in which we are living. To get our affairs in hand, to feel a grip on them, to become free, we must learn, and practice, I am sure, the methods of collective control. To this task we can all devote ourselves. At the same time that we are selling goods or making goods, or whatever we are doing, we can be working in harmony with this fundamental law of lie. We can be assured that by this method, control is in our power.
(Follett 1937: 169)

An important thinker who brought her formidable intellect to bear on many aspects of organizational life, Mary Parker Follett remains one of the seminal figures in management thinking in the twentieth century. Her work had a direct impact on the formation of the human relations school, and indirectly influences management thinking today. Her work can be criticized on the grounds that it is over-philosophical and lacks attention to key principles, but such criticisms are perhaps unfair; Follett never sought to provide managers with tools for their hand, but urged instead that they should alter their ways of thinking. Hers is a philosophical approach, and none the less valid for that. In the early twenty-first century, Follett's approach to the problems of coordination and control still provides food for thought for management practitioners.

BIBLIOGRAPHY

Follett, M.P. (1896) *The Speaker of the House of Representatives*, New York: Longmans Green.

——— (1918) *The New State–Group Organization: The Solution for Popular*

Government, New York: Longmans Green.

Follett, M.P. (1924) *Creative Experience*, New York: Longmans Green.

———— (1937) 'The Process of Control', in L. Gulick and L.F. Urwick (eds), *Papers on the Science of Administration*, New York: Institute of Public Administration, 159–69.

Graham, P. (ed.) *Mary Parker Follett: Prophet of Management*, Boston, MA: Harvard Business School Press.

Metcalf, H.C. and Urwick, L.F. (eds) (1941) *Dynamic Administration: The Collected Papers of Mary Parker Follett*, Bath: Management Publications Trust.

Urwick, L.F. (ed.) (1949) *Freedom and Coordination*, London: Management Publications Trust.

———— (1956) *The Golden Book of Management*, London: Newman Neame.

Urwick, L.F. and Brech, E.F.L. (1949) *The Making of Scientific Management*, vol. 1, *Management in British Industry*, London: Management Publications Trust; repr. Bristol: Thoemmes Press, 1994.

MLW

FORD, Edsel (1893–1943)

Edsel Ford was born in Detroit, Michigan on 6 November 1893, the only son of Henry FORD and his wife Clara. He died of stomach cancer at his home in Grosse Pointe, Michigan on 26 May 1943. He married Eleanor Clay in 1916; they had four children. He was educated at Detroit University School but did not attend university, and in 1912 joined Ford Motor Company. At his father's instruction, he apprenticed in a number of different departments of the company, learning the details of the business. This apprenticeship was short; when James COUZENS resigned from the board in 1915, Edsel Ford, then aged twenty-two, was promoted into his place as company secretary. In 1919 he became president of the company, and held this position until his death.

Edsel Ford was the temperamental opposite of his father. He appreciated the arts and design, becoming a notable collector and patronizing leading artists such as the Mexican muralist Diego Rivera; from a design perspective, he pressed repeatedly and without success for Ford's cars to become more 'stylish' and better able to compete with the products of General Motors. He opposed the latter's increasingly autocratic and heavy-handed management methods; his own views of labour relations were enlightened, and he did not oppose trade unions. However, Henry Ford continued to dominate both the company and his son, and Edsel Ford's views were seldom if ever allowed to prevail. Through the 1930s the two were on increasingly bad terms personally, with the autocratic Ford bullying and hectoring his son, who in turn became more and more withdrawn. Edsel Ford did have a few successes: in 1927, after a long struggle, he finally persuaded his father to drop the outmoded Model T and replace it with the more up-to-date Model A, and in 1940 he overcame Henry Ford's reluctance to convert part of Ford's production facilities to military aircraft manufacture.

In 1922 Ford acquired the Lincoln Motor Company, which became Edsel Ford's personal fief. Free of the interference of his father, he was able to put into practice his own views on labour management and design. Hiring in top designers, he helped Lincoln produce some of the most stylish and attractive cars yet built, including the famous Lincoln Continental, which appeared just before the Second World War. Although Edsel Ford's influence on the Ford Motor Company was minimal, many of his ideas were picked up after the war by his son and successor, Henry FORD II, who helped turn Ford's fortunes around.

BIBLIOGRAPHY

Nevins, A. and Hill, F.E. (1957) *Ford: Expansion and Challenge*, New York: Scribner.

—— (1962) *Ford: Decline and Rebirth*, New York: Scribner.

MLW

FORD, Henry (1863–1947)

Henry Ford was born on a farm near Dearborn, Michigan on 30 July 1863, one of eight children of William and Mary Ford. He died at his Detroit home, Fair Lane on 7 April 1947. He was educated in the local public school, where he learned mathematics and also a little reading and writing. Barely literate when he finished school in 1879, he was fascinated by machinery and determined to find work as a mechanic. At the age of sixteen he apprenticed at Flower Brothers Machine Shop in Detroit, and later at the Detroit Drydock Company; he also took a part-time job as a watch repairman. The three years he spent in Detroit gave Ford considerable practical experience in various aspects of engineering. He himself was particularly interested in watches and gears, and seems at one time to have considered going into watchmaking as a business.

Returning home in 1882, Ford first set up a small machine shop and carried out work for neighbouring farmers, and later took a job with Westinghouse as a district engineer, travelling and servicing steam engines. In 1888 he married Clara Bryant; they had one son, Edsel Bryant FORD, in 1893. Now determined to make a career in engineering, Ford moved his family back to Detroit that same year and he found a job with the Edison Illuminating Company; he was promoted rapidly, and by 1893 was chief engineer for the Chicago area.

By the 1890s invention fever was sweeping the United States. Inspired by the examples of Thomas EDISON and Alexander Graham BELL, whose work was already changing the nature of American life and culture, thousands of amateur engineers built workshops and tried to invent working examples of new devices such as aeroplanes and motor cars. Ford was one of these. What exactly directed his attention to cars is not known, but his early experience with watches and gears helped him solve one of the major problems: how to convert the motive power provided by a steam or internal combustion engine into drive through the wheels. His simple design for a transmission led to his development of a working automobile in 1896. The car, which he called a quadricycle, ran on bicycle wheels and weighed just 227 kilograms (500 pounds) in total. Ford promptly sold it to raise capital for further experiments, and continued to make and sell experimental prototypes in this fashion for some years. He later recalled a chance meeting with Thomas Edison at which the latter quizzed him about his designs and encouraged him to carry on; the meeting, Ford said, was a great inspiration to him. Later he and Edison became close friends, and they and Harvey FIRESTONE used to go on 'boy's own' camping expeditions into the Michigan wilderness; a rare form of relaxation for this driven man.

In 1899, with capital provided by a Detroit lumber dealer, William Murphy, Ford established the Detroit Automobile Company and resigned from Edison to become the new firm's superintendent in charge of production. This first attempt by Ford at producing motor cars on a commercial basis was a total failure, largely because Ford knew nothing about production and managed to make only a handful of cars. Undeterred, Ford and his backers tried again, setting up the Henry Ford Company in 1900. Again, few cars were actually built, but one of these proved to be a successful racing car. Ford became suddenly enthusiastic about motor racing and neglected his business, and accordingly was fired from the Henry Ford Company in 1902 (the company went on to become the Cadillac Motor Car Company and eventually became part of General Motors). Ford joined the former racing car driver Tom Cooper in a partnership which built the 999, a car which set a world land speed record and also made its driver Barney Oldfield a national hero. Among Cooper's associates was the young draughtsman Charles SORENSON, who was talent-spotted by Ford and rose to become one of his most trusted and effective managers.

His racing car triumphs under his belt, Ford seems to have come to his senses and gone back to his original plan, which was to build cheap, efficient cars which could be widely sold on an affordable basis. With fresh backing, this time from the Detroit coal dealer Alexander Malcolmson, and with more engineering talent in the person of Childe Harold Willis, Ford established the Ford Motor Company in Detroit in June 1903. Partners included John and Horace Dodge, who supplied Ford's original engines, and James COUZENS, a Malcolmson employee who acted as treasurer. Ford provided the engineering and production knowledge, and was appointed vice-president and general manager. The new company was almost immediately embroiled in a patent suit with the Association of Licensed Automobile Manufacturers (ALAM), backed by rivals such as Packard and Olds Motor Company, which claimed to have sole rights to manufacture gasoline-powered automobiles. Ford, who had earlier applied to join ALAM and been turned down, decided to fight the suit. He eventually won his case in 1911; in the meantime, typically, Ford continued on with his own plans as though the problem did not exist. These plans, for the production of small, cheap cars that could be sold to ordinary people, led to yet another problem, this time with his chief backer Malcolmson, who advocated the strategy adopted by most other car-makers, producing expensive luxury models for the high end of the market. Ford bought out Malcolmson in 1906 and went ahead with the development of the Model N, a cheap runabout that went on sale later that year for $600.

To cut costs, Ford began a policy of vertical integration by taking over some of his main suppliers, beginning with the John R. Keim steelworks in Buffalo, New York. With Keim, Ford acquired the services of yet another talented manager, William KNUDSEN. Together, Knudsen, Sorenson and Couzens formed one of the greatest management teams the world has yet seen; with Ford, they made the mass production of motor cars happen and propelled Ford into a position of utter dominance in the industry, far outstripping rivals such as the fledgling General Motors (GM) of William C. DURANT; for the next decade, only John North WILLYS at Overland ever seriously threatened Ford's dominance.

That dominance was founded on two factors: the Model T, launched in 1908, and the building of the assembly line production plant at Highland Park, Michigan, which began production in 1910. Designed by Ford and Wills, the Model T, or 'Tin Lizzie' as it was nicknamed by affectionate drivers, first went on sale for $825, but Ford constantly sought to drag the price down, trading volume of sales for unit profits; in the mid-1920s prices fell as low as $275 for a new Model T. With a twenty-two-horsepower engine and advanced chassis and steering design, the car was technologically advanced when first launched, yet its design was so simple that interchangeable parts could be easily mass produced and then assembled. Between 1908 and 1927, seventeen million Model Ts were sold, more than all other models of car put together at the time.

Designed by architect Albert Kahn and purpose-built for the production of the Model T, the Highland Park plant covered sixty-two acres. It featured the largest assembly line yet seen in the world, and had been carefully engineered to increase car production to speeds beyond anything yet attempted; instead of twelve to fourteen hours to assemble a finished car, the previous norm, Model Ts could now be assembled from stocks of finished parts in an hour and a half.

The opening of Highland Park sent a shock through the US business world. Visitors from other companies and even other countries flocked to see it; among those who learned from Ford's production methods was the Czech shoemaker Tomas Bat'a, who would later establish his own revolutionary approach to management in Europe. Ford won plaudits not only for his mechanical engineering but for his attention to detail and carefully engineered production system, which was based in large part on the methods of scientific management advocated by Frederick W. TAYLOR, but also owed much to earlier mass production systems such as that developed by Cyrus Hall MCCORMACK. In terms of worker relations, too, Ford was seen as a visionary. In 1914 he cut the working day to eight hours, believing this to be the optimum working day for worker efficiency, and also initiated the famous $5 daily wage, nearly double the going rate in the industry.

The period 1910–20 was Ford's heyday. He was feted as a hero in the United States, where his goal of bringing cheap motoring to the masses had brought about a transport revolution in society, in which even clerks and manual workers could afford a car. Ford had democratized transport, and changed the face of America in the process; the country's long love affair with the automobile had begun. Overseas he became an almost mythical figure. Strangely, Communist Russia was full of admiration for Ford – Lenin and Trotsky admired his methods, *Pravda* serialized his books and delegations of Soviet officials and factory managers came to Detroit to study 'Fordism' in action, and the philosophies of both Ford and Taylor were transplanted into Soviet industry. In Britain, on the other hand, attitudes were more ambivalent: by the 1920s Ford's public image and egotism were beginning to attract

more attention than his cars, and Aldous Huxley went on to satirize Ford in *Brave New World*, where the deity is known as 'Our Ford' rather than 'Our Lord'.

Cracks had already begun to appear during the First World War. Ford was a convinced pacifist, and in 1915 chartered a 'Peace Ship' to sail to Europe to try to resolve the war by negotiation; he also attempted to hand out pacifist literature with each car he sold. This led to a break with James Couzens, the talented administrator and salesman in charge of Ford's marketing effort, who left in 1915 to take up a career in politics. Knudsen was the next to go, resigning in 1921 over Ford's refusal to countenance a replacement for the ageing Model T; he joined Ford's rival General Motors, now being capably run by Pierre DU PONT and Alfred SLOAN, and played a key role in developing the Chevrolet, the low-priced competitor that ultimately drove the Model T out of the market. Sorenson and Edsel Ford, who had succeeded Couzens, were unable to make much headway against Ford's growing autocracy.

By 1920 the pace of innovation at Ford was slowing. Convinced that his original recipe for success was the correct one, Ford failed to see that times had moved on; indeed, he himself had been responsible for much of the change. The novelty of car travel was wearing off; now people wanted more features from their cars and, indeed, were developing different sets of needs and motivations for buying cars. GM was willing to cater to these different needs; Ford was not. His famous remark, 'a customer can have a car of any colour he wants, so long as it is black', may be apocryphal but is indicative of a mindset. When Chevrolet began cutting into Ford's market, Ford's only method of fighting back was to cut prices still further, which meant that Charlie Sorenson, now in sole charge of production, had to find new ways of cutting costs. The atmosphere in Ford factories changed, too. Wages were cut by nearly half; worker education and many other benefits were done away with; Ford's famous sociological department which had studied worker motivation was closed down; strict discipline was enforced which prevented workers from whistling or even talking during shifts.

In the mid-1920s Ford showed signs of change once more. Sorenson and Edsel Ford finally persuaded Ford to drop the now almost moribund Model T and bring out a new model, the Model A. Ford plants shut down production while the new car was quickly designed and marketed (400,000 advance orders were received before the first car was ever produced). The Model A was nothing like as revolutionary as the Model T, but it showed some response to consumer needs and was successful; and it helped keep Ford in business, though now lagging third in numbers of cars sold behind GM and Chrysler. The opening of the great River Rouge plant in 1927 to produce the Model A also had favourable results in terms of impact and profitability. Diversification began for the first time. The development of an aircraft industry was a limited success, although the Ford Trimotor was a very advanced and efficient design, but production ceased in the 1930s. The acquisition of Lincoln Motor Company was more successful; under the direct guidance of Edsel Ford, Lincoln became the maker of the USA's most luxurious cars.

The 1930s saw continued decline. Edsel Ford, bullied by his father and increasingly ill, had lost all influence. Even Sorenson could do little to reason with the old man. Ford's new confidante was Harry Bennett, a former prize-fighter who was connected to the Mafia in Chicago, and who now ran the Ford Service Department, a group of informers and thugs who enforced discipline among the work force with an iron hand. The workers, tried beyond any reasonable limits of loyalty, finally rebelled and tried to unionize; when Bennett's men beat up several union organizers, the workers struck in 1941 and compelled recognition of the United Auto Workers. Ford suffered a stroke in 1938, and from then on was both physically and mentally ill, paranoid

and, in the words of the normally loyal Sorenson, suffering from hallucinations. In 1940 Ford refused to participate in the government's aircraft manufacturing programme largely because of a paranoid delusion that President Franklin D. Roosevelt was out to destroy him (the fact that William Knudsen was in charge of the programme probably did not help to allay Ford's suspicions). Edsel Ford and Sorenson finally persuaded him to take part, and the Willow Run production plant was established near Ypsilanti, Michigan to make heavy bombers; even so, Ford would never go near the plant, convinced he would be assassinated by government spies. Harry Bennett was now virtually in control of both the company and Ford himself; Charlie Sorenson recalls the sight of Clara Ford in tears at the thought of what 'that monster' was doing to her husband.

Edsel Ford's death in 1943 brought about a crisis, as Ford insisted on resuming the presidency of the firm. Clara Ford and her widowed daughter-in-law now staged a rebellion of their own, threatening to sell their shares to outsiders unless the octogenarian leader stood down. He finally gave way; intervention at the top levels of government secured the release of Edsel's son, Henry FORD II, from military service and he returned home to take up the presidency. Despite no management training or background whatever, Ford proved adept at his job, and in the immediate postwar years assembled a team which included future senior Ford executives Ernest R. Breech, Lee IACOCCA and Robert McNAMARA, and began turning the beleaguered company around.

Ford has assumed an almost mythical status in the history of American business and in the national epic more generally. The two images, however, are sharply at variance. In US history, he is the man who democratized the automobile; he played a key role in the concept of 'freedom' in American society, in which freedom of mobility granted through the car plays a large part. He is a folk hero on a par with Edison or COLT. In business history, however, it has become fashionable to compare Ford unfavourably with his rivals at GM, notably Alfred Sloan. GM was progressive and innovative, Ford was conservative and unreceptive to change; GM was focused on the market, Ford was focused on production; GM was divisionalized and efficient, Ford was centralized and inefficient; and most of all, GM was managed by professionals with a separation of ownership and control, while Ford was managed by its family owners.

All of these theses are challengeable, of course, especially the last. GM initially had little separation of ownership and control, especially under Durant and du Pont, while Ford, in the early stages at least, had a number of brilliant managers on his senior staff. The problem, as Nevins and Hill (1957) point out in the second of their highly detailed studies of Ford, is that most comparisons are valid depending when they are made. The Ford of 1934 is by no means the same as the Ford of 1914. That Ford himself went on too long is undeniable; equally, it is hard to deny his successes in his early years, or his impact on management both in the car industry and more generally.

Nevins and Hill describe Ford's basic managerial insight as being based on five related facts:

> that the American people needed cars in millions; that a single durable inexpensive model could meet that demand; that when new technological elements were woven together to create mass production, they could furnish millions of cheap vehicles; that price reduction meant market expansion; and that high wages meant high buying power. This was as obvious, when demonstrated, as Columbus's art of standing an egg on its end. Until then it was so far from clear that Ford had to battle his principal partner and the current manufacturing trend to prove it. A special kind of genius lies in seeing what everybody admits

to be obvious – after the exceptional mind thinks of it; and Ford had that genius. It changed the world.
> (Nevins and Hill 1957: 614)

He was also a brilliant engineer, one who was probably at his happiest when designing. Dearborn Engineering, the corporate research and development group centred around Ford himself was, in the years before 1920 at least, was a hive of activity and ideas. These ideas concerned process as well as product. Highland Park was every bit as revolutionary as the car it created; River Rouge, though more control-oriented, still contained its share of technological and engineering wizardry; Willow Run, though plagued with initial problems, later achieved the unheard of feat of producing one four-engined B-24 bomber every hour. To the end of his days, Ford possessed an almost intuitive understanding of production engineering and process flows. Virtually every mass production system ever developed in the world since owes at least something to Ford and his ideas.

That Ford himself gave much thought to both what he was doing and his purpose in doing it is clear from his writings. Although these must be used with care, as their primary purpose was often self-aggrandisement, there are frequent passages where he muses to his co-author Samuel Crowther on his purpose and goals. The following, from *Moving Forward* (1931) is interesting on a number of levels:

> Through all the years that I have been in business I have never yet found our business bad as a result of any outside force. It has always been due to some defect in our own company, and whenever we located and repaired that defect our business became good again – regardless of what anyone else might be doing. And it will always be found that this country has nationally bad business when business men are drifting, and that business is good when men take hold of

their own affairs, put leadership into them, and push forward in spite of obstacles. Only disaster can result when the fundamental principles of business are disregarded and what looks like the easiest way is taken. These fundamentals, as I see them, are:

(1) To make an ever-increasingly large quantity of goods of the best possible quality, to make them in the best and most economical fashion, and to force them out onto the market.

(2) To strive always for higher quality and lower prices as well as lower costs.

(3) To raise wages gradually but continuously – and never to cut them.

(4) To get the goods to the consumer in the most economical manner so that the benefits of low-cost production may reach him.

These fundamentals are all summed up in the single word 'service' ... The service starts with discovering what people need and then supplying that need according to the principles that have just been given.
(Ford and Crowther 1931: 2–3).

As a statement of philosophy, this shows both the strengths and weaknesses of Henry Ford's approach to management. On the one hand there is the attention to quality, to the product and, despite his critics, to the needs of the market. On the other hand, there is the ignoring of competition and the centring of responsibility on the manager himself. Part Frederick Winslow Taylor, part Friedrich Wilhelm Nietschze, here is a portrait of the executive as superman, capable of solving all problems through authority and control. It is a philosophy which, like the man himself, is full of contrary aspects and is not capable of being sustained for long.

Certainly at the time these words were written, Ford had abandoned large parts of this philosophy in practice. He became increasingly autocratic in manner, driving away most members of his brilliant management team and losing access to the talent pool that had made the early company successful. His bullying and humiliation of his son scandalized all around him; the normally loyal Sorenson is highly critical of Ford on this point and calls Ford's handling of his son his greatest failure. His paranoia and suspicion of all around him changed his relationship with his work force from one of happy cooperation to one of fear. There are two faces to Fordism, just as there were two faces to Ford himself. Sorenson commented that Ford feared and shunned ostentation, and never seemed at home in the luxurious mansion he had built for himself at Fair Lane, yet that paradoxically he craved the limelight and did all he could to stimulate the growth of the Ford myth. By 1920, if not earlier, he had begun to believe his own mythologizing. Like Napoleon, he went on too long.

BIBLIOGRAPHY
Burlinghame, R. (1949) *Backgrounds of Power: The Human Story of Mass Production*, New York: Charles Scribner's Sons.
Ford, H. (1929) *My Philosophy of Industry*, London: Harrap.
Ford, H. and Crowther, S. (1922) *My Life and Work*, New York: Doubleday.
Ford, H. and Crowther, S. (1926) *Today and Tomorrow*, New York: Garden City.
—— (1930) *My Friend Mr Edison*, London: Ernest Benn.
—— (1931) *Moving Forward*, New York: Garden City.
Nevins, A.N. and Hill, F.E. (1954) *Ford: The Times, the Man, the Company*, New York: Charles Scribner's Sons.
—— (1957) *Ford: Expansion and Challenge, 1915–1933*, New York: Charles Scribner's Sons.
—— (1962) *Ford: Decline and Rebirth*, New York: Charles Scribner's Sons.
Sorenson, C. and Williamson, S.T. (1957)

Forty Years with Ford, London: Jonathan Cape.

Sward, K. (1948) *The Legend of Henry Ford*, New York: Rinehart.

MLW

FORD, Henry, II (1917–87)

Henry Ford II was born on 4 September 1917 in Detroit, Michigan, the son of Edsel FORD and his wife, Eleanor Clay, and the grandson of Henry FORD. He died in Detroit of legionnaire's disease on 29 September 1987. He married three times: to Anne McDonnell in 1940, to Maria Austin in 1965 and to Kathleen Duross in 1980; there were three children from the first marriage. After schooling, he attended Yale University but did not take a degree. He joined the US Navy in 1941 and served with the rank of ensign, though did not go overseas. In 1943, following the death of his father, Ford received his discharge from Secretary of the Navy Frank Knox to enable him to return to Detroit and assist his ageing grandfather in the management of Ford Motor Company, which was playing a critical role in the war effort. Ford became a vice-president in 1943, and president of the company in 1949.

Ford took over the company at a time when labour relations were poor, productivity was low and the company was losing $9 million a month. He shook up Ford's moribund management team, dismissing many of the older men who had served under his grandfather, promoting new talent such as Lee IACOCCA and hiring in outsiders such as Ernest R. Breech from General Motors, and also Charles Thornton and Robert McNAMARA. He overhauled Ford's design and marketing programme, encouraging his executives to become market-oriented; the company was not in the business of selling cars, he said, but in the business of selling 'personal mobility'. Not all the new designs were successful – the Edsel, in particular, was an over-engineered and costly failure – but the company was able to compete successfully against General Motors and the Japanese auto-makers through the 1950s and 1960s.

Perhaps Ford's most important management initiative was to encourage the company to become more international. Before 1945, Ford presence outside the United States had been limited to Britain and one or two other countries; Henry Ford II gave the company a global presence and re-established its worldwide brand identity. He looked abroad for alliances and investments; in the 1970s he came close to merging Ford with Giovanni Agnelli's Fiat, and later in the decade he bought a stake in the Japanese car-maker Mazda. This international presence helped saved the company when the domestic car market collapsed in the 1970s.

Ford began withdrawing from active management in the late 1970s. His later years were unhappy; two marriages had failed and he suffered from problems with alcohol. An autocrat by nature, he quarrelled with Iacocca and others, who then departed to work for his competitors. Nonetheless, he had achieved what many had believed to be impossible: with virtually no management experience or training, he had rescued the failing Ford Motor Company from almost certain bankruptcy and had restored it to a position as one of the top three car-makers in the United States. How much this achievement was due to Ford himself and how much depended on talented juniors such as Iacocca and McNamara is difficult to say; but team-building is generally agreed to be an important aspect of management, and in this respect, in his early years at least, Ford was highly successful.

BIBLIOGRAPHY
Hayes, W. (1990) *Henry: A Life of Henry Ford II*, New York: Grove Weidenfeld.

MLW

FORRESTER, Jay Wright (1918–)

Jay Wright Forrester was born in Arnold, Nebraska on 14 July 1918 and spent his early life on his family's cattle ranch. He studied electrical engineering at the University of Nebraska, and became a research assistant at the Massachusetts Institute of Technology (MIT) in 1939, where he began his career as an electrical engineer working on servo mechanisms for radar and weapons. He was awarded his masters degree from MIT in 1945, and shortly after was made director of MIT's digital computer laboratory, where from 1946 to1951 he was responsible for the design and construction of one of the first high-speed digital computers. He rapidly became one of the nation's leading engineers in the design and applications of computers. He was made head of the digital computer division at MIT's Lincoln Laboratory in 1952, where he developed his patent for magnetic core memory. Believing that computers would have significant benefits in a number of applications, he began to use his computing expertise to address the problems of corporate industry.

Forrester was made professor of management of the Sloan School at MIT in 1956, and there spent the next thirty-three years of his career exploring the dynamic structures of social systems. Beginning in 1957 he developed methods of industrial dynamics as a way to understand and design corporate policy. His engineering expertise led him to identify the concept of feedback in industrial systems and to study their subsequent dynamic behaviour. While working with General Electric, he discovered that managers' interventions in inventory control and staffing levels were producing counter-intuitive effects, due precisely to the combination of feedback loops in operation. He used his experience with modelling systems and building simulations to develop an approach to managing the behaviour of social systems. Forrester proposed that 'feedback concepts can provide a sound theoretical foundation and integrating framework for diverse observations on the behaviour of social systems' (Forrester 1961).

Forrester brought together ideas from control engineering (including concepts of feedback and system self-regulation) with cybernetics (the nature of information and its role in control systems) and organizational theory (the structure of human organizations and the mechanisms of human decision making) to build the field of system dynamics. He used these concepts to develop techniques for representing and simulating complex, non-linear, multi-loop feedback systems. This work found a broad range of real-world applications. In 1961 he published *Industrial Dynamics*, in which he put forward his new approach to systems analysis which later became known as system dynamics. This became immediately controversial, receiving both enthusiastic praise and vicious condemnation. The three main features of the system dynamics approach are (1) feedback loops operating in the system; (2) computer simulation that could map out the changing behaviour of the interaction of multiple feedbacks; and (3) an engagement with people's mental models. Forrester held that the most important information about social systems is people's assumptions about what causes what. This was an unusual contribution for a systems engineer, and the emphasis he placed on mental models undoubtedly contributed to the wide uptake of his approach to dealing with systems.

In 1968 Forrester extended the approach with colleagues to study the growth and stagnation of urban areas, producing his book *Urban Dynamics* (1969), in which he demonstrates how different parts of the system become dominant at different times and, again, the counter-intuitive behaviour of social systems. His subsequent major books expanded on the scope of system dynamics from the analysis of an industrial firm to an unlimited field of application, including specifically the entire world. He called for the development of a new profession, that of social dynamics, with structures of training and theory, experiments and principles. He used his vantage point to highlight the need for the exploration of alternative political and economic rationales that would be compatible with a finite world. He asserted that only by discovering how the ethical, political, physical, technical, economic and social forces of society interact with one another can we understand the alternative patterns of future development. This thinking was a clear forerunner to the more recent work on sustainable development. It was his hope that system dynamics could be the unifying framework and vehicle for interdisciplinary communication in finding the alternatives to growth: 'Not only is system dynamics capable of accepting the descriptive knowledge from diverse fields but it also shows how present policies lead to future consequences' (Forrester 1975). His concern was to find a path for both industrial and underdeveloped nations through the transition from growth to 'viable equilibrium'.

Forrester was a member of the Club of Rome, a private group of members meeting to find ways to better understand the changes occurring in the world, now understood as the *global problematique*. The renowned *Limits to Growth* study grew out of the club's planned programme to explore the alternatives to the *problematique* driven by manifestations of stress in the world system such as excessive population, rising pollution and increasing inequality in standards of living. This study was based on Forrester's system dynamics approach. The publication of this work in *World Dynamics* (1971) received much attention in the press, principally attracting support from environmentalists who shared similar concerns, and from engineers who understood the methods and approach. The work made explicit Forrester's belief that forces within the world system must and will rise far enough to suppress the power of growth. It also attracted significant criticism from economists, who believed variously that the model was incomplete and were concerned about the costs and feasibility of halting economic growth, although Forrester notes that the debate shifted soon after to what strategy should be used to slow economic growth rather than whether it should be slowed.

His model of the world as a system paid particular attention to the interrelationships between parts of the system in an attempt to avoid undesirable and unintended consequences of our actions. It was a dynamic model of population, capital investment, geographical space, natural resources, pollution and food production. Forrester emphasized that as with other models, important variables had to be omitted, that aggregation lost distinctions between developed and underdeveloped countries, and that the concepts were rooted in the attitudes and concerns of the time. However, he defended the use of models (even though they are poor representations) with reference to the fact that humans act at all times on the models and mental images they have formed personally. In striving to ensure that the most acceptable model was also the best model, he urged that the best existing model should be identified at each point in time, that it should be used in preference to traditional models, and that there should be continual effort to improve available world models. This call was answered by a growing field of researchers working in the field of global modelling.

Forrester noted that 'all systems seem to have sensitive influence points through which the behaviour of the system can be improved ... however these influence points are usually not in the locations where most people expect them to be' (Forrester 1975), and understood that simple direct actions would not result in a desired outcome, whereas acting upon feedback loops may be more effective. His thinking was an early foreshadow of contemporary complexity theory and its understanding of 'control parameters'.

Forrester's significant contribution to systems thinking and to management practice has been acknowledged with many awards and honours. In 1968 he received the Inventor of the Year Award from George Washington University, and in 1969 the Valdmer Poulsen Gold Medal from the Danish Academy of Technical Sciences; in 1972 the IEEE awarded him both the medal of honour and the Systems, Man and Cybernetics Society Award for outstanding accomplishment. He was inducted into the US National Inventors Hall of Fame in 1979. Later in his career, having retired from the Sloan School in 1989, Forrester was able to pursue his long-time interest in the application of system dynamics to learning, and worked to create learning materials to help teachers and students from kindergarten age upwards to adopt 'learner-directed learning' across the curriculum.

Essentially a man of action and practicality, Forrester was anti-utopian in his approach to the future. He was prepared to work with pragmatic, imperfect tools in order to get a job done. He was also of the conviction, however, that the traditions of civilization could be altered to become compatible with global equilibrium. His work in combining computer simulation with feedback thinking was a major advance in the field, and had a wide application from adverting strategy to managing the growth of start-up companies and the US national economy. His work underpins much of the current work done on modelling social systems.

BIBLIOGRAPHY

Forrester, J.W. (1961) *Industrial Dynamics*, Portland, OR: Productivity Press, 215–19.
——— (1969) *Urban Dynamics*, Portland, OR: Productivity Press.
——— (1973) *World Dynamics*, 2nd edn, Cambridge, MA: Wright-Allen Press.
——— (1975) *Collected Papers of Jay W Forrester*, Cambridge, MA: Wright-Allen Press.
Lane, D. (1998) 'Forrester, Jay Wright', in M. Warner (ed.), *IEBM Handbook of Management Thinking*, London: International Thomson Business Press, 215–19.
Legasto, A.A., Forrrester, J.W. and Lyneis, J.M. (eds) (1980) *System Dynamics*, Amsterdam: North Holland.
Meadows, D.H. and Robinson, J.M. (1985) *The Electronic Oracle*, New York: John Wiley and Sons.

AJ

FRIEDMAN, Milton (1912–)

Milton Friedman was born in Brooklyn, New York on 31 July 1912. He was the son of Jeno Saul Friedman and Sarah Ethel Friedman, Jewish immigrants from the western Ukraine. In 1925 the family moved to Rahway, New Jersey, not far from New Brunswick, the site of what was then Princeton College. In 1928 Milton Friedman began to attend Rutgers, obtaining his BA in economics in 1932. At Rutgers, he was a pupil of Arthur Burns, the future Chairman of the Federal Reserve and an influence in shaping Friedman's own economic views.

Friedman entered the University of Chicago, from which he obtained his MA in 1933. After writing a master's thesis on railway stock prices, he soon began to publish pieces in the *Quarterly Journal of Economics* and other journals. Between his masters degree and doctorate he worked in Washington as an economist, where he contributed to a 1939 government study of consumer expenditures in the United States. By 1941 he was working as a tax economist with the United States Treasury. Friedman began his Ph.D. work at Columbia University in 1943, graduating in 1946 after completing a dissertation on income from independent professional practice. By 1946 Friedman was teaching economics at the University of Chicago, where he remained until 1980.

At Chicago, Friedman established a friendship with the noted Austrian economist

Friedrich von Hayek. More than anyone else, Hayek's free market views shaped Friedman's own. By the end of the 1950s, Friedman had become the best known member of an emergent Chicago School of economics, which challenged the Keynesian orthodoxy dominant in most university faculties. During the 1950s Friedman turned the University of Chicago into a renowned bastion of market-oriented thinking. Not all of the Chicago faculty, however, were as libertarian in their thinking as Friedman or Hayek: Paul Douglas was a Democrat, Oskar Lange a market-oriented socialist.

The Nixon administration very much disappointed Friedman. He considered Nixon to be a most intelligent man in his grasp of economics, but one too willing to compromise his principles. The wage and price controls which Nixon imposed to protect the US dollar in August 1971 appalled him. Ronald Reagan, whom Friedman served as a policy adviser, impressed him far more as one who stuck to his market principles, deregulating prices of oil and gas.

By the middle of the 1970s, events were beginning to discredit the economics of John Maynard Keynes. In the aftermath of the Yom Kippur War of 1973, the oil-producing countries began to raise prices. The traditional Keynesian remedies no longer seemed to be working. According to Keynesian logic, governments should not have to face inflation and unemployment at the same time. Attempts by both the Nixon administration and the British government of Edward Heath to control inflation via a price and incomes policy were failing. In Chile, the policies of a Marxist government brought the country to the point of economic disaster, leading to a rightist military coup. By 1975 New York City hovered on the verge of bankruptcy, for which many blamed its social welfare policies.

According to Yergin and Stanislaw (1999), Friedman offered alternative policies to those of Keynesianism, and it seemed that many were now willing to consider them. His credibility was further enhanced when his mentor Hayek was a joint winner of the Nobel Prize for Economics in 1974. By 1975 Margaret Thatcher was leader of the British Conservative party, which she transformed according to monetarist principles, employing Friedman as her adviser. In Chile, the regime of General Augusto Pinochet turned to some of Friedman's followers from the University of Chicago to restructure the Chilean economy on free market lines.

Friedman's ideas received wide exposure in a television mini-series aired in 1976 entitled *Free to Choose*, which was turned into Friedman's most popular book (Friedman and Friedman 1980). *Free to Choose* signalled that free market economics had rapidly entered the mainstream and was becoming the new economic orthodoxy. It taught Friedman's monetarist and libertarian economics in a persuasive popular form, using everyday examples. The book was an instant success.

In *Free to Choose*, Friedman, a practical libertarian, nonetheless expressed his ideal concept of the role of government. Citing Adam SMITH, he insisted that government had four legitimate functions:

1. Protecting life and property from violence, including national defence.
2. Setting forth laws and administering justice through the court system.
3. Providing for public works such as transportation and communication.
4. In a limited manner, taking care of those not able or responsible enough to care for themselves.

Friedman traced American success to the minimal government devised by Jefferson and the free market economics of Smith. The source of many problems, he argued, was the attempt to move from equality of opportunity to equality of outcome.

Friedman looked upon the history of the nineteenth century in a very positive light. In

Britain between 1846 and 1897, living standards improved dramatically for all classes while the level of government spending fell from 25 per cent to 10 per cent of GDP. After the turn of the century, however, many were seduced into embracing the notion that big government, in the right hands, would make life much better. Nineteenth-century America, for Friedman, was not a gilded age of 'robber barons' but a time of golden opportunity in which farmers and workers, as well as immigrants, steadily improved their lot. Government spending did not exceed 12 per cent of national income before 1929, and only 3 per cent of this was federal spending. Private charities such as the Salvation Army flourished. Internationally, the century from 1815 to 1914 was the most peaceful and prosperous in human history, said Friedman, largely due to free trade and free world markets, which also provided a counter to domestic monopolies.

As an individualist, Friedman insisted that market and fairness were often mutually exclusive: 'Life is not fair. It is tempting to believe that government can rectify what nature has spurned. But it is also important to recognize how much we benefit from the very unfairness we deplore' (Friedman and Friedman 1980: 137). Should government spend billions to give every one boxing lessons to make them the equal of Muhammad Ali? What if at the end of an evening in a casino the winners had to pay the losers? If individuals bore the consequences, they should make the decisions. One could not rely upon the price mechanism without accepting unequal income as the result: 'If what a person gets does not depend on the price he receives ... what incentive does he have to seek out information on prices or to act on the basis of that information?' (Friedman and Friedman 1980: 23). Why work hard, accumulate capital, or seek the best bargain if the result was all the same in the end? The system of personal risk and responsibility created Ford and Standard Oil. Friedman was certainly not against philanthropy, so long as it was voluntary, but

utterly rejected any efforts to equalize outcome. He believed that academics and bureaucrats who preached egalitarianism were living a double standard, as they were highly paid.

As far as Friedman was concerned, collectivist and redistributionist economics was morally corrupting as well. When a society such as Britain taxed earned income at over 80 per cent in the top bracket and unearned income at 98 per cent, this encouraged tax evasion, which in turn undermined lack of respect for law, and resulted in higher crime and fraud everywhere. In contrast, the more free the market, the more equality would result.

Friedman also stirred controversy with his views on business ethics. He rejected not only government intervention, but also the concept that business had social responsibilities that were not dictated by the market. In an article written for the *New York Times Magazine* of 13 September 1970 he criticized executives who felt they had a social duty to provide jobs, end discrimination or avoid pollution. To Friedman, this concept was 'pure and unadulterated socialism' disguised as free enterprise (Friedman 1970).

Friedman insisted that only individuals had responsibilities, not companies. An executive was responsible to his directors and shareholders. Spending money on anti-pollution equipment or training the hardcore unemployed would mean higher prices to consumers, lower dividends for shareholders and lower wages for employees, which Friedman saw as an onerous form of taxation without representation. In effect, it reduced the executive to the role of public employee. Adam Smith had condemned the notion of 'trading for the public good' and so did Friedman, who felt that morally this would bolster the view that profits were immoral:

But the doctrine of 'social responsibility' taken seriously would extend the scope of the political mechanism to every human activity. It does not differ in philosophy from the most explicitly collectivist doctrine. It differs only by professing to believe that collectivist ends can be attained without collectivist means. That is why, in my book 'Capitalism and Freedom,' I have called it a 'fundamentally subversive doctrine' in a free society, and have said that in such a society, 'there is one and only one social responsibility of business – to use its resources and engage in activities designed to increase its profits so long as it stays within the rules of the game, which is to say, engages in open and free competition without deception or fraud.

(Friedman 1970)

During the 1980s Friedman's policies appeared to be meeting with success, further enhancing his reputation. The Thatcher government effected a social revolution in Britain, curbing both inflation and the power of the militant unions by controlling the money supply and deregulating markets. Despite the harshness of its regime, Chile slowly began to move back to economic prosperity. In the United States, the monetarist policies of the Federal Reserve under Paul Volcker and Alan Greenspan helped end inflation and pave the way for a major economic boom.

Friedman, still articulate and writing, lives near San Francisco. According to an interview with the American C-Span network in September 2000, he remains the chief free market economist in the world. He declares that he is not a conservative, but 'a small-l libertarian' who supports the Republicans rather than the Libertarian Party as the more appropriate vehicle for his views. His libertarianism is tempered, however, by a strong sense of the practical. In his ideal state, the role of government would be sharply pruned back from taking 40 per cent of Americans' earnings to a mere 10 per cent. He would fully privatize social security, allowing people to decide what fraction of their income they would devote to their own retirement. Friedman would provide a basic safety of food and shelter for the very poor through a negative income tax. A gold standard is not realistic, he says, when the state controls such a large part of the economy. Any government surplus would be used to reduce taxes.

While he admired the libertarian Austrian economists, he considered Friedman Hayek's mentor Ludwig von Mises a bit too doctrinaire for his liking. Though he regarded Mises, as he did Ayn RAND, as a remarkable free market thinker, he considered him and many other libertarians to be too 'intolerant'. Friedman felt and still feels that free market thinkers needed to be learners, not rigid disciples of a frozen creed. He admires those such as Federal Reserve Chairman Alan Greenspan, a former disciple of Ayn Rand, whom he considers to be the most outstanding Federal Reserve Chairman in the bank's history.

BIBLIOGRAPHY
'Friedman, Milton' (1969) in C. Moritz (ed.), *Current Biography*, New York: H.W. Wilson Company, 151–4.
Friedman, Milton (1957) *A Theory of the Consumptive Function*, Princeton, NJ: Princeton University Press.
—— (1962) *Capitalism and Freedom*, Chicago: University of Chicago Press.
—— (1970) 'The Social Responsibility of Business Is to Increase Its Profits', *The New York Times Magazine*, 13 September; text in Free University of Berlin, 'Warum Neoliberalismus?' (Why Neoliberalism?), http://userpage.fu-berlin.de/~comtess/neolib/corp-resp.html, 17 May 2001.
—— (2000) 'In Depth', *C-SPAN2 Booknotes*, televised interview aired on Sunday 3 September.
Friedman, M. and Friedman, R. (1980) *Free to Choose: A Personal Statement*, New York: Harcourt, Brace, Jovanovich.
Yergin, D. and Stanislaw, J. (1999) *The*

*Commanding Heights: The Battle
between Government and the
Marketplace that is Remaking the*
Modern World, New York: Simon and
Schuster.

DCL

G

GALBRAITH, John Kenneth (1908–)

John Kenneth Galbraith was born in the town of Iona Station, Ontario on 15 October 1908, the son of a farmer who had also been a teacher and worked as an insurance salesman. Originally intending to be a farmer and husbandman, Galbraith entered the Ontario Agricultural College in Guelph, Ontario in 1930, just as the Great Depression descended upon Canada. Canadians suffered severely as their country was highly dependent on exports. Galbraith was drawn to the study of economics by the realization that he could learn to be the best farmer in the world, but it would avail him nothing if he could not sell his crops or his hogs (Galbraith 1994). In 1934 Galbraith was awarded a scholarship in agricultural economy to attend the University of California at Berkeley. He graduated in 1937, and was teaching at Berkeley when he was offered a position at Harvard University. The salary was substantially more than he was earning at Berkeley, and he accepted.

In his study of economics Galbraith had read *The Wealth of Nations* by Adam Smith, whom he admired, and was taught, as was every other student of economics, from the *Principles of Economics* (1890) of Alfred Marshall. In the 1930s and 1940s Galbraith broadly accepted the standard classical model of market competition in which all firms were subject to market forces regardless of their size, derived from Smith and Marshall.

Another economist who profoundly affected Galbraith's thought was John Maynard Keynes, whose *General Theory of Employment, Interest and Money* (1936) helped Galbraith understand the Great Depression of the 1930s. He became a Keynesian and New Dealer. In 1937 Galbraith went to study at Cambridge University, hoping to learn from Keynes, but was unable to do so as his mentor had suffered a heart attack. Later, during the Second World War, Keynes paid Galbraith a surprise visit, but the two men did not become close.

During the war Galbraith, now a US citizen, worked with the National Defense Advisory Commission and then became deputy administrator for the Office of Price Administration. After the war, in 1946 he served as director of the Strategic Bombing Survey and the Office of Economic Security. He had also served as editor of *Fortune* magazine from 1943 to 1948. In 1949 he resumed teaching at Harvard as a full professor of economics. He was already well known as a writer. In his earliest works, *Modern Competition and Business Policy* (1938), *A Theory of Price Control* (1952) and *American Capitalism* (1952), he was already questioning Marshall's textbook models of free competition. In *American Capitalism*, he contended that big corporations could be balanced by other big corporations and above all by Big Labour. In *The Great Crash: 1929* (1955), Galbraith attributed the disaster of the Wall Street Crash of 1929 to reckless speculation.

Galbraith's visit to India in 1955 also affected his thinking. Working as an adviser to the Indian Statistical Institute, he developed a strong love and affinity for the peoples of India and their cultures. Returning to Harvard, Galbraith concluded that the economics he was teaching needed also to be adapted for students from the developing world. The contrast between the poverty of India and the affluence of 1950s America helped inspire one of Galbraith's most controversial books. In *The Affluent Society* (1958), he sought to shift the economic debate from issues of poverty to those relating to a country in which a majority of the population were middle-class consumers and in which the poor were a minority. In India the relationship between increased production and happiness was never in doubt, but in the United States that relationship could be questioned. Galbraith was increasingly critical of a society in which gross national product was being treated as an end in itself. Billions of dollars were now being spent upon wants and luxuries, encouraged by advertising, in the private sector, while important public concerns such as education, welfare, urban renewal and transportation were starved for funds. Galbraith described the discrepancy between private consumption and public expenditure as the 'social balance'. He was also one of the first American writers to express concern over what economic growth might do to the environment. *The Affluent Society* was not well received by a generation that had endured the Great Depression, enjoyed the stability of suburbia and did not mind having secure jobs. Nonetheless, the book helped focus attention on the persistence of poverty in urban ghettos, the Deep South and West Virginia, particularly after the Democratic Party came to power in 1961.

Galbraith had been a personal friend of Senator John F. Kennedy, who sometimes phoned him for advice. When Kennedy became president, he appointed Galbraith ambassador to India at the latter's request.

Galbraith served in India from 1961 to 1963, returning to Harvard after Kennedy's death. The new administration of Lyndon B. Johnson sought to address Galbraith's concerns over poverty, but Galbraith himself became further disillusioned by the Vietnam War. During this period he completed what is probably his most important book, *The New Industrial State* (1967).

Building upon *American Capitalism*, *The New Industrial State* called for a reconsideration of traditional theories of market competition. In an age of giant corporations and economic concentration, the traditional formulas of supply and demand did not apply as they once did. True, there were still hundreds of thousands of small entrepreneurs whose prices, wages and profits fluctuated according to the laws of supply and demand as Adam Smith and Alfred Marshall taught that they had. Companies like General Motors, American Telephone and Telegraph, IBM or General Electric, on the other hand, operated by a different set of rules. One had to qualify the notion of free enterprise when a thousand corporations accounted for half of all American goods and services. Instead of being subject to market forces, the big corporations were powerful enough to dictate them. They could organize preferential markets through defence contracts, collude to fix prices and create their own demand through advertising. Suppose Ford or Chrysler wanted to market a new car: Galbraith argued that they would do so knowing what the price would be in five years, what the demand would be and what the costs would be. This ability to plan meant the elimination of uncertainty and the supercession of the market; corporations control the market, not the consumer. The corporations are run by managers, who create and occupy the technostructure which controls planning; the managers do not directly reap profits, which go instead to distant shareholders. Some of the arguments in *The New Industrial State* had to some extent been heard before, notably in BURNHAM's *The Managerial*

Revolution in the 1940s, and concerns about vertical integration and excessive control had been voiced by Lewis HANEY in the 1920s. Galbraith, however, pulls these various strands of thought together in a powerful critique of corporate culture.

Further books such as *Economics and the Public Purpose* (1973), *Money* (1975) and *The Age of Uncertainty* (1977) reinforced Galbraith's reputation as the major economist of the American left and the chief academic opponent of Milton FRIEDMAN. The intellectual tide, however, was beginning to run strongly in Friedman's direction by the mid-1970s as the Keynesian remedies preached by Galbraith seemed unable to distribute shares of what seemed to be a shrinking pie. In spite of the neoclassical revival, Galbraith remained a Keynesian throughout the 1980s and 1990s. In an interview in 1994 he reiterated his belief that economies did not automatically operate on their own but needed some governmental direction (Galbraith 1994). In hard times, government should stimulate demand, and should restrain it during boom times. Underneath the new vogue of conservatism, Galbraith insisted that most American presidents, including Ronald Reagan, were still Keynesians even if they would not admit it.

In the 1990s Galbraith was still proud to call himself a 'liberal' at a time when even Democratic candidates shunned the label (in the United States the term 'liberal' connotes not a free market individualist as it sometimes does in Britain but rather a mildly collectivist position akin to that of New Labour or the Liberal Democrats). For Galbraith, the term connoted someone who supported the market where it worked and called for government action where it was needed, without being bound by any fixed ideology. When asked in 1994 what contribution he most wished to be remembered for, Galbraith replied that it would be his theory on how the corporate economy often operated in defiance of the laws of the market.

BIBLIOGRAPHY

Galbraith, John Kenneth (1938) *Modern Competition and Business Policy*, Cambridge, MA: Harvard University Press.

—— (1952) *A Theory of Price Control*, Cambridge, MA: Harvard University Press.

—— (1952) *American Capitalism*, Boston: Houghton Mifflin.

—— (1955) *The Great Crash: 1929*, Boston: Houghton Mifflin.

—— (1958) *The Affluent Society*, Boston: Houghton Mifflin.

—— (1967) *The New Industrial State*, Boston: Houghton Mifflin.

—— (1973) *Economics and the Public Purpose*, Boston: Houghton Mifflin.

—— (1975) *Money*, Boston: Houghton Mifflin.

—— (1977) *The Age of Uncertainty*, Boston: Houghton Mifflin.

—— (1981) *A Life in Our Times: Memoirs*, Boston: Houghton Mifflin.

—— (1992) *The Culture of Contentment*, Boston: Houghton Mifflin.

—— (1994) interview with Brian Lamb, C-Span, Booknotes, 13 November 1994, http://www.booknotes.org/transcripts/10076.htm, 13 December 2000.

Hession, C.H. (1972) *John Kenneth Galbraith and His Critics*, New York: W.W. Norton and Co.

Lamson, P. (1991) *Speaking of Galbraith: A Personal Portrait*, New York: Ticknor and Fields.

Rutherford, D. (1998) 'Galbraith, John Kenneth', in M. Warner (ed.), *Handbook of Management Thinking*, London: International Thomson Business Press, 238–42.

DCL

GALVIN, Robert William (1922–)

Robert William Galvin was born on 9 October 1922 in Marshfield, Wisconsin, into a devoted family of modest means which later became one of the wealthiest in the United States. Paul Galvin, Robert's father, suffered bankruptcy shortly after the birth of his only child. The family then moved to Chicago where, after experiencing another bankruptcy, Paul Galvin founded the Galvin Manufacturing Corporation in 1928 to manufacture battery eliminators. Located at 847 West Harrison Street, the concern employed only five workers upon opening. Within months, however, Galvin's new enterprise appeared doomed, as the market for battery eliminators evaporated. The older Galvin then astutely moved the company into an entirely new product line, the car radio. What was an unheard of and high-risk innovation in 1930 soon became commonplace in the expanding automobile culture which was sweeping the car-crazed United States. Galvin's first commercial automobile radio was dubbed the 'Motorola', a name signifying both motion and the radio. The product's popularity ultimately convinced Paul Galvin to rename the company Motorola in 1947.

Robert Galvin grew up in the Rogers Park neighbourhood on the north side of Chicago and Evanston, a suburb just north of the city. From the age of seven, he accompanied his father to company meetings and business trips across the country, which proved to be informal training for his eventual succession as head of Motorola. He attended Notre Dame University for two years before joining the US Army Signal Corps in 1942. At the end of the Second World War he returned to his father's company, working first as a stockboy and eventually as a production-line troubleshooter. By then Galvin Manufacturing was located on the west side of Chicago at 4545 West Augusta Boulevard. Galvin quickly advanced within the ranks before being promoted to executive vice-president

in 1948, and to president in 1956, only three years before his father died.

When Robert Galvin assumed the presidency of Motorola, the firm was earning $227 million a year manufacturing car radios, walkie-talkies, solid-state colour televisions and phonographs. Over the ensuing three decades, Galvin transformed Motorola into an $11 billion per year electronics colossus, employing over 100,000 people. As the president or chairman of Motorola, Inc. from 1956 to 1990, Galvin was the leading electronics executive in the United States. He was an advocate of 'virtual perfection', a manufacturing and production theory emphasizing 'total quality' for the final product. Proponents sometimes referred to this as the 'six sigma' philosophy. As a manufacturing strategy, virtual perfection marked a dramatic departure from the scientific management techniques developed by Frederick Winslow TAYLOR early in the twentieth century.

Motorola's success and longevity rested, in part, on Galvin's ability to adapt to changing conditions in the American economy. Like his father more than half a century earlier, Galvin completely abandoned historically successful but declining product lines for newer, high-risk commodities. In the mid-1980s, he led Motorola's move into miniaturizing pagers and cellular phones, just before those markets took off. By 1990 Motorola had jettisoned television production and was the leading manufacturer of two-way radios, cellular phones, pagers and advanced dispatch systems for commercial automobile fleets. The company was the fourth largest maker of semiconductors in the United States. Unlike International Business Machines (IBM), which faltered upon entering a new technological phase (moving from mainframe computers to personal computers), Motorola nimbly moved from conventional two-way radios and televisions to cellular radios and pagers.

In the second half of the twentieth century, Galvin was the foremost proponent of virtual perfection. In 1978, after a Motorola general sales manager pointed out numerous poor features in Motorola's product line, Galvin began emphasizing 'total quality'. Galvin sought to create a corporate and production culture that did as much as possible to please the customer. In the 'six sigma' philosophy, Galvin sought a production goal in which all variations remained within six standard deviations from norm, or achieving a quality level of 3.4 defects per million; hence the label 'virtual perfection'. Galvin was influenced by the ideas of Joseph JURAN and other postwar industrial theorists, but in the end insisted that Motorola developed its own production philosophy and system.

Virtual perfection departed dramatically from the scientific management techniques developed by Taylor. Galvin believed the Taylor approach was outdated and a top-down phenomenon, evaluating and measuring factory-floor production at the level of the individual worker. By contrast, Motorola organized workers into independent, self-directed teams with no formal supervisor. Galvin sought 'to determine from the bottom up' what were the needs for production. He believed that virtual perfection ultimately saved immense amounts of time while producing a better quality product. Characteristically, there was never a single time-clock in any Motorola plant.

In the latter years of his career, Galvin became a proponent of new and innovative forms of industrial and business education. Beginning with the Motorola Training and Education Center, a corporate training department which opened in 1981, Galvin was one of the first to introduce continuous training programmes for employees in his American factories. Along with Motorola University and the Galvin Center for Continuing Education (1986), Motorola employed new delivery technologies such as computer-based training, electronic publishing, satellite communications and other interactive training systems to serve as both classroom facilities and electronic distribution points. Galvin envisioned Motorola University supplementing the existing system of higher education and enabling Motorola employees to attend in-depth seminars without leaving their work locations. Satellite-transmitted seminars soon replaced business trips. By 1985 Motorola devoted over one million hours to training 25,000 of its 90,000 employees worldwide, an investment of $44 million.

Motorola's success generated political appointments for Galvin. In 1970 he served on the US President's Commission for International Trade and Investment. From 1982 to 1985 Galvin chaired the Industry Policy Advisory Committee to the US Special Representative to the Multilateral Trade Negotiations. Galvin was also active in the Republican Party, serving as the finance chairman in several electoral campaigns of US Senator Charles Percy of Illinois.

By the 1980s Galvin was a leading advocate increasing trade relationships with Asian nations. During that time, Motorola attacked Japanese producers for 'dumping' cellular phones in the United States, a charge later upheld by the International Trade Commission, while restricting access to United States corporations in Japan. Galvin was later identified as a key architect in opening up the Japanese semiconductor market in 1986, and in leading Motorola's expansion elsewhere in Asia. In 2000 Motorola received permission to construct two additional large factories in China valued at $1.9 billion, making the firm the largest private corporation in China.

In 1990 Galvin retired as Motorola's chairman and was later succeeded by his son Christopher. Robert Galvin remained involved in long-term corporate planning as the head of Motorola's executive committee. He was inducted into the National Business Hall of Fame (1991) and received the National Medal of Technology (1991) and the Marshall Field Making History Award of the Chicago Historical Society (1995). Just prior to his retirement as chairman, Galvin was named one of the first recipients of the Malcolm

Baldridge National Quality Award from the Department of Commerce (1988). He is described by business reporters as 'the elder statesman of Chicago business' (*Chicago Sun-Times*, 9 July 2000).

BIBLIOGRAPHY

Galvin, R.W. (1991) *The Idea of Ideas*, Schaumberg, IL: Motorola University Press.

McKenna, J.F. (1991) 'Bob Galvin Predicts Life After Perfection', *Industry Week* 240, 21 January: 12–15.

Petrakis, H.M. (1965) *The Founder's Touch*, New York: McGraw-Hill.

Thompson, K.R. (1992) 'A Conversation with Robert W. Galvin', *Organizational Dynamics* 20(Spring): 56–9.

TG

GANTT, Henry Laurence (1861–1919)

Henry Laurence Gantt was born on a plantation in the state of Maryland on 18 May 1861, not long after the outbreak of the American Civil War. He died at his home in New York on 23 November 1919. The family home was several times in the path of one of the warring armies which fought across Maryland and northern Virginia from 1861 to 1865, and much of their farm was ruined; Gantt, indeed, grew up in an atmosphere of some hardship. The family fortunes later recovered somewhat and Gantt was educated at the McDonagh School, going on to Johns Hopkins University in Baltimore, where he received his AB degree in 1880. He returned to the McDonagh School and taught natural science and mechanics there for three years. In 1884 he secured a job as a draughtsman with an iron foundry and also attended the Stevens Institute of Technology, graduating in 1884 with a degree in mechani-

cal engineering, a year after Frederick Winslow TAYLOR graduated with the same degree.

In 1887 Gantt joined the Midvale Steel Company in Philadelphia as an assistant in the engineering department. He then served for a little under two years as assistant to Taylor, then chief engineer, and worked with Taylor on the early development of the latter's famous system of management. Gantt was then promoted to superintendent of the casting department, and in 1893 left Midvale to take up a variety of technical and consulting positions around Philadelphia; his contact with Taylor became infrequent. In 1899, however, Taylor was called in to undertake his now famous consultancy project at Bethlehem Steel, and sent at once for Gantt. From 1899 to 1902 Gantt worked closely with Taylor and Carl BARTH on the consultancy. He remained at the plant for some months after the dismissal of Taylor and the subsequent purchase of Bethlehem by Charles M. SCHWAB, finally resigning in late 1902.

From 1902 to 1919 Gantt engaged in private consultancy work, initially in association with Taylor or one of the other members of his circle. His consultancy clients included Westinghouse, Canadian Pacific Railways, Union Typewriter, American Locomotive Company and a number of textile mills. Gantt also became friendly with Frank GILBRETH and his wife Lillian GILBRETH, and was particularly interested in their work on motion study. He played a leading role in the promotion of scientific management; indeed, it was at his New York apartment in 1913 that supporters of the movement agreed to adopt the term to cover all their work. Significantly, Taylor was not present at the meeting, and relations between him and Gantt worsened as the latter grew closer to the Gilbreths. Gantt was also increasingly unwell, but this did not prevent him from undertaking war work in 1917, working with Frankford Arsenal and the Emergency Fleet Corporation.

Gantt's best-known work was undertaken at Bethlehem in partnership with Taylor. He is most known for two achievements: the development of the 'task and bonus' system and the invention of graphic charts for production control, the famous 'Gantt charts'. The task and bonus system actually has its origins in Taylor and Gantt's work at Midvale, and has been described as an improvement on Taylor's differential rate system. Under Gantt's system, the worker was given a specific stated reward if he or she could perform a task within the time allotted, and then a further bonus if he or she could significantly better that time. Like Taylor's system, the task and bonus system depended on management's first making an accurate study of the time required to perform a task. However, it was much simpler to administer and was perceived to be more equitable; Drury (1915) comments that by 1915 his wage system had largely replaced that of Taylor.

The first Gantt chart, known as a 'daily balance chart', was developed at Bethlehem for the purpose of describing the process of work. Updated daily, the chart showed how work was progressing and, says Urwick, facilitated 'continuous pre-planning of production' (Urwick 1956: 90). Gantt went on to develop other charts to depict costs and expenses graphically. 'The final evolution, the bar-chart which bears his name, made the important change of planning production programmes in terms of *time* instead of quantities. Nothing could be simpler than the Gantt Chart, yet nothing could at the time have been more revolutionary' (Urwick 1956: 90).

Because Gantt worked so closely with Taylor, he is often overshadowed by the latter and his work is frequently seen as just another form of Taylorism. In fact, Gantt had important views on industrial relations that were recognized by Robert HOXIE, who treated Gantt's approach to labour as partially independent of that of Taylor, particularly with respect to the concept of justice for workers (Hoxie 1916). Gantt is now widely considered to be one of the founding fathers of the American industrial democracy movement. His own best-known book, *Work, Wages and Profits* (1910), takes as its theme the utilization of scientific management for the common good of both worker and employer:

> Those who have given even superficial study to the subject are beginning to realize the enormous gain that can be made in the efficiency of workmen, if they are properly directed and provided with proper appliances. Few, however, have realized another fact of equal importance, namely, that to maintain *permanently* this increase of efficiency, the workman must be allowed a portion of the benefit derived from it.
>
> (Gantt 1910: 23)

He goes on:

> To obtain this high degree of efficiency successfully, however, the same careful scientific analysis and investigation must be applied to every labor detail as the chemist or biologist applies to his work. Wherever this has been done, it has been found possible to reduce expenses, and, at the same time, to increase wages, producing a condition satisfactory to both employer and employee.
>
> (Gantt 1910: 23)

Gantt's thesis is simple: a properly conducted scientific investigation into the nature of work at each plant will inevitably establish facts concerning the nature and value of the labour required to carry out those tasks. Once these facts have been established, labour and management can come to an easy agreement on the best form of remuneration. There will no longer be any need for a confrontational approach by labour to management, and vice versa, as the main sources of disagreement will have been removed.

For all his emphasis on science, Gantt's is not a rigid mind. He is opposed to cross-industry standards for judging work, and believes that each factory is an individual environment with its own standards and needs; investigations should not be applied generally, but should be conducted in each workplace separately. He is particularly adamant that scientific management is about principles, not rules:

> The man who undertakes to introduce scientific management and pins his faith to rules, and the use of forms and blanks, without thoroughly comprehending the principles upon which it is based, will fail. Forms and blanks are simply the means to an end. If the end is not kept clearly in mind, the use of these forms and blanks is apt to be detrimental rather than beneficial.
>
> (Gantt 1910: 8)

This may seem ironic coming from the inventor of the most famous process chart of all time, but Gantt was always adamant that the purpose of his charts was to provide information on which managers could make decisions, not to make the decisions for them. Even by 1910 he was aware of the potential straitjacketing effect which the use of charts and forms could have on less sophisticated managerial minds. Much of his later work argues for greater sophistication, creativity and training in management.

Personally, Gantt was a likeable man, much more successful as an apostle of scientific management than his dour colleague Taylor. Observers spoke of his flexible mind and adaptable outlook; a mutual friend commented that whereas Taylor would simply bore through an obstacle, Gantt would find a way around it, or even change goals altogether (Drury 1915). His work and writing both betray a strong concern for the human element in both work force and management. In 1929 the American Society of Mechanical Engineers and the Institute of Management jointly established the annual award of the Henry Laurence Gantt Gold Medal for distinguished achievement in industrial management as a service to the community. The first award was made, posthumously, to Gantt himself.

BIBLIOGRAPHY

Drury, H.B. (1915) *Scientific Management*, New York: Longmans Green.

Gantt, H.L. (1910) *Work, Wages and Profits*, New York: Engineering Magazine Co.; 2nd edn, 1913.

—— (1916) *Industrial Leadership*, New Haven, CT: Yale University Press.

—— (1919) *Organizing for Work*, New York: Harcourt, Brace.

Hoxie, R.F. (1916) *Scientific Management and Labor*, New York: D. Appleton and Co.

Urwick, L.F. (1956) *The Golden Book of Management*, London: Newman Neame.

MLW

GATES, William Henry, III (1955–)

Bill Gates was born in Seattle, Washington on 28 October 1955 to William Henry Gates, Jr and Mary Gates. As home of the Boeing Corporation (see BOEING), Seattle in the early 1960s was already a city of the future. The Seattle World's Fair of 1962, with its Space Needle, took the theme of technology of the twenty-first century. The exhibits of the fair made a strong impression upon six-year-old Bill Gates. There he saw giant IBM mainframes, and an exhibit on the World of Tomorrow in which a futuristic office forecast inventions that could send electronic mail and machines that could talk to one another. The General Electric pavilion envisioned wall-sized television screens, videocassette recorders and personal home computers.

As a youth, Bill Gates was small and thin. Younger than his classmates, he still stood out in terms of mathematic and general intellectual ability. He had an IQ of 160–70 and a competitive, nonconformist manner that later helped to make him a successful entrepreneur. In 1967 Gates entered the all-male Seattle Lakeside School. Students here formed their own cliques, and Gates was remembered as a serious but talkative member of the maths and science clique. Maths and science students such as Gates tended to keep to themselves at Lakeside, but in the autumn of 1968 Gates made a discovery that would ultimately change the world for ever. In the maths and science building, Gates discovered an old teletype machine. With its keyboard, printer and telephone modem, it resembled the personal computer of the future.

When Gates first encountered computers, they had been in existence for thirty years without playing a dominant role in the economy. The first commercial computer of the early 1950s, the Universal Automatic Computer (UNIVAC) of Remington Rand, used vacuum tubes and was affordable only by the federal government and a few big firms such as General Electric. Transistors made it possible for IBM, Honeywell and a few others to build smaller machines in the late 1950s, but these were still cumbersome. Their application in business was limited until new computer languages such as COBOL (Common Business-Oriented Language) and FORTRAN (Formula Translator) let computers operate not just with binary digits but words and formulae. By the time Bill Gates was in secondary school, computers were using printed circuits, running several programs at the same time, and being used by companies in systems analysis. Gates joined the computer revolution when it was still in its infancy. Even though renting time on the teletype was expensive, its availability gave him the opportunity to pursue what soon became his overwhelming passion: writing programs.

While still a teenager, Bill Gates was already entering the world of business. At Lakeside he had made friends with another young computer enthusiast, Paul Allen. Both were very good at creating programs in a simple language called BASIC, and were hired to work for the school's Computer Centre Corporation, or C-Cubed. By 1971 Allen and Gates, both still in their teens, had set up their own company, Traf-O-Data. According to his own account in his book *The Road Ahead* (1995), Gates already had both a love for computers and a belief that they would one day become small, economical and powerful.

Gates entered Harvard in 1973, and, after completing his first year, went to work for Honeywell in the summer of 1974. By this time the world was on the verge of the personal computer revolution. By 1964 a new generation of computer hardware included the integrated circuit and with it, by the end of the 1960s, the silicon computer chip. The first Intel microchips were produced in 1971. As early as 1972 Gates was experimenting with the Intel 8008 microchip to see if it could be made to run BASIC programs. The 8008 was too small, but the 8080, introduced in the spring of 1974, had ten times its power. While still not powerful enough, it enabled Gates to envision a different kind of computer that would be affordable and that would give himself and Allen a whole new marketing niche:

> Computer hardware, which had once been scarce, would soon be readily available, and access to computers would no longer be charged for at a high hourly rate. It seemed to us people would find all kinds of new uses for computing if it was cheap. Then, software would be the key to delivering the full potential of these machines. Paul and I speculated that Japanese companies and IBM would likely produce most of the hardware. And why not? The microprocessor would change the structure of the industry. Maybe there was a place for the two of us.
>
> (Gates 1995: 15)

From his Harvard dormitory, Gates sent letters to the major computer firms, offering to write them a version of BASIC for the new Intel chip. No one responded to his offer.

Bill Gates's genius was not so much in making his own inventions, however, as in bringing together the technology of others. He invented neither the microchip nor the desktop computer, but in 1975 he and Paul Allen married them for life in a way that would change the world. In January 1975 *Popular Electronics* magazine announced that a company called Model – later Micro, Instrumentation and Telemetry Systems (MITS) – had invented a small computer called the Altair 8080.

The Altair had no monitor or keyboard, and operated by flipping switches and flashing lights. Gates noted its limitations, for it lacked software, could not be programmed and was more a novelty than a tool. But he also sensed its potential, and the danger of not acting on that potential. His reaction was 'Oh no! It's happening without us! People are going to go write real software for this chip.' Although this 'would happen sooner rather than later', Gates wanted to be involved from the start: 'The chance to get in on the first stages of the PC revolution seemed the opportunity of a lifetime, and I seized it' (Gates 1995: 16).

Gates and Allen set to work without either an Altair or an 8080 chip, but in the winter of 1975 they were able to write a BASIC program for the Altair within five weeks. The result was the birth of a company which Gates and Allen first called Micro-Soft, and eventually Microsoft. First based in Albuquerque, New Mexico, the firm soon relocated to Seattle. To make it work, both took risks: Allen left his programming job at Honeywell and Gates dropped out of Harvard in 1976. He felt it was worth the risk, for 'the window of opportunity to start a software company might not open again' (Gates 1995: 18).

In the beginning, Microsoft was a bare-bones operation in which Gates and Allen financed everything themselves. According to

Gates, the key to Microsoft's success lay in their vision that there would soon be cheap computers everywhere, and that they would be in the right place at the right time to write the software for them:

> We got there first and our early success gave us the chance to hire many smart people. We built a worldwide sales force and used the revenue it generated to fund new products. From the beginning we set off down a road that was headed in the right direction.
>
> (Gates 1995: 18)

MITS was soon receiving many orders for its Altair computer. BASIC software began to spread, sometimes through pirated versions. By the end of 1976 Microsoft had contracts with several firms, including General Electric, and was grossing $100,000 a year. By 1977 and 1978 Microsoft was beginning to diversify, writing programs in COBOL and FORTRAN for microcomputers produced by Tandy, Commodore and others.

Gates advanced on the broadest of fronts, signing licensing agreements for his software with a number of computer companies in the late 1970s. His next client was Steve JOBS, who had founded Apple Computers in 1976. In April 1977 Jobs brought out his Apple II, which contained a spreadsheet called VisCalc and a word-processing program called WordStar. Gates recognized that people's decisions to buy computers were often based on the applications that came with them.

With Microsoft grossing $4 million per year by 1979, Gates now entered the applications market. The computer industry was beginning to standardize, and small businesses were now beginning to buy personal computers on a large scale in a market dominated at first by Radio Shack and Apple. According to Michael Flint (2000), the windfall for Gates and Microsoft came in 1980 when John Opel of International Business Machines (IBM) determined to enter the personal computer market.

While utterly dominating the market in main-frames, IBM's executives recognized the threat of the microcomputer. Traditionally internal-izing research, marketing and sales, IBM, in a race against time, was compelled to outsource its development of software.

The coming of the IBM personal computer would accelerate the standardization of the industry exponentially. IBM's team built its hardware from existing components that were readily available, permitting other companies to 'clone' the IBM technology. IBM used microchips from Intel, and licensed the oper-ating system and applications from Microsoft. Gates worked closely with IBM technicians to produce the Microsoft Disk Operating System, or MS-DOS.

In August 1981 the IBM personal computer, backed by the giant's brand name, went on sale. Microsoft granted, for a one-time fee, the right to MS-DOS for IBM as its standard operating system. IBM sold DOS with its IBM 360 and later computers for only $60. This was smart marketing on the part of Gates, who saw far more long-term gains in defining the technical rules of the software market:

> Our goal was not to make money directly from IBM, but to profit from licensing MS-DOS to computer companies that wanted to offer machines more or less compatible with the IBM PC. IBM could use our software for free, but it did not have any exclusive license or control of future enhancements. This put Microsoft in the business of licens-ing software platform to the personal-computer industry.

> (Gates 1995: 49)

The IBM personal computer quickly began to capture the microcomputer market. By 1982 software companies were writing all sorts of applications compatible with it. Not only Microsoft Word and Excel, but Lotus Development's Lotus 1-2-3 were now written for both IBM and DOS. Any computer firm not compatible with this software began to go out of business. By 1984 DEC, Texas Instruments, Xerox and all others save Apple and the IBM clones had fled the personal computer market. The number of personal computers rose from two million to five million. By 1985 Microsoft was earning $150 million annually and employing 1,000 people.

Although Microsoft and IBM now domi-nated the market, Gates was never one for complacency. Apple, IBM's sole serious com-petitor, was creating a market for its popular Macintosh computers. The 'Mac', as it is known, was an extremely user-friendly machine. When one logged on to an IBM computer, one had to access files and appli-cations via a cumbersome DOS code that used a confusing array of letters, numbers and punctuation marks. A Mac user turned on his machine and slid a device called a graphic user interface – or more popularly, a 'mouse' – across his or her desk. The mouse was con-nected to a pointer on the screen. Files were listed on the screen by pictures called icons. To open a file, all one had to do was move the pointer over the icon and click on it. The file opened up as a window, several of which could be open at the same time. Gates knew by 1983 that both Microsoft and IBM would have to replace DOS with a similar type of operating system. By 1984 Microsoft Windows 1.0 was on the market and an instant success, preserving the dominance of the IBM-compatible computer.

By 1990 Microsoft was the world's largest software firm, a $1-billion corporation with offices in Britain, France, Germany, Ireland, Australia, Singapore, Indonesia and Malaysia. Windows 3.0, released in 1990, became standard software on most IBM-compatible computers, of which there were now at least fifty million. During the 1990s Microsoft earnings reached almost $6 billion in 1995, and $14 billion in 1998, by which time Microsoft was the most admired company in the United States, employed over 28,000 people, and had entered the entertainment industry through its merger with Dreamworks SICG and the creation of the MSNBC online news network. When Windows 95 was released in 1995, it was a major media and news event.

The next major challenge facing Microsoft was the coming of the Internet. This created an even more explosive revolution than the personal computer. From half a million online users in 1991 the number of had grown tenfold by the middle of the decade, when private providers began to take over the World Wide Web. This number grew tenfold again, to over forty million by 1998. Once again Gates faced a new challenge with the marketing by Netscape of Netscape Navigator, a browser software allowing users to connect with the World Wide Web. In August 1995 Microsoft released its own Internet Explorer 1.0, following it with Internet Explorer 2.0 in November 1995 and version 3.0 in August 1996. During 1997 Gates made an agreement with Apple in which the latter would install Internet Explorer as its default browser.

While Microsoft was the most admired corporation, and was surpassed in market value in 1997 only by General Electric and Coca-Cola, many compared it to the Morgan Bank or Standard Oil. Chief among these was the US Department of Justice, which in 1994 began investigating Microsoft for alleged monopolistic practices. On 21 May 1998 the federal government and twenty state governments filed an anti-trust action against Microsoft. The Department of Justice's Anti-trust Division argued that Microsoft was a clear monopoly that controlled 90 per cent of the software market. In November 1999 Federal Judge Penfield Jackson ruled that 'Microsoft engaged in a concerted series of actions designed to protect its monopoly power' (Cohen 1999: 63). The government alleged that the firm bound its browser into its Windows 98 operating system to shut out Netscape, pressured Intel out of the software market, and also sought to use its market advantage to coerce IBM, Compaq, Apple and others. The judge insisted that Microsoft, in its zeal to suppress its competitors, was depriving consumers of the new innovations a more open market would have brought. Appeals against the judgement are continuing.

In their defence, Gates and his attorneys argued that they had broken no law and acted only because they saw the new technologies of Netscape, Intel, Upstart Linux and Java as a potential threat in a highly competitive business in which today's software giant may be tomorrow's dinosaur. If Washington resorted to draconian anti-trust actions, no company would be able to protect its trade secrets from its rivals or itself from government regulation. The situation has not been fully resolved at time of writing.

In 1999 Gates published a second book, *Business @ the Speed of Thought: Using a Digital Nervous System*, in which he outlined his management philosophy. Business, he predicted, would change more in the next decade than in the last fifty years. The key issue in the 2000s would be about *velocity*, about how quickly the nature of business itself would change. A company will have to adjust to market shifts in a matter of hours, not weeks. Gates argued that those business leaders who are able to react most quickly to rapid change and can empower their units and line employees to do the same will survive and prosper. Many decisions will no longer be made at the centre. Workers will need access to smart machines at their desks. Everything in a company will be put into digital form, for now, business decisions have to move at the pace of electronic markets' (Gates 1999: 412).

Regardless of the outcome of the anti-trust action, Bill Gates remains in a position to shape if not dominate the course of the age of e-commerce. The richest and most influential business figure in the world in the 1990s, he is the unquestioned leader of the digital revolution.

BIBLIOGRAPHY
Cohen, A. (1999) 'Bill Gates' Monopoly: The Findings of Fact', *Time* 154(20): 60–69.
Flint, M. (2000) 'Microsoft History', in 'Microsoft and the Freedom to Subjugate', http://www.geocities.com/free2 subj/mshist.html, 28 November 2000.
Gates, B. (1995) *The Road Ahead*, with N. Myhrvold and P. Rinearson, New York: Viking Penguin.
—— (1999) *Business @ the Speed of Thought: Using a Digital Nervous System*, with C. Hemingway, NewYork: Warner Books.
Manes, S. and Andrews, P. (1994) *Gates: How Microsoft's Mogul Reinvented an Industry and Made Himself the Richest Man in America*, NewYork: Touchstone.

DCL

GAY, Edwin Francis (1867–1946)

Edwin Francis Gay was born in Detroit, Michigan on 27 October 1867, the son of Aaron and Mary Gay. He died at Pasadena, California on 8 February 1946. His father was a prosperous timber merchant. Gay was educated at schools in Michigan and in Europe before taking an AB in philosophy and history from the University of Michigan in 1890. He then went to the University of Berlin for graduate study in medieval history. Becoming attracted to the scholar's life, he remained in Europe for the next twelve years, studying at various universities including Leipzig, Zurich and Florence, and finally completing his Ph.D. at Berlin in 1902. He had married his university classmate Louise Randolph in 1892; a notable scholar herself, she accompanied Gay to Europe and worked with him. Both the Gays would later recall this as an idyllic time in which they were able completely to immerse themselves in their passion for study.

In 1902 Gay returned to the United States and took up a post as instructor in economics at Harvard University. Both his intellectual power and hitherto undiscovered administrative talents marked him out as a rising star, and he was made professor and chairman of the department of economics in 1906. When Harvard's president, Charles Eliot, began developing his plan for a business school, Gay was one of his key advisers in the run-up to the school's establishment in 1908.

Eliot's first choice for dean of the new school was William Lyon Mackenzie King, formerly an instructor in economics at Harvard and now deputy minister of labour in the Canadian government. King turned the post down (he went on to become Canada's longest serving prime minister), and in February 1908 the post was offered to Gay, who accepted with reluctance. Once having taken up the post, however, he worked indefatigably to make Harvard Business School a success, winning the admiration of the school's supporters and opponents alike. After his initial reluctance was overcome, Gay came to see the School as a chance to combine scholarship and action:

> To fashion, build, and manage a school which would train men for business as a profession; to bring his wide range of knowledge to bear on planning and guiding that training; to inculcate an awareness of the social obligations and consquences of business enterprise; and to do this for a country that was travelling fast toward economic maturity and preeminence – here indeed was a call to active service that could not be declined.
>
> (Heaton 1952: 69)

His commitment to Harvard Business School was total; as Charles Eliot later said, 'he transferred himself body and soul to the new School, put all his time and strength into it' (Heaton 1952: 74).

Gay was working with no models to guide him; only the universities of Pennsylvania and Dartmouth had previously established graduate schools of business (the Wharton and Tuck schools, respectively). No matter how much managerial and academic talent he was able to recruit to the school, the blueprint for it had to be his own. It was Gay who determined the guiding philosophy of the school, which he saw as resting on two key ideas. First, he defined the task of the business manager as 'making things to sell at a profit (decently)'. Second, he defined the school's own task as 'to experiment and to learn what the *content* and *form* should be for the training of mature students primarily for "making" or "selling"' (Heaton 1952: 76). The key qualities necessary in a successful manager were courage, judgement and sympathy, and it was the school's role to inculcate and strengthen these in students through education.

It was Gay who determined that the degree offered by the school would be called 'Master of Business Administration', a title which became adopted around the world. It was Gay too who adapted the case system pioneered by Harvard Law School to the study of management. This proved to be a difficult task, as there was no pre-existing body of case material. A key ally here was the publisher and writer Arch W. SHAW, an early and enthusiastic supporter, who was tasked by Gay with building up a bank of case studies. Innovatively, Shaw began developing 'living' case studies as well as written ones, giving students a chance to study 'live action' problems. Shaw was also a moving force behind the establishment of the Bureau of Business Research, one the initial functions of which was to supply case study material.

Most important of all, Gay sought to move away from the traditional format of classroom lectures, towards teaching methods that would involve and challenge students and stimulate their imaginations. Melvin COPELAND, who was recruited by Gay in 1909 and asked to begin teaching a marketing course at thirty-six hours notice, later recalled encountering Gay a couple of weeks after teaching had begun. When the dean asked how the course was going, Copeland replied, 'I have found enough to talk about so far.' 'That is not the question,' replied Gay. 'Have you found enough to keep the students talking?' Copeland, taking the broad hint, abandoned his lecturing style for one of classroom discussion, and followed this through the rest of his career. Much later, he realized that Gay had selected him as a 'guinea pig' for introduction of classroom discussion and the case method in marketing (Copeland 1958: 59–60).

By his own admission, Gay had no business or management experience. He proved adept, however, at finding people who had such experience and winning them over to his cause. This was not altogether easy: many of the captains of industry approached proved to be inadequate teachers, while others lacked the time to commit to the venture. Gay several times approached Frederick W. TAYLOR, the founding father of scientific management, but was repeatedly rebuffed; he then turned his attention to Taylor's associate Carl BARTH, and by dint of persistence eventually persuaded Barth to give a course of lectures. Barth was won over, and so too was Taylor, who taught occasionally at the school until his death. Gay also recruited the important academic figures who would be the cornerstone of Harvard Business School in its early years, such as W.J. Cunningham and especially Paul CHERINGTON, the school's first professor of marketing. Realizing early on that established academics would have difficulty adapting to his methods, he also sought out new talent, recruiting men such as Melvin Copeland and inculcating them with his vision. Other important figures like Arch Shaw, T.W. Lamont and the economist Wesley Clair MITCHELL became key supporters.

By 1917 the school was beginning to prosper and Gay, exhausted, resigned as dean. He served as adviser to the US Shipping Board during the First World War. In 1919, deciding not to return to Harvard, he accepted an offer from Lamont to take over the editorship of the New York *Evening Post*, which the latter owned. This move was not a success, and in 1924 the newspaper went bankrupt. Gay then returned to Harvard as a professor of economic history, where he remained until he retired in 1936. Moving to California, he served on the research staff of the Huntingdon Library until stricken with pneumonia in January 1946. He died the following month.

Gay's achievements at Harvard Business School were considerable. The pedagogic methods he developed there were widely imitated: the case method remains standard at most business schools today. Gay's philosophy of business education likewise remains at the heart of most thinking on the subject. His personal managerial accomplishment in getting the school off the ground should not be overrated; the progenitor of the case study could himself be regarded as a useful case example of developing and carrying through a highly successful innovation. Heaton's tribute to him is by and large an accurate assessment of his character and methods:

> The early history of the School had something of the flavour of a cause, a crusade, or a movement beyond the frontier of educational settlement, with Gay as leader, inspirer, and challenger. He never told his colleagues what to do, for he would not have known what instructions to give. Instead he sent them off to explore, with a double piece of advice: to remember that there were no experts in this new field and that the printing of a statement did not make it authentic. His own faith, resourcefulness, and expenditure of energy impelled them to give the best that was in them, so that each man made his full contribution to the policies and programs that were a team

product rather than the achievement of any one person.

(Heaton 1952: 81)

Yet Gay himself, in his later years, regarded his own career as a failure. In 1908 he had departed from the historical and economic research that he loved, and was never able to recapture the passion for his work that he had felt in his youth. He wrote to a friend in 1935: 'It is one of my serious regrets that I ever undertook the deanship of the Business School' (Heaton 1952: 6).

BIBLIOGRAPHY
Copeland, M. (1958) *And Mark the Era: The Story of Harvard Business School*, Boston: Little, Brown.

Heaton, H.K. (1952) *A Scholar in Action: Edwin F. Gay*, Cambridge, MA: Harvard University Press.

MLW

GENEEN, Harold Sydney (1910–97)

Harold Sydney Geneen was born in Bournemouth, England on 22 January 1910 to Samuel and Aida Geneen. He died in New York on 25 November 1997. His father, a merchant, was of Portuguese Jewish ancestry, his mother was Italian. Harold himself was raised as a Catholic. In December 1910 the Geneens emigrated to the United States. By 1915 they had separated, with Samuel pursuing a business career, Aida a singing career, and Harold placed in a boarding school.

According to biographer Robert Schoenberg (1985), Geneen had a relatively happy youth in spite of his broken home, although he found it hard to trust others as he felt deserted by both parents. Attending the

Suffield School near Hartford, Connecticut from 1917 to 1926, he excelled in mathematics. He could not at first afford to enter college, so he began working as a page on the New York Stock Exchange. During the 1920s the work was profitable, but Geneen saw little future in it for himself. He wanted something more steady.

Between 1928 and 1934 Geneen put himself through night school at New York University, majoring in accounting. By 1932 he was working for the Mayflower Associates, landing a job even at the worst of the Great Depression. His degree helped him find work, and in 1934 he moved on to Lybrand, Ross Brothers, and Montgomery, where he worked until 1942. Geneen distinguished himself from the others around him by his single-minded dedication to his work. He loved figures for their own sake, for they told him the whole story of a company. He took the profit and loss of his clients, says Schoenberg, personally and seriously.

By the time the United States entered the Second World War in December 1941, Harold Geneen was bored with his job and sought a more challenging position with a producing industry. He found it in January 1942 with Amertorp, a subsidiary of the American Can Company. By May he was hard at work designing an accounting system for the firm's plant in Forest Park, Illinois. His next task was setting up a cost control system at the firm's St Louis plant. This system had to track the cost of every component in every torpedo. Geneen's system sent an envelope with every part and punched a ticket at every operation. The system made it possible to pinpoint any production defect, slowdown or problem.

When Geneen really wanted more than all else, according to Schoenberg (1985), was a career in which he would have complete control and responsibility. He achieved this dream in stages. His next career move was to Bell and Howell in 1946, but within a year he had moved to the steel firm of Jones and

Laughlin, where he remained for twelve years. Here Geneen further developed his accounting methods, partly inspired by those of Alfred P. SLOAN of General Motors, for turning around a struggling firm. Geneen wanted to know the profit on each product line, and organized accounting as far down as he could in the production chain. Steel production was a volatile business, and managers would often lay off workers at random, or whole departments, during a downturn. Geneen had a much more practical approach: every division should have a downsizing plan for every 10 per cent of lost returns. These plans would involve more than layoffs, and include shift reductions and other economies.

A bigger challenge waited Geneen when he was hired by the Boston technological firm of Raytheon in June of 1956. Managed by Charles Francis Adams, Jr, Raytheon was a company in trouble. Even though it had $175 millon in revenues, its stock had recently plummeted to one-quarter of its former value. Raytheon, a firm of brilliant scientists and unprofitable managers, managed to stay afloat thanks to its military contracts for the Hawk and Sparrow tactical missiles.

Geneen discovered that the non-military sector of the company was losing money badly. The management was rigidly centralized and had little idea how each of the divisions were doing. The key to Geneen's approach was improving the ratio between returns and expenses, and eliminating any calculation not concerned with profit. He met with the firm's engineers in order to explain to them that greater profits meant more resources for their research. Geneen worked systematically to slash inventory costs by requesting the armed forces pay more in advance. By subcontracting, he passed fully 50 per cent of Raytheon's inventory costs on to the subcontractors.

As he had done before, Geneen set up profit and loss accounting in the smallest divisions possible. The company was to be run systematically on the basis of what Geneen called *competitive ratios.* Geneen calculated the ratio of sales/personnel and sales/profit, and applied these ratios throughout all Raytheon operations. He then set the goal of 3 per cent net profit on sales, 10 per cent on civilian contracts, and 18 per cent on shareholder investment.

One of Geneen's most unique innovations was the monthly financial and operating meeting. Here he would scrutinize closely the detailed reports of his managers. These reports were not mere ledgers, but contained explanations of the figures. A management policy group met once a month, where full reports from every unit were submitted. Every division knew what was going on in every other division. Geneen would pick up details from these memos that no one else could. He wanted all management problems to be aired in the open. Norman Krim, a Raytheon manager, quotes Geneen:

> Above all it is important that there be no 'covering up' of our problems at any management level ... If I were to look for any single indication of management's strength *or ability in any company* ... the degree of 'openness and objectivity' in appraising its own performance would be the single most important index of management's strength.
>
> (Schoenberg 1985: 89)

According to Schoenberg (1985) and Sampson (1974, 1996), Geneen was seen as intrusive and heavy-handed by many in the firm, who resented his tampering with Raytheon's paternalistic culture which seemingly minimized the importance of profit. He pressured employees to work nights, and to put the firm above even their families. But the figures spoke for themselves. Geneen's techniques freed over $30 million in money for profitable investment. Sales rose from $175 million to $375 million between 1956 and 1958. Raytheon became the top employer in Massachusetts.

Geneen's controversial but remarkable success finally enabled him to acquire a presidency of his own, in a firm much bigger than Raytheon. On 10 June 1959, Harold Geneen became president of International Telephone and Telegraph, better known as ITT. On the surface, says Anthony Sampson in his *Sovereign State of ITT* (1974), ITT looked formidable, a giant conglomerate with 116 plants in over twenty countries and sales of almost $766 million. Geneen's keen eye nonetheless saw the clay feet of the giant. ITT's management structure was very loose. It was more a loose collection of uncoordinated companies than a single firm. The European companies were totally separate from the North American and Latin American branches. The United States accounted for only one-fifth of ITT's $29 million profits; politically volatile Latin America accounted for one-third of all ITT earnings. No one knew what ITT earned in profits until the end of a business year.

Wherever he looked, Geneen found lack of organization, duplication of effort and many unprofitable contracts. The European ITT firms basically depended upon servicing the government telephone monopolies of their various countries, which kept rates down while preventing investment in new systems. In Latin America, ITT monopolized the telephone systems in Brazil, Chile and Peru, as well as Puerto Rico and the Virgin Islands.

Geneen's maxim was that managers ought to *manage.* He fired many of the unprofitable managers and brought in some of his associates from Raytheon. Managers, he felt, ought to lead instead of merely reacting to problems. They needed a conscious long-term strategy as to what their firm should achieve, and where it ought to be one, two or five years in the future. Unlike his predecessor, Sosthenes Behn, who ran ITT from his home, Geneen moved the firm's headquarters into a tall office tower on New York's Park Avenue. Here he set up what Anthony Sampson described as 'the most intricate and rigorous system of' financial control that the world has ever seen'

(Sampson 1974: 70). The Raytheon system of regular meetings, systematic reports, ratios, targets, five-year plans and close oversight by Geneen was applied to ITT on a much bigger scale.

In March of 1963 Geneen prepared a memo in which he was quite pessimistic about the investment climate in Europe. He saw the governments there becoming more hostile to the United States and more nationalistic. With over 80 per cent of its trade and investments overseas, Geneen wanted ITT to be more American. The large amount of investment in Latin America was a cause of concern to him, especially when Fidel Castro expropriated the ITT phone company in Cuba. Geneen proposed that ITT begin to acquire American firms, so that by 1970 a majority of its earnings would come from domestic, not foreign sources. He began to buy companies in many diverse fields which he thought would be profitable. Geneen, however, had a particular interest in service companies with transferable technology.

During the 1960s, according to Sampson, the multinational enterprise truly came into its own, as did the conglomerate form of business organization in which totally unrelated companies were joined together in a single corporate organization. ITT was the prime example of this trend. Geneen first made an alliance with the Lazard Frères investment bank, whose capital it used to acquire a number of companies. First, there was the car rental firm Avis, followed by Sheraton Hotels, Continental Insurance, the publisher Howard Sams, William Levitt's housing firm, Pennsylvania Glass Sand, Continental Baking and many others.

Under Geneen, ITT's revenues grew from $765 million in 1959 to a gargantuan $22 billion in 1978. The conglomerate operated 400 companies in seventy countries and employed 425,000 people by 1974. Not everyone was happy with Geneen's formula for success. Robert Townsend of Avis, bought out by ITT, lamented what he saw as the

rigidity of Geneen's business culture and its detrimental impact upon small, creative individualistic firms. When ITT tried to acquire the American Broadcasting Corporation in 1966, it was blocked from doing so by the United States Justice Department.

When the Justice Department also sought to prevent ITT from acquiring Hartford Insurance, the company lobbied against it and gave the Republican Party $400,000 for it 1972 campaign. This revelation, published in early 1972, tarnished ITT's image. The revelations regarding ITT activity in Chile were even more damaging. Geneen, conscious of the fact that 12 per cent of ITT's profits came from its Chilean telephone company, offered the Central Intelligence Agency $1 million to prevent the Marxist government of Salvador Allende from expropriating ITT's holdings. Allegations of similar activities in Indonesia, Iran, Mexico and other countries eventually surfaced as well, further undermining ITT's reputation (Sampson 1996).

The Chile revelations of 1973 were the beginning of the end of Geneen's career with ITT (Schoenberg 1985). The conglomerate's stock plunged from sixty dollars to twelve. The United States Internal Revenue Service ruled that ITT's acquisition of Hartford Insurance was not tax free, and that it owed the agency $100 million. Mergers no longer granted ITT the huge growth they had in the 1960s. While the company was still making money, the rate of profit began to decline. Avis and Levitt began to lose money, and Europe entered a long period of economic stagnation. ITT's image was now tarnished, its meetings picketed and its offices bombed on several occasions.

Geneen remained a brilliant manager to the end, but as he faced the possibility of a perjury indictment (which was never filed), ITT's board of directors decided not to renew his contract, and, aged sixty-seven, on 1 January 1978, he surrendered the presidency to Lyman Hamilton. His own health failing due to palsy, Geneen nevertheless worked as an independent investor until his death.

Shortly before his death in late 1997 Geneen, at the age of eight-seven, published *The Synergy Myth, and Other Ailments of Business Today*. In this work, he summarized his lifelong management philosophy. As in his 1984 book *Managing*, he reiterated that there was 'no secret, no magic formula' to business success save 'the old-fashioned virtues of hard work, honesty, and risk taking' (Geneen 1997: xii). Management fads such as Theory Z and Total Quality Management were in his mind 'baloney'. The biggest flaw in managers was the unwillingness to take risks. This, in Geneen's mind, was as bad for business as laziness and dishonesty. He felt particular disdain for the term 'synergy', which he felt was nothing but hope that somehow a merger would be greater than the sum of its parts.

Geneen continued to defend the usefulness of the conglomerate, in spite of the fact that only ITT, General Electric and two others were now listed by the *Wall Street Journal* as being such. Reflecting upon ITT, he made the point that its very diversity gave it choices which more focused companies lacked. General Motors lives and dies by cars, but ITT could sell both telephone service and bread: 'The conglomerate is the ideal vehicle for exploiting the rich possibilities of risk taking without jeopardizing the corporation's survival.' If risk was like a bucking bronco, 'a conglomerate is the vest way to enjoy the ride' (Geneen 1997: xvi).

One of the most effective managers in history, Harold Geneen contributed to the art of management the ability to coordinate and operate a huge multinational with many component firms and effectively integrate the smallest part with the whole. He was the epitome of scientific management and control accounting carried to its logical extent. After Geneen, even though the large centralized conglomerate form began to lose its appeal, the science of detailed budgeting and planning would be regarded as an absolute necessity for a competitive firm (Schoenberg 1985).

BIBLIOGRAPHY
Barnet, R.J. and Müller, R.E. (1974) *Global Reach, The Power of the Multinational Corporations*, New York: Simon and Schuster.
Geneen, H. with Moscow, A. (1984) *Managing*, Garden City, NY: Doubleday.
——— (1997) *The Synergy Myth, and Other Ailments of Business Today*, with B. Bowers, New York: St Martin's Press.
Sampson, A. (1974) *The Sovereign State of ITT*, Greenwich, CT: Fawcett Publications.
——— (1996) *Company Man, The Rise and Fall of Corporate Life*, London: HarperCollins Business.
Schoenberg, R.J. (1985) *Geneen*, New York: W.W. Norton and Company, Inc.

DCL

GETTY, Jean Paul (1892–1976)

Jean Paul Getty was born on 15 December 1892 in Minneapolis, Minnesota and died of a heart attack, while suffering from prostate cancer, at Sutton Place in Surrey on 6 June 1976. He was the son and sole surviving child of George Franklin Getty, an insurance attorney and oil investor, and Sarah Catherine McPherson Risher. In 1903 his father purchased 1,100 acres near Bartlesville, Indian Territory (now Oklahoma) and, after striking oil on this land in 1904, moved his family to the town of Bartlesville. Despite his youth, Getty quickly displayed an astute sense of business enterprise, and developed a keen interest in the oil industry and in his father's oil-prospecting firm, which had been incorporated as the

Minnehoma Oil Company. George Getty decided in 1906 for personal reasons to relocate his family from the Indiana Territory to southern California, but Jean Paul Getty spent time each summer as a teenager working in his father's oil fields around Tulsa. After graduating from high school in 1909, he took a job with his father's oil-prospecting firm.

Getty briefly attended the University of Southern California before transferring to the University of California at Berkeley in 1911, but later withdrew and enrolled at Oxford University. In 1913 he sat for and earned a noncollegiate diploma in economics and political science, and then embarked on a tour of Europe before returning to the oil fields of Oklahoma. As a student, he had a reputation for being less interested in study than in travel and in achieving the means that would permit him to pursue the life he imagined for himself.

In September 1914 Getty was surveying oil fields and, with his father's backing, started buying up low-priced oil leases in the so-called red-beds area of Oklahoma. Contrary to prevailing wisdom, these leases proved to be rich in oil deposits, and by buying and selling these oil leases and drilling wildcat oil wells in Oklahoma, Getty made his first million dollars by June 1916. After achieving economic success, including being named a director in his father's oil company, he left Tulsa for Los Angeles. He remained in southern California for two years, where it was presumably much easier to pursue another of his life's interests – women. In 1918 Getty returned to the family's Oklahoma-based oil business, but encouraged his father to enlarge the firm's oil business to the new oil fields in California. By 1922 the Gettys' Californian oilfields were a significant part of the family business. In March 1923 his father suffered a heart attack and during his absence, Jean Paul assumed the role of supervisor at George F. Getty, Inc. It was also during this period that the tensions between father, mother and son became more strained and more public.

Upon his father's death in 1930, Getty assumed the presidency and became general manager of George F. Getty, Inc. In 1933 he acquired complete control when he purchased 18,000 shares of stock from his mother. Getty pursued an expansionary strategy throughout the 1930s and acquired a majority interest in Pacific Western, California's largest oil company at the time. The economic crisis of the Great Depression in the United States provided Getty with the opportunity to buy up the stock of rival oil companies at depressed prices. He embarked on a campaign to acquire Tidewater Associated Oil Company, but was opposed by Standard Oil. Since Standard Oil controlled Tidewater through the Mission Company, Getty began buying stock in Mission and had purchased 40 per cent of Mission's stock by 1936. Getty would ultimately acquire Tidewater, but did not achieve that control until 1951.

In 1937 Getty acquired Skelly Oil. One of the subsidiaries that Getty acquired with Skelly was Spartan Aircraft. After the United States entered the Second World War, Getty telegraphed the under-secretary of the navy, James V. Forrestal, to offer his services. The navy declined his offer for active duty but did encourage Getty to gear up his industrial capacity for the war effort. During the war, Spartan Aircraft manufactured spare parts and trainers for the military. Getty personally supervised this wartime production, and boasted of Spartan's reputation and record of wartime production. In the years after the war, Spartan converted its manufacturing capacity and profitably produced mobile homes.

Like other aspects of his life, there are alternative interpretations of Getty's motives. Since he had toured Europe widely throughout the 1930s and had developed friendships with some officials in Nazi Germany, there were those who questioned his loyalties and judgement. Accordingly, his commitment to the American war effort was interpreted by some as evidence of his patriotism, while others cynically dismissed his efforts as an attempt to rehabilitate a damaged reputation.

In 1949 Getty, through Pacific Western, moved to expand his oil business into the Middle East by obtaining a sixty-year lease from King Saud of Saudi Arabia for a concession in the lands, known as the Neutral Zone, between Saudi Arabia and Kuwait. Getty was assuming significant risk since oil had not yet been discovered in this particular region. Getty agreed to a compensation scheme that required sizeable payments even if oil remained undiscovered. After a number of initial dry wells and an investment of some $30 million, a substantial oil reserve was discovered in February 1953, and Getty's fortune went from millions to billions.

After having finally gained control of the Mission Company and having become its president, Getty renamed Pacific Western the Getty Oil Company in 1956. Getty also purchased the first supertankers to transport oil, increased the number of retail gas stations and built a new refinery in Delaware. As well as his holdings in oil, real estate and manufacturing made Jean Paul Getty one of the world's richest men. Getty's holdings would ultimately include some 200 companies, with around 12,000 employees. *Fortune* magazine's 1957 pronouncement that Getty was the world's richest man brought him a level of celebrity that drew attention to his life and personality. Admired by some for his relentless and even ruthless business practices, and detested by others for these same practices, as a celebrity Getty became an icon of what was either good or bad about American business. For example, there is the often repeated story of the billionaire Getty installing pay phones in his country mansion. Getty claimed he did this so that his guests would not feel they were imposing on him; others interpreted it as a miserly act worthy of a character similar to Charles Dickens's Scrooge.

Beginning in the 1930s, Getty was a celebrated collector of fine art, including paintings, sculpture, carpets, tapestries, eighteenth-century French furniture and English silverware, and rare and first-edition books. He founded the J. Paul Getty Museum in Malibu, California in 1953. In 1970 construction began on a new structure for the museum, which was completed in 1974 at a total cost of around $1 billion. After his death in 1976, Getty's will endowed it with an additional $1.2 billion after probate, making it one of the world's richest museums. His country estate, where he lived for the last twenty-five years of his life, became the Getty Arts Centre.

Despite his many business achievements and the accumulation of vast personal wealth, Getty's personal life was marked by few enduring relationships and hardship. He was married and divorced five times and had five sons, one of whom died in adolescence and another of whom committed suicide as an adult. In July 1973 Getty's seventeen-year-old grandson J. Paul Getty III was kidnapped in Italy and held for ransom for five months before he was released, minus his right ear. The celebrity of the Getty name helped make this one of the world's most infamous kidnapping cases. Getty had initially rejected the kidnappers' demand, insisting that any payment would create an incentive to harm his other fourteen grandchildren. Ultimately he loaned his son, Eugene Paul, enough money to pay the kidnappers.

In the years after the Second World War Getty spent little time in the United States, living and controlling many of his businesses from hotel suites in Paris and London. In 1959 he moved to Sutton Place, a sixteenth-century Tudor mansion in Surrey, so as to remain close to his lucrative Middle Eastern oil interests. As he grew older, Getty became increasingly reclusive and dysfunctional, and misery seemed to haunt his descendants. When asked about his legacy, Getty quipped, 'money doesn't necessarily have any connection with happiness. Maybe with unhappiness.' At the time of his death, Getty's personal wealth was estimated at $2–4 billion.

BIBLIOGRAPHY

Getty, J.P. (1965) *How to be Rich*, New York: Jove.

Getty, J.P. (1976) *As I See It: The Autobiography of J. Paul Getty,* Englewood Cliffs, NJ: Prentice-Hall.

Lenzner, R. (1985) *The Great Getty: The Life and Loves of J. Paul Getty, Richest Man in the World*, New York: Crown Publishers.

Miller, R. (1985) *The House of Getty*, New York: Henry Holt.

TES

GIANNINI, Amadeo Peter (1870–1949)

Amadeo Peter Giannini was born in San Jose, California on 6 May 1870 and died in San Mateo, California on 3 June 1949. Giannini was the son of Italian immigrants. He attended school through the eighth grade, and then began working for his stepfather's wholesale produce company. Giannini was so successful in this business that he became a partner by the age of nineteen. In 1901 Giannini sold his interest in the firm to his employees and retired. A year later, however, he was asked to manage his recently deceased father-in-law's large estate, which included a seat on a bank board in San Francisco's North Beach area. This experience gave Giannini insight into the business potential of meeting the financing needs of small borrowers, and in 1904 he organized the Bank of Italy to meet this goal. Initially, the bank made small loans mostly to Italian merchants, farmers and labourers, and his direct contact with customers and then unconventional promotions expanded the bank to nearly $1 million in assets within two years.

The banking crisis caused by the Panic of 1907 convinced Giannini that only large banks were truly safe, but most large banks of the day did not attend to the needs of small customers. To make his bank bigger in a way that would still serve small borrowers, he successfully pushed for state banking laws to permit branch banking. During the 1910s he acquired several small banks and made them into branches of the Bank of Italy. In 1928 Giannini took advantage of liberalized banking regulations created by the McFadden Act of 1927 to expand and reorganize his banking interests. He formed a holding company, Transamerica Corporation, and converted Bank of Italy to a national charter. This conversion allowed Giannini to buy banks with strong branch networks in other states, and within a year his banking operations stretched from California to New York, as well as Italy. In 1930 he reorganized his bank holdings into two firms, the nationally chartered Bank of America National Trust and Savings Association, and the state-chartered Bank of America for his California operations. In 1933 changes in the law allowed Bank of America National Trust and Savings Association to absorb the state-chartered bank as well. The Bank of America built its business primarily by serving small businesses and individuals. It was also the first to create an extensive branch banking system. It was one of the largest and most innovative banking firms in the world, and its work helped transform modern banking practices.

Giannini left Transamerica shortly after this reorganization, but soon returned to help guide the firm through the banking crises of 1932–3. His leadership helped the company weather the Great Depression, and by 1939 the total assets of the bank had doubled to $1.6 billion. The growth of Giannini's banking business, however, drew increased criticism from competitors, and in 1949 the Federal Reserve Board held anti-trust hearings that eventually forced Transamerica to sell all its banking stock except that of Bank of America.

Giannini did not live to see the partial dismantling of his banking empire, but at the time of his death Bank of America was the world's largest commercial bank, with over 500 branches in California, and offices worldwide. Transamerica Corporation was also a large diversified conglomerate controlling banks, financial institutions, real estate and industrial companies. Although it never reached his goal of a worldwide network of branch banks, Giannini's bank was important in the economic growth of California and the Pacific coast region.

BIBLIOGRAPHY
Bonadio, F.A. (1994) *A.P. Giannini: Banker of America*, Berkeley, CA: University of California Press.
Nash, G.D. (1992) *A.P. Giannini and the Bank of America*, Norman, OK: University of Oklahoma Press.

DM

GILBRETH, Frank Bunker (1868–1924)

Frank Bunker Gilbreth was born in Freeport, Maine on 7 July 1868 to Hiram and Martha Gilbreth. He died in Montclair, New Jersey, on 14 June 1924. Gilbreth attended Boston English High School. While he was an average student, he had a mechanically adept mind and passed his entrance examinations for the Massachusetts Institute of Technology. However, he chose instead to go to work for Whidden and Company Construction, where he was hired in a quasi-management training position. Later, from 1895 through 1911, he was president of Frank Gilbreth Construction, and, starting in 1912, he and his wife formed Gilbreth Consulting, Incorporated. In February 1921 he was honoured by being asked to display his motion study work at the Olympic Exposition in London. He also received an honorary LLD from the University of Maine in 1920.

At Whidden Construction, his first assignment was as a bricklayer's apprentice, but he was not satisfied with merely learning a skill. He wanted to know why his instructors laid a brick using one set of motions when working on their own, and different motions when they were teaching him. These observations were the beginning of Gilbreth's pioneering work in motion study and ergonomics, and led to his first invention. At the age of twenty-four, he was granted the first of many patents for what he called his 'non-stooping scaffold'. This scaffold was designed to improve the rate at which bricks were laid. However, the truly significant fact was that the design intentionally reduced the amount of stress and fatigue on the workers' backs. Prior to his invention, bricklayers spent most of their time bending over to pick up bricks and then mortar, both of which were kept beside the worker's feet. With Gilbreth's scaffold, a second level was added, at the worker's waist height, for the storage of materials. The scaffold would be raised so that the top of the wall, being built, was always even with the worker's torso. In this way, the worker could lay more brick in a day and would be less fatigued, particularly in terms of back strain.

In 1895 Frank Gilbreth formed his own construction company, which built projects all over the United States. With little in the way of formal management training, the success of his company was the result of a growing system of acquired knowledge, which Gilbreth called his 'field system'. He was once advised that he did not have a system unless it was written down, and he took this advice to heart. The field system was a written set of rules and standards. These standards were based on past experience of what methods worked and what did not. His long-standing rule was that anyone could make an alternative suggestion, but this change would have to be evaluated and found to be more efficient before it was adopted. If the new rule was accepted, the developer was paid for the suggestion and a new standard established.

The summer of 1903 marked two important events in the history of business management. Frederick W. TAYLOR presented his paper called 'Shop Management' before the American Society of Mechanical Engineers, and Frank Gilbreth first met his future wife and business partner, Lillian Moller (see Lillian GILBRETH). These two events led to the later formation of Gilbreth Consulting Engineers. During their courtship, Frank told Lillian that he wanted two things from their marriage. First, he wanted her to be not only his wife but also his business partner. He needed someone who could learn the business and help him with improvements. His second desire was that they should have twelve children, and more specifically six boys and six girls. The often comical aspects of the Gilbreth 'dozen' were made famous by the books *Cheaper by the Dozen* and *Belles on Their Toes* written by two of their children.

Gilbreth later read Taylor's paper on shop management. In this paper, he thought he found the epitome of his own efforts to systematize the operation of his construction company. This inspired the Gilbreths to write their first books: *Field System* (1908a) and *Concrete System* (1908b) and later, *Bricklaying System* (1909). Frank Gilbreth became almost obsessed with Taylor and his system, which later came to be known as scientific management. Taylor in turn became interested in Gilbreth's work in bricklaying improvements, where the output of bricklayers had been increased from an average of 125 bricks per hour to 350. Taylor later included a chapter on Gilbreth's work in his book *Principles of Scientific Management*, first published in 1911.

While he was an ardent supporter of Taylor and his system, Frank Gilbreth believed that he and Lillian, who was then studying for her doctorate in psychology, could help to improve the Taylor system, using their motion study work and by developing a greater emphasis on the human factor, an element largely absent from Taylor's system.

Unknown to Gilbreth, the last thing Taylor wanted was what he called 'those damned improvements'. Taylor felt that his system, as written, was perfect and should not be tinkered with. Indeed, Taylor and his disciples on several occasions did everything they could to squelch the Gilbreths' consulting practice.

Ironically, after Taylor's death, these same disciples (notably Sanford Thompson and Horace Hathaway) then tried to take credit for many of the Gilbreths' innovations and even claimed that Taylor first came up with the idea of motion study. This notion is negated by two letters exchanged between Frank Gilbreth and Frederick Taylor, in 1913. In a letter to Taylor, Gilbreth, who had just patented his micromotion study apparatus, offered to give the system to Taylor. Taylor, who felt the system was no more than a gadget, replied that Gilbreth was the better man to develop the system.

In modern parlance, people talk about 'time and motion studies' as if they were somehow linked as a system. However, the two systems were never used together until more than twenty-five years after Frank Gilbreth's death (Jaffe 1984). Taylor's time study was a part of a system to optimize the output of workers. He would study the basic tasks performed, using a stopwatch to measure the times of the best workers. These times would then be used to formulate piecework pay to reward workers able to meet the new standard. In contrast, the Gilbreths' system of motion study did not establish time standards, but instead established standards for how materials and tools could best be designed and arranged to fit the abilities of the human worker. In his free moments Gilbreth championed causes ranging from the rights of the disabled to the Simplified Spelling movement.

As with his early experiences in bricklaying, Frank Gilbreth believed that there was One Best Way to perform a task, not one best time, as Taylor's system promoted. The Gilbreths later would call their system 'The One Best Way To Do Work'. Their book, *Motion Study*

(1911), was significant in that it contained detailed lists of various physical, mental and sociological attributes of the individual. This study drew two important conclusions: (1) that with the wide variety of attributes and exponential combinations of these attributes, there was no such thing as an average worker, but (2) there were some commonalties which could be addressed. The first of these common aspects the tackled by the Gilbreths was fatigue.

Studies and papers examining fatigue were numerous during Gilbreth's lifetime. However, these studies either focused on measuring the worker's physical endurance or called for reducing the length of work days (which in this era ranged from twelve to sixteen hours per day). In their book *Fatigue Study* (1916), the Gilbreths asked, why should we measure the limits of fatigue (which they knew would vary from person to person); why not simply eliminate *all unnecessary fatigue* by eliminating wasted motions and make the remaining work as simple as possible? In this way, a business would provide optimum conditions, which would allow each worker to perform at their best.

A prime example of their fatigue work involved modifying chairs and workbenches to meet the individual statures of the workers. They recognized that excessive reaches for tools and parts caused unnecessary fatigue, and they designed many simple appliances to reduce this overexertion. Recognizing that fatigue was also caused by remaining in one position all day, they invented the concept of the 'sit-stand' workstation.

The final piece of the motion study system developed when the Gilbreths became interested in ways to employ disabled workers. They found that by analysing the essential elements of a task, and with minor design accommodations, the majority of jobs could be performed by people with almost any type or combination of disabilities. Not only was this ground-breaking work in the movement to employ the disabled, it drove home the point that, no matter the condition or need,

the workplace could and should accommodate the physical needs of the worker.

Frank Gilbreth developed numerous methods for studying the motions of workers. He first employed the fledgling field of motion pictures, where films of work tasks were studied frame by frame. Owing to the great expense of this method, he invented the cyclegraph and chronocyclegraph. These methods used time-exposed photographs in combination with flashing lights attached to the workers' hands or head. The results showed not only the path of travel of the motion, but the time it took to complete. Charts and other analysis methods were also developed to track unnecessary or overly fatiguing motions. In order to set standards in the study of motions, the Gilbreths identified seventeen different motions, which they called *Therbligs* (the name derived from rearranging the letters of Gilbreth). By charting the Therbligs of each hand, they could identify long reaches, unnecessary pauses or redundant motions. From these studies, the Gilbreths developed numerous devices which today are considered mainstays of ergonomic design. For example, in their typing studies, they were the first to propose a redesign of the keyboard (later developed by August Dvorak), the wrist rest, the shift-lock key and the copy holder. With no modern test instruments or detailed ergonomics studies, the Gilbreths were able to identify the best biomechanical abilities of the human form, and design tools and work to fit them.

Frank Gilbreth also invented the process chart, a form of 'macro-motion study', whereby the manufacturing process was traced from raw materials to finished product. The process chart used symbols to characterize types of work activities, so that redundant or unnecessary steps could be discovered and eliminated. Not only has the process chart, with minor variations and improvements, remained an important tool in business efficiency, it has also given birth to other applications. Remarkable similarities can be found in methods such as fault tree analysis as well as systems safety techniques.

One important legacy of Frank Gilbreth's work can be found in modern hospital operating theatres. Then, as now, it was recognized that the shorter the duration of an operation, the better were the chances for the patient's recovery. Using motion study, Gilbreth found that contemporary operations were grossly inefficient, in that the doctor spent half of the operating time looking for the next instrument he needed. Frank felt that a superior method would be to have the doctor signal or call for his next instrument and to have the nurse place it in his hand. While we easily recognize this technique as common practice today, Gilbreth had to fight long and hard for its acceptance. Many of his other methods of reducing motions and achieving greater speed were also adopted. Just a few examples include using the *Therblig* of 'prepositioning' a tool, whereby the nurse would place the instrument in the doctor's hand in the position in which it would be used. Gilbreth's packet principle, was also developed, according to which nurses arranged instruments on a tray in the order in which they would be used, thus saving further time. Today, hospital emergency rooms are stocked with prearranged instrument trays, each designated to perform specific procedures.

The successes of Frank and Lillian Gilbreth received sporadic recognition while Frank was alive, but he did not receive proper recognition for much of his pioneering work until many years after his death. Recognition was further muddled by some of Taylor's followers, who were quick to condemn Gilbreth's methods and equally quick to take credit for his accomplishments. However, thanks to the efforts of Lillian Gilbreth, the pioneering work of Gilbreth, Incorporated was not forgotten. Next to raising and educating her family, her main objective was to see that Frank received proper credit for his work. She also ensured that their papers were preserved at Purdue University.

Despite the many Gilbreth innovations already in use, there are many more yet to be adopted. A large portion of the business community is still opposed to ergonomics as being too costly, despite the proof that the Gilbreths offered of dramatic increases in production. Businesses whose workers put in long hours are just now recognizing the benefits of providing these employees with places to take short naps to improve their alertness, a proposal made by the Gilbreths in 1911. And most of all, the Gilbreths' call for inclusion of the 'human factor' into the way employers deal with employees remains a challenge for managers everywhere.

BIBLIOGRAPHY

Note: the first four works listed below were published under Frank Gilbreth's name alone, but were in fact co-authored with Lillian Gilbreth. Her name began appearing on the covers from 1912 on.

Gilbreth, F. (1908a) *Field System*, New York: Myron C. Clark.

—— (1908a) *Concrete System*, New York: The Engineering News Publishing Company.

—— (1909) *Bricklaying System*, New York: Myron C. Clark.

—— (1911) *Motion Study*, New York: Van Nostrand Company.

Gilbreth, F. and Gilbreth L. (1912) *Primer of Scientific Management*, New York: Van Nostrand Company.

—— (1916) *Fatigue Study*, New York: Sturgis and Walton.

—— (1917) *Applied Motion Study*, New York: Sturgis and Walton.

—— (1920) *Motion Study for the Handicapped*, New York: Macmillan.

Gilbreth, F.B., Jr and Carey, E.G. (1949) *Cheaper by the Dozen*, London: William Heinemann.

—— (1950) *Belles on the Their Toes*, London: William Heinemann.

Jaffe, W. (1984) 'Standardisation and Scientific Management', *Mechanical*

Engineering (April): 56–9.

Yost, E. (1949) *Frank and Lillian Gilbreth: Partners for Life*, New Brunswick, NJ: Rutgers University Press.

DF

GILBRETH, Lillian Evelyn Moller
(1878–1972)

Lillian Evelyn Moller was born on 24 May 1878 in Oakland, California, where her German-American parents owned a hardware and plumbing supply business. She died on 2 January 1972, in Phoenix, Arizona. During her childhood, in her own words, she was 'an introvert by inclination ... she lived most happily in her books' (Gilbreth 1998: 57). Her love of reading led her to enter the University of California at Berkeley, against some opposition from her parents, who felt that young ladies had no need of college. She received her BA in 1900 and her master's degree in 1903, both in literature, hoping for a future in teaching or college administration. Upon completion of her undergraduate degree, Lillian was chosen as the first woman to deliver a commencement address at Berkeley. This period was also one of her first experiences with blatant gender discrimination: when she achieved the same score as a young man in competition for the Phi Beta Kappa Key, she was told that the man would in fact receive the award because he had more use for it (Gilbreth 1998: 72)

In 1903 she met Frank Bunker GILBRETH, then the president of his own construction company. They married in October 1904, with a plan to raise twelve children and to be full partners both at home and in Frank's business. Together the Gilbreths developed techniques for finding the one best way to do work, starting with the various tasks of building construction. By 1911 Lillian was already establishing herself as a leading advocate of applying psychology to the job of management; she took a Ph.D. in psychology from Brown University in 1915. Upon their two specialities – motion study and the psychology of management – the Gilbreths built a distinctive management system which they offered to businesses from 1912 to 1924 as an alternative to Frederick TAYLOR's more famous system. Although they started out as allies of Taylor, differences arose and by 1921 they were arguing that their industrial management system was both more scientific and more humane than Taylor's time study system.

In 1924 Frank Gilbreth was invited to Europe to help launch the First International Management Congress, but he died of a heart attack a few days before they were due to sail. Lillian Gilbreth found herself on her own with eleven children to raise. She set about achieving two major goals. First, she had to generate a living that would not only keep the family together, but also see to it that all the children were able to attend university. Second, she wanted to see that her husband received proper credit for his work and that this work was carried on. Her first step in this latter venture was to attend the International Management Congress in Frank's place and to deliver his speech.

Upon returning home, she found that almost all of their clients had either cancelled or failed to renew their contracts. Even though she had been an equal working partner in Gilbreth, Inc., most of the firm's clients had little faith that she could undertake consulting work alone. Some businessmen still sought her counsel but, in order to avoid ridicule, they consulted with her by phone or mail rather than in person. Nonetheless, Gilbreth was able to keep the family afloat financially by starting, in late 1925, to teach a motion study course in her home to representatives from various businesses. At the same time, she pursued consulting contracts with firms employing women such as a secretarial training school, a sandwich-making company and department stores such as Macys, where she worked without pay or even a signed contract (this work ultimately did lead to paying contracts with other retailers, however).

Gilbreth soon began to recognize that she would need to reinvent Gilbreth, Inc. in such a way that a woman management expert would be considered acceptable, even preferable. As a person, Lillian Gilbreth tried to avoid confrontation. In the partnership, she had always been the quiet peacemaker who countered Frank's sometimes less than diplomatic approach. It is no surprise, then, that she chose not to take up the battle for women's rights. Instead, she took a pragmatic approach to improving women's lives. With recent advances in both household technology and child development research, she thought she could offer useful advice to American homemakers. In two household advice books in the mid-1920s, *The Homemaker and Her Job* (1927) and *Living With Our Children* (1928), she brought the ideas and methods of scientific management to bear on homemaking. Even though these books were not the first to extend business management methods to homemaking, Gilbreth's writings were the first to show homemakers how to conduct their own motion studies, and psychological studies of themselves and their children.

These books helped to establish Gilbreth as a homemaking expert, drawing on her increasingly public persona as a domestic whiz/mother of eleven. This led to contracts with utility companies and women's magazines designing efficiency kitchens. For example, she designed 'The Kitchen Practical' for the Brooklyn Borough Gas Company in 1929 and several other efficiency kitchens for the *New York Herald Tribune Magazine* in 1930. Efficiency kitchens promoted Gilbreth's engineering methods and expertise, applying motion study and psychology, to homemaking,

but they also promoted the latest kitchen appliances and the utilities that powered these appliances. Thus, these projects brought Lillian into a commercial realm during a period when middle- and upper-class kitchens changed from large rooms accommodating several servants to small, technologically up-to-date workspaces perfect for the solitary homemaker. She emphasized correct heights of work surfaces and a circular workspace that would minimize reaching, walking, bending and lifting. In effect, the principles of Gilbreth-style scientific management were made operational in the kitchen. Lillian's personal story as a struggling, widowed mother of eleven added a fascinating backdrop to the spectacle offered by these kitchens and attracted consumers to the philosophy, as well as the appliances on display. These kitchens were toured by thousands of women and publicized in women's magazines. By 1930 the income she was earning from these commercial projects allowed her to stop teaching her motion study courses.

In 1929, at the onset of the Great Depression, her friend and fellow engineer President Herbert Hoover called her to Washington to head up the women's division of his Emergency Committee on Unemployment. She was by that time a recognized spokesperson on women and work, and, thanks to opinion research she carried out for such firms as Johnson and Johnson, she was also considered capable of doing sophisticated research on the needs and desires of women nationwide. American women became better understood by government and private companies thanks to her efforts.

In the early 1930s she was offered a part-time professorship at Purdue University, where first her husband and then she had given annual lectures for many years. There she founded the 'work simplification' curriculum in the school of home economics, and established a motion study laboratory in the school of management. She commuted by train from her home in New Jersey to Purdue (in West Lafayette, Indiana), staying about a month at a time and living in a girl's dormitory. Her children were all of school age by that time, but she still worried about them constantly and sometimes requested the advice of her college-age dorm-mates when one of her children was having a problem.

The 1940s, 1950s and 1960s saw Gilbreth pursue a variety of research topics and speaking engagements, often on the topic of household scientific management. Home economics departments, such as the one at the University of Connecticut in Storrs, borrowed her services to set up their practice kitchens and work simplification courses. Companies such as Maytag invited her as special guest and speaker at their annual banquets. Engineering professor Alan Mogenson invited her to do a series of annual talks on this subject to his students in Lake Placid, New York. She travelled around the world studying management advances and delivering speeches on the pioneers of scientific management and what their historical legacy can offer the contemporary world; a gifted speaker, she became an unofficial ambassador to the world's business community, promoting the exchange of management knowledge. During the New Deal era and the Second World War, Gilbreth remained on call to the Women's Bureau of the Department of Labour. Her success in mobilizing women's clubs during the Depression stood as evidence of her insight into the needs of women and their social groups. In all, she served in posts for six consecutive US presidents, beginning with Herbert Hoover in 1929.

Gilbreth considered her greatest achievement to be her efforts to design kitchens and other accommodations for disabled homemakers. This was an extension of her work with Frank in designing workspaces for disabled war veterans. It attracted the interest of such organizations as the American Heart Association, which called upon her to design a 'Heart of the Home Kitchen' for homemakers with heart conditions. Mothers who had suffered from polio required specially engineered clothes for themselves and their small children, and she contributed to these advances behind the scenes. Looking back at these efforts from the present era with the Americans With Disabilities Act becoming part of the business mindset, her efforts might seem minute; but for individuals with disabilities in the 1940s and 1950s, her work was probably viewed as a godsend that male engineers might never have provided.

From a management historian's point of view, perhaps Gilbreth's greatest historical contribution was to the human factors approach in modern management. To the new field of personnel management, she offered pioneering words on the subject of individual differences as well as practical methods for ascertaining, measuring and adjusting placement of workers in ways that capitalized on these differences. In the 1930s, for example, she often wrote on the topic of job satisfaction, arguing that different types of work can be found satisfying to different types of individuals. The key was to match individuals to the type of work that fit their natural attributes. This was a far more advanced image of the worker than that espoused by Frederick Taylor and his associates in the early days of management; and it was a view that recognized the need to improve the work experience in many jobs so that no worker was expected to waste his or her special talents and skills.

Lillian Gilbreth's legacy to women worldwide is not limited to her professional contributions. Over the course of her life, and especially after the publication of the famous books about her family (*Cheaper By the Dozen* and *Belles On Their Toes*), she provided a role model that inspired thousands of women to hold onto the dream of having a career and a family in spite of the obstacles that persist in a patriarchal society. She had a remarkable and distinguished career as 'America's First Lady of Engineering', along with a large, well-adjusted and successful family. Her marriage to Frank Gilbreth set high standards for modern couples, long before the two-earner family became the norm. Then, from 1924 onward, she did it all without the help of a husband, and with only a handyman and occasional secretary in her employ. Women of today, with comparatively normal careers and small, manageable families, still stand in awe of this woman. She was a prototype of the modern superwoman, balancing family and career, and somehow remaining humble and personable in the process. Many women in science, engineering and management today cite Lillian Gilbreth as an influence on their own decision to have a career.

As to her pledge to see that Frank Gilbreth received credit for his work and that that work was carried on, she kept her promise. In the 1930s she began to prepare her own and Frank's papers for donation to Purdue University. The Gilbreth Collection is an important historical record which can still provide ideas and inspiration. As to Frank's favourite invention, motion study, she continued to teach the techniques in her early classes in Montclair and later at Purdue. She also played a major role in later work in motion study by the likes of Anne Shaw (in England), Ralph Barnes and Alan Mogenson. It is through her students and colleagues that her intellectual legacy continues to shape managerial practice and the work experience around the world.

Aside from her doctorate in industrial psychology, she received twenty-three honorary degrees and twenty-six awards in her lifetime.

BIBLIOGRAPHY

Gilbreth, F.B, Jr (1994) *Ancestors of the Dozen*, private printing.

Gilbreth, F. and Gilbreth, L. (1912) *Primer of Scientific Management*, New York: Van Nostrand Co.

—— (1916) *Fatigue Study*, New York: Sturgis and Walton.

—— (1917) *Applied Motion Study*, New York: Sturgis and Walton.

—— (1920) *Motion Study for the Handicapped*, New York: Macmillan.

Gilbreth, L.M. (1914) *The Psychology of Management*, New York: Sturgis and Wilton.

—— (1924) *Quest for the One Best Way*, Chicago: Chicago Society of Industrial Engineers.

—— (1927) *The Homemaker and Her Job*, New York: D. Appleton.

—— (1928) *Living With Our Children*, New York: W.W. Norton.

—— (1998) *As I Remember*, Norcross, GA: Engineering and Management Press

Gilbreth, L.M. and Cook, A.R. (1947) *The Forman and Manpower Management*, New York: McGraw Hill.

Gilbreth, L.M. and Yost, E. (1944) *Normal Lives for the Disabled*, New York: Macmillan.

Gilbreth, L.M., Thomas, O.M. and Clymer, E. (1954) *Management in the Home*, New York: Dodd, Mead and Co.

LG
DF

GIRARD, Stephen (1750–1831)

Stephen Girard was born in Bordeaux, France on 20 May 1750, the son of a French naval officer. He died near Philadelphia on 26 December 1831. Though blind in one eye from birth, he resolved on a career at sea. At the age of fourteen he sailed as a cabin boy on a trading ship to the West Indies. Remaining in the West Indies for some years, he became involved in trade and was appointed a ship's captain in 1773, aged twenty-three. On a visit to New York in 1774, however, he decided to give up the sea and became instead a partner in a merchant business. He moved to Philadelphia in 1776, just before the outbreak of the American Revolution. He married Mary Lum in 1777. The couple had no children; she later became mentally ill and was institutionalized until her death in 1815.

Girard seems to have prospered despite the conflict, and after the end of the war began engaging in foreign trade and buying ships. He quickly amassed a fortune, and, like many rich traders before him, invested some of his capital in banking. The private Bank of Stephen Girard, established in Philadelphia in 1810, quickly became one of the more important financial institutions in Pennsylvania, even (illegally) issuing its own bank notes. Now one of the most important financiers in the country, in 1812 Girard entered a syndicate along with John Jacob ASTOR to sell government bonds to finance the war of 1812. After the war he was a founder director of the Bank of the United States, but resigned after disagreement with the bank's president. A philanthropist, he established Girard College, a large private school near Philadelphia.

One of the most successful bankers in US history, Girard is the outstanding example of the early nineteenth-century accumulator of capital who prospered, largely through trade, and did much to lay the foundations on which the first large American corporations were built later in the century. The astonishing successes of the American financial community in the nineteenth century have often been overlooked, but it seems clear that this success was critical to the later rapid growth of industry. The railways and other large firms which emerged after the American Civil War could not have done so without capital, and it was men like Girard who launched the financial institutions which provided that capital.

BIBLIOGRAPHY

Macmaster, J.B. (1918) *The Life and Times of Stephen Girard*, 2 vols, Philadelphia: J.B. Lippincott.

MLW

GOIZUETA, Roberto Crispulo (1931–97)

Roberto Crispulo Goizueta was born in Havana, Cuba on 18 November 1931 to a relatively wealthy family. He died on 18 October 1997 in Atlanta, Georgia. Goizueta grew up in one of the nicest neighbourhoods in the capital city. He attended Belen Academy, a Jesuit institution that has been called 'a veritable fortress of wealth and power for the aristocratic class of prerevolutionary Cuba' (Greising 1998: 8). While a student he visited the United States for summer camps, and then spent a year in prep school at Cheshire Academy in Connecticut. Accepted by several elite universities, Goizueta chose Yale and majored in chemical engineering. Soon after graduation in 1953 he married Olguita Casteleiro, whom he had begun dating while at Belen.

After graduating from Yale, Goizueta spent about a year working for his father in the family firm which dealt in architecture, real estate and sugar refining. Soon, however, he decided that he wanted to prove himself outside the family's business. In mid-1954 Goizueta spotted a classified advertisement for an unnamed company seeking a recently graduated chemical engineer with good English skills – precisely his qualifications. The employer was Coca-Cola, and he got the job. Believing that the young man should have a personal stake in the company, Goizueta's father loaned him $8,000 to buy 100 shares of the Atlanta-based soft drink giant. Fortuitously, the shares were placed in a custodial account in New York City.

The young engineer quickly became a key figure in technical matters such as quality control for the five Coke bottling plants in Cuba. He made several trips to Atlanta and even met Robert W. Woodruff, the president and personification of Coca-Cola. When Fidel Castro, also a Belen Academy graduate, took control of the country in 1959, Goizueta, like many among Cuba's elite, left for the United States. By mid-1960 nationalization of Coke's plants seemed imminent, and the Castro government was restricting the export of money and technical information. In order not to reveal that the family intended to emigrate, Roberto and Olguita departed in early October 1960 with only a couple of hundred dollars and clothes suitable for a vacation. Like most early Cuban émigrés, Goizueta assumed that he would some day return when the Castro regime collapsed. He even compiled from memory an inventory of the physical assets of Coca-Cola's Cuban plants to use as evidence in future claims proceedings.

Goizueta had established himself well enough in the company that he had a new job assignment as soon as he reached Miami, an advantage that most fellow Cubans in the United States did not have. At first, the Goizueta family lived in a modest Miami apartment, but soon their fortunes began to rise. Attached to Latin American technical operations and working out of an office in Nassau, Goizueta travelled throughout the region. Spurning offers from other companies, he made important contacts that would serve him well as he climbed Coke's corporate ladder.

In 1964, new Coke president Paul Austin brought Goizueta to Atlanta to work at company headquarters. Austin had met Goizueta in pre-Castro Havana, and the Cuban fit with Austin's plans to emphasize international operations. Austin put the engineer to work analysing the structure of company decision making, first in technical operations and then in other fields. The early confidence that Austin placed in 33-year-old Goizueta was the career turning point that moved him from purely engineering concerns to broader management issues. Goizueta was the first immigrant to be given such a critical headquarters task. His supreme confidence, impeccable grooming and gentlemanly, even aristocratic, demeanour helped Goizueta move comfortably among executives much his senior.

Goizueta's first major report on management restructuring called for a more centralized approach to formulating technical standards and providing expertise, while still allowing for decentralized decision making consistent with those standards. Greising (1998: 36) believed that this approach 'would become a hallmark of Goizueta's approach to broader management and strategic challenges as chief executive of the company'. On the basis of this work Goizueta was promoted to vice-president of technical research and development, becoming at the age of thirty-five the youngest vice-president in company history. Already closely linked to the rising Austin, Goizueta now had opportunity for occasional visits with Woodruff, still known as 'the Boss', and learned to flatter Woodruff as a key means to further advancement.

Goizueta's career took a leap forward in 1974, when a senior executive suffered a debilitating heart attack. Goizueta moved into the gap, and Austin made him senior vice-president of the technical division. Importantly, Goizueta now became one of only two executives who knew the secret formula for concocting Coca-Cola syrup. At this time the relationship between Austin and Woodruff was becoming strained, primarily over Austin's efforts to diversify through corporate acquisitions. Although 'the Boss' was no longer president or chairman, he remained the most influential force in the company through his domination of the finance committee and by virtue of the fact that he remained the single largest stockholder. Goizueta had to negotiate a fine line between loyalty to Austin, his mentor, and courting the favour of Woodruff. He proved especially adept at the latter.

By the end of 1979 there was intense competition among top executives to succeed the ageing Austin. Most outside observers did not see Goizueta as a leading candidate to move up, but his competitors inside were well aware that the Cuban was an astute corporate politician. The leading candidates for the top job appeared to be Ian R. Wilson, a South African who was then heading Far East operations, and Donald R. Keough, who was in charge of US operations. Wilson was cosier with Woodruff even than Goizueta, and he was also Austin's choice as successor. His abrasive style, his principally international emphasis, his status as a white South African, and perhaps most of all, Robert Woodruff's and the board's growing disenchantment with Austin all worked against Wilson. In early 1980 Keough and Goizueta formed an alliance, each agreeing to appoint the other as number two if he should win the top spot.

In May 1980 Woodruff, still in control of a majority of the board despite his ninety years and failing health, informed Austin that he had decided that Goizueta would be the successor. Goizueta quickly assumed the position of president while Austin, for the time being, remained CEO and chairman of the board. In twenty-six years, the supremely self-confident Cuban engineer had gone from answering a blind 'help wanted' ad in a Havana newspaper to the presidency of one of the world's best-known companies. But his ascendancy to the chairmanship and full control was not yet complete.

The key to Coca-Cola's operations in the United States and abroad was the independent bottler system. These companies bought Coke syrup, mixed it with carbonated water and distributed the finished product. Many of the US bottlers were not pleased with the choice of Goizueta. They tended to prefer Keough, who was more attuned to the marketing than the technical side of operations. Even Woodruff was not sure that he wanted Goizueta to have full control. Goizueta realized this weakness, and he quickly set out to ingratiate himself with the bottlers, especially with the financially stronger ones that could be expected to absorb smaller, poorer performing firms. This strategy, along with strong support from key members of the board of Atlanta's Trust Company Bank, worked. The untimely death of a potential Woodruff-backed figurehead chairman sealed the contest. Only 100 days after they had named him president, the Coca-Cola board designated Roberto Goizueta as chairman and chief executive officer, to be effective from early 1981. The new CEO stood by his agreement to make Donald Keough the clear second in command as president and chief operating officer.

Goizueta moved quickly to put his mark on Coke's elderly and conservative board of directors. He pushed through age and term restrictions that would eventually move Woodruff's old cronies aside. More importantly, he wrested control of the all-important finance committee from 'the Boss'. Goizueta still courted Woodruff's blessings for major moves such as borrowing money to buy out bottlers, but no one doubted any longer that the Cuban was firmly in charge.

The new chairman faced several challenges, the most troubling of which was that his flagship brand was losing domestic market share to arch-rival Pepsi-Cola. Also needing attention were inefficiencies in overseas operations and a generally unprofitable collection of diversified subsidiaries. Coke's stock value had seriously lagged, and many of company's biggest investors, including Trust Company Bank, had backed Goizueta in the hopes that he was the leader who could restore shareholder value. The chairman understood that challenge at the most basic level because he still held the original 100 shares that he obtained in 1954 when he first went to work for Coke in Havana in 1954. Although technically a hired hand, Goizueta thought and acted like an owner.

Goizueta made it clear to bottlers and executives that he held no reverence for 'sacred cows', not even the secret formula. As a chemical engineer, he regarded the formula as a chemical compound that could be altered and improved. As a corporate engineer of sorts, he regarded the 'Coke' name as an asset that could be leveraged for greater profit. These two assumptions led him to one of his greatest triumphs and to his most public disaster.

The triumph was Diet Coke. The company's diet cola Tab sold well, but its once rapid growth rate had flattened by the early 1980s. Tradition and fear of legal technicalities had kept the company from using the 'Coke' name on any product save the original concoction. In fact, Goizueta had looked favourably on the Diet Coke project in the 1970s, but he chose not to champion it while he was jockeying for executive leadership. Paul Austin, in one of his last major decisions as CEO, pulled the plug on Diet Coke, but now that he was in charge Goizueta quickly revived the effort. Tradition did not concern Goizueta, and the legal fears proved to be considerably overstated. Confident that the Coke brand would make the product a success, and assured that company chemists had formulated a beverage that tasted better than other diet drinks, including Tab, Goizueta was ready to move. Again using his charm to bring Woodruff over to his side, Goizueta released Diet Coke in the summer of 1982. It was an immediate success: by the end of 1983 it was the nation's fourth most popular soft drink behind only Coke, Pepsi and 7-Up. Diet Coke's slogan 'just for the taste of it' symbolized a whole new market for low-calorie sodas.

In his next assault on a sacred cow, Goizueta learned that taste was not enough. Pepsi mounted an advertising campaign based on taste tests that showed their product winning in head-to-head consumer comparisons. Coke's secret replications of the tests showed Pepsi to be right. And sales figures showed Pepsi gaining, more from minor brands than from Coke, but gaining nonetheless. Executives were worried, and rightly so.

As in the case of Diet Coke, Goizueta had encouraged laboratory work on the formula while he was head of the technical division, but he had not pushed for implementation while he worked at that level. The laboratories and test marketers worked feverishly, and secretly, to find a formula that consumers would prefer. It was not an easy task.

Everyone knew that Pepsi tasted sweeter, but simply adding more sugar to Coca-Cola would not do the trick. Ironically, in the meantime Pepsi had quit using taste tests in its advertising because the campaign was getting old and the 'Cola War' was costing too much in price cuts.

Coca-Cola market researchers were aware that loyal Coke drinkers might resist a new formula for reasons of emotion as much as palate. But, as it turned out, they underestimated the depth of those feelings. Clinical taste tests were not enough because, as Frederick Allen, author of the company history *Secret Formula*, later wrote: 'taste buds would always be compromised by the thoughts and emotions and associations that the name of the product conjured up in their minds. Knowing what they were drinking would always affect the taste' (Allen 1994: 401). Goizueta knew that no one was more emotionally attached to Coca-Cola than Robert Woodruff. According to Allen, the CEO gently hinted to 'the Boss' about the possible need to tinker with the formula but never told him point blank that a change was in the works because Woodruff would have 'hit me over the head' (Allen 1994: 408).

While the new Coke project was brewing, Goizueta was making other moves that, coupled with Diet Coke's success, enhanced corporate profits and substantially raised stock prices. In early 1982 he purchased Columbia Pictures. The Hollywood diversification quickly turned a profit with some box office successes, and Coke was able to divest itself of Columbia for a sizeable capital gain. The Columbia deal, at first widely criticized, helped give Goizueta a reputation for financial as well as technical brilliance. In the meantime, Goizueta also jettisoned Coke's wine and coffee lines and other subsidiaries.

By 1984 Coke's chemists and marketers were convinced that they had a product that would consistently beat Pepsi, and original Coke itself, in head-to-head taste tests. For a combination of legal, ethical and marketing reasons, Goizueta and his team rejected the idea of just quietly making the change and not announcing it. Also, there was a vigorous internal debate about whether to retire original Coke or to market both a new and regular product. The main problem with the two-brand strategy was that it would likely divide market share and assure first place for Pepsi even if the two products combined outsold the rival. According to Allen, Goizueta had to be convinced to add the word 'new' to the actual name of the beverage and he had to be persuaded not to mention explicitly the Pepsi challenge in the initial press conference and early promotion of the change. In retrospect, the CEO would have been better off to have gone with his initial approach.

Despite the Herculean efforts at secrecy, word had leaked out, and Pepsi was ready with a vigorous, and effective, response to the announcement of New Coke in April 1985. Pepsi simply declared that they had won the 'Cola War'. In Pepsi's view, Coca-Cola was not just introducing a reformulated product, they were admitting that they had been beaten. Much of the press accepted this explanation, and a surprisingly inept initial press conference by Goizueta and Keough probably made matters worse rather than better. As Allen succinctly put it, 'Long before they had ever tasted a sip of it, millions of Americans decided they *hated* New Coke ... Many people didn't *want* to like New Coke. The were unable to give it a fair chance' (Allen 1994: 413–14). Editorial cartoonists, late night comedians and even the respected conservative radio commentator Paul Harvey ridiculed the change. The public outcry was nearly unanimous.

As an engineer who believed in facts and figures, Goizueta had a difficult time comprehending that consumers would make such a non-rational decision. But as an executive, Goizueta could recognize a mistake, and he was not afraid to admit it and fix it. In mid-summer, less than three months after the introduction of New Coke, Goizueta bowed

to public pressure and announced that 'Classic Coke' was back. Personally, Goizueta preferred New Coke and continued to drink it even after Coke Classic returned, but he was the exception. For a brief few months Pepsi gained sales leadership, but by early 1986 Coca-Cola Classic was back on top. Meanwhile, Diet Coke passed 7-Up to capture third place. Pepsi had won a battle but not the war. As CEO, Goizueta shouldered blame for the initial decision, and it would stay with him for the rest of his career; but all was forgiven by Coca-Cola stockholders as their net worth climbed sky high in the late 1980s and 1990s. Goizueta knew that competition was the driving force of the free market system. 'If Pepsi-Cola didn't exist,' he told a reporter years after the New Coke episode, 'I would try to invent it. It keeps us, and them, on our toes and keeps us lean' (Roush 1996).

In fact, increasing stockholder value was Goizueta's primary goal to which all other goals were subordinated. Unlike during Paul Austin's leadership, Coca-Cola under Goizueta carefully cultivated Wall Street. Along with Keough, he met often with financial executives and portfolio managers. One of the tactics for increased value was to increase per capita consumption in global markets where Coca-Cola was one of the world's two or three best-known brand names. International sales expanded rapidly, especially in newly opened Eastern Europe and in Japan. In a highly publicized coup, Goizueta convinced Venezuela's leading bottling company to switch from Pepsi to Coke. Wall Street responded very positively, and values soared. Among the major investors showing confidence in Coke was financial genius Warren Buffet, whose stake grew about fourfold in only three years from 1989 to 1992. Goizueta himself became famously rich thanks to generous stock options that the board granted him. The size of his compensation package attracted the attention of the business press, but few stockholders complained because he had made them rich too.

The market value of Coke when he took the reins was just over $4 billion; the value at his death stood around $150 billion. Goizueta had engineered a thirty-fourfold increase in sixteen years. He died as the wealthiest Hispanic in the United States with a personal worth of $1.3 billion in Coca-Cola stock, $3 million of which came from the original $8,000 worth of shares he bought in 1954 (*Los Angeles Times*, 19 October 1997; *Fortune*, 13 October 1997).

Even though the Coca-Cola board had induced Goizueta to serve past the normal retirement age of sixty-five, he knew that he needed to prepare the next generation of leadership. About a year before his death the veteran chairman told an *Atlanta Constitution* writer,

> My No. 1 task right now, as opposed to 1980 and 1981 when I kind of cleaned house, is to acquire and identify talented people and ensue they are developed and to have the systems in place to move this company to a higher plateau of achievement.
>
> (Roush 1996)

The Cuban CEO who had succeeded native Georgian Paul Austin spent several years grooming another native Georgian, M. Douglas Ivester, to be his successor. Shortly before Goizueta's death *Fortune* magazine described their relationship as 'an almost perfect partnership – Ivester managing the business ... and Goizueta managing big-picture strategy and Coke's marvelous relationship with the Street'. A stock analyst was quoted as predicting that 'the transition will be seamless' (Sellers 1997). Only days after this article appeared, Goizueta died of cancer, and the analyst's prediction proved accurate.

Following his death, former President Jimmy Carter declared, 'perhaps no other corporate leader in modern times has so beautifully exemplified the American dream' (Associated Press, 19 October 1997). Indeed,

Goizueta lived a twentieth-century version of the Gilded Age rags-to-riches stories of 'robber barons' such as Andrew CARNEGIE. A young, nearly penniless immigrant, a refugee from Castro's Cuba, he rose to the zenith of American business.

BIBLIOGRAPHY

Allen, F. (1994) *Secret Formula: How Brilliant Marketing and Relentless Salesmanship Made Coda-Cola the Best-known Product in the World*, New York: HarperBusiness.

Barry, T. (1998) 'Georgia's Most Respected CEO for 1998', *Georgia Trend* (May): 18ff.

Cline, K. (1989) 'Roberto Goizueta and the Cola Revolution', *Atlanta Business Chronicle* (10 April): 1ff.

Greising, D. (1998) *I'd Like the World to Buy a Coke: The Life and Leadership of Roberto Goizueta*, New York, John Wiley and Sons.

Huey, J. (1997) 'In Search of Roberto's Secret Formula', *Fortune* (29 December): 230ff.

Morris, B. (1995) 'Roberto Goizueta and Jack Welch: The Wealth Builders', *Fortune* (11 December): 80ff.

Oliver, T. (1986) *The Real Coke, the Real Story*, New York: Random House.

Roush, C. (1996) 'Coca-Cola's Guiding Light', *Atlanta Constitution* (24 November): H1, H3.

Sellers, P. (1997) 'Where Coke goes from Here', *Fortune* (13 October): 88–91.

BR

GOLDWYN, Samuel (1882–1974)

Samuel Goldwyn was born Schmuel Gelbfisz (altered to Samuel Goldfish) on 27 August

1882 – the date is also quoted as 1884 and as possibly July 1879 (Gomery 1999: 216; Berg 1989: 5) – in Warsaw to Aaron David Gelbfisz, a peddler, and Hannah Reban Jarecka (other sources give his parents' names as Abraham and Hannah Goldfish). He died on 31 January 1974 in Los Angeles. He emigrated to Gloversville, New York as a teenager. He had some orthodox Jewish education in Poland, and one year of night school at the Gloversville Business College. He married Blanche Lasky in 1910, and the couple had one daughter; he later married Frances Howard in 1925, and they had one son.

Goldwyn started working in a glove factory and rapidly rose to become a partner in the firm. He was a highly successful glove salesman. Through his marriage to Blanche Lasky, he met Jesse Lasky, a vaudeville producer. The two men formed the Jesse L. Lasky Feature Picture Play Company in 1913, and produced the first American-made feature-length film, *The Squaw Man*, which was directed by Cecil B. DeMille in his directorial debut. Goldwyn and Lasky merged their company with Adolph Zukor's Famous Players, and Goldwyn eventually sold out for $900,000. In 1917 Goldwyn joined with the Selwyn brothers, who were Broadway producers. They dubbed their new venture Goldwyn Pictures Company. Goldwyn liked the name (a combination of Goldfish and Selwyn) so much that he adopted it as his legal name. Eventually their company merged with Metro pictures and became Metro-Goldwyn-Mayer (MGM). Goldwyn became an independent producer in 1922, although he temporarily aligned his efforts with United Artists.

Goldwyn's management style included tolerance of 'yes men': as he admitted, 'I'll take 50 per cent efficiency to get 100 per cent loyalty' (Krebs 1974: 34). As a producer, he 'coddled actors, writers, and directors, but when he felt they were not producing what he had expected of them, he switched tactics and

heaped invective upon them' (Krebs 1974: 34). One writer, Ben Hecht, found that Goldwyn's treatment of him was similar to 'an irritated man shaking a slot machine' (Krebs 1974: 34). Goldwyn was known for seeking strong scripts, refusing to use outside funding and making high-quality films. He refused to underestimate his audience: 'Entertainment ... does not automatically exclude thought. The minds of an intelligent audience do not stop working even when they are most relaxed' ('Goldwyn, Samuel' 1944: 248). His films were popular, including *The Best Years of Our Lives* and *Wuthering Heights*, and during a twenty-year period his films drew more than 200 million customers. Unfortunately, his last film, *Porgy and Bess*, flopped amidst criticism of its portrayal of blacks. He also had difficulty with the changing mores of Hollywood films, being disgusted with the free-wheeling depictions of sex in the 1960s.

Goldwyn had an ability to discover stars, including Tallulah Bankhead, Robert Montgomery, Gary Cooper, Teresa Wright, Ronald Colman, Rudolph Valentino and Eddie Cantor. Unfortunately, he let Cooper go from his studio and later had to pay large sums to get him back. He also misjudged the potential of actress Anna Sten, whom he first characterized as having 'the face of a sphinx', but saying later: 'She's colossal in a small way' (Krebs 1974: 34).

As Goldwyn once described himself: I was a rebel, a lone wolf. My pictures were my own; I financed them myself and answered solely to myself. My mistakes and my successes were my own. My one rule was to please myself, and if I did that, there was a good chance I would please others.

(Krebs 1974: 34)

BIBLIOGRAPHY
Berg, A. (1989) *Goldwyn: A Biography*, New York: Alfred A. Knopf.
'Goldwyn, Samuel' (1944) *Current*

Biography, Who's Who and Why, New York: H.W. Wilson and Co., vol. 5: 246–9.

Gomery, D. (1999) 'Goldwyn, Samuel', in J.A. Garraty and M. Carnes (eds), *American National Biography*, New York: Oxford University Press, vol. 9, 214–16.

Krebs, A. (1974) 'Samuel Goldwyn Dies at 91', *New York Times* 123(42,377), sect. 1: 1, 34.

DS

GOODRICH, Benjamin Franklin (1841–88)

Benjamin Franklin Goodrich was born in Ripley, New York on 4 November 1841 and died in Manitou Springs, Colorado on 3 August 1888. Goodrich was an ambitious man who came into the business world following a brief career as a physician. He graduated from the Cleveland Medical College in 1860, and served in the Union army as a surgeon during the American Civil War. After the war, Goodrich tried establishing a medical practice in several locations. These efforts were apparently not successful, for Goodrich sought a personal fortune in the burgeoning postwar economy. His restless ambition led him to leave the medical field in favour of a business position in New York City, where he worked briefly in the shipping department of an oil firm.

While in New York, Goodrich became involved in several real estate ventures with some success. Intrigued by the possibilities of rubber manufacturing, Goodrich and a friend, John Morris, invested $10,000 in the Hudson River Rubber Company in 1869. This firm, however, proved burdened by debt, worn-out machinery and intense competition. Soon these problems led Goodrich to look for a

western location that might allow him to escape the intense competition of New York, while satisfying newer customers in the expanding economy. His travels took him to Akron, Ohio, where local business and civic leaders were willing to help Goodrich establish a new firm. They pledged an investment of $15,000 to help the young manufacturer relocate to Akron. The Goodrich, Tew Company began in 1870 as an Akron partnership, the first rubber manufacturing firm west of the Appalachian mountains. (In 1880 the firm became the B.F. Goodrich Company.) Akron proved to be a good location, with canal and rail connections to raw material supplies and, in particular, the markets of growing Midwestern industries. Eventually other entrepreneurs invested in Akron rubber manufacturing establishments, and the city became known as the world's rubber capital.

As an entrepreneur, Goodrich established a diversified strategy, one that continued to characterize his firm long after his death. The firm's principal products were fire hoses and machinery belts, but it also manufactured rubber goods ranging from jar rings to washing-machine rollers. (Goodrich avoided rubber shoe manufacturing, however, as this was an intensely competitive business.) Hoses and belts were especially profitable products in the Midwestern markets of growing cities and expanding railroads, mines and factories. In 1881, after its first full year of operation as a corporation, the B.F. Goodrich Company made profits of $69,000 on sales of $319,000; its assets were only $233,000. Shortly before Goodrich's death in 1888, the firm had assets of $564,000, earning an annual profit of $107,000.

Goodrich was also personally involved in the business. He worked in a small laboratory on the compounding of rubber, trying various formulae – and keeping them secret and proprietary – in an effort to improve rubber products. In fact, science was an important part of successful rubber manufacturing, and the B.F. Goodrich Company, shortly after the founder's premature death from tuberculosis, established one of the nations first industrial laboratories.

Goodrich's personal legacy was a business strategy of diversified manufacturing aimed at a variety of industrial and consumer markets supported by careful scientific development of rubber compounds. The B.F. Goodrich Company continued as a diversified manufacturer for a century following its founder's death. It also was known as a scientifically innovative firm, pioneering new plastics and rubbers.

BIBLIOGRAPHY
Blackford, M.G. and Kerr, K.A. (1996) *B.F. Goodrich: Tradition and Transformation, 1870–1995*, Columbus: Ohio State University Press.

KAK

GORDY, Berry, Jr (1929–)

Berry Gordy Jr was born on 28 November 1929 in Detroit, Michigan. Born and raised in a ghetto area of Detroit, Gordy tried his hand at professional boxing before deciding – after ten wins and four losses – that the ring was too tough and the featherweight class was not profitable enough. He tried running a jazz specialty record store, but went bankrupt. He then directed his attention towards the emerging field of R&B, promoting his talents as a songwriter and record producer. In 1957 Gordy scored his first commercial breakthrough when R&B star Jackie Wilson turned his song *Reet Petite* into a minor pop hit for Brunswick Records. Follow-up hits for Wilson and Brunswick consolidated Gordy's reputation as Detroit's leading songwriter.

In 1959 Gordy founded Motown Records as a vehicle for independently producing and marketing his own music, and also for marketing the songwriting and performing talents of Detroit's bright young black singers and musicians. He chose the name in acknowledgement of Detroit's popularly designated status as 'Motor Town', home of the Ford Motor Company and other major car manufacturers.

In 1960 Gordy signed to his label a teenage quintet, Smokey Robinson and the Miracles, who produced two major hits, 'Way Over There' and 'Shop Around'. With the ensuing profits, Gordy expanded his label's talent roster. His ability to spot a commercial prospect never failed; over the next two years he signed such promising newcomers as Mary Wells, the Supremes, the Marvelettes, Martha and the Vandellas, the Temptations, Marvin Gaye and the hit-oriented songwriting team of Lamont Dozier, Eddie Holland and Brian Holland. In the years following, Gordy added such talents as Stevie Wonder, the Four Tops, and Jr Walker and the All Stars. Diana Ross, who graduated from lead singer of the Supremes to solo stardom, became known as Motown's first all-around entertainer.

The result was huge success, artistic and financial, for Motown Records. which grew to become the United States' largest black-owned entertainment conglomerate. In the process, Gordy moved black 'rhythm and blues' music (R&B) into the popular mainstream and rendered obsolete the old US *Billboard* magazine practice of listing R&B and 'Top 100' as separate, race-segregated pop music categories. A key factor in this success was Gordy's insistence on taking personal responsibility for what he called 'quality control'. This meant that songs could not emerge from the recording studio as finished product until they were up to what he considered 'Motown standards'.

For much of the 1960s, the number of records Motown released, relative to the company's size, was one of the lowest in the music industry. However, the percentage of these that became hits was one of the highest.

In 1966 alone, it was estimated that fully 75 per cent of Motown releases made the US pop charts.

In 1971 Gordy moved Motown to Hollywood and diversified into motion pictures, television programmes and theatrical productions. During the 1970s many of Motown's top artists defected to other labels, but the company retained its position as an important independent label with the recordings of Stevie Wonder, the Commodores and Rick James. In the 1980s, however, Motown Records struggled. Ross signed with RCA and Gaye with Columbia. Some disenchanted former employees sued Motown, alleging failure to pay royalties. Gordy by this time was more interested in producing television programmes such as *Lonesome Dove* than in making hit records. In July 1988 he sold Motown Records to MCA and Boston Ventures for $61 million. In 1990 he was inducted into America's Rock and Roll Hall of Fame. Joe McEwen and Jim Miller wrote in *Rolling Stone* magazine that 'through a combination of pugnacious panache, shrewd judgement and good taste, Gordy became the mogul of the most profitable black music concern in the world' (Miller 1980: 235).

BIBLIOGRAPHY

Miller, J. (ed.) (1980) *The Rolling Stone Illustrated History of Rock & Roll*, New York: Random House.

Stambler, I. (1977) *Encyclopedia of Pop, Rock and Soul,* New York: St Martin's Press.

BB

GOULD, Jay (1836–92)

Jason Gould was born on 27 May 1836 and died in New York on 2 December 1892. Born to John and Mary Gould, poor farmers in Roxbury, New York, Gould's youth was very much shaped by his poverty as well as his poor health His mother died when he was four, and Gould himself almost died from pneumonia and typhus. His unhappy youth helped, according to O'Connor (1962), to condition his Darwinian outlook on life. In Gould's mind there was no excuse for being poor, for poverty meant sickness, starvation and death. Gould, however, had all the attributes of a future entrepreneur: he was bright, quick-witted, a self-starter and persistent. He would stop at nothing to become rich. He taught himself accounting and surveying, then went into business as a tanner. But by the time Gould was twenty, around 1857, he had found his life's calling as a Wall Street financier. Gould quickly mastered the new art of finance capital, becoming one of the most successful brokers in history.

On Wall Street, Gould's strategy was to take over ailing businesses and make them profitable. In 1874 he bought the Pacific Mail Steamship Company and then the Union Pacific Railroad, which was poorly managed and tarnished by political scandal. Gould was not able to fix the Union Pacific, however, and sold his holdings in the railway. He then set out to create his own railway by merging part of the Kansas Pacific, the Missouri Pacific, the Wabash, and the Denver and Rio Grande between 1879 and 1881. He extended this system into parts of the Midwest, New York and New England, so that by 1881 Gould controlled 21,000 kilometres (13,000 miles) of track, more than the New York Central or the Pennsylvania. That same year, Gould also bought the Western Union telegraph network.

In control of both the giant Missouri Pacific and Western Union, Gould was now as powerful, if not more so, than Standard Oil, Carnegie Steel or the New York Central. His effort to corner the gold market in 1884 triggered a panic which endangered his empire, but it survived. His health began to fail, but he continued to be active, even repurchasing the Union Pacific in 1890.

When he died in 1892 Gould left behind both a successful empire in transportation and communication, and a reputation for questionable dealings that would, more than anything else, help to shape the image of Gould as a Robber Baron. Historians have not been kind to Jay Gould. To Josephson (1962) among many others, he was an unscrupulous manipulator who ran the Erie Railroad, watered stock and bribed state legislators. But in the 1990s, an age of corporate restructuring and shareholder value, Gould came to be seen in a more favourable light (see for example Klein 1999) as a master financier and successful business leader who could turn around ailing corporations.

BIBLIOGRAPHY
Josephson, M. (1962) *The Robber Barons: The Great American Capitalists, 1861–1901*, New York: Harcourt, Brace, Jovanovich.
Klein, M. (1986) *The Life and Legend of Jay Gould*, Baltimore, MD: Johns Hopkins University Press.
—— (1999) 'Gould, Jay', *American National Biography*, ed. J.A. Garraty and M.C. Carnes, New York: Oxford University Press, vol. 9, 344–7.
O'Connor, R. (1962) *Gould's Millions*, Garden City, NY: Doubleday.

DCL

GRAHAM, Katharine (1917–)

Katharine Meyer was born in New York City on 16 June 1917, the fourth of five children born to Eugene Meyer, a wealthy Wall Street businessman, and Agnes Elizabeth (Ernst) Meyer, an author and philanthropist.

Growing up in Washington, DC, Katharine Meyer showed an early interest in journalism. She wrote for the school magazine while attending Madeira, a private boarding school in Virginia. After her father purchased the moribund *Washington Post* for $825,000 at a bankruptcy auction in 1933, Katharine held occasional summer jobs at the paper while completing a BA in history at the University of Chicago. She spent a year working as a labour reporter for the *San Francisco News* after graduating from university. She then accepted her father's invitation to join the *Washington Post*. Because as publisher's daughter she would have felt awkward working as a reporter, she opted to write editorials instead.

In June 1940 she married Philip Graham, a Harvard Law School graduate who worked as a clerk for two Supreme Court justices and dreamed of entering politics. After serving in the US Army Air Corps during the Second World War he abandoned his political ambitions and – at his father-in-law's request – accepted the position of associate publisher at the *Washington Post*. At that point Katharine stopped working at the *Post* and devoted herself to raising her daughter and three sons.

Philip Graham found the *Post* to be a struggling paper that barely broke even, and helped put it on a firmer financial footing after becoming publisher in 1948. He merged the *Post* with one of its rivals, the money-losing *Washington Times-Herald*, and added *Newsweek* magazine to the company's growing stable of holdings. He also expanded radio and television holdings and helped establish an international news service.

In August 1963 Philip Graham – who suffered from manic depression – committed suicide. Katharine Graham became president of the Washington Post Company, and later publisher of the newspaper. At first awkward and insecure in her role as principal owner of the company, she publicly asserted herself as a strong newspaper executive in 1971, when she decided that the *Post* should defy a US court order and publish excerpts from a classified

Pentagon study of US military involvement in Vietnam. The following year, she supported her editor, Benjamin C. Bradlee, in his position that the *Post* should investigate a seemingly innocuous burglary at the Democratic National Committee headquarters at Washington's Watergate apartment complex. The investigation, conducted by *Post* reporters Bob Woodward and Carl Bernstein, ultimately led to the indictment of several White House officials and to the resignation of President Richard Nixon in August 1974.

Graham held the title of publisher until 1979, and was generally considered the most powerful woman in US newspaper publishing. The *Post* grew in influence and stature under her leadership until it joined the elite, along with the *New York Times* and *Los Angeles Times*. It was read and consulted by presidents and prime ministers, and exerted a powerful influence on American political life. In 1979 Graham turned the title of publisher over to her son Donald, but as chairman of the Washington Post Company until 1991 she remained active in all areas of the business, from advising on editorial policy to devising strategies for diversifying the company's holdings. In 1988 *Business Month* magazine listed the Washington Post Company as one of the 'five best managed companies' in America. Two years later, Graham received *Fortune* magazine's Business Hall of Fame award, having proven herself to be a stronger corporate head than either of the two men who influenced her earlier life, her father and her husband.

Graham retired in 1991, and published her memoirs in 1997. Known as a forceful and courageous publisher, she knew when to rely on the expertise of her editors and when to assume responsibility for decisions. Mike Wallace, a reporter for the US public affairs television programme *60 Minutes*, told the *Post* on the occasion of her seventieth birthday in 1987 that 'she is a woman who in effect, I suppose, came to the job unprepared and turned out to be one of the giants of journalism in the last quarter century' (*Dictionary of Literary Biography* 1993: 110).

BIBLIOGRAPHY
Davis, D. (1979) *Katharine the Great: Katharine Graham and the Washington Post*, New York: Harcourt Brace Jovanovich.
Dictionary of Literary Biography (1993) Volume 127: American Newspaper Publishers, 1950–1990, Detroit: Gale Research.
Felsenthal, C. (1993) *Power, Privilege and the Post: The Katharine Graham Story*, New York: Putnam's.
Graham, K. (1997) *Personal History*, New York: Random House.

BB

GROVE, Andrew Stephen (1936–)

Andrew Stephen Grove was born Andras Grof in Budapest on 2 September 1936, the son of George Grof, a businessman, and his wife Maria, a bookkeeper. He grew up in a Hungary during the Second World War and under the postwar communist regime, and left the country after the abortive Hungarian Revolution of 1956, arriving in the United States in 1957. He became a US citizen in 1962. Grove's higher education was all undertaken in the United States; he took a BA from City College, New York in 1960, and a Ph.D. in chemical engineering from the University of California at Berkeley in 1963. He married Eva Kastan in 1958; they have two children.

Following his Ph.D., Grove joined the Fairchild Semiconductor Research Laboratory in San Jose, California, where he was a member of technical staff from 1963 to 1966, section head in surface and device physics from 1966 to 1967, and assistant director of research and development from 1967 to 1968. Here he worked under Gordon Moore and Robert NOYCE, who had been the first to discover how effectively to use silicon chips in making semi-conductors. When Moore and Noyce left Fairchild to set up Intel in 1968, they invited Grove to join them. Here he served as vice-president and director of operations from 1968 to 1975, executive vice-president from 1975 to 1979, and chief operating officer from 1976 to 1987; he became president in 1979 and chief executive officer in 1987. A man of great energy, he also lectured at Berkeley from 1966 to 1972, and for many years he wrote a news-paper column for the San Jose *Mercury*.

Although Noyce and Moore had founded Intel, it was under Grove's leadership that the company rose to occupy a position of domi-nance in its industry. Jackson describes how Grove has transformed the company:

From being an innovator, it became a company whose objective was to deliver – to make sure its good ideas were turned into practical products that customers could use, products that arrived on schedule and at prices that fell consistently year by year. This transformation was no mean feat. It forced Intel to become rigorously organized and focussed, and to find a balance that allowed it to keep firm control over its oper-ations without jeopardizing the creativity of the scientists who were its greatest assets. The result of this transformation was that Intel rose to domination of its industry.

(Jackson 1998: xiii)

Intel chips are now used in the vast majority of PCs made around the world. Grove himself believes in technology as a kind of unstop-pable force: in technology, he says, 'what can be done will be done' (Grove 1996: 5). Like Noyce, he links technological development with social progress.

Grove has a strong management philoso-phy, which he has set out in several books. He sees information as being at the heart of the management process. In his own working life, he constantly collects and filters information, and he encourages all his employees to do the same. He believes too in the need for emotion and belief in work – intuition is as important as analysis. He does not believe in continuous hands-on management, although he is less *laissez-faire* in this regard than was Robert Noyce; but he argues that as managers have limited time and energy, they should concen-trate on doing those things that will have the maximum impact, moving to the point where their leverage will be greatest.

High Output Management (1983) is aimed at middle managers, whom Grove sees as 'the muscle and bone of every sizeable organiza-tion', but often ignored by theorists (1983: ix). The book, which is amusingly written in a light tone, sets out to define what it is that managers *do*. In one metaphor, he compares the doing of management to a waiter serving breakfast: both have the same basics of production, 'to build and deliver products in response to the demands of the customer at a *scheduled* delivery time, at an *acceptable* quality level, and at the *lowest* possible cost (1983: 3). He argues that man-agerial activity should not be confused with output. Planning, negotiation, allocating resources and training are things that managers *do*; the output is what they actually *produce*. At Intel, he says, the managerial output is not ideas, it is silicon wafers; the outputs of high-school principals are students, the outputs of surgeons are healed patients, and so on. A manager's output is the output of his own orga-nization (1983: 38). This means that manage-ment is a team activity, and so 'the single most important task of a manager is to elicit peak performance from his subordinates' (1983: 145). Managers need to know what motivates their employees; here Grove refers specifically to MASLOW's hierarchy of needs, and argues that managers need to be aware of how these needs motivate employees and subordinates.

Only the Paranoid Survive (1996) is both sharper and more thoughtful. Writing in the aftermath of a disastrous incident in which half a billion dollars worth of defective Pentium chips had to be recalled and replaced, Grove warns against managerial complacency:

I believe in the value of paranoia. Business success contains the seeds of its own destruction. The more successful you are, the more people want a chunk of your business and then another chunk and then another until there is nothing left. I believe that the prime responsibility of a manager is to guard constantly against other people's attacks and to inculcate this guardian attitude in the people under his or her management.

(Grove 1996: 3)

He conceptualizes change in the business environment not as a continuous process but as a series of flash points or 'strategic inflection points', times when the fundamentals by which a business has existed and operated suddenly change. These strategic inflection points have some similarity to the paradigm shifts described by T.S. KUHN. The appearance of one of these points can mean new opportunities, or it can mean the beginning of the end, depending on how the business responds. Formal planning cannot anticipate these kinds of change, and therefore manages have to be able to respond to the unanticipated.

One of the difficulties in dealing with strategic inflection points is recognizing them when they arrive: how can the manager distinguish signals from noise (1996: 101)? The answer, says Grove, is for managers to engage in vigorous debate, sharing information and generating new ideas. Always challenge the data, he says; ask what it is really telling to you; listen to everyone around you. Everyone must be encouraged to speak; fear of punishment, in many organizations, is the great inhibitor of discussion, and this in turn leads to signals being missed. He recognizes that many managers will not find this easy: 'With all the rhetoric about how management is about change, the fact is that we managers loathe change, especially when it involves us. Getting through a strategic inflection point involves confusion, uncertainty and disorder' (1996: 123).

Getting through a strategic inflection point is tense and chaotic; there are no rules here, precisely because the ground rules themselves are changing. But, says Grove,

at some point you, the leader, begin to sense a vague outline of the new direction. By this time, however, your company is dispirited, demoralized or just plain tired. Getting this far took a lot of energy from you; you must now reach into whatever reservoir of energy you have left to motivate yourself and, most importantly, the people who depend on you so you can become healthy again.

(Grove 1996: 139)

Change is almost like a sickness, and companies need strength and stamina to recover. Now is the time to make sense of the picture, to rein in chaos, and proceed towards goals. In another metaphor, Grove describes passing a strategic inflection point as like crossing the Valley of Death.

BIBLIOGRAPHY
Grove, A.S. (1967) *The Physics and Technology of Semiconductor Devices*, New York: Wiley.
—— (1983) *High Output Management*, New York: Random House.
—— (1996) *Only the Paranoid Survive: How to Exploit the Crisis Points that Challenge Every Company and Career*, New York: HarperCollins.
Jackson, T. (1998) *Inside Intel: Andy Grove and the Rise of the World's Most Powerful Chip Company*, London: Penguin.

MLW

GUGGENHEIM, Daniel (1856–1930)

Daniel Guggenheim was born in Philadelphia on 9 July 1856, the son of Meyer and Barbara Guggenheim. He died at his home on Long Island, New York on 28 September 1930. Guggenheim's father had emigrated from Switzerland and set up a lace-importing business in the United States; Guggenheim joined the family firm at the age of eighteen and then went himself to Switzerland, where he worked as a lace buyer for the next eleven years. The family business prospered during those years, and M. Guggenheim and Sons became involved in silver and lead mining in the American West. Returning from Switzerland, Daniel Guggenheim pushed for the firm to focus on refining and smelting rather than ore extraction, seeing the former as more profitable and less risky. He also pressed for the adoption of new technologies to achieve greater cost savings and efficiency. Taking over the firm when his father retired, Guggenheim ploughed much of his profits back into the firm and expanded rapidly. In 1890 he moved into Mexico, negotiating concessions from Mexican president Porfirio Diaz and establishing smelters and a highly profitable copper mine.

During the 1890s firms in many industries moved to consolidate and form combines. Smelting firms merged into the American Smelting and Refining Company (ASARCO) in 1899, and pressure was placed on Guggenheim to join the combine. He resisted, however, until he could secure terms favourable to himself and his business; when ASARCO finally bought out Guggenheim in 1901, he became the combine's chairman. More rapid expansion followed, with mines and smelters all over North America as well as in Chile and the Belgian Congo. Guggenheim turned to J.P. MORGAN for fresh supplies of capital, which was then invested in new technologies on a continuous basis. Under Guggenheim, ASARCO became the world's largest, most technologically advanced and most efficient mining corporation.

The transformation from labour-intensive work to highly skilled and mechanized processes in mining and smelting led to labour unrest. Initially confrontational, Guggenheim, like other mine-owners, advocated breaking strikes by force. Around 1910, however, he seems to have had a change of heart. Hoyt (1967) suggests that there was something of a conversion on the road to Damascus, with Guggenheim, having achieved great wealth, now beginning to consider his social responsibilities. Impetus may have come from his wife Florence, whom he had married in 1884; a noted philanthropist, Florence Guggenheim saw to it that much of the Guggenheim fortune was spent on good causes. However, a wave of violent strikes which swept the mining industry from 1911 to 1913 certainly had a strong impact. With miners and security men fighting and killing each other, Guggenheim believed that the only way to avoid anarchy was to achieve labour peace. He began trying to set an example, reducing working hours and providing housing and medical benefits for workers. He also began making direct contacts with the leaders of the labour movement. With John D. ROCKEFELLER, Jr, Guggenheim arranged a meeting with Samuel Gompers at which a plan for labour peace, at least for the duration of the First World War, was worked out. The plan appears to have been only partially successful, with some of Guggenheim's subordinates preferring confrontation to cooperation, and the violence continued.

Whatever his initial motives, Guggenheim became deeply interested in the sociological and psychological aspects of labour relations, and in his later years he seems to have made a real attempt to understand worker motivation, in particular the motivation to strike or create unrest. In 1915 he stunned the United States Industrial Relations Commission, before which he was testifying, when he said that employees were justified in organizing, as many capitalists were too arbitrary in their treatment of their workers:

There is today too great a difference between the rich man and the poor man. To remedy this is too big a job for the state or the employer to tackle single-handed. There should be a combination in this work between the Federal government, the state, the employer and the employee. The men want more comforts – more of the luxuries of life. They are entitled to them. I say this because humanity owes it to them.

(Hoyt 1967: 236)

In an article published that same year, Guggenheim openly called for state intervention in the labour market to protect workers. Among the measures he advocated were minimum wages and working conditions, compulsory profit sharing and compulsory measures to promote industrial democracy. He did not believe that corporations – including, it seems, his own – could undertake such reforms unaided, and that only the government could achieve lasting labour peace. The necessity for such measures, he believed, was clear:

I think the difference between the rich man and the poor man is very much too great, and it is only by taking steps to bridge the gulf between them that we shall be able to get away from the unrest now prevailing among the working classes.

(Guggenheim 1915: 210).

Guggenheim also continued to be interested in new technology. He was an early backer of the aircraft industry, and funded the first American school of aeronautics. In the 1920s he became involved in nitrate mining in Chile, in a joint venture with Chilean government, but this went badly wrong when nitrate prices collapsed in 1929; at the time of Guggenheim's death, the company was suffering heavy losses. The Chilean government dissolved the joint venture in 1933. The company survived, but lost its world preeminence.

BIBLIOGRAPHY

Guggenheim, D. (1915) 'Some Thoughts on Industrial Unrest', *Annals of the American Academy of Political and Social Science* 59(May): 209–11.

Hoyt, E.P. (1967) *The Guggenheims and the American Dream*, New York: Funk and Wagnalls.

MLW

GULICK, Luther Halsey, III (1892–1993)

Luther Halsey Gulick III was born in Osaka, Japan on 17 January 1892 and died in New York on 10 January 1993, a week short of his 101st birthday. His family background was remarkable. His grandparents, Luther and Louisa Gulick, were among the first missionaries to Hawaii and Micronesia; they later worked in China and Japan, where Dr Gulick translated the Bible into Japanese. Their son, Luther Halsey Gulick, Jr, became one of the founders of the modern physical education movement; he served as secretary of the physical training department of the Young Men's Christian Association (YMCA) from 1887 to 1903, during which time he devised the YMCA's famous triangular emblem, worked tirelessly to promote the organization and, along with James Naismith, developed and promoted the game of basketball. He and his wife, Charlotte Vetter Gulick, travelled widely in the course of these and other activities, and it was on one such trip to Japan that Luther Halsey Gulick III was born.

Like his father, Gulick attended Oberlin College, graduating with an AB in 1914. His father, after leaving the YMCA, had served as an adviser to a number of public health departments, and it may have been this that prompted Gulick towards a career in public administration. In 1916 he joined the research staff of the Bureau of Municipal Research in New York. This organization had been established in 1906 to provide staff support for the New York City municipal government and had been immediately recognized as a success; it was imitated in many other large American cities. In 1911 the New York bureau had added a training school for public servants to its facilities, and in 1914 the economic historian Charles Beard, then a professor at Columbia University, was appointed as the training school's director. Beard, one of the most respected intellectuals of his day, seems to have been a considerable influence on Gulick, although he was far from sharing the former's pacifist views.

In 1917, when the United States entered the First World War, Gulick joined the US Army while Beard resigned from the faculty of Columbia in protest at the university's decision to support the war and suppress dissent. This divergence seems not to have harmed the two men's working relationship, however; Beard was named director of the bureau in 1918, and he appointed the returning Gulick to succeed him as head of the training school in 1919. Beard's tenure as director does not seem to have been a success, in part because of the cloud of suspicion that hung over his pacifist activities; in 1919, in a minor precursor of the McCarthy anti-communist campaign of the 1950s, Beard was one of several intellectuals named by US military intelligence as a suspected foreign agent. He was forced to resign in 1921 and Gulick, just twenty-nine years old, was his chosen successor.

Over the course of the next decade, Gulick oversaw the transformation of the bureau from an urban to a global organization. Immediately after his appointment, he completed the bureau's reorganization under its new name, the National Institute for Public Administration (NIPA). The training school was hived off to Syracuse University in 1924, and under Gulick's leadership NIPA began focusing on national and, increasingly, international problems of administration. At home, clients included the federal government and several state and city governments; overseas, Gulick followed in his family's footsteps in Japan, advising on the establishment of the Institute of Municipal Research in Tokyo – which was modelled on NIPA – and conducting a study of the reconstruction of Tokyo following the 1923 Kanto earthquake. In 1927–8 NIPA carried out studies for the government of Yugoslavia, and from 1929 to 1930 it advised the Chinese government of Chiang Kai-shek on fiscal reform (though without much effect). In recognition of its increasing international role, NIPA dropped the word 'National' from its title and became simply the Institute for Public Administration (IPA).

By the 1930s Gulick was probably the world's leading authority on public administration. US and foreign governments consulted him frequently. In 1931 he was named Eaton Professor of Municipal Science and Administration at Columbia University, a post which he held until 1942. He was a prime mover in the establishment of the Public Administration Clearinghouse. He was invited to serve on the Brownlow Committee, chaired by Louis F. Brownlow and charged by President Franklin D. Roosevelt with reorganizing the office of the president. After the Second World War he was active in further national and international work, including consultations with the city of Calcutta on developing a new water supply, and with President Nasser on a new constitution for Egypt. He retired in 1961, but continued to write and lecture. Over the course of his career he wrote or co-authored some fifteen books and more than 200 articles; the first of these was published in 1920 and the last seventy years later, when Gulick was ninety-seven.

Most of Gulick's works are practical and focused on particular issues; they include an astonishing number of reports of commissions and committees of inquiry which he chaired. In three particular works, however, Gulick sets out his philosophy of administration clearly. The first of these is his introduction to *Papers on the Science of Administration* (1937), edited by himself and Lyndall Urwick. This book, a management classic, was conceived of by Gulick and published by the IPA in New York; as well as essays by Gulick and Urwick, it contains contributions by such notables as Henri Fayol, Mary Parker FOLLETT and James MOONEY. The second book, *Administrative Reflections from World War II* (1948), is a thought-provoking attempt to apply some of the lessons learned during the war to peacetime administrative practices. The third, *The Metropolitan Problem and American Ideas* (1962), is based on a series of lectures on government and administration which Gulick gave at the University of Michigan the year he retired; it is largely based on the other two works, but does contain some new insights.

Like his contemporaries in the scientific management movement, Gulick believed that public administration could be made more effective if it were practised according to a set of guiding principles. He saw no essential difference between public sector administration and private sector business management, believing that the processes and practices involved were identical: both had strategic goals and targets, both sought greater efficiency and both developed organizations as a method of reaching their goals. This last point is particularly important. Gulick believed that organizations were tools, means of achieving an end. Rather than building an organization and guiding it towards a goal, the goal should be firmly fixed in the first instance and the organization then configured to meet that goal. Gulick can here be seen as occupying a middle point between Fayol's earlier 'top down' concept of organizations being designed and guided according to grand principles, and, later, CHANDLER's famous dictum that 'structure follows strategy'. Systematic purpose and clear policy, said Gulick, would always achieve desired ends, so long as the organization was technically capable of reaching those ends.

Thus while scientific management's focus, initially at least, was on the task and the worker, Gulick's primary concern was the organization as a whole. His choice of collaborators for *Papers on the Science of Administration* shows clearly his interests and influences: they include Mooney's investigations into the roots of organization, Follett's work on the social nature of organizations, Fayol's grand principles and Urwick's development of the line and staff concept.

Gulick's own contribution is a conceptualization of organization that is both simple and dynamic. All organizations, he says, are characterized by a tension between the need for division and the need for coordination. The 'division' to which Gulick refers is the classical concept of the division of labour as described by Petty and Adam Smith, among others, and which Gulick now sees as the root of all organizations: 'Work division is the foundation of organization; indeed, the reason for organization' (Gulick and Urwick 1937: 3). The classical economic – and scientific management – view that efficiency is achieved through the division of labour is one with which Gulick agrees. However, he says, it is important to recognize that there are limits beyond which labour cannot usefully be divided. Technology and custom provide some limits, although there may be ways of overcoming these. Nor does it make sense to divide labour to the point where defined tasks require the labour of less than one person; this would mean less, rather than more, efficiency. There are also organic limitations to the division of labour. It might, says Gulick, be more efficient to have the front half of the cow in the pasture grazing while the rear half is in the barn being milked, but any attempt to divide the cow in this fashion would, for obvious reasons, fail.

Divided labour makes for efficiency, but only if the labour and its outputs are harmonized with the organization's goals. This is achieved, says Gulick, through a seemingly opposed process, that of coordination. In any system or organization which relies on the division of labour, there must be some person or persons whose primary function is to ensure the coordination of all the organization's component parts. That role Gulick assigns to the organization's leaders (there are clear reflections here of the line and staff principle). The leader should also be the organizational architect: to him or her falls responsibility for both designing the system by which labour is divided – that is, the structure and organization of the various work units, together with the assignation of tasks to each – and for the ongoing coordination of these units.

Work units can be coordinated in four ways: by purpose (that is, the aims of the work unit), by process (what the unit actually does, such as engineering or accounting), by persons or things dealt with or served (products made, customers served and so on) and by geographical place or location (Gulick and Urwick 1937: 33–4). Each of these four methods requires a different form of coordinating activity:

> If all the departments are set up on the basis of purpose, then the task of the chief executive will be to see that the major purposes are not in conflict and that the various processes which are used are consistent ... If all the departments are set up on the basis of process, the work methods will be well standardized on professional lines, and the chief executive will have to see that these are co-ordinated and timed to produce the results and render the services ... If place be the basis of departmentalization, that is, if the services be decentralized, then the task of the chief executive is ... to see that each of these services makes use of standard techniques and that the work in each area is part of a general programme and policy.
>
> (Gulick and Urwick 1937: 33–4)

In fact, it is seldom that departments are defined according to one of these four criteria

alone. Frequently, two, three or all four criteria will apply. This of course renders the task of the chief executive still more complex. Departments may overlap in one or more of these areas; work units which can be neatly segregated by process may overlap in geographical terms, or vice versa. A critical task of the chief executive is to reduce as far as possible the friction that such overlaps may cause.

To reduce friction, the chief executive has a further weapon at his disposal. As well as coordinating the organization through purpose, process, product/service and place, he or she can also coordinate the organization through ideas. It is this method, says Gulick, that allows the frictions and conflicts between work units to be smoothed out and the whole organization to be brought to bear on a consistent course towards its goals. Indeed, *without* coordination by ideas, the organization will fail:

> Any large and complicated enterprise would be incapable of effective organization if reliance for co-ordination were placed in organization alone. Organization is necessary; in a large enterprise it is essential, but it does not take the place of a dominant central idea as the foundation of action and self-co-ordination in the daily operation of all parts of the enterprise. Accordingly, the most difficult task of the chief executive is not command, it is leadership, that is, the development of the desire and will to work together for a purpose in the minds of those who are associated in any activity.
>
> (Gulick and Urwick 1937: 37)

Ideally, each organization should have a single guiding idea, one which is universally understood throughout the organization; it was this sense of a single uniting purpose, more than any other single factor, which led to US and Allied victory in the Second World War (Gulick 1948). In the end, it could be argued that Gulick sees ideas as more potent and more powerful than organizations. People need ideas, to motivate them and to give them purpose; their performance will improve and they will make greater sacrifices if their minds as well as their physical labour is committed to the task in hand. One of top management's key jobs, then, is the dissemination and diffusion of this idea, 'the translation from purpose to programme' (Gulick 1948: 78). Summing up the lessons of the US war effort, he argues that:

> Organizations and the men who direct them are expendable. In a world of unprecedented emergencies and uncharted experiences, many things must be tried. When some fail to meet the situation, or when they have served their immediate purpose, they must be superseded. They are casualties, sacrificed in the process of institutional running.
>
> (Gulick 1948: 31).

Ultimately, however, just as there are limits to the division of labour, so also there are limits to coordination. Five factors, says Gulick, combine to limit the ability of leaders to achieve full coordination. These are (1) uncertainty concerning the future; (2) lack of knowledge on the part the leaders; (3) lack of administrative or management skills on the part of the leaders; (4) a general lack of knowledge and skills on the part of other members of the organization; and (5) what Gulick calls 'the vast number of variables involved and the incompleteness of human knowledge, particularly with regard to man and life' (Gulick and Urwick 1937: 40). It is noteworthy that all five of Gulick's limits to coordination revolve around some form of knowledge, or rather, the lack of some of these forms of knowledge. If division is limited by organic and technical constraints, then coordination is limited in large part by lack of knowledge.

The need, then, is to get a balance between division and coordination. Excessive division will pull the organization apart centrifugally; excessive coordination will result in compression and concentration, and a corresponding loss of efficiency. Coordination, says Gulick, must be managed with a delicate hand; he is strongly in favour of decentralization and of allowing work units to work with minimal control, preferring coordination by 'guiding ideas' to that by command and constraint.

So powerful should these guiding ideas be, says Gulick, that individual members of the organization should be prepared to sacrifice themselves for the greater good; even, if necessary, serving as scapegoats. In a controversial passage written after the Second World War, he says:

> the prestige of top management must be maintained even though this involves a certain shifting of responsibility for individual failures and successes to subordinate organizations and men. This is cruel to those organizations and men, but it preserves the integrity of total management in a world of trial and error. In administration, as in baseball, it is the batting average that counts, not the occasional strikeout. Top management must be held accountable for the total record, not each segment.
>
> (Gulick 1948: 32)

This is a sentiment with which many in top management might agree, but the statement opens something of a gap in Gulick's thinking where human motivations are concerned. What sort of motivation is required for people to sacrifice their own careers and livelihoods in this fashion? In wartime, where survival is at stake, such selflessness occurs. In the peacetime world of business, the stakes are lower and such selflessness is correspondingly more rare. Just as there are limits to the leader's span of control, so too are there limits to employees' willingness to become totally involved with their organization.

Yet it is this mix of attitudes, part authoritarian and part humanist, part American and part European, which makes Gulick as a thinker so fascinating. He did not fully resolve the conflicts inherent in his own ideas, but we can see in him the beginnings of a global thinker, drawing his influences not only from the recent American past but from the broader and older context of Europe; and influenced too, even if only in subtle ways through his family connections, by the thought of the Far East. Unlike many of his American contemporaries, he did not believe there was one best way to manage organizations; there were universal principles of organization, but it was up to each group and its leaders to chart their own strategy towards their own goals.

One of the outstanding figures in the history of public administration, Gulick guided what was essentially a new discipline through its formative years in the 1920s, and gave it a philosophy and a framework in the 1930s and 1940s. He was one of the first to realize that public administration could – and indeed must – learn from new developments in business management, especially new systems of thought such as scientific management and the human relations school. But for Gulick, the link between private sector and public sector management was a two-way street; each could contribute to the other.

His collaboration with Lyndall Urwick resulted in a management classic; his own work is often strictly practical, but he never lost sight of the ultimate goals and aims of management in either sphere.

BIBLIOGRAPHY

Fitch, L.C. (1997) *Make Democracy Work: The Life and Letters of Luther Halsey Gulick, 1892–1993*, Berkeley, CA: Institute of Government Studies.

Gulick, L.H. (1948) *Administrative Reflections from World War II*, University, AL: University of Alabama Press.

—— (1962) *The Metropolitan Problem and American Ideas*, New York: Alfred A. Knopf.

Gulick, L.H. and Urwick, L.F. (eds) (1937) *Papers on the Science of Administration*, New York: Institute of Public Administration.

Institute of Public Administration (2000) 'Timeline of Events in IPA's History', http://www.theipa.org, 19 April 2001.

MLW

H

HAAS, Robert Douglas (1942–)

Robert Douglas Haas was born in San Francisco on 3 April 1942, the son of Walter and Evelyn Haas; his family are descended from a nephew of Levi STRAUSS, founder of the clothing manufacturer of that name. He married Colleen Gershon in 1974; they have one daughter. Haas took his BA at the University of California in 1964, and then served as a volunteer with the Peace Corps in the Ivory Coast (1964–6). Returning home, he took his MBA from Harvard Business School in 1968, and was then a fellow at the White House from 1968 to 1969, before joining McKinsey and Company from 1969 to 1972. He then joined Levi Strauss in 1973. He was the company vice-president for corporate planning and policy from 1978 to 1980, chief operating officer from 1981 to 1984, president and chief executive officer from 1985 to 1990, and has been chairman since 1990, stepping down as chief executive officer in 1999. He has held a number of other posts including trustee of the Brookings Institution and member of the Trilateral Commission.

During his tenure at the top of Levi Strauss, Haas led a turnaround of the once moribund company. Sales and profit grew rapidly, especially in the 1980s, on the back of new brands such as Dockers and Slates, whose creation Haas had closely managed. He also greatly developed Levi Strauss's overseas markets, turning the company into a global business and giving its brands international status. In 1985 he made the company private through a leveraged buyout, one of the largest such buyouts attempted up to that time. Haas has provided strong leadership coupled with a clear global vision. His career to date shows how the application of strong management can turn around ageing companies and give them a new lease of life, apparently in defiance of corporate life-cycle theory.

HALSEY, Frederick A. (1856–1935)

Frederick A. Halsey was born in Unadilla, New York on 12 July 1856, the son of a doctor. He died on 20 October 1935 in New York City. After receiving a bachelor's degree in mechanical engineering from Cornell University in 1878, Halsey took a job as an engineer with the Rand Drill Company, where he worked from 1880 to 1990. He married Stella Spencer in 1885, and the couple had two daughters. Halsey was promoted to the position of engineer and general manager of Canadian Rand Drill Company in 1890. In 1894 he joined the staff of *American Machinist* as associate editor; he was promoted to editor in 1907, and became editor emeritus in 1911.

Halsey's most notable achievement was the development of the wages and efficiency system known as the premium plan, first presented in a paper to the American Society of

Mechanical Engineers in 1891 (see Drury 1915: 41–50 for a detailed summary). Halsey, like many of his fellow engineers, saw wage systems as a way of increasing industrial efficiency. The best way of achieving efficiency, it was felt, was to provide incentives for employees to work more efficiently, and the best way of doing this was to link wages with output.

Prefacing his description of the premium plan, Halsey noted that the two most common incentive systems then in use, piecework and profit sharing, were both flawed. Profit sharing tended to reward all workers equally, so that the idle benefited at the expense of the industrious; also, profits could arise from causes other than increased efficiency. For both these reasons, profit sharing did not always provide a strong incentive. In piecework systems, the problem was rather the opposite: as soon as workers increased output, employers tended to cut the piece rate, so that the workers ended up doing more for the same wage. Again, there was no lasting incentive.

Halsey's premium plan was a revised version of the piece-rate system which was intended to solve the problem of rate-cutting. It consisted of paying, in addition to a basic day wage, a premium based on time saved per task. Each task had a standard benchmark in terms of time required to complete it; if the worker could complete the task more quickly, he or she would then earn the premium rate on top of the day rate. The premium rate itself was usually fixed at about one-third the day rate; Halsey was emphatic that the premium rate should never go as high as the day rate. The one-third figure, says Halsey, is generally ideal in that it provides sufficient incentive for the workers without tempting employers into cutting rates. If they were to do so, the workers could simply reduce their rate of output and fall back on their basic day rates, rather than being trapped into working harder as they would be in a piece-rate system.

There is evidence that, nonetheless, employers did sometimes try to cut premium rates. A modified form of the premium plan called the Rowan plan, developed by the marine engine-maker David Rowan and Company in Glasgow around 1900, attempted to counter this by introducing a slightly more complicated scheme in which day rates as well as premium rates could be raised to reward increased output. Thus even if premium rates were cut, a higher day rate would still obtain.

Although Halsey developed the premium plan while working for Rand Drill Company, curiously, the system appears to have been first tried out in another firm, the Springer Torsion Balance Company, in 1888 (Drury 1915: 48). The plan proved to be very effective, with studies showing that the time to complete standard tasks was often reduced by as much as 30–40 per cent. By 1902 the premium plan was in use in factories all over North America and in several European countries, including Britain and Germany. The premium plan was just one of several such systems developed in the 1880s, the other notable example being the gain-sharing plan of Henry R. TOWNE. Both were an influence on Frederick Winslow TAYLOR, as he makes clear in his early papers on his differential rate system (itself a modified piecework system). Generously, Halsey later commented that Taylor's system was superior to his own and recommended that employers should use the Taylor system.

From 1900 onward Halsey was increasingly preoccupied with campaigning against the metric system. He became one of metrification's most impassioned opponents, arguing that (1) the metric system was no more efficient than the present system; (2) the introduction of the metric system would mean great costs for no discernible gain in efficiency; and (3) governments were behaving immorally in compelling adoption of the metric system. His efforts were a major factor in the rejection of the metric system by the US Congress in 1906. Halsey wrote nine books and a large number of articles on various subjects to do with engineering and management, and few miss the chance to attack the metric system still further. One quote will give an idea of his views:

Nowhere has the system made material progress in industry except when backed by the policeman's club ...With their system of weights and measures as a foundation, the English-speaking peoples have built up the greatest commercial and industrial structure the world has known. This system they are asked to abandon for the benefit of others at a cost that is beyond estimate, and for compensating advantages that to themselves are wholly trivial and imaginary. They are asked to enter the slough of despond in which metric Europe wallows in order to help metric Europe out.

(Halsey 1904: 12)

BIBLIOGRAPHY

Drury, H.B. (1915) *Scientific Management*, New York: Columbia University Press.

Halsey, F.A. (1904) *The Metric Fallacy*, New York: D. Van Nostrand and Co.

—— (1905) 'The Premium Plan of Paying for Labour', in J.R. Commons (ed.), *Trade Unionism and Labour Problems*, Boston: Ginn and Co.

—— (1914) *Methods of Machine Shop Work*, New York: McGraw-Hill.

MLW

HAMEL, Gary (1954–)

Gary Hamel attended Andrews University in Michigan, taking a BSc in 1975, and then University of Michigan, where he received an MBA in 1976; he later received a Ph.D. in business from Michigan in 1990. While still working on his thesis, Hamel joined the faculty of the London Business School, where he remains visiting professor of strategy and international management. With C.K. Prahalad, with whom he has collaborated professionally for many years, he founded the management consultancy group Strategos. The two authors have collaborated on seven articles for *Harvard Business Review*, two of which won the McKinsey prize for best article to be published in the journal that year, and a best-selling book, *Competing for the Future* (1994). Hamel remains one of the most popular management gurus in the world, and is widely sought after as a speaker.

Hamel is probably most famous for his work with Prahalad on strategy, and in particular on the concept of 'core competencies'. The latter are often defined as being simply 'what a company is good at', but in reality, Hamel and Prahalad say, there is much more to it. Core competencies are not what the corporation values about itself; they are what customers value about the corporation. The define a core competency as a unique skill or attribute which customers value highly, which cannot be easily transferred out of the corporation, but which can be replicated across a range of products/services/markets with which the company is engaged. Any definition of core competences must begin with the customer's point of view; any attribute which cannot be seen to be desired by the customer is *ipso facto* not a core competence.

This is a deceptively simple concept, but one which has great importance for strategy and strategic development. In *Competing for the Future*, Hamel and Prahalad develop on this basic premise to explain what companies and managers should be doing today if they are to win out over their competitors in the future. They believe that companies should always be trying to go a step beyond their rivals, seeking revolutionary rather than evolutionary advances. Hamel has returned to this last theme in his most recent book, *Leading the Revolution* (2001).

240

BIBLIOGRAPHY
Hamel, G. (2001) *Leading the Revolution*, New York: McGraw-Hill.
Hamel, G. and Prahalad, C.K. (1989) *Competing for the Future: Breakthrough Strategies*, Boston, MA: Harvard Business School Press.

MLW

HAMILTON, Alexander (1757–1804)

Alexander Hamilton was born on the Caribbean island of Nevis on 11 January 1757, the illegitimate son of James Hamilton, a Scottish merchant, and Rachel Lavien, a Huguenot shopkeeper. He was mortally wounded in a duel with Republican politician Aaron Burr at Weehawken, New Jersey on 11 July 1804, and died in New York the following day.

His father deserted the family shortly before his mother died in 1368. A local Presbyterian minister raised funds to send Hamilton to school in New York, where he attended King's College (now Columbia University) in 1774. On the outbreak of the American Revolution, Hamilton joined the rebels, fighting with distinction at the battles of White Plains and Trenton. He was rewarded with an appointment as aide-de-camp to General George Washington, an event which marked the beginning of his political career. After the war Hamilton became a member of Congress and was instrumental in drafting the Constitution of the United States; under Washington's presidency, he was appointed the first US Secretary of the Treasury in 1789, and was instrumental in establishing the administrative machinery of government in the USA. He married Elizabeth Schuyler in 1780; the marriage produced eight children.

During his time as Secretary of Treasury, Hamilton developed plans for reviving the United States economy. He saw the national economy and national security as strongly linked. Unlike many writers then and since, Hamilton believed that commercial growth and prosperity made war more likely, not less; commerce did not inevitably lead to peace. The commercial interests of the United States thus had to support its military interests, and vice versa. To this end, Hamilton was a strong believer in an integrated economy with a diverse industrial portfolio. A protectionist, he particularly favoured government support for small but strategically important industrial sectors which would enable them to grow rapidly (what is now known as the 'infant industry' concept).

Hamilton's vision of the growth of the US economy was largely adopted by political and business leaders throughout the nineteenth century, although the pendulum of fashion oscillated (then as now) between protectionism and free trade. His economic approach can be summed up as viewing what is good for business as good for the nation, and vice versa. This outlook shaped the views of American managers and business leaders for generations, and was particularly well suited to the polyethnic character of American business, leading to a sense of corporate solidarity and a view that personal enrichment was a social and moral good (in contrast with the paternalist ethos prevalent in most European societies). It also led to the close relations between big business and government in the USA, sometimes verging on corporatism, which persisted at least into the 1960s. Not himself a businessman, Hamilton was both a talented administrator and a powerful influence on the shaping of managerial culture in the United States.

BIBLIOGRAPHY
Frisch, M.J. (1991) *Alexander Hamilton and the Political Order*, Lanham, MD: University Press of America.
McKee, S. (ed.) (1934) *Papers on Public Credit, Commerce and Finance by*

Alexander Hamilton, New York: Columbia University Press.

Mitchell, B. (1976) *Alexander Hamilton: A Concise Biography*, New York: Oxford University Press.

MLW

HAMMER, Armand (1898–1990)

Armand Hammer was born in New York City on 21 May 1898, the son of Julius Hammer, a Russian immigrant, and his wife Rose. He died in Los Angeles on 10 December 1990. He married three times: to Olga von Root in 1925, to Angela Zevely in 1943, and to Frances Tilman Barrett in 1956; the first two marriages ended in divorce, and there was one son from the first marriage. After high school in New York, Hammer studied medicine, graduating from the Columbia College of Physicians and Surgeons in 1921. However, he had concurrently been working as a manager in his father's pharmaceutical business, and was already a millionaire by the age of twenty. He abandoned medicine for a career in business.

Hammer's opportunity came in the 1920s, in the newly established USSR. While Western governments and companies ostracized the communist government, Hammer used family connections in Russia to get into Moscow and meet top officials, eventually securing a meeting with Lenin. He settled in Moscow for a time and became an important East–West business conduit, exporting Russian products such as asbestos, and importing foodstuffs and machinery. The rise of Stalin meant the end of his business in Russia, however, and he returned to New York, where for a time he ran a successful business dealing in art and artefacts; he also became a noted collector of artworks, and founded a major gallery in New York. After the repeal of prohibition he also invested in a number of distilleries, and then after the Second World War he moved into cattle ranching.

In 1957 Hammer changed direction yet again, acquiring a controlling interest in the financially troubled Occidental Petroleum Company. Rebuilding the company and putting it on a sound financial footing required some years, but in 1966 Occidental struck a very large oil field in the deserts of central Libya, propelling the company into the ranks of major oil producers. When the government of Colonel Moammar al-Qadafi came to power in 1969, threatening nationalization of the oil industry, Hammer struck a bargain which allowed the government a majority share in the profits and gave Occidental a virtual monopoly on oil production. As he had done with Lenin fifty years earlier, Hammer now became a window on the world for the otherwise isolated Libya, facilitating imports and exports and sometimes assisting in negotiations with other powers. Hammer had also maintained his contacts with Russia over the decades, again helping to facilitate East–West negotiations on a number of occasions; he became a personal friend of the last communist leader, Mikhail Gorbachev, and one of Hammer's last public acts was to fly medical teams to the Ukraine to assist in the aftermath of the Chernobyl nuclear disaster.

Hammer was a master of relationship management. He understand better than most twentieth-century business leaders the relationship between politics and business; his talent was to be able to persuade political leaders of all persuasions, ranging from Western liberals to Soviet communists to Islamic revolutionaries, of his views and to gain their trust. This ability to make and maintain relationships at the highest level – often in the face of his home country's public opinion – marks Hammer out as an intelligent and courageous manager and business leader.

BIBLIOGRAPHY
Hammer, A. and Lyndon, N. (1987)
Hammer, New York: Putnam.
Weinberg, S. (1989) *Armand Hammer: The Untold Story*, Boston: Little, Brown and Co.

MLW

HAMMER, Michael (1948–)

After taking his bachelor's, master's and Ph.D. degrees at Massachusetts Institute of Technology (MIT), Michael Hammer joined IBM as a software engineer before returning to MIT as a professor of computer science. In the late 1980s he participated, with Thomas Davenport, in the PRISM research project run by the Index consulting group, which developed the concepts that were to launch him as one of the most influential management 'gurus' of the early 1990s. In articles published in the 1990 volumes of the *Sloan Management Review* and *Harvard Business Review* respectively, Davenport and Hammer discussed their findings in terms of a new approach to management that they called business process redesign, or reengineering. This proclaimed that the power of modern information technology provided an opportunity for corporations to reinvent themselves around business processes and achieve dramatic performance improvements. Hammer's article, characteristically entitled 'Reengineering Work: Don't Automate, Obliterate', achieved rapid recognition and his subsequent book (*Reengineering the Corporation: A Manifesto for Business Revolution*) with James Champy of CSC Index topped the best-seller lists on its publication in 1993.

Hammer's definition of reengineering is 'the fundamental rethinking and radical redesign of business processes to achieve dramatic improvements in contemporary measures of business performance', of which the key words are seen to be 'radical', 'dramatic' and 'process'. 'Radical' is taken to indicate that redesign should start with a blank slate: throw out all the old processes and assumptions and start again. Reengineering is a new beginning. 'Dramatic' refers to reengineering's performance improvement targets. In contrast to the incremental approach of total quality management, reengineering aims for step changes rather than marginal improvement. Finally, 'process' indicates that businesses should be organized around horizontal processes, 'collections of activities that take various kinds of input and create an output that is of value to a customer' (Hammer and Champy 1993: 35), rather than on traditional, vertical functional lines.

Hammer's claims for reengineering in these works were nothing if not bold. Reengineering was described as the biggest breakthrough in management thinking since Adam Smith, and readers were assured that performance improvements such as 'taking 78 days out of an 80-day turnaround time, cutting 75% of overhead and eliminating 80% of errors' (Hammer 1990: 112) could be achieved by any organization following its precepts. Reengineering was also seen to create a 'new world of work' involving shifts: from functional departments to process teams; from simple tasks to multidimensional work; from control to empowerment; from training to education; from payment for activity to compensation by results; from promotion by performance to advancement based on ability; from protective to productive values; from managers as supervisors to managers as coaches; from hierarchical to flat organizational structures; and from executives as scorekeepers to executive leadership.

If, as critics such as Grint (1994) argued, few, if any, of these ideas were quite as novel or radical as Hammer suggested, they certainly seemed to have remarkable appeal to managers at the time. Thus in his second book (*The Reengineering Revolution*, with Steve Stanton), published in 1996, Hammer reported that more than three-quarters of America's largest companies were said to be undertaking reengineering projects in 1994, while Davenport (1995) estimated the size of the market for reengineering consultancy and related services to be $51 billion in 1995.

Perhaps because of this remarkable success, reengineering also attracted its fair share of critics. While some, such as Grint (1994), focused on accounting for the concept's exceptional popularity (given its unexceptional content), others questioned its efficacy, noting that, as with PETERS and Waterman's *In Search of Excellence* (1982), many of Hammer's reengineering exemplars had subsequently fallen on hard times. In this they were assisted by a (later much regretted) statement in 'Reengineering the Corporation', that 50 to 70 per cent of organizations undertaking reengineering failed to achieve the dramatic results they intended. Although Hammer sought to dismiss this 'myth' in *The Reengineering Revolution*, arguing that reengineering was not inherently risky – indeed, success was 'guaranteed' for those who followed its principles correctly – doubts about reengineering's effectiveness continued to grow.

A more substantive concern was raised by writers such as Davenport (1995), Hammer's erstwhile colleague on the PRISM project, who argued that reengineering's treatment of the human side of organizations was seriously deficient. Having himself likened reengineering to a neutron bomb that destroys people and leaves structures standing, and having advocated an aggressive top-down approach to reengineering implementation, sweeping away old practices and eliminating many jobs, Hammer was forced to concede that reengineering might have been 'insufficiently appreciative of the human dimension', a fault that he attributed to his engineering background (White 1996). He continued to resist, however, suggestions that reengineering was simply a euphemism for mindless downsizing.

In retrospect, it would seem that 1995 marked the turning point in the fortunes of reengineering. Although Hammer continued to promote reengineering (Hammer 1996; Hammer and Stanton 1999), albeit emphasizing the enduring contribution of its process orientation in an age of enterprise systems and e-commerce rather than the more extravagant claims of its unique solution to the problems of modern management, the concept seems to be popularly viewed as having been a passing fad. Indeed, Hammer's 1996 book was entitled *Beyond Reengineering*.

Hammer's achievement, therefore, is that of having captured, for a period in the early 1990s at least, the popular imagination with a simple, but arguably derivative, message about how companies should, and could, organize themselves around processes rather than functions. As Jones (1994) notes, this has been attributable in no small measure to his effectiveness as a writer and speaker. Citing business leaders, American cultural, sporting and political figures as well as classic writers to support and illuminate the ideas, his writing is studded with catch phrases such as 'paving the cowpaths', 'rearranging the deckchairs on the Titanic', or 'dusting the furniture at Pompeii', and supported by alliterative lists and enumerated 'principles'. The language is simple, direct and supremely self-confident. As a speaker, his evangelical style of delivery is also frequently remarked upon. Indeed, he has himself described reengineering as a theology. It is unclear, therefore, whether in the longer term reengineering will be seen as a phenomenon of primarily historical and sociological interest, or as having made a significant contribution to management. Hammer's role in promoting the concept and thereby perhaps providing the rationale for significant programmes of organizational restructuring in the early 1990s, however, would seem undeniable.

BIBLIOGRAPHY

Davenport, T.H. (1995) 'The Fad that Forgot People', *Fast Company* (November): 70–74.

Grint, K. (1994) 'Reengineering History: Social Resonances and Business Process Reengineering', *Organization* 1(1): 179–201.

Hammer, M. (1990) 'Reengineering Work: Don't Automate, Obliterate', *Harvard Business Review* (July–August): 104–12.

—— (1996) *Beyond Reengineering*, London: HarperCollins.

Hammer, M. and Champy, J. (1993) *Reengineering the Corporation: A Manifesto for Business Revolution*, London: Nicholas Brealey.

Hammer, M. and Stanton, S. (1996) *The Reengineering Revolution*, London: HarperCollins.

—— (1999) 'How Process Enterprises Really Work', *Harvard Business Review* (November–December): 108–18.

Jones, M.R. (1994) 'Don't Emancipate, Exaggerate: Rhetoric, "Reality" and Reengineering', in R. Baskerville, S. Smithson and J. DeGross (eds), *Information Technology and New Emergent Forms of Organizations*, Amsterdam: North-Holland, 357–78.

White, J.B. (1996) 'Reengineering Gurus take Steps to Remodel their Stalling Vehicles', *Wall Street Journal*, 26 November: A1.

MJ

HANEY, Lewis Henry (b. 1882)

Lewis Henry Haney was born in Eureka, Illinois on 30 March 1882. He took his AB in economics at Dartmouth College in 1903, and his Ph.D. at the University of Wisconsin in 1906. He taught economics at the University of Iowa from 1906 to 1908, then was assistant professor at the University of Michigan from 1908 to 1910 and professor at the University of Texas from 1910 to 1916. He was a member of the Economic Advisory Board of the Federal Trade Commission (1916–20) and was then briefly director of research for the South Wholesale Grocers Association (1920) before taking up a post as chief of the cost marketing division of the US Department of Agriculture in 1921. He also returned to academia, taking up an appointment as professor of economics at New York University in 1921 and director of business research at the university from 1921 to 1930.

Haney's economics, which show strongly the emphasis of Alfred MARSHALL, led him to a consideration of the role of human agency rather than a strict mechanical approach to the market. His *History of Economic Thought* (1911) was a highly influential work and was widely cited by business economists of the day. Haney traces the development of economic ideas and systems as far back as Mosaic and Vedic law, and examines their development through classical Greek and Roman philosophy, through the Middle Ages, and so on up to his own time. The thrust of his work was to show that economics is an evolutionary rather than a revolutionary process, and that forms of economic behaviour change only slowly.

Business Organization and Combination (1913) applied economic analysis to activities of the business corporation. Particularly noteworthy is a chapter which examines the internal workings of organizations, especially the role, nature and function of management. Haney develops what he calls an 'hourglass' model of the large corporation, in which the interests of large and diverse groups of shareholders and employees are funnelled together in the space occupied by a comparatively small group, the corporation's executives and managers. Management exists to serve the interests of both these groups, but divergences in their interests can lead to conflicting loyalties. In terms of organization, Haney was a functionalist and a supporter of the line and staff principle; he argued that management, like labour, needed to be divided to achieve maximum efficiency.

A largely conservative thinker, Haney was opposed to 'integrated marketing', the growing trend in the early twentieth century among large corporations to integrate downstream and manage their own distribution networks. He saw this trend as tending to increase producer power over both retailers and consumers, leading to abuses such as 'excessive' advertising and price fixing. He was vigorously opposed in this view by his fellow economist L.D.H. WELD, then serving as director of research for the meat-packing firm of Swift; their debate was played out in the pages of *American Economic Review* over the course of 1920–21. The issues raised during the debate remain live ones in terms of both business ethics and the economics of the market-place.

BIBLIOGRAPHY

Cattell, J.M., Cattell, J. and Ross, E.E. (1941) *Leaders in Education*, 2nd edn, Lancaster, PA: The Science Press.

Haney, L.H. (1911) *History of Economic Thought*, New York: Macmillan; revised edn 1922.

—— (1913) *Business Organization and Combination*, New York: Macmillan.

—— (1920) 'Integration in Marketing', *American Economic Review* 10: 528–40.

—— (1921) 'Integration in Marketing: Reply to L.D.H. Weld', *American Economic Review* 11: 487–9.

Weld, L.D.H, Haney, L.H. and Gray, L.C. (1921) 'Is Large-scale Centralized Organization of Marketing in the Interest of the Public? Roundtable Discussion', *American Economic Review* 10(suppl.): 215–24.

MLW

HARMAN, Willis Walter (1918–97)

Willis Walter Harman was born in Seattle, Washington on 16 August 1918, the son of Fred Harman, an engineer, and his wife Marguerite. He died in Stanford, California on 30 January 1997. His formal education and early career were technical. He received a BS in electrical engineering in 1939 from the University of Washington. After the Second World War, during which he was on active service for five years as a naval reserve officer, he gained an MS in Physics and a Ph.D. in electrical engineering, both from Stanford University in 1948. He married Charlene Reamer in 1941, and they had four children.

Harman began his academic career at Stanford University as assistant professor in electrical engineering in 1948. After three years as associate professor at the University of Florida, he returned to Stanford as a professor in 1952, teaching electronics, communication theory and systems analysis. During his time there as professor of engineering–economy systems, he became interested in the 'sensitivity training' and 'human potential' movement. This convinced him of the importance of the task of self-discovery, and he consequently developed his teaching around this philosophy. Shortly after, in 1958, he received the George Washington Award for his outstanding contribution to engineering education from the Society for Engineering Education.

Harman was greatly influenced by the work of Alfred M. Hubbard, Humphry Osmond, Aldous Huxley and others in their attempts to build a systematic study of consciousness. They believed that this new understanding could play an important role in the steering of society. These influences are evident in his *An Incomplete Guide to the Future* (1976), in which Harman explores new images of the human, and makes challenges to definitions of knowledge governed by scientific orthodoxy. The book is an eloquent call to futures studies at a deeply human level, while at the same time setting out much of the pioneering thinking of futures studies. Harman succinctly illustrates some of the key dilemmas facing the transforming of industrial society, including the growth dilemma, the distribution dilemma, and what he describes as the work-roles dilemma – the inability of industrialized societies to provide enough satisfying work roles to meet the needs and expectations of their citizens. Drawing on a wide range of philosophy, images and poetry, the book is an exemplar of the multidisciplinary approach Harman advocates.

As he became more involved and interested in social questions, Harman moved into social policy analysis and in 1966 joined the Stanford Research Institute (SRI). The following year he became director of the Educational Policy Research Center at SRI. The centre was asked to investigate alternative future possibilities for the society and their implications for educational policy as part of a US government programme in 1968. Under Harman's direction the centre developed a new, multidisciplinary approach to identify and assess the plausibility of a vast number of future possibilities for society. Part of the approach was to construct sequences of these possible futures, which came to be known as 'future histories'. The policy implications they explored revealed that only a handful of possible futures were at all desirable. Furthermore, due to the interrelatedness of the *problematique*, the desirable futures required fundamental changes in the industrial culture.

SRI developed a Center for the Study of Social Policy to continue the work, of which Harman became director. He went on to assess the conceptual foundation of thinking and doing that might support a benign transition to such a future, choosing to focus on images of the nature of people in relationship with the universe. One of the most important projects was published as *Changing Images of Man* (1982). During the fourteen years of the work of the futures research group at SRI, Harman played a central role in the evolution of the group's ideas and approaches.

Harman also developed, with Joe Armstrong, a functional strategy and framework for conducting technology assessments (TA). TA are generally described as a type of policy studies which examines the widest possible scope of impacts and consequences in society of the introduction of new technologies. Harman's was a significant early contribution to the development of the field.

Harman's *Global Mind Change* (1988) penetrated to the heart of the global predicament and moved it forward to a transformed world. Slaughter sums up the character of this book: 'His treatment of three metaphysical perspectives is exemplary in its understated economy, and the book opens out the prospect of cultural recovery on a global scale' (Slaughter 1995: 192). In general, Harman's work was clear-sighted, persuasive and accessible. His contribution to addressing complex social problems and to studying the future should be more widely acknowledged.

BIBLIOGRAPHY
Harman, W.W. (1976) *An Incomplete Guide to the Future*, Stanford, CA: Stanford University Press.
—— (1988) *Global Mind Change*, Indianapolis, IN: Knowledge Systems, Inc.
Markley, O. and Harman, W.W. (1982) *Changing Images of Man*, Oxford: Pergamon Press.
Slaughter, R.A. (1995) *The Foresight Principle*, Twickenham: Adamantine Press.

AJ

HATHAWAY, Horace King (1878–1944)

Horace King Hathaway was born in San Francisco on 9 April 1878, and died in Palo Alto, California on 12 June 1944. Trained at the Drexel Institute in Philadelphia, he worked with Midvale Steel Company from 1896 to 1902, working his way up from apprentice to foreman. From 1902 to 1904 he was superintendent of the Payne Engine Company at Elmira, New York. He then joined the Link-Belt Company in Philadelphia, where he worked with Carl BARTH and Frederick W. TAYLOR to bring in a production system based on scientific management. In 1905 Hathaway and Barth performed a similar task at the Tabor Manufacturing Company in Philadelphia with great success: by 1910 the failing company had been turned around and output had more than trebled. Hathaway ultimately became vice-president of the company.

In 1907 Hathaway joined Taylor's consulting practice in Philadelphia, where – apart from a period of service with the US Army from 1917 to 1919 – he remained until 1923. He also lectured at Harvard Business School, the Massachusetts Institute of Technology and the Wharton School at the University of Pennsylvania. In 1923 Hathaway returned to the West Coast for several years, working as a consulting engineer; in 1927 he joined the Mallinckrodt Chemical Works in St Louis, where he remained until 1941, when he returned to San Francisco and set up a consulting practice. From 1937 until his death he was a lecturer at the School of Business at Stanford University.

The youngest of the Taylor team, Hathaway was also one of the most active of its members in terms of teaching and writing. He published a number of important articles describing the Taylor system.

BIBLIOGRAPHY

Drury, H.B. (1915) *Scientific Management*, New York: Columbia University Press.
Hathaway, H. (1911) 'Prerequisites to the Introduction of Scientific Management', *Engineering Magazine* 41; repr. in C.B. Thompson (ed.), *Scientific Management*, Cambridge, MA: Harvard University Press, 1914.
——— (1912) 'The Planning Department: Its Organization and Function', *Industrial Engineering* 12; repr. in C.B. Thompson (ed.), *Scientific Management*, Cambridge, MA: Harvard University Press, 1914.
Urwick, L.F. (ed.) (1956) *The Golden Book of Management*, London: Newman Neame.

HEARST, William Randolph (1863–1951)

William Randolph Hearst was born on 29 April 1863 in San Francisco, California and died at his estate San Simeon, California on 14 August 1951. He was the son of George Hearst, a mine developer and US senator, and Phoebe Apperson. He first became involved in journalism while attending Harvard College during the 1880s, working for the *Harvard Lampoon* and Joseph PULITZER's New York *World*. In 1886 he took charge of the *San Francisco Examiner*, a weak paper owned by his father, and made it a commercial success. Nine years later he acquired the New York *Morning Journal*, which placed him in direct competition with Pulitzer.

Hearst's main contribution to newspaper publishing was his willingness to invest money in the media, and his was the first fortune based on newspapers and magazines. Using his father's wealth, Hearst spared no expense to buy newspapers and hire journalists from competitors. By 1913 Hearst owned seven daily newspapers, five magazines, two news services and a film company. One reason for Hearst's success was that his publications appealed to people across class and ethnic lines by extensive use of pictures and an eclectic mix of articles.

Hearst was best known for his use of emotionally charged stories to attract readers. Dubbed by the press as 'yellow journalism', after the Yellow Kid cartoon figure created by Richard Outcault, these stories not only boosted circulation but also shaped public opinion. The most famous use of this writing style occurred in 1898 when Hearst whipped up public hatred of Spain and support for Cuban rebels. The sinking of the battleship USS *Maine* was sensationalized to such an extent that President McKinley was essentially forced to declare war on Spain, and Hearst publicly took credit for this decision.

Hearst was also involved in Democratic Party politics, and actively supported the causes of organized labour, the urban working class and Progressive Era reformers. Although he served from 1903 to 1907 in the US House of Representatives as a Democrat from New York, Hearst lost several other attempts to hold office, including mayor of New York City in 1905 and 1909, lieutenant governor of New York in 1906, and the Democratic presidential nomination in 1904. Hearst's private life was also complex. He married several times, and used his vast personal fortune to build his palatial mansion at San Simeon, and assemble one of the largest private art collections in the country. In 1937 Hearst was the subject of Orson Welles's movie *Citizen Kane*.

By the 1920s Hearst's business acumen was failing, as evidenced by his decision to pursue market share for his publications at the expense of profitability. Although his papers accounted for 14 per cent of all daily circulation and nearly a quarter of the Sunday papers sold in the 1930s, he was so deeply in debt that he was forced to give up control of his holdings. New professional managers sold unprofitable media and real estate, and by 1940 only seventeen of the forty-two papers Hearst had bought or established remained. At the end of his life, Hearst still headed the largest news conglomerate in the USA with sixteen dailies, two Sunday papers and nine magazines. He controlled 10 per cent of daily circulation after the Second World War.

BIBLIOGRAPHY
Nasaw, D. (2000) *The Chief: The Life of William Randolph Hearst*, Boston: Houghton Mifflin.
Swanberg, W.A. (1961) *Citizen Hearst: A Biography of William Randolph Hearst*, New York: Scribner.

DM

HEFNER, Hugh Marston (1926–)

Hugh Hefner was born in Chicago on 9 April 1926, the son of Glenn and Grace Hefner. Graduating from high school in 1944 he joined the US Army, where he served as a clerk and also drew cartoons for an army newspaper. Discharged in 1946, he attended the Chicago Art Institute, then enrolled in the University of Illinois, where he graduated with a BA in well under the normal time through enrolling in extra classes; he largely paid his way through university by work as a cartoonist, and also found time to edit the university's student newspaper, where one of the features he introduced was 'Co-ed of the Month'.

Graduating in 1949, Hefner worked briefly as an assistant personnel manager and an advertising copywriter. In 1951 he took a job as a copywriter with *Esquire* magazine, but promptly lost it when the magazine relocated its head office to New York. Hefner now resolved to start a magazine of his own. He correctly forecast that the economic boom of the 1950s would lead in time to a social revolution, and that prewar trends towards more relaxed social mores and a freer attitude to sex would continue, and it was in this direction that he decided to fashion his market niche. The result was *Playboy*, the first issue of which was laid out on Hefner's kitchen table and which went on sale in December 1953; he did not commission a subsequent issue because he had no money to pay for it. The magazine sold 50,000 copies within days, making Hefner's fortune.

Apart from its obvious features – the first issue featured the famous centrefold picture of the then model Marilyn Monroe, who went on to Hollywood stardom and notoriety of her own – the magazine also developed a reputation for incisive, sometimes cutting-edge journalism. During the 1950s and 1960s it became a 'must read' for American men, despite violent opposition in the Bible Belt states and by conservatives everywhere. Its radical edge dulled in the 1970s, but by then it had established a place in American folklore. Hefner used his profits to diversify into other ventures such as music promotion and nightclubs, and to fashion a playboy lifestyle for himself. He remains an outstanding example of how marketing success can be ensured simply by being in the right place at the right time.

HEINZ, Henry John (1844–1919)

Henry John Heinz was born in Pittsburgh, Pennsylvania on 11 October 1844, the eldest of eight children of German immigrants, Henry and Margaretha Heinz. He died at his mansion, Greenlawn, in Pittsburgh on 14 May 1919. He grew up in Sharpsburg, Pennsylvania, where his father owned a small brickworks. From an early age he displayed an entrepreneurial bent, and from the age of eight began selling surplus vegetables from the family garden. Finding he was making a profit, he embarked on the business more seriously, setting up hothouses and acquiring more land. By the time he was sixteen, Heinz was employing local women to sell for him and was also supplying vegetables on contract to greengrocers in Pittsburgh.

In 1859 Heinz took a course at Duff's Business College in Pittsburgh, one of a number of small business training colleges which had sprung up around the United States in the 1840s and 1850s; they taught accounting and bookkeeping and also some rudimentary management skills, and were in many ways the forerunners of today's business schools. Armed with these skills, in 1865 Heinz used his profits from the grocery business to buy a half share in his father's brickyard. Here he made some minor adjustments to the kilns and drying apparatus which improved the quality and output of bricks. Alberts (1973) notes that Heinz maintained a lifelong interest in bricks, and in later years visitors to his office were sometimes surprised to see piles of brick samples stacked on his desk.

In the meantime his developing food business continued. He became a specialist in the production of horseradish, and in the first of many marketing innovations, began packaging and selling horseradish in clear glass bottles so that consumers could see both the quantity and quality of the product they were getting. In 1869 he and a friend, L.C. Noble, set up a partnership to produce and sell horseradish and other food products in Pittsburgh. In the same year he married Sarah Sloan Young, an Irishwoman whose family had emigrated to the United States from County Down; they went on to have five children. Heinz and Noble expanded quickly into other products such as vinegar, pickles and sauerkraut, and branched out as far afield as Chicago and St Louis. However, although Heinz was a capable financial manager, he was unable to cope with the combination of falling agricultural prices and tight credit in the summer of 1875, and by the end of the year, Heinz, Noble and Company had been forced into bankruptcy. Heinz later paid his share of the firm's debts in full.

Despite the financial problems, Heinz knew he was onto a winning business formula. He formed a new partnership in 1876 with his brother John and cousin Frederick Heinz, and himself became general manager of the new firm F. and J. Heinz Company. Investing heavily in food preparation equipment, Heinz specialized in the production of pickles and produced a range of products that began winning awards for quality. By 1879 he had paid off the company's debts. Heinz was one of the first to realize the vast potential of the newly invented process for preserving food in tinned metal containers, and in 1881 made further investments in this technology. Throughout the 1880s he launched range after range of canned foods, including such modern staples as canned vegetables, canned spaghetti and canned beans.

In 1888 Heinz bought out the shares of his partners and re-established the business as H.J. Heinz and Company. His was now one of the leading food-processing businesses in the United States. He built a vast new factory on the banks of the Allegheny River, designed in what Alberts (1973: 91) describes as 'solid Pittsburgh Romanesque'. Other factories followed as the company expanded; by the middle 1890s it was the largest canning and pickling business in the world. By 1900 Heinz was making 200 products in nine factories, and had a branch house in London and agencies worldwide. Highly vertically integrated, the business made its own bottles and cans, owned its own railway cars and had 16,000 acres of directly owned land, as well as importing agricultural produce from all around the world.

In 1905 the company incorporated, with Heinz and the other managing partners, including his son Howard, becoming the sole shareholders. He continued to be actively involved in the management of the firm until the last years of his life. In the early 1890s he built a mansion in Pittsburgh, which he called Greenlawn, and became friendly with others of the Pittsburgh millionaires' set including Henry Clay Frick and George WESTINGHOUSE. Heinz's wife died in 1894; he himself died in 1919.

Heinz's early management training at Duff's Business College, slight though it was by today's standards, was of some importance in shaping his management outlook. From Duff's he gained an appreciation of the importance of financial management skills; in the early stages of his businesses, Heinz often served as bookkeeper and accountant himself, and later continued to monitor closely the basic financial indicators. Yet Heinz was not a cost-cutting manager; he balanced financial requirements with the other needs of his business, and used accounting information to help determine where the most profitable opportunities lay. Heinz was one of those rare and imaginative managers who used accounting and financial data to explore opportunities for growth. He always had a strict regard for business fundamentals; as McCafferty, for many years his private secretary, said: 'He was not a dreamer or a visionary, who went into business and by chance made a success. He was a businessman by origin, by preference, and by training' (McCafferty 1923: 137).

One of Heinz's most imaginative arrangements was related to the maintenance of product quality standards. He appreciated from the beginning that his products would be successful if he could maintain high and consistent quality. In the 1880s Heinz began developing purchasing arrangements with farmer, especially growers of cucumbers and cabbage used in making pickles and sauerkraut. By these arrangements, Heinz would agree to purchase the farmer's entire output of a given crop at a previously agreed price, usually well above the average market rate; for their part, the farmers had to allow inspection of crops by Heinz technicians and to plant and harvest specific crops at specific times to ensure the best quality of output. Heinz got the quality he needed, the farmers were well paid, and the agricultural community of the Midwest learned more about scientific farming methods (Heinz's farming technicians were hired from the country's leading agricultural colleges). Heinz and his managers were constant advocates of higher standards in the food industry; he supported the Pure Food Crusade of the 1890s and the Pure Food and Drug Act of 1906, a position which brought him into conflict with other food producers.

It is for his advances in marketing and branding, however, that Heinz is best remembered, and here it seems that his own intuition rather than training was his chief guide. McCafferty tells the story of how Heinz 57 varieties, one of the most famous brands in American history, was conceived:

Its origin was in 1896. Mr Heinz, while in an elevated railroad train in New York, saw among the car-advertising cards one about shoes with the expression: '21 Styles'. It set him to thinking, and as he told it: 'I said to myself, "we do not have styles of products, but we do have varieties of products." Counting up how many we had, I counted well beyond 57, but "57" kept coming back into my mind. "Seven, seven" – there are so many illustrations of the psychological influence of that figure and of its alluring significance to people of all ages and races that "58 Varieties" or "59 Varieties" did not appeal at all to me as being equally strong. I got off the train immediately, went down to the lithographers, where I designed a street-car card and had it distributed throughout the United States. I myself did not realize how highly successful a slogan it was going to be.'

(McCafferty 1923: 147)

Previously, in heavily branded industries such as soap, the practice had been to brand each product or product line separately. In Heinz's case this would have been so expensive as to be impracticable. His inspiration was to create a single corporate brand that could be applied across all products.

Even before the development of this famous brand, however, Heinz had shown himself to be an innovative marketer. His sales staff used then untried methods such as product demonstrations and free samples given away at public events; these methods were expensive, but they were also highly effective. At the Chicago World's Fair in 1893, Heinz hit on another give-away: setting up a Heinz pavilion, he gave each visitor a free 'pickle pin' as a memento. Alberts calls this 'one of the most famous giveaways in merchandising history', and notes that so many people crowded into the pavilion that the floors began to sag and had to be reinforced (Alberts 1973: 123). He opened the Allegheny works to visitors and set up guided tours; at the height of the tourist season, the works saw as many as 20,000 visitors a year.

In 1900 Heinz sponsored the first advertising billboard lit by electric light bulbs; the sign featured 1,200 light bulbs, 'at a time when a single bulb was a curiosity' (Alberts 1973: 128). The *New York Times* called it a 'work of advertising genius', and the billboard itself became an important tourist attraction until its demolition a few years later to make way for the construction of the Flatiron Building.

Perhaps the most splendid of all Heinz's promotional efforts was the Heinz Ocean Pier in Atlantic City, New Jersey, sometimes called the 'Crystal Palace by the Sea' and sometimes, less reverently, 'The Sea Shore Home of the 57 Varieties'. Nine hundred feet in length, the pier featured a glass pavilion with a sun room and reading room, and of course a kitchen giving out free samples of Heinz products. At the height of its popularity before the First World War, the pier was attracting over 20,000 people a year. Its popularity declined in the 1930s, however, and the pier was finally abandoned after being badly damaged by a hurricane in the autumn of 1944. The pier, splendid though it was, never really paid back its cost to the company, and is the one aberration in Heinz's otherwise shrewd career of cost-effective marketing.

Heinz's enlightened approach to business extended also to his relationships with his employees. Strongly paternalistic in approach, he believed in hiring employees young, training them in his business methods and promoting on merit; he believed that all employees ought to feel part of the Heinz family. McCafferty, who knew him well (although he is obviously biased in his favour), writes of how Heinz's business philosophy was a comingling of ethics and sound business principles, and of how he sought to infuse this personal view into the organization:

> A cardinal article of his faith was that men can be trusted, that most men would rather do right than wrong. He perceived that the reason they did not adhere to their best inclinations was that they were afraid they could not succeed that way in business. His big deed of human leadership was to show men that they did not need to be afraid.
>
> (McCafferty 1923: 127)

Heinz, says McCafferty, emphasized welfare work not to head off industrial unrest, but because he thought it was right. His was one of the first companies in the United States to introduce free life insurance for employees.

Robert Alberts, author of what remains the best study of Heinz to date, summarizes Heinz's philosophy of business in what he calls the eight 'Important Ideas'. These ideas are a balanced mix of sound business principles, an approach to the market based on a mixture of intuition and common sense, and an ethical view which is embedded at the heart of his approach. The eight principles are summarized as follows:

1. Housewives are willing to pay someone else to take over a share of their more tedious kitchen work (Alberts 1973: 7).

2. A pure article of superior quality will find a ready market through its own intrinsic merit – if it is properly packaged and promoted (1973: 7).

3. To improve the finished product that comes out of the bottle, can or crock, you must improve it in the ground, when and where it is grown (1973: 47).

4. Our Market is the World (1973: 79).

5. Humanize the business system of today and you will have the remedy for the present discontent that characterizes the commercial world and fosters a spirit of enmity between capital and labour (1973: 90).

6. Let the public assist you in advertising your products and promoting your name (1973: 123).

7. Good foods, properly processed, will keep without the addition of preservatives (1973: 171).

8. If people could work together in religion, then lasting peace might be found (1973: 191).

Like many of the great business leaders of his day, Heinz had strong social principles. He was deeply religious, although his faith had different varieties, and he seems at times to have been a Lutheran, an Episcopalian, a Methodist Episcopalian and a Presbyterian, to the baffled amusement of his Ulster Protestant wife. He was for twenty-five years a Sunday school superintendent, and later served on the executive council of both the International Sunday School Association and the World Sunday School Association. He took his Christian values into both civic and business life. He served as vice-president of the Pittsburgh Chamber of Commerce and on a number of other civic bodies. He was also a noted art collector and philanthropist; among his many civic roles in later life was the presidency of the Pittsburgh branch of the Egyptian Exploration Fund.

Heinz left behind him a solid business and an enduring brand name. A marketing innovator, he was also a very able all-round manager, able to balance commercial needs with ethical behaviour, financial controls with marketing costs in a way that led to a high degree of both efficiency and effectiveness. He remains one of the outstanding managerial figures of his generation.

BIBLIOGRAPHY

Alberts, R.C. (1973) *The Good Provider: H.J. Heinz and His 57 Varieties*, London: Arthur Barker.
McCafferty, E.D. (1923) *Henry J. Heinz: A Biography*, New York: Bartlett Orr Press.

MLW

HERZBERG, Frederick Irving (1923–2000)

Frederick Irving Herzberg was born in Lynn, Massachusetts on 18 April 1923, the son of Lithuanian immigrants Lewis and Gertrude Herzberg. He died in Salt Lake City, Utah on 19 January 2000. He married Shirley Bedell in 1944; they had one son. Herzberg grew up in New York City and was educated at City College New York. His studies were interrupted by the Second World War, where he served as a noncommissioned officer in the US Army, winning the Bronze Star for valour; he was also one of the first Allied soldiers to enter Dachau concentration camp, and was assigned the task of providing food and medical care to the survivors immediately after the liberation. Returning to academic life, Herzberg completed his BS degree in 1946 and went on to take an MS and Ph.D. in psychology at the University of Pittsburgh. He was research director of psychological services at Pittsburgh from 1951 to 1957, and professor of psychology at Case Western Reserve University in Cleveland from 1957 to 1972. In 1972 he was appointed professor of management at the College of Business, University of Utah, where he remained until his retirement in 1995.

Herzberg's reputation is built upon a theory of motivation at work in organizations, also known as 'actualization-atmosphere' factors, based upon the hierarchical human needs approach and on the great biblical myths of Adam and Abraham. The actualization factors are the work itself and all forms of acknowledgement of work done. Acting upon these factors enables an individual's behaviour at work to be shaped over the long term. Atmosphere factors include remuneration, job security, management policy in the company and relations between colleagues. Acting on these leads to short-term satisfaction. The implicit hypothesis in this theory is that the individual should grow through their work. His research as applied to company organization had considerable success in the 1970s. He led management policy towards job enrichment and enlargement of tasks, of multitasking and of job rotation, and was critical of TAYLOR's view of the individual at work.

According to the so-called theory of 'needs', human beings are comparable to animals in that they are governed by needs. For humans there is a hierarchy of needs, with that of self-accomplishment made possible through work at the top. Moreover, the great Judaeo-Christian myths express motivations shared by all humanity. The story of Adam teaches us that the first man was created perfect in all aspects, but that God drove him out of earthly Paradise once he ate the fruit from the tree of knowledge. From there comes the notion of guilt and of humans having to pay the penalty, leading him to try to escape from uncomfortable situations in his environment. In the world of work, individual strives to improve his or her working conditions; however, this improvement does not permit the individual at work to satisfy his or her need for self-fulfilment. It is therefore necessary to search elsewhere. The other story which gives an alternative picture of mankind is that of Abraham. Abraham was assured by God of attaining the Promised Land, provided he obeyed God, got up and followed. This vision signified that humans are resourceful beings as they have been given innate positive attributes. It is a dynamic perspective in which humans are seen as being full of potential but in need of guidance to demonstrate it.

These two natures of being human equate to two outlooks on humanity. One falls within a pessimistic tradition of human nature, in which humans, pinioned by the consequences of original sin, must be supervised and guided. The other outlook, this time optimistic, sees humans as beings full of positive attributes provided that their environment enables them to unlock and activate them.

Herzberg finds confirmation of this dual theory of motivation in the empirical research he has led. He maintains it has enabled him to discover and define factors of satisfaction or discontent at work. The first of these, the actualization factors, which emanate from Abraham's nature and lead to satisfaction at work, are achievement, recognition for achievement, work itself, responsibility and the possibility for development or growth. Factors of discontent, or atmosphere factors, arising from Adam's nature, are management policy in the company, management (its qualities and failings), remuneration, work conditions, relations between people (management, employees, equals), prestige, job security and personal factors (where work affects personal life, such as in the case of relocation).

Actualization factors provide a sense of lasting satisfaction. Having a fulfilling job (not routine or lacking interest), receiving recognition for work done, being given responsibility are all actions leading to lasting changes in attitude. Actions such as increase in salary, change of manager, alteration in human resource management, improvement of working conditions, provision of a job guarantee and intervention in workplace relations all tend only towards a lowering of tension, albeit a noticeable one, but they do not alter behaviour deep down.

In his empirical research, carried out in organizations across the world and in all professional fields, Herzberg has shown that individuals always recall positively actions relating to actualization factors ('I had a more interesting job', or 'my boss congratulated me on this job') whereas they always recall negatively actions relating to atmosphere factors ('I had a rise in salary; it's better, but it doesn't equate to what the company should have done', etc).

Amongst the examples put forward by Herzberg, that of the work organization of the secretaries at the Bell Telephone Company has become famous. These secretaries had to answer letters from shareholders of the company. The standardized replies were checked by supervisors. The secretaries' morale was low, absenteeism high and errors numerous. Several atmosphere factors (increase in salary, changes to and development of the hierarchy and planning of the work environment) failed to change anything. It was decided to change the way the work was organized. Each secretary was put in charge of a specific area, in which she became an expert, able to advise her colleagues. Supervision was reduced. Each wrote and signed letters herself. They themselves organized the day's workload. The result was a significant rise in productivity and a quality of response never before achieved.

Managerial policy on task enrichment and enlargement and job rotation from 1960 to 1970 owe much to the theories of Herzberg. Until that time the dominant ideas had been those of Taylor, namely that the individuals at work essentially demanded high salaries, thereby acknowledging more or less openly that they could work without necessarily being interested in the work they were doing. In this vision, the nature of the work and that of the tasks took second place. The period from 1960 to 1980 was a time when disaffection with work and the rejection of unskilled work (the absenteeism record of unskilled workers, disregard for quality almost to the extent of sabotage, rejection of work through lack of interest) became important concerns for managers and politicians in charge. Movements such as those of the hippies on the west coast of the United States, or the student movements of 1968 in Europe appeared to threaten a society built upon industrial order and seemed to be signs of rejection of a society that was supposed to confer well-being but alienated those who served it.

One response to these threats from within Herzberg's body of work was an explanation of the crisis being due to the failure to take the fundamental needs of human nature into consideration. Many managers, politicians and trade union leaders accepted this explanation. Policies to improve working conditions, above all for unskilled workers in large organizations, arose out of Herzberg's work. In order to make the work more attractive and to motivate operators and employees, new tasks were added to repetitive tasks (minor adjustments, maintenance, cleaning, customer despatch, rotation of jobs between operators, etc.). Workstations were re-examined in order to give more responsibility to salaried employees, responsibility that the Taylor division of work had removed.

The success of Herzberg's motivational theory is linked to the contribution of the sociocultural movement from the psychologically, even psychoanalytically orientated work of the Tavistock Institute in London. The central idea is that in order to alter an individual's behaviour, one must act on the group. When members of a small work group are given autonomy and when confidence is shown in them (semi-autonomous groups), they will behave much more productively than under the old system. The concept of the semi-autonomous group was a great success, just when Herzberg's ideas were becoming well known. The two movements combined to exert their influence. In the 1970s, changes in the enrichment and enlargement of tasks were combined with semi-autonomous groups.

Various celebrated reforms were put into place in line with Herzberg's theories. The first was undoubtedly that of the Volvo factories in Kalmar, Sweden at the beginning of the 1970s. A poor social climate had developed (very high absenteeism rate, lack of quality) so management decided to do away with the car assembly line and to replace it with production organized by units. Car parts brought to the reduced workshops were assembled by a team of workers who themselves organized how the work was shared out, ensured it was done in the given time and controlled quality. The tasks were therefore enlarged and enriched, and the workers gained versatility. The results were wholly positive: improved social climate, sharp decline in the absenteeism rate, spectacular rise in quality. Observers from around the world came to visit the factory where the management had dared to do away with the traditional assembly line.

Many other measures were put into effect over the same period in other European countries, often by government bodies. In Germany, the 'Humanisierung der Arbeit' (Work Humanizing) programme, launched by the Social Democrat government (at the beginning of the 1970s), was at the forefront of important research and measures centred on the reorganization of the workplace. In France, in 1974, the government created l'Agence Nationale pour l'Amelioration des Conditions de Travail (National Agency for the Improvement of Work Conditions) in order to encourage social innovation and to launch research programmes. Many innovations aimed at improving conditions and the organization of work were aided and followed through by the agency, and used as an example in its publications.

In Britain, even if the movement has been less important (the country has a long history of industrialization, with greater emphasis given to professional abilities, and a higher degree of autonomy and control in the workshops), many new work systems (enriched and enlarged work, autonomous groups) have been introduced in organizations. In the

United States, even though the movement has been reined in by the tradition of collective bargaining, whose rules, such as the seniority rule and job description, are extremely difficult to change, numerous projects connected with the quality of workplace life have been carried out. New systems for the organization of work have been introduced by management, not without great resistance from the trade unions. Herzberg's ideas have contributed towards launching an important movement of work reorganization and change within companies and in industrial relations.

Herzberg has greatly contributed towards rejection of the ideas of Taylor and FORD on human nature. He reminds us strongly that the workers are motivated by their interest in what they do, that they can buy into and interest themselves in their work. He contributed to reducing excess division of labour, gave autonomy to the least qualified workers, and saw beyond work conditions, bringing to the fore the organization of work itself, in the sense of lessening its traditional division. In this sense, he was an instigator of more flexible, supple organizations, of networked companies as we now know them.

Despite this, Herzberg's theses have aged a lot. There is a theoretical weakness in the theory of needs and their formation into a hierarchy – needs defined independently of the workplace situation and without considering the actual individual. There is a real behavioural determinism operating here. No one has since proved that fulfilment at work should be a universal and permanent motivation. Each individual chooses the way in which he or she will achieve fulfilment, and that way can undergo change. There are thousands of ways of fulfilling oneself at work: strikes, sabotage, industrial action, absenteeism, retirement, etc. In its universal attempt to explain behaviour and to do this away from where the action is taking place, the theory of needs is self-limiting. The advice given by Herzberg has above all consisted of proposing an improved organization. However, the central assertion of his theory, that of people's need for fulfilment in work, is false.

BIBLIOGRAPHY
Bernoux, P. (1998) 'Herzberg, Frederick', in M. Warner (ed.), *IEBM Handbook of Management Thinking*, London: International Thomson Business Press, 294–300.
Herzberg, F. (1959) *Managerial Choice: To Be Efficient and To Be Human*, New York: Dow-Jones Irwin.
——— (1966) *Work and the Nature of Man*, Cleveland, OH: The World Publishing Company.
'Obituary: Frederick Irving Herzberg' (2000) *Salt Lake City Tribune*, 23 January; http://www.siop.org/tip/backissues/TipApril00/31Obituaries.html, 16 April 2001.

PB (trans. Susan Nevard)

HEWLETT, William (1913–2001)

William Hewlett was born in Ann Arbor, Michigan on 20 May 1913. He died at his home in Palo Alto, California on 12 January 2001. The son of a doctor who taught medicine at the University of Michigan, Hewlett grew up in San Francisco after his father became a professor at the Stanford Medical School. He described his childhood as 'busy and happy', and fondly recalled family vacations spent in the Sierra Nevada, where he developed a love for the outdoors that he retained for the rest of his life (Packard 1995: 19).

Hewlett revealed an early curiosity about the way things worked, and often conducted home-made experiments to find out. Some involved explosives, and Hewlett later counted himself lucky not to have killed himself. While science came easy to him at school, he had great difficulty reading and writing, and that hampered him in other subjects. He overcame his dyslexia by developing the ability to listen carefully and memorize his schoolwork.

When Hewlett was twelve years old, his father died of a brain tumour. He said later that if his father had survived, he might have chosen a career in medicine. Instead, he chose electrical engineering.

Because he did so poorly in almost all high school subjects except the sciences, Hewlett had difficulty gaining admission to Stanford. He believed he was accepted only because his father had taught there. He met David PACKARD in his freshman year, and the two had become close friends by the time they were seniors. Both were influenced by their engineering professor, Frederick Terman, who promoted a relationship between the scientific and engineering community of Stanford and the emerging high-tech industries of what eventually became California's Silicon Valley. Terman advised Hewlett and Packard to gain experience and knowledge before taking steps to start their own business.

Both travelled eastward after graduation. Packard worked at General Electric in Schenectady, New York, and Hewlett continued his studies at the Massachusetts Institute of Technology (MIT). He received his master's degree in electrical engineering from MIT in 1936. Hewlett then returned to Stanford, where Terman helped him win a contract to construct an electronic device for recording brainwaves. When Packard opted to leave General Electric and return to California in 1938, Terman arranged a research fellowship for him at Stanford and encouraged the two engineers to open their own business. He suggested that Hewlett's invention of a resistance-capacity audio oscillator for testing sound equipment should be the kernel of the business.

The garage of the house that Hewlett and Packard were renting in Palo Alto, California became their first business address. In 1939 Hewlett received an engineering degree from Stanford and the partners made their first commercial sale to the Walt Disney Studios, which purchased eight of Hewlett's oscillators for use in making the animated film *Fantasia*. The two entrepreneurs moved from their garage to a rented building in Palo Alto, where they swept the floors, kept the books and took the inventory themselves, as their product line of electronic measuring and testing instruments expanded.

During the Second World War, the company developed products for military applications that were important enough to earn Packard a draft exemption. He ran the company by himself while Hewlett served in the US armed forces, first as a signal officer and then as head of the electronics division of the War Department's special staff. Hewlett was discharged in 1945 and returned to Hewlett-Packard to lead its research and development efforts, while Packard retained responsibility for the company's business. By the time Hewlett-Packard incorporated in 1947, the company had 111 employees on its payroll and was reporting annual sales of $679,000.

With Hewlett serving as engineering team leader, the company became a mecca for America's bright young scientists and engineers. The best talent at such eastern US institutions as MIT and Bell Labs took notice, and the western migration of America's technological community began. At Hewlett-Packard they found an environment conducive to encouraging technological innovation. 'There is a feeling that everyone is part of a team, and that team is H-P,' said Hewlett. 'It is an idea based on the individual. It exists because people have seen that it works, and they believe that this feeling makes H-P what it is' (Peters and Waterman 1982: 233).

Within the business, David Packard was the management strategist who devised ways to keep their company functioning like a small, close-knit family as it expanded internationally. Hewlett was the technological guru who believed that employees with innovative engineering and scientific ideas should be front and centre in the operation of the company as it adapted to meet changing market demands. With Hewlett motivating and encouraging them, the scientists and engineers kept Hewlett-Packard at the forefront of technological development in the United States. When he challenged them to develop a computer that would fit in his desk drawer, they invented the HP 9100 calculator, the first computer of its type to be as small as a typewriter. Hewlett then challenged them to go one step further, asking them to make a calculator that would fit in his pocket. They responded with the HP 35, a hand-held calculator that turned out to be the company's first real consumer product, selling well to the general public. Prior to its introduction in 1972, Hewlett-Packard had marketed its products solely to the scientific and engineering communities.

Hewlett spent forty years with Hewlett-Packard. In accordance with the company's plan for management succession, he retired as chief executive officer in 1978, when the company had 57,000 employees and was producing annual revenues of $3 billion. But he still retained an active interest in the company. That became clear to the American business community in 1990, when he and Packard, then both in their late seventies, reasserted themselves in Hewlett-Packard's operations. They used their influence to revamp the company's management structure, which they viewed as having become too bureaucratic and too centralized, and succeeded in arresting the downward movement of the company's profits.

Along with his continuing interest in the business operations of Hewlett-Packard, Hewlett maintained his interest in technological advancements. In 1985 he was awarded America's highest scientific honour, the National Medal of Science. In 1991 he received the Silicon Valley Engineering Hall of Fame Award, and the following year he received the National Inventors Hall of Fame Award.

A series of strokes in the late 1990s slowed Hewlett's movements and limited his ability to participate in the business culture he had created. However, even from his hospital bed he continued to demonstrate his prowess as a mathematician. When a female friend, by way of small talk during a visit to his hospital bedside, told Hewlett about her concern that her high heels might leave marks on a parquet floor, Hewlett responded by asking her how much she weighed. He then proceeded to calculate – one day after suffering a stroke – whether the pounds per square inch she exerted on the floor would be enough to make an impression. The 'garage genius' still had a problem to solve.

BIBLIOGRAPHY

Packard, D. (1995) *The HP Way: How Bill Hewlett and I Built Our Company*, New York: HarperCollins.

Peters, T.J. and Waterman, R.H. (1982) *In Search of Excellence*, New York: Warner Books.

BB

HILL, James Jerome (1838–1916)

James Jerome Hill was born in Rockwood, Eramosa Township, Ontario on 16 September 1838 and died of peritonitis in St Paul, Minnesota on 29 May 1916. One of three surviving children, he was fourteen when his father died, and he was forced to quit school for work in a country store. While still a teenager, he left Canada for the United States, where he took up residence in Saint Paul in Minnesota Territory. There he soon became an integral figure in the transformation of Minnesota from a raw frontier to an economically diverse region. Active in the steamboat trade on the Mississippi and Red rivers, he expanded into warehousing and the fuel business, and later invested heavily in Minnesota's Iron Range and the mining industries of Iowa, Montana and Washington state.

Approaching middle age, he entered into the railroad business, in 1877 joining with Norman Kittson, John S. Kennedy, and Canadians Donald Smith and George Stephen to complete the St Paul and Pacific railway from Minneapolis–St Paul to the Canadian border. Subsequently he built to the west, finally completing what became the Great Northern Railway from St Paul to Seattle in 1893. Alone among US transcontinental lines, the Great Northern remained solvent and avoided bankruptcy in the hard times of the 1890s.

Through his founding and leadership of the Great Northern Railway, Hill dominated rail transportation and played a significant role in the economic development of the American Northwest during the late nineteenth and early twentieth centuries. Allying himself with the nation's preeminent investment banking firm, the house of J.P. MORGAN, Hill obtained control of the Northern Pacific and Chicago, Burlington and Quincy railroads. He became one of the leading figures in the rise of 'big business' in the United States. Following a dramatic conflict with Edward H. Harriman, Hill presided over the Northern Securities holding company (1901–1904), the largest railroad organization of its day, which included the 'Hill Lines' controlled by himself and Morgan. Although the US Supreme Court ordered the dissolution of Northern Securities under provisions of the Sherman Anti-trust Act, the same railroads merged again in 1970 to become the Burlington Northern (now Burlington Northern Santa Fe) system.

After 1900 Hill involved himself in a wide variety of other pursuits. He delivered countless public addresses on a broad range of topics, including international trade, agronomy, finance and the environment. He remained an important adviser to US presidents from the 1880s until his death. He ran model experimental farms in Minnesota to develop superior livestock and crop yields for settlers locating near his railroads. His philanthropic interests were wide-ranging and included significant support for educational, religious and charitable organizations throughout Minnesota, the Northwest and the nation. In his adopted home town, he constructed the James J. Hill Reference Library, which houses his personal papers, to encourage individual self-improvement. When he died suddenly in 1916, James J. Hill was still at work, penning his thoughts on the wisdom of the nation's military 'preparedness' in light of the First World War.

BIBLIOGRAPHY
Hidy, R.W., Hidy, M.E., Scott, R.V. and Hofsommer, D.L. (1988) *The Great Northern Railway: A History*, Boston: Harvard Business School Press.

Hill, J.J. (1910) *Highways of Progress*, New York: Doubleday and Page.

Malone, M.P. (1996) *James J. Hill: Empire Builder of the Northwest*, Norman, OK: University of Oklahoma Press.

Martin, A. (1976) *James J. Hill and the Opening of the Northwest*, New York: Oxford University Press.

Pyle, J.G. (1916-1917) *The Life of James J. Hill*, 2 vols, Garden City, NY: Doubleday and Page.

WTW

HILTON, Conrad Nicholson (1887–1979)

Conrad Nicholson Hilton was born in San Antonio, New Mexico on 25 December 1887, the son of Augustus and Mary Hilton. He died in Santa Monica, California on 3 January 1979. He married three times: to Mary Barron in 1925 (divorced 1934), to actress Zsa Zsa

Gabor in 1942 (divorced 1946) and to Mary Frances in 1976; these marriage produced four children. He attended military schools in Albuquerque and Roswell, New Mexico and later St Michael's College in Santa Fe and the New Mexico Institute of Mining. He joined his father, a general storekeeper, as a partner in business, served in the New Mexico state legislature from 1912, and was an officer in the US Army quartermaster corps in France in 1917–18. He helped to found the New Mexico State Bank in 1913. After the death of his father in 1918 he took over the business with the intention of moving into banking, but instead saw a business opportunity in the run-down Mobley Hotel in Cisco, Texas. Finding the hotel business profitable, Hilton began to expand. Lacking capital, his initial strategy was to buy run-down hotels and renovate them. As the business grew, however, he began building new hotels on leased land, starting in Dallas and gradually expanding across Texas and the Southwest. By 1930 he owned eight hotels.

The operation remained under-capitalized, and the Depression forced Hilton close to bankruptcy, but he managed to put together a partnership with two other hoteliers that kept them all afloat. In 1934 the merger failed, and Hilton went his own way again with five hotels. This time he had access to sufficient capital and resumed his expansion. He began buying prestige hotels such as the Waldorf in New York, and then moved on to purchasing existing chains. In 1948 he moved overseas to Puerto Rico, establishing Hilton International Corporation. He also diversified into related businesses, setting up the Carte Blanche credit-card company and a car rental chain. By the time of his death there were 260 Hilton hotels around the world, either directly owned or franchised, and Hilton himself was worth half a billion dollars. He retired in 1966, handing over control to his son Barron Hilton.

Hilton's success was founded on several key factors. First, he had a strong sense for the best strategic locations, and knew where to place or buy hotels to attract the maximum number of travellers. Second, he built a strong brand identity for Hilton, with large advertising campaigns and standardized service offerings that guaranteed quality and consistency. Third, he worked to build up staff morale, encouraging them to feel involved in the business and to treat customers as guests. His autobiography *Be My Guest* (1957) was for many years distributed free to customers.

BIBLIOGRAPHY
Hilton, C. (1957) *Be My Guest*, Englewood Cliffs, NJ: Prentice-Hall.

HOLLERITH, Herman (1860–1929)

Herman Hollerith was born in Buffalo, New York on 29 February 1860 and died in Washington, DC on 17 November 1929. He was educated in New York and attended the Columbia School of Mines, from which he graduated with a distinction at the age of nineteen. In 1879 he became a special agent for the industrial census with the Census Bureau in Washington, DC. During his tenure, the Census Bureau undertook the 1880 US population census. The monumental task of tabulating the census made a deep impression on Hollerith; a peak work force of nearly 1,500 clerks required seven years to complete the task, almost entirely without benefit of office machinery.

In 1882 Hollerith became an instructor in mechanical engineering at Massachusetts Institute of Technology, where he began, in his own time, to develop a machine for census tabulation. He returned to Washington after a year to become a patent agent. In 1888, in preparation for the upcoming decennial population census, the Census Bureau held a competition for an improved system to expedite the tabulation. Following a number of trials,

Hollerith won the competition with his Electrical Tabulating System. In the Hollerith system, the schedule for each individual in the census was transcribed onto a card as a set of set of punched holes. Once punched, the cards could be automatically sorted and tabulated by the census machinery. Altogether, some 62 million cards were punched for the census, which took two and one-half years to complete. Although the cost of tabulating the 1890 census was higher than in the previous census, the greater volume of useful tabulations and the speed with which they were produced meant that there would never be a return to manual methods.

In 1896 Hollerith incorporated the Tabulating Machine Company (TMC) to supply the census system to other nations, and to develop machines for commercial use. The Hollerith machines were rented, providing a constant income stream, while the cards were sold, providing a second very lucrative source of income. (This basic revenue model was to sustained TMC, and later IBM, until the latter's 1956 anti-trust consent decree, when it agreed either to sell or to lease its machines and to permit the use of non-IBM cards.)

In 1905 the Census Bureau decided to develop its own tabulating system, rather than pay what it considered to be the extortionate prices demanded by Hollerith. From this point on, Hollerith put all his energies into developing the commercial market, creating a range of fully automatic equipment. The tabulating system consisted of three basic machines: a card punch for recording data onto cards, a sorting machine for arranging cards into numerical sequence, and the tabulator for totalling the data on the cards. The new equipment facilitated full-scale commercial accounting operations as well as statistical tabulations. By 1911 TMC was supplying data-processing systems to a hundred of the largest firms in the United States.

In 1911, while Hollerith was in ill health, TMC was sold for $2.3 million in a merger organized by the trust builder Charles R. Flint. TMC thus became the principal constituent of the Computing-Tabulating-Recording Company (C-T-R). Hollerith personally received $1.2 million from the sale, which allowed him to retire in considerable luxury. He continued to serve as a technical consultant to C-T-R, but after a few years his contributions were taken over by the experimental department created within the company to improve and develop the machines. C-T-R was renamed International Business Machines (IBM) in 1924, and its subsequent rise to become the leading global supplier of data-processing equipment was largely due to its president, Thomas J. WATSON, Sr. Hollerith's achievement was essentially that of an inventor-entrepreneur, creating the technology and establishing it in the market-place.

BIBLIOGRAPHY
Austrian, G.D. (1982) *Herman Hollerith: Forgotten Giant of Information Processing*, New York: Columbia University Press.
Pugh, E.W. (1995) *Building IBM: Shaping an Industry and Its Technology*, Cambridge, MA: MIT Press.

MC-K

HOXIE, Robert Franklin (1868–1916)

Robert Franklin Hoxie was born in Edmeston, New York on 29 April 1868, the son of Solomon and Lucy Hoxie. He committed suicide in Chicago on 22 June 1916. He married Lucy Bennett in 1898; they had no children. Hoxie took his bachelor's degree from Cornell University in 1893, and then served as an instructor in economics, first at Cornell College, Iowa and then at Washington University in St Louis, before returning to teach at Cornell University in 1903. He took a Ph.D. from the University of Chicago in 1905, where one of his professors was Thorstein VEBLEN. In 1906 he was appointed associate professor of political economy at Chicago, a post which he held until his death. In 1914 he was appointed special investigator to the US Commission on Industrial Relations, and it was in this capacity that he produced his most important works, the books *Scientific Management and Labor* (1915) and *Scientific Management and Social Welfare* (1916). In later life Hoxie suffered from severe depression, and this illness led to his suicide.

Hoxie's work on scientific management arose out of an increasing concern that the techniques of scientific management, particularly as expounded and practised by Frederick W. TAYLOR and his associates, although designed to make the life of the worker easier, were actually leading to labour unrest. A strike at the Watertown Arsenal following the introduction of the Taylor system led some congressmen to call for the use of the stopwatch (used in time studies) to be banned in factories. Faced with a growing labour and political problem, the government set up the Commission on Industrial Relations and invited Hoxie to conduct an investigation into the problem.

Scientific Management and Labor is a remarkable book, not least in that it is one of the few fair and impartial works on scientific management to have been written contemporary with the movement itself. Hoxie's report follows two themes: (1) the claims of scientific management relative to labour, and (2) the objections raised by trades unions to scientific management. He discusses both these themes through a detailed and critical look at the nature and practices of scientific management in the workplace. In terms of the claims of scientific management, he makes a critical distinction between the systems espoused by Taylor, Henry GANTT and Harrington EMERSON (appendices spell out the differing views of each man in full). He notes Taylor's

claims that scientific management leads to both greater efficiency and greater democracy, and then sums up the claims by trade unions to the opposite effect, namely that scientific management is undemocratic, inefficient and not even particularly scientific; and moreover, that the tight controls required to make the system work lead to higher levels of labour unrest.

After analysing these claims, Hoxie concludes that both have some merit. In defence of scientific management, he accepts that some of its measures and practices are crude, but that the discipline is still young and refinement is ongoing. The impact of scientific management in terms of eliminating waste and improving business efficiency is undoubted, and on this merit alone the system should be considered and adopted. However, Hoxie finds that scientific management does not *per se* provide any greater protection for the worker, nor that there is any inbuilt tendency towards industrial democracy. Workers under scientific management, he concludes, are at the mercy of employers who are guided variously by their 'ideals, personal views, humanitarianism or sordid desire for immediate profit with slight regard for labor's welfare' (Hoxie 1915: 138). It follows, therefore, that labour must organize in order to counterbalance the power of management. To the tension this would cause in the workplace Hoxie saw no immediate solution; he regarded that tension as the price that would have to be paid for industrial progress.

BIBLIOGRAPHY
Hoxie, R.F. (1915) *Scientific Management and Labor*, New York: D. Appleton and Co.
—— (1916) *Scientific Management and Social Welfare*, New York: Survey Books.

MLW

HUNTINGTON, Henry Edwards
(1850–1927)

Henry Edwards Huntington was born in Oneonta, New York on 27 February 1850 and died in Philadelphia on 23 May 1927. He was the son of Solon Huntington, a merchant, land speculator and farmer, and Harriet Saunders, but his business career developed through his close relationship with his uncle, railway magnate Collis Huntington. In 1871, Huntington began working for Collis at a variety of positions primarily with his eastern railroads. In 1892 Huntington moved to San Francisco, where Collis was president of the Southern Pacific Railroad, and advanced within the company so that by 1900 he appeared ready to succeed his uncle. When Collis died that year, however, the majority stockholders blocked his election. Although Huntington was already wealthy enough to retire, he instead moved to Southern California where he controlled the Los Angeles Railway, and focused on real estate development.

Huntington realized that to build a real estate empire in and around Los Angeles he needed to accomplish two basic objectives. First, to add value to the agricultural land in Southern California, he had to build a comprehensive rail system that would connect it to businesses in Los Angeles. Second, he wanted to develop this land as suburban communities and build utilities to attract homebuyers. In 1901 Huntington and several investors formed the interurban Pacific Electric Railway, that would connect small outlying communities to downtown Los Angeles and his Los Angeles Railway. A year later, he formed the Huntington Land and Improvement Company to purchase, subdivide and sell land for residential use, as well as the Pacific Light and Power Company to supply electricity for his trolley system, with excess power sold to other consumers.

Huntington's strategy for developing Southern California proved very successful and profitable. By 1910 his railroads consisted of over 1,900 kilometres (1,200 miles) of track that blanketed the region, while his power company supplied nearly 20 per cent of the electricity in the city of Los Angeles. More importantly, as one of the largest landowners in Los Angeles County, Huntington played a critical role in the geographic, social and economic development of this metropolitan area. Based on this work and skilful promotions, Los Angeles grew from a population from 50,395 in 1890 to more than 576,000 thirty years later.

In 1910 Huntington began to disengage himself from his business concerns and became a serious collector of rare books and paintings. Huntington purchased several individual collections, and to preserve them and promote their use, in 1919 he endowed a trust that established the Huntington Library, Art Collections and Botanical Gardens, all at his estate in San Marino, California. Henry Huntington's name remains prominent throughout Southern California, as evidenced by Huntington Beach, Huntington Park, Huntington Drive, the Huntington Hospital and the Huntington Hotel.

BIBLIOGRAPHY
Friedricks, W.B. (1992) *Henry E. Huntington and the Creation of Southern California*, Columbus, OH: Ohio State University Press.
Thorpe, J. (1994) *Henry Edwards Huntington: A Biography*, Berkeley, CA: University of California Press.

DM

I

IACOCCA, Lee (1924–)

Lee Iacocca was born as Lido Anthony Iacocca in Allentown, Pennsylvania on 15 October 1924. His parents, Nicola and Antoinette Iacocca, had immigrated from Italy. They were a family of entrepreneurs who lost almost everything during the Great Depression. By the time Iacocca had graduated from high school in Allentown in 1942, he had determined to become an auto company manager. His health exempting him from military service (he had suffered from rheumatic fever), Iacocca entered Lehigh University in Bethlehem, Pennsylvania. Doing poorly in physics, he switched from mechanical to industrial engineering. He nevertheless graduated with high grades in 1945, earned a master's in mechanical engineering from Princeton in 1946, and went to work for the Ford Motor Company in August 1946.

Iacocca began as an engineer but soon moved to a role which better fit his personality: sales. Over the following decade Iacocca worked his way up through the ranks of Ford sales in Pennsylvania. During 1956 he turned the sales figures in the Philadelphia district from the lowest in the nation to the best. From there his rise as Ford's top salesman was meteoric. By 1960 he was in charge of marketing all Ford cars and trucks, and in that year succeeded Robert MCNAMARA as vice-president of the Ford division.

One of Iacocca's greatest talents was his almost intuitive ability to know what the public wanted to buy. As the boom generation entered their teens, he knew Ford needed a stylish car that would appeal to them. The Ford Mustang, unveiled in March 1964, was a triumph of both design and brilliant marketing. It sold 400,000 in one year and earned Iacocca promotion to vice-president of all North American auto operations in 1967. The same genius that produced the sporty Mustang now created the Mercury Cougar for the sports car market, the Mercury Marquis for the medium price market, and the Lincoln Mark III for the luxury market.

Iacocca's progressive management philosophy stressed intuition and initiative as well as careful accounting. One could spend a lot of time, he said, gathering facts on markets, but one could listen too much to the accountants, who by their very nature 'tend to be defensive, conservative, and pessimistic' while salesmen like himself were 'aggressive, speculative, and optimistic'. Both were necessary: 'If the bean counters are too weak, the company will spend itself into bankruptcy. But if they're too strong, the company won't meet the market or stay competitive' (Iacocca and Novak 1986: 46). It was important, moreover, that a manager set the tone for his firm: 'Business, after all, is nothing more than a bunch of human relationships.' One needed to 'start with good people, lay out the rules, communicate with your employees, motivate them, and reward them if they perform' (Iacocca and Kleinfeld 1988: 74).

In December 1970 Iacocca was named sole president of the entire Ford Motor Company by Henry FORD II. His first act was to embark on a programme of cost-cutting measures and downsizing of non-automotive lines. Iacocca's successes, however, made him appear a threat to Henry Ford II, who harassed and eventually fired him in July 1978.

Iacocca lost no time in finding a new job as president and chief executive officer of Chrysler Corporation. By the late 1970s, the smallest of the Big Three was in very serious trouble. Rising oil prices, federal anti-pollution regulations and intense Japanese competition, when combined with deficient management, threatened to doom the company. In the third quarter of 1978 Chrysler lost $158 million. Iacocca faced a seemingly impossible task. Chrysler's accounting system had no financial controls, rewarded overproduction, and its Plymouths and Dodges were poorly engineered. The first thing Chrysler needed was money, so Iacocca sold off its non-automotive properties and all operations outside North America. Japanese inventory techniques were also introduced.

Chrysler's situation became even more desperate in the wake of the Iranian Revolution of 1979. As gasoline became scarce, sales of trucks and 'gas-guzzling' cars which used large amounts of fuel plummeted. Iacocca turned to Washington, obtaining a $1.5 billion loan from Congress. He then applied all his management and public relations skills to rescuing the valuable corporation. It is likely that no one but Lee Iacocca could have inspired Chrysler's employees and shareholders to accept the drastic measures he took. Almost 60,000 of Chrysler's 130,000 workers were laid off, twenty out of sixty plants were eliminated, salaries and wages were cut (including that of Iacocca himself, who set an example). Union leader Douglas Fraser of the United

Auto Workers was appointed to the board of directors.

Iacocca went on television with a series of commercials urging consumers, 'If you can find a better car [than Chrysler's], buy it.' New models were introduced – the Dodge Aries and the Plymouth Reliant, frontwheel-drive K-Cars which were economical but roomy. By 1981 they had captured a fifth of the compact auto market and were praised by *Motor Trend* magazine as cars of the year. Under Iacocca, Chrysler not only recovered but triumphed in the 1980s. In 1983 Chrysler paid back the federal loan in full. The introduction of the minivan guaranteed Chrysler's success in a vast new niche. In 1984 Chrysler posted a profit of $2.4 billion and, by 1988, a healthy US market share of almost 15 per cent.

In his later years Iacocca continued to innovate, creating the Dodge Viper and restructuring Chrysler's vehicle manufacturing procedures on the basis of Swedish-style platform teams in which each division had considerable autonomy. He even hinted at what his successor – Robert Eaton, who took over in December 1993 – would accomplish: a global business alliance with a major German or Japanese auto-maker. It is as the creator of the Mustang and the saviour of Chrysler, however, that Iacocca will be most remembered.

BIBLIOGRAPHY
Iacocca, L. and Kleinfeld, S. (1988) *Talking Straight*, New York: Bantam Books.
Iacocca, L. and Novak, W. (1986) *Iacocca: An Autobiography*, New York: Bantam Books.

DCL

J

JAQUES, Elliott (1917–)

Elliott Jaques was born in Toronto on 18 January 1917. He studied at the University of Toronto, obtaining a BA and an MA before going on to Johns Hopkins Medical School. He served as a major in the Royal Canadian Army Medical Corps in the Second World War, and completed a Ph.D. at Harvard before moving to Britain and becoming a founding member of the Tavistock Institute of Human Relations in London. He became a psychoanalyst in 1951, and set up the Brunel Institute of Organisation and Social Studies (BIOSS) at Brunel University in Britain in 1970. Since 1985 he has lived in the United States, where he is visiting research professor in management studies at George Washington University, Washington, DC.

Jaques's understanding of human nature, his highly empirical approach and his wish to put social science on a proper scientific footing are grounded in medicine, psychiatry and psychoanalysis. Soon after the war he and his colleagues began what was to become a thirty-year project with the Glacier Metal Company in Britain. He has worked extensively in the United States, Australia and Canada, and his work has had a significant impact on the US military. Jaques's models were further codified with his colleagues in BIOSS, and his ideas continue to be elaborated and applied through its work in private, public, religious and military organizations across the world.

Jaques is a prolific writer of books and articles about his key concept of 'requisite organization' – an organization in which people can work and be together in ways that all feel to be fair. The title of his first book, *The Changing Culture of a Factory* (1951), was one of the earliest uses of 'culture' in reference to the workplace. The essence of his early thinking was distilled in *Measurement of Responsibility* (1956), and the profound insights of this early work were elaborated into a system for designing, managing and leading 'felt-fair' organizations, for example, in *Requisite Organization* (1988).

In collaboration with colleagues at the Tavistock Institute, Jaques developed 'social analysis', an approach to understanding the life of an organization through attentive listening and analytical feedback. Consultants offered analyses, but made no recommendations and never arrogated to themselves the responsibilities of the people in the organization who had initiated the study. At the heart of the process lay 'listening to the music behind the words', with acute sensitivity to every aspect of what each person said and to every hint of what could, with encouragement, be articulated (Rowbottom 1977).

This attentive listening created a climate in which people could voice the subtleties of experience they lived but had not articulated; the tacit knowledge of which Michel Polanyi speaks. They found themselves able to say how they felt about the process of their work, about the decisions they were called upon to make and the anxiety of waiting to see how they turned out, about the reward they felt would be fair for the level of responsibility they were asked to carry, about their working relationships with others and how they felt about the fairness of their working conditions.

Jaques's approach to people, work and the design of organizations is best understood in the light of his belief that people working together should be treated as people. From this it follows that organizations should be designed in such a way as to provide conditions that induce confidence, trust and competence, and to remove those that produce anxiety, confusion and incompetence. In a requisite organization, people work together in ways that strengthen bonds of mutual trust and fairness, enhance imagination and innovation, and reduce suspicion and mistrust; the organization achieves its purposes and contributes to the health of the wider society. 'Anti-requisite' organizations support autocratic coercion and destructive anxiety, and thus inhibit creativity. Although they may appear to be effective for some years, they eventually flounder.

When Jaques originally communicated his ideas about the nature of work and of people, they were not fully heard. Fifty years later, changes in the environment and in society have created a more receptive climate. In particular, globalization and the growth of knowledge work have helped to focus attention on the economic value of what people treated as individuals bring to work, and on the conditions that encourage them and make the most of their contribution.

A key idea is Jaques's 1956 definition of work as 'the exercise of discretion within prescribed limits to reach a goal within a stated completion time'. The contemporary phrase for 'exercising discretion' is to 'make the call' – to choose a course of action when one does not emerge from analysis. From his attentive listening and his psychoanalytic understanding, Jaques came to see that the discretionary content of work has a special feel for people

because it is about the fine judgements they make when they do not and cannot know what to do. As Jaques put it, this is a

> sphere of psychological activity which, although extremely familiar, remains ... ill-defined. There is no satisfactory ... language for it. We speak about judgement, intuition, nous ... We cannot put into words what it is that we are taking into account in doing what we are doing, and in that sense we do not know that what we are doing will get us where we want to go, will achieve the result we want to achieve. We judge that it will, we think it will, but we are not sure *and only time will tell*.
>
> (Jaques 1988: 156)

If this discretionary content is not bounded, there can be no coherence in the work people do together, and an individual could be completely overwhelmed by expectations. It is the manager's responsibility to 'prescribe' limits, to set rules objectively in the form of policies (written and unwritten), procedures and physical controls which must be obeyed. By defining the field, these limits free the person to use his or her discretion in coping with uncertainties, vicissitudes and unknowns as they feel towards the wisest way of forwarding the work for which they are responsible (Jaques 1956; Evans 1979).

Characteristic of Jaques is his sensitivity to how it *feels* to adhere to prescribed limits: the person is responding to choices someone else has made, and can assess and control his or her contribution by reference to objective standards. Appraisal and control of how we exercise our discretion has no immediate reference external to ourselves; we can evaluate it only through reference to intuitively sensed internal standards until completion time, when the effect of our decisions can be externally reviewed.

Completion time, when the quality of decisions is revealed, is an important aspect of Jaques's thinking. Throughout his writing (especially *The Form of Time*, 1982) he has drawn attention to the significance of time and uncertainty for human behaviour, and to the anxiety of waiting to see the fruits of one's decision making. The external corollary of this individual anxiety is the manager waiting for sufficient feedback to be confident that each of the people working for him or her is making decisions that are robust over time. In some projects this reassurance is forthcoming in weeks, in others it may be five years before the quality of the decision making can be evaluated. As Jaques gathered more and more evidence of the span of time that had to elapse before the quality of decisions could be seen, he realized that there was a consistent pattern. Decisions about some kinds of work could be evaluated in three months; decisions about other kinds needed a year; some – especially when improvement was involved – could not be evaluated before two years had passed; and others – where completely new ways of approaching production, customers, a market had to be developed – required five years to completion time. Still others – where a new combination of product, process, research, technology, markets had to come into being – could not be evaluated for ten years. Beyond that, global institutions made decisions about changes, critical masses of capital, people and positioning, where fruits could not be seen for twenty or more years.

Jaques used this evidence to construct a framework of levels of complexity of work in which authority is distributed and managers can be held to account in ways they feel to be fair. Despite the pace of change and decisions fifty years later and the pressure for quick completion, these time-scales remain robust as measures of the evolving life and complexity of an organization.

Another significant contribution to the requisite organization in which people are more likely to be creative and responsible is Jaques's hypothesis that the capacity in each individual to use their judgement to make decisions grows over time at broadly predictable rates.

This hypothesis arose from extensive studies of earning progression of individuals that yielded an array of curves similar in structure to the curves generated by mathematical studies of growing organisms.

As Jaques realized that people made consistent links between their earnings, their responsibilities and exercising discretion, it occurred to him that the progression curves might also reflect a consistent pattern of growth in the capacity to exercise discretion: 'capability'. This hypothesis has been systematically tested over twenty five-years in longitudinal studies of 'capability' in a wide range of organizations and cultures in developed and developing economies. These studies demonstrate that capability does grow at broadly predictable rates and that, if each individual is to use it to the full, this growth must be paced with growth in responsibility. To be prevented from working at full capacity by being asked to carry too much or too little responsibility is constricting, degrading and finally persecuting. The studies make it clear that there are no differences in distribution of capability with regard to gender, race or educational opportunity (Stamp 1986).

Much of Jaques's thinking has become common currency in organizations: 'discretion', 'judgement calls' and 'time-horizons' are widely used. 'Flattening' of organizations more often than not leads to a pattern of levels as defined by him, and when 'downsizing' removes a level of work that is necessary, it soon creeps back in. Interest in 'empowering' people at work is an attempt to gain access to the discretionary energy of people. In a requisite organization, each person will be 'empowered' to use their discretion within a framework of prescribed limits; one of the fundamental tenets of such an organization being that each person is able to use his or her capability to exercise discretion to the full, both as it is and as it grows.

Research into the cognitive unconscious (Reber 1993) provides support for Jaques's emphasis on the direct connection between the processes involved in work and unconscious mental activity:

Industrial society ... has overvalued ... the critical, the conscious, the verbal, the brain ... everything to do with knowledge ... It has lost its ability sufficiently to value and to feel secure in relying upon the other side of the human equation – the side that contains intuition, judgement, flowing unverbalised sense, the feel of the situation, the deeper sense of simply understanding what is right and wrong or fair or just, the sense of the reasonable, the ability to sit back and reflect and remember and to feel a part of one's past and present, and to identify with other human beings, to feel empathy and sensitivity ... what Keats has called 'negative capability' ... being in uncertainties, mysteries, doubts without any irritable reaching after facts and reason.

(Jaques 1982: 221)

BIBLIOGRAPHY

Evans, J. (1979) *The Management of Human Capacity*, London: MCB Publications.

Jaques, E. (1951) *The Changing Culture of a Factory*, London: Tavistock Publications.

—— (1956) *Measurement of Responsibility*, London: Tavistock Publications.

—— (1961) *Equitable Payment*, London: Heinemann Educational Books.

—— (1976) *A General Theory of Bureaucracy*, London: Heinemann.

—— (1982) *The Form of Time*, London: Heinemann Educational Books.

—— (1988) *Requisite Organization*, Falls Church, VA: Cason Hall and Co; 2nd edn, *Requisite Organization: A Total System for Effective Managerial Organization and Managerial Leadership for the 21st Century*, 1997.

—— (1990) *Creativity and Work*, Madison, CT: International Universities Press.

Jaques, E. and Brown W. (1965) *Glacier Project Papers*, London: Heinemann.

Jaques, E. and Cason K. (1994) *Human Capability*, Falls Church, VA: Cason Hall and Co.

Jaques, E. and Clement, S. (1991) *Executive Leadership*, Falls Church, VA: Cason Hall and Co.

Jaques, E., Gibson, R. and Isaac, J. (1978) *Levels of Abstraction in Logic and Human Action: A Theory of Discontinuity in the Structure of Mathematical Logic, Psychological Behaviour and Social Organization*, London: Heinemann.

Reber, A. (1993) *Implicit Learning and Tacit Knowledge: An Essay on the Cognitive Unconscious*, Oxford: Oxford University Press.

Rowbottom, R. (1977) *Social Analysis*, London: Heinemann.

Stamp, G. (1986) 'Some Observations on the Career Paths of Women', *Journal of Applied Behavioural Science* 22(4): 385–96.

—— (1992) *Day of Judgment: In Festschrift for Elliott Jaques*, Falls Church, VA: Cason Hall and Co.

Stamp, G. and Stamp, C. (1993) 'Well-being at Work: Aligning Purposes, People, Strategies and Structures', *The International Journal of Career Management* 5(3).

GS

JOBS, Steve (1955–)

Steve Jobs was born in San Francisco, California on 24 February 1955. The adopted son of machine-shop technician Paul Jobs and his wife Clara, he grew up in the working-class communities of Mountain View and adjoining

Los Altos, which are located in the area of northern California that came to be known as Silicon Valley when the original American developers of the miniature transistor turned the area into a centre for high-technology research and manufacture. An early interest in electronic gadgets prompted Steve Jobs to attend after-school lectures by engineers and scientists at the Hewlett-Packard electronics firm, where, at the age of thirteen, he landed his first summer job, working on an assembly line. Demonstrating the brashness that would become the hallmark of his character, Jobs phoned company co-founder Bill HEWLETT at home to ask for electronic parts. A bemused Hewlett acquired the parts for him and offered him a summer internship.

Also employed at Hewlett-Packard at that time was Steve Wozniak, five years Jobs's senior. Despite the age difference, the two became friends. They also became partners in crime when, as a prank, they designed and marketed for profit a 'blue box' system for making long-distance phone calls without payment. In 1972 Jobs finished high school and enrolled in Reed College, a liberal arts junior college in Portland, Oregon. He grew his hair long, experimented with psychedelic drugs, embraced Zen Buddhism, became a vegetarian, and lived in a rural commune, where he subsisted on a diet of apples, pears and other fruit. In early 1974 he returned to California and worked as an electronics technician for Atari, a company that manufactured shopping-arcade video games. He left after three months to visit India in search of spiritual enlightenment. When he returned, he resumed employment with Atari.

In January 1975 *Popular Electronics* magazine in the United States ran a cover story on a newly developed computer kit for hobbyists called the Altair, and announced that the era of personal computing was at hand. Jobs and Wozniak joined a local computer hobbyists' club and started talking about ways to turn this emerging technology into a product with mass appeal. They formed a partnership, calling themselves Apple Computer after Jobs's favourite fruit. Working in the garage of Jobs's parents' home, Wozniak and Jobs designed and built a prototype of the Apple I, a preassembled computer circuit board. A local electronics equipment retailer ordered fifty of the boards, and sold them at $666.66 apiece, more than twice what it cost the two young entrepreneurs to build them.

Because the Apple I came without a keyboard, monitor, power supply or case, it appealed only to hobbyists and electronics enthusiasts. The Apple II followed, with features more suited to the general user. Microcomputers from other manufacturers appeared on the market at the same time, but the Apple II quickly outpaced its competitors. The marketing drive and missionary zeal of Steve Jobs, coupled with his ability to attract media attention, became key factors in the early success of his company. At the age of twenty-one, invariably dressed in shorts, T-shirt and sandals, the bearded Jobs was hailed by the media as something of a prophet: a technological visionary who stood as a symbol of something larger. As Young notes,

> his youth and good looks, his ability to say the quotable thing ... and an American public looking for a hero ... combined to make this one slender, intense young man a mythic figure amid the revitalized economy of post-Vietnam America.
>
> (Young 1988: 128)

At the age of twenty-three, Jobs was a millionaire. At twenty-four, he was worth $10 million; by the age of twenty-five his net worth was over $100 million. He was the youngest person ever to make the *Forbes* magazine list of America's richest people, and one of only a handful to have done so without inherited wealth.

But not everything he touched turned to gold. The Apple III had to be withdrawn because of design flaws. Another failure was the Lisa, a $10,000 computer aimed at the small business market, which Jobs named after his daughter. Jobs eventually cancelled the Lisa project when it took longer than projected to succeed. He did bounce back with the Macintosh, a machine that simplified computing for the ordinary consumer because it used the graphics-based, 'point and click' technology of a hand-held 'mouse' for its various functions, rather than relying on cumbersome, text-based keyboard commands. However, because the Macintosh was considerably more expensive than the lines of personal computers being developed by other manufacturers – particularly those using 'clones' of an operating system developed by Bill GATES's Microsoft software company for the giant International Business Machines (IBM) corporation – the Apple machine soon acquired the image of an elitist product, not one developed for the mass consumer market. The cheaper machines lacked the sophisticated friendly' features of the Macintosh, yet they flourished in the market-place while Apple faltered.

In 1985 continuing poor sales and internal problems at Apple Computer led to a restructuring of the company and the forced resignation of Jobs. He started a new company called NeXT, and spent the next four years developing a home computer for scholars and scientists that proved to be elegant, innovative and powerful but – with a price tag of $10,000 – so expensive that it had to be repositioned as a business computer. NeXT struggled until Jobs closed the hardware division and turned the company into a software firm. He purchased the digital animation division of Lucasfilm Ltd – a small motion picture studio owned by the film director George Lucas – to create Pixar Animation Studios.

By 1995 Jobs's star was on the rise again. Pixar, in conjunction with the Disney Corporation, released Toy Story, the first computer-generated feature film, and it became a box office hit. Apple Computer, meanwhile, was losing money and market share following the release of Microsoft's popular Windows 95, an operating system with a graphics-based interface technology similar to that of the Macintosh. Eager to develop a new operating-system strategy, Apple bought NeXT for $400 million in late 1996 and made Jobs a consultant to the company he had co-founded. Six months later, the executive board of Apple ousted the company's chief executive officer (CEO) Gil Amelio and appointed Jobs as 'interim' CEO.

In 1998 Jobs re-emerged publicly as a computer visionary, and Apple regained its reputation as a profitable trend-setter with the introduction of the iMac, a stylish, candy-coloured, one-piece computer that boosted Apple's share of the American home computer market from 6 to 12 per cent. In early 2000 Jobs agreed to drop the word 'interim' from his title and resume the role of permanent CEO. He received a salary of only $1 a year but was awarded options on ten million shares of Apple stock and a Gulfstream V jet plane for his personal use. Twenty-five years after starting his quest to change the fabric of American life with his consumer-oriented computing machines, Jobs was still pursuing his dream of building computers for people, not for corporations. More than just marketing hardware and software, he was marketing a symbol: an image of American life in which the computer becomes an empowering cultural force.

BIBLIOGRAPHY

Butcher, L. (1988) Accidental Millionaire: The Rise and Fall of Steve Jobs at Apple Computer, New York: Paragon House.

Deutschman, A. (2000) The Second Coming of Steve Jobs, New York: Broadway Books.

Young, J.S. (1988) Steve Jobs: The Journey is the Reward, Glenview, Illinois: Scott, Foresman and Co.

BB

JOHNSON, Howard Dearing (1896–1972)

Howard Dearing Johnson was born in Boston, Massachusetts on 2 February 1896 (some sources indicate that he was born in 1897 or 1898, although the day and month are not in dispute), the son of John Hayes Johnson and Olive Bell Wright. He died on 20 June 1972 in New York City. Johnson's family lived and worked in the greater Boston area, where his father was a cigar merchant. John Johnson was of Swedish descent and Olive Johnson was of Scottish and Irish heritage. Howard's parents lived in Boston for the first several years of marriage before moving to Wollaston, a suburb of the city, in 1902. Howard was an only son but had three sisters, and early accounts suggest that John Johnson tried to assure that his son would be raised as a 'man' amidst a family dominated by females. Boxing matches, sledding incidents, name calling and the accompanying bruises and scars were not uncommon in the Johnson household. Speculation is that these early traumas contributed to the young Howard's independence, cockiness and resilience.

After leaving school at a young age (following yet another disagreement with his father), Johnson went to work for his father in his tobacco business. Records indicate that he helped build the business through the introduction of new products and time spent on the road as a travelling salesman. The First World War interrupted his tobacco career and Johnson entered the military, where he provided medical operations with supplies. Upon his return, he rejoined his father in the family business. His father's premature death less than two years later would have an impact on his career direction. He sold the store after reducing its debt, and moved on to other things.

Howard Johnson's early entry into the food service industry is well documented. He began with the purchase of the Walker-Barlow's drug store in Wollaston. The store came complete with a soda fountain from which ice cream was sold. Following his initial disappointment with the quality of the ice cream, he made some adjustments to the recipe and was eventually satisfied. He soon recognized the popularity and profitability of the ice cream compared to the other product lines, and, upon the advice of his accountant, promoted this particular aspect of his business. Expanding, he opened a series of ice-cream stands on the beach, for which he recruited youngsters to sell the product. These satellite operations generated over $200,000 in one summer of operation. Beginning with only chocolate and vanilla ice cream, he continued to add new flavours until he reached the then famous twenty-eight varieties. Again recognizing opportunity when it presented itself, he expanded his offerings to include frankfurters and other sundries. Having grown his beach food-service operation, his next step was to open a full-fledged restaurant.

Johnson's first restaurant was located in Quincy, Massachusetts, south of Boston. He opened it in 1928 in an office building. The restaurant had a typically 'down-east' menu which included Boston baked beans, frankfurters, clam chowder and fried clams. These were to become, along with his premium ice cream, the restaurant's signature items that helped to establish the restaurant company as an integral part of the American landscape. Eventually the Howard Johnson menus would grow to some 700 items, most of which were supplied by a central commissary, also owned by the company. Simply prepared food, value, firm standards and vision allowed his business to grow. He was a stickler for quality; this attention to quality is attributed to his days as a tobacconist, when he had more than one encounter with suppliers who tried to provide him with substandard product.

Perhaps one of Johnson's greatest contributions to the international hospitality industry came with his decision to franchise his operation (after opening only one store). While not the first in the industry to franchise, he approached the notion of franchising with a formalized plan, one that encompassed standards for the entire restaurant operation from the menu to the architecture. His first franchise was opened in Orleans on Cape Cod in 1935, and within a year he had opened a total of seventeen restaurants.

From the beginning, Howard Johnson's vision was founded on a belief that the automobile would rule, a belief reflected in the growth of the company in eastern Massachusetts to his dominance of the American turnpikes in the second half of the century. His seventeen restaurants had grown to 200 by the coming of the Second World War. Johnson then had to re-evaluate his strategy: 90 per cent of his restaurants closed as a direct result of the war and subsequent rationing. This, ironically, led to other opportunities for the entrepreneur. His business acumen allowed him to survive the war by a variety of means: continuing to make ice cream for other retail operations, and becoming the food-service provider for colleges and military operations.

Following the war, Johnson picked up where he had left off. He grew the chain from twelve units in wartime to 200 once again in a few short years. By the 1950s he had opened 400 restaurants. He then decided to diversify and enter the lodging business. He opened his first hotel in Savannah, Georgia in 1954, and grew this chain as well. The company expanded over the next two decades to 1,000 restaurants by its peak in the mid-1970s; and in addition to the signature restaurant chain, the company also controlled over 500 motor lodges and two smaller food-service chains: Red Coach Grill and Ground Round. Until at least 1958 (a year before he stepped down as president of the company) Johnson maintained the company's corporate offices in Wollaston, Massachusetts, where it all began. In 1959 he turned the company over to his son, who eventually took it public and then sold it. Johnson remained for some time as treasurer and chairman of the company he built. He had married, to Bernice Manley, and they had one son and one daughter.

Howard Johnson has been characterized as hard-working, independent and a stickler for detail, although he was known to label himself as a promoter and nothing else. Various quotations attributed to him portray a man who was no-nonsense, detail-oriented and introspective. He will best be remembered for building a business (several times over); helping to develop the franchise restaurant system as we know it today; creating the concept of the 'turnpike' restaurant; and perfecting a frozen-food distribution system (through which he supplied all of his restaurants). In short, he changed the way that the restaurant and lodging industries were operated as well as the way in which they were perceived by the public.

Most Americans born prior to 1970 are familiar with the name of Howard Johnson and the famous orange roofs that sit atop his restaurants. He has been referred to as 'probably the best known name to ever appear in the restaurant business' (Lundberg 1976). At the very least, Howard Johnson was an innovator, entrepreneur and pioneer in the hospitality industry. From humble beginnings, he made his mark on the hospitality industry in a variety of ways.

BIBLIOGRAPHY

Alexander, J. (1958) 'Host of the Highways', *Saturday Evening Post*, 19 July.

Baird, C. (2000) Personal communication with director and archivist, Conrad Hilton College, University of Houston, 19 September.

Clark, W.H. and Moynahan, J.H.S. (1955) 'Howard Dearing Johnson: The Roadside Host', in *Famous Leaders of Industry*, Boston: L.C. Page and Co.

Howard Johnson Hotels and Inns, *Brand History*, www.hojo.com/ctg/cgi-bin/ HowardJohnson/brand_history, 15 May 2001.

Howard Johnson International (2000) Personal communication with Andrew

Miller, Public Relations, Cendant Corporation, 8 September.

Lundberg, D.E. (1976) *The Hotel and Restaurant Business*, Boston: Cahners Books International.

'Obituary: Howard D. Johnson' (1972) *New York Times*, 21 June, 46.

CB

JOHNSON, John Harold (1918–)

John Harold Johnson was born in Arkansas City, Arkansas on 19 January 1918, the son of Leroy Johnson, a mill worker, and Gertrude Jenkins. His father was killed in a mill accident when Johnson was six, and although his mother remarried, the family lived in considerable poverty. In 1933 Johnson and his mother moved to Chicago hoping to find a better life. A bright student, Johnson was educated at Du Sable High School in Chicago's South Side; fellow pupils included Harold Washington, later mayor of Chicago, and the future jazz musician Nat 'King' Cole.

In 1936 Johnson enrolled at the University of Chicago, financing his studies through part-time work at Supreme Liberty Life Insurance, the largest black-owned insurance company in the United States. Supreme Life's president, Harry H. Pace, was Johnson's early mentor, and while at Supreme Life Johnson learned how black businessmen like Pace were able to capture the increasingly affluent black market – not because of their colour but because they understood the needs of the market better than did their white counterparts. He also became friendly with Earl Dickerson, another Supreme Life executive who was also active in Chicago politics. In 1941 Johnson married Eunice Walker; they had two children.

In the late 1930s Johnson had become interested in publishing, and was appointed assistant editor of Supreme Life's monthly newsletter. It was while working on this project that Johnson conceived of the idea of a black equivalent to *Reader's Digest*. Raising a loan of $500 with his mother's furniture as collateral, Johnson launched his first magazine, *Negro Digest*, in 1942. Ingham and Feldman (1994) note that the take-up was slow at first, until Johnson hit on an idea for a series, 'If I Were a Negro', in which prominent white people were invited to contribute articles. One of the first contributors was Eleanor Roosevelt, wife of President Franklin D. Roosevelt. This coup resulted in a trebling of the journal's circulation almost overnight.

In 1943 Johnson quit Supreme Life to devote himself full-time to publishing. In 1945 he launched his second journal, this one based on the very successful picture journal *Life*, published by Henry LUCE. Johnson's version of *Life* was *Ebony*, a glossy magazine which aimed to 'mirror the happier side of life – the positive, everyday achievements from Harlem to Hollywood' (Ingham and Feldman 1994: 372). The portrayal of a positive image had an immediate impact on its black audience, and *Ebony* quickly reached a circulation of 400,000. The next step was to gather advertising; in the early years *Ebony* lost money despite its massive circulation, and had to be supported by its sister publication the *Negro Digest*. Johnson's breakthrough came when he persuaded radio-maker Zenith to advertise in *Ebony*; Zenith's president, Eugene McDonald, not only remained a steady advertiser but persuaded other big names to advertise as well. *Ebony* was now in profit.

More journals followed, including *Jet*, a weekly news magazine, and *Tan*, a 'true confessions' type magazine. Johnson also branched out into book publishing and other ventures, of which easily the most successful was Fashion Fair Cosmetics, which produced a range of cosmetics and skincare products for black women. By the end of the 1980s Fashion Fair products were being sold in more than 1,500 stores across the country (Ingham and Feldman 1994: 374). Johnson also owns radio and television stations, and later bought his old employer, Supreme Life.

It has been estimated that Johnson's publications reach 60 per cent of the black adult market in the United States (Davis 1987). *Ebony* now has a circulation of over 1.5 million. Johnson himself has his critics: civil rights leaders have attacked him for not taking a harder line over racist issues, and closer to home he has been described by employees as an autocrat and a hard taskmaster. Johnson rebuts these criticisms, particularly the former. But there is little denying that he has a genius for finding and exploiting market niches. His understanding of the cultural needs of African-Americans has been matched by his ability to design and bring to market products to meet those needs. He is one of the outstanding entrepreneurs of twentieth-century America.

BIBLIOGRAPHY

Davis, W. (1987) *The Innovators: The Essential Guide to Business Thinkers*, London: Ebury Press.
Ingham, J.N. and Feldman, L.B. (1994) *African-American Business Leaders: A Biographical Dictionary*, Westport, CT: Greenwood Press.

MLW

JUNGK, Robert (1913–94)

Robert Jungk was born Robert Baum in Berlin on 5 November 1913, the son of a writer. He died in Salzburg, Austria on 14 July 1994. A Jewish student at the University of Berlin when Hitler came to power, he was arrested soon after the Reichstag fire for anti-Nazi activities, and had his citizenship revoked. Thanks to the intervention of his friends he was released shortly after, and went on to continue his degree studies at the Sorbonne in Paris. Two years later he returned to Germany to work illegally for a subversive press service, but again had to flee, this time to Czechoslovakia in 1933, where he set up another anti-Nazi agency. When Prague fell in 1939 he transferred his activities to Paris, and when Paris fell he moved to Switzerland. Even there he was arrested and jailed, as his anti-Nazi writings were not tolerable to the neutral state. He was released thanks to a powerful American friend, and became the Central European correspondent for the London *Observer* from 1944 to 1945, in which capacity he covered the Nuremberg Trials. He completed his education, taking his Ph.D. in Zurich with a thesis on the resistance of the Swiss press to censorship. In 1945 he returned to Germany and worked as a correspondent in Yugoslavia and Hungary, later moving to the United States as correspondent for Swiss newspapers. He became a US citizen, but later moved back to Europe and settled in Salzburg. He married Ruth Suschizky in 1948, and had two sons.

Jungk's experiences and observations of persecution left him feeling deeply powerless about the Holocaust, particularly when he was unable to persuade other journalists to write about it. This frustration became the source of his lifelong drive to devise ways in which ordinary people can participate, fight back and influence the course of events. He demonstrated a long resistance to tyranny, and was sensitive to oppression in all its forms. He was a renowned and passionate humanist, and wrote compelling accounts of the impacts of nuclear holocaust. He was a long-time opposer of nuclear arms, lecturing and demonstrating all over the world. This work against the nuclear threat was an important part of his life's work, dedicated to the future and to peace.

Jungk's early experiences forged the major themes of his work: the power and potential destructiveness of modern technologies, the corresponding need for careful foresight and the struggle to preserve human qualities in the changing postwar world. He was awarded numerous prizes, including the Prix de la Resistance in 1960, the International Peace Prize in 1961 and the German Conservation Prize in 1978.

His book *Tomorrow is Already Here* (1954) attacked the materialism of the Western world. He challenged the prevalent view that the future was the promise of a world of technological achievement, 'where research and development would constantly increase humanity's feelings of omnipotence'. A later book, *The Everyman Project* (1976) provided constructive responses to what he saw as the deepening dilemmas of the West. Jungk believed passionately that we should not go blindly into the future, and actively called for citizen imagination and involvement in the invention of new social institutions; the invention of nonviolent methods of bring about social, political and economic change; the inventions of alternative occupations; new goals and values; and the creation of a creative society. This urging became the inspiration for the development of the Institute for Social Inventions based in London, of which he later became president. He became a pioneer in the field of futures studies as a means of responding to these challenges. In 1953 he founded the first Institute for Research into the Future; later, with Johan Galtung, he co-founded the International Conference on Futurism in 1967, out of which emerged the World Futures Studies Federation. In 1987 he established the Robert Jungk International Futures Library with the support of the city of Salzburg.

Jungk made significant and practical contributions to the development of the humanist and ecological perspective, in futures studies particularly, but also management. His principal contribution to management thinking was his development of a democratic (participatory) approach to enable people to become involved in developing creative ideas and projects to shape their own futures, 'the futures workshop'. Jungk was driven by the ideal of real participation in decisions. He challenged the common practice of inadequate consultation and participation where it came too late to have any impact. It was the initial stages of problem definition which he identified as the most important for people to participate in.

His approach was eminently practical and lively, and was built upon a strong philosophy of openness and inclusivity. He describes the workshop as having three phases after the preparation phase. The first is a critique phase to bring out all the grievances and negative experiences relating to the topic. This is followed by a fantasy phase, in which ideas, desires and fantasies, and alternative views are expressed. The ideas are developed by working groups into solutions and brought into the implementation phase, where the present constraints and power structures are examined. Imaginative solutions are sought to get around these and to develop a plan of action. He drew on the creative thinking techniques of de Bono, amongst others, for this part of the process.

Jungk's techniques have become widely used in Europe (particularly in Austria, Denmark and Switzerland) and had particular success in influencing social and political change in particular regions, as well as exploring the future of particular industries. This has impacted on the philosophy of public sector decision-making processes and planning, and community development. He saw his future workshop techniques being used to solve problems in businesses, schools and voluntary organizations, in designing individual and community development plans, and for enlivening meetings and seminars. Jungk's work brought together the work and philosophies of de Jouvenel, Kenneth and Elise Boulding, Galtung and McHale, and it continues to hold a significant place in the field of futures studies. His methods continue to be developed and applied by futurists throughout the world.

Jungk's aim was to capture what he believed was the most neglected and most important of all resources: people's imaginations. In 1962 he was among the first to organize methods of drawing on imagination as a means to solve problems and specifically to focus on bringing about desirable change. His success was partly due to his insight into psychology and the realization that much of people's passivity is to be explained by the hostility of our social environment to anything from the realms of our imagination. He gave future workshops the task of righting the damage done by what he called the 'mass suppression of the imagination', noting that negative future expectations more often end up as self-fulfilling prophecies, while positive images of a future bring better prospects of its attainment.

Jungk was driven by the conviction that the future was colonized by a tiny group of people, and that citizens were too often moving into a future shaped by this elite. He equally believed, however, that it was possible for small groups to bring about significant change. He was committed to activism, although he noted that it was 'just as essential for people to know what they were fighting for, not just what they were fighting against'. He was awarded a Right Livelihood Award ('the alternative Nobel Prize') in 1986 for his work on future workshops, and for fighting for sane alternatives and ecological awareness.

BIBLIOGRAPHY
Jungk, R. (1954) *Tomorrow is Already Here*, trans. M. Waldman, London: Hart-Davis.
—— (1976) *The Everyman Project: Resources for a Humane Future*, London: Thames and Hudson.
Jungk, R. and Mullert, N. (1987) *Future Workshops: How to Create Desirable Futures*, London: Institute for Social Inventions.
Right Livelihood Awards (2001) *Robert Jungk – 1986*, http://www. rightliveli-hood.se, 15 March 2001.
Slaughter, R.A. (1994) *Robert Jungk, Futurist and Social Inventor*, Brisbane: World Futures Studies Federation.

AJ

JURAN, Joseph Moses (1904–)

Joseph Moses Juran was born in Braila, Romania on 24 December 1904. When he was five his father departed for America, seeking a better life for the family. Three years later, in 1912, the rest of the family joined his father in Minnesota. Growing up in Minnesota, Joseph Juran helped his family make ends meet by doing whatever jobs he could find: 'Joe drove a team of horses, he worked as a laborer, a shoe salesman, bootblack, grocery clerk and as a bookkeeper for the local icehouse' (Butman and Roessner 1995: xxvi). He excelled in school and advanced three years ahead of boys his age. Having a sharp tongue and being the youngest in his class, he often became the prey for classroom bullies. 'The grind of school, poverty, never-ending jobs and chores at home' (Butman and Roessner 1995: xxvi) were challenges that helped toughen this very young high school graduate. At the time, his self-esteem was not particularly high; however, this would change thanks to a favourable change in his environment.

Enrolling at the University of Minnesota in 1920, he became the first member of his family to attend college. Becoming a good chess player, Juran found an activity that challenged his analytical mind. In time he became the University of Minnesota chess champion and also performed well in state-wide competitions. His success at chess enabled him to improve his self-esteem. 'Gradually, he shed the image of the skinny misfit and outsider; now he knew that his difference was in the nature of a gift, rather than a curse' (Butman and Roessner 1995: xxvi).

In 1924 Juran completed his studies at the University of Minnesota, graduating with a BS in electrical engineering. Finding employment at Western Electric, he was assigned to the Inspection Department of the Hawthorne Plant near Chicago. At that time the Hawthorne Plant employed about 40,000 workers, with approximately 5,000 of them devoted to inspection. Working on the function of inspection, Joseph Juran enthusiastically began his lifelong quest for quality products, and advanced through a series of management and staff positions. He eventually became a key member of the newly formed Inspection Statistical Department: 'It was one of the first such departments established in industry in this country. In retrospect, the greatest significance of this department may have been that it set Juran firmly on the path toward his life's work' (Butman and Roessner 1995: xxviii).

In 1928 Joseph Juran wrote his first work about quality. Entitled *Statistical Methods Applied to Manufacturing Problems*, it discussed the role of sampling in analysing and controlling the quality of manufactured products. Later it became part of the *AT&T Statistical Quality Control Handbook*, still in use today. As might be expected, the number of managers, administrators and line workers at the Hawthorne Plant decreased substantially during the Great Depression. While many were let go, others who had proven themselves to be particularly able were relocated to other necessary positions within Western Electric. Juran had not only proven himself, but he also had the ability to improve quality and productivity at Western Electric at a time when any gains in efficiency were critical. Because of these talents, Juran was relocated to New York City in 1937, where he assumed an enviable position as head of Industrial Engineering at Western Electric's corporate headquarters. In this capacity, he exchanged ideas about industrial engineering with many other companies. While visiting General Motors in Detroit, he got the idea for the now famous concept known as the 'Pareto Principle'.

While quality managers today teach and use Pareto analysis, many of them are unaware that Juran conceptualized this approach and that Pareto had little to do with it. Essentially, when Juran worked with company-wide quality committees, his approach was to work on the most critical problems first. Indeed, he encouraged focusing on what he called the 'vital few' before attempting to solve many other trivial problems. Years later, Juran acknowledged that this was an improper attribution to Vilfredo Pareto, an Italian economist of the late 1800s and early 1900s: 'Proper attribution would be to Max Otto Lorenz, who developed the "Lorenze Curve", which displays the deviation of a sample from the standard' (Wren and Greenwood 1998: 215–6).

The Pareto principle is widely used now in the quality management field and is sometimes described as the 80/20 rule. In this case, it is thought that 80 per cent of the problems are caused by 20 per cent of operations. The application of this concept places a high priority on solving the vital few problems without diverting attention unnecessarily towards trivial problems. Another application of Juran's Pareto principle (often referred to as Pareto analysis) is that customers in a sales effort, for example, can be categorized into vital few customers and useful many customers. Although both of these categories of customers are important, they may need to be treated differently. In this regard, Pareto analysis helps identify and focus attention on the needs of different groups. Graphic presentation of this analysis is often presented with Pareto charts: 'Pareto charts are useful after brainstorming and then constructing a cause-effect diagram to identify those items that could be responsible for the most impact' (Brocka and Brocka 1992: 299).

At the start of the Second World War, Juran departed from Western Electric to serve as an assistant administrator with the Lend-Lease Administration in Washington, DC. This organization managed the shipment of material to friendly nations at the beginning of the war . 'Here, Juran became enmeshed in managing governmental processes, including a massive problem in what today might be called "renumerating government", or "business process engineering"' (Butman and Roessner 1995: xxx). As this organization expanded, Juran led a multi-agency team that cut government red tape and paper log-jams that bogged down important shipments that were stranded on the docks. As the war progressed, Juran's team redesigned far-reaching shipping processes that sped up the movement of essential lend-lease war materials to the United States' allies.

At the conclusion of the Second World War, Juran decided to forgo working for corporate America and government, and instead launched his own efforts as an independent person. His intentions at the time were to use the balance of his life to philosophize, research, write, lecture and consult on management. Initially, he served as chair of the Department of Administrative Engineering at New York University. In time he built a consulting practice, wrote books and developed quality management lectures for the American Management Association. In 1951 the publication of his *Quality Control Handbook* helped establish Juran's reputation as an authority on quality and, because of this reputation, he received numerous requests to lecture and consult. This book, now known as *Juran's Quality Control Handbook*, is in its fourth edition. The first three editions sold in excess of 350,000 copies, cumulatively.

During the last two decades of the twentieth century, W. Edwards DEMING was often considered the primary expert on quality management, while Joseph Juran was never considered less than second in an array of countless champions of the quality movement. Although Deming worked with large groups of executives in Japan starting in the summer of 1950, Juran joined the effort in 1954. It should be emphasized that both men respected each other and got along very well; however, Deming claimed that 'Juran tended to issue "far-out statements and platitudes" about management. Juran thought Deming was wrong, for instance, to tell management to "drive out fear." Juran believes "fear can bring out the best in people"' (Cortada and Woods 1998: 33–4). 'Juran [also] felt that Deming was basically a statistician who had spent much of his life without direct corporate experience and responsibilities, while Juran had more of a managerial viewpoint' (Wren and Greenwood 1998: 217).

Both Deming and Juran played a major role in helping the Japanese overcome their reputation as a producer of poor quality products. Japan had a period of rapid economic growth from the mid-1950s through the 1960s. This was also a time of significant progress in the effectiveness of Japan's quality control efforts. In the normal course of events, Juran's reputation from of his *Quality Control Handbook* came to the attention of Ken-ichi Koyanagi, then managing director of the Union of Japanese Scientists and Engineers (JUSE). In 1952 Deming arranged for Ken-ichi to meet Juran at an American Society for Quality Control meeting held in Syracuse, New York. Two years later, Juran accepted JUSE's invitation and made his first visit to Japan from 4 July to 17 August 1954. Although some of Juran's material was not new to the Japanese, many of his ideas and approaches were both needed and fresh. For example, Juran's Pareto principle of the vital few and useful many was well received. During his factory visits in Japan during 1954, Juran noticed what seemed to be an overemphasis on statistical tools and a corresponding shortage of the application of managerial tools. 'It is important to emphasize that the content of Juran's lectures differed from that of the lectures given by Deming. In particular, it should be remembered that while Deming's field was statistics, Juran's field was management' (Nonaka 1995: 540). Consequently, Juran's visits were significant in changing Japan's emphasis from statistical quality control to the management of quality and company-wide quality control.

When Juran visited Japan for the second time in November and December 1960, he conducted courses for top executives and chiefs of divisions and sections in Tokyo and Osaka. Returning to Japan on numerous occasions after 1960, Juran continued to make a substantial contribution to Japan's industrial renaissance. In reflecting on the assistance that he and Deming had given to the Japanese, Juran seemed to minimize its importance and related 'if Deming and I had never gone there, the Japanese quality revolution would have taken place without us' (Juran 1994: 10). Deming had similar thoughts when he considered his own efforts in helping the Japanese; he felt 'that he did not cause the great transformation that occurred in Japanese management and manufacturing. Rather, the Japanese caused these changes themselves' (Petersen 1987: 136). Beyond the modesty of both Juran and Deming, we find that these men were very instrumental in helping the Japanese achieve their own industrial renaissance. In fact, the Japanese appreciate the splendid efforts of both. In the years to follow, the emperor of Japan awarded each of them the Second Order Medal of the Sacred Treasure, the nation's highest award presented to foreigners.

Back in the United States during the 1980s, many leaders had difficulty in defining quality. Some confused quality with luxury and wondered if it was really critical. Juran defined quality as 'fitness for use' (Juran 1989: 15). It should be recognized that Juran emphasized 'that it is the user who is really the concern, not some abstract ideal of quality' (Sashkin and Kiser 1993: 55). In this instance consumers, for example, receive what they expect. This is the opposite of what marketers sometimes call

'bait and switch'. A suitable example of not being fit for use are the poor quality Firestone tyres that caused serious automobile accidents at the start of the twenty-first century. These consumers did not expect luxury tyres, but they did expect tyres that were 'fit for use'. Unfortunately for Firestone, this was not the case. Had Juran's approach to quality management been followed, Firestone and Ford could have saved themselves a considerable loss in time, money and reputation.

Throughout his efforts to improve quality, Juran criticized two mistaken opinions that have prevented many American managers from producing quality products and services. The first is that many managers 'have not yet accepted the fact that they, not the workers, must shoulder most of the responsibility for the performance of their companies' (Hunt 1992: 66). Another mistaken opinion is that managers 'fail to realize the great financial gains to be made once quality becomes their top priority' (Hunt 1992: 66).

As Juran's philosophy about quality management evolved further, many of his earlier concepts developed into additional practical approaches suitable for the workplace. Juran defined quality management as 'the process of identifying and administering the activities needed to achieve the quality objectives of an organization' (Juran and Gryna 1993: 7). It became obvious to Juran that individual piecemeal efforts would accomplish little in attempting to improve the quality of an organization's output. Instead, he insisted on a company-wide quality effort. This systematic approach used throughout a company would be 'quite similar to the method long used to set and meet financial goals' (Juran 1988a: 244–5). Getting more specific, Juran urged that quality operations 'require some form of coordination that has enough force to put company performance ahead of departmental goals' (248). This level of company-wide quality management would be necessary for effective joint planning, project teams, early warning systems and genuine employee participation.

One of Juran's first steps for achieving quality is to conduct a company-wide assessment of quality. According to Juran, this assessment furnishes a starting point for understanding the size of the quality issue, and the specific areas requiring attention. This assessment consists of four elements:

1. Cost of poor quality.

2. Standing in the marketplace.

3. Quality culture in the organization.

4. Operation of the company quality system.

(Juran and Gryna 1993: 15)

In organizing for quality, Juran visualizes that coordination of quality activities requires coordination for control and coordination for creating change. In addition, 'to achieve quality excellence, upper management must lead the quality effort' (Juran and Gryna 1993: 155). Further, a quality council consisting of upper managers should develop a quality strategy and guide its implementation. In addition, 'middle management executes the quality strategy through a variety of roles [and] inputs from the work force' (Juran and Gryna 1993: 155). Quality teams create change; however, the implementation of the quality strategy occurs through the chain of command in the line organization instead of a staff quality department. Throughout this overall effort is an emphasis on company-wide quality control.

Juran's method for the management of quality consists of three processes. They are quality planning, quality control and quality improvement. These three processes, taken together are referred to as the Juran trilogy, and are shown in more detail below:

Steps in Juran's quality planning process

1. Determine quality goals.

2. Develop plans to meet these goals.

3. Identify the resources to meet these goals.

4. Translate the goals into quality.

5. Summarize 1 to 4 into a quality plan.

(Flood 1993: 18–19)

Steps in Juran's quality control process

1. Evaluate performance.

2. Compare performance with set goals.

3. Take action on the difference.

(Flood 1993: 19)

Steps in Juran's quality improvement process

1. Establish the infrastructure needed to secure annual quality improvement.

2. Identify the specific needs for improvement – the improvement *projects*.

3. For each project, establish a project team with clear responsibilities for bringing the project to a successful conclusion.

4. Provide the resources, motivation, and training needed by the teams to (a) diagnose the causes, (b) stimulate establishment of a remedy, and (c) establish controls to hold the gains.

(Cortada and Woods 1995: 195)

After the Second World War, when Juran decided to work on his own he intended to philosophize, research, write, lecture, and consult about management. Juran not only developed theory about quality management, but was also able to teach how to apply this theory.

Like others who made significant contributions to business and society, Juran is not without critics. The critics tend to dwell on issues one would expect to be directed towards someone born about ninety-five years ago; that is that he is old-fashioned, lacks an understanding of modern human relations, and does not understand bottom-up leadership and motivation. Robert Flood's remarks are typical; he considers that Juran's emphasis on management's responsibility 'fails to get to grips with the literature on motivation and leadership' (Flood 1993: 21). In addition, 'the contribution that the worker can make is undervalued, rejecting in principle bottom-up initiatives in the west' (Flood 1993: 22). In discussing the human dimensions further, Flood adds that Juran's methods 'in many ways are traditional and old fashioned' (Flood 1993: 22). Counter to the views of Flood, one could argue that Juran *does* recognize the human element. Indeed, according to Juran, 'An understanding of the human situations associated with the job will go far to solve the technical ones; in fact, such understanding may be a prerequisite of a solution' (Brelin *et al.* 1995: 183). Based on his work, Juran should also be credited with being a flexible and capable change agent. With regards to his outlook on adapting to change, Juran furnished his thoughts about being stuck in a traditional routine: 'by dozing on our habitual square we can lose touch with reality and the changing environment. Norms and standards are helpful, but inadequate if they fail to adapt or follow requirements' (Teboul 1991: 32). He added: 'Nothing can be justified by the mere fact of its existence' (Teboul 1991: 32).

It would be difficult to state where Juran made his most significant contribution. An observation by Warren Schmidt and Jerome Finnigan credits Juran for his significant work with the Japanese, but in commenting on his work in the United States they add that 'his work was better received in Japan' (Schmidt and Finnigan 1993: 174). Schmidt and Finnigan are probably correct in terms of Juran's current notoriety, but one could also argue that the long-term effect of Juran's philosophy in the United States is more profound. In spite of the collapse of the fad connected with total quality management, Juran's ideas and approaches for quality management are still alive in some segments of business and industry. The Juran Institute is also keeping alive Juran's philosophy and the application of his ideas. He founded the Juran Institute in 1979 to pursue his quality management goals:

'The Institute offers consulting and management training in quality management' (Mitra 1993: 57). Located in Wilton, Connecticut, it 'offers a video-based training program which is a structured project-by-project process designed to produce an improvement in quality and reduction in quality-related costs' (Evans and Lindsay 1989: 454).

In 1987 Juran relinquished his leadership of the Juran Institute and is now chairman emeritus. After his last series of lectures in 1993–4, entitled 'The Last Word', he stopped all public appearances to devote time to writing and his family. Time will give the definitive assessment of Juran's long-term impact.

BIBLIOGRAPHY

Brelin, H.K., Davenport, K.S., Jennings, L.P. and Murphy, P.F. (1995) *Focused Quality: Managing for Results*, New York: John Wiley and Sons.

Brocka, B. and Brocka, M.S. (1992) *Quality Management: Implementing the Best Ideas of the Masters*, Homewood, IL: Business One Irwin.

Butman, J. and Roessner, J. (1995) 'Foreword', in J.M. Juran (ed.), *Managerial Breakthrough: The Classic Book on Improving Management Performance*, New York: McGraw-Hill.

Cortada, J.W. and Woods, J.A. (1995) *The McGraw-Hill Encyclopedia of Quality Terms and Concepts*, New York: McGraw-Hill.

—— (1998) *The Quality Yearbook*, New York: McGraw-Hill.

Evans, J.R. and Lindsay, W.M. (1989) *The Management and Control of Quality*, St Paul, MN: West Publishing Company.

Flood, R.L. (1993) *Beyond T.Q.M.*, New York: John Wiley and Sons.

Hunt, V.D. (1992) *Quality in America: How to Implement a Competitive Quality Program*, Homewood, IL: Business One Irwin.

Juran, J.M. (1988a) *Juran on Planning for Quality*, New York: The Free Press.

Juran, J.M. (1988b) *Juran's Quality Control Handbook*, 4th edn, New York: McGraw-Hill.

—— (1989) *Juran on Leadership for Quality: An Executive Handbook*, New York: The Free Press.

—— (1994) 'Quality Advisor: A Century of Quality', *Manufacturing Engineering* (September): 10–11.

Juran, J.M. and Gryna, F.M. (1993) *Quality Planning and Analysis*, New York: McGraw-Hill.

Mitra, A. (1993) *Fundamentals of Quality Control and Improvement*, New York: Macmillan.

Nonaka I. (1995) 'The Recent History of Managing for Quality in Japan', in J.M. Juran (ed.), *A History of Managing for Quality: The Evolution, Trends, and Future Directions of Managing for Quality*, Milwaukee, WI: ASQC Press, 517–52.

Petersen, P.B. (1987) 'The Contribution of W. Edwards Deming to Japanese Management Theory and Practice', *Academy of Management Best Paper Proceedings 1987* (11 August): 133–7.

Rao, A. *et al.* (1996) *Total Quality Management: A Cross-Functional Perspective*, New York: John Wiley and Sons.

Sashkin, M. and Kiser, K.J. (1993) *Putting Total Quality Management to Work*, San Francisco: Berrett-Koehler.

Schmidt, W. and Finnigan, J.P. (1993) *TQ Manager: A Practical Guide for Managing in a Total Quality Organization*, San Francisco: Jossey-Bass.

Teboul, J. (1991) *Managing Quality Dynamics*, New York: Prentice Hall.

Wren, D.A. and Greenwood, R.G. (1998) *Management Innovators: The People and Ideas that have Shaped Modern Business*, New York: Oxford University Press.

PP

K

KAISER, Henry John (1882–1967)

Henry John Kaiser was born in Canajoharie, New York on 9 May 1882, the son of cobbler Frank Kaiser and his wife Mary, both of whom had immigrated from Germany. He died on 24 August 1967. Coming from a poor family, Kaiser entered the work force at the age of thirteen. He began working in a dry goods store and as a photographer's apprentice. He was a hard worker, and an entrepreneur from the beginning. He had to support his family as well as himself. Quickly learning the photographer's trade, he soon saved enough to purchase his employer's business in 1902. After the turn of the century Kaiser decided to further his technical and business education by studying at the University of Nebraska and the Montana School of Mines.

In 1906, aged twenty-four, Kaiser moved to the Pacific Northwest, settling in Spokane. The following year he married a Virginian, Bessie Fosburgh. Working at first as sales manager of a hardware store, Kaiser was soon drawn to the world of construction. He was hired by a road-building firm which did business in both Washington state and British Columbia, and then went into the business for himself. By the time of the First World War Kaiser's construction firm was expanding down the Pacific coast. Even before the 1920s he was doing well in a very high-risk business (Adams 1997). Construction firms often faced high labour costs and uncertain opportunities in a very competitive market in which, all

too often, too many companies were chasing too few contracts. Not many would survive a tough downturn.

Kaiser, despite a strong free enterprise creed, knew that bidding on state and federal contracts for roads and other public works was essential to his prosperity. Highways were not as easily financed by market forces as were railroads (Hugill 1993). The only way that highways in the United States could be built was if state and federal governments levied taxes to pay for them, and then hired private contractors to build and pave them. In 1916 and again in 1921 Congress passed Highway Acts, and by 1924 the federal government was paying half the cost of new roads while the states paid the other half, about $15,000 per mile. During the middle of the 1920s a huge network of several hundred paved highways joined the United States from Maine to California.

In the 1920s, as the auto age gained momentum, Kaiser the road-builder expanded his contracts not only in the United States, where paved highways for Model T and Chevrolet cars were now criss-crossing the landscape, but in Canada and Cuba as well. He was innovative as a construction entrepreneur. He knew better how to cut costs than did most of his competitors: when he built roads he used fuel-efficient diesel tractors and steam shovels, and put tyres on wheelbarrows pulled by his tractors. He tried as far as possible to give his highly skilled employees something unheard of in the construction industry: a measure of job security. Before one job was finished, Kaiser was already lining up another.

Kaiser also knew how to seek new markets outside road construction and even outside the United States. When the Great Depression of the 1930s descended, Kaiser's firm survived by taking part in the construction of several large dams, most notably that authorized by President Herbert Hoover. The Department of the Interior's Bureau of Reclamation awarded a contract to the Six Companies combine that Kaiser had organized. Kaiser began to divert the Colorado River in 1932, and to lay the huge prefabricated concrete blocks into place at the Boulder Canyon dam site where Nevada, Arizona and California joined in 1933. There was enough concrete in the dam to pave a highway from New York to California. Kaiser's consortium built its own town, Boulder City, to house the 5,000 workers of the Six Companies. It took them just two years to construct Boulder Dam: the dam (later called Hoover Dam) was dedicated in 1935, and its generators were installed in 1936 and 1937. Kaiser's engineering feat created America's largest artificial lake, Lake Mead, 176 kilometres long. Of the vast amount of power generated by the dam, 56 per cent went to California and the rest to Arizona and Nevada. The prosperity of the American Sunbelt would have been impossible without the electricity supplied by Kaiser's dam.

As his reputation as a builder grew, Kaiser went on in the 1930s to manage other consortia. In 1933 he took charge of Bridge Builders, Inc. and later bridged San Francisco Bay with a suspension bridge linking San Francisco and Oakland. In 1934 he headed the Columbia Construction Company to build the Bonneville Dam in Oregon. In 1939 he led Consolidated Builders in creating the Grand Coulee in Washington State, the biggest dam of all. During all of these mega-projects, Kaiser never abandoned his businesses in sand, gravel and cement.

Kaiser and his firms did well under Republican Presidents Warren Harding, Calvin Coolidge and Herbert Hoover, but it was the successive administrations of Franklin D. Roosevelt that afforded him his greatest opportunities. In tackling the Great Depression, Roosevelt first tried a government/industry partnership under the National Recovery Administration (NRA), until that was nullified by the Supreme Court. Although Roosevelt had stabilized the economy, lifted morale and probably prevented an anti-democratic revolution in the United States, he soon found business had turned against his New Deal policies. Roosevelt granted labour unions full collective rights, and brought in unprecedented welfare and regulatory measures. At first he sought anti-trust measures against corporate monopolies, but soon he discovered a more practical solution: using federal power to promote rather than stifle enterprise by directly encouraging new entrepreneurs to enter monopolistic markets (Adams 1997). As far as Roosevelt's New Deal was concerned, Kaiser's new firms were ideal candidates for government contracts. By 1939 Europe was once again at war and Roosevelt was deeply concerned about the threat of Nazi Germany. The need to rearm and the need to promote free competition in industries such as construction came together in the person of Kaiser. With a fresh government contract signed in August 1939, Kaiser organized his dam-builders into the Permanente Corporation to undersell the big cement companies.

Kaiser was the first important representative of a new breed of businessperson described by Adams (1997) as the 'government entrepreneur'. Firms like the Permanente Corporation depended upon markets and demand created by federal contracts in defence, social welfare and public works. Kaiser and others in his position began to send lawyers and agents to Washington, DC, giving birth to the city's large corporate lobbies.

The contracts won by Kaiser's new cement firm led directly to his role in the production effort in the Second World War. Not only did he begin supplying cement to naval bases in Hawaii, Guam and Wake Island, but he entered the realm of shipbuilding. Henry Kaiser had never built so much as a rowboat before 1940, but he entered into a partnership with the Todd Shipbuilding Company, in which Kaiser would supply the skilled and unskilled labour. The new corporation, which began making thirty freighters for the British merchant marine, began operations in San Francisco Bay in January 1941.

Kaiser's greatest accomplishments came during the war. One of the most critical parts of that struggle was the Battle of the Atlantic. Hitler's U-boats were sinking British and, later, American merchant ships at some periods in the war faster than the shipbuilding industry could replace them. Unless the United States could supply Britain with food and arms faster than the German submarines could sink the convoys, victory in Europe would be impossible. In addition, the defeat of Germany and Japan required supplying nearly a hundred US and fifty British divisions across the Atlantic and the Pacific.

Kaiser came to the rescue in one of the most remarkable feats of mass production in history. By 1942 he had added three more shipyards, two in Richmond, California, and one in Los Angeles. Kaiser was now faced with the task of creating the largest merchant marine ever, capable of waging a total, global war. He solved the problem with the invention of the Liberty Ship, based upon British tramp steamer designs. Liberty Ships had a range of up to 22,000 kilometres on a single voyage. Most importantly, they were cheap and easy to produce. Kaiser's shipyards prefabricated them: the ships were put together in sections, which were then assembled. Kaiser was soon making 3.5 ships a week, fourteen per month – 600 in 1942 alone. By 1943 he was making ships far quicker than Hitler could sink them; by the end of the war his yards had produced almost 1,500 Liberty Ships (Casdorph 1991).

Kaiser was now a national hero. He was one of the most distinguished of the many businesspeople whose efforts during the war had enabled America to out-produce the Axis by far, and wage a successful two-front war. His role in business history was particularly important as a symbol of a new social contract between American business, labour and government. In 1965 he was the first business executive ever to be formally honoured for his treatment of labour by the American Federation of Labor–Congress of Industrial Organizations (AFL–CIO).

During the 1920s entrepreneurs such as Henry FORD and even Kaiser himself had been idolized. Business could do no wrong: as Calvin Coolidge observed, it was 'the business of America'. Ideas of personal responsibility, minimal government and *laissez-faire* were almost universally accepted in rhetoric, if not in reality. During the 1930s, however, the image of businesspeople was transformed into that of uncaring enemies of labour and the public good. The Second World War enabled Kaiser and many like him to regain public respect once again, through partnership with Washington, recognition of labour and combining profitability with national goals.

Henry Kaiser was already thinking of the long term before the end of the war. He applied his genius for prefabrication to the new suburban America that emerged in the late 1940s. Still active in steel and concrete, Kaiser now diversified into appliances and even into building homes. Foreseeing an America that would be linked by superhighways, he envisioned a light, economical car which could challenge the General Motors/Ford/Chrysler triad. He and auto salesman Joseph W. Frazer set up the Kaiser-Frazer Corporation to build an innovative new car at the government's Willow Run plant in Detroit. The stylish Kaiser-Frazer car was, sadly, ahead of its time and could not carve out a lasting market share. The last models were produced in 1955.

One further contribution of Henry Kaiser needs to be noted – his role in creating the first and largest American health maintenance organization: Kaiser Permanente. According to the company's official Internet history, a physician named Sidney Garfield wished to provide medical care to the thousands of workers labouring on the Los Angeles Aqueduct. Refusing to turn anyone away, Garfield soon found his hospital unable to meet its expenses. He then adopted the suggestion of an engineer, Harold Hatch, that allowed workers to prepay a premium of five cents per day. The scheme worked and soon Garfield was able to insure 6,500 workers on the Grand Coulee. When the war came, Henry Kaiser, wishing to insure his 30,000 shipyard workers, formed an association with Garfield. After the war, the scheme was opened to other investors. By 1955 Kaiser Permanente insured 300,000 policyholders and by 2000, the Oakland-based company covered eight million.

Henry Kaiser spent his later years in Hawaii. His legacy was formidable. More than any other executive, he helped redefine the role of business in American culture. When Kaiser first went into business early in the century, hostility to unions, welfare and government intervention was an integral part of a highly individualistic business culture. By the 1940s, however, Kaiser was in the forefront of a revolution in management which now recognized the need to regard labour as a partner, government as a benefactor, and the public good as an essential part of business.

BIBLIOGRAPHY

Adams, S.B. (1997) *Mr. Kaiser Goes to Washington: The Rise of a Government Entrepeneur*, Chapel Hill, NC: University of North Carolina Press.

Casdorph, P.D. (1991) *Let the Good Times Roll: Life at Home in America During World War II*, New York: Paragon House.

'Henry J. Kaiser' (1999) *McGraw-Hill Encyclopedia of World Biography*, Detroit, MI: Gale Research, Inc., vol. 8, 412–13.

Hugill, P.J. (1993) *World Trade Since 1431: Geography, Technology, and Capitalism*, Baltimore, MD: Johns Hopkins University Press.

'Kaiser, Henry J.' (1971) *Current Biography, Who's Who and Why, 1942*, ed. M. Block, New York: The H.W. Wilson Company, 431–4.

Kaiser Permanente (2000) 'Kaiser Permanente History', http://www. greenislandgraphics.com/kp_fujitsu/learn/kphist.html, 1 November 2000.

Schwarz, J.A. (1988) 'Kaiser, Henry John', *Dictionary of American Biography*, New York: C. Scribner's Sons, suppl. 8, 307–10.

United States Department of the Interior, Bureau of Reclamation (2000) 'Hoover Dam–How it All Works', http://www. hooverdam.com/workings/main.htm, 1 November 2000.

—— (2000) 'The Chronology', http://www.hooverdam.com/History/chrono.htm, 1 November 2000.

DCL

KANTER, Rosabeth Moss (1943–)

Rosabeth Kanter was born Rosabeth Moss on 15 March 1943 in Cleveland, Ohio, the daughter of Nelson Moss, an attorney, and his wife Helen. She married Stuart Kanter in 1963; following his death in 1969 she married Barry Stein in 1972. After taking a BA *magna cum laude* from Bryn Mawr College in 1964, she undertook graduate studies at the University of Michigan, receiving an MA in 1965 and a Ph.D. in 1967. She was assistant professor of sociology at Brandeis University from 1967 to 1973 and, after a year as a visiting faculty member at Harvard, associate professor of sociology at Brandeis from 1974 to 1977. She then joined Yale University as associate professor of sociology (1977–8) and then professor of sociology (1978–86). Since 1986 she has been professor of management at Harvard. Kanter edited *Harvard Business Review* for three years from 1989 to 1992. Among many other professional roles, she was a founding committee member of the International Women's Forum.

As well as her work in the world of business, Kanter has had some influence on public policy. A Democrat, she collaborated in 1988 with Governor Michael Dukakis of Massachusetts on *Creating the Future*, an analysis of the Massachusetts 'economic miracle' of the 1980s, which had been achieved in part through cooperation between state agencies and private enterprise. The book, which shows some influence of Kanter's Harvard colleague Robert REICH, formed the philosophical underpinning for Dukakis's unsuccessful campaign for the presidency that year; the victor, the Republican George Bush, instead adopted more non-interventionist policies, but Kanter's ideas came back into favour with the election of the Democrat Bill Clinton in 1992.

A sociologist by training, Kanter in her early writings focused on issues relating to work and the family (Kanter 1976, 1977a, 1977b). This led her to consider the sociology of organizations, particularly business corporations. Her view has been that corporations have a powerful effect on the lives of people everywhere, especially in the developed world, and that anyone interested in the functioning of society must consider the role that corporations play. This led her to a closer examination of corporations in her two most notable works, *The Change Masters* (1983) and *When Giants Learn to Dance* (1989). Both these works were bestsellers, and during the 1980s and early 1990s Kanter was one of the world's most sought after management gurus. She remains a powerful and persuasive speaker and writer on issues of management and organization.

Kanter's aim in her work is not only to understand and explain corporations but also to provide guidance on how to make them both more effective businesses and better places to work. She believes that corporate structures tend to impede communication and innovation. To become more efficient and to compete more effectively, corporate managers need to break down these barriers and make communication flows smoother and faster, and to introduce greater flexibility. Innovation, in her view, is the key to success, for individual businesses and for nations and cultures. Writing in the early 1980s, when the US economy seemed to be floundering in the face of dynamic foreign competition, she argued that the only way forward was for the United States to innovate its way past the competition, and to take a leading-edge position in terms of both technology and organization. Her view was taken seriously, and to Kanter must go some of the credit for stimulating the technological and economic boom experienced in the United States during the 1990s, itself based on a twin platform of high-technology innovation and flexible organization.

In *The Change Masters* Kanter discussed how organizations approach innovation. The fundamental problem, she says, is that most organizations are unused to managing innovation. In Western society, especially American society, innovation has traditionally been something that is carried out by inventor-entrepreneurs (examples might include Thomas EDISON or Samuel COLT) or, more latterly, Silicon Valley entrepreneurs such as William HEWLETT and David PACKARD. She argued in *The Change Masters* that, to survive, corporations needed to learn how to create internally the kind of climate in which these inventor-entrepreneurs could flourish, to 'create conditions even inside larger organizations, that make it possible for individuals to get the power to experiment, to create, to develop, to test – to innovate' (Kanter 1983: 23). This is what is needed, she says, but the reality in most corporations is the opposite: innovation is restricted and slowed.

The key to innovation, in turn, is communication. Businesses must make the free flow of information and knowledge a priority. If lines of communication are poor, employees in the lower levels feel cut off from the decision makers above them. From a sociological perspective, she sees workers responding to this feeling of isolation in one of two ways: either they strive for promotion, to get into the upper ranks themselves, where they will have access to information and perhaps some influence on the decision-making processes; or they slip into what she calls a static state, in which motivation and productivity decline in equal measure.

How to be free of this problem is the focus of much of her work. At heart, her solution centres around the breaking down of organizational barriers and the creation of a corporate culture where the circulation of knowledge, through both formal and informal channels, is encouraged and stimulated. There is a strong emphasis in her work on employee participation, coalitions and teamwork, concepts which were to become part of mainstream management theory in the 1990s, all of which lead to closer contact between the separate elements and individuals that make up the organization. Coordination and cooperation are essential; in the complex environment of modern business there is no longer any room for the 'lone wolf' entrepreneur, as few single individuals have sufficient span of control to manage at the required level of complexity. Instead, we are moving into a 'post-entrepreneurial' world, in which only cooperation and coordination will yield any certainty of success.

The Change Masters sounded a warning to America's big businesses that they needed to change their thinking. *When Giants Learn to Dance*, published six years later, was a much sharper admonition to corporations to clean up their act. The future, says Kanter, will require corporations to achieve more with

less: 'This constitutes the great corporate balancing act. Cut back and grow. Trim down and built. Accomplish more, and do it in new areas, with fewer resources' (Kanter 1989: 31). She accepted the prevailing view that coporations needed to become 'leaner and fitter', but she argued strongly against what she saw as the thoughtless slashing of costs and structures without regard for the consequence; there was a difference between trimming away fat, and cutting into the bone. Downsizing and delayering were in many cases necessary, but could not be conducted randomly; instead, they needed to be conducted according to what she called 'the post-entrepreneurial principles of management', which should:

• Minimize objectives and maximize options. Keep fixed costs low and as often as possible use 'variable' or 'contingent' means to achieve corporate goals.

• Find leverage through influence and combination. Derive power from access and involvement, rather than from full control or total ownership.

• Encourage 'churn'. Keep things moving. Encourage continuous regrouping of people and functions and products to produce unexpected, creative new combinations. Redefine turnover as positive (a source of renewal) rather than negative.

(Kanter 1989: 354)

The corporation of the future, Kanter believes, will be a much more flexible place, one where jobs are designed around products rather than schedules. There is an obvious consequence in human terms, and Kanter acknowledges the tension between the corporate need for flexibility and the needs of employers and managers for security; in this her work bears some resemblance to that of Charles HANDY, who also considers the problems of personal insecurity in a dynamic working environment.

Kanter's solution is for employees to find security not through association with a specific job or company but through employability – the knowledge that they can always find employment. Work structures also need to become more flexible. Kanter describes three organizational strategies which should lead to greater flexibility: (1) the development of greater synergy, with more internal cooperation and better integrated organization; (2) the establishment of alliances with other organizations; and (3) the development of 'newstreams', new business possibilities to take the organization into the future. The result, she says, will be the demise of bureaucracy and the emergence of more cooperative, interactive organizations better able to meet the challenges of the future: 'These three post-entrepreneurial strategies can change sluggish organizations into agile athletic champions in the global corporate Olympics. They can show bloated, elephantine corpocracies how to dance' (Kanter 1918: 35).

Kanter has continued to teach these lessons in her subsequent work and also in her extensive career as a consultant. Her work encompasses several domains, and overlaps with that of some of her contemporaries. As noted, she shares in common with Handy an emphasis on the human aspects of the organization, and the need to balance human needs with corporate goals. Like Peter DRUCKER, she emphasizes innovation, flexibility and responsiveness. Like Tom PETERS – though less dogmatically – she insists on the need to do away with rigid structures, to create a 'small company' mindset that transfers the virtues of entrepreneurship into the heart of corporate empire. Her vision of a post-entrepreneurial world in which cooperation and alliances are essential features is widely shared, not just in the United States. In the late 1990s the e-commerce boom and the rise of 'dotcom' companies appeared to herald a return of the entrepreneurial age; the subsequent failure of many of these small firms and the knock-on consequences for the US economy in 2000–2001 appear to vindicate Kanter's original view.

BIBLIOGRAPHY
Kanter, R.M. (1976) *Work and Family in the United States: A Critical Review and Research and Policy Agenda*, New York: Russell Sage Foundation.
—— (1977a) *Another Voice: Feminist Perspectives on Social Life and Social Science*, New York: Doubleday.
—— (1977b) *Men and Women of the Corporation*, New York: Basic Books.
—— (1983) *The Change Masters: Innovation for Productivity in the American Corporation*, New York: Simon and Schuster.
—— (1989) *When Giants Learn to Dance: Mastering the Challenge of Strategy, Management and Careers in the 1990s*, New York: Simon and Schuster.
—— (1995) *World Class*, New York: Simon and Schuster.
Kanter, R.M. and Dukakis, M.S. (1988) *Creating the Future: The Massachusetts Comeback and Its Promise for America*, New York: Summit Books.
Kanter, R.M. and Stein, B.A. (1980) *A Tale of 'O': On Being Different in an Organization*, New York: Harper and Row.
Witzel, M. (1998) 'Kanter, Rosabeth Moss', in M. Warner (ed.), *IEBM Handbook of Management Thinking*, London: International Thomson Business Press, 341–4.

MLW

KAPOR, Mitchell David (1950–)

Mitch Kapor was born in Brooklyn, New York on 1 November 1950. His father, Jesse

Kapor, was the owner of Corrugated Paper Products Incorporated of Brooklyn. The family lived on Long Island, where Kapor attended public schools and graduated from high school in 1967. He attended Yale University, studying psychology, linguistics and computer science, specializing in cybernetics, and graduating with a BA in psychology in 1971. After graduation, Kapor made a living as a disc jockey, a stand-up comic and a mental health counsellor, and became involved with transcendental meditation (TM).

In 1976 Kapor moved to Switzerland to enrol in an 'Enlightenment-or-Bust' programme to further his studies in TM. Prior to this move, he had been a TM instructor in Cambridge, Massachusetts, and Fairfield, Iowa. After a gruelling five months of study, Kapor decided to leave Switzerland and return home to the United States, even though he had severed all ties with his home. According to Kapor, upon leaving the programme, 'I felt like I was crossing from slavery into freedom, from one intolerable situation into the great unknown' (Kapor 1994).

Upon his return, Kapor enrolled in Beacon College in Boston, where he obtained an MA in psychology in 1978. In that same year, the price of the Apple II computer fell within Kapor's means. Learning how to use the computer himself, he then began offering tutoring in computer use at five dollars an hour. Kapor had entered the world of computers and business.

His rise in the field of computers began when he met the inventors of Visi-Calc, the first spreadsheet software. Kapor took this idea further when he created Visi-Plot, a spreadsheet software that could plot and graph results. Visi-Plot was an instant success. Building on this experience, Kapor co-developed a further software program, Lotus 1-2-3, which was designed to attract business users. Lotus Development Corporation was founded in 1982 to market Lotus 1-2-3. Kapor, along with his partner Jonathan Sachs,

saw Lotus prosper with a $53-million profit in the first year; by its third year of operation the company was netting $225 million. But after four years with Lotus Kapor resigned, explaining that, 'I like starting things, the hands-on aspect of it. But the job was different now' (Schneider n.d.). However, Kapor continued to serve as a director of Lotus until 1987.

From 1987 to 1990 Kapor served as chairman and CEO of a new business, On Technology Corporation, which developed software applications for support networks. In 1990 Kapor and John Perry Barlow, a former lyricist for the Grateful Dead, founded the Electronic Frontier Foundation (EFF). This non-profit civil liberties organization was founded to protect privacy, free expression and access to public records and information online. Today, EFF is supported by many established businesses including Microsoft, AT&T, Bell Atlantic and Apple. On behalf of EFF, Kapor has testified at numerous congressional hearings and has been credited for the drafting of the blueprint for the National Information Infrastructure.

In 1992 Kapor created his own investment firm, Kapor Enterprises Incorporated, in Cambridge, Massachusetts. This firm has invested in several start-up companies, including UUNET Technology and RealNetworks; Kapor has also served as a director on the boards of several of these firms. In 1999 Kapor joined Accel Partners where he directed the sourcing of new investments and assists management of the Accel Portfolio companies. Aside from his business activities, Kapor is also engaged in philanthropic work. From 1984 to 1998 he was a trustee of the Kapor Family Foundation, and in 1997 he founded the Mitchell Kapor Foundation, dedicated to creating a more socially just and ecologically sustainable future.

Mitch Kapor has proved to be an extremely successful businessman with the creation of three profitable companies. In creating EFF, he has helped to fight for the civil liberties of people online. He continues to assist struggling new businesses and research. Not only was Mitch Kapor one of the most important software innovators of the last two decades of the twentieth century, but he continues to be a driving force in the computer world of the twenty-first century.

BIBLIOGRAPHY
Kapor, M. (1994) 'Mitchell Kapor on Dharma, Democracy and the Information Superhighway', in *TRICYCLE: The Buddhist Review*, Summer, http://www.kapor.com/homepages/mkapor, 5 March 2001.
Schneider, S. (n.d.) 'Biography', http://128.173.40.129/~history/Kapor.Schneider.html, 5 March 2001.

JW

KEARNEY, Andrew Thomas (1892–1962)

Andrew Thomas Kearney was born in Brockway, Pennsylvania on 5 July 1892, the son of James and Margaret Kearney. He died in Chicago on 11 January 1962. He married Harriet Mohr in 1926, and they had one daughter. After taking his BS degree at Pennsylvania State College in 1916, he undertook graduate study there and at Northwestern University in Illinois from 1919 to 1925. In 1920 he joined the commercial research department at Swift, where he worked with L.D.H. WELD; Kearney took over the department in 1926, and managed it until 1930. Leaving Swift, he joined James McKINSEY's consultancy firm in Chicago as a partner. When McKinsey stepped aside from the business in 1935 to become chairman of the board of Marshall Field, Kearney became a senior partner; in 1939, two years after McKinsey's death, he became managing partner of the firm, now known as McKinsey,

Kearney and Company. In 1946 he left to set up a new business, A.T. Kearney and Company, which still exists today.

Kearney was a prominent figure in McKinsey's at an important period in the company's growth, and was responsible for much of day-to-day management in the early 1930s; after McKinsey's death he was also responsible for strategy and direction, and led the company's work in consulting with manufacturers and engineers during the Second World War. He did much to lay the foundations for the modern McKinsey's organization, and for the whole field of modern management consultancy. His reasons for leaving in 1946 are not known; the new firm he established remained small during his lifetime, and did not even establish an office outside Chicago until the year before his death.

Kearney also taught marketing at Pennsylvania State College from 1919 to 1920, and lectured on business at the University of Chicago from 1925 to 1931. He led the American Production Mission to China in 1945, foreshadowing his firm's later involvement with the Far East. He was awarded the Medal of Freedom in 1946.

KELLEHER, Herbert David (1931–)

Herbert David Kelleher was born in Camden, New Jersey on 12 March 1931, the son of Harry and Ruth Kelleher. He married Joan Neeley in 1955; they have four children. After a BA at Wesleyan University in 1953, Kelleher took his law degree from New York University in 1956 and was called to the bar in New Jersey in 1957. He served as clerk of the New Jersey Supreme Court until 1959, then went into private practice. He moved to San Antonio, Texas in 1961, where he again worked in private practice. In 1967 he was one of the co-founders, along with Rollin

King, of Southwest Airlines, based in Dallas, Texas. His first job was to ensure that the company got off the ground, in a literal sense: when Southwest Airlines applied for certification its rivals in Texas, Braniff and Texas International, claimed that the market was already saturated and opposed certification. Kelleher, as the corporate lawyer, fought his rivals through the courts for four years, often providing his services free as funds began to run low, and won; in September 1971, Southwest Airlines made its first flight between Dallas and Houston.

From this unpromising beginning, Southwest Airlines grew rapidly. Kelleher, who went on to become president and CEO, adopted a 'guerilla war' strategy, refusing to challenge his larger rivals head-on at the major airports, and instead moved into the state capitals and smaller commuter airports of the Midwest and Southwestern states. This strategy has paid off; in 2000 Southwest Airlines was worth around $1.2 billion, served fifty-five cities and had over 300 aircraft in operation.

Southwest Airlines is one of the most studied companies in history, familiar to an entire generation of business school students largely through the famous series of case studies produced by Christopher Lovelock at Harvard Business School in 1975. The fascination with Southwest Airlines stems from the unorthodox approach of its leader. Kelleher has broken almost every rule of management in airline operation. He abandoned the 'hub and spoke' method of operation for a series of direct flights between cities within his network; this system should be inefficient, but it is not. Most routes do not have a reservation system; passengers turn up and go, as they would on a bus. The airline does not sell tickets through travel agents; it does not offer through ticketing with other airlines, and no in-flight meals are served. Services between major centres run nearly as frequently as a bus as well; at one point in the 1990s, Southwest was running seventy-eight flights a day between Houston and Dallas. Planes often fly half full.

But, as the Lovelock cases and many later studies point out, Kelleher had got his market almost exactly right. By concentrating on volume and generating revenue, he could afford to accept costs that other airlines could not. Also, and this is seldom mentioned, Southwest Airlines is perhaps the most efficient airline in operation, with simple low-tech systems on the ground and the latest, most fuel-efficient engines in the USA on its aircraft, yielding cost savings which can be used effectively in other areas. By providing a cheap and reliable service, Kelleher has generated thousands of loyal customers; the mayors cities not covered by Southwest Airlines write regularly to Kelleher to invite him in. As well as securing a large market for itself, Southwest Airlines has grown the market for air travel in the United States.

Behind Southwest Airlines' record of success – despite its spartan service, it won national service quality awards five times in the 1990s – is a powerful corporate culture, the central figure of which is Kelleher himself. An inspirational leader who has led the company through many crises, he places much emphasis on the company's history and is himself the focus of much of that history. Southwest Airline employees are also among the best paid in the industry and have high levels of employee share ownership; their capacity for loyalty can be seen in the very low staff turnover figures, among the lowest of any airline.

Through his career in airlines, Kelleher has been a maverick: he has done almost everything contrary to industry norms, and has seen his unorthodoxy pay off with the building of a company that, measured by any standard, is highly successful. Small wonder that his career is so widely studied. What remains to be seen is whether Southwest Airlines can continue this success under his eventual successor.

BIBLIOGRAPHY

Freiberg, K, Freiberg, J. and Peters, T. (1998) *Nuts! Southwest Airlines' Crazy Recipe for Business and Personal Success*, New York: Bantam.

Lovelock, C.H. (1975) 'Southwest Airlines Cases A–D', Cambridge, MA: Harvard Business School.

MLW

KELLOGG, William Keith (1860–1951)

William Keith Kellogg was born in Battle Creek, Michigan on 7 April 1860 and died there on 6 October 1951. He was the seventh of the ten children of John Preston Kellogg, and the fifth child of John's second wife, Ann Janette Kellogg. The family had settled in Battle Creek in 1856, completing a series of moves that had drawn John Preston Kellogg from New England to Michigan in search of lumber and cheap land.

John Preston Kellogg was a broom-maker, and Willie Kellogg began working for his father as a stockboy when he was only seven years old. He had little formal schooling. He first attended the Number Three Ward School until the age of ten, and then a Seventh Day Adventists sectarian select school until after the age of thirteen. By that time he had completed sixth grade and John Preston did not insist that his son. attend school. Instead, he went to work full-time for his father as a broom salesman. 'W.K.', as he was often known, was remarkably successful, applying himself assiduously and developing his talents for analysis, memorization, tenacity, customer service and persistence. Unlike his brother John Harvey, eight years his senior, who was sent to medical school and postgraduate work, Willie was thought to be a slow learner. Years later, it was determined that his slowness was attributable to poor eyesight, not lack of intelligence.

The Kellogg family belonged to the Seventh Day Adventist Church, centred at that time in Battle Creek. The leaders of the church, James and Ellen White, were close friends of the Kellogg family, even supporting two of Kellogg's older brothers, Merritt G. and John Harvey Kellogg, in their medical studies, and later employing them at the Western Health Reform Institute.

For a few months during 1877–8, Kellogg was put in charge of the broom factory when his father broke a hip. Aged just seventeen, he did exceedingly well. Shortly thereafter, James White, the Seventh Day Adventist leader, and George King, a businessman, established a broom factory in Dallas, Texas. After six months of production problems, they hired Kellogg to run the factory. Kellogg spent the better part of a year in Dallas; while there, in 1879, he began writing a diary that is preserved today at the W.K. Kellogg Foundation archives. James White had been a poor businessman, and Kellogg had to borrow from one source or another to meet the company payroll on several occasions. But he ran the factory and the business well, and developed a keen business sense. Towards the end of the year, however, Kellogg's homesickness became too much, and he returned to Battle Creek in November 1879.

By 1880 Kellogg had decided that he needed more formal education. He first attended a business college in Battle Creek, but the course seemed too slow for him. Next, he went to Parson's Business College in Kalamazoo, and explained that he wanted a business education fast. Kellogg was allowed to complete the work as quickly as he could and acquired his certificate as a qualified bookkeeper and accountant in less than three months. Shortly thereafter, at the age of twenty, Kellogg married Ella Davis, the daughter of a grocer/clock repairman. They had four sons and one daughter: Willie Keith, who died at the age of four, Karl, John Leonard (Lenn),

Elizabeth (Beth), and Irvin Hadley, who died the year after his birth.

Kellogg began working at the Battle Creek Sanitarium for his brother John in 1880, with a starting salary of $6 a week. Never, in the twenty-five years he worked there, did Kellogg ever earn more than $87 a month. Kellogg called himself John Harvey's flunkey, often doing duties such as shining his brother's shoes or giving him a shave. In reality, Kellogg had many administrative duties, including all responsibility for bookkeeping and correspondence received by the Sanitarium, or any other one of John Harvey's companies. This amounted to some sixty to a hundred pieces of mail each day. Additionally, Kellogg interviewed people who were in need of medical attention but unable to afford it, determining whether they received treatment. Kellogg declined the position of business manager for the Sanitarium, offered to him by the board. During the quarter century he worked at the 'San', Kellogg never had a title, but it was well known that he did all the behind the scenes work and eventually became resentful towards his brother for never sharing any of limelight.

During these years, Kellogg became indebted with a mortgage and the financial responsibilities of a family. He was unable to meet his expenses with the small salary that he received, and worried that he would always be a poor man. Around 1893 Kellogg was offered a side job by his brother John Harvey, selling his brother's books and retaining 25 per cent of the profits. Kellogg, replicating his first job as a broom salesman, was successful and finally became debt-free after thirteen and a half years.

It would be impossible to present a full biography of Kellogg and the history of the cereal industry without discussing the Health Reform Institute and Dr John Harvey Kellogg (1852–1943). The famous Battle Creek Sanitarium, originally called the Western Health Reform Institute, was the vision of Ellen White, an early leader of the Seventh

Day Adventist religion. With an initial stock issue of $11,000, the institute purchased a two-storey farmhouse and eight acres in Battle Creek and began operation. Merritt G. Kellogg, the oldest Kellogg boy, was the first family member to serve on the institute's staff. Later, Dr John Harvey Kellogg joined as the physician-in-chief and changed the name of the institute to the Battle Creek Sanitarium, coining the word 'sanitarium'. In addition to running the 'San', John Harvey founded over thirty companies and publications over a fifty-year period.

The San was more like a hotel or a spa than a hospital, although there were excellent doctors and a wide variety of medical services, even surgeries. In addition to traditional medical interventions, a number of health treatments were developed by Dr Kellogg based on Seventh-Day Adventist values, including water treatments (external and internal), massage and electric therapy. Individuals came to learn how to lead healthier lives by diet, exercise and changing their lifestyles. Sunlight and exercise were important, as were daily baths in an era when weekly baths were more than the norm. The diet for all was strictly vegetarian and calorie-controlled, emphasizing the importance of whole grains, vegetables and nuts, not meats. Alcohol, tobacco, meat and sex were forbidden. The San was a tremendous success during the late 1800s and early 1900s. Thousands stayed there, including Johnny Weismuller, Henry FORD, Thomas EDISON, John D. ROCKEFELLER and Will Durant.

Dr John Harvey Kellogg was the opposite of his younger brother William. Whereas W.K. was introverted, quiet, detail-oriented, circumspect and meticulous in his work, John Harvey was extroverted, flamboyant, self-promoting, gregarious and spontaneous. W.K. possessed excellent business acumen, financial skills and a photographic memory, whereas John Harvey had few of these skills. Although a famed surgeon and gifted writer, he was the victim of scams, his own grandiose schemes and his inability to manage even his best ideas. John Harvey, who stood about 5 feet 2 inches (157 centimetres), in later years dressed only in white at all times of the year; W.K., who stood about 5 feet 7 inches (170 centimetres), always dressed neatly but conservatively. The brothers complimented each other, yet were incompatible and litigious, particularly in later years. Many believed that it was the hard work, long hours and honesty of W.K. Kellogg that kept the San afloat and prosperous, but it was John Harvey who received all the fame and notoriety. Certainly, Kellogg never prospered monetarily while employed at the San.

Both Kellogg brothers spent a considerable amount of time in the San's experimental kitchens searching for tasty and nutritious food for the patients. Beverages made from grain, not coffee or tea, were developed, as were peanut butter and other nut products to substitute for animal fat. John Harvey Kellogg established the Sanitas Food Company as a way to sell some of the health foods they developed by mail order, putting W.K. in charge of the business and financial end, and paying him 25 per cent of the company profits. Patients often visited the San's kitchens, where they could learn about the food and how to prepare it when they left. One patient, C.W. Post, was inspired by what he saw at the San and started the Post Cereal Company selling Postum, a grain-based coffee substitute, and Post Grape Nuts.

The brothers searched for a ready-to-eat breakfast cereal. After several failed experiments, they accidentally left a pot of boiled wheat on the stove for an extended period of time. The wheat mixture was put through double rollers anyway, and the result was wheat flakes. They had accidentally discovered the principal of tempering, which equalizes the moisture throughout the wheat and causes the wheat to flake. The cereal, and similar cereal made from other grains, particularly corn, were popular with San patients and many wanted it even after they left. A significant business in mail-order breakfast cereal began.

John Harvey Kellogg did not want his name on any packaging for food sold by the Sanitas Food Company, or his name directly associated with the company, feeling it would be a violation of medical ethics for him to be selling health foods. Additionally, he was opposed to any national advertising. W.K. had a different idea. He did not want to sell corn flakes by mail; he wanted to sell them by the train carload.

With corn flakes as the driving force, the Sanitas Food Company grew and Kellogg became its general manager. After twenty-two and a half years of work at the Sanitarium, Kellogg left in 1901 to further pursue the development of the Sanitas Nut Food Company. Six months later, however, when fire destroyed the Sanitarium, Kellogg returned to work at the San, without salary, to help rebuild the institution by securing financing and overseeing much of the rebuilding effort. All together, Kellogg gave twenty-five years of dedicated service to the Sanitarium.

During the years 1900–1905, more than forty-two competing cereal companies operated in Battle Creek. This proved to be tough for the Sanitas Nut Food Company, because other companies were advertising more thoroughly and selling their products through a variety of outlets. Kellogg developed an unofficial partnership with Arch SHAW, a long-time friend and business adviser, to increase sales. Despite the wishes of John Harvey, Kellogg and Shaw made the cereal taste better by adding sugar and malt, and then sought to increase sales through a Sanitas advertising campaign: 'Will you live the Battle Creek life for thirty days?' The company offered an assortment of Sanitas foods that could be purchased through direct mail. On 22 January 1906, with the help of St Louis financiers, Kellogg secured the rights to sell corn flakes from his brother John Harvey for $170,000, and the new Battle Creek Toasted Corn Flake Company went public with its stock. This business would become the Kellogg Company in 1922.

On 4 July 1907 the factory was destroyed by fire. This was a devastating blow, for it coincided with a decline in the cereal boom in Battle Creek. Kellogg never lost his drive, and within twelve hours had architects working on plans for a new, fireproof factory at a new location, ideally situated between the Grand Trunk and the Michigan Railways, positioning the company to ship out on either line. With something like the vision of Henry Ford, Kellogg wanted railcars to come in full of raw materials and to be shipped out full of finished cereal.

Although Kellogg was a cautious man by nature, in advertising he was inventive and fearless. With Arch Shaw working from Chicago, Kellogg created campaigns and promotions that have become legendary. Advertising became the key driving force for company success and, later, success within the industry. Door-to-door sampling campaigns spread knowledge of corn flakes; company representative handed out free samples to the occupants of the house along with promotions, coupons and slogans. Shortly thereafter, Shaw and Kellogg developed another advertising promotion to offset new competition. Kellogg's signature was added to the cereal boxes with the words, 'Beware of imitations, none original without this signature.' This promotion, combined with the new four-colour printing process developed by Arch Shaw, which made food look attractive, set the business in motion.

Other noteworthy campaigns included Kellogg's full-page advertisement in the *Ladies Home Journal* in 1906, asking people to stop buying corn flakes and let the company catch up on its orders. The ad was a gamble, costing one-third of the annual operating budget of the company. Sales skyrocketed. Another campaign suggested women wink at their grocers on Wednesday to receive a free box of corn flakes. In 1912 Kellogg installed the world's largest electric sign in Times Square,

New York to advertise corn flakes. Portraits of children and beautiful, wholesome women were also used extensively in advertising campaigns.

In addition to advertising, Kellogg introduced notable innovations in packaging and production. From the start the company relied on a mass production system, automated from product to packaging. The first package in 1906 sold for fifteen cents and contained eight ounces of corn flakes. In 1914 the Waxtite system was added, first as an exterior wax wrapping for each cereal box, then later changed to an interior wax paper wrap to ensure quality and consistency in the product. Kellogg also pioneered the use of coupons to promote sales, and employed slogans, premiums and dynamic packaging all to sell cereal. He encouraged new cereal and new products, such as Rice Krispies and All-Bran, and constantly looked for innovative machinery for more efficient and more automated production.

Through good products, effective advertising, and efficient mass production the Kellogg Company prospered and grew. Kellogg wanted most to have a family succession for running the company. In 1908 he turned the company over to his second son, John L. Kellogg, an inventive and mechanical genius who became the driving force moving the company forward until 1921. An economic downturn hurt profits; Kellogg blamed his son, forced his resignation and assumed control of the company again in 1925. He next placed his hopes for a Kellogg dynasty on his grandson John L. Kellogg, Jr. As a boy, Kellogg tutored him in the business and, after graduation from college, John Jr was made vice-president. Unfortunately, the grandson could not live up to his grandfather's expectations. A high-strung individual, John Jr was demoted and left the company; he committed suicide in 1938.

Perhaps Kellogg's greatest legacy is the W.K. Kellogg Foundation, one of the world's largest foundations in terms of assets, annual grants and total giving over the years. The foundation, originally established in 1930 as the W.K. Kellogg Child Welfare Foundation, became the W.K. Kellogg Foundation Trust in 1934. Through it, the foundation was given stock in the Kellogg Company which represented 57.5 per cent of the outstanding stock; Kellogg himself retained a 2.5 per cent share. His other lifetime and estate contributions totalled $47 million (W.K. Kellogg Foundation 1955).

As for directing the Foundation, Kellogg stated 'I don't want to restrict you in any way. Use the money as you please, so long as it promotes the health, happiness, and well being of children' (Powell 1956: 308). Kellogg preferred that long-term solutions to people's problems be developed, as opposed to giving handouts that would last only a short time. The mission statement of the foundation reads, 'To help people help themselves through the practical application of knowledge and resources to improve their quality of life and that of future generations.' Its programming interests in the United States are health, education, philanthropy and volunteerism, food systems, agriculture, youth, special opportunities, and greater Battle Creek programmes. The generosity Kellogg practised all his life continues in the work of the foundation he created.

Kellogg disliked the terms 'philanthropy' and 'philanthropist', particularly when applied to his work and himself. In sympathy to his feelings, the foundation used the term 'helpful endeavours' for the work they performed through Kellogg's generosity (W.K. Kellogg Foundation 1955: 6). The thrust of foundation efforts, its 'helpful endeavours', is in areas related to Kellogg's work or interests. For example, the dependence of the Kellogg business on raw material from farms led to many efforts on behalf of people living in rural communities; Kellogg's understanding of the power of advertising and communication led the foundation to work in the area of information dissemination; Kellogg's lack of

educational opportunities led to investments in improving educational opportunities for others; and Kellogg's own troubled eyesight and the physical problems of his grandson Kenneth led to foundation work in health.

Kellogg rarely made unsolicited suggestions about foundation activities, and maintained a strong interest without active involvement. A key to the success of the foundation can be attributed to Kellogg's foresight in giving the foundation trustees responsibility and authority. In contrast with his normal authoritarian style of management in business activities, the foundation received his generosity, his interest and his wisdom but never his interference. Kellogg minutely examined financial statements, some eliciting comments such as why it was 'necessary to make long distance phone calls to give money away' (Powell 1956: 309), but the Foundation had independence of action even during Kellogg's life, well preparing it to continue its functions as capably as before after his death (W.K. Kellogg Foundation 1955).

Many of Kellogg's achievements, acquisitions and accomplishments ended in public service. His wealth laid the basis of the W.K. Kellogg Foundation, and his largest homes became estates dedicated to public benefit. For example, in 1925 Kellogg decided that he and his second wife, Dr Carrie Staines, needed a more appropriate Michigan home for their needs. Kellogg acquired thirty-two acres of property on Gull Lake, near Battle Creek, and oversaw the building of a Tudor estate costing $747,000, completed in October 1926. Much detail was devoted to the estate structures, which included a pagoda, a Dutch windmill imported from the Netherlands, a guesthouse and accompanying buildings, a boathouse and more. In style and intent it reflected the popular taste of other successful businessmen of the period, such as Henry Ford and Edsel FORD. Although Kellogg often said, 'I never learned to play' (Powell 1956: 24), many of the features of the estate were devoted to play and leisure activities for guests and relatives (Stanford 1983).

Kellogg transferred the Gull Lake estate to the W.K. Kellogg Foundation in 1930, with a life lease for himself and his wife; it was subsequently used by the Coast Guard and the US Army until 1950. In 1952 the former Gull Lake estate became the property of Michigan State University and the Kellogg Gull Lake Biological Station for academic training and ecological research. 'In the end, his private and public worlds intermeshed. His formal estate – a home for the elite – became a treasure for many' (Stanford 1983: 45).

In a similar manner, Kellogg gave his other two significant homes to the public. The W.K. Kellogg ranch in the Pomona Valley was constructed under the guidance of architect Charles Gibbs. Its 800 acres housed many building, all of Spanish design, including top facilities for the development of the pure-bred Arabian horse. These were the third largest Arabian stables in the United States, yet Kellogg knew little about the Arabian horse; he hired the talent. During his visits to the ranch Kellogg would entertain top celebrities, and his Arabian horses, with riders in full Bedouin regalia, were traditional participants in the new year's day Tournament of Roses parade. The ranch was deeded to the University of California in 1932, after an elaborate ceremony hosted by Will Rogers, to become the W.K. Kellogg Institute of Animal Husbandry. Later, the ranch was deeded to the US Army, and then transferred to the Department of Agriculture. Eventually, through an Act of Congress, the ranch was deeded to the State of California for educational use through the California State Polytechnic College. Similarly, Kellogg's Italian villa in Dunedin, Florida became the Dunedin Marine Base for quartering and training Marines during the Second World War.

Kellogg's influence on the food business was enormous. He is credited with developing the cereal business and was often dubbed the 'King of Cereal'. The company he founded is today the largest producer of cereal foods in the world. Kellogg's makes twelve of the fifteen best-selling breakfast cereals in the world. His success rested on a number of personal traits and sociological factors. As an individual, Kellogg operated from a base of religious and moral principles he acquired as a young man. He was modest, shy and taciturn, but possessed enormous determination and willpower. He spoke directly, used few words, and valued time. He always made decisions quickly, and headed an organization that had only one leader. That enabled the Kellogg Company to react quickly and decisively as the industry grew and developed. Kellogg was the first to recognize the importance of advertising in the industry and the importance of appealing to a mass market. His prodigious memory and interest in details gave him a wide-ranging grasp of Kellogg operations and the industry in its entirety.

As a leader, Kellogg was autocratic but benevolent; his company was paternalistic and well established in the community. His need to control and direct and his tendency to make swift decisions proved less satisfactory in his personal life. Nonetheless, his generosity, love of family and strong morals won him warm relationships with most of his relatives and long-time friends such as Arch Shaw and A.W. Harris, founder of the Harris Trust and Savings Bank of Chicago.

It was also Kellogg's good fortune to make corn flakes at a time when breakfast habits were starting to change. People were rejecting lard, bacon and fried food in favour of convenience and food reputed to be healthy. What had been health food soon became accepted as healthy food, by millions throughout the world, through the activities of W.K. Kellogg. Thus, Kellogg created both a company and an industry.

BIBLIOGRAPHY
Butler, M., Thornton, F. and Ashley, M. (1955) *The Best to You Each Morning:*

W. K. Kellogg and the Kellogg Company, Battle Creek, MI: Heritage Publications.

Folsom, B. (1997) 'Corn Flakes and Greatness', *Mackinac Center for Public Policy* 5: 97–127.

Gould, W. (1997) *Business Portraits: Kellogg's,* Lincolnwood, IL: NTC Publishing Group.

Kalamazoo Writing and Video Company (1990) *Legacy: The Life of W. K. Kellogg,* video, Battle Creek, MI: W.K. Kellogg Foundation.

'Kellogg's Corn Flakes' (1952) *Modern Packaging* (February).

Powell, H.B. (1956) *The Original Has This Signature,* Englewood Cliffs, NJ: Prentice-Hall.

Stanford, L.O. (1983) *W. K. Kellogg and His Gull Lake Home: From Eroded Cornfield to Estate to Biological Station,* Hickory Corners, MI: W.K. Kellogg Biological Station, Michigan State University.

W.K. Kellogg Foundation (1955) *The First Twenty-five Years: The Story of a Foundation,* Battle Creek, MI: W.K. Kellogg Foundation.

—— (1979) *I'll Invest My Money in People,* Battle Creek, MI: W.K. Kellogg Foundation.

RG

KIMBALL, Dexter Simpson (1865–1952)

Dexter Simpson Kimball was born in New River in the Canadian province of New Brunswick on 21 October 1865. He died in Ithaca, New York on 1 November 1952. He grew up in California, where his parents had moved from Canada, and in 1881 began an apprenticeship as an engineer. Completing his training, he worked for Union Iron Works in San Francisco from 1887 to 1893. In 1893 he went to Stanford University, completing an AB in mechanical engineering in 1896. He spent two more years with Union Iron Works, then took a post teaching machine design at Cornell University from 1898 to 1901. He worked again in industry from 1901 to 1904, but then returned permanently to Cornell, taking the position of professor of machine construction (later professor of machine design and construction). In 1915 he became professor of industrial engineering, and from 1920 to 1936 served as dean of the College of Engineering at Cornell; on two occasions he also served as acting president of the university. He did war work in the Second World War, advising the Office of Production Management and teaching on the Federal War Training Programme and at the US Naval Academy in Annapolis, Maryland. Throughout this period he was active as a consultant to industry and a leading member of many professional bodies, including the American Society of Mechanical Engineers, of which he was president in 1922.

Kimball's main contribution to management was through his teaching. As a progressive engineer, he was well aware of the developments in management being made by Frederick W. TAYLOR and his colleagues, and built these into his courses. In 1904, on returning to Cornell, he designed and taught an elective course on works administration, which Urwick (1956) says was the first course to be offered at any American university which was based on scientific management. Kimball supplemented his teaching with a series of textbooks, most notably *Principles of Industrial Organization* (1913), the first textbook in the field and one which remained in use in some quarters until after the Second World War. He later wrote on plant management industrial economics.

Like many textbooks of the day, *Principles of Industrial Organization* takes a broad approach to its subject. Kimball devotes the first five chapters to a study of the growth and development of industrial organizations, tracing their evolution as far back as the Middle Ages (again like the work of many writers of the day, his account of production methods in the Middle Ages is not wholly accurate). As well as the principles of organization *per se*, he also covers methods of administration and control. A chapter on standardization gives a clear summary of the methods developed by Taylor and GILBRETH, and may also contain the first description of combined time and motion studies. Wage systems, including those advocated by Taylor, GANTT, HALSEY and EMERSON, are also discussed, and there is a sizeable chapter on industrial relations.

In general, Kimball advocates a 'scientific' approach to organization, which is founded in part on a study of Taylor and in part on an appreciation of the work of Harrington Emerson, particularly the latter's advocacy of the line and staff model of organization. Although he advocates the division of labour, he notes that excessive division and control can impair the functioning of the organization, as it is difficult to find supervisors

with vision, intelligence and leadership, and while no doubt some form of organization must always be employed, especially for the rank and file of the workers, care should be exercised that the administrative methods do not throttle the initiative and enthusiasm of even the lowest subordinate. Genius does not work well in harness, and men are always more important than machines or methods.

(Kimball 1913: 158–9)

BIBLIOGRAPHY
Kimball, D.S. (1911) *Industrial Education*, Ithaca, NY: Cornell University Press.
—— (1913) *Principles of Industrial Organization*, New York: McGraw-Hill.
—— (1919) *Plant Management*, New York: Alexander Hamilton Institute.
Kimball, D.S. (1929) *Industrial Economics*, New York: McGraw-Hill.
Urwick, L.F. (ed.) (1956) *The Golden Book of Management*, London: Newman Neame.

MLW

KNIGHT, Philip (1938–)

Philip ('Phil') Knight was born on 24 February 1938 in Portland, Oregon, the son of William Knight, a newspaper publisher, and Lota (Hatfield) Knight. He graduated with a bachelor's degree in accounting from the University of Oregon in 1959 (where he was also an athlete, training with the prominent track and field coach, William Bowerman) and an MBA from Stanford University in 1962. He worked as an accountant for Price Waterhouse in Portland and taught at Portland State University. He married Penelope Parks and has two sons, a daughter and a foster daughter.

While working on his MBA, Knight wrote a paper describing how high-quality athletic shoes could be made cheaply overseas due to the lower cost of labour, and then sold in the United States for a healthy profit. Knight decided to test this idea. With Bowerman as his partner, Knight imported Tigers, athletic shoes made in Japan. Knight started by selling the shoes from his car at local high school track meets. The shoes and selling prices proved popular, and Knight began hiring former runners and other athletes as salespeople. He sought and received endorsements from prominent athletes. By 1972 Knight had decided that the company should manufacture its own shoes using overseas labour. He renamed the company Nike (after the goddess of victory).

Nike's ascent during the 1970s and 1980s was meteoric. From his initial $500 initial investment, Knight currently has an estimated $5 billion net wealth (Newcomb 1999: 296). His business philosophy has been called 'anti-establishment' (Lane 1996: 44). He often eschews micro-level management and frequently allows subordinates to operate freely, as long as they improve productivity and do not 'mess up'. He also recognizes that he is not in the business of selling shoes, but rather is in the business of selling the 'athletic ideals of determination, individuality, self-sacrifice and winning' (Lane 1996: 44).

Nike became the world's largest seller of athletic shoes by the mid-1980s. However, in perhaps its greatest mistake, Nike misjudged the burgeoning aerobics market. Knight reacted to Reebok's successful capture of this new segment of the market by disavowing his former reluctance to advertise. He hired the Wieden and Kennedy advertising agency, after first greeting them with, 'Hi, I'm Phil Knight and I don't believe in advertising' (DeFord 1993: 66). Knight and Nike struck back at Reebok with a series of advertisements using basketball star Michael Jordan and rising filmmaker Spike Lee. The business world took note of the new approach: 'Nike scores points for attitude, for irreverence' (Lane 1996: 42).

Nike has also reversed the usual marketing tactic of producing a good product and then getting athletes to endorse it. In many cases, Nike signs an athlete and then models the product around him or, increasingly, her, thus branding the product by its association with the athlete. By the turn of the millennium, Nike was aggressively expanding not only the geographic spread of its company but also the range of its products. Soccer and other international sports are growing parts of the company's business. In addition, Nike has begun to represent athletes in order to control the marketing of them. Some critics believe that players are more loyal to Nike than to their teams.

Nike and Knight have attracted other criticisms. A long-running controversy concerning Nike's use of cheap overseas labour has dogged the company for years. Despite Knight's large donations to his Alma Mater, the University of Oregon, a vocal group of students there have protested at labour conditions at Nike manufacturing plants throughout the world.

BIBLIOGRAPHY

DeFord, F. (1993) 'Running Man: How did Phil Knight turn Nike from a Tiny Company making Sneakers with a Waffle Iron into the $3.7 billion Juggernaut that has given us Michael Jordan and Bugs Bunny, Just Do It, and the Swoosh that Conquered the Planet?', *Vanity Fair* 56(8): 52–72.

Lane, R. (1996) 'You Are What You Wear: Nike's Phil Knight isn't Selling Shoes. He's Selling Attitude', *Forbes* 158(9): 42–6.

Newcomb, P. (ed.). (1999) 'The Forbes 400: The Richest People in America', *Forbes* 164(9): 169–426.

Willigan, G. (1992) 'High-Performance Marketing: An Interview with Nike's Phil Knight', *Harvard Business Review* 70(4): 90–101.

DS

KNOEPPEL, Charles Edward (1881–1936)

Charles Edward Knoeppel was born in Milwaukee, Wisconsin on 15 April 1881 and died in Philadelphia on 29 November 1936. He went to school in Buffalo, New York, where his family had moved, but lack of money prevented his attending college. He worked briefly as a journalist, then took a job as a labourer in an iron works. His intelligence and ability won him promotion to posts as a draughtsman and designer, and by 1904 he was in a management position with the Parkhurst Boiler Works in Oswego, New York. Here his primary responsibility was the implementation of a system of production management based on the contemporary work of Frederick W. TAYLOR. Knoeppel was familiar with Taylorism, and in this early stage of his career was its keen proponent. From 1905 to 1909 he worked as a consultant, for part of the time in partnership with his father, implementing Taylor systems.

In 1909 his career changed course when he joined the staff of Emerson Engineering, the New York consultancy firm set up by Harrington EMERSON. He spent two years with Emerson, time which had considerable impact on his ideas. He continued to work as a consultant, and in 1914 set up C.E. Knoeppel and Company, Industrial Engineers, in New York. He ran this business until 1925, when he left to join a Boston-based firm of engineers; a spell as a consultant in Cleveland followed; and finally in 1933 Knoeppel settled in Philadelphia, where he continued to work as a consultant until shortly before his death.

Knoeppel started his career as a consultant as a fairly narrow technical functional specialist, absorbed primarily in problems of production. Exposure to Emerson and also to Herbert CASSON, who worked with Emerson around the same time, broadened his view to a more holistic approach to organization. His best-known work, *Organization and Administration* (1918), originally designed as a textbook for teaching organization, is notable as one of the first books to focus squarely on the principles of organization. In this work, Knoeppel switches the focus of organization to narrow issues of control, as was primarily the case in scientific management, to a more human-centred and holistic view of the organization, which paved the way for the introduction of sociological and psychological theory in the 1920s by scholars such as Mary Parker FOLLETT and Elton MAYO.

Like Follett, Knoeppel emphasizes coordination over simple control. Coordination and control are, he says, mutually interdependent and neither can exist without the other; but he gives primacy to coordination, as it is only through the latter that the efforts of the organization can be harnessed to achieve its product. Like Emerson and Casson, but in more detail, he uses biological metaphor to explain how organizations work. He shows how organization between the key elements of the human body – the brain (as guide and controller), the senses (as expert acquirers and processors of information), and the organs and limbs (as performers of functional tasks) – results in the entire body being harnesses to achieve its goals, and develops at length how organizations can do likewise. Based on this biological metaphor, Knoeppel sets out what he calls his 'six principles of organization':

First: INVESTIGATION: Finding out what to do.

Second: ORGANIZATION: Building the machine that will properly carry out what should be done.

Third: RECORDS: Gathering facts and statistics to be used by this organization in arriving at the right kind of conclusions in carrying out what should be done.

Fourth: PLANNING: Logically arranging and co-ordinating all details so that the various steps can be rapidly and efficiently carried out.

Fifth: STANDARDIZATION: Carrying out the steps determined or actually doing the work in a proper manner.

Sixth: INCENTIVES: The results of the successful application of the other five.

(Knoeppel 1918: 58)

Knoeppel's work was very highly regarded, and along with Dexter KIMBALL he was considered one of the leading writers on organization of his day. His thought stands midway between that of the pioneers of scientific management and the later developments of the human relations school; it partakes somewhat of both, and is important in that it argues for a balance between humanistic and technical concerns in management.

BIBLIOGRAPHY

Knoeppel, C. (1915) *Installing Efficiency Methods*, New York: Engineering Magazine Co.
—— (1916) *Industrial Preparedness*, New York: Engineering Magazine Co.
—— (1918) *Organization and Administration*, New York: McGraw-Hill.
—— (1920) 'Most Effective Type of Industrial Organization', *Industrial Management* 60: 61–5.
—— (1923) *Profit Engineering: Applied Economics in Making Business Profitable*, New York: McGraw-Hill.
Urwick, L.F. (ed.) *The Golden Book of Management*, London: Newman Neame.

MLW

KNUDSEN, William Signius (1879–1948)

Signius Wilhelm Poul Knudsen was born in Copenhagen, Denmark on 25 March 1879, the son of Knud Peter and Augusta Knudsen. He died in Detroit, Michigan on 27 April 1948. His father, a customs official, struggled to support a family of twelve. Knudsen was a hard worker from a very early age, and did well in mathematics at the Danish Government Technical School. Between 1894 and 1898 he began his business education as an apprentice in a wholesale hardware firm. His next field of endeavour was the bicycle business, where he worked his way up from clerk and mechanic to warehouse manager.

Knudsen saw America as his land of opportunity. Having managerial experience and a good technical background, he sailed for New York in 1900. He arrived in the United States as a well-educated immigrant, highly skilled in mathematics and able to read English, German and French. Aided by the Lutheran mission, he was soon able to find work in the shipyards of Morris Heights, New Jersey.

Changing his name to William Signius Knudsen, he worked in the rail industry before joining the steel firm John R. Keim in Buffalo, New York in 1902 or 1903. This came at a time when Keim was shifting from manufacturing bicycles to automotive parts. Working at Keim brought Knudsen into contact with the new horseless carriages; he worked with early steam-car engines and other steel products when the cycle market became glutted. Some of his first orders involved components such as brake drums for Oldsmobiles.

By his early twenties Bill Knudsen was already a self-starter, dedicated to improving his business skills. He took a course in steel-making and helped his boss, William H. Smith, perfect a method of applying steel-making to auto parts. He and Smith personally went to Henry FORD and won from him a huge contract for axle housings. By 1908 the Keim firm was an important supplier for Ford.

In 1911 Knudsen married Clara Elizabeth Euler. They had four children, one of which would later become a senior manager with both General Motors (GM) and Ford. In that same year, Keim was bought out by Ford. Knudsen felt that he could assemble Model T bodies at Keim plants, and Ford gave him that responsibility. Labour troubles then broke out in Buffalo. When Keim's workers went on strike, Ford, notoriously anti-labour in his attitudes, moved the entire Buffalo operation by rail to Detroit. By 1916 Knudsen, settled in Detroit, was managing not only Ford's Detroit assembly plants but over two dozen other Ford plants, scattered across the country along railway lines. At each of these plants Model Ts, partially assembled in Detroit, were quickly put together.

Knudsen quickly earned a reputation as one of Henry Ford's most gifted managers. The outbreak of the First World War brought a further challenge. While America was neutral, many American factories were producing for Britain and France, and this meant that Ford was soon running short of sheet metal. Knudsen set out to find new sources of sheet steel, and was so successful that when the United States entered the war in 1917, Henry Ford appointed him the company's war production manager. Knudsen demonstrated his talent for combining bold technical innovation with sound general management. Halberstam (1986) describes him as the most able man in the Ford Motor Company. In 1917 German U-boats were sinking Allied merchantmen faster than the Allies could build them. The tide was turned by the adoption of the convoy system, but convoys needed escorts. Ford helped produce them in the form of the Eagle Boat. Knudsen did not have enough skilled shipyard workers, but got around the problem with a mass production facility which had three assembly lines, each of which could make seven boats. The parts would be stamped, numbered and prefabricated, and then shipped to the plant for assembly.

After the war, Ford put Knudsen in charge of all production, where he worked under the tutelage of Ford lieutenants Charles SORENSON and P.E. Marshall. In this new position, however, the big, earthy Danish immigrant, standing over two metres tall and weighing over 100 kilograms (230 pounds), soon clashed sharply with the austere and moralistic Henry Ford. According to Halberstam (1986), the Ford Motor Company in 1919–20 was no longer the creative pioneer it had been a decade earlier. Henry Ford now ran the company rigidly and would not tolerate any criticism. He still continued to produce the same Model T, treated his workers harshly and managed his subordinates through intimidation. This was too much for Knudsen, who began to suspect that Ford envied his abilities and considered him a threat. Ford was also paying no attention to the changing tastes of a growing class of car consumers. Giving up his $50,000 salary, Knudsen resigned from Ford in 1921.

Ford's loss was to be GM's gain. The year after he left Ford, GM vice-president Alfred P. SLOAN offered Knudsen a position. Within three weeks, GM president Pierre S. DU PONT had made him vice-president in the Chevrolet Division. When Sloan succeeded du Pont as president in 1924, Knudsen was promoted to president of Chevrolet. The low-priced Chevrolet was to be GM's answer to the Model T. In 1921 this seemed a forlorn hope: for every Chevrolet sold, about 200,000 in total, Ford was selling six or seven Model Ts. Charles Kettering, GM's engineer, wanted to make the Chevrolet an air- or copper-cooled car. Knudsen, after working on the project for over a year, finally recognized that the concept was a very bad investment into which the company had already sunk over $7 million. Knudsen bluntly told Kettering:

this car isn't any good. You and the people you have working on it down in Dayton ... aren't automobile people. This car isn't strong enough, the rear axle isn't any good, and even if you get these things worked out so they are good, the car will cost too much for Chevrolet to make.

(Langworth and Noble 1986: 82)

The air-cooled Chevrolet was $200 more expensive than earlier models, and, despite Knudsen's opposition, du Pont was only deterred from marketing it by Knudsen's threat to resign. Production was abandoned after only 759 out of a proposed 50, 000 of the cars were made, and these were pounded into scrap or dumped into Lake Erie.

Knudsen set to work to produce a Chevrolet that would not only be marketable, but eventually able to challenge the Model T. Knudsen fixed the defective rear axle, proposed a six-cylinder engine, and stressed improving the Chevrolet's overall quality and appearance.

Sloan gave Knudsen more leeway under GM's revolutionary decentralized management structure. In 1924 Chevrolet sold 280,000 cars versus 1,750,000 Model Ts; but by 1925 Chevrolet was producing 441,000 cars and by 1926, 500,000. The affordable Chevrolets were available in a variety of colours and, at a price that even a clerk could afford in the booming 1920s, were cutting sharply into the Model T's market. Ford was now selling only two of his black Model T's, unchanged since 1908, for every Chevrolet. Knudsen so devastated Ford's market that in the end he drove the Model T out of business. Ford, after dominating the economy car market for two decades, had to shut down his plants in 1926 order to retool them to build the Model A.

Knudsen rapidly sensed victory. While Ford's plants were idle, GM was continuing to make and sell Chevrolets, allowing the latter briefly to overtake Ford by producing 787,000 cars in 1928. Ford recaptured much of his market in 1929, but the coming of the Great Depression sealed GM's victory. In contrast to Henry Ford's rigid, highly paternalistic management style, Sloan's General Motors used systematic control accounting and long-term budget planning which enabled it to better weather the Depression. GM made a profit every year during the 1930s, and sales of Chevrolets overtook those of Fords.

How was Knudsen able to produce cars more efficiently than Ford? Flexibility was a major factor. According to Flink (1999), GM plants had general purpose machine tools that could be rapidly converted from making parts for one model to making parts for another. Knudsen and other division managers also bought many of their components instead of making them. This technique of flexible mass production was to be Knudsen's major contribution to management, and would eventually be copied by both Ford and Chrysler.

Knudsen was rewarded with the executive vice-presidency of all GM's North American car manufacturing in 1933 and became the president of GM itself in 1937. Out-producing the seemingly invincible Henry Ford was but an apprenticeship for Knudsen to out-produce an even more formidable competitor: the Axis powers during the Second World War. President Franklin D. Roosevelt was so impressed with Knudsen's management skills that he asked him, in May 1940, as the German army was over-running France, to help advise the Council of National Defense. Knudsen gave up a $459,000 salary to serve with the council for nothing. By 1941 he was directing the Office of Production Management, and by 1943 was in charge of war production for the Department of War; he became director of the Air Technical Service Command in 1944. He was awarded the Distinguished Service Medal in the same year.

Returning to General Motors in 1945, Knudsen was forced to retire by Sloan, which deeply depressed him. He died in 1948. His skills in marketing and in production, when combined with Sloan's accounting and management, made Chevrolet the leading low-priced car in America, and General Motors the world's leading car company.

BIBLIOGRAPHY

Beasley, N. (1947) *Knudsen, a Biography*, New York: McGraw-Hill.

Crabb, R. (1969) *Birth of a Giant: The Men and Incidents that Gave America the Motorcar*, Philadelphia, PA: Chilton Book Company.

Flink, J.J. (1999) 'Knudsen, William Signius', in J.A. Garraty and M.C. Carnes (eds), *American National Biography*, New York: Oxford University Press, vol. 22, 843–4.

Halberstam, D. (1986) *The Reckoning*, New York: Avon Books.

Langworth, R.M. and Norbye, J.P. (1986) *By the Auto Editors of Consumer Guide: The Complete History of General Motors: 1908–1986*, New York; Beekman House.

Sloan, A.P. (1990) *My Years with General*

Motors, ed. J.D. McDonald and C. Stevens, New York: Currency Doubleday.
'William S. Knudsen' (1999) *The McGraw-Hill Encyclopedia of World Biography*, Detroit, MI: Gale Research, vol. 9, 67–8.

DCL

KOCHAN, Thomas A. (1947–)

Thomas Kochan was born in the Midwestern state of Wisconsin on 28 September 1947. Between 1969 and 1973 he graduated with three degrees (BBA, MS, Ph.D.) from the University of Wisconsin, an institution that has long held an enviable reputation in industrial relations. In 1973 he was appointed assistant professor (later associate professor) in Cornell University's School of Industrial and Labor Relations, taking leave in 1979–80 to work at the US Department of Labor. His Ph.D. research examined public sector bargaining, and he continued to focus on public sector industrial relations in the 1970s.

Following this formative work, it was the publication of *Collective Bargaining and Industrial Relations* in 1980 that established Kochan's reputation. This book was a departure from the institutional framework with which much of the study of industrial relations had traditionally been preoccupied. Kochan tried to 'integrate' this framework with 'advances in theory building and empirical research from the behavioural sciences and economics' (Kochan 1980: viii). An important element of Kochan's work was the use of quantitative research methods, which until then had not been so widely used in the study of industrial relations. Many leading industrial relations scholars participated in the debate that followed this publication; a leading journal, *Industrial Relations*, devoted a review issue to the discussion (see also Chelius and

Dworkin 1990). In the same year, Kochan was appointed professor at the Sloan School of Management, Massachusetts Institute of Technology (MIT). He subsequently became the George M. Bunker Professor of Management there.

In 1986, in collaboration with Harry Katz and Bob McKersie, Kochan published *The Transformation of American Industrial Relations*, a work that tried to build on the 'systems' model of industrial relations developed by Dunlop (1958). In this book, the authors sought to explain why union density was in decline and why the 'New Deal' model of industrial relations seemed to have lost its relevance. They argued that unions, governments and managers no longer shared the similar perspective that had underpinned industrial relations since the Second World War. The decline of union power, they contended, had allowed management to exercise a greater degree of 'strategic choice' in employment relations. They identified a number of levels at which management could exercise strategic choice, from the geographic location of a business's physical plant to the nature of work organization at individual workplaces. According to Kochan *et al.* (1986), the increased availability of strategic choices had led some managers to shift away from traditional collective bargaining. Another strategy being used more frequently, they argued, was based on new work organization systems combined with human resource management techniques that had largely been developed in non-union enterprises.

Although the book was widely acclaimed, the arguments in *The Transformation of American Industrial Relations* were not accepted by all. The most substantial criticisms centred on the extent to which the authors' conclusions could be supported by empirical evidence. Nevertheless, one of Kochan *et al.*'s central propositions – that the *locus* of industrial relations was shifting to the individual enterprise or workplace – has been confirmed by subsequent events. So too has been their observation that many unions do not appear to have a viable strategy for maintaining their roles within transformed employment relations systems.

Many of the propositions advanced to support the concept of strategic choice had theoretical application in all industrialized countries. Accordingly, Kochan and his colleagues initiated and led a series of international, comparative studies to examine the extent to which other countries' industrial relations systems were being transformed in similar fashion to those in the United States. The MIT group coordinated a team of international researchers who examined key industries including banking, car manufacturing, airlines, steel and telecommunications. Research focused on employment relations practices such as patterns of skill formation and training, work organization systems and methods of remuneration. The research, reported in Locke *et al.* (1995), found at least three international trends: a tendency to decentralize employment relations to the enterprise or workplace level, increased attention to team-based work organization, flexibility and communication, and greater emphasis on skill development and training. These developments were associated with attempts to empower workers and encourage them to make a greater contribution to the performance of the enterprise. This international project has spawned a number of other comparative studies, in some of which Kochan continues to participate (for example, Kochan *et al.* 1997).

The increasing global perspective of Kochan's research led him to investigate, with colleagues, the relationship between economic development and employment relations. One study examined developments in some of the newly industrializing countries in Asia (Verma *et al.* 1995). The authors concluded that while there was no single 'Asian model' of employment relations, the countries that had been most successful economically were those that had learnt from innovation and modified their

employment relations practices to suit their changing market circumstances.

Following the publication of the *Transformation* book (Kochan *et al.* 1986), Kochan led a number of projects concerned with particular aspects of employment relations, including occupational health and safety, and quality of working life. One interest was in so-called 'high performance work systems', in connection with which he examined work organization at General Motors's Saturn plant. Subsequently he played a key role in the MIT International Motor Vehicle Program. The first findings published as an outcome of this programme were that 'lean production' (as developed by Toyota) was the most effective way to manufacture cars (Womack *et al.* 1990). However, as part of a research team that tested this finding in an international study, Kochan argued that production systems are determined in a complex way by many factors and that there may not be a single 'best' work system (Kochan *et al.* 1997). The team found that the car manufacturing industry around the world was moving towards lean production techniques, but that the interaction of global competitive pressures and the strategies adopted by firms, governments and work forces was inducing varying extents and rates of implementation in different contexts.

Kochan has a long history of participation in collegial activities at the scholarly and public policy levels. He was president of the International Industrial Relations Association from 1992 to 1995, and president of the Industrial Relations Research Association (IRRA) from 1999 to 2000. From 1993 to 1995 he served as a member of President Clinton's Commission on the Future of Worker–Management Relations, chaired by John DUNLOP. His own proposals for change in the 1990s centred on improving employment relations through *The Mutual Gains Enterprise* (Kochan and Osterman 1994), in which the authors promoted the desirability of experimenting with different approaches to worker participation and representation. In 1995 he was a centennial visiting professor at the London School of Economics; in 1996 he received the Heneman Career Achievement Award; and in 1997 he was elected a Fellow of the National Academy of Human Resources.

Most recently, Kochan has argued in papers and conferences that the transformation of work has outpaced change in employment relations institutions and policies. According to Kochan, the resulting mismatch has damaged the 'social contract' that underpins work in industrialized countries. He has attempted to stimulate a public debate in the United States about the changes that are necessary to repair this damage. On behalf of the IRRA, he initiated and jointly edited a new journal for practitioners, *Perspectives on Work*.

Kochan has made a notable contribution to theory and practice in the field of employment relations, a field whose concepts he himself has done much to identify and explain. The international comparative studies that he has initiated have demonstrated how an interdisciplinary approach can be adopted to the study of relationships at work. His development of the concept of strategic choice has provided a robust framework within which to conduct extensive empirical research. Kochan has followed earlier University of Wisconsin alumni such as John COMMONS as an active participant in public debates that had as their purpose the improvement of managerial practices and employment relations. He is a respected intellectual in the United States, and his international work has established for him recognition and influence in other industrialized countries and in the newly industrialising countries of Asia.

Kochan is one of the most influential contemporary scholars in the field of international and comparative employment relations, as well as a respected commentator on public policy in the United States. He has been a leader in the development of employment relations as an interdisciplinary approach to the study of industrial relations and human resource management. Kochan advocates the need for social science scholars to engage with practitioners in industry and public policy. He has acted as an adviser to American governments and continues to stimulate public discussion and debate about the direction of workplace change.

Acknowledgement
For a fuller discussion about Tom Kochan, see Bamber and Lansbury (1998). It is acknowledged that to some extent this present article draws on that longer article. The author is also grateful to Ken Lovell for research assistance.

BIBLIOGRAPHY
Ancona, D., Kochan, T., Scully, M., Van Maanen, J. and Westney, D.E. (1996) *Managing for the Future: Organizational Behavior and Processes*, Cincinnati: South-western Publishing.
Bamber, G., and Lansbury, R.D. (eds) (1998) *International and Comparative Employment Relations: A Study of Industrialised Market Economies*, 3rd edn., Sydney: Allen and Unwin and London: Sage.
—— (1998) 'Kochan, Thomas', in M. Poole and M. Warner (eds), *IEBM Handbook of Human Resource Management*, London: International Thomson Business Press, 355–60.
Bamber, G.J., Park, F., Lee, C., Ross, P.K. and Broadbent, K. (eds) (2000) *Employment Relations in the Asia-Pacific: Changing Approaches*, London: Thompson.
Chelius, J. and Dworkin, J. (1990) *Reflections on the Transformation of Industrial Relations*, Rutgers, NJ: Institute of Management and Labor Readings, State University of New Jersey.
Dunlop, J. (1958) *Industrial Relations Systems*, New York: Holt, Rinehart and Winston.

Katz, H.C. and Thomas, A.K. (2000) *An Introduction to Collective Bargaining and Industrial Relations*, 2nd edn., Boston: McGraw-Hill.

Kochan, T. (1980) *Collective Bargaining and Industrial Relations: From Theory to Policy and Practice*, Homewood, IL: Irwin.

Kochan, T. and Osterman, P. (1994) *The Mutual Gains Enterprise*, Boston: Harvard Business School Press.

Kochan, T. and Useem, M. (1992) *Transforming Organizations*, New York: Oxford University Press.

Kochan, T., Katz, H.C. and McKersie, R.B. (1986) *The Transformation of American Industrial Relations*, New York: Basic Books.

Kochan, T., Lansbury, R.D. and MacDuffie, J.P. (1997) *After Lean Production: Changing Employment Practices in the World Auto Industry*, Ithaca, NY: Cornell University Press.

Locke, R., Kochan, T. and Piore, M. (eds) (1995) *Employment Relations in a Changing World Economy*, Cambridge, MA: MIT Press.

Rubinstein, S.A. and Kochan, T.A. (2001) *Learning from Saturn: Possibilities for Corporate Governance and Employee Relations*, Ithaca, NY: Cornell University Press.

Verma, A., Kochan, T. and Lansbury, R.D. (eds) (1995) *Employment Relations in the Growing Asian Economies*, London: Routledge.

Womack, J.P., Jones, D.T. and Roos, D. (1990) *The Machine that Changed the World*, New York: Rawson/Macmillan.

GB

KOONTZ, Harold (1908–84)

Harold Koontz was born in Findlay, Ohio on 19 May 1908, the son of Joseph Koontz, a schoolteacher, and his wife Harriet. He died at Encino, California on 11 February 1984. He married Mary Learey in 1935; they have two children. After taking an AB at Oberlin College in 1930, Koontz took his MBA at Northwestern University in 1931 and his Ph.D. at Yale University in 1935. He was successively instructor in business administration at Duke University (1933–4), instructor in accounting and transportation at the University of Toledo (1934–5) and assistant professor of economics at Colgate University (1935–42). He served on the War Production Board in Washington from 1942 to 1944, and with the Association of American Railroads from 1944 to 1945.

Following the war Koontz went into the aircraft industry, and from 1945 to 1948 was assistant to president and director of planning at Trans-World Airlines (TWA). From 1948 to 1950 he was director of sales for Consolidated Vultee Aircraft Corp. in San Diego, California. He then returned to academia, taking up a post as professor of business policy and transportation at University of California, Los Angeles (UCLA) from 1950 to 1962; he was Mead Johnson Professor of Management at UCLA from 1962 to 1975, and then professor emeritus, teaching part-time until 1981. In addition to teaching, he was president of the Institute for Administrative Research from 1966 to 1970 and served on the boards of several companies; he was consultant to, among others, Lockheed, Bank of America and Nippon Management Association.

Koontz was one of the leading mid-twentieth-century writers on management, and his work was well known in Europe and Japan as well as across the United States. *Principles of Management* (Koontz and O'Donnell 1955) was his major work and cemented his reputation, becoming a standard textbook and for a time surpassed in popularity only by Peter DRUCKER's *The Practice of Management*, which had appeared the previous year. Like Drucker's work, *Principles of Management* is in essence an attempt to analyse what it is that managers do, although the approach used in the two books is radically different. Koontz's work attempts to deconstruct management, seeing it as being in essence a bundle of different but related tasks. In a schema that owes something to Henri FAYOL's theory of administration, Koontz includes among these tasks such elements as organization, staffing, directing, planning and control.

Koontz's fundamental definition of management is management as coordination:

The coordination of human effort is the essence of all grouped activities, whether the objectives are business, military, religious, charitable, educational, or social. The fundamental component of this association is management – the function of getting things done through others. In bringing about this coordination of group activity, the manager plans, organizes, staffs, directs, and controls the activities of subordinates.
(Koontz and O'Donnell 1955: 3)

He believes that 'the organization of human beings for the attainment of a common purpose is as old as civilization itself' (Koontz and O'Donnell 1955: 3). However, management has grown to become more important as business enterprises have grown in size and scale, and this has led to an increasing separation of ownership and control. Koontz here draws on the work of BERLE and MEANS, and also of James BURNHAM, to show how and why that separation has been accomplished.

Although – or perhaps because – organization is a universal human activity, the management of organizations requires fundamental guiding principles. In the debate about scientific management, Koontz says that management partakes of the nature of both science

and art; moreover, the two need not be mutually exclusive, as there can be principles in art as well as in science. Principles, says Koontz, are not just there to increase efficiency; they also help to focus thinking and cystallize the purpose of management. He sees the use of guiding principles as being a means of channelling management activity towards basic social objectives, such as happiness, well-being, peace, security and freedom:

Among the many reasons for our failure to channel our tremendous accumulation of knowledge and resources has been our inability to coordinate people so that individual objectives will be translated into group attainments. This, in a broad sense, is the job of management. Extensions of the frontiers of management science, by increasing the efficiency of management, would unquestionably have revolutionary impact on the cultural level of our society.
(Koontz and O'Donnell 1955: 11)

Koontz goes on to make the point that: 'The primary function of business in society is to produce and distribute those goods and services necessary for material welfare' (Koontz and O'Donnell 1955: 11). This leads to an observable phenomenon, that those countries with the highest standard of living are those with the highest quality of management. Good management, he says, as much as the availability of markets or resources, has been responsible for American economic growth.

Koontz does not subscribe the 'revolution' theory of the development of management, and believes, along with Oliver Sheldon, that the principles and practices of management have been evolving almost indefinitely. Koontz himself greatly admired Charles Babbage as a pioneer of modern management thinking. Unusually for a management writer in the 1950s, he urged readers to go back to earlier thinkers and writers such as Sheldon, Henry DENNISON, Lyndall Urwick, Mary Parker

FOLLETT and Ordway TEAD, all of whom had contributed to our understanding of what management is.

Appraising Managers as Managers (1971) revisits some of these themes. The book, which is dedicated to Koontz's friend Lyndall Urwick, looks at what managers do from a perspective of appraisal, but makes it clear that how well managers perform depends in large part on the environment in which they must perform; the manager is inseparable from the organization. Some of the environmental factors that lead to better management performance include commonality of understood purpose, whereby managers are clear about the organization's goals; an intentional structure of roles, with duties and responsibilities clearly designed and set out; a supportive and enabling climate which assists managers to perform rather than hindering them and setting barriers; and an environment of clarity, in which knowledge is freely available. A balance needs be struck between making clear what a manager's duties are and excessive proceduralism, which can turn into a straitjacket: he remarks that 'it is a difficult thing to be clear without being detailed' (Koontz 1971: 6).

Koontz provides an excellent, clear synthesis of thinking on management up to the mid-twentieth century. His call for a more historical approach and for a recognition of the traditions of management that have led to the development of present-day approaches is unusual for its time and place. He continues to be worth reading for his clear and pragmatic approach to the functions and tasks of management.

BIBLIOGRAPHY

Koontz, H. (1941) *Government Control of Business*, New York: Houghton.
—— (1964a) *Toward a Unified Theory of Management*, New York: McGraw-Hill.
—— (1964b) *Requirements for Basic and Professional Education for Scientific Management*, London: British Institute of Management.
Koontz, H. (1967) *The Board of Directors and Effective Management*, New York: McGraw-Hill.
—— (1971) *Appraising Managers as Managers*, New York: McGraw-Hill.
Koontz, H. and O'Donnell, C. (1955) *Principles of Management*, New York: McGraw-Hill.
—— (1974) *Essentials of Management*, New York: McGraw-Hill.

MLW

KOTLER, Philip (1931–)

Philip Kotler was born in Chicago on 27 May 1931. After taking a BA at De Paul University in 1950 he went on to take an MA in economics at the University of Chicago, where he studied under Milton FRIEDMAN; his Ph.D. came from the Massachusetts Institute of Technology in 1956, where his supervisor was Paul SAMUELSON. He was thus exposed to contrasting approaches to the subject. He was associate professor of economics at Roosevelt University from 1957 to 1961, spending the last year as a postdoctoral research fellow at Harvard University. In 1962 he was invited to join the faculty of the Kellogg Graduate School of Management at Northwestern University, but chose to teach marketing rather than economics. From thenceforth marketing became his field of study and work; he was appointed associate professor in 1965 and full professor in 1969. He is currently Johnson & Son Distinguished Professor of International Marketing at Northwestern, maintaining the long tradition of marketing thought at that university which began with Fred CLARK and Walter SCOTT eighty years ago. He has written fifteen books including *Marketing Management*, first published in

1967, which has gone through a number of editions and has been continuously in print since first publication, and more than seventy-five articles for major journals. He remains the recognized doyen of the international marketing academic community.

Kotler's contribution to marketing and to management generally has been threefold. First, he has done more than any other writer or scholar to promote the importance of marketing, transforming it from being a peripheral activity 'bolted onto' the more 'important' work of production. Second, he has continued and enlarged on a trend in marketing activity since the Second World War of shifting the emphasis in marketing away from price and distribution issues to a greater focus on meeting customer needs and on the bundle of benefits the customer receives from a product or service. Third, he has broadened the concept of marketing from mere selling to a much more general process of communication and exchange, and has shown how marketing can be extended and applied to non-profit organizations, charities, political parties and a whole variety of non-commercial situations.

Although marketing had been studied as an academic subject at US universities and business schools almost since the beginning of the century, and although the concept had already been the subject of lengthy work by scholars beginning with Clark, Scott, Paul CHERINGTON, Melvin COPELAND, L.D.H. WELD and others in the 1920s, when Kotler became involved in marketing in the mid-1960s it was still the Cinderella branch of business. Many companies did not have marketing departments; others had them but treated them primarily as research departments, with marketing as a subordinate function to sales. Kotler, observing the variations on this theme, classified approaches to marketing on five levels of increasing sophistication. First, there is the *production concept*, which 'holds that consumers will favor those products that are widely available and low in

cost. Management in production-oriented organizations concentrates on achieving high production efficiency and wide distribution coverage' (Kotler 1967: 17). Demand is assumed, and sales will ensue if the product can be got cheaply to the customer. Second, there is the *product concept*, which 'holds that customers will favor those products that offer the most quality, performance, and features. Management in these product-oriented organizations focus their energy on making good products and improving them over time' (Kotler 1967: 17). Although the emphasis here has switched from price to the bundle of benefits the consumer receives when making the purchase – in other words, from price to value – this is still a passive approach to the market.

Third, Kotler says, there is the *selling concept*. This 'holds that customers, if left alone, will ordinarily not buy enough of the organization's products. The organization must therefore undertake an aggressive selling and promotion effort' (Kotler 1967: 19). Here there is a switch from a passive to an active engagement with the market. There are various forms of selling, from the 'soft sell', which emphasizes educating the customer about the product and allowing the latter to make a free decision, to the aggressive 'hard sell', which emphasizes completing the transaction. Selling, says Kotler, is a risky business unless backed up by many other activities including research into customer needs, preferences and so on.

Fourth comes the *marketing concept*, which 'holds that the key to achieving organizational goals consists in determining the needs and wants of the target markets and delivering the desired satisfactions more efficiently and effectively than competitors' (Kotler 1967: 22). This approach, which had been outlined as long ago as the 1920s, had been developed in more detail by scholars and practitioners in the 1950s and 1960s, and was the prevailing academic orthodoxy in the late 1960s, even if few organizations had yet become so sophisticated in their approach. This approach requires some active engagement by both parties, and assumes, as Copeland had once argued, that the basic goal of both parties in an exchange is to complete a transaction; it falls to the marketer to find out what the needs of the customer are and to attempt to deliver a product that meets as many of those needs as possible, making the transaction as satisfactory as possible.

Fifth, however, Kotler offers what he calls the *societal marketing concept*. This 'holds that the organization's task is to determine the needs, wants, and interests of target markets and to deliver the desired satisfactions more effectively and efficiently than competitors in a way that preserves or enhances the consumer's or society's well-being' (Kotler 1967: 29). This concept, which is Kotler's own, introduces a solid ethical core into marketing, and links ethical behaviour with both the profit motive and the satisfaction of consumer wants, seeking a balance between all three.

The societal marketing concept has been controversial since the beginning and is part of Kotler's more general campaign to broaden the concept of marketing, which he introduced in his seminal *Harvard Business Review* article with Sidney Levy in 1969, 'Broadening the Concept of Marketing'. Here, Kotler and Levy argued that marketing was not just about commercial transactions; it was also about social values. Every product that is made and sold performs some sort of social function; every transaction has some social aspect; social values are part of all exchanges. Marketing is, whether it likes it or not, a social function. So much of marketing is about communication – of needs, of wants, of offerings, of price and features – and all communication is value-laden. This was radical enough in 1969, but Kotler and Levy went further: it is possible to apply the value principles of marketing to non-commercial exchanges, such as services and products which are provided on a non-profit basis or even for free; more, it is

possible to apply them to communications situations where no formal transaction takes place at all, such as elections of political candidates.

Kotler and Levy's articles caused something of a sensation, and distinguished marketing academics of the day rushed rebuttals into print. The most common criticism was that Kotler and Levy had 'broadened' marketing so far that it had disappeared; if the principles of marketing could be applied to all forms of exchange, commercial or otherwise, why bother calling it 'marketing' at all? But Kotler, notably in his later work with Alan Andreasen (see Kotler and Andreasen 1996), has pointed out that while non-profit marketing and commercial marketing differ in many aspects, they remain based on the same fundamental principles. Marketing, Kotler continues to insist, is 'a social process by which individuals and groups obtain what they need and want through creating and exchanging products and value with others' (Kotler 1967: 4).

This process has several elements. First, Kotler begins with needs, wants and demands, the starting point for all marketing analysis and research. He makes some distinction between the three terms: *needs* are the realization of the lack of some basic requirement; *wants* are specific requests for products or services to fill needs; *demands* are wants backed up by the desire and ability to pay or otherwise make exchange. Second, Kotler considers products, including services, an umbrella term; in some circumstances, products can also be people, places, organizations, activities or ideas (Kotler 1967: 5). In the most general sense, products are those things which satisfy needs, wants and demands; they are the seller's offering to meet the buyer's demand.

Two further important concepts in Kotler's theory of marketing are value and satisfaction. Customers, faced with competing products (bearing in mind the definition above), make their choice based on perceived value. They may engage in a variety of information-gathering activities in order to try to assess more accurately what that value might be. Following Copeland and Scott and many other earlier writers, Kotler acknowledges that value is a highly complex concept, one which varies between people and products and over time. Satisfaction is the extent to which actual value realized by the purchase or acquisition of the product matches the pre-purchase assessment of value: if actual value is equal to or greater than perceived value, satisfaction will result; if not, then dissatisfaction will result.

When people have demands, products are available, value has been perceived and a choice has been made, both parties then proceed to the exchange phase. For an exchange to take place, Kotler says, five conditions must be in force (Kotler 1967: 8):

1. There must be at least two parties.

2. Each party must have something that is of value to the other party.

3. Each party must be capable of communication and delivery.

4. Each party must be free to accept or reject the offer.

5. Each party must believe it is appropriate and desirable to deal with the other party.

This simplified schema is at the heart of Kotler's concept of what marketing *is*. To *do* marketing, however, is much more complex, and has two related requirements: the devotion of sufficient resources to manage marketing effectively, and the positioning of marketing at the heart of the company's strategy and philosophy. A market orientation – or better, a societal marketing orientation – is an essential prerequisite. Marketing should be part of the philosophy of all managers in that all should be focused on the needs and wants of the customer and be prepared to satisfy his or her demands. In structural terms, the marketing department must be at the heart of the organization, not on its periphery.

The activities required for marketing are complex and can be costly. First, there is a need for research and analysis, which includes broad environmental scanning, and focus on current and potential customers. Marketing intelligence and marketing research systems should aim to measure the size of the market, forecast potential demand, engage in identifying market segments and defining the demand potential of each, and either targeting potential segments for the firm's existing products or working to develop new products that will meet the needs of profitable segments (and where possible, engaging in both). Marketing planning is another essential activity, which gauges the life cycle of current products, estimates when they will need to be phased out and plans new products to replace them. Kotler was one of the first to define marketing strategy as a subset of strategy in its own right. He then turns to the tactical and operational levels of marketing, such as the management of pricing, marketing channels and distribution, and communications and promotion.

Kotler's view of marketing presents marketing as a complete set of activities encompassing awareness of consumer demands and formulation of response. Although the activities required are complex, the framework of desire and response is beautifully simple, and as he himself has shown, applies equally well to commercial and non-commercial situations. Under Kotler's influence, first US businesses and later those in Europe and Japan changed their approach to marketing; marketing departments subsumed sales departments rather than vice versa, marketing directors occupied board-level positions and marketing has become a core function in most major organizations: new organizational models such as team management tend to include at least one marketing person in every product or service team, and much greater awareness of marketing is being gradually instilled in all managers. Not only has Kotler changed the nature of marketing as a discipline but he has also, through his teaching and writing, worked a quiet revolution in the thinking of managers worldwide.

BIBLIOGRAPHY

Kotler, P. (1967) *Marketing Management*, Englewood Cliffs, NJ: Prentice-Hall, 1997.

Kotler, P. and Andreasen, A. (1996) *Strategic Marketing for Nonprofit Organizations*, Englewood Cliffs, NJ: Prentice-Hall.

Kotler, P. and Levy, S.J. (1969) 'Broadening the Concept of Marketing', *Journal of Marketing* (January): 10–15.

MLW

KOTTER, John P. (1947–)

John P. Kotter was born in San Diego, California. He attended Massachusetts Institute of Technology (MIT), graduating with a BSc in electrical engineering in 1968; he then attended MIT's Sloan School of Management, where he took his MBA in 1970. He then moved to Harvard University, where he received a Ph.D. in organizational behaviour in 1972, under the supervision of Paul LAWRENCE. He joined the teaching faculty at Harvard, being made full professor in 1980; at time of writing he is Konosuke Matsushita Professor of Leadership, Organization Behaviour and Human Resource Management at Harvard Business School.

Most of Kotter's work over the past two decades has focused on aspects of managerial behaviour. His book *The General Managers* (1982) is an important work which looks at how general managers work and function. Kotter concludes that although there are similarities in the ways in which general managers work, there are also important differences, and he questions whether 'general management' can be conceptualized as a discipline. Much of a manager's effectiveness, says Kotter, is dependent on how he or she builds relationships with others inside and outside the organization. The most important relationships are often ones which have nothing to do with the structure or hierarchy of the business; managers engage in what is effectively a form of alliance-building with colleagues and others who they believe will support them and enable them to achieve their goals. The book and its supporting research thus reinforce early organization behaviour research from the 1920s and before, which conceptualized organizations as human entities and suggested that management functions as a series of human interactions.

Kotter's most significant and controversial work, however, has been on the subject of leadership. In *A Force for Change* (1990) he argues that leadership and management differ, and should be considered separately. He identifies four principal areas of difference between the two, the general thrust of which is that management tasks are focused on execution and control, whereas leadership tasks are focused on planning and vision. He goes on to argue that modern organizations need less management and more leadership. He differs from some other authorities in the field by believing that leadership comprises a set of skills that can be taught; in other words, leaders are made, not born. Much of Kotter's subsequent work has focused on how training for leaders can best be provided in order to ensure an adequate supply of future business leaders.

BIBLIOGRAPHY

Kotter, J.P. (1982) *The General Managers*, New York: The Free Press.

—— (1985) *Power and Influence: Beyond Formal Authority*, New York: The Free Press.

—— (1988) *The Leadership Factor*, New

York: The Free Press.

Kotter, J.P. (1990) *A Force for Change: How Leadership Differs from Management*, New York: The Free Press.

—— (1996) *Leading Change*, Boston, MA: Harvard Business School Press.

—— (1997) *Matsushita Leadership*, New York: The Free Press.

MLW

KRAVIS, Henry (1944–)

Henry Kravis was born in Tulsa, Oklahoma on 6 January 1944. The son of Ray Kravis, an oil engineer and one-time oil business partner of Joseph P. Kennedy, Kravis graduated from Claremont-McKenna College in California, majoring in economics. After college he got a job at the Madison Fund, a closed-end mutual fund in New York. While working at the Madison Fund he attended Columbia University, where he earned an MBA in 1969. After graduation, Kravis joined the investment banking firm Bear Stearns, where his cousin George R. Roberts was also employed. Both Kravis and Roberts worked for corporate finance manager Jerome Kohlberg, Jr, who taught them what he called 'bootstrap' acquisitions. The goal of this type of investment finance was to help the management of undervalued small companies, or undervalued operations within larger companies, to borrow the capital to buy the business for themselves. Although Kohlberg felt there were great opportunities for this type of financing, Bear Stearns would not appropriate funds for these projects, and in 1976 he and his two associates resigned to form Kohlberg Kravis Roberts and Company (KKR).

The leveraged buyout structure developed by KKR involved forming a limited partnership, often with company management, to acquire the equity in a publicly traded company and take it private. KKR usually contributed 10 per cent of the buyout price from its own funds, and borrowed the balance from investors by issuing so-called 'junk bonds', a type of debt issue initially developed by Michael Milken at the investment bank Drexel Burnham Lambert. Once KKR took control of the firm, it tried to streamline the company through layoffs, and/or by disposing of assets or unprofitable subsidiaries. While most leveraged buyouts were intended to help existing management control the firm as a private corporation, in some instances KKR made a company private long enough to make it lean and profitable before offering its stock to the public again. KKR's transactions helped dismantle many conglomerate businesses, and the profits they generated became part of the high-flying investment banking community culture of the 1980s.

Initially, nearly all KKR transactions were made on a friendly basis with the cooperation of the management. In 1986, however, the firm departed from its role as 'white knight' when it intervened in a struggle over Beatrice Companies, a conglomerate based on a food-processing business. KKR outbid the other competitors, offered the management generous retirement packages and proceeded to sell off most of the subsidiaries. While this acquisition was not exactly hostile, it was aggressive, and this approach became known as the 'bear hug' acquisition. Although KKR made large profits from this deal, Kohlberg was not comfortable with making these types of acquisitions. When KKR became involved in the 1987 acquisition of Owens-Illinois, which involved the same approach as used with Beatrice, Kohlberg resigned from the firm.

The most famous KKR leveraged buyout was the 1988 five-week bidding war to control RJR Nabisco. This giant tobacco and food conglomerate owned some of the most recognizable brands in the world, and the takeover battle received significant media attention. Ultimately, Kravis won control of the company by bidding more than $25 billion, an amount nearly double the previous record price of a commercial enterprise.

Since its inception, KKR has acquired more than forty-five companies and spent more than $73 billion. KKR was the first to take a major company listed on the New York Stock Exchange private in a leveraged buyout, led the first billion-dollar buyout, and was responsible for the creation of the public tender offer.

BIBLIOGRAPHY
Bartlett, S. (1991) *The Money Machine: How KKR Manufactured Power and Profits*, New York: Warner Books.
Gross, D. (1996) *Forbes Greatest Business Stories of All Time*, New York: John Wiley and Sons.

DM

KROC, Raymond Albert (1902–84)

Ray Kroc was born in Oak Park near Chicago, Illinois on 5 October 1902 and died in San Diego on 14 January 1984. His father was a long-time employee of the Western Union company. After a brief formal education, he went to work at his uncle's drugstore soda fountain, preparing and dispensing soft drinks. Having a distinctly entrepreneurial nature, he was soon in business for himself, selling sheet music as well as harmonicas and ukuleles.

During the First World War Kroc served briefly with the US Army, where he shared a barracks with future cartoonist and leisure park promoter Walt DISNEY. After the war, he went back to sales work, but also worked part-time as a pianist, including a stint playing in a bordello (Kroc 1977: 19–21). After a

short interlude selling real estate during the Florida land boom, Kroc found a long-term vocation as a paper-cup salesman with the Lily Cup company, where he developed a nationwide network of soda fountain and restaurant customers. In the mid-1930s Kroc took on sales for the 'Multi-Mixer', a blender that could simultaneously prepare five milkshakes, which he sold to restaurants all over the United States. This work brought Kroc into contact with the nascent fast-food industry through sales to companies such as Dairy Queen and Tastee-Freeze.

By the late 1940s sales of the 'Multi-Mixers' had begun to taper off and Kroc was on the lookout for another business opportunity. Curious to discover how a small restaurant chain in southern California had become his biggest 'Multi-Mixer' customer, he went to meet its owners, the brothers Maurice and Richard McDonald. This visit was a Damascene experience. Kroc was astonished with the McDonald's restaurant operation, which he considered an epitome of efficiency, simplicity and cleanliness. As he recalled later, 'I felt like some latter day Newton who'd just had an Idaho potato caromed off his head' (Kroc 1977: 66). What impressed him most was the extent to which the McDonald brothers were able to streamline their food preparation system.

In this system, food preparation jobs had been broken down into simple repetitive steps easily taught to unskilled labour, creating a fast-moving assembly line operation. The menu had been strictly limited to hamburgers, french fries, milkshakes and soft drinks. Food was delivered in disposable paper wrappers, and customers served themselves. Combining this system with low prices, the McDonald restaurants generated huge volumes, far out of proportion to their actual size (Love 1986: 66).

Kroc gave careful thought to what he had seen. With the right kind of management, the prospects for this business seemed limitless and 'visions of McDonalds restaurants dotting cross-roads all over the country paraded through my brain' (Kroc 1977: 9). He soon convinced the McDonald brothers to grant him a licensing agreement and, at the age of fifty-two, set off to spread McDonald's restaurants throughout the country. The first of Kroc's outlets was opened in Des Plaines, Illinois during 1956 and, despite a field crowded with competitors, many more soon mushroomed around the United States and then abroad. Kroc kept the McDonald brothers' architectural concept of the 'Golden Arches', which soon became a ubiquitous sight across both American and foreign landscapes. By 1999 there were more than 28,000 outlets worldwide.

One important competitive advantage which Kroc had over his rivals was the fact that his restaurants stressed a wholesome family atmosphere. Unlike other fast food outlets, McDonalds banned pay phones, juke boxes and vending machines. Not only did this make for a more pleasant environment, but it also removed incentives for customers to linger any longer than necessary (Fishwick 1986: 41). A key factor in the chain's ability to generate repeat business rested in its overall reputation, rather than the quality of any single outlet or operator. The aim was to ensure that, no matter what McDonald's restaurant one entered, the food would look and taste the same as that in all the others. This was accomplished by a continuing programme of education and a steady review of operator performance. To reinforce this, Kroc created 'Hamburger University', a special training school for his managers.

The McDonald's restaurant chain has its critics, including those who question the nutritional value of its food. These critics received much publicity in London during the so-called 'McLibel' trial that lasted from 1994 to 1997. Nor did Kroc himself escape political controversy. Holding decidedly conservative political views, he donated $250,000 to Richard Nixon's election campaign in 1972. This led to accusations that he was trying to influence the Federal Price Commission regarding the cost of a 'Big Mac' hamburger. Towards the end of his career, Kroc created his own foundation in order to devote some of his considerable private fortune to philanthropy. He also branched off into professional sports, purchasing the San Diego Padres baseball team in 1974.

BIBLIOGRAPHY

Boas, M. and Chain, S. (1976) Big Mac: The Unauthorized Story of McDonald's, New York: E.P. Dutton.

Fishwick, M. (ed.) (1986) Ronald Revisited: The World of Ronald McDonald, Bowling Green, OH: Bowling Green University Popular Press.

Kroc, R. (1977) Grinding it Out: The Making of MacDonald's, Chicago: Henry Regney Co.

Love, J.F. (1986) McDonald's: Behind the Arches, New York: Bantam Books.

Ritzer, G. (1993) The McDonaldization of Society, Thousand Oaks, CA: Pine Forge Press.

Vidal, J. (1997) McLibel. Burger Culture on Trial, London: Macmillan.

SK

KUHN, Thomas Samuel (1922–96)

Thomas Samuel Kuhn was born in Cincinatti, Ohio on 18 July 1922, the son of Samuel Kuhn, an industrial engineer, and his wife Minette. He died of cancer in Cambridge, Massachusetts on 17 June 1996. He married Kathryn Muhs in 1948 (they divorced in 1978), and they had three children; he later married Jehane Burns in 1982. After taking his bachelor's degree in physics from Harvard University in 1943, Kuhn worked with the US Office of Scientific Research and Development from 1943 to 1945, returning to Harvard to take his master's degree in 1946 and his Ph.D. in 1949. He was a junior fellow at Harvard (1948–51), and then instructor and assistant professor of general education and the history of science from 1951 to 1956. He then went to the University of California at Berkeley as an associate professor of history and philosophy, being made professor of the history of science in 1961. From 1964 to 1979 Kuhn was professor of the history of science at Princeton University, and from 1979 to 1983 he was professor of philosophy and the history of science at the Massachusetts Institute of Technology, retiring as professor emeritus from 1984 until his death.

Although he initially trained as a physicist, Kuhn became interested in the history of science from an early date. His first work in this field, *The Copernican Revolution* (1957), described the change in Western scientific thinking that resulted from the changing views of astronomy and cosmology that followed Copernicus's work. Following on from this, Kuhn began to examine how scientific thinking evolves and moves forward in the light of new discoveries. The result was *The Structure of Scientific Revolutions* (1962), a revolutionary work in both the history and philosophy of science, and the book which introduced the word 'paradigm' to contemporary thinking.

According to Kuhn's study, fields of scientific thought begin with a period of competition between rival schools and theories, each of which has its own view of how the world (or the universe, etc.) works. Gradually the schools are either eliminated as their positions are proved unsound or begin to converge towards a so-called 'exemplary solution', which all parties agree is an acceptable model of how their discipline functions (Einstein's theory of relativity is one such exemplary solution). The scientific research and thought which is practised in accordance with the model solution Kuhn terms 'normal science'; the overall picture including exemplary solution and the normal science which revolves around it is the 'paradigm' or dominant mode of thought on the subject at hand (arguments about the exact definition continue, and Kuhn himself uses the term in a number of different senses). However, no exemplary solution is perfect, and anomalies in the paradigm remain which researchers come in time to explore. Eventually, one or more of these anomalies reaches a point of significance, when it effectively disproves the exemplary solution and renders the paradigm null. At this point, new schools of thought emerge and the process repeats itself.

Variants of paradigm thinking are found in most intellectual disciplines today, including business and management; many writers, for example, represent the information revolution and the trend towards e-commerce as the beginning of a new 'paradigm', while others regard the development of scientific management at the beginning of the twentieth century as paradigmatic in nature. Whether these shifts conform to Kuhn's basic concept of paradigm is not at all clear, but to some extent this is irrelevant. Kuhn's real contribution to business thinking has been to make managers and researchers alike aware of the potential transience of all things: markets, customers, forms of organization, legal frameworks, financial instruments and so on. Kuhn paints a dynamic picture of historical development which can be applied just as easily to business and management as to science. Most managers are familiar with the word 'paradigm', but are less certain of how to recognize one. The chief danger inherent in applying paradigm theory to business lies in too eagerly anticipating the next paradigm and perhaps 'jumping the gun'; the rise and fall of so-called 'dotcom' companies in 1999–2000 may be an example of searching too hard for a paradigm that has not yet arrived. A new appreciation of what Kuhn really meant might be useful in helping businesses forecast when and how new trends develop, thus separating some of the signals from some of the noise.

BIBLIOGRAPHY

Kuhn, T.S. (1957) *The Copernican Revolution: Planetary Astronomy in the Development of Western Thought*, Cambridge, MA: Harvard University Press.

Kuhn, T.S. (1962) *The Structure of Scientific Revolutions*, Chicago: University of Chicago Press.

MLW

L

LAND, Edwin Herbert (1909–91)

Edwin Land was born in Bridgeport, Connecticut on 7 May 1909, the son of a Russian immigrant, Harry Land, and his wife Matha. He died in Cambridge, Massachusetts on 1 March 1991. He married Helen 'Terre' Maislen in 1929; they had two daughters. The Land family name was originally Solomonovich; the name 'Land' stems from the arrival of the family at Ellis Island in 1880, who misunderstood the immigration officer who asked them their names and told him they had just 'landed'. Land, who as a boy was nicknamed 'Din' by his sister and went on to use this name for the rest of his life, grew up in Connecticut, where his father ran a thriving scrap metal business. As a small boy he became fascinated with optics, particularly after reading one of the leading books on the subject, Robert W. Wood's *Physical Optics*, which had been published in 1905. Land went to Harvard University in 1926 to study physics, already experimenting with stereoscopes and the polarization of light. At Harvard, according to McElheny (1998), Land also read Oswald Spengler's *The Decline of the West* and was inspired by the latter's vision of a future dominated by technology and engineers.

In 1928, while still an undergraduate, Land borrowed money from his father to set up a laboratory, and in 1929 filed a patent application for a polarizer. In 1932 he set up a business in partnership with a Harvard graduate, George B. Wheelwright III, to manufacture polarizers for two applications: to be applied to car windscreens so as to diffuse the dazzling beams of oncoming headlights during night driving, and for the making and viewing of three-dimensional cinema films. The former market never took off, the car manufacturers of the day deciding that the resulting safety benefits would not be worth the cost of installing polarized windscreens; 3D films, despite a brief period of popularity, never really caught on. However, many other applications were developed from the original technology. By the end of the 1930s there was a burgeoning market for polarizing sunglasses, and Land also developed devices such as the vectograph, for viewing three-dimensional photos such as could be taken from the air by reconnaissance aircraft, which was widely adopted by the US Army during the Second World War.

Following the war, Land's Polaroid Corporation led the way in the development of colour photography, but a chance conversation with his daughter led him on to his next major innovation – instant photography. By 1947 Land had a working model, but picture quality was far too poor to be marketable. Some years were to pass before first black-and-white and then colour instant cameras were perfected. It was not until 1972 that the famous Polaroid SX-70 camera came on the market.

Land was also involved in national scientific and defence work, and in the 1950s played a major role in the development of the high-altitude reconnaissance aircraft, the U-2. His work in such high-profile fields as 3D cinema and instant cameras made him something of a celebrity figure: tall and darkly handsome, with a distinct facial resemblance to Cary Grant, he became an apostle of science to the American public, who hailed him as a hero. Within Polaroid, however, dissatisfaction with Land's management style was rising; there were product quality and cost problems with the SX-70 which Land did not appear to be addressing. In 1980 a boardroom coup led by his old friend and lawyer Julius Silver and non-executive directors including Ken OLSEN forced Land to step down as chief executive officer and president; by 1985 he had sold his last remaining shares in Polaroid and severed all connections with the company, devoting himself to research for the remaining years of his life.

Land had a number of well-documented failings as a manager, including lack of attention to costs and a reluctance to abandon a project even when it had little or no chance of success. He did, however, have a strong vision of the role of science, technology and knowledge in making business enterprises successful, and it was this vision that carried him and Polaroid through the years of growth from the 1930s to the 1960s. Land conceived of the ideal business of the future being what he called a 'science-based corporation', in which the core of the corporation was a team of researchers whose sole function was to generate knowledge and potential new products. The exploitation of these products would then be carried out by management teams centred around each product line. Polaroid itself was structured along these lines, and it is possible that this model was the partial inspiration for Ken Olsen's 'matrix organization' model, which he developed at Digital Equipment Corporation (DEC) in the 1950s. But, as at DEC, the model only worked as long as rapid growth and high profits were being generated; in times of slow growth, the costs of maintaining the scientific core, rather than the benefits to be expected from research, were what tended to obsess directors (Olsen was removed from presidency of DEC in very similar circumstances in 1991).

But although the specific model may have had its functional problems, the core concept of science generating knowledge which could be turned into commercial advantage has been and remains a very powerful one, and has played a major part in the development of new high-technology industries and sectors around the world in the 1990s and up to the time of writing. Land was not just a prophet of a new age of scientific commerce, he was also an inventor and entrepreneur who played a leading role in bringing that age about.

BIBLIOGRAPHY

McElheny, V.K. (1998) *Insisting on the Impossible*, New York: Perseus.

MLW

LAWRENCE, Paul Roger (1922–)

Paul Roger Lawrence was born in Rochelle, Illinois on 26 April 1922, the son of Howard and Clara Lawrence. The family later moved to Grand Rapids Michigan, where Lawrence attended Grand Rapids Junior College from 1939 to 1941; he received his AB from Albion College in 1943. Following service as a lieutenant in the US Navy from 1943 to 1946, Lawrence worked for a time on the assembly line at an automobile parts manufacturing plant to gather experience of working life on the factory floor, and then went to Harvard Business School, where he took his MBA in 1947. He went on to do a doctorate in organization studies under the tutelage of Professor Fritz ROETHLISBERGER, completing this in 1950. He was appointed assistant professor at Harvard in 1951, associate professor in 1956 and professor in 1961; in late 1967 he succeeded Roethlisberger as Wallace Brett Donham Professor of Organization Behaviour, which post he held until he retired in 1991.

Lawrence married Martha Stiles in 1948; they have two children.

Lawrence was initially motivated to study human relations. Growing up in Michigan, he saw at first hand much of the damaging labour unrest in that state's automotive plants and believed it ought to be possible to find a solution to these problems. Interest in this subject, however, took him the relatively short step into the field of organization behaviour, as he began probing the reasons behind why people in organizations behave as they do and, subsequently, how organizations are structured and function.

As a researcher, Lawrence's tastes have been quite catholic, ranging from motivation and control, intra-organization integration, change management, governance and rejuvenation of mature firms and sectors. He has rarely worked alone, and seems to prefer the stimulus of working with colleagues, particularly those in different disciplines; his collaborators have included figures as diverse as John KOTTER and Amitai ETZIONI. His most fruitful and memorable collaboration, however, has been with his Harvard colleague Jay LORSCH. In the late 1960s and early 1970s Lawrence and Lorsch published several path-breaking works, notably *Organization and Environment* (1967).

In *Organization and Environment*, Lawrence and Lorsch attacked the idea that there was one best form of organization which could be suited to all businesses across all industries and environments. Their study of high-performing firms revealed that successful businesses used a variety of organizational forms. Variances could depend on the industrial/business sector in which the firm was operating, the necessary relationships between departments and functions of the firm, the personalities and relationships between top managers, or any of a number of other variables. In an aspect of their study which has since received much attention (for example, Mallory 1998), they described the methods of organizational integration used by high-performing firms in different sectors, and found

that there were both similarities and differences. That is, some methods (paper systems, direct contact between managers, formal reporting along hierarchical lines) were common to all the firms studied, but some employed additional elements, such as temporary integrating teams or permanent departments whose prime function was to manage integration. As all the firms studied were performing equally well, Lawrence and Lorsch concluded that all the approaches studied could be seen to be equally valid, given the circumstances in which they were employed.

The result was their development of what is generally known as 'contingency theory', which suggests that the nature of the organization will vary depending on the task which the organization is trying to perform. Organizations, they suggest, are built along two guiding principles: the division of the organization into specialist departments and teams, each with its own task to perform, and the integration of these subunits into an organizational whole which is focused on the organization's central task or goal. This approach, which resembles in some respects the division and recombination of labour discussed by BURNS, means that different combinations may be assembled depending on (1) the diversity of the organization and the number of tasks and subtasks it must accomplish, and (2) the level of integration required between each function or department. A variety of different integration modalities may be employed to achieve goals between these functions and departments, depending on their own tasks and working styles.

In his later work with other collaborators, Lawrence has carried some of these ideas forward. He has continued to examine the components of organization and how these may be combined for best effectiveness. In Davis and Lawrence (1983), for example, the authors advocate the use of matrix organizations in which elements may be reconfigured and recombined according to need. In Lawrence and Kotter (1975), the authors studied the workings of the office of mayor in large American cities, looking at four key variables: the mayors' personalities, their agendas, their ability to mobilize crucial resources to meet those agendas, and the cities' organizational and socioeconomic traits. They developed what they call 'co-alignment theory', showing that urban government works best when all four factors are aligned. Lawrence's work, with Lorsch and subsequently, should be counted alongside that of writers such as Burns, CHANDLER, and MILES and SNOW, all of whom argue from various perspectives that organizational structure should be aligned with the organization's needs and goals rather than designed according to preset principles.

BIBLIOGRAPHY

Davis, S.M. and Lawrence, P.R. (1983) *Matrix*, New York: Basic Books.

Lawrence, P.R. and Dalton, G.W. (1971) *Motivation and Control in Organizations*, Homewood, IL: Irwin.

Lawrence, P.R and Dyer, D. (1983) *Renewing American Industry*, New York: The Free Press.

Lawrence, P.R. and Etzioni, A. (1991) *Socio-Economics: Toward a New Synthesis*, Armonk, NY: M.E. Sharpe.

Lawrence, P.R. and Glover, J.D. (1960) *A Case Study of High Level Administration in a Large Organization: The Office of the Assistant Secretary of the Air Force (Management) 1947–1952*, Cambridge, MA: Harvard Graduate School of Business Administration, Division of Research.

Lawrence, P.R. and Kotter, J. (1975) *Mayors in Action: Five Approaches to Urban Governance*, New York: John Wiley.

Lawrence, P.R. and Lorsch, J. (1967) *Organization and Environment: Managing Differentiation and Integration*, Cambridge, MA: Harvard University Press.

Lawrence, P.R. and Lorsch, J. (1969) *Developing Organizations: Diagnosis and Action*, Reading, MA: Addison-Wesley.

—— (ed.) (1972) *Organization Planning: Cases and Concepts*, Homewood, IL: Irwin.

Lawrence, P.R. and Ronken, H.O. (1952) *Administering Changes: A Case Study of Human Relations in a Factory*, Cambridge, MA: Harvard Graduate School of Business Administration, Division of Research.

Lawrence, P.R. and Vlachoutsicos, C.A. (1990) *Behind the Factory Walls: Decision Making in Soviet and US Enterprises*, Cambridge, MA: Harvard Business School Press.

Lawrence, P.R., Lane, H.W. and Beddows, R.G. (1981) *Managing Large Research and Development Programs*, Albany, NY: State University of New York Press.

Lorsch, J. and Lawrence, P.R. (1970) *Studies in Organizational Design*, Homewood, IL: Irwin.

Mallory, G. (1998) ' Lawrence, Paul Roger and Lorsch, Jay William', in M. Warner (ed.), *IEBM Handbook of Management Thinking*, London: International Thomson Business Press, 376–9.

MLW

LEE, Ivy Ledbetter (1877–1934)

Ivy Ledbetter Lee was born in Cedartown, Georgia on 16 July 1877, the son of the Reverend James Lee, a Methodist minister, and his wife Emma. He died of a brain tumour in New York on 9 November. He attended Emory College and then Princeton University, graduating with an AB from the latter in 1898, and went on briefly to attend Harvard Law School. Lee showed an early talent for writing, and in part paid his way through university by writing for Princeton student newspaper; near the end of his degree his work was picked up by several New York newspapers as well. In 1899 he moved to New York and found a job as a reporter with the *Morning Journal*; he later went on to work for the New York *Sun* and then for Joseph PULITZER at the New York *World*; his time at the *World* coincided with that of Herbert CASSON.

During Lee's period at the *World* he became sympathetic to the problems of large corporations, in an atmosphere where public opinion was increasingly turning against them; other journalists such as Ida TARBELL were actively criticizing large businesses and their impact on American society. Lee felt that businesses needed to tell their own side of the story, and conceived of a commercial opportunity for himself in doing so. In 1903 he left the *World* and became publicity manager for the Democratic Party's candidate for mayor of New York, and in 1904 established his own business as a public relations consultant, doing more publicity work for the Democratic Party and also for a firm of New York stockbrokers.

In 1912 Lee took on his first major client, the Pennsylvania Railroad. His work with them was spectacularly successful, and he managed not only to obtain highly favourable coverage for the company on several occasions, but also to mitigate the worst public relations effects of problems and accidents such as train crashes. In 1915 he met John D. ROCKEFELLER and was appointed the latter's public relations officer; other clients acquired around this time included Daniel GUGGENHEIM and Walter CHRYSLER. During the First World War Lee worked without fee to handle publicity for the American Red Cross, and during the 1920s did unpaid work for a number of other charities. In the late 1920s he sparked controversy by visiting the Soviet Union and reporting in highly favourable terms on what he found there; he was then accused of being a secret agent for the Soviet government. He was the founding father of modern public relations.

BIBLIOGRAPHY

Lee, I. (1925) *Publicity: Some of the Things It Is and Is Not*, New York: Industries Publishing Company.
——— (1929) *The Press Today*, New York, n.p.

LEVITT, Theodore (1925–)

Theodore Levitt was born in the United States in 1925 and educated at Antioch College (AB, 1949) and Ohio State University (Ph.D. in economics, 1951). After a period as assistant professor of economics at the University of North Dakota, he joined the faculty of Harvard Business School in 1949, receiving a professorship in 1964 and retiring in 1990.

As professor of marketing at Harvard, Levitt wrote a number of highly influential articles and books; he was at one time the best-known marketing academic in the United States, and continues to be widely referred to. His most famous work remains the article 'Marketing Myopia' which appeared in *Harvard Business Review* in 1960. Here Levitt describes how companies which fail to focus on their customers are doomed to eventual extinction. The American railroad industry, for example, declined because the railway companies perceived themselves as being in the railroad business. They failed to realize that their customers perceived them as being in the transportation business; and when other competing forms of transportation proved quicker and cheaper, customers moved to them. Levitt's lesson is that companies should always try to find out how their customers perceive them, and adapt according to customer needs and demands.

In this article and in subsequent articles and books, notably *Innovation in Marketing* (1962), Levitt repeated his call for customer focus, an issue that was subsequently taken up and developed by Philip KOTLER. Together, Levitt in the 1960s and Kotler in the 1970s changed management perceptions of marketing from a peripheral activity to a core activity within all businesses. Levitt was also influential in his discussion of customers as assets, and wrote extensively on globalization, which he saw as having a homogenizing effect on market; he believed that in time there were would be a global convergence of markets with national and cultural characteristics being gradually ironed out under the impact of global marketing and brands.

BIBLIOGRAPHY

Levitt, T. (1960) 'Marketing Myopia', *Harvard Business Review* (July–August): 45–56.

——— (1962) *Innovation in Marketing: New Perspectives for Profit and Growth*, New York: McGraw-Hill.

——— (1983) *The Marketing Imagination*, New York: The Free Press.

MLW

LEWIN, Kurt (1890–1947)

Kurt Lewin was born in Moligno, Germany (now in Poland) on 9 September 1890, the son of Leopold Lewin, a shopkeeper, and his wife Recha. He died of a heart attack on 11 February 1947 in Newtonville, Massachusetts. He married Maria Landsberg in 1917; they divorced in 1928 and he married Gertrud Weiss later that same year. There were two children from each marriage. Lewin was educated at the Berlin Gymnasium, graduating in 1909, and studied at the Universities of Freiburg and Munich before going on to study philosophy at the University of Berlin under Ernst Cassirer. Here he became interested in psychology, and on completing his degree enrolled at the Berlin Psychological Institute, where he completed his Ph.D. in 1916. He then joined the German army and was commissioned as a lieutenant, serving on the Western Front and winning the Iron Cross for valour.

Returning the to the Psychological Institute after the war, he joined the faculty as a *privatdozent*. Here he came under the influence of the *Gestalt* psychologists Max Wertheimer and Wolfgang Köhler, and won an international reputation for his work on behaviour and motivation. In 1929 he was invited to lecture at the International Congress of Psychology at Yale University, and subsequently lectured in Tokyo and Moscow. In 1933, following the election of Adolf Hitler as chancellor of Germany, Lewin resigned from the institute and emigrated to the United States, where he found a post as acting professor of education in the school of home economics at Cornell University. In 1935 he joined the State University of Iowa as professor of child psychology. In 1944 he moved to the Massachusetts Institute of Technology (MIT), where he founded the Research Center for Group Dynamics, the first research institute with the specific goal of examining the behaviour of groups. He worked on developing the research programmes of this centre up until the time of his death.

Lewin's early work in Germany focused on individual motivation. On moving to the United States, however, he became more interested in the behaviour of groups, initially of children but later of adults in the context of formal organizations and the workplace. His focus through the 1940s was on group decision making and the management of change. He was particularly interested in systematizing group behaviour and developing schema whereby such behaviour could be understood. In a late piece of work (Lewin 1954) he developed a three-stage theory of change. The first stage he calls 'unfreezing', in which previously held beliefs, patterns of behaviour, etc. are dissolved or removed preparatory to the actual process of change. The second stage, 'moving', is the transition from one state to another. The third stage, 'freezing', is the validation and embedding of the new state or mode of behaviour. Lewin also conducted a number of studies into the motivation for change, and concluded that personal success depends on the ability of people to set their own levels of aspiration at a realistic level: too high and the person will fail to meet his or her goals and become discouraged, too low and underachievement will be the result.

Lewin's studies of group dynamics not only led to greater understanding of how people interact and behave in groups but also of how leaders emerge and exert authority over others.

Among his work at MIT was the development of the theory of what he called 'action research'. This again involves a three-stage process. First, the researcher plans his or her research, determining what knowledge is needed at each stage of the project. Second, the researcher executes the programme, gathering data. Third, the researcher evaluates the data and feeds this back into the next stage of the planning process. This cyclical approach to learning had a later influence on the development of 'action science' by Chris ARGYRIS and Donald SCHÖN.

One of the most influential psychologists of the twentieth century, Lewin has had a considerable impact on the study of group and organizational dynamics, decision making and leadership. His work remains at the foundation of much later thinking and theorizing on these and other subjects.

BIBLIOGRAPHY

Cattell, J.M., Cattell, J. and Ross, E.E. (1941) *Leaders in Education*, 2nd edn, Lancaster, PA: The Science Press.

Lewin, K. (1935) *A Dynamic Theory of Personality*, New York: McGraw-Hill.

Lewin, K. (1936) *Principles of Topological Psychology*, trans. F. Heider and G.H. Heider, New York: Mc-Graw Hill.

——— (1954) 'Studies in Group Decision', in D. Cartwright and A. Zander (eds), *Group Dynamics: Research and Theory*, London: Tavistock.

Marrow, A.J. (1969) *Practical Theorist: The Life and Work of Kurt Lewin* New york: Teachers' College Press.

MLW

LIKERT, Rensis (1903–81)

Rensis Likert was born in Cheyenne, Wyoming on 5 August 1903 and died in Ann Arbor, Michigan on 3 September 1981. He attended the University of Michigan and graduated with an AB degree in economics and sociology in 1922. He later studied psychology at Columbia University and received his Ph.D. in 1932. As a student at the University of Michigan, Likert met Jane Gibson, whom he later married during his years at Columbia. They had two daughters, Elizabeth and Patricia. In addition to being partners in marriage, Rensis and Jane Likert were professional colleagues until the death of Rensis in 1981.

Likert taught in the department of psychology at New York University from 1930 to 1935 (Campbell 1988). He became director of research for the Life Insurance Agency Management Association in Hartford, Connecticut in 1935. While at the Life Insurance Agency Management Association, he started a programme of research on the effectiveness of different styles of supervision. In 1939 he was appointed director of the Division of Program Surveys in the Bureau of Agricultural Economics of the US Department of Agriculture in Washington, DC. In 1946 the University of Michigan requested that Likert set up an interdisciplinary institute for research in the social sciences. He founded and then directed the Institute for Social Research until he retired in 1970. After retirement, Likert worked as a private consultant on problems of organization and management, and continued his research on the comparative effectiveness of participative management until his death (Campbell 1988).

The foundations for Likert's career as a psychologist and statistician were laid during his years in graduate school, when he became interested in the newly emerging field of social psychology (Campbell 1988). He had a vision for survey research which he first expressed in his dissertation, *A Technique For The Measurement of Attitudes* (1932). He sought to develop procedures and methods for studying people's attitudes and the variables that influence them. One product of this study was the creation of what would become the most widely used scale for attitude measurement, the Likert scale. Structurally, this attitude scale is anchored by two extremes, ranging from favourable to unfavourable, with a neutral midpoint for each statement (Likert 1932). The scale's values range from 1 to 5 or 7; the mid-point of the scale is reserved to reflect an undecided position. Likert-scale responses are tabulated and a statistical procedure is applied to determine the relative significance of each attitudinal statement.

As noted above, Likert moved to Washington, DC in 1939. The US Department of Agriculture had established the Division of Program Surveys to provide a conduit through which farmers and other citizens could communicate to the department their experiences with the various federal programmes. Existing procedures of information gathering were crude and in need of improvement. Likert, along with Morris H. Hansen and others from the Department of Agriculture, the Bureau of the Census and Iowa State University, collaborated to develop a method for sampling households and individuals based on the identification and listing of small units of land throughout the country. Likert's underlying theory for this procedure, and the specific selection techniques his team developed, provided the basis for what later became known as probability sampling.

Early in his tenure at the Division of Program Surveys, Likert realized that more reliable methods for obtaining information from individual respondents were required. The standard practice of the day among government agencies was to use a reporting form that specified only the types of information desired; interviewers were given free rein to ask whatever questions they thought best to obtain that information. This uncoordinated practice of interviewing was highly susceptible to interviewer bias. To avoid or reduce such bias, the Division of Program Surveys adopted formalized questionnaires that interviewers were instructed to follow without deviation. Likert also introduced the concept of open-ended questions as part of these interviews. In contrast to forced-choice questions which offer a limited set of

response options, this approach allows the respondent to answer the question in his or her own words. These and other interview techniques pioneered by Likert have since become standard practices for survey research (Campbell 1988).

In 1946 the University of Michigan extended and Likert accepted an offer to establish an interdisciplinary institute for research in the social sciences. Likert used this opportunity to found the Institute for Social Research (ISR). He directed the ISR until his retirement. Although the ISR was not the first such institute in the United States, its structure and interdisciplinary approach distinguished the ISR from those that preceded and followed it (Campbell 1988). To achieve cross-disciplinary involvement, the ISR was located administratively outside the established schools and departments of the University of Michigan. The members of the ISR's research staff held their primary appointments within the institute, rather than the teaching departments of the university. Financial support for the ISR came from grants and contracts, foundations, government agencies and private-profit and non-profit organizations.

Rensis Likert's role in establishing and guiding the ISR, particularly during its early formative years, was critical to its success. As the institute's representative for grant and contract proposals and negotiations, Likert's enthusiasm and powers of persuasion provided the ISR with a distinct advantage during a time of intense competition for research support. His unfailing optimism and his refusal to believe that any obstacle could possibly impede the growth and progress of the ISR inspired and encouraged his colleagues. His leadership of the ISR contributed immensely to its rapid growth. Within a few years of its founding, the ISR had become the largest university-based organization for research in the social sciences in the United States (Campbell 1988).

At the ISR, Likert built upon his earlier research into the problems of organizing human resources. Central to this effort was a focus on leadership. To Likert, leading the human component was the most important responsibility of managers because it set the stage for all of the remaining tasks. Under Likert's direction, the ISR initiated a series of empirical studies within a variety of organizations for the purpose of determining the types of organizational structuresand leadership principle that best contributed to high levels of productivity and job satisfaction, while simultaneously achieving low levels of absenteeism and turnover (Wren 1994).

This programme of research resulted in the identification of two distinct leadership orientations: (1) an employee orientation, in which the supervisor focused on the interpersonal relationships on the job; and (2) a production orientation, in which the supervisor stressed production and the technical aspects of the job. Moreover, an employee orientation, when combined with general rather than close supervision, was shown to produce higher levels of productivity, morale and group cohesion, and lower levels of worker turnover and anxiety. Supervisors achieved these favourable outcomes by showing concern for workers, building team spirit, and moving away from a close, production-centred leadership style, to a looser, employee-oriented and supportive leadership style (Wren 1994).

Building on this early research, Likert refined his ideas into his participative management theory (Likert 1961). Using funds provided by the Office of Naval Research, the initial research for this theory began in 1947. For the underlying theory and design of this study, Likert drew heavily on the research of associates such as Angus Campbell, Dorwin Cartwright, Daniel Katz, Robert L. Kahn, Stanley Seashore and Floyd Mann (Campbell 1988). The impetus for Likert's theory of participative management stemmed from his recognition that a fundamental change was taking place in Western societies. A perception of greater freedom resulted in a basic change in how employees expected to be treated; such expectations became manifest in higher levels of involvement, initiative, and autonomy (Likert 1961). He also realized that

the need for cooperation and participation in managing modern organizations was greater than was the case in earlier days when technologies had been simple and the head of the organization had possessed much of the requisite technical knowledge. Likert was especially interested in identifying the leadership characteristics that distinguish highly effective mangers from their less effective counterparts. Ultimately, this search led to his conclusion that there are important differences in the basic assumptions that such managers make about the best ways to manage people (Campbell 1988).

Likert's ideas regarding participative management culminated in the publication of *The Human Organization: Its Management and Value* (1967). While these ideas were derived primarily from the problems and successful practices Likert observed in business enterprises, he believed that other institutions, such as schools, labour unions, and professional and voluntary organizations, would have little difficulty in applying the general principles of his theory. Drawing on his earlier research, Likert distinguished between four types of leader behaviour: (1) System 1, 'exploitative authoritative'; (2) System 2, 'benevolent authoritative'; (3) System 3, 'consultative'; and (4) System 4, 'participative group'. Likert conceptualized System 4 as the embodiment of the participative management approaches he observed being used by the most effective managers. Three key concepts provide the foundation for System 4 management: (1) the principle of supportive relationships; (2) group methods of supervision and decision making; and (3) the establishment of high-performance goals by the organization (Wren 1994).

To fulfil the principle of supportive relationships, the leader must ensure that relations among organizational members are supportive and based upon feelings of trust, respect and personal worth. Such support results in a high degree of group loyalty, as well as favourable attitudes and trust among peers, superiors and subordinates. The second concept involves group decision making and a form of interlocking group structure. Each group is linked to the rest of the organization by persons who serve as 'linking pins', due to their membership in more than one group. Positive effects attributed to this structure include high levels of reciprocal and coordinated influence, efficient and effective communication, and the distribution of relevant information needed for each decision and action to appropriate locations in the organization. The third concept is reflected in the high-performance expectations expressed by System 4 managers, as well as all work group members. Employees are integrally involved in setting the challenging goals required for satisfaction of their achievement needs. Moreover, participation is used to establish organizational objectives that integrate the needs and desires of all organizational members with those of persons who are functionally related. Together, these three concepts of System 4 management combine to produce a highly effective social system for interaction, problem solving, mutual influence and organizational achievement.

Likert also contributed to the study and development of human asset accounting (Likert 1967). This approach enables managers to make reasonably accurate estimates of the current values of the human organization and customer goodwill. Likert believed that it would take from five to ten years and many millions of dollars to collect the data and to make the computations required before human asset accounting procedures could be fully developed. Determining the original investment in human assets was similar to assessing the original cost of a fixed asset. While this procedure was relatively simple, there remained the problem of estimating the current value of the human organization. Historical measures indicate the earning power of the human organization at the time the variables were measured, but the measurement of subsequent earnings may not be achieved until later. Likert warned of the danger of using only present earnings as an estimate of the value of human resources. This present value may be distorted when one considers that, at the same time that profits are high, the actual value of the human

asset may decline due to adverse events, such as increased employee turnover, and other dysfunctional outcomes. Likert suggested that the same basic concepts and methods employed in human asset accounting could be applied to estimate the value of customer goodwill.

In his last book, *New Ways of Managing Conflict* (1976), co-authored with his wife Jane, Likert proposed System 5, a more complex, sophisticated and effective system of management that he expected to emerge as the social sciences matured. In System 5, a reciprocal system of influence and participation would replace the hierarchy of authority, causing the organization chart to look more like a fishnet than a pyramid. When conflict arose, overlapping group memberships ('link pins') would facilitate the cooperation required to reach a consensus solution. Employees would be known as 'associates' (formal organizational titles would be eliminated), and leadership would arise from feelings of 'oneness' and a 'shared sense of purpose' (Wren 1994).

As a colleague, Likert exhibited a warmth towards others and an infectious enthusiasm for his work that permeated his writings. His style of leadership was consistent with what he preached: his office and his home were always open, and all were welcome. Moreover, as he espoused in his theory of participative leadership, Likert ensured that the feedback he directed towards others was always positive and constructive (Kahn 2000).

BIBLIOGRAPHY

Campbell, A. (ed.) (1988) *International Encyclopedia of the Social Sciences, Biographical Supplement*, New York: The Free Press.

Kahn, R. (2000) Personal communication, 20 October.

Likert, R. (1932) *A Technique for the Measurement of Attitudes*, New York: McGraw-Hill.

—— (1961) *New Patterns of Management*, New York: McGraw-Hill.

—— (1967) *The Human Organization: Its*

Management and Value, New York: McGraw-Hill.

Likert, R. and Likert, J. (1976) *New Ways of Managing Conflict*, New York: McGraw-Hill.

Wren, D. (1994) *The Evolution of Management Thought*, 4th edn, New York: Wiley.

JCH

LINDBLOM, Charles Edward (1917–)

Charles Edward Lindblom was born in Turlock, California. He received his BA in economics and political science from Stanford University in 1937, and his Ph.D. from the University of Chicago in 1945. He came to the Institute for Social and Political Studies at Yale University in 1946, where he is currently Sterling Professor Emeritus in Economics and Political Science. During his career, he has received many honours and has been a fellow at such institutions as the Center for Advanced Study of Behavioral Science, the RAND Corporation and the Guggenheim Foundation. His major works include books such as *Politics, Economics and Welfare*, with Robert Dahl (1953), *A Strategy of Decision* with D. Braybrooke (1963), *The Intelligence of Democracy* (1965) and *Politics and Markets* (1966), as well as articles such as 'In Praise of Political Science' (1957), 'The Science of Muddling Through' (1959) and 'Still Muddling, Not Yet Through' (1979).

Throughout his work, Lindblom has been a consistent critic of rational choice theory; the 'rational comprehensive' approaches to decision making and planning. In the rational perspective, the decision makers are assumed to be able to rank their values, analyse all means of achieving desired ends, and then ultimately choose the outcome that maximizes outputs at lowest cost. As also argued in the behavioural approach

of Herbert SIMON and James G. MARCH (March and Simon 1958), Lindblom finds the rational model impractical and unrealistic, and argues that effective decision makers in the real world do not even attempt to approximate the idealized schema of rational choice. Instead, decision makers simplify their tasks in the process of finding satisficing solutions that lie close to existing policy or experience. A satisficing solution thus ends the search for alternatives, and the decision maker does not try to optimize or maximize through further search. In the end, Lindblom finds, decision makers, planners and administrators are much better off with such decisions than with results of the attempt to follow rational models of decision making.

At the centre of Lindblom's argument are the ideas of 'incrementalism' and 'partisan mutual adjustment'. The idea of incrementalism emphasizes that small steps are the way to progress. Decision makers and political administrators, Lindblom finds, will normally focus on only a limited range of options, due to their satisficing nature. Incrementalism dictates that this step-by-step process should build on the current situation and only represent modest departures from existing decision-making procedures. The idea of 'partisan mutual adjustment' emphasizes the advantages of a fragmented decision process, in which groups of decision makers adjust their conduct to each other's behaviour. Lindblom finds that these processes may be more 'rational' than attempts consciously to coordinate all action from a single planner. Both these ideas were present in 'The Science of Muddling Through' (1959), and were subsequently extended and revised.

In a later essay, Lindblom distinguished various sorts of 'incrementalism' (Lindblom 1979). He distinguishes first 'incremental politics' (the politics of change through small steps) from 'incremental analysis' (policy analysis reliant upon simplifying assumptions). He then proceeds to provide three different meanings of 'incremental analysis': 'simple incrementalism' (analysis that explores policy options which differs only incrementally from existing practice); 'disjointed incrementalism' (a particular decision strategy that invokes a specific set of simplifying assumptions); and 'strategic analysis' (any conscious strategy radically to simplify analysis of policy choices). 'Disjointed incrementalism' is, according to Lindblom, one form of 'strategic analysis', a form which invoked 'simple incrementalism' as a simplifying device.

The main argument for using 'strategic analysis' is that we can never fully comprehend the world in all its complexity and, hence, we can never fully analyse the complex problems and interactions that are necessary for optimal policy making. Lindblom argues that policy makers and decision makers should avoid seeking 'comprehensive' or 'synoptic' analysis, because by trying to accomplish an ideal which is unattainable, decision makers will 'fall into worse patterns of analysis and decision' than those who pursue 'the guiding ideal of strategic analysis' and 'knowingly and openly' muddle 'with some skill' (Lindblom 1979: 518).

Although present in all political systems, 'partisan mutual adjustment' is typical of decision processes in contemporary democracies. This is discussed in Lindblom's *The Intelligence of Democracy*. The main goal of this book is to 'undertake a systematic comparative analysis of centrality and partisan mutual adjustment among various kinds of political officials and leaders as competing methods for rational coordination of government decisions' (Lindblom 1965: 9). Coordination is defined as a set of incremental decisions (Lindblom 1959: 154), and partisan mutual adjustment is defined as the adaptive processes through which independent decision makers can coordinate independent decisions without anyone's coordinating them, without a dominant common purpose, and without rules that fully prescribe their relations to each other (Lindblom 1959: 3). Thus, interaction among participants will aid coordination in the absence of a central planner, and policy making becomes possible through partisan mutual adjustment. In this process, each decision maker acts according to his or her own goals and specialized interests, in an incremental way.

To Lindblom, incrementalism is also an empirical success story, and his views on incrementalism are now widely used in political science as a decision-making device. This is particularly so because incrementalism can support 'calculated, reasonable, rational, intelligence, wise – the exact term does not matter – policy making' (Lindblom 1959: 294). The reason for this is that partisan mutual adjustment motivates policy makers to pursue their own goals and hence to accept satisficing decisions (Lindblom 1959: 148). Another advantage of the sequential decision process is that it can adjust to change, and emerging problems and ideas. As Lindblom noted,

if decision making is remedial and serial, anticipated adverse consequences of any given policy can often be better dealt with if regarded as new and separate problems than if regarded as aspects of an existing problem. And unanticipated adverse consequences can often be better guarded against by waiting for their emergence than by often futile attempts to anticipate every contingency as required in synoptic problem solving.

(Lindblom 1959: 150–51)

With these and other ideas, Lindblom contributed not only to economics, but also to political science, sociology and management, the main ingredients in his work being economics and political science. Lindblom's skills exceed those of the domain of economics, and his work should be read as being truly interdisciplinary in spirit, linking economics to political science problems, and political science to management and problems of welfare. His aim is to contribute to the broad understanding of the science of human action.

BIBLIOGRAPHY

Braybrooke, D. and Lindblom, C.E. (1963) *A Strategy of Decision*, New York: The Free Press.
Dahl, R. and Lindblom, C.E. (1953) *Politics,*

Economics and Welfare, New York: Harper and Bros.

Lindblom, C.E. (1959) 'The Science of Muddling Through', *Public Administration Review* 19(Spring): 79–88.

—— (1965) *The Intelligence of Democracy*, New York: The Free Press.

—— (1966) *Politics and Markets: The World's Political Economic Systems*, New York: Basic Books.

Lindblom, C.E. (1979) 'Still Muddling, Not Yet Through', *Public Administration Review* 39: 517–26.

March, J.G. and Simon, H.A. (1958) *Organizations*, Oxford: Blackwell.

MA

LITTLE, Arthur Dehon (1863–1935)

Arthur Dehon Little was born in Boston on 15 December 1863, the son of an army officer, and died in Northeast Harbor, Maine on 1 August 1935. He displayed an early interest in chemistry: at the age of twelve he nearly blew up his parents' house, and at thirteen he built his first chemical laboratory. He was educated at Berkeley High School, New York City, and then at Massachusetts Institute of Technology (MIT), where he co-founded and edited the student newspaper. He had to leave MIT in 1884 without taking a degree, as his parents had run into financial problems, and took a job as a chemist with the Richmond Paper Company. In 1886 he and a partner, Roger Griffin, left to set up a chemical analysis and consulting firm, Griffin and Little, working primarily with firms in the paper industry; they also registered a number of patents, including one for rayon. The partnership ended when Griffin was killed in a laboratory accident in 1893.

On his own, Little made several attempts to set up industrial ventures during the period 1893–1905. He finally decided to go back to what he was good at, namely industrial research and consultancy. Founding the Arthur D. Little Company in Boston near the MIT campus – from this institution he hired most of his scientists and engineers – Little developed a business that began with industrial research but gradually encompassed product and process issues such as product development and plant design. The company was highly successful, attracting a range of blue chip clients including the US Forestry Service, the United Fruit Company, the Canadian Pacific Railway and General Motors, from whom Little's firm built a research laboratory. Later, marketing and environmental consultancy work was added to the portfolio, and Arthur D. Little became the world's first all-round management consultancy (as opposed to the specialist consultancy businesses established by the scientific management gurus).

Little was a strong believer in the links between research and progress: research was, he believed, the sole guarantee of continued profitability for companies and of growth for countries. A prolific writer and speaker, he did much to popularize science and persuade business leaders to make scientific research a priority. His most famous publicity event was in 1921, when he and his chemists actually made a silk purse from sows' ears. The ears boiled and rendered into glue, which was then chemically treated to make fibres; the fibres were then woven and sewn together to make the purse.

BIBLIOGRAPHY
Kahn, E.J. (1986) *The Problem Solvers: A History of Arthur D. Little, Inc*, Boston: Little, Brown.

LIVINGSTON, Robert (1654–1728)

Robert Livingston was born in Ancrum, Scotland on 13 December 1654 and died at his home near Albany, New York on 1 October 1728. His father was a Presbyterian minister, and the family spent a number of years in Rotterdam, forced out of Scotland by religious persecution. During this time Livingston learned the Dutch language, and also gained some commercial experience. In 1672 Livingston returned briefly to Scotland, and in 1673 he sailed to Massachusetts, where he established a business partnership with a local merchant. He moved inland to Albany, New York in 1674. Albany had only recently come under British control, and commerce remained in the hands of the Dutch community. Livingston's fluency in Dutch and his commercial acumen gave him a unique advantage as the only merchant who could negotiate with and build relationships with the Dutch merchants in their own language. He became fully integrated with the Dutch merchant community, and became particularly close to the prominent Van Rensselaer family; he married Alida van Rensselaer in 1679.

With wealth, Livingston also began to develop political power. He became a member of the New York Assembly in 1709, and speaker in 1718; here he helped reform the colony's administration and built political bridges with the Dutch community, just as he had in commerce. He also developed a good rapport with the Native American tribes: he seems to have learned to speak Iroquois, and developed a number of business contacts with the Six Nations. He also advised successive governors of New York on native affairs. The most powerful businessman in New York and one of its leading politicians, Livingston founded a dynasty that remained prominent in business politics until the American Revolution (1775–83) and after.

In his ability to establish networks, to work between and across cultures, to move easily between the worlds of politics and business, and to act if necessary as a power broker between competing interests, Livingston's career foreshadows that of many later American business leaders. He successfully adapted his European skills and outlook to the changed conditions of the New World, and played a small but important role in the establishment of American business culture.

BIBLIOGRAPHY
Kierner, C.A. (1992) *Traders and Gentlefolk: The Livingstons of New York, 1695–1790*, Ithaca, NY: Cornell University Press.

LORSCH, Jay William (1932–)

Jay William Lorsch was born in St Joseph, Missouri on 8 October 1932, the son of Hans Lorsch, a business manager, and his wife Serina, a librarian. He took an AB at Antioch College in 1955 and a master's degree from Columbia University in 1956. He then served for three years in the US Army as a lieutenant. Returning to civilian life, he took a doctorate in business administration from Harvard Business School in 1964. In that year he was appointed associate professor of organization behaviour, and was made professor in 1972; he is currently Louis E. Kirstien Professor of Human Relations at Harvard. Married, he and his wife Annette have three children.

Lorsch began as a student of organization behaviour, and first made his name in a collaboration with Paul LAWRENCE in the late 1960s and 1970s. Their most notable work was *Organization and Environment* (1967), which developed the idea of 'contingency theory' with regard to organizations. In essence, Lawrence and Lorsch argue that there is no one best form of organization, no one particular organizational structure which serves better than all the others. Instead, the optimum form of any organization will depend on a number of factors, most notably the level of diversity within the organization (more particularly, the number of subunits or divisions the organization has, and how diverse their tasks and goals are) and the level of integration required between the different subunits or divisions in order to achieve organizational goals. Lawrence and Lorsch showed that organizational form must be contingent on the organization's needs.

Lorsch has carried forward the contingency approach into his later works, along with an appreciation of the kinds of constraint under which organizations and managers operate. In Lorsch and Morse (1975) he looks at the attitudes of individuals to the organizations of which they are a part, and suggests that these too can vary depending on the individuals' needs and goals. Individuals need to be motivated by the organization, but at the same time, from the organization's point of view, they need to be integrated with the organization's goals and structure. Again, the manner of this integration is contingent on both the nature of the organization and the individuals.

The needs and desires of individuals can also have an impact on the goals they are meant to be working towards. Donaldson and Lorsch (1983) show how strategic choice, though apparently free, is in fact highly constrained. The expectations of shareholders and customers and the organization's financial goals are major constraints, but so too are the organization's psychology and culture. The authors suggest that top management will often choose strategic options that are in alignment with their psychology and culture, rather than taking the much harder option of attempting cultural change so as to align culture with more desirable goals. In an important chapter, 'Who are the Corporate Managers?', they look at the motivations of top managers. They find that traditional motives such as monetary reward and the drive to excel are important, but they also note that with older managers in particular there is also a drive to perpetuate. Some chief executives would like to see their children succeed them at the top, others more generally want to see the company grow and become a permanent monument to themselves. The importance of making a mark or registering some lasting achievement is one of the most important psychological motivations of top managers and can be regarded as an important factor in the nature of strategic choice.

BIBLIOGRAPHY

Donaldson, G. and Lorsch, J. (1983) *Decision Making at the Top: The Shaping of Strategic Direction*, New York: Basic Books.

Lawrence, P.R. and Lorsch, J. (1967) *Organization and Environment: Managing Differentiation and Integration*, Cambridge, MA: Harvard University Press.

—— (1969) *Developing Organizations: Diagnosis and Action*, Reading, MA: Addison-Wesley.

—— (ed.) (1972) *Organization Planning: Cases and Concepts*, Homewood, IL: Irwin.

Lorsch, J. (1965) *Product Innovation and Organization*, New York: Macmillan.

—— (1978) *Understanding Management*, New York: Harper.

—— (ed.) (1987) *Handbook of Organization Behaviour*, Englewood Cliffs, NJ: Prentice-Hall.

Lorsch, J. and Allen, S.A. (1973) *Managing Diversity and Interdependence: An Organizational Study of Multidivisional Firms*, Cambridge, MA: Harvard University Press.

Lorsch, J. and Lawrence, P.R. (1970) *Studies in Organizational Design*, Homewood, IL: Irwin.

Lorsch, J. and Morse, J.J. (1975) *Organizations and Their Members: A Contingency Approach*, New York: Harper.

MLW

LUCE, Henry Robinson (1898–1967)

Henry Robinson Luce was born in Tengchow Province, China on 3 April 1898 and died at Phoenix, Arizona on 28 February 1967. His parents were missionaries for the Presbyterian church in China. Luce was educated at the Chefoo School, a British boarding school in China, at Hotchkiss in Lakeville, Connecticut and at Yale University, where he graduated in 1920. In 1918 he served with the Yale Student Army Training Corps and was commissioned a second lieutenant. After Yale he spent a year studying at Oxford before returning to the United States as a reporter, first for the *Chicago Daily News* and then for the *Baltimore News*.

On 3 March 1923 Luce and Briton Hadden, a fellow Yale graduate, launched *Time* magazine. *Time* provided busy Americans with a capsule summary of the week's news, broken down into twenty-two departments and written in a terse, flippant and entertaining style. It proved successful with young businessmen and the expanding market of college-educated readers. Within two years circulation had passed 100,000, and the magazine was turning a regular profit.

Following Hadden's untimely death in 1929, Luce launched his second magazine, *Fortune*, in 1930. Despite being launched just as the country was sinking into the Great Depression, Luce's glossy paean to America's business civilization succeeded. Luce introduced his third major magazine, *Life*, in 1936. *Life*, the nation's first magazine fully to exploit the power of pictures, became the largest circulating and most profitable magazine in America. *Time*, *Fortune* and *Life* formed the core of a media empire that included radio and television stations, the 'March of Time' newsreel, other magazines (including *Sports Illustrated*, introduced in 1954), paper mills and the popular Time–Life book series.

Luce's influence as a journalist was considerable. The news summary initiated an ongoing process of trimming the news into smaller and smaller pieces. The early *Time*'s use of language, especially its tendencies to coin new words ('newsmagazine'), to popularize words from other languages ('tycoon', from Japanese),

and to use descriptive adjectives ('strong-jawed', 'horse-faced'), made an indelible mark on the American language. Luce also pioneered 'group journalism', bringing assembly-line techniques and the division of labour to journalism by breaking the journalist's job into independent tasks for the researcher, writer and editor. Group journalism was the most significant of his attempts to make journalism more efficient and effective, and also to have his magazines speak with a single corporate voice.

From the very beginning, *Time* dispensed with the professed goal of objectivity. While providing both sides of an issue, *Time* would 'clearly indicate which side it believes to have the stronger position' (Elson 1968: 8). As Luce aged, he became more willing to use his magazines to advocate his core beliefs. These ranged from his early idealistic hopes that American business leaders would develop a service ethic to his later staunch anti-communism and unremitting support for Chiang Kai-shek's rule in China. Luce formulated many of these beliefs in his most important essay, his 1941 call for America to play a more expansive international role in the 'American century'.

Easing himself out of the day-to-day operations of his magazines, Luce stepped down as editor-in-chief in 1964. He died of a coronary occlusion at his home in Phoenix.

BIBLIOGRAPHY
Baughman, J.L. (1987) *Henry R. Luce and the Rise of the American News Media*, Boston: Twayne.
Elson, R.T. (1968) *Time Inc.: The Intimate History of a Publishing Enterprise, 1923–1941*, New York: Atheneum.
Luce, H.R. (1941) *The American Century*, New York: Farrar and Rhinehart.
Swanberg, W.A. (1972) *Luce and His Empire*, New York: Scribner's.

RV

M

MARCH, James Gardner (1928–)

James Gardner March was born on 15 January 1928 in Cleveland, Ohio. He graduated from high school in 1945 in Madison, Wisconsin, where the March family had moved in 1937. After earning a baccalaureate degree in political science at the University of Wisconsin, March received a doctorate in the same field from Yale University. Interaction with political scientists such as Robert Dahl and V.O. Key, economists such as Charles LINDBLOM, anthropologists such as George Peter Murdoch, and sociologists such as Fred Strodtbeck awakened in March a broad interest in the social sciences. Determined to analyse and understand human decision making and behaviour, he felt comfortable with the tools of mathematics and statistics early on, and felt these tools were important for model building in the social sciences. At the same time, however, March also had a deep concern for empirical data, and for historical and institutional approaches to economics, political theory, psychology and other social sciences. This interdisciplinary and cross-disciplinary interest had been fostered early on; he grew up in Wisconsin with a father who had been a student of J.R. COMMONS.

March's interdisciplinary approach made him an interesting candidate for the new behavioural perspective on human decision making which was then beginning with the work of Richard CYERT and Herbert SIMON at the Carnegie Institute of Technology (later Carnegie Mellon University). After a job interview with Simon, who was recruiting for the Carnegie Institute's school of industrial administration, March left Yale for Pittsburgh, where he helped shape the development of Carnegie Mellon University's new graduate school of industrial administration. Carnegie Mellon University in the 1950s and 1960s proved to be a very stimulating and productive place, where several important ideas were fostered. March, along with Richard Cyert and Herbert Simon, developed the field of behavioural economics, which has proved an important alternative to neoclassical economics (Earl 1988). It was, furthermore, the place where several other modern developments in economics and organization theory were initiated, such as rational expectations theory, transaction cost theory and evolutionary economics.

At Carnegie, March worked mostly on organizations (March and Simon 1958), the behavioural theory of the firm (Cyert and March 1963) and the concept of power in the study of social systems. March stayed at Carnegie as a professor of industrial administration and psychology until 1964, when he went to the University of California, Irvine to become a professor of psychology and sociology, and dean of the school of social sciences. While at Irvine, (along with Charles Lave) he developed a set of ideas about the art of modelling (Lave and March 1975). Along with Michael D. Cohen, he also began a study of leadership and ambiguity in the context of American college presidency (Cohen *et al.* 1972). This book discusses the loose coupling between decision-making problems and solutions to these problems, and gives reasons for leaders to encourage ambiguity, rather than prediction and control. The idea that choice is fundamentally ambiguous is a central theme to ideas about 'garbage can decision processes' (Cohen *et al.* 1972) which also emphasize the temporal sorting of problems and solutions.

In 1970 March came to Stanford University, where he is currently a professor emeritus in business, political science, sociology and education. In addition to his professional books and articles, he is the author of five books of poetry.

For more than four decades, March has crossed many disciplinary boundaries to address questions relating to decision making, learning and human behaviour (in organizations and elsewhere) (Augier and Kreiner 2000). Starting in political science and then moving through several disciplinary domains such as political science, management theory, psychology, sociology, economics, organization theory and institutional theory, March's academic career has been focused on understanding and analysing human decision making and behaviour. The basic thesis that he pursued was that human action is neither optimal (or rational) nor random, but nevertheless reasonably comprehensible (March 1978, 1994, 1999). The ideas that were developed in order to understand human behaviour in organizations in March's early work on the analysis of how people deal with the uncertain and ambiguous world were, among other things, the concepts of bounded rationality and satisficing (March and Simon 1958). These ideas led him into more careful studies of decision making and to his work on the behavioural theory of the firm (Cyert and March 1963), an attempt to provide a set of concepts that could be used to understand actual decision making in firms. March sees the firm as an *adaptive political coalition* (March 1962; Cyert and March 1963), thus as confronting internal conflicts of interest. According to Cyert and March:

Since the existence of unresolved conflict is a conspicuous feature of organizations, it is exceedingly difficult to construct a useful positive theory of organizational decision-making if we insist on internal goal consistency. As a result, recent theories of organizational objectives describe goals as the result of a continuous bargaining-learning process. Such a process will not necessarily produce consistent goals.

(Cyert and March 1963: 28)

The firm is also seen as an adaptive system which, through learning, search and experimentation, adapts to its environment. The experience of the firm is embodied in a number of 'standard operating procedures' (routines); procedures for solutions to problems which the firm in the past has managed to solve. As time passes and experience changes, so the firm's routines change through processes of organizational search and learning. As a result, the firm is seen not as a static entity, but as a system of slack, search and rules that change over time in response to experience, as that experience is interpreted in terms of the relation between performance and aspirations. This view of the firm was important to modern developments such as evolutionary theory and transaction cost economics, which both bear intellectual debts to the ideas in the behavioural theory of the firm. For example, the ideas of bounded rationality and conflict of interest are now standard in the transaction cost theory of Oliver WILLIAMSON (1985, 1996) in particular; elements of the thoughts of the firm as an adaptive political coalition can be found in both the theory of teams (Marschak and Radner 1972) and game theory, and the view of the firm as a system of rules which adapt to its changing environment is important in the evolutionary theory put forward by Richard NELSON and Sidney WINTER (1982).

The behavioural theory of the firm was an attempt to make understandable how individuals make decisions and behave in the real world. Like classical economists, March saw action as involving statements, or 'guesses', about future consequences of actions as well as preferences for those actions (March 1978, 1994). However, he believed that neoclassical orthodoxy gave too little attention to the institutional and cognitive constraints on economic and organizational behaviour and on individual decisions, and too little room for human mistakes, foolishness, the complications of limited attention and other results of bounded rationality. March and his early co-authors thus proposed to include the whole range of limitations on human knowledge and human computation that prevent organizations and individuals in the real world from behaving in ways that approximate the predictions of neoclassical theory. For example, decision makers are sometimes confronted by the need to optimize several, sometimes incommensurable, goals (Cyert and March 1963). Furthermore, instead of assuming a fixed set of alternatives among which a decision maker chooses, March postulated a process for generating search and alternatives and analyzing decision processes through the idea of aspiration levels (March and Simon 1958), a process that is regulated in part by variations in organizational slack (Cyert and March 1963). Finally, individuals and organizations often rely on routines or rules of thumb learned from experience or from others, rather than seeking to calculate the consequences of alternatives.

Relying on these behavioural principles, March later developed his ideas on human imagination and decision intelligence, thereby further elaborating the behavioural perspective. One key theme in his later work has been the problems of achieving a balance between 'exploration' and 'exploitation' (March 1991, 1996a). Exploiting existing capabilities is full of rewards in the short run, but does not prepare people for changes in technologies, capabilities, desires, tastes and identities. For such preparation, exploration is necessary. Exploration involves searching for things that might come to be known, experimenting with

doing things that are not warranted by experience or expectations. Thus, March advocates a 'technology of foolishness' (1971), and advises us to engineer choice in such a way as to strike for a balance between exploration and exploitation (1991, 1996a). He has also examined the determinants of risk-taking behaviour, particularly the ways in which risk taking is a situational, rather than trait, phenomenon, and the effects of adaptive aspirations, learning, and competition on risk taking (March 1988b, 1991, 1996a; March and Shapira 1987, 1992).

Another idea, central to March's later work on institutional and political theory (March and Olsen 1989, 1995), is to see institutions and organizations as fundamentally social in nature, embedded in the larger institutional and historical contexts of which they are part, and to discuss the role of these institutions in the political scene. The notion that rules are central is brought to the fore through an emphasis on action as stemming not from a calculation of consequences, but from matching a situation to rules of behaviour associated with an identity or an organizational code. This focus on rule and identity-driven behaviour leads naturally to a concern with the ways in which rules change over time. In recent work with Martin Schulz and Xueguang Zhou, March has explored the development of rules through a quantitative study of rule change over an extended period of time (March et al. 2000).

March's ideas have taken hold in many of the disciplinary fields in which he has worked. He is also the winner of many prestigious awards. What sets him apart are his visions and analyses of 'the pursuit of intelligence' by individuals and organizations (March 1999; Augier and Kreiner 2000). Achieving what one wants is a wonderfully complex, even paradoxical quest in a world where consequences are impossible to predict, where preferences are unstable and where people are limited in their rationality. Evaluating the intelligence of behaviour involves mediating between the long run and the short run, and between the needs of a collectivity and the needs of its sub-units. March's main effort has been less to explain how intelligence can be achieved and more to understand how individuals and organizations struggle to act sensibly in the face of the difficulties posed by the indeterminate nature of intelligence and the limitations of human beings and human experience. March's book *A Primer on Decision Making* (1994) encapsulates the themes he has elaborated in his work on the pursuit of intelligence in decision making. It exercises concepts and ideas such as bounded rationality, rule following and the logic of appropriateness, search patterns, the allocation of attention, uncertainty, indeterminance, ambiguity, coupling, variable risk preferences and the temporal sorting of problems, all of which have been essential to March's work.

BIBLIOGRAPHY

Augier, M. and Kreiner, K (2000) 'An Interview with James G. March', *Journal of Management Inquiry* 9(4): 284–97.

Cohen, M.D., March, J.G. and Olsen, J.P. (1972) 'A Garbage Can Model of Organizational Choice', *Administrative Science Quarterly* 17(1): 1–25.

Cyert, R. and March, J.G. (1963) *A Behavioral Theory of the Firm*, Oxford: Blackwell, 1992.

Earl, P. (ed.) (1988) *Behavioral Economics*, Aldershot: Edward Elgar.

Lave, C. and March, J.G. (1953) *An Introduction to Models in the Social Sciences*, New York: Harper and Row.

March, J.G. (1953) *Autonomy as a Factor in Group Organization: A Study in Politics*, Ph.D. dissertation; New York: Arno Press, 1980.

March, J.G. (1962) 'The Business Firm as a Political Coalition', *Journal of Politics* 24 (2): 662–78.

—— (1971) 'The Technology of Foolishness', in J.G. March (ed.), *Decisions and Organizations*, New York: Basil Blackwell, 253–65.

March, J.G. (1978) 'Bounded Rationality, Ambiguity and the Engineering of Choice', *Bell Journal of Economics* 9(2): 578–608.

—— (ed.) (1988a) *Decisions and Organizations*, New York: Basil Blackwell.

—— (1988b) 'Variable Risk Preferences and Adaptive Aspirations', *Journal of Economic Behavior and Organization* 9 (1): 5–24.

—— (1991) 'Exploration and Exploitation in Organizational Learning', *Organization Science* 2(2): 71–87.

—— (1994) *A Primer on Decision-making*, New York: Free Press.

—— (1995) 'The Future, Disposable Organizations and the Rigidities of Imagination', *Organization* 2(3): 427–40.

—— (1996a) 'Continuity and Change in Theories of Organizational Action', *Administrative Science Quarterly* 41(2): 278–87.

—— (1996b) 'Learning to Be Risk Averse', *Psychological Review* 103(3): 309–19.

—— (1999) *The Pursuit of Intelligence in Organizations*, Oxford: Blackwell.

March, J.G. and Cohen, M.D. (1974) *Leadership and Ambiguity*, Boston: Harvard Business School Press, 1986.

March, J.G. and Olsen, J.P. (1989) *Rediscovering Institutions: The Organizational Basis of Politics*, New York: The Free Press.

—— (1995) *Democratic Governance*, New York: The Free Press.

March, J.G. and Shapira, Z. (1987) 'Managerial Perspectives on Risk and Risk-taking', *Management Science* 33: 1404–18.

March, J.G. and Shapira, Z. (1992) 'Variable Risk Preferences and the Focus of Attention', *Psychological Review* 99(3): 172–83.

March, J.G. and Simon, H.A. (1958) *Organizations*, Oxford: Blackwell.

March, J.G., Schulz, M. and Zhou, X.

(2000) *The Dynamics of Rules: Change in Written Organizational Codes*, Stanford, CA: Stanford University Press.

Marschak, J. and Radner, R. (1972) *Economic Theory of Teams*, New Haven, CT: Oxford University Press.

Nelson, R. and Winter, S. (1982) *An Evolutionary Theory of Economic Change*, Cambridge, MA: Bellknap Press.

Williamson, O.E. (1985) *The Economic Institutions of Capitalism*, New York: The Free Press.

—— (1996) 'Transaction Cost Economics and the Carnegie Connection', *Journal of Economic Behavior and Organization* 31 (4): 149–55.

MA

MARRIOTT, John Willard (1900–85)

Bill Marriott was born in Marriott, Utah on 17 September 1900 to Hyrum Willard Marriott and Ellen Morris Marriott. He died in hospital near his summer home in New Hampshire on 13 August 1985, leaving his wife and two sons. He had seven siblings, and was the fourth generation of his family to live in Utah. His forebears had moved West with other followers of the Church of Jesus Christ of Latter-day Saints (the Mormons). His early years were spent working on his family's ranch, selling clothes and serving as a missionary for the Mormon church. Looking beyond ranching life, he attended Webber College and then the University of Utah, from which he graduated in 1926.

Marriott's vision was evident as early as 1927, when he opened his first hospitality venture, a nine-seat A&W root-beer outlet in Washington, DC. Beginning with his belief in the company and helped by his choice of locations, a career was born. He had left Utah

earlier that year with only a small amount of capital (a couple of thousand dollars, by most accounts). Although root-beer sales did not initially meet his projections, he developed the business as he saw fit. It slowly expanded until it eventually became a Hot Shoppe, which offered a full menu and car hop service. The Hot Shoppes were eventually to develop into a 100-unit chain that became an important part of the Marriott business portfolio. However, the Great Depression caused Marriott to put his expansion plans on hold, as did his own illness; he was diagnosed with Hodgkin's Disease in 1933, but made a full recovery following an extended vacation. The improving financial conditions and his own improved health allowed him to continue his expansion.

Under Marriott's direction, his company focused exclusively on food service related ventures between 1927 and 1957. During this time, lines of business ranged from the Hot Shoppe concept to turnpike restaurants to industrial feeding and in-flight food-service operations. It was not until 1957 that the company began branching out into other areas of the hospitality industry. Marriott opened his first hotel in that year in Arlington, Virginia. His company eventually expanded the lodging division, purchasing and developing additional restaurant chains, and expanding its contract catering division. It even ventured into cruise ships and theme parks, but sold these a short time later. Rapid expansion caused the company to become truly international, with operations in twenty-six countries by the mid-1980s. At the time of Marriott's death, the company consisted of multiple lines of business and was generating $3.5 billion in annual revenues. At the time of writing, fifteen years after his death, his legacy is a company with a total turnover of $20 billion annually.

As a manager, Marriott was known as a caring employer. This was evidenced by the importance he placed on learning his many employees' names and travelling extensively to his various properties. His company was

343

among the first in the hospitality industry to offer a full range of employee benefits. Another event that reflects his care for people was the decision to open his Virginia restaurants to black customers in 1960, a move that seemed revolutionary at the time.

Marriott continued to direct the company (which formally became the Marriott Corporation in 1967), with his wife Alice as a director and son J.W. Marriott, Jr as president, until 1972. He remained active in the company as chairman of the board until his death.

Simply to chronicle what Marriott accomplished during his eighty-four years would not do the man justice. He not only created and grew a company through his vision, but his professional career had a profound impact on the hospitality industry as we know it today. It would not be inaccurate to suggest that during his career he influenced every single segment of the hospitality and tourism industries, and the way that they now operate. But there was more to his life than business. Throughout his career, his devotion to his family and the Mormon church did not waver. His family was always an important part of his business: his three brothers, wife and two sons would work with him at different points in his career. The church was also a beneficiary of his financial success: a large percentage of his earnings were always donated to the Mormon church. There seemed to be little separation between the three entities (family, church and career) in the way that he lived his life and ran his business.

BIBLIOGRAPHY

Hospitality Industry Hall of Honor (n.d.) 'J. Willard Marriott', http://www.hrm.uh.edu/ hallofhonor, 5 March 2001.
Lundberg, D.E. (1976) *The Hotel and Restaurant Business*, Boston: Cahners Books International, Inc.
Marriott International (2001) http://www.marriott.com, 5 March 2001.
New York Times (1985) 'Obituary – J. Willard Marriott', 15 August, D23.
O'Brien, R. (1989) *Marriott: The J. Willard Marriott Story*, Salt Lake City: Desert Book Company.

CB

MASLOW, Abraham Harold (1908–70)

Abraham Harold Maslow was born in New York City on 1 April 1908, the son Samuel Maslow, a barrel repairman, and his wife Rose, both immigrants from Russia. He died in Menlo Park, California on 8 June 1970. He married Bertha Goodman in 1928, and they had two children. He studied psychology at the University of Wisconsin-Madison, earning a BA in 1930, an MA in 1931 and a Ph.D. in 1934. He was a research associate at Columbia University from 1935 to 197, and from 1937 to1951 was associate professor of psychology at Brooklyn College. In 1951 he helped establish the psychology department at Brandeis University, and chaired it until 1961. He held research fellowships at several research centres in California in the 1960s, and was resident fellow at the W. Price Laughlin Charitable Foundation in Menlo Park at the time of his death.

Maslow was a founding figure of what became known as the humanistic school of psychology, which rejected both the psychoanalytical and behaviourist schools. The humanistic school sought explanations for human motivation in an inner core of instinct and feeling that all humans possess. This inner core is not genetic – Maslow strongly rejects biological determinism – but is composed instead of a complex of feelings, emotions, instincts, desires, needs and wants. This basic core is common to all people, but manifests itself in each individual in different ways and at different times. Although Maslow's early work was highly controversial and led to his virtual ostracism within the psychological community in the 1950s, he was later recognized as a pioneering psychologist and his work on human motivation informs many fields of research.

Among those who did give serious attention to Maslow's theories from an early date were psychologists working in fields connected with organization studies, notably Rensis LIKERT, Frederick HERZBERG and Douglas MCGREGOR. For these scholars and others like them, Maslow's views on motivation solved several puzzles concerning organization behaviour, especially with regard to the apparently complex motivations of workers and how these motivations appear to shift and change over time. Later Maslow's theories were also examined by marketing researchers seeking clues to consumer behaviour. The theories have been found to be broadly applicable in both fields.

Maslow laid out his theory of motivation in full at an early date in *Motivation and Personality* (1954). The chapter of this work entitled 'A Theory of Human Motivation' has become a fundamental text for most students of motivation in business settings. Maslow himself begins by stating the influences that helped him develop this theory, mentioning the pragmatic philosophy of William James and John Dewey, the Gestalt theories of Wertheimer and Goldstein, and other psychologists including Freud, Reich and Adler. He describes motivation as stemming from what he calls a 'hierarchy of needs', which consists of five sets of basic needs: (1) physiological needs, (2) safety needs, (3) belongingness and love needs, (4) esteem needs and (5) self-actualization needs.

At the most basic level, the physiological needs are the needs we have for the things that help us to live: air, water, food. These needs are, says Maslow, the most pre-potent of all needs, and override all others further up the hierarchy: 'A person who is lacking food,

safety, love, and esteem would most probably hunger for food more strongly than for anything else' (Maslow 1954: 37). He then goes on to note how a dominant need can colour one's entire outlook on life:

Another peculiar characteristic of the human organism when it is dominated by a certain need is that the whole philosophy of the future tends also to change. For our chronically and extremely hungry man, Utopia can be defined as a place where there is plenty of food. He tends to think that, if only he is guaranteed food for the rest of his life, he will be perfectly happy and will never want anything more. Life itself tends to be defined in terms of eating. Anything else will be defined as unimportant. Freedom, love, community feeling, respect, philosophy, may all be waved aside as fripperies that are useless, since they fail to fill the stomach. Such a man may fairly be said to live by bread alone.

(Maslow 1954: 37)

But as the need for food and other basic necessities for life to continue are filled, that outlook changes. As soon as physiological needs are met, then 'at once other (and higher) needs emerge, and these, rather than physiological hungers, dominate the organism' (Maslow 1954: 38). Note, says Maslow, 'that gratification becomes as important as deprivation in motivation theory, for it releases the organism from the domination of a relatively more physiological need, permitting thereby the emergence of other more social goals' (Maslow 1954: 38). The next set of needs along this path from the physiological to the social is safety needs. These can be generally described as the need for physical security for ourselves and those we are close to, and manifest themselves in desire for security, stability, desire for law and order, and freedom from physical threat. In civilized societies where the threat of physical violence is comparatively rare, we can still see safety needs manifested in areas such as desire for job stability and security, the need for protection against illness and old age through insurance and pensions, and so on. Safety needs also manifest themselves more generally in a common preference for familiar over unfamiliar things, and an avoidance of situations where we are uncertain or do not know how to react.

Once physiological and safety needs are satisfied, there then emerges a third set of needs, for belongingness and love (in some later writing Maslow refers to these more generally as social needs). Next comes the need for self-esteem, actually a complex set of needs in its own right which Maslow breaks down into two parts:

> first, the desire for strength, for achievement, for adequacy, for mastery and competence, for confidence in the face of the world, and for independence and freedom. Second, we have what we may call the desire for reputation and prestige ... status, fame and glory, dominance, recognition, attention, importance, dignity, or appreciation ... Satisfaction of the self-esteem need leads to feelings of self-confidence, worth, strength, capability, and adequacy, of being useful and necessary in the world. But thwarting of these needs produces feelings of inferiority, of weakness, and of helplessness.
> (Maslow 1954: 45)

Ultimately, says Maslow, failure to satisfy these needs when they are dominant can lead to neurosis and personality breakdown.

Last of all, says Maslow, there is the need for self-actualization. Even if our physical and social needs are met, even if we are well fed, safe and secure, love and are loved, and have respect and sense of worth, there exists something more: a need to do what we feel we are called to do. He borrows the term 'self-actualization' from Kurt Goldstein (similar terms exist in Daoist and Buddhist psychology), but uses it specifically to 'refer to man's desire for self-fulfilment, namely, to the tendency for

him to become actualized in what he is potentially' (Maslow 1954: 46). This need emerges more or less strongly in individuals, powerfully in some, not at all in others. In general, however, humanistic psychology takes self-actualization to be the end goal of every human, and the highest of all needs in the hierarchy.

Although the hierarchy of needs is a simple concept, there are complicating factors. Apart from these basic needs there are also others: Maslow lists, for example, the desire to know and understand, and also aesthetic needs (for beauty, attractive surroundings, and so on). He also points out that the hierarchy of basic needs is not fixed: for some people, for example, self-esteem needs are more important than social needs and will be actualized earlier. In most cases, however, these variances in the hierarchy are indications of pathological personalities. Needs can also be influenced by culture; that is to say, the relative importance and nature of various needs may depend on the culture into which the individual has been born or is currently living. Finally, he points out that a need does not have to be 100 per cent satisfied for the next need in the hierarchy to become dominant: a starving man does not have to satiate his hunger completely before he begins to consider his needs for safety. This leads to situations where multiple needs may be present in varying degrees; this is particularly true as we move more towards the social end of the scale.

Despite these added complexities, however, the hierarchy of needs remains a very powerful tool for understanding human motivation in business contexts. Researchers on organization behaviour have pointed out the strongly social needs of workers. The fundamental reason for taking a job may be to earn money to buy food (physiological) and pay rent or a mortgage (safety), but for most people in most workplaces there are other factors that motivate one to work, including camaraderies or team spirit (belongingness) and pride in one's work and a sense of worth (self-esteem).

It has been noted that when the higher order needs can be met successfully, the result is usually greater levels of loyalty and trust, greater team spirit and better team working, and higher productivity and efficiency (not to mention fewer problems in labour relations). The concept of the organization existing to fill the needs of its members remains a powerful one, and has been the subject of many investigations.

Marketers too have become interested in the hierarchy of needs. In the 1920s Melvin COPELAND had established a basic division between rational and emotional needs, but Maslow's hierarchy provides a much more sophisticated concept. It has led in particular to the development of the concept of 'bundle of benefits', in which it is perceived that consumers buy a product or service to satisfy not one but several needs, and will usually buy the one capable of satisfying the greatest number of needs simultaneously. Thus a car buyer who considers safety as his or her primary need will buy the car that has the most safety features (or alternatively, the cheapest car so as to minimize financial risk); the buyer who emphasizes belongingness needs will buy the car that will earn him or her the greatest admiration and respect of friends, family and colleagues; and the buyer who emphasizes self-esteem needs will buy the car that makes them feel good about himself or herself. Motivation theory has been applied in this way in both consumer research and in the design of advertising and promotions.

Although by no means a complete explanation for motivation, and at times complex to use in practical situations, Maslow's hierarchy has nonetheless become an investigatory tool of major importance in the fields of marketing and organization studies. His work forms the basis for much subsequent theory and practice.

BIBLIOGRAPHY

Maslow, A. (1954) *Motivation and Personality*, New York: Harper and Bros.

Maslow, A. (1962) *Towards a Psychology of Being*, Princeton, NJ: Van Nostrand.

Rose, M. (1978) *Industrial Behaviour: Theoretical Development Since Taylor*, London: Penguin.

MAYER, Louis B. (1885–1957)

Louis B. Mayer was born Lazar Meir on 4 July 1885 (this is likely incorrect, but it is the date that Mayer chose) in Minsk, Russia to Jacob (who ran a scrap-iron salvage business) and Sarah Metzler. The family emigrated to New Brunswick, Canada in 1888, and Mayer graduated from St John High School in 1902. He married Margaret Shenberg, with whom he had two daughters; he later married Lorena Danker. He died in Hollywood on 29 October 1957.

Mayer moved to Massachusetts in 1904. After working briefly at buying and selling cotton waste, he acquired a burlesque theatre in Haverhill, Massachusetts for a $600 down payment. He emphasized that his theatre was suitable for good families by debuting with a religious film. Throughout his career, he believed that films had the potential to influence the public's morality (Schulberg 1998: 82). From his first theatre, he went on to purchase several other theatres and later went into partnership with Nat Gordon. Since the demand for appropriate films outstripped the supply, Mayer decided to form a distribution agency in 1914, and then set up a production company, Louis B. Mayer Pictures Corporation, in 1918. He hired Irving Thalberg as his production head, who improved the quality of movies being produced. Mayer emphasized 'slick, extravagant and sure-fire dramatic films built around newly created stars' (*New York Times* 1957). 'He likes vast, glittering sets. He approves of gorgeous gowns, pretty girls, lingerie sequences, and expensive assignations. In brief, it is Mayer's influence which sends shop girls crowding into the theatre where MGM pictures are shown' (*Current Biography* 1943: 523). He disdained 'sophistication' in his films, and promoted star appeal. He produced films such as *Ben Hur*, *The Big Parade*, *The Good Earth* and *Grand Hotel*.

In 1924 Mayer merged with Marcus Loew and Goldwyn Pictures Corporation to form Metro-Goldwyn-Mayer Corporation (MGM). He was vice-president, and soon produced several major films and recruited many big stars, including James Stewart, Greta Garbo, Katharine Hepburn, Spencer Tracy, Clark Gable and Judy Garland. Mayer eventually became directing head of MGM, and essentially ran the business side of the company. MGM became the world's largest motion picture company, and he became the 'highest-paid American' for seven consecutive years, making $1,296,503 in pre-tax salary in 1937 (*New York Times* 1957).

Mayer became one of Hollywood's most powerful figures, sometimes being referred to as the 'King of Hollywood'. Allegedly, he was powerful enough to be able to make or break careers throughout Hollywood, although he preferred to project a fatherly persona to his stars, directors and producers (Schulberg 1998: 84). He was also renowned for entertaining important visitors to Hollywood. Although he produced flamboyant films, he himself maintained a conservative appearance. Mayer also founded the Academy of Motion Picture Arts and Sciences and was its president from 1931 to 1936. Using this position and his clout as MGM head, he helped dictate industry-wide policies regarding wages, fashion and politics.

While MGM continued to produce hit movies throughout the 1930s and 1940s, including *The Thin Man*, *Mutiny on the Bounty*, *Gone with the Wind* and *Mrs. Miniver*, Mayer was unable to resist the growing popularity of television. With the movie industry declining in the late 1940s and with continuing feuding with Nicholas

Schenck, president of Loew's, Inc., Mayer was forced to resign from MGM in 1951. He might have gained satisfaction from the knowledge that MGM's fortunes did not improve with his departure. His own comebacks with other studios were frustrated by lack of finances, however, and he never produced another film.

BIBLIOGRAPHY
Block, M. (1943) 'Mayer, Louis B.', in *Current Biography, Who's Who and Why*, New York: H.W. Wilson Co., vol. 4, 521–4.
Higham, C. (1993) *Merchant of Dreams: Louis B. Mayer, M.G.M., and the Secret Hollywood*, New York: Donald I. Fine.
'Louis B. Mayer, Film Maker, Dies' (1957) *New York Times* 107(36, 439), sect. 1: 29.
Schulberg, B. (1998) 'Louis B. Mayer: His MGM was a Film Factory, with Stars as Assembly-line Workers and a Hit Formula: Chaste Romance, Apple Pie and Andy Hardy', *Time* 152(23): 82–6.

DS

MAYO, George Elton (1880–1949)

Elton Mayo was born in Adelaide, South Australia on 26 December 1880 and died in Guildford, Surrey on 1 September 1949. He was the second child of a respected colonial family; his father was a civil engineer, and his mother Henrietta Mary *neé* Donaldson was devoted to her children's education and success. Elton was expected to follow his grandfather into medicine, but failed at university studies and was sent to Britain. Here he turned to writing, wrote on Australian politics for the *Pall Mall Gazette* and taught at the Working Men's College in London. He then returned to Australia to work in an Adelaide publishing business where his radical management practices were not appreciated. He returned to university and became the most brilliant student of the philosopher Sir William Mitchell, won prizes for scholarship and in 1912 was appointed a foundation lecturer in philosophy and education at the newly established university in Queensland. Here he married Dorothea McConnel, who had been educated in landscape art at the Sorbonne and frequently visited Europe. They had two daughters, Patricia Elton Mayo, who would follow her father's management thinking and had an interesting sociological career, and Ruth, who became a British artist and novelist and took the name Gael Elton Mayo.

Mayo taught philosophy, ethics, metaphysics, economics, education and the new psychology of Freud, Jung and especially Pierre Janet. From the beginning he trained himself in public speaking, and became an outstanding lecturer. He spoke at Worker's Education Association classes and tutorials, and addressed unions and professional bodies. He much impressed Bronislaw Malinowski when they met in 1914, and they became good friends. During the First World War he served on government bodies, advised on the organization of work for the war effort, wrote and lectured on industrial and political psychology and psychoanalysis, and contributed a lively piece (Mayo and Booth 1916) to *Lady Galway's Belgium Book*. He was made a professor of philosophy in his university's reorganization after the war.

With a young Brisbane doctor, Thomas R.H. Matthewson, who had sought advice on the management of patients suffering war neurosis, Mayo refined his clinical skills in psychotherapy. He began to apply his observations on Matthewson's patients, and the ideas of the new psychology to political and industrial problems and political agitators (Trahair 1981, 1982). He felt he could trace society's ills to psychological causes (Bourke 1982).

Mayo applied unsuccessfully for a directorship of adult education at the University of Melbourne, and went there to lecture on psychoanalysis before taking sabbatical leave to Britain in 1922. He intended to visit the United States on his way to the UK to work with a medical scholar at Oxford. However, from the moment he landed in San Francisco he was sought as a speaker on many social psychological topics, attracted the attention of industrialists and industrial psychologists for his thoughts on psychological causes of industrial unrest, and readily explained America's industrial problems by reference to understandable irrationalities among workers, the poor skills of managers and the inhuman conditions of work that made for an insane society (Mayo 1919, 1922a, 1922b).

When his university refused to extend Mayo's unpaid sabbatical leave, it forced his resignation. Destitute in the United States, he vigorously sought help from those who had led him to believe there was support readily available for his ideas and industrial research plans. Unexpectedly, he was promised an income for six months by the philanthropist John D. ROCKEFELLER, and given a temporary post at the University of Pennsylvania in 1923. There he researched the value of rest pauses on worker productivity in various textile firms. In one study he introduced regular pauses from the back-breaking work in a cotton-spinning mill and saw improvements in worker productivity. The practice was assiduously opposed by the foremen who, when Mayo was absent from the plant, returned workers to past practices. The effect of their intervention was a dramatic fall in productivity, thus illustrating the effectiveness of Mayo's rest pauses. Mayo drew attention to this quasi-experiment to support his view on the value of treating employees humanely. Using these data, and the psychological and sociological ideas in his *Democracy and Freedom* and related papers (Mayo 1919, 1922a, 1922b), and his remarkable gift for public speaking, Mayo attracted much attention from notable American psychologists for his views on the value of the new psychology, in particular, the role of mental reveries for understanding variations in individual behaviour and social interaction at work.

Within two years he was offered a choice of the directorship of the new psychological laboratory at McGill University or a research professorship in the recently invigorated Harvard Business School, with enormous support from the Rockefeller Foundation. He chose the latter. In Boston, he wanted to study the impact of changed working conditions on the physical and psychological welfare of employees. To do this, he aimed to validate an index of blood pressure which correlated with the workers' psychological and physical states of fatigue. This, he believed, he could then relate to both the social and psychological welfare of employees at work, at home and in community life. His efforts to secure research sites were supported in principle by higher management, and in person by employees, but were rejected by middle managers. Meanwhile he taught occasionally at Harvard Business School, and took on assistants and some young scholars who seemed in need of counselling as well as research supervision (Roethlisberger 1977).

In March 1928 Mayo was approached by the Western Electric Company's controller of manufacturing to give his views on an unusual research finding which showed that in some cases employees' productivity varied inversely with variations in the rest pauses they were expected to adopt. Mayo was asked if organic differences between workers could explain these odd findings. He concluded that attitude to work seemed to affect the behaviour of the employees. This led management to introduce a large-scale interviewing programme at a plant in Chicago, to establish what the workers felt and thought about their work. When he learned of the programme in September 1928, Mayo became interested in the training of interviewers.

By March 1929 the company wanted Mayo to take full responsibility for the programme of interviewing 10,000 employees. He suggested the firm could train its own interviewers with a little guidance and encouragement from him. His guidance was simple: give your full attention to the interviewee, and make it evident that you are doing so; listen and do not talk; never argue or give advice; listen for what the interviewee wants to say, does not want to say, and cannot say without help; as you listen plot tentatively, and for subsequent correction, the pattern of experience that is being presented before you; to test your grasp of the pattern summarize cautiously and clearly what has been said without twisting it; and finally, treat what has been said in confidence. These rules became the basis of Mayo's clinical technique for data collection, and his sociological training for humane management. For three years, Mayo collaborated with the researchers at the Hawthorne Works in Chicago. He nurtured the relations he had founded between them and the Harvard Business School, and sought to protect the work from both professional criticism and the business depression.

On his annual journeys to Europe during the 1930s to be with his wife and daughters, Mayo took every opportunity at university meetings, academic conferences in Britain and on the European continent, and at informal gatherings with colleagues to outline and discuss the work at the Hawthorne Works, and when he returned alone to the United States he would tell the management at the Hawthorne plant and their superiors at company headquarters in New York how impressed were his British and European contacts with their research. In this way the Hawthorne studies became synonymous with Mayo's research, and many textbook writers later assumed Mayo had been the director of what would become groundbreaking research in American industrial sociology and applied social psychology.

In fact, he was a counsellor and guide to the management's conduct of the research, and an interpreter of their findings. When the 1930s Depression put paid to this unusual and costly research, Mayo agreed to write up and publish the findings in several books. Ill health made this impossible; the task was given to

Mayo's assistant Fritz ROETHLISBERGER and to Bill Dickson from the company (Roethlisberger 1977); and Thomas North WHITEHEAD, a British engineer, took on the task of presenting the statistical – and to some degree qualitative – analysis of the work (Whitehead 1938). It fell to Mayo to summarize and interpret the work in his Lowell lectures at Harvard (Mayo 1933).

The major book (Roethlisberger and Dickson 1939) was finished in 1936 but nothing could be published until Western Electric's senior managers were satisfied that they had met advice relating to legal problems the firm was facing in the mid-1930s. The book was not expected to be a great success. But after its review, sales took off and remained high for almost twenty years. Entitled *Management and the Worker*, the book appeared on managers' shelves, and attracted study and analysis on both sides of the industrial conflict. Many academic critics attacked the work when it appeared. It was not until 1991 that there appeared a most comprehensive study of the research and its shortcomings by an Australian historian (Gillespie 1991).

During the late 1930s Mayo was primarily interested personally in clinical psychology and anthropology, and taught his few students the techniques of interviewing and understanding how individuals defined their social situations. He was about to begin a study of the social context of industrial organization at a plant in Newcastle, but the Second World War ended that and he was instead drawn into research on teamwork and absenteeism in aircraft companies in southern California. In addition, the Rockefeller grant had to be renegotiated. In late 1941 and early 1942 Mayo endured many personal losses, and decided to retire. He spent his time giving talks and writing his final works (Mayo 1945, 1947a, 1947b). On retiring he did not return to Australia but chose to live in England, his wife's favoured place, and after talking with the few industrial psychologists in Britain, agreed to join a group at the National Institute of Industrial Psychology to encourage ways for managers to integrate technical with

social skills in industry, and to establish adaptive view of society to help Britain overcome the devastation of war and rebuild industry. But funds for this research were not provided by the British government; in fact, it was his daughter Patricia Elton Mayo and her research work at the British Institute of Management that attracted government funds. Nevertheless, Mayo began an arduous round of lecturing, but he overstepped the limits of his health. He had serious stroke in December 1947, was unable to work, and after a few years of retirement in an apartment at the National Trust's manor of Polesden Lacey, in Surrey, he died.

Mayo wrote on many topics other than industrial matters, and a complete list appears in Trahair (1984a). The central theme in his industrial work was that the too rapid and poorly planned application of new technologies to work had given rise to excessive strains at work, disturbed the relation between work and community, made workers feel alien to their traditional employment, and sent them home physically exhausted and psychologically spent. Their response was adequate to this situation: they ruined their families, founded unions, went on strike, and in too many instances became evermore irrational, childish and endangered the social order with demands not for reform but revolution.

In his day, Mayo's view were too startling and not always attractive or well understood by technically trained but interpersonally unsophisticated managers, who used money alone to resolve employment problems. Mayo saw similar views among union leaders. To him, the solution to conflict was to integrate intelligently the technology of work with the social skills needed to maintain people at work. Education was the means to integrate the technology if human organization of work was to be productive and gratifying. For this reason he advocated collaborative and adaptive relations, and taught that much could be learned from the study of small groups of effective workers in diverse cultures. Anthropology could be a great boon, social psychology was important, and much could be learned about mental ill health from psychiatry. Above all the modern manager and administrator ought to learn the skills of listening and observing, and bringing goodwill to the problems of industrial civilization.

After the Second World War, human relations became a popular term to direct conflict resolution at work, and a vital topic for the training of middle managers and the education of senior mangers; but the phrase took on diverse meanings, led to a variety of manipulative practices, and today it has been replaced with a new language for the application of psychology to work itself as well as work organization. Nevertheless, modern forms of human relations at work still emphasize the value of participative decision making and personal autonomy for productive and gratifying employment.

BIBLIOGRAPHY

Bourke, H. (1982) 'Industrial Unrest as Social Pathology: The Australian Writings of Elton Mayo', *Historical Studies* 20(79): 217–33.

Gillespie, R. (1991) *Manufacturing Knowledge*, London: Cambridge University Press.

Mayo, E. (1919) *Democracy and Freedom: Essays in Social Logic*, Workers' Educational Series No. 1, Melbourne: Macmillan.

—— (1922a) 'Civilisation and Morale; Industrial Unrest and Nervous Breakdown; the Mind of the Agitator; the Will of the People; Revolution', *Industrial Australian Mining Standard* 67(January–February): 16, 59–60, 63, 111, 263.

—— (1922b) *Psychology and Religion*, Melbourne: Macmillan.

—— (1933) *The Human Problems of an Industrial Civilisation*, New York: Macmillan.

Mayo, E. (1945) *The Social Problems of an Industrial Civilisation*, Boston: Division of Research, Graduate School of Business Administration, Harvard University.

Mayo, E. (1947a) *The Political Problems of an Industrial Civilisation*, Boston: Division of Research, Graduate School of Business Administration, Harvard University.

—— (1947b) *Some Notes on the Psychology of Pierre Janet*, Cambridge, MA: Harvard University Press.

Mayo, E. and Booth, A. (1916) 'Ring Down the Curtain', in M.C. Galway (ed.), *Lady Galway's Belgium Book*, Adelaide: Hussey and Gillingham, 40–48.

Roethlisberger, F.J. (1977) *The Elusive Phenomena*, Boston: Division of Research, Harvard School of Business Administration.

Roethlisberger, F.J. and Dickson, W.J. (1939) *Management and the Worker*, Cambridge, MA: Harvard University Press.

Trahair, R.C.S. (1981) 'Early Contributions to the Political Psychology of Elton Mayo', in J. Walter (ed.), *Reading Life Histories: Griffith Papers on Biography*, Canberra: Australian University Press, 56–69.

—— (1982) 'Elton Mayo and the Political Psychology of Harold D. Lasswell', *Political Psychology* 3: 170–88.

—— (1984a) *The Humanist Temper: The Life and Work of Elton Mayo*, New Brunswick, NJ: Transaction.

—— (1984b) 'The Life and Work of Elton Mayo', in B.J. Fallon, H.P. Pfister and J. Brebner (eds), *Advances in Industrial Organizational Psychology*, Amsterdam: Elsevier Science Publishers, 1–9.

Whitehead, T.N. (1938) *The Industrial Worker: A Statistical Study of Human Relations in a Group of Manual Workers*, Cambridge, MA: Harvard University Press, 2 vols.

RT

McCLELLAND, David C. (1917–98)

McClelland was born in Mt Vernon, New York on 20 May 1917 and died in Lexington, Massachusetts on 27 March 1998. After completing a Ph.D. in psychology at Yale University in 1941, he was professor at Wesleyan University in Connecticut from 1942 to 1956, and American Friends Service Committee and Instructor at Bryn Mawr College, Pennsylvania from 1943 to 1945. He was Programme Director at the Ford Foundation from 1952 to 1953. He began his long association with Harvard University in 1949 to 1950, returning to Harvard in 1956 as a full-time faculty member until 1987; he was chairman of the Department of Social Relations from 1962 to 1967. From 1987 to 1998 he was professor emeritus at Harvard and also a professor at Boston University. He founded the consulting firm McBer and Company in 1963. McClelland married twice, first to Mary Sharpless in 1938 and second to Marian Adams in 1984; there were five children by the first marriage and two by the second.

Few scholars have had as much impact as McClelland on research about and the practice of management. There have been four major themes in his work directly related to management. One was the creation of a theory of human motives and enlightening empirical base, most notably addressing the Needs for Achievement, Affiliation, Power and the Leadership Motive Profile. A second theme was the definition of motivational change, establishment of empirical support for this theory and the inspiring application projects at the individual, organizational, community and national levels in every continent except Antarctica. A third theme was the development of tests and operant methods, such as the Thematic Apperception Test, the Behavioral Event Interview and the Test of Thematic Analysis, which have been used in research and applications. A fourth theme was the development of job-competency studies, methods and applications as a way to link human capabilities to performance.

Human motivation, in David McClelland's perspective, is 'a recurrent concern for a goal state or condition as measured in fantasy which drives, directs and selects the behavior of the individual' (McClelland 1985: 590). Building on the work of Henry Murray (1938), he focused on three particular motives: the Need for Achievement (N Ach); the Need for Affiliation (N Aff); and the Need for Power (N Pow). Most of his work focused on N Ach from the late 1940s through the 1960s (McClelland et al. 1953; McClelland 1961; McClelland and Winter 1969). N Pow emerged as a focal point of research in the late 1960s and through to the 1990s (McClelland et al. 1972; McClelland 1975, 1985).

The Need for Achievement is an unconscious drive to do better toward a standard of excellence. People with strong N Ach assess themselves to measure progress toward goals. They set goals, strive to take moderate risks, prefer individual activitie, prefer recreational activities during which a person can get a score, such as golf, and prefer occupations with performance data clearly available, such as sales positions.

The Need for Power is an unconscious drive to have impact on others. People with strong N Pow often assert themselves by taking leadership positions, and gambling, drinking alcoholic beverages and committing aggressive acts; they have high blood pressure, prefer interpersonally competitive sports, such as football, like to collect prestige possessions, and prefer occupations in which they can help or have impact on others, such as working as teachers, ministers or managers.

The Need for Affiliation is an unconscious drive to be a part of warm, close relationships, like friendships. People with strong N Aff choose to spend time with close friends or significant others, write letters or telephone friends or family, prefer to work in groups, are sensitive to others' reactions, prefer collaborative activities, and prefer occupations in which they work closely with others, such as elementary school teachers and counsellors.

McClelland's work and that of his colleagues established the importance of a person's 'pattern' of these motives. Everyone has some level of each motive, but the relative dominance varies. The pattern of a person's motive strength is indicative of occupational performance. For example, high N Ach, low N Aff, and moderate N Pow are characteristic of successful entrepreneurs throughout the world. High N Pow, moderate to low N Aff, moderate N Ach and high Activity Inhibition (i.e., a measure of self-control) are characteristic of effective leaders, middle-level and executive managers (McClelland and Boyatzis 1982). In addition to studying the motives of individuals, McClelland initiated a series of studies of motivational trends in societies. He established an empirical link between motivational themes in cultural modes of expression (e.g., hymns, myths and children's books) and national events (e.g., the rise and fall of an economy, social movements and wars) (McClelland 1961, 1975).

McClelland's concept of changing motives was simple: a person changes his or her motives by changing the ways in which he or she thinks and acts. After years of experiments in countries throughout the world, he made several observations: people can change the shape of their motive profile; people will only change if they want to change; change cannot occur without a change in the person's environmental supports; and any of these attempts at motivational change increases a person's sense of efficacy.

The earliest efforts by McClelland were to stimulate business and economic development by training small business owners in achievement thinking and behaviour. It worked in India and other countries (McClelland and Winter 1969) and then with minority owned and operated small businesses in the United States (Miron and McClelland 1979). The method was extended to the power motive in efforts to help alcoholics (McClelland et al.

1972), and then executives and middle-level managers in industry (McClelland and Burnham 1976), even within the context of community development (McClelland et al. 1975).

McClelland summarized his approach in an article published in 1965: (1) give people feedback about their current thinking patterns (i.e., motives) and behaviour; (2) help them to understand the research on the relationship between motives and successful performance; (3) encourage them to set goals and plan for experimentation with new thought patterns and new behaviours; and (4) attempt to create supportive systems, what we would now call support groups, learning teams or self-designing study groups, and then ask them to re-evaluate progress toward their goals periodically.

These discoveries about motives and motivational change would not have been possible without operant measures. David McClelland had been an advocate of operant methods (i.e., tests where a person must generate thoughts or actions). He contrasted their rich data to the more traditional scores a person gets from 'respondent' tests (i.e., tests calling for a true/false, rating or ranking response). A person demonstrates thought, emotion, action and choices through operant measures. For example, in the Thematic Apperception Test, a person creates and tells a story about what is happening after looking at a picture for about a minute. The pictures are selected to be somewhat ambiguous and allow the person to project. In the Behavioral Event Interview, a person is asked to 'tell about a time, recently, when you felt effective in your job'.

McClelland developed compelling evidence to show that operant methods, as compared to respondent methods, consistently show: (1) more criterion validity; (2) less test-retest reliability; (3) greater sensitivity (i.e., discriminate mood changes, style differences and other somewhat subtle, dynamic aspects of human thought and behaviour); (4) more uniqueness and are less likelihood of suffering from multic-ollinearity; and (5) increased utility in applications to human or organizational development (McClelland 1985).

The key to rigorous research and ethical use of operant methods is the process of coding the raw information. McClelland extended thematic analysis from a highly unreliable, clinical art form to a legitimate research method (Smith *et al.* 1992; Boyatzis 1998). To achieve validity, the coding of the raw information requires consistency of judgement, or inter-rater reliability. It is difficult, if not impossible, to achieve reliability without a clear, explicit codebook. The use of codebooks and reliable coding opened the doors to many new measures. These measures, in turn, allowed creative inquiry into a wide range of people's behaviour and outcomes.

Operant methods revealed a level of insight in assessment of a person's talent. McClelland *et al.* (1958) conceptualized a broad array of skills as a reflection of a person's capability. Reviving his earlier personality theory (McClelland 1951), McClelland and his colleagues at McBer and Company expanded the search for competencies in the early 1970s (skills, self-image, traits and motives: see Boyatzis 1982) in many occupations (Spencer and Spencer 1993). In this approach, the definition of a job competency differs from many behaviourist approaches to the identification of skills in that the job competency definition requires that the person's intent be understood, not merely observation of the person's actions. Therefore, there is an emphasis on characteristics of the 'person', rather than just on the tasks involved in the job.

Using operant methods to explore the differences in thoughts, feelings and behaviour of superior performers as compared to average or poor performers, competency models were developed and validated against performance in a job. Studies were completed on bank tellers, social workers, police, priests, generals and admirals, executives, sales representatives, scientists, programmers, project managers and so forth.

The competency assessment methods developed a picture of how the superior performer thinks, feels and acts in his or her work setting. This contextual and concrete picture provided case studies and models for how to help anyone in a job, or aspiring to one, develop their capability. As professionals in organizations were trained in the techniques of job competency assessment, they developed competency-based training programmes, career path systems, developmental assessment programmes, coaching and guidance programmes, and recruiting, selection and promotion systems. In his last published work, McClelland extended understanding of the impact of competencies on performance by postulating a 'tipping point'. In addition to knowing which competencies are needed to be effective in a job, he examined a way to determine how much of each competency was sufficient to attain outstanding performance (McClelland 1998).

McClelland personally trained and developed legions of scholars, consultants and leaders, stimulating their curiosity, guiding and often provoking them to contribute to the field of and practice of management. He was a founder or influential director of over fourteen for-profit and not-for-profit consulting companies, the most notable of which is McBer and Company, now a part of the Hay/McBer Group.

BIBLIOGRAPHY
Boyatzis, R.E. (1982) *The Competent Manager: A Model for Effective Performance*, New York: John Wiley and Sons.
—— (1998) *Transforming Qualitative Information: Thematic Analysis and Code Development*, Thousand Oaks, CA: Sage Publications.
McClelland, D.C. (1951) *Personality*, New York: William Sloane Associates.
—— (1961) *The Achieving Society*, New York: Van Nostrand.
—— (1964) *The Roots of Consciousness*,

New York: Van Nostrand.

McClelland, D.C. (1965) 'Toward a Theory of Motive Acquisition', *American Psychologist* 20: 321–33.

—— (1973) 'Testing for Competence Rather than Intelligence', *American Psychologist* 28: 1–14.

—— (1975) *Power: The Inner Experience*, New York: Irvington.

—— (1979) 'Inhibited Power Motivation and High Blood Pressure in Men', *Journal of Abnormal Psychology* 88: 182–90.

—— (1984) *Motives, Personality, and Society: Selected Papers*, New York: Praeger.

—— (1985) *Human Motivation*, New York: Cambridge University Press.

—— (1998) 'Identifying Competencies with Behavioral Event Interviews', *Psychological Science* 9(5): 31–339.

McClelland, D.C. and Boyatzis, R.E. (1980) 'Opportunities for Counselors from the Competency Assessment Movement', *Personnel and Guidance Journal* 58: 368–72.

—— (1982) 'The Leadership Motive Pattern and Long-term Success in Management', *Journal of Applied Psychology* 67(6): 737–43.

McClelland, D.C. and Burnham, D.H. (1976) 'Power is the Great Motivator', *Harvard Business Review* 54: 100–11.

McClelland, D.C. and Winter, D.G. (1969) *Motivating Economic Achievement*, New York: Free Press.

McClelland, D.C., Rhinesmith, S., and Kristensen, R. (1975) 'The Effects of Power Training on Community Action Agencies', *Journal of Applied Behavioral Sciences* 11: 92–115.

McClelland, D.C., Atkinson, J.W., Clark, R.A. and Lowell, E.L. (1953) *The Achievement Motive*, New York: Appleton-Century-Crofts.

McClelland, D.C., Baldwin, A.L., Bronfenbrenner, U. and Strodbeck, F.L. (1958) *Talent and Society*, New York:

Van Nostrand.

McClelland, D.C., Davis, W.N., Kalin, R. and Wanner, E. (1972) *The Drinking Man: Alcohol and Human Motivation*, New York: Free Press.

Miron, D. and McClelland, D.C. (1979) 'The Impact of Achievement Motivation Training on Small Business', *California Management Review* 21(4): 13–28.

Murray, H. (1938) *Explorations in Personality*, New York: Oxford University Press.

Smith, C.P., Atkinson, J.W., McClelland, D.C. and Veroff, J. (eds) (1992) *Motivation and Personality: Handbook of Thematic Content Analysis*, New York: Cambridge University Press.

Spencer, L.M., Jr and Spencer, S. (1993) *Competence at Work: Models for Superior Performance*, New York: John Wiley and Sons.

Winter, D.G. and McClelland, D.C. (1978) 'Thematic Analysis: An Empirically Derived Measure of the Effects of Liberal Arts Education', *Journal of Educational Psychology* 70: 8–16.

Winter, D.G., McClelland, D.C. and Stewart, A.J. (1981) *A New Case for the Liberal Arts: Assessing Institutional Goals and Student Development*, San Francisco: Jossey-Bass.

RB

McCORMACK, Mark H. (1930–)

Mark McCormack was born in Chicago, Illinois to Ned and Grace (Wolfe) McCormack on 6 November 1930. He grew up in Chicago, where his father published a farm journal. McCormack started playing golf as a teenager as therapy for injuries he suffered in an automobile accident. He was the number one golfer on his William and Mary collegiate team. During a match with rival Wake Forest, he met the professional golfer Arnold Palmer. After receiving his bachelor's degree from William and Mary College in 1951, McCormack earned a law degree from Yale University in 1954, served in the army, and joined the law firm of Arter and Hadden in Cleveland. He married twice: first, Nancy Breckenridge and second, former tennis pro Betsy Nagelsen. There were three children by the first marriage.

McCormack started booking exhibitions for professional golfers during the late 1950s. His first real coup occurred when Arnold Palmer asked McCormack to review his endorsement contracts. McCormack recognized an untapped market: corporations paying to be associated with top athletes. McCormack's success at earning Palmer unprecedented amounts of money from endorsements induced Gary Player and Jack Nicklaus to sign with him as well. With these three top golfers on his books, McCormack's success as a golf agent was assured.

However, McCormack combined competence with vision. He quickly recognized that athletes had a worldwide appeal, and his company, aptly named International Management Group (IMG), began signing top athletes from all around the world including French skier Jean-Claude Killy, Swedish tennis star Björn Borg, and Scottish racing driver Jackie Stewart. McCormack's strategy of signing top athletes gave him influence with the top international sporting events, which he gradually used to create vertical integration. He promoted Wimbledon, the Olympics, major tennis and golf tournaments, and skiing events. IMG does not limit itself to sports stars, as the company has also promoted the Pope (John Paul II's 1982 tour of Great Britain), the Nobel Foundation, Itzhak Perlman, the Mayo Clinic and the Ringling Brothers Circus. In order to occupy his athletic clients during slack times in their schedules, McCormack created what some critics called 'trash sports'

events such as golf's Skins Game, *Battle of the Network Stars* and *American Gladiators*. He continues to dominate the representation of top athletes, having signed golfer Tiger Woods, and has diversified by signing team sports stars. McCormack himself now has a net worth of $700 million (Newcomb 1999: 332).

McCormack's success has drawn criticism. Some observers fear that his simultaneous promotion of events and representation of individual athletes create a conflict of interest. In his best-selling book, *What They Don't Teach You at Harvard Business School*, McCormack dismissed this:

> I have no doubt, if we wanted to, we could make an impact on the way the sport is structured and the way it is governed. That would be very short-sighted. Our long-term interest is in enhancing any sport in which we are involved, doing everything we can to help it grow. This is not because we are 'good sports' but because we are good businessmen.
>
> (McCormack 1984: 172)

Perhaps the best characterization of McCormack comes from *Sports Illustrated* writer E.M. Swift, who described him as someone who 'foresaw the future and, in the best tradition of American industrialists, prepared to meet it' (Swift 1990: 121).

BIBLIOGRAPHY
McCormack, M. (1984) *What They Don't Teach You at Harvard Business School*, New York: Bantam Books.
Newcomb, P. (ed.) (1999) 'The Forbes 400: The Richest People in America', *Forbes* 164(9): 169–426.
Swift, E. (1990) 'The Most Powerful Man in Sports', *Sports Illustrated* 72(21): 99–121.

DS

McCORMICK, Cyrus Hall (1809–84)

Cyrus Hall McCormick was born in Rockbridge County, Virginia on 15 February 1809, the son of Robert McCormick and Mary Anne Hall. He died in Chicago on 13 May 1884. McCormick's father, a prosperous farmer, was also a mechanic and an inventor who tried for some two decades to develop a reaping machine, without success. Cyrus McCormick, who had worked as his father's assistant and received his technical training in the latter's workshop, was described by a contemporary as 'a natural mechanical genius' (Casson 1909: 27). He took up the mechanical reaper project and completed his first successful prototype in 1831, patenting the machine in 1834. In 1837, after a venture into iron mining had failed, McCormick turned his attention to making and selling reapers on a commercial basis. Takeoff was slow at first, with only fifty reapers sold by 1844, but by 1847 McCormick had raised enough capital to relocate to Chicago, which had good transport links and was close to the developing markets of the American Midwest.

In 1848 McCormick's patent expired. Attempts to protect his intellectual property resulted in a series of legal battles, in which Abraham Lincoln first made his name as a lawyer for McCormick's opponents. Losing the patent suit meant that McCormick now faced intense competition; by 1860 there were more than 100 companies making reaping machines. McCormick, however, had two advantages: his machines were of demonstrably better quality than their rivals, and his marketing methods enabled him to sell more machines than his competitors. In 1860 McCormick was selling 5,000 reapers a year in the United States and had begun to penetrate the European and other overseas markets. Continuous improvements to the basic machine helped him keep his technological and marketing advantage.

In the 1870s and 1880s the population of the United States grew rapidly and millions of acres of land, especially in the Midwest and West, were put under cultivation. The market for reapers grew rapidly. The great Chicago fire of 1871, which destroyed McCormick's factory, was a blessing in disguise, for he was able to build a new, far larger plant which used mass-production methods greatly to increase production. By 1885 the plant was producing 50,000 machines a year and selling around the world.

McCormick was elected to the French Academy of Sciences in 1879 in recognition of his contributions to agriculture, and received a number of other awards from the scientific community. He became involved in Democratic politics in Chicago, and was considered as a candidate for vice-president of the United States in 1876. A devout Presbyterian, he gave much money to church and other social organizations including the McCormick Theological Seminary and the YMCA. His wife, Nancy Fowler, whom he married in 1858, was also a noted philanthropist.

A successful inventor, McCormick's claim to fame lies also in his pioneering business methods. According to Casson, McCormick did not just invent the reaper, 'he invented the business of making reapers and selling them to the farmers of America and foreign countries' (Casson 1909: 47). He developed an early model of mass production; of the major American manufacturers, only COLT had developed mass-production techniques earlier than him. McCormick's factory system was widely imitated in later years. His marketing methods were likewise in advance of their time. Creative advertising and demonstrations of his machines were backed up by methods such as warranties and extension of credit to customers, which later became standard features in the car industry. Ambitious and entrepreneurial, McCormick also had a strongly ethical outlook derived from his Presbyterian faith. The successful development and marketing of the reaper revolutionized agriculture and made it possible to feed the rapidly growing cities of America.

McCormick's son, Cyrus McCormick, Jr, took over the business after his father's death and ran it successfully, overseeing its combination with its rivals to form the farm machinery giant International Harvester in 1906. He was managing director of International Harvester until 1919 and then chairman until 1935, overseeing the firm's growth into a global giant with assets of $350 million by 1935. He died in 1936.

BIBLIOGRAPHY

Casson, H.N. (1909) *Cyrus Hall McCormick*, Chicago: A.C. McClurg.
Hutchinson, W.T. (1930–35) *Cyrus Hall McCormick*, 2 vols, New York: Century.

MLW

McGREGOR, Douglas Murray (1906–64)

Douglas Murray McGregor was born in Detroit, Michigan on 16 September 1906 and died at Emerson Hospital in Concord, Massachusetts on 13 October 1964, following a heart attack at his home in Acton, Massachusetts. He was a committed family man, very religious and sensitive to the plight of the less privileged. He married Caroline Ferris in 1928 in Poughquag, New York, and they had two children: a daughter, Patricia Jane Colvard, and a son, Peter Murray.

McGregor's education began at the Thirkell School, and he graduated from Northwestern High School in 1923. Later in 1923 he began classes at City College of Detroit, now know as Wayne State University, where he received his AB degree in 1932. McGregor worked in several capacities from the time he started college until his graduation, as a night watchman, filling station attendant, and finally as district manager of Buffalo Grey Auto Stations from 1927 to 1930. In 1930 he began work for his father, Murray McGregor, who was the director of the McGregor Institute in Detroit. The institute was a mission home for transient labourers in the Detroit area providing food and shelter. By 1932, while working for the Public Welfare Department in Detroit, McGregor had organized and supervised a feeding station for 5,000 unemployed workers who were casualties of the Great Depression. In 1933 he returned to Oberlin College in Ohio, where he had attended classes in 1926, to complete work on his AM degree. Following a successful year at Oberlin, McGregor enrolled at Harvard University, where he completed his Ph.D. in psychology in 1935.

McGregor remained at Harvard for two years, where he worked as an instructor and tutor in social psychology. He then joined the faculty at Massachusetts Institute of Technology (MIT) as an assistant professor of psychology in 1937. During the Second World War he served the Labor Department as an analyst and arbitrator in war industry disputes. By 1940 he had established a consulting relationship with the Dewey and Almy Chemical Company, and was their director of industrial relations from 1943 to 1945. In 1945 he also provided consulting services to the US Manpower Commission. A full professor at MIT in 1948, he was then offered and accepted the position of president of Antioch College in Yellow Spring, Ohio. From 1948 to 1954 he served the school, known for its liberal traditions, by challenging the students and faculty alike to be active participants in the educational process. During his presidency at Antioch, McGregor began a long and prosperous relationship with Standard Oil Company as a consultant. MIT brought him back as professor of industrial management in 1954, and meanwhile his list of consulting clients grew to include the Champion Paper and Fibre Company, the Bell Telephone Company of Pennsylvania, Union Carbide Corporation and Imperial Chemical Industries of the UK. In 1962 he was named a Sloan

Fellows Professor at MIT, a position he held until his untimely death two years later.

The Human Side of Enterprise (1960) was McGregor's only book. The greatest contribution of that work was the introduction of Theory X and Theory Y. These theories summarized how managers viewed their employees' human nature, and how managers assumed employees felt about work. Theory X represented the traditional view of control, and its assumptions were basically that employees dislike work, are lazy, avoid responsibility, lack ambition and need direction. In contrast, McGregor introduced his Theory Y as a 'modest beginning for new theory with respect to the management of human resources' (McGregor 1960: 34). Theory Y assumed that employees liked work, had self-control, accepted responsibility and showed creativity. McGregor proposed that if managers held employees to Theory Y assumptions, existing industrial practices would be improved. Employees would respond positively to being treated well at work and become more productive. This viewpoint was in stark contrast to the mindset of the day, and contributed to a revolution of how management viewed employees.

A collection of McGregor's essays was published in 1966, edited by two of his former students and influential management figures in their own right, Warren BENNIS and Edgar SCHEIN. McGregor's wife Caroline also contributed to the collection, entitled *Leadership and Motivation*. In the following year his unfinished book, *The Professional Manager*, was published after it had been completed by Caroline McGregor and Warren Bennis. This book was an attempt to show ways to implement the theories introduced in *The Human Side of Enterprise*. Here McGregor went into great detail concerning the process that managers go through when dealing with others and how to manage problems that arise on a daily basis.

At the time that Theory X and Theory Y were introduced, organizations were beginning to find new faces in the work force; a work force more diverse in race, sex, nationality, religious beliefs and background. The civil rights movement in the United States was gaining momentum, and employers were faced with situations and circumstances with which they were unfamiliar. McGregor's Theory Y gave managers a new way to approach employees, and it worked. Theory Y allowed employers to give their employees more freedom, to show them more respect and to foster creativity. Employees, in turn, accepted the new responsibilities and showed self-control that facilitated better relationships between the manager and his or her subordinates. These improved relationships led to a more motivated and productive workforce. The employees felt a greater sense of self-worth through their work and the employers gained invaluable assets: satisfied, motivated and productive employees.

McGregor's impact and influence are still evident today. The notion of Theory X and Theory Y is discussed in virtually all introductions to management and organizational behaviour textbooks. His Theory Y is reflected in modern management practices such as empowerment, satisfaction and responsiveness, to name just a few. Although McGregor's theory was quite simple, it shed new light on the previous work of scholars and philosophers such as Robert Owen, Abraham MASLOW and Mary Parker FOLLETT. While others had talked about different styles of management, he was the first to describe his theory in a manner that both academicians and practitioners found appealing. McGregor was able to articulate his thoughts and ideas and integrate them with the previous discoveries by others. By doing this, he was able to show managers that if they could get employees committed to achieving organizational objectives, then their own objectives would simultaneously be achieved.

BIBLIOGRAPHY

Bennis, W. and McGregor, C. (eds) (1967) *The Professional Manager*, New York: McGraw-Hill.

Bennis, W. and Schein, E. (eds) (1966) *Leadership and Motivation*, Cambridge, MA: Massachusetts Institute of Technology Press.

McGregor, D.M. (1960) *The Human Side of Enterprise*, New York: McGraw-Hill.

CC

McHALE, John (1922–78)

John McHale was born in Glasgow on 19 August 1922 and died in Houston, Texas on 2 November 1978. He served in the Royal Navy from 1941 to 1946. He then trained as a sociologist, attending Nelson Hall College and Yale University. McHale was undeniably a polymath, and as such his career had many strands. On leaving the Royal Navy, he followed a career as an artist, designer, filmmaker, writer and lecturer in London. He left London in 1962 to take up the position of director of World Resources Inventory at Southern Illinois University, where he also completed his Ph.D. He moved to the State University of New York in 1968 to head the Center for Integrative Studies, where he stayed for nearly ten years. He was appointed professor of sociology and director of the Center for Integrative Studies at the University of Houston in 1977. He was made a special fellow of Yale University School of Art in 1955, a senior research fellow of the East–West Centre, University of Hawaii in 1973, and a presidential fellow of the Aspen Institute of Humanistic Studies in 1977. He also acted as a consultant to the US government and the United Nations.

McHale had a broad range of interests and deep knowledge on a number of subjects, illustrated by his publication of numerous books. Notable among these were *The Future of the Future* (1969), *The Ecological Context* (1970), *World Facts and Trends* (1972), *The Changing Information Environment* (1976) and *Women in World Terms: Facts and Trends*, with his wife, Magda Cordell McHale (1975). He was an advocate of Buckminster Fuller's ideas on design and synergy, compiling and editing a volume on his work. He drew on this thinking in his systems approach to exploring the future of world resources. He, along with his wife Magda, another noted artist, and Aurelio Peccei created the Center for Integrative Studies with the aim of providing a focus for studying the interrelationships between parts of the global system.

The Future of the Future was a classic text of its time, setting out his humanist philosophy, and the rationale and importance of studying the future. McHale was one of the first to clarify that thinking about the future was an essential part of being human. The book's starting point was the urgent threat to our future brought on by environmental degradation. This book and *The Ecological Context* both called for massive redistribution of global energy flows, and networks of strategic planning that transcended the traditional political structures in the pursuit of efficient allocation of resources. Although he summed up humans' dilemma in two stark alternatives – that of collaborating with nature to create a better life for everyone, or of abusing nature and ultimately destroying the Earth and all humanity – McHale was relentlessly cheerful, claiming that humans had never been in a more fortunate position to manipulate their environment and to make the necessary important decisions.

McHale's early work has been echoed in the mainstream environmental sustainability movement, and was praised for its balanced, practical and pragmatic warnings, and for being informative on a breadth of issues. McHale expressed his arguments not in terms of philosophy but in terms of the specifics of global ecology and world resources, and this unsentimental approach contributed to the success of the work. McHale, along with Elise BOULDING, de Jouvenel, JUNGK and others, is regarded as one of the pioneers of a major strand of action-oriented futures studies which emerged in the early 1960s, focusing on creating desirable futures and social inventing. He contributed significantly to the substantive field of futures studies and, in particular, alerted the world to the emergence, and importance, of a global society.

His art also reflected his futurist orientation and his fascination with the mechanized world, incorporating images of modern machines, often arranged into human shapes with a robot-like appearance. These were designed to convey positive non-threatening messages about technology, which echoed his belief in the ability of automation to free humankind from a restrictive and stagnant society. In 'Man Plus', a key chapter of *The Future of the Future*, meaning people accessorized by technology, such as prosthetics, McHale described his hope for technology to amplify and diversify the human organism.

McHale was awarded the Medaille d'Honneur en Vermeil from the Société d'Encouragement au Progrés in 1966, was made a Knight Commander of the Order of St Dennis and was given an honorary doctorate from Ripon College in 1977. His work was noted for its humanist perspective, lack of sentimentality and pragmatism. He was one of the leading pioneers of futures studies.

BIBLIOGRAPHY
Hasiotis, G.M. (ed.) (1984) *The Expendable Ikon: Works by John McHale*, Buffalo, NY: Buffalo Fine Arts Academy.
Masini, E.B. (1998) 'The Role of Futures Studies in a Global Society', *Society and Economy* 20(3), http://www.lib.bke.hu/gt/index.html.
McHale, J. (1969) *The Future of the Future*, New York: George Braziller.
—— (1970) *The Ecological Context*, New York: George Braziller.
McHale, J. (1972) *World Facts and Trends*, New York: Collier.
—— (1976) *The Changing Information Environment*, London: Elek.
McHale, J. and McHale, M.C. (1975) *Women in World Terms: Facts and Trends*, New York: Macmillan.

AJ

McKINSEY, James Oscar (1889–1937)

James Oscar McKinsey was born near Gamma, Missouri in 1889 and died of pneumonia in Chicago in 1937. Originally training as a teacher, he went on to study at the University of Arkansas and then the University of Chicago, where he took a BPhil degree in 1917. Service in the US Army followed, but after the First World War McKinsey returned to Chicago to take his MA, and in 1919 also qualified as a certified public accountant. He lectured on accounting at Columbia University from 1920 to 1921, and then joined a private accountancy practice from 1921 to 1924, during which time he wrote a number of standard textbooks on accounting and budgetary control. In 1925, however, sensing that the principles he was describing had application far beyond the field of accounting, he set up his own management consultancy practice, McKinsey and Company, in Chicago, where he was senior partner from 1925 to 1935; he also taught business policy and economics at the University of Chicago during this period. In 1935 one of his clients, the department store Marshall Field and Company, was so impressed by his consultancy work that the board offered McKinsey the position of chief executive officer. He accepted, handing over the consultancy business to A.T. KEARNEY, but died of pneumonia two years later. He was also chairman of the American Management Association at the time of his death.

McKinsey is an important figure in the history of financial management, in that he was one of the first to develop a systematic approach to costing and budgeting. Unlike many accountants, however, he realized that such a systematic approach to financial matters had broader implications for business strategy. During his ten years with McKinsey and Company, he developed a holistic approach to business which, though founded on financial fundamentals, looked at production and marketing issues as well as part of a larger business picture. This whole-firm approach, which is visible in some of his writings, notably McKinsey (1924), was later widely adopted by other management consultants, and represents a break from the system-specific consultancies which had appeared during the earliest period of scientific management.

BIBLIOGRAPHY
McKinsey, J.O. (1922) *Budgetary Control*, New York: The Ronald Press.
—— (1924) *Business Administration*, Chicago: Southwestern Publishing Co.

McKNIGHT, William Lester (1887–1978)

William Lester McKnight was born in Brookings County, South Dakota on 11 November 1887, the son of Joseph and Cordelia McKnight. He died in Miami Beach, Florida on 4 March 1978. His father was a farmer, and after high school McKnight also took a job on a farm to pay his way through Duluth Business University in Minnesota. This was one of a number of small business colleges that had sprung up around the United States near the end of the nineteenth century, teaching elementary skills to young men and (in some cases) women interested in a career in business; at Duluth, McKnight learned bookkeeping, business letter-writing and penmanship. While still at the college he was recommended for a bookkeeping job at the Minnesota Mining and Manufacturing Company (3M). After an interview which he thought he had failed, he was offered the job. What McKnight did not know was that 3M, whose major product was sandpaper, was badly managed and almost bankrupt.

McKnight proved to be a good and conscientious bookkeeper and soon won promotion to cost accountant and then to manager of the company's Chicago office. In 1911 3M's sales manager resigned and the board, unable to secure a qualified replacement, turned in near desperation to one of its few young managers who seemed to have any real talent: McKnight.

When he was appointed sales manager of 3M at the age of twenty-four, McKnight had never worked in sales in his life. He proved quickly that lack of experience was not a handicap: intuitively, he grasped the nature of the sales problems facing 3M, and set about rectifying them. Until then 3M's sales staff had dealt primarily with purchasing agents, competing with other manufacturers. This competition was especially difficult for 3M, as its products were inferior in quality to those of the competition. McKnight pushed his salesmen to go into workshops and talk directly to the workers using the sandpaper, demonstrating the product and also gathering information which could be used to help improve quality. He strengthened communications between the factory and the salesmen. He urged his colleagues in the production department to improve quality, and suggested means of doing so. Finally, he suggested to top management that the firm should get out of some of its most competitive markets and diversify into areas where the pressure was less intense. It was at McKnight's instigation that the company developed and marketed a new type of sandpaper in 1914, the success of which turned the company's fortunes around;

in 1916 it was able to pay a dividend for the first time in many years.

In 1914 McKnight suggested that 3M should appoint a general manager to coordinate sales and production. The board agreed, and gave McKnight, aged twenty-seven, the job. He was made vice-president a year later, president in 1929, and chairman in 1949.

McKnight stamped his authority and ideas on 3M in a wide variety of ways. One of his first important policies was to increase research and development so as to improve the quality of existing products, and develop new ones. Through the 1920s he led the company in successful product diversification into areas such as masking tape and cellophane tape; he also directed the associated marketing effort which led to Scotch brand tape becoming one of the most famous brands in America. During the 1930s he continually increased the company's spending on research and development, using new products to keep ahead of the competition even through the worst of the Great Depression. After the Second World War he turned his attention to the company's organization: 3M had, he felt, become too big for its chief executive to control directly, and McKnight shifted the company to a decentralized M-form organization of the type developed earlier by Du Pont and General Motors, among others.

It was said of McKnight that he led his subordinates but drove himself. He stressed the importance of innovation, and encouraged employees to participate and come forward with ideas. He lived for his work, and had few hobbies apart from his passion for horse racing. He had married Maude Gage in 1915, and they had one child. After Maude's death he married Evelyn Franks in 1973. When McKnight retired in 1966, the couple devoted themselves to philanthropy and to a new hobby, financing Broadway musicals. McKnight's legacy to 3M was a culture of innovation which survives to this day and which has led the company to develop many other profitable new products, most famously Post-It Notes in the 1980s.

BIBLIOGRAPHY

Hamburger, S. (1999) 'McKnight, William Lester', in J.A. Garraty and M.C. Carnes (eds), *American National Biography*, New York: Oxford University Press, vol. 15, 131–2.

Huck, V. (1955) *Brand of the Tartan: The 3M Story*, New York: Appleton-Century-Crofts.

MLW

McNAMARA, Robert Strange (1916–)

Robert Strange McNamara was born in San Francisco on 9 June 1916, the son of Robert James and Claranell McNamara. His father was an Irish-American of working-class origins; his mother was a strong but loving disciplinarian. Graduating near the top of his high school class, McNamara entered the University of California, Berkeley in 1933 at the age of seventeen. Here he discovered his passion for both mathematics and logic. According to biographer Deborah Shapley, 'he began, at that point in his life, to talk and think in numbers; it was a consciously adopted style' (Shapley 1993: 13).

As he went from Berkeley to the Harvard Business School, McNamara longed to apply his superb mathematical logic to solving the problems of society. His seminars were models of precise, orderly presentation. He began to learn the latest management techniques of finance, developed by Pierre S. Du Pont, which were taught at Harvard by Ross Graham Walker. Walker taught McNamara how a manager could calculate return in relation to volume over a given period of time.

Companies could now have a common yard-stick in measuring divisional performance. This would allow them to plan more efficiently. McNamara could see this action in the 1930s with General Motors (GM), which was able to turn a profit every year during the depression.

McNamara, now married and, from 1940, a Harvard instructor, saw his calling as one of raising the ethical standards of business. The goals of large companies did not necessarily have to be opposed to broader social and civic goals. The coming of war reinforced this belief. When the United States entered the Second World War, the Army Air Force had just a handful of aeroplanes. Soon it would be mass producing thousands of aircraft. General H.H. 'Hap' Arnold, the Army Air Force commander, recruited a team of managers who could teach statistical control to his officers. The team, headed by Charles Bates 'Tex' Thornton, included McNamara. Given the rank of captain, McNamara went to work in Britain, drawing up flow charts of aircraft and their parts, as well as of casualties. He also helped train other officers in setting up control teams. He quickly encountered the entrenched traditions of military life; pushing for results, the logical McNamara often clashed with his superiors. Generally, however, his work produced excellent results.

In 1943 McNamara was posted to Kansas to work on Boeing B-29 production. By 1944 he was in India, working for Twentieth Bomber Command. Here McNamara studied the flights of American bombers going over the Himalayas to supply Nationalist Chinese forces fighting the Japanese. This route, known as the 'Hump', was perilous and not very cost-effective. McNamara calculated deliveries and losses, and found the operation was costing more in downed planes and pilots than it was worth, although it was politically important in terms of US–China relations. Earning the Legion of Merit for his work, McNamara drew a number of conclusions on the waste-fulness of military spending. His final task during the war was to manage the reduction of aircraft production.

McNamara's reputation as a brilliant cost manager was such that, after the war, he was quickly recruited, along with the rest of the Thornton team by Henry FORD II. The Ford Motor Company, once the giant of car production, was in dire straits in 1945. Henry Ford senior was now senile and set in his ways; his son Edsel FORD, who had sought to reform the company's outdated management practices, had died in 1943. General Motors, with its innovative management practices, had long ago captured the lion's share of the auto market. Ford may have been saved only by the coming of war. Now McNamara was given the opportunity to resuscitate a company that had not made a profit in almost a decade. What McNamara found horrified him. Ford was losing $10 million dollars per month; the company had no credit and was running out of money; warehouses and factories were filled with unlabelled parts. Nobody knew what the company's balance would be six months in the future, or even what it cost to make a single car.

Ford's senior auto manager, Ernest Breech, set up a central policy committee to create a coordinated management structure. Breech assigned McNamara to reorder Ford's finances. McNamara and the others on the former Army Air Force team, nicknamed the 'Whiz Kids' by Ford personnel, quickly moved to split Ford into divisions. They brought in control accounting, borrowing the techniques that had made GM so effective. Peter F. DRUCKER's *The Concept of the Corporation* (1946), which praised the GM system, became required reading on Breech's staff. All costs were to be itemized using a common system.

By 1949 McNamara was Ford's financial controller, exercising central management over the company's money, budget forecasts and plans. Slowly but surely, Ford came back from the financial brink. By 1949 a new, stream-lined Ford, produced in its own division, sold 800,000 cars, double the 1948 model.

Shrewdly, the new Ford was available in showrooms three months before the 1949 Chevrolet, making a serious dent in a low-priced car market GM had previously controlled.

McNamara and the other 'Whiz Kids' quickly became famous, as business schools cited the turnaround they were accomplishing at Ford. Nevertheless, McNamara was a bit of an anomaly within the company he was helping to save. Ford culture was highly conservative and conformist, even more than that of GM. A Ford manager lived in the right place, dressed the right way, had a proper wife and always voted Republican. Especially when the senior Ford was alive, eccentric behaviour was censured. McNamara, however, was a Democrat who lived among the academics of Ann Arbor, Michigan. This behaviour was tolerated only because of McNamara's great value to the company.

McNamara slowly began to rise within the ranks during the early and mid-1950s, becoming first deputy general manager and then, in 1955, general manager of the Ford division. Ford continued to recover as a company. The 1954 Thunderbird sold particularly well. By this time Henry Ford II and several others in the company felt it was time to challenge GM. They aimed to set up a new division and market a brand new medium-priced car. This car was the famous Edsel, which reached showrooms in the fall of 1957. A striking car with a distinctive vertical grille and broad, curved tail-lights, the Edsel was so badly designed and outlandish that consumers avoided it in droves. Dealers lost millions.

McNamara was not responsible for the Edsel. When he took over as group vice-president in the fall of 1957, he privately planned to phase it out. The car had cost Ford $350 million, and its failure helped ensure that Ford would not overtake GM. The failure of the Edsel, however, ensured that McNamara was able to rise even higher in Ford's ranks as his rivals were discredited. In contrast to the Edsel, the Ford Falcon represented the progressive values McNamara himself held. Frugal in his lifestyle, McNamara wanted to make a car that was affordable, fuel-efficient and an alternative to an increasingly popular Volkswagen. The 1960 Falcon sold 400,000, making it a great success for both Ford and McNamara, who was heavily involved with its design and development.

As a manager, McNamara was admired for his photographic memory and his computer-like efficiency. He centralized planning and control while decentralizing responsibility. He concentrated a great deal of power in his own hands. When budgetary estimates were presented to him, he was able to make instant mental calculations and query them. He did, however, provoke criticism for a management style that some saw as intimidating. He sometimes treated those under him as antagonists. In many ways, too, he was very much ahead of his time. A decade before Ralph NADER, McNamara installed seat belts in the 1956 Ford; but the innovation did not catch on.

In 1960 McNamara succeeded to the presidency of the automotive giant he had rescued a decade before. His tenure there was very brief. Always seeing business as a means to higher civic goals rather than an end in itself, McNamara accepted an invitation to become secretary of defence in the administration of John F. Kennedy in 1961. He now sought to apply his systematic management style to the defence sector. He saw great similarities in the management of any large organization, whether it be Ford, the Roman Catholic Church or the department of defence. According to an interview McNamara gave at Berkeley in 1996, he once approached Kennedy and, as he talked with him, drew him a flow chart of the presidency in which the Y axis stood for power and the X axis for his time in office.

Some of McNamara's management philosophy was set out in his 1968 book, *The Essence of Security*. In his mind, a manager could be either reactive or proactive, and he himself preferred to be the latter. The former 'waits until subordinates bring him problems for solution or alternatives for choice'. A proactive manager, on the other hand, 'immerses himself in his operation, leads, and stimulates an examination of the objectives, the problems, and the alternatives' (McNamara 1968: 88). He built up American missile and conventional forces and then sought to implement management reforms designed to make defence cost-effective. In July of 1962 he proposed a five-year cost-reduction programme designed to end waste and duplication among the three armed forces.

The army was preparing for a long war; at the same time the air force envisioned a short nuclear exchange. McNamara insisted that the services coordinate their strategies. His budgeting grouped the units that would have to fight together in a war, the navy's Polaris with Air Force B-52s and Minuteman ICBMs, naval task forces with the Marines and the Tactical Air Command. McNamara did not want to waste money on weapons that would be obsolete by the time they were perfected. Much to the anger of air force generals, he scrapped the $10 billion B-70 bomber project. There should not be, he felt, too many weapons systems which might prove unreliable and overly costly. The F-111, for example, could be used by both the navy and the air force as a fighter and a bomber. McNamara's changes in the departmental budgeting system not only endure to this day but were also the model for reforms throughout much of the federal government. A planning, programming and budgeting system based upon systems analysis allowed the services to know exactly where their money was going. Separate intelligence agencies were brought under the jurisdiction of the Joint Chiefs of Staff. Logistics and supply agencies were consolidated and merged.

McNamara's concepts of management were put to the test in Vietnam. At first he felt that the North Vietnamese and the National Liberation Front (Viet Cong) could be defeated by a scientifically managed war of pacification, attrition and nation building. While American firepower caused enormous casualties to the Vietnamese communists, however, the war remained stalemated, as Hanoi matched every escalation by Washington. By 1967, McNamara, blamed by many for the war, had privately begun to doubt that further escalation was of any value. The failure of pacification confirmed his growing suspicion that American management models were inapplicable in a highly nationalistic and traditional Vietnamese culture. 'We viewed the people and leaders of South Vietnam in terms of our own experience', he wrote in retrospect (Mc Namara 1995: 322). He began to question the conduct of the war, and commissioned the study that eventually became the Pentagon Papers. His departure from the government in early 1968 was in part his own decision and in part that of President Johnson.

In fact, McNamara had already set his sights upon a position that was more in accord with his essentially humanitarian philosophy. President of the World Bank was McNamara's final managerial role, and his most successful. Even as he was involved in the war in Vietnam he realized, and expressed in an address in Montreal in May 1966, that 'in a modernizing society security means development' as well as military power, and that 'without development there can be no security' (Kraske et al. 1996: 168). McNamara saw the World Bank as his weapon in fighting world poverty and hunger.

Under McNamara's dynamic leadership, the World Bank expanded in its size, role and influence. In April 1968, he set up a five-year lending programme as the basis for the bank's strategy. He then drew up an elaborate system of statistical tables that quantified in great detail the hard facts of life expectancy, nutrition, income and death rates. He was, however, anything but dispassionate about what those numbers revealed; he looked upon the struggle against poverty as a genuine war to be fought with zeal and determination. He felt deeply about the multitudes he was trying to help. In an interview with the *Washington Post* in 1980, he dwelt upon the importance of the tables. The bank was in the business of advancing over 2 billion people, but 'you have to see whether you're doing it'. It was important whether the life expectancy of a Chadian was longer than it had been twenty-five years ago: 'We are in the business of dealing in numbers – numbers of people, numbers of dollars, numbers of tons of food produced. How on earth can you run this place without thinking in those terms?' (Kraske *et al.* 1996: 173).

McNamara instituted his programming and budgeting system and set goals. In 1972 he replaced the system of checks and balances in the World Bank with a centralized hierarchy of regional vice-presidents with well-defined responsibilities. He expanded the staff from 1,600 in 1968 to 5,700 by 1981, bringing in many international people to change the bank's American image. Its commitments grew from $1 billion to $13 billion. He used the massive statistics the bank's researchers were now gathering to try to formulate the question: what best can be done to help the populations of the developing world? He first concluded that promoting agriculture and education were most important. He soon began to see that despite a 5 per cent growth rate, the gap between rich and poor was still widening. The reason, he deduced, was that the distribution of wealth within developing countries was still highly inequitable and that land reforms and measures to improve the lot of the small farmer were imperative.

In 1973 McNamara set forth the World Bank's second five-year plan, which increased lending by 40 per cent and targeted peasant agriculture. The bank became the leading world agency for rural development. McNamara began to see the bank as a world, not an American, institution. He sometimes advocated courses of action that would bring him into conflict with US national interest as defined by the state department. When the Organization of Petroleum Exporting Countries (OPEC) quadrupled prices in 1974, McNamara obtained commitments of $2 billion from them to the bank to help developing countries cope with the rocketing oil prices. The oil shock of 1979 following upon the Iranian revolution was even worse. McNamara felt that the only way to deal with this was to aid countries in a fundamental restructuring to strengthen their private economies, savings and investment.

In June 1980 McNamara announced that he would be turning the reins of the World Bank over to a new and younger leader who could offer some continuity in leadership for the 1980s. When he retired in 1981 he left a World Bank that was much larger, more international and more effective in the cause of development than its predecessor had once been.

In his forty-year career Robert McNamara illustrated what scientific management could and could not accomplish. His systems analysis techniques revitalized several major American institutions. He helped Ford recover its major role in the American auto industry, and rationalized and modernized the accounting and administrative structure of the department of defence. In Vietnam, McNamara could not, in his own opinion, wage a successful counter-insurgency or promote a nation-building experiment in a radically different culture. But his combination of the accountant's reason and the reformer's passion was more successful in his transformation of the World Bank into the major global agency for international development.

BIBLIOGRAPHY

Halberstam, D. (1986) *The Reckoning*, New York: Avon Books.

Kraske, J., Becker, W.H., Diamond, W. and Galambos, L. (eds) (1996) *Bankers with a Mission: The Presidents of the World Bank, 1946–91*, New York, Oxford University Press.

McNamara, R.S. (1968) *The Essence of Security: Reflections in Office*, New York: Harper and Row.

——— (1995) *In Retrospect: The Tragedy and Lessons of Vietnam*, New York:

Times Books.
Shapley, D. (1993) *Promise and Power: The Life and Times of Robert McNamara*, Boston. MA: Little, Brown.

DCL

MEADOWS, Donella Hager (1941–2001)

Donella (Dana) Hager was born in Elgin, Illinois on 13 March 1941. She died in Hanover, New Hampshire on 20 February 2001. She trained as a scientist, obtaining a degree in chemistry from Carleton College in 1963 and a Ph.D. in biophysics from Harvard University in 1968. As a research fellow at Massachusetts Institute of Technology (MIT), she was a protégé of Jay Wright FORRESTER, learning his approach to systems dynamics. She taught environmental systems, ethics and journalism at Dartmouth College in Hanover, New Hampshire for twenty-nine years. In 1983 she resigned her tenured professorship to devote more time to international activities and writing, remaining as adjunct professor. In subsequent years she took up visiting scholar positions at institutions in Honolulu, Oslo and Vienna.

Meadows is known for her work on global modelling and integrated systems analysis. Although she was also an advocate of sustainable development and a prolific writer, she described herself as a farmer and writer only. One of her most important works was the renowned *The Limits to Growth* (1972), which sold more than three million copies in twenty-three languages. In this work, Meadows and her colleagues reported the work of the Club of Rome's 'World3 Project' undertaken at MIT. The World3 model was based on an ecological view of the global system and had a specific motivating concern with limits. The probability that limits of the

global system exist and would be reached sometime was part of the initial problem definition. World3 was the computer model developed by Forrester that was used to integrate the global data and to work through their long-term implications.

The *Limits to Growth* study produced three central conclusions. First, if the present growth trends in population, industrialization, pollution, food production and resource depletion continue unchanged, the limits to growth on the planet will be reached within the next 100 years. The most probable result will be a sudden and uncontrollable decline in both population and industrial capacity. Second, it is possible to alter these growth trends and establish a sustainable economic stability. The state of global equilibrium can be designed so that the basic material needs of each person on Earth are satisfied and so that each person has an equal opportunity to realize his or her individual human potential. Third, the sooner people begin working to attain this outcome, the greater the chance of achieving it.

The Limits to Growth generated considerable controversy. It was seen to be unjustifiably pessimistic, and indicative of the fact that estimates of the world's carrying capacity are (and must be) extremely subjective and connected to the individual's culture, ideology and identity. Much of the criticism stemmed from a decision to publish a popularized version of the findings before the detailed work had been scrutinized by the academic community. The book began a debate about the limits of the Earth's capacity to support human economic expansion that continues to this day.

Meadows subsequently worked on a number of studies of social, environmental, energy and agriculture systems, publishing *Toward Global Equilibrium* (1973) and *The Dynamics of Growth in a Finite World* (1974). As a consequence of her contributions to systems theory and global trend analysis, her work has been a formative influence on many other academic and policy studies, and international agreements. She chronicled the emerging field of global modelling in *Groping in the Dark: The First Decade of Global Modelling* (1981), and further critiqued the state of the art of social system modelling in *The Electronic Oracle: Computer Models and Social Decisions* (1983). A realistic advocate of modelling, she was not blind to its failings. She asserted 'that the purpose of a model is to simplify the system until it is comprehensible, not to duplicate the system in every detail' (Meadows *et al.* 1982), and made it quite clear that the validity of the model is subjective. She was openly concerned with the failings of modelling, the dominance of the computer elite and the unquestioning acceptance of technocracy in this field of research.

Meadows' view was that global models can at best provide conditional, imprecise predictions within a given set of policies. The essence of the global model is simplification that can lead to understanding rather than the answering of specific questions. Furthermore, she advocated plurality in the use of models, saying that 'the best global models will be those that are carefully constructed to answer a finely defined set of questions, that means that there should be very many global models' (Meadows *et al.* 1982). In her opinion, models have value in serving as clear representations of points of view, as cross-cultural and cross-disciplinary communications devices, and in identifying inconsistencies and gaps in knowledge of a given system.

Meadows returned to *Limits of Growth* twenty years after its first publication to produce an update. In *Beyond the Limits* (1992), she, along with her co-authors, discovered that many of the growth trends had continued over the intervening two decades to a point where many resource and pollution flows had grown beyond their sustainable limits. Yet they also discovered that, although some options for a sustainable future had disappeared, others had emerged from new technologies and institutions:

The limitless features of the model are human inventiveness and the number of generations we should feel responsible for. The challenge identified is to feed and provide for not only the present, but all future generations from the earth's finite flow of natural resources, where our inventiveness may create ideas and policies that will contribute to that.

(Meadows *et al.* 1972)

The pertinence and wisdom of the challenge made in *Beyond the Limits* was widely acknowledged by economists and environmentalists alike.

Meadows was a prolific writer and for sixteen years wrote a weekly newspaper column, 'The Global Citizen', for which she received awards and nominations. In recognition of her work she was awarded a three-year Pew Scholarship in Conservation and the Environment in 1991, which she used to support her work in resource management. The Swiss Federal Institute of Technology presented her with an honorary doctorate in 1992, and she was awarded a five-year fellowship by the MacArthur Foundation in 1994.

Throughout her life, Meadows was driven by the concerns of the sustainability movement, an international effort to reverse damaging trends in the environment, the economy and social systems. Meadows not only wrote prolifically on the subject but also was very much an activist, and advocated the value of 'hands-on' experience. It was her long experience of living and working on a communal, organic farm in New Hampshire that gave her much insight into the practicalities of sustainable resource management. She was actively involved in establishing and contributing to organizations to develop sustainability thinking and practice. In 1981 she founded and coordinated the International Network of Resource Information Centers (INRIC) with her former husband Dennis Meadows. The group was very successful in facilitating collaboration among hundreds of leading sustainability academics, researchers and activists. Through her work with the group, she developed training work-shops and games for resource management. Most recently Meadows founded the Sustainability Institute in Vermont, USA, which she described as a 'think-do tank' working on research in global systems and practical demon-strations of sustainable living, notably the development of an ecological village and organic farm in Vermont. She was a tireless contributor to systems modelling, education and policy reform, with particular respect to resource management, economic progress and environmental ethics. She continually demon-strated her willingness to innovate in both her intellectual and practical lives.

BIBLIOGRAPHY

Balaton Group (2001) Donella Meadows – Obituaries, Hartland, VT: Sustainability Institute.
Meadows, D.H. Meadows, D.L. and Randers, J. (1972) The Limits to Growth: A Report for the Club of Rome's Project on the Predicament of Mankind, New York: Universe Books.
——— (1992) Beyond the Limits: Global Collapse or a Sustainable Future, London: Earthscan.
Meadows, D.H. and Robinson, J.M. (1983) The Electronic Oracle: Computer Models and Social Decisions, Chichester: John Wiley.
Meadows, D.H., Richardson, J. and Bruckman, G. (1982) Groping in the Dark: The First Decade of Global Modelling, Chichester: John Wiley.

AJ

MEANS, Gardiner Coit (1896–1988)

Gardiner Coit Means was born in Windham, Connecticut on 8 June 1896 and died quietly at home near Vienna, Virginia on 15 February 1988. The son of a Congregational minister, he was raised in a social environment that accepted the existence of the large business enterprise. Moreover, as a group, Congregational ministers advocated a more rational system of social and economic inter-action that downplayed the traditional roles accorded to individualism and competition. They saw as integral to this system the role of government regulation of big business, and intervention in the affairs of business as being necessary for the promotion of the social and economic well-being of the society as a whole. With this background, it is not surprising that Means's contribution to management lies in his work on the modern corporation and its impact on the American economy, and on the corresponding need for government interven-tion in the economy.

Means spent his pre-college days growing up in Massachusetts and Maine. He entered Harvard University in 1914, at the age of eighteen, and majored in chemistry. With the outbreak of war in 1917, he enlisted in the army and was sent to an officer's training camp in Plattsburgh, New York. Although he had not completed the course work required for a degree, Harvard, in keeping with the patriotic fervour of the time, awarded BA degrees to him and all other members of the class of 1918 who had joined the armed forces. After receiving his commission, he was trained as a reserve military aviator and was sent to Texas. While there, Means took pictures of flights, crashed planes and other items of interest, which he then sold as packets to his fellow aviators.

When Means was discharged from the army in 1919, he joined the Near East Relief and was sent to Harput (now Elizaer), Turkey to provide technical training and industrial exper-tise to the industrial activities set up by Near East Relief for the Armenian (and Greek) orphans under its care. Working in a pre-Industrial Revolution economy, he developed a putting-out system of children knitting wool stockings, sweaters and caps on machines sent from the United States; he also supervised shoe shops, hand-weaving and hand-spinning shops, a dye shop, a tailor shop, a blacksmith shop, a tin shop and a carpentry shop. Finally, he developed a putting-out system for cotton and wool spinning. In addition, Means had to work with the local merchants who imported the raw materials for the shops. The merchants had a fixed amount of stock on hand, of which he required only part, and the prices he paid for the raw materials were determined in the transaction itself. Thus Means had to bargain with the individual merchants as to both price and quantity, and the particular figures arrived at were specific to the transaction.

Returning to the United States in 1920, Means entered Lowell Textile School (now University of Lowell) in Massachusetts in September, a decision prompted by his exposure to hand-weaving in Turkey. After two years of studying wool manufacturing, he left in March 1922 to set up Means Weave Shop to make a high-quality (and high-priced) hand-woven blanket of his own design that was very different from any made by other blanket manufacturers. Means marketed his blankets through many small shops instead of seeking a large retailer that could leave him high and dry if its order was not renewed, and would affect his small staff of workers for whom he preferred steady work. Through the running of his business enterprise, Means became well acquainted with the Boston wool market and the textile machinery market, and quickly came to the conclusion that American industrial life was very different than what he had experienced in Harput. In particular, he found himself setting his price prior to any transaction in the market and then engaging in many sequential transactions at this price, even though his costs and sales varied, selling many thousands of blankets. When Means did change his price in 1929, he did so more in response to a fall in the price of wool than to a decline in sales, and the subsequent price was also administered to the market.

While managing his shop, Means became interested in learning more about business methods and about the operation of the economy, such as the causes of business depressions and unemployment. Thus, he enrolled as a graduate student in Harvard's department of economics in 1924. His subsequent exposure to neoclassical economic theory convinced him that it had little relevance to the modern corporate economy of twentieth-entury America and more in common with the pre-industrial economy he had experienced in Turkey. By the time he received his MA in 1927, Means had become quite disappointed with orthodox theory. Soon afterwards he was approached by Adolf BERLE to assist him in his research project on the modern corporation. Means collected the statistical evidence and provided the economic analysis, while Berle provided the legal analysis. The result of this collaborative effort was their book *The Modern Corporation and Private Property* (1933). In particular, Means developed the tripartite distinction between ownership, control and management. He also spelled out the economic arguments regarding the implications of the separation of ownership from control for the traditional theoretical roles of private property, of wealth and the profit motive in directing economic activity and increasing social welfare, and of enterprise size for the coordination of economic activities by the forces of supply and demand in the market-place.

Soon after he completed his work with Berle, Means became involved in James Bonbright's research on holding companies. His contribution to their book, *The Holding Company* (1932), consisted of searching for early examples of pure holding companies and providing the analysis for the economic consequences of holding companies. Means's work on the modern corporation and holding companies became the basis of his Harvard doctoral dissertation, 'The Corporate Revolution: The Modern Corporation and its Effect on Certain

Fundamental Economic Postulates'. He obtained his Ph.D. in 1933.

The publication of *The Modern Corporation* propelled Means into his career as a government and political economist. The book's impact on public opinion resulted in Means being recruited in 1933 to the position of Economic Advisor on Finance to Henry Wallace, Roosevelt's secretary of agriculture. In taking the position, Means took it for granted that he would be trying to develop policies and instruments that would make the economy work more effectively. However, he found that his suggestions were not taken seriously by the policy makers. Therefore, he undertook an empirical study of wholesale prices and used the results to explain why Roosevelt's economic policies failed to produce economic recovery. The study was published in 1935 as *Industrial Prices and their Relative Inflexibility*. The impact of the study on the thinking of economists and policy makers was significant, and Means used this fame to get transferred to the National Resources Committee (NRC), which had been set up to engage in indicative economic planning. While at the NRC he initiated a research project to develop a model of the US economy that could be used for economic planning. The fruits of the project were published in *The Structure of the American Economy*, part I: *Basic Characteristics* (1939). However, the rise in popularity of US Keynesianism resulted in the project being closed down before Means was able fully to develop the model.

Means left the NRC in 1940 and joined the Bureau of the Budget; however, differences of opinion about the impending inflation threat with the coming of war, combined with his failure to shape the economic advice sent to Roosevelt led him to leave the bureau in 1941. In 1943 he obtained the position of associate director of research for the Committee for Economic Development (CED), a business-sponsored, private research group originally concerned with government policies to ensure a full-employment transition to a peacetime economy. While at the CED he instigated the collection of statistical series on money flows, now regularly published by the Federal Reserve Board in its flow of fund accounts. Means retired from the CED in 1958, and spent his remaining years writing and lecturing on the modern corporation and public welfare and its destructive implications for orthodox economic theory, and testifying before congressional committees on administered prices and administrative inflation.

Means's impact on the world of business came through his influence on national economic policy from the 1930s to the 1970s. His writings on the modern corporation and holding companies contributed to the emerging liberal political environment that resulted in the passage of the Securities Exchange Act of 1934 and the Public Utility Holding Company Act of 1935. His work on inflexible prices and their relationship to the size of the business enterprise contributed to the growing disenchantment with big business by Congress and the public, which eventually lead in 1938 to the establishment of the Temporary National Economic Committee and to a renewed antitrust campaign headed by Thuman Arnold. Finally, his work on administered prices and administrative inflation contributed to the establishment of the Hearings on Administered Prices and Economic Concentration before the Senate Subcommittee on Anti-trust and Monopoly (1957–69) for the purpose of developing legislation to regulate big business and its monopolistic power. However, this impact was not entirely of his choosing. Although economists, such as John Blair and Walter Adams, and politicians, such as Rexford Tugwell, Estes Kefauver and Phillip Hart, used his work to attack business leaders and the modern corporation, Means never thought of the modern corporate enterprise as being an inherently monopolistic, economically inefficient institution which required the application of anti-trust laws or detailed regulation by government; nor did he think that business leaders were robber barons. Rather,

Means believed that the corporate enterprise could be efficiently organized and managed on a large scale, and that the separation of ownership from control did not have any impact upon the motivation of business leaders. Moreover, he argued that the modern corporation could make a positive contribution to the social welfare of all Americans, if business leaders and politicians realized that government involvement in the economy via indicative national economic planning, for example, could lead to the full utilization of all economic resources.

Means based his arguments on the fact that the advent of the large modern corporation rendered many of the fundamental concepts of orthodox economics obsolete, with the result that new concepts had to be forged and a new picture of economic relationships had to be created. In particular, his work on the modern corporation clearly established that the corporation was a significant and important institution in the American economy. To show this, Means created the concepts of the top 200 (or 100) largest enterprises and the four-firm concentration ratio as ways to indicate the quantitative and qualitative significance of the large business enterprise in the economy, as well as in individual markets. Moreover, he developed a picture of the modern corporation where ownership, control and management were important features of its organizational structure; where corporate management could make pricing and investment decisions independently of the market-place and not based on profit maximization; and where the decisions of corporate management have an impact beyond the enterprise, and on the social welfare of the American economy at large. Means combined this picture with his concepts of administered prices and administrative inflation to delineate an alternative theory to orthodox economics: his doctrine of administered prices. The doctrine delineated the forces that affected the coordination of economic activity, and determined the actual manner in which the modern corporate economy

operated. Central to the doctrine was the argument that the under-utilization of economic resources was a problem of social organization that could only be corrected through social or governmental industrial policy making.

Means acknowledged that his doctrine, if accepted, would mean the rejection of orthodox economic theory, its views of the role of the business enterprise in the economy, and its recommendations for national economic policy. Consequently, orthodox economists have vigorously attacked the doctrine and prevented it from being taught to university students, the future business leaders and politicians of the United States. Moreover, because the doctrine delineates a positive role for government involvement in the economy that would involve some constraints on business leaders' decision making, conservative groups within the business community have vigorously opposed it. Consequently, business and economic students graduate from university with no knowledge of Means and his work, orthodox economists ignore him and belittle, reject and suppress his work, and business leaders reject his doctrine and continue to accepted the orthodox picture of how the economy operates. Perhaps in future Means's work will form an important component of the thinking and worldview of business leaders; but this would require an intellectual revolution in economic thinking not seen since the 1930s. For the moment, Means's contribution to the modern management paradigm remains marginal.

BIBLIOGRAPHY

Berle, A. and Means, G. (1933) *The Modern Corporation and Private Property*, New York: Macmillan.

Bonbright, J. and Means G. (1932) *The Holding Company*, New York: McGraw-Hill.

Lee, F. (1998) *Post Keynesian Price Theory*, Cambridge: Cambridge University Press.

Means, G. (1935) *Industrial Prices and Their*

Relative Inflexibility, Washington, DC: GPO.

Means, G. (1939) *The Structure of the American Economy*, part I: *Basic Characteristics*, Washington, DC: GPO.

—— (1962a) *The Corporate Revolution in America*, New York: Crowell-Collier Press.

—— (1962b) *Pricing Power and the Public Interest*, New York: Harper and Brothers.

—— (1991) *The Heterodox Economics of Gardiner C. Means: A Collection*, ed. F. Lee and W. Samuels, Armonk, NY: M.E. Sharpe.

Samuels, W. and Medema, S. (1990) *Gardiner C. Means' Institutional and Post-Keynesian Economics: An Interpretation and Assessment*, Armonk, NY: M.E. Sharpe.

FSL

MELLEN, Charles Sanger (1851–1927)

Charles Sanger Mellen was born in Lowell, Massachusetts on 16 August 1851 and died in Concord, New Hampshire on 17 November 1927. Mellen was educated in the public schools of Concord, New Hampshire and began his railway career at the age of eighteen in the cashier's office of the Northern New Hampshire Railroad. He advanced through positions in the Central Vermont, Northern New Hampshire and Boston and Lowell railway lines, and then became general purchasing agent for Union Pacific in 1888.

In 1892 Mellen was made general manager of the New York and New England Railroad, and then vice-president of the New York, New Haven and Hartford Railroad, often referred to simply as the New Haven system. Chartered in 1872, the merger between the three railway companies had resulted in a long-desired rail

link between Boston and New York, and precipitated a series of additional mergers. More than a hundred small independent railroads built in New England between 1850 and 1860 were absorbed over the years into the New Haven system.

The local railroad lines that became part of the New Haven system were built in response to local business and transportation needs. In this respect, they differed from the rail lines in the western United States, which preceded and shaped settlement. The New Haven lines served primarily to link existing towns, business and markets. This system thus developed through consolidations and mergers. By 1890 company revenue exceeded $100 million per year, and the firm employed 4,000 people to serve twelve million passengers annually.

Mellen's advance from 1897 onward was due largely to the influence of New York financier J.P. MORGAN, who initially installed him as president of Northern Pacific and then, in 1903, made him president of the New Haven system. Leaving the financial affairs largely in the hands of the company's directors and bankers, Mellen improved the rolling stock, added new track, built stations, beautified the yards, electrified rail lines between Hartford and New Haven, and built a power generating plant in Connecticut. These accomplishments, however, were overshadowed by Mellen's ambitious schemes to dominate all modes of transportation in New England.

By 1910, in addition to being president of the New Haven system, Mellen was also controlling the Boston and Maine Railroad and its cog railway, Maine Central. In a spirit of unrestrained commercial expansion, he bought up steamboat lines, trolley systems and other railroad lines regardless of price, and incorporated them into the New Haven system. In what seemed like a particularly foolhardy venture, he attempted to build an electric trolley line to the summit of Mount Washington.

A series of train accidents brought to a head a growing public resentment against Mellen's attempts to achieve a virtual monopoly of New England transportation. The Interstate Commerce Commission, after an investigation, called the Mellen management 'one of the most glaring instances of maladministration revealed in all the history of American railroading'. To be fair, the poor financial practices were probably only partly his fault, but as president he had to assume the responsibility. The public outcry plus a long series of governmental investigations finally caused Mellen's resignation in 1913. Former colleagues remembered him as a hard worker with a driving personality, but frosty in his human contacts, dictatorial to his subordinates and subservient to his superiors.

BIBLIOGRAPHY

Howe, N.S. (2000) *Not Without Peril: 150 Years of Misadventure on the Presidential Range of New Hampshire*, Boston: Appalachian Mountain Club Books.

BB

MERCK, George Wilhelm (1894–1957)

George Wilhelm Merck was born in New York on 29 March 1894 and died in West Orange, New Jersey on 9 November 1957. He graduated with an AB from Harvard University in 1915, and then went to work for his father's pharmaceuticals firm, Merck and Company. He married Josephine Cary Wall in 1917, and they had two children; after a subsequent divorce he married Serena Stevens in 1926, with whom he had three children. Merck spent the period 1915–25 working in various parts of the firm, learning how the business functioned. When his father resigned for health reasons in 1925, Merck took over as president. Under Merck, the company grew from being a small regional manufacturer to one of the giants of the US pharmaceutical industry.

Merck was convinced of the value of science to industry, and vice versa. He constantly stressed the need for more research, believing that accumulations of scientific knowledge would be both good for the company and good for society. He built a number of specialist research facilities, ranging from the Merck Institute for Therapeutic Research in New Jersey to Experimental Plantations Incorporated, a subsidiary based in Guatemala and Costa Rica dedicated to developing medicines from tropical plants; the latter, in particular, was well in advance of its time. The results for the company was a stream of new products which were marketed with great commercial success. Among Merck and Company's major accomplishments was the synthesis of a number of vitamins, including B1 (thiamin) and E, and the first commercial sales of vitamins C, K and riboflavin. Merck also led the way in the development of penicillin, researching and bringing the drug to market in just two years, and then following this up with the development of another major antibiotic, streptomycin. The company developed over 1,000 new products over the course of three decades.

Merck believed that scientific knowledge gained through research should be made public, and he sponsored or produced many important publications such as the Merck Index of drugs and chemicals. The company also funded many academic research projects and scholarships. Merck himself served as a US government adviser on biological warfare, and on the National Research Council.

BIBLIOGRAPHY

Vicary, E.Z. (1999) 'Merck, George Wilhelm', in J.A. Garraty and M.C. Carnes (eds), *American National Biography*, New York: Oxford University Press, vol. 15, 333–4.

MEYER, André Benoit Mathieu
(1898–1979)

André Benoit Mathieu Meyer was born in Paris on 3 September 1898, the son of Jules and Lucie Meyer. He died in Lausanne, Switzerland on 10 September 1979. His father was a small businessman. Meyer left school in 1914 to take a job as a bank messenger, and later worked for the Paris Bourse. In 1922 he married Bella Lehman; they had two children.

In 1925 Meyer was invited to join Lazard Frères, a leading Paris bank. He quickly made a name for himself as an investment banker. He worked with the car-maker André Citroën during the later 1920s; when Citroën went bankrupt during the Great Depression it was Meyer who came to the rescue, negotiating with the tyre manufacturer Michelin and arranging for the latter to take over Citroën. Meyer was later awarded the Legion of Honour for helping save Citroën and other companies.

In 1940 Meyer and his family left France and settled in New York. He joined the New York branch of Lazard and took charge of reorganizing the firm, becoming senior partner in 1944. In a few years he had transformed Lazard into what Martel (1999: 397) calls 'the most venturesome investment bank in America'. He remained in the United States after the war, taking out US citizenship in 1948 and becoming the virtual king of the financial deal-makers in the 1950s and 1960s. Lazard was not heavily capitalized, so Meyer moved instead into venture capital, usually taking a stake in whatever deal he was putting together. By the 1960s his reputation as a financial wizard was second to none, and he was working for companies such as Atlantic Richfield, R.J. Reynolds and RCA. He had a particularly strong relationship with ITT and its chief executive, Harold GENEEN, and helped Geneen manage the takeovers of Avis and Hartford Fire Insurance. The latter led to Securities and Exchange Commission (SEC) suits against ITT and Lazard, and Meyer came close to being sued personally. Eventually, like Geneen, Meyer negotiated a settlement with the SEC.

David SARNOFF of RCA 'observed that at the heart of Meyer's success was his lightning-quick, almost intuitive analytical powers that enabled him to grasp the subtleties and implications of even the most complicated transactions while others were still thinking things over' (Martel 1999: 398). Many observers commented on Meyer's love of complex problems: he sometimes referred to his work as 'financial engineering', but in fact he treated it more like puzzle-solving. His mind relished complexity (Reich 1983), and he enjoyed the challenge of his work as much as the wealth it brought him. His personal management style was tight and authoritarian: subordinates worked strictly to his direction, and the other partners of Lazard usually fell into line with his wishes. His nickname at Lazard was 'Zeus', which summed up both his Olympian stature and his tendency to anger when contradicted or balked.

His network of friendships with the rich and powerful spanned the globe, and included politicians such as Georges Pompidou and Lyndon Johnson, as well as industrialists such as Giovanni Agnelli. He was particularly close to the Kennedy family, and was romantically linked to Jacqueline Kennedy before her remarriage to Aristotle Onassis. A lover of art, Meyer amassed a considerable collection at his homes in the United States and Switzerland. As with Agnelli, his friendships and collections were not just a source of personal pleasure; they were also an essential part of his networking and deal-making activities.

Meyer managed financial transactions tightly, combining strong analytical abilities, superb networks and close attention to detail. As Martel (1999: 208) says, 'under his leadership Lazard essentially invented modern aggressive deal making and dominated the field as the most important investment house in mergers and acquisitions during the 1950s and 1960s'. Meyer influenced not only the financial community but business management more widely. He played a leading role in the wave of mergers and acquisitions during this period, but he was also partly responsible for the trend: the activities of Meyer and other investment bankers helped grow the market for mergers and acquisitions. The profit motive of men like Meyer should always be considered part of the calculus when studying merger and acquisition activity.

BIBLIOGRAPHY

Martel, C.M. (1999) 'Meyer, André Benoit Mathieu', in J.A. Garraty and M.C. Carnes (eds), *American National Biography*, New York: Oxford University Press, vol. 15, 397–8.

Reich, C. (1983) *Financier: The Biography of André Meyer*, New York: John Wiley and Sons.

MLW

MILES, Raymond E. (1932–)

Raymond Miles was born in Texas on 2 November 1932. He received a BA from North Texas State University in 1954, followed by an MBA (1958) and Ph.D. (1963) from Stanford University. He joined the faculty of the University of California, Berkeley in 1963 and has remained there since, becoming professor of business administration in 1971 and serving as dean of Berkeley's school of business administration from 1983 to 1990. Now retired, he remains professor emeritus at the university.

Miles's main aim, both in his earlier solo work and in later writing with his collaborator, Charles SNOW, has been to synthesize various theories of management and develop at least the outlines of an overall theory. In particular, he has sought to harmonize and find common ground between theories of strategy and theories of organization. In his *Theories of Management* (1975), Miles concluded that the key organizational variables are threefold: goals, technology and structure. The first concerns the organization's destination, the second two the means by which it gets there. All three are intimately connected, and should not be considered in isolation.

This theory was developed much more fully in Miles's later work with Charles Snow, *Organizational Strategy, Structure and Process* (1978). Referring to organizational variables, Miles and Snow first ask how and why these variables come to exist. They conclude that the variables are generated within organizations as part of an 'adaptive process' whereby each organization struggles to come to terms with its environment in a unique way, and develops characteristics accordingly. The reason why such responses differ is in turn due to the complexities of the environment, which they see as

> not a homogeneous entity but rather ... a complex combination of factors such as product and market conditions, industry conditions and practices, governmental regulations, and relations with financial and raw material suppliers. Each of these factors tends to influence the organization in its own unique way.
>
> (Miles and Snow 1978: 18)

Organizations attempt to respond to these pressures by attempting to ensure that their own organization (structure) and technology (process) are closely aligned with the strategy they must pursue in order to respond effectively to their environment. This concept, known as 'organizational fitness for purpose', is now widely referred to in literature on organizations.

Miles's writing output has been comparatively small; he confessed once that he had little taste for writing books, and his enthusiasm for the subject 'tended to drop off after about twenty pages' (Miles 1975: 2). But the work that he has produced has been of high quality, and has made a considerable contribution to modern understanding of how and why organizations behave and react as they do.

BIBLIOGRAPHY

Miles, R.E. (1975) *Theories of Management: Implications for Organization Behaviour and Development*, New York: McGraw-Hill.

Miles, R.E. and Snow, C.C. (1978) *Organizational Strategy, Structure and Process*, New York: McGraw-Hill.

—— (1984) 'Fit, Failure and the Hall of Fame', *California Management Review* 26(3): 10–28.

Witzel, M. (1998) 'Miles, Raymond E. and Snow, Charles C.', in M. Warner (ed.), *IEBM Handbook of Management Thinking*, London: International Thomson Business Press, 455–60.

MLW

MITCHELL, Wesley Clair (1874–1948)

Wesley Clair Mitchell was born in Rushville, Illinois on 5 August 1874, the son of John and Lucy Mitchell. He died in New York City. He married Lucy Sprague in 1912; they had four children. He attended the University of Chicago, taking his AB there in 1896 and his Ph.D. in economics in 1899, studying under John Dewey and Thorstein VEBLEN. He was instructor in economics at Chicago from 1900 to 1902, then assistant professor of commerce at the University of California from 1902 to 1908 and, after a year's interval as lecturer at Harvard, professor of political economy at the University of California from 1909 to 1912. He then joined Columbia University as professor of economics, where he remained until his retirement. He directed the New School for Social Research at Columbia from 1919 to 1931. His most notable institutional achievement was the founding of the National Bureau for Economic Research (NBER) in 1920; he remained associated with NBER until his death, trained many of its future leaders including Arthur Burns, and helped make the organization into one of the most high-profile economic research bodies in the United States. Mitchell was also loosely associated with Harvard Business School, and was a friend and supporter of its founding dean, Edwin GAY.

Mitchell belongs to the institutionalist school of economics, members of which also include John R. COMMONS. Mitchell himself remains best known for his work on business cycles, which not only influenced economic thinking but was also widely read in management circle; *Business Cycles*, first published in 1913, is frequently referred to in management literature over the next decade In 1927 Mitchell heavily revised the book, taking into account both new research of his own and developments by others, notably the wave theory of Nikolai Kondratieff. This book, *Business Cycles: The Problem and its Setting*, is the most refined statement of Mitchell's views, although he did produce a later joint work with Burns, *Measuring Business Cycles* (1947), which updates the work still further.

The observation of business cycles and fluctuations, Mitchell says, is not new. He cites J.C. Sisimondi as being the first to make any systematic analysis of this phenomenon; Sisimondi, and after him Marx, believed that cycles were an inevitable part of capitalism. John Stuart Mill, on the other hand, sought an explanation in the behaviour and judgement of people as economic actors, what Mitchell calls a 'psychological' explanation; W. Stanley Jevons believed that business cycles were controlled by solar radiation (Mitchell mentions this and passes on without comment), while other writers including Clement Juglar and Lord Overstone developed a theory of cyclical oscillations that anticipates Kondratieff.

Mitchell's own observation is that these fluctuations are a relatively new phenomenon in economic terms, and that less advanced economies suffer less from fluctuations. Further, in advanced economies, it is those sectors such as transportation, commerce, manufacturing and banking which, by the time of his writing, were most economically sophisticated and were dominated by large business organizations that suffered the most severe effects of these fluctuations or cycles. Sectors where small-scale organizations were more prevalent exhibited less fluctuation (Mitchell includes agriculture in this latter category, saying that while farming does have cycles, their causes are linked to factors such as weather and crop yields which do not have economic causes). His hypothesis, then, is that there is a link between large business organizations and business cycles.

Cycles, says Mitchell, run through four phases: prosperity, recession, depression and revival. An economy which passes through all four of these phases can be said to have completed a cycle. Mitchell makes a distinction between 'cycles' and 'crises', which are one-off events usually having more severe consequences than cycles. Yet the effect of cycles is increasingly steadily, and the fluctuations are growing noticeably larger: booms are getting higher, depressions are getting deeper. Mitchell attributes this change to two factors. First, large commercial organizations are becoming increasingly interdependent, both in terms of ownership and in terms of economic and commercial activity, meaning that the declining profitability of one sector creates a 'drag' effect which pulls other sectors down as well. Second, the economies of nations are also becoming increasingly interdependent. Formerly, the economies of developed nations exhibited quite different cyclical patterns as a result of different economic, political and social factors at work in those economies. By the early nineteenth century,

however, international influences were becoming increasingly prominent, leading to a cyclical alignment or convergence; thus when the economy of a dominant nation such as the United States entered a downturn, it would drag other economies down as well. The events of 1929 were to illustrate Mitchell's point very graphically indeed.

In searching for causes for business cycles, Mitchell rejects the view that cycles are inherent in capitalism itself. Rather, he sees them as stemming in part from the growing interdependence and influence of large organizations. What start off as cycles in the activities of individual businesses, caused by the economic activity and behaviour of their managers and owners, becomes in large organizations an institutional cycle, stimulated by the ways in which organizations behave and act as economic entities. Those behaviours, in turn, are a result of both internal organizational dynamics and the interactions between organizations and their environments. Thanks to interdependence, as noted above, what starts as a downturn (or boom) in one sector spreads to others and creates a general movement. The regularity and frequency of cycles, Mitchell believes, can also be explained in part by reference to the actions and reactions of economic institutions.

Mitchell's business cycle theory was referred to by academics and writers in many business fields. Marketers, for example, used business cycle theory to explain fluctuations in consumer demand; even if all other factors remained equal, consumer demand for a given product would still rise during times of prosperity and fall during times of recession and depression. Finance theory also took business cycles into account when discussing the availability of money and credit. His methods of gathering and analysing statistical data were also influential. Business cycle theory had – and continues to have – its critics, as Mitchell noted in his 1927 edition of *Business Cycles*, but the mass of statistical and anecdotal evidence he assembles to support his theory is often overwhelming. Although the theory is only a partial one and does not offer a full explanation of the causes of business cycles, Mitchell paved the way for generations of further scholarship.

BIBLIOGRAPHY

Cattell, J.M., Cattell, J. and Ross, E.E. (1941) *Leaders in Education*, 2nd edn, Lancaster, PA: The Science Press.

Mitchell, W.C. (1913) *Business Cycles*, Chicago: A.W. Shaw.

—— (1927) *Business Cycles: The Problem and its Setting*, New York: National Bureau of Economic Research.

Mitchell, W.C. and Burns, A.F. (1947) *Measuring Business Cycles*, New York: National Bureau of Economic Research.

MLW

MOONEY, James David (1884–1957)

James Mooney was born in Cleveland, Ohio on 18 February 1884, the son of James and Mary Mooney. He died some time in September 1957 at his home on Long Island. He married twice, to Leonora Watson in 1914 (three children) and to Ida McDonald in 1929 (three children). After taking a bachelor of science degree at New York University, Mooney then attended the Case Institute of Technology, where he took a bachelor's degree in mining and metallurgy; he later took a master's degree and a doctorate in engineering from Case. After a period with mining exploration teams in California and Mexico, Mooney worked at a succession of jobs with companies including Westinghouse, B.F. Goodrich and finally Hyatt Roller Bearing Company, rising to a management position with the latter. During the First World War he joined the US Army and served with the expeditionary force in France, posted to an artillery regiment and rising to the rank of captain.

Demobilized after the war, Mooney joined the Remy Electric Company, a small subsidiary of General Motors (GM), as president and general manager. An intelligent and perceptive man and an original thinker, he was quickly headhunted by GM's head office following the company's take-over by Pierre DU PONT, and in 1922 was appointed vice-president of GM and president of GM Overseas. This was already a large division, and Mooney proceeded to make it much larger, expanding GM's business into more than 100 countries. Always aware of local cultural sensitivities, Mooney adapted US working practices and ideas where necessary to fit in with local markets. As the executive in charge of all GM plants and service outlets outside North America, Mooney travelled widely and became acquainted with many heads of state and senior government officials, and there seems little doubt that it was his ambassadorship for the company that allowed GM to grow its overseas business so dramatically during the 1920s and 1930s.

Mooney became an important figure in GM; Pierre du Pont respected him and listened to his advice, and Alfred SLOAN relied upon him. Mooney is sometimes referred to as Sloan's *eminence grise*, the deep thinker on the GM board whose ideas on strategy and organization were listened to with respect. His ideas on management and especially on organization theory were among the most advanced of their time, and as well as commanding the respect of heads of state and government Mooney was also on friendly terms with many of the leading management intelligentsia, such as Lyndall Urwick, Luther GULICK and Mary Parker FOLLETT.

GM had several subsidiaries in Germany, an important market, and by the time of the outbreak of the Second World War Mooney was familiar with many senior officials in the German government. He seems to have become convinced that the war could be ended if a neutral third party were prepared to mediate between the belligerents in Europe, and volunteered to undertake the task. He had little time for diplomats, who he reckoned treated diplomacy as a strategic contest with little thought for the lives of those involved on either side. In December 1939 and January 1940 Mooney met with President Franklin D. Roosevelt and made his offer to serve as a mediator. Roosevelt granted permission for Mooney to hold exploratory talks with the German and Italian governments, and Mooney accordingly flew to Germany. His contacts in German industrial circles and on the staff of Reichsmarshal Hermann Goering were able to arrange meetings for him, and Mooney met with Adolf Hitler on 4 March 1940 and with Goering a few days later; he then travelled to Italy for a meeting with Mussolini. Although he was received amicably and was able to present his views, he received no concessions and no further meetings were held.

In retrospect, Mooney must be seen as naive in this regard. It is astonishing that he could have been so close to affairs in Germany and not have realized the true nature of the Nazi regime, yet it seems this was so. His efforts, although made in good faith, were kept secret at first, but eventually news leaked out and in the summer of 1940 the Chicago-based *PM* magazine ran a series of articles accusing Mooney of Nazi sympathies, and linking his meeting with Hitler to his earlier receipt of the German Order of Merit for services to industry in 1938. Mooney sued the magazine and won, but he never again attempted to intervene in affairs of state. Resigned to the inevitability of war, he left GM Overseas and set up a group of directors to begin planning the conversion of the corporation's facilities to wartime production. Already an officer in the US Naval Reserve, Mooney was called up once the United States entered the war, serving with the bureau of aeronautics, then in staff posts in Europe, and finally on the staff of the chief of naval operations; he finished the war with the rank of captain in the navy. After the war he

returned only briefly to GM, and in 1946 became chairman and president of Willys Overland, taking over the post from Charles SORENSON. He later retired from this post and set up a consulting firm, J.D. Mooney Associates, in New York, working with this firm until the time of his death.

As well as his work, Mooney is noted for a single book, *Onward Industry! The Principles of Organization and Their Significance to Modern Industry*, later reprinted simply as *Principles of Organization*. The book is co-written with Alan C. Reilley; in the foreword Mooney notes that he himself had long been considering the ideas in the book and was about to start writing when he fell into a discussion with Reilley and realized the latter had many of the same thoughts. Although the book is a joint effort, it seems clear from other solo writings that the core philosophy derives from Mooney.

Mooney begins by stating his view that organization is a constant: 'Organization is as old as human society itself' (Mooney and Reilley 1931: xiii). In a view which strongly echoes the thinking of John DAVIS, he sees organization as an essential part of all human activity: 'Organization is the form of every human association for the attainment of a common purpose' (Mooney and Reilley 1931: 10). This does not mean that all organizations are alike; in fact, there are as many different types of organization as there are purposes for them to achieve. However, underlying all types of organization there are basic or first principles, concepts to which all successful organizations adhere, and it is these that he sets out to identify.

His approach to organization, like that of Davis, is strongly historical. Mooney sees the roots of modern business organization as being found in two previous organizational types: the medieval monastic orders, and eighteenth- and nineteenth-century professional military organization. He and Reilley describe in some detail how and why both these organizational forms emerged, and the principles on which they are based. Through these descriptions he high-lights many similarities with modern business organizations, most notably the simultaneous need for coordination and control, and the links between successful achievement of purpose, strong leadership and sound organizational structure.

Mooney also takes a holistic view of organization, and makes reference to the biological metaphor which had been developed by KNOEPPEL and others. He criticizes some writers (he does not name them) who conceptualize organization solely as the framework of the business; this, says Mooney,

> implies that organization refers only to the differentiation and definition of individual duties, as set forth in the familiar organization charts. But duties must relate to procedure, and it is here that we find the real dynamics of organization, the motive power through which it moves to its determined objects. Organization, therefore, refers to more than the frame or skeleton of the industrial edifice. It refers to the completed body, with all of its correlated functions. And it refers to these functions as they appear in action, the very pulse and heart beats, the circulation, the respiration, the vital movement, so to speak, of the organized unit.
>
> (Mooney and Reilley 1931: 12–13)

He goes on to draw a distinction between the terms 'organization' and 'management'. If organization is the body as described above, then management is the 'vital spark' that animates it and moves it; he likens management to a 'psychic force'.

> The technique of management, in its human relationships, can be best described as the technique of handling or managing people, which should be based on a deep and enlightened human understanding. The technique of organization may be described as that of relating specific duties or functions in a completely coordinated scheme. This statement of the difference between managing and organizing clearly shows their intimate relationship. It also shows, which is our present purpose, that the technique of organizing is inferior, in logical order, to that of management. It is true that a sound organizer may, because of temperamental failings, be a poor manager, but on the other hand it is inconceivable that a poor organizer may ever make a good manager ... The prime necessity in all organization is harmonious relationships based on integrated interests, and, to this end, the first essential is an integrated and harmonious relationship in the duties, considered in themselves.
>
> (Mooney and Reilley 1931: 14–15)

Mooney is an advocate of the line and staff principle of management first developed by Harrington EMERSON. In such a system, the organization is divided between the 'line' functional departments involved in production, supply, marketing and so on, and the staff, a corps of generalists usually found near the top of the organization who engage in planning, analysis, monitoring and coordination activities. Line management is about achieving targets; staff management is about deciding what the targets are to be and setting them. But Mooney does not fall into the trap common to other writers of the period in thinking that the staff in some way governs or controls the line. On the contrary:

> the line not merely dominates but includes and contains the staff ... They must not be thought of as segregated functions. The idea of a staff that simply recommends, or of a line that simply does what the staff recommends, would be an absurdity in organization.
>
> (Mooney and Reilley 1931: 494)

Line managers not only are more important than staff managers – it is on the former that the productivity and profitability, and hence the existence, of the firm depends – they also have more knowledge: in their own specialized departments, they are far more knowledge-able and skilled than the staff. The ultimate purpose of the staff, then, is quite simply to *transmit knowledge*, to ensure that the spe-cialized knowledge which accumulates in the departments is shared out through the organi-zations and, most importantly, reaches the highest levels of the organization where it can influence analysis and decision making.

Coordination is an ever-present problem in organizations. There is a need to decentralize control as far as possible, as tightly centralized control is not efficient; but at the same time, too much decentralization and independence lead to divisions wandering off on their own and failing to work towards the overall goal. In his professional life Mooney often saw this in practice, as GM, a sometimes unstable coali-tion of formerly competing car firms, often had difficulty in persuading refractory division chiefs to pull together. Only the strong lead-ership of Alfred Sloan and his successors could achieve this, and Mooney duly devotes con-siderable attention to the need for leadership to overcome the problems of coordination. In a later article, Mooney argued that good lead-ership achieves authority without imposing it:

Here we come to what I conceive to be a vital distinction; that between authority as such, and the form of authority that projects itself through leadership. The difference may be seen in their relation to the organization itself. It takes supreme co-ordinating author-ity to create an organization; leadership, on the other hand, always presupposes the organization. I would define leadership as the form in organization through which authority enters into process; which means, of course, that there must be leadership as the necessary directive of the entire orga-nized movement.

We know how leadership functions in the direction of this movement, and we are all familiar with the structural form through which it operates. We call it delegation of duties, but few realize how absolutely nec-essary to an orderly and efficient procedure is a sound application of this delegating prin-ciple.

(Mooney 1937: 93)

There is one organizational principle more important than all others, however, and it is this: all organizations have a goal, and every organization's sole purpose is the achievement of that goal. It is imperative, he says, to focus on the goal, and not to confuse the goal itself with the means required to meet it. Although he is a supporter of scientific management and the efficiency movement, Mooney expresses some concern with what he sees as a growing trend towards seeing these as ends in them-selves. Efficiency, says Mooney, is never more than a means to meeting a goal:

Worthiness in the industrial sphere can have reference to one thing only, namely the con-tribution of industry to the sum total of human welfare. On this basis only must industry and all its works finally be judged ... The lessons of history teach us that no effi-ciency of procedure will save from ultimate extinction those organizations that pursue a false objective; on the other hand, without such efficient procedure, all human group effort becomes relatively futile.

(Mooney 1937: 97–8)

Onward Industry! was a very popular book in its day, sufficiently so for the author to revise and reissue it later in the decade. Its popular-ity may of course have been a reflection of Mooney's high position and considerable rep-utation; managers have historically tended to buy books by other managers whom they respect. But in fact the book performed a con-siderable service in correlating a number of fairly academic theories and bringing them to a popular audience. It also articulated most forcefully a view that has gone out of fashion today: that organization is a constant in human society and that there is much to be gained by studying historical forms of organization. Mooney is now appreciated by only a handful of business historians; but many of his views on organization still resonate today.

BIBLIOGRAPHY
Mooney, J.D. (1937) 'The Principles of Organization', in L.H. Gulick and L.F. Urwick (eds), *Papers on the Science of Administration*, New York: Institute of Public Administration, 91–8.
Mooney, J.D. and Reilley, A.C. (1931) *Onward Industry! The Principles of Organization and Their Significance to Modern Industry*, New York: Harper and Bros.

MLW

MORGAN, John Pierpont (1837–1913)

John Pierpont Morgan was born in Hartford, Connecticut on 17 April 1837, the son of Junius Spencer Morgan and Juliet Morgan. He died in Rome on 31 March 1913. Unlike Andrew CARNEGIE and John D. ROCKEFELLER, Morgan was himself the product of a wealthy family. Junius Morgan, a dry goods merchant, was the established descendant of Welsh immigrants who had arrived in Massachusetts in 1636. Moving to Boston in 1851, Junius taught his son the art of business and money management at a very early age. The young Pierpont Morgan kept a ledger of his candy and ice-cream purchases, and charged other children admission to see a diorama of Columbus's discovery of America.

In 1854 Junius Morgan became a partner in the London-based firm of George Peabody and Company. Here he dealt in foreign exchange, commodities and securities, many of which were connected with American railroads. Pierpont Morgan went with his father to London, and from there to the Continent to further his education. After attending grammar and public school in Hartford and Boston's English High school, from which he graduated in 1854, Pierpont studied at the Institution Sillig in Vesey, Switzerland (1854–6) and then Göttingen University in Germany (1856–7). He quickly showed an aptitude for the practical and mathematical over the theoretical.

Pierpont Morgan returned the United States in late 1857, where, at the age of twenty, he began work with Duncan, Sherman and Company, Peabody's New York agents. Junius Morgan was grooming his son to be his heir in hope that the Morgans would follow the Baring/Rothschild tradition of family banking. Essential in this tradition was the role of trust. In order that foreign clients honour Morgan credit, the Morgan name had to become known as a trustworthy brand. Heredity and refinement played a role in establishing that brand.

Morgan had also just started with Duncan, Sherman when both the American and British economies crashed in the Panic of 1857. The emerging global economy contracted in the aftermath of the Crimean War (1854–6) and investment in railways dried up. American banks quickly ran into trouble and defaulted on their payments to Peabody. Morgan's bank survived because his father's bank came to its aid, and his father's bank survived in turn because the Bank of England and the prestigious Barings house had come to Peabody's aid with a loan of £800,000. The Panic of 1857 made a deep impression on both Junius and Pierpont Morgan. The father, like the Rothschilds and Barings, detested price competition and passed this disdain on to his son. Pierpont, at the age of twenty, learned the importance of caution in finance and lending, plus a healthy scepticism about the virtues of cut-rate competition in banking, which he came to see as ruinous to financial stability.

Morgan set up his own office in 1860. In 1861 he married Amelia Sturges, daughter of a railway baron; she died of tuberculosis during their honeymoon. The following year, he organized J.P. Morgan and Company, Bankers. He continued to work with his father in a Transatlantic business alliance which lasted until 1894; the new Morgan bank served as an agent for the Peabody bank. The Morgan bank was much influenced by English precedents. It formed syndicates that jointly underwrote new issues of bonds or stock. Morgan usually took as much as 50 per cent of an issue, allowing the other houses to divide the rest.

The Civil War and the railroad boom of the late 1860s and early 1870s turned Morgan into a financial power to be reckoned with. Paying a surrogate to join the army in his place (a common practice among those who could afford it), Pierpont bought and sold securities, bills of lading, grain and iron. He also dealt in currencies and in gold, and served as a source of market intelligence for his father. With his father in charge of the Peabody bank – now J.S. Morgan and Company – both Morgan banks were funnelling British capital into the American rail industry. The Morgans, both in London and New York, were especially active in dealing in government securities. In 1864 Pierpont Morgan took in partners and expanded his firm to become Dabney, Morgan and Company. Together with his father's firm, they floated American government notes in 1866–8 and also notes for Chile and Peru, and funded the French government after its defeat in the Franco-Prussian War (1870–71) by Bismarck's Germany.

Dabney, Morgan and Company made much of its fortune underwriting investments in railroads. Some of these, such as the New York Central, Pennsylvania, and Baltimore and Ohio (B&O) were fairly sound. Others, like the Erie, were a high-risk investment which could only profit by capturing market share from other railroads. The Central, led by Cornelius VANDERBILT, the Pennsylvania, led by Thomas Scott, the B&O and even the Erie joined in collusion, fixing their rates and fares. Free enterprise sounded good in theory, but unrestrained market competition in practice endangered the profits of the established lines. At the Erie, however, Jay GOULD and his ally James Fisk at first joined in and then cut their rates at an opportune moment so as to undercut their rivals. Morgan repeatedly came to the defence of the established lines.

The competition between the Erie and the New York Central, Pennsylvania, and B&O lines led to rate wars which endangered all of them. J.P. Morgan himself was plunged into one of these in 1869. He had underwritten the Albany and Susquehanna Railroad, which linked Albany and Binghamton, New York. The railroad, however, soon fell under attack from the Erie's speculators, Fisk and Gould. Morgan bought his way onto the Albany and Susquehanna board and used his position to save the railway from the Erie's control, enhancing his own reputation as a financier.

In 1871 Morgan created a new partnership when he merged with Drexel and Company, an investment bank in Philadelphia which underwrote both the Pennsylvania and the B&O. The new firm was called Drexel, Morgan and Company. Morgan also became closely allied with the powerful New York Central, which, under Cornelius Vanderbilt, was now the largest company in the United States. The aggressive elder Vanderbilt died in 1877, and his more cautious son William VANDERBILT, stung by adverse publicity surrounding his vast wealth and his father's dealings, commissioned Drexel, Morgan to sell New York Central shares. In 1879 J.P. Morgan became a New York Central director, and a lasting alliance was forged between the Vanderbilt railway and the Morgan bank. The Central deal of 1879 was followed by that involving the Northern Pacific, which ran from Minnesota to Oregon. The railway, once bankrupt in the early 1870s, was now able to expand. Morgan was again allowed to place directors on the board of the railroad. He was now at the centre of railroad finance in the United States.

Morgan had helped defeat the challenge of Gould, but he faced a new one in the 1880s, when the Pennsylvania encouraged a group of railwaymen directly to enter the Central's market. According to Chernow (1990), as the Penn's allies built a rival line along the west bank of the Hudson, terrible rate wars broke out between the Penn and the Central. Vanderbilt retaliated by building a line in Pennsylvania. Morgan was appalled, and recognized that nobody could win. He met with the heads of both railway giants on his yacht, the *Corsair*, in July 1885, and negotiated an end to the rate war. According to the terms of the deal, the Central would control both Hudson lines and the Penn would take over the Central's line in Pennsylvania. Neither would encroach on the territory of the other. Both lines benefited and saw their stocks soar, but nobody won more than Morgan, whose influence was now even greater.

In an age of limited government, Morgan became the regulator of the big railroads. He was behind the refinancing and reorganization of lines such as the Baltimore and Ohio, Chesapeake and Ohio, and the Reading. He reorganized the Richmond Terminal Railroad in Virginia. Morgan installed his own employees on the boards of the railways he reorganized, and used his influence to promote pooling and other anti-competitive arrangements. For example, he underwrote both the Northern Pacific and its rival, the Great Northern.

A great deal has been written about Morgan in the past, much of it portraying him in negative terms. He has usually been described as a selfish 'robber baron', out to rule the country. In particular, he was vilified by the Populists of the 1890s. Morgan, in their view, was an agent of the British and the Rothschilds, responsible for maintaining the gold standard and for deflationary economic policies. To the farmers of the Great Plains he was responsible for the hard money that made it difficult for them to pay their debts and keep their farms. He owned, in their minds, the railroads that charged them high rates.

This traditional portrait of J.P. Morgan has been retouched by Jean Strouse (1999). Originally critical of Morgan, Strouse gained more sympathy for her subject as she uncovered the uncatalogued archives of the Pierpoint Morgan Library. What emerged was a Morgan with a strong sense of *noblesse oblige*, deeply concerned about preserving the stability and soundness of the American economy. The gold standard had to be maintained at all costs, and destructive competition minimized. If the railways went bankrupt, they would drag much of American industry down with them. If the free silver the Populists wanted was coined, foreign investors would cash it in for gold, draining the American gold reserve and causing the collapse of the national currency. In the absence of the interventionist state, Morgan had to fill the vacuum, and attracted resentment for doing so.

The United States had no central bank after Andrew Jackson dissolved the Bank of the United States in the 1830s. Banks were controlled by the individual states, with no nationwide control over either the issuing of bank notes or other forms of credit. In 1889 the balance of payments in gold turned against the United States. When the terrible depression of 1893 struck, this situation aggravated a crisis that only Morgan could resolve.

Morgan's most dazzling feat, according to Chernow (1990), was to save the gold standard and control the flow of gold in and out of the United States. The crisis was the result of a banking crash in Britain, where Barings was devastated by the failure of the Argentinian wheat crop, and J.S. Morgan and Company had to rescue them. British investors, however, then began a run on American gold, which brought about the Panic of 1893 on Wall Street and the worst depression in American history before 1929. More gold was fleeing the country than was coming in. The Sherman Silver Purchase Act of 1890 aggravated this situation. The gold drain continued to worsen throughout 1894, as Congress wanted to maintain a silver standard while President Grover Cleveland insisted upon gold. British and European investors had no confidence in American policy, and treasury gold reserves sank from $107 million in February 1894 to $68 million in January 1895. By then, gold was ebbing from the US Treasury at an alarming rate, and President Cleveland was powerless to stop it. Morgan, meanwhile, had become alarmed. He had offered Cleveland assistance; this was turned down, as the president did not wish to be seen publicly doing deals with unpopular bankers. Morgan then went to the White House; when Cleveland refused to see him, Morgan refused to leave until he did. Finally, when the US Sub-Treasury vault in New York was down to $9 million and a draft for $10 million was presented, Cleveland turned in desperation to Morgan.

Morgan offered a plan according to which he and the Rothschilds would gather a large stock of gold, much of it from European vaults, in return for $65 million in gold bonds. In return, the gold in the US Treasury would not be allowed to flow out. In essence, he was promising to rig the gold market. This was legalized through recourse to an 1862 law, which had allowed President Lincoln emergency powers to buy gold. The markets calmed and the dollar was saved. Morgan, however, was more than ever vilified as the alleged tool of British finance.

Morgan's next major goal was the reorganization of American railroads. He did not believe that unrestrained free competition was beneficial to the economy:

The American public seems unwilling to admit ... that it has a choice between regulated legal agreements and unregulated extralegal agreements. We should have cast away more than 50 years ago the impossible doctrine of protection of the public by railway competition.

(Sinclair 1981: 146)

The passage of the Interstate Commerce Act of 1887 resulted in a further enhancement of Morgan's power. The Act sought to maintain fair rates and outlaw pooling; the result was a series of conflicting railway associations unwilling to cooperate with one another. In 1889 Morgan moved to keep the peace once again by trying to set up a cartel, the Western Traffic Association, both to enforce the Interstate Commerce Act and to maintain reasonable rates. He was also prepared to join with other banking houses in refusing to underwrite the construction of parallel lines and other unprofitable overbuilding. Morgan clearly thought he had furthered the public good.

The association was ordered dissolved by federal courts in 1897. Morgan, meanwhile, moved first to consolidate rail systems and then to create regional alliances between the consolidated systems. One by one, he began to reorganize the railroads: the Philadelphia and Reading, the Baltimore and Ohio, and the Chesapeake and Ohio in the late 1880s, then the Southern railways, the Erie, the Lehigh Valley, and finally the Northern Pacific and Santa Fe after 1895. Morgan's control of the coal-carrying railways in New York and Pennsylvania allowed him efficiently to set price and production schedules. He had the New York Central and the Pennsylvania invest in the other railroads. In the western states, meanwhile, E.H. Harriman and James J. HILL were consolidating other lines, which Morgan then combined into the Northern Securities Company (dissolved by the Supreme Court in 1904). In 1906 Morgan still retained influence over the New York Central, Pennsylvania and Great Northern systems.

Morgan expanded his investments beyond railways, making major investments in the organization of several of what later became important American firms, such as General Electric, American Telephone and Telegraph and International Harvester. The most important of these, however, was United States Steel. The steel industry in 1900 was dominated by

Andrew Carnegie. Morgan controlled a rival company, Federal Steel. A lawyer named Elbert Gary proposed combining a number of smaller firms with Federal to rival Carnegie Steel. In the end, however, rather than creating a rival to Carnegie Steel, Morgan bought the mammoth firm, organizing it and the others into the largest company in the world: the $1.4-billion United States Steel.

Morgan was now seen as the virtual owner, along with the Rockefellers, of the United States. Finley Peter Dunne's Irish-American character Mr Dooley satirized his power:

> Pierpont Morgan calls in wan iv his office boys, th' prisidint iv a national bank, an' says he, 'James,' he says, 'take some change ou iv the'damper an'run out an'buy Europe f'r me,' he says. 'I intind to re-organize it an'put it on a paying basis,' he says. 'Call up the Czar an' th'Pope an' th'Sultan an' th'Impror Willum, an'tell thim we won't need their savices afther nex'week.'
> (Quoted in Brands 1999: 76)

Morgan himself, says Strouse (1999), was an extremely private person, and destroyed many of his personal papers. His reputation for secrecy was legendary: 'Money talks; Morgan doesn't.' The reasons for his silence, however, were more professional than personal. Given his enormous power – not unlike that of a central banker of today – his every utterance would send stocks soaring or plummeting. Whatever Morgan said or did affected the market, and so the less he said the better. His appearance also affected his personality. His large deformed nose, instantly noticeable, inhibited many of his social relationships. He had a gruff personal manner, but he was eminently fair and recognized merit when he saw it; he hired people on that basis.

When Morgan set up the Northern Securities Corporation to rationalize the railroads in the Pacific Northwest, he aroused the wrath of President Theodore Roosevelt, who launched an anti-trust suit against Northern

Securities, and won. Morgan was now frightened by the new interventionist tone of Progressive Era politics, and his fears were confirmed in 1907, when the stock market crashed. The spectre of another 1893 dampened Roosevelt's anti-trust ardour, and, for the final time, Morgan was called upon to be the saviour of his country. Morgan created another syndicate that saved the market, and a depression was averted. In 1912 Morgan was called before the Pujo Committee of the American Congress, which was investigating corporate power. Its findings led in 1913 to the creation of the Federal Reserve System. Morgan's own death symbolized both the end of one era, and the dawn of a new one of public control of monetary policy.

John Pierpont Morgan was the most famous investment banker in American history. and arguably the most powerful man (save the president of the United States) in the late nineteenth- and early twentieth-century United States. He controlled most of the country's railways, which, as Alfred CHANDLER and other later observers recognized, not only made the astonishing American economic growth of the late nineteenth and early twentieth centuries, but also developed the rudimentary models of management which other emerging large companies copied and improved upon. He also reorganized the steel and other industries, in which, again, modern management was beginning to emerge. In addition, he was the saviour of the American economy during the financial panics of 1895, 1901 and 1907. In effect, he served as America's central banker in an era when there was no Federal Reserve.

BIBLIOGRAPHY
Brands, H.W. (1999) *Masters of Enterprise: Giants of American Business from John Jacob Astor and J.P. Morgan to Bill Gates and Oprah Winfrey*, New York: The Free Press.

Chernow, R. (1990) *The House of Morgan: An American Banking Dynasty and the*

Rise of Modern Finance, New York: Atlantic Monthly Press.

Kirkland, E.C. (1967) *Industry Comes of Age: Business, Labor and Public Policy, 1860–1897*, Chicago: Quadrangle Books.

Salsbury, S. (1999) 'Morgan, John Pierpont', in J.A. Garraty and M.C. Carnes (eds), *American National Biography*, Oxford: Oxford University Press, vol. 15, 833–9.

Sinclair, A. (1981) *Corsair: The Life of J. Pierpoint Morgan*, Boston: Little, Brown and Co.

Sobel, R. (1968) *Panic on Wall Street*, New York: Collier Books.

Strouse, J. (1999) *Morgan, American Financier*, New York: Random House.

DCL

MORSE, Samuel Finley Breese (1791–1872)

Samuel Finely Breese Morse was born in Charlestown, Massachusetts on 27 April 1791, the son of Jedidiah Morse, a Calvinist clergyman, and died in New York on 2 April 1872. He attended Phillips Academy at Andover in 1799, and then Yale University from 1805 to 1810, where he first learned about electricity. Morse's first desire was to become an artist, and he made a living as a painter in the 1810s and 1820s. Saddened by the death of his wife Lucretia and his parents between 1825 and 1827, he left the United States and travelled in Europe from 1829 to 1832.

Returning to the United States in 1832, Morse entered into a discussion with Dr Charles Jackson of Boston, who convinced him a device could be made which could send messages over long distances via electric wires. Morse became obsessed with the idea; on his return home, his brother Sidney recorded that Samuel was 'full of the subject of the telegraph during the week from the ship, and for some days afterward could scarcely speak about anything else' (Standage 1998: 30). From 1832 to 1838 Morse worked on his idea, with few results. Poverty was a constant problem; despite having a professorship at New York City University, he was paid no salary. He often had to choose between eating and spending money on his telegraph, built on an artist's frame, that could send messages only a few feet.

In late 1837 a chemistry professor, Leonard Gale, showed Morse how, by use of several batteries and wire turned around a magnet, he could send electricity as far as 16 kilometres (10 miles). Morse, Gale and Alfred Vail, a wealthy student and son of an iron-maker, then formed a partnership to share any profits from the telegraph. The new invention now began to take familiar form. Messages were turned into impulses through a simple key, and recorded at the other end by a moving pen. Words were turned into a code of dots and dashes, the famous Morse Code, in which the simplest letters would have the simplest signatures.

As in the case of his contemporary Charles Babbage, few were prepared to accept that Morse's work had practical value, and it was not until 1843 that the US Congress voted $30,000 to build an experimental telegraph line from Baltimore to Washington, DC. When the line was finished on 24 May 1844, the sentence 'What Hath God Wrought?' was transmitted between the two cities. In spite of coverage in the newspapers, most still saw the telegraph as a mere curiosity. But Morse was enough of a visionary to see the potential of his device. Thwarted by governmental scepticism, he organized a private firm called the Magnetic Telegraph Company. Business saw the potential of his invention if government did not. By late 1845 lines were being strung out of New York City. New York and Philadelphia were joined in 1846. A score of other companies began to build lines as well.

Like the Internet of the 1990s, the telegraph web in America grew explosively, as others applied Morse's invention. In 1846 there were 60 kilometres (40 miles) of telegraph line; by 1848 there were 3,000 kilometres (2,000 miles) and by 1850 almost 20,000 kilometres (12,000 miles) operated by some twenty firms. By 1852 there were almost 50,000 kilometres (30,000 miles) of line operational or under construction, and the United States Census reported that 'numerous lines are now in full operation for a net-work over the length and breadth of the land' (Standage 1998: 58). The first cable under the Atlantic was laid in 1858, and the first line to California was completed in 1861. Beyond his innovation, Morse did not personally play a major role in the telegraph business, generally licensing his patents to others. He remarried in 1847 and helped found Vassar College. By the time of his death in 1872 he had changed the world beyond measure. Ideas, thoughts, business records, news, all could now be sent long distances in a matter of seconds.

Morse recognized this would eventually change humanity's entire way of life. In the late 1830s he had a vision of a wired world in which messages would flow instantly back and forth between Europe and America: 'If it will go ten miles without stopping, I can make it go around the globe' (Standage 1998: 40). His telegraph made a national market and national and multinational corporations possible. It created the foundations for global economy, and made possible instant world and financial news. Without the telegraph, there would have been no giant firms led by Andrew CARNEGIE (who began his own career as a telegraph operator), John D. ROCKEFELLER or John Pierpont MORGAN, no Union victory in the Civil War, no Gilded Age, no telephone and no Internet. Like Tim BERNERS-LEE in our own time, Morse helped change the way management was thought and practised.

BIBLIOGRAPHY
Finn, B.S. (1999) 'Morse, Samuel Finley Breese', in J.A. Garraty and M. Carnes (eds), *American National Biography*, New York: Oxford University Press, vol. 15, 940–42.
Standage, T. (1998) *The Victorian Internet: The Remarkable Story of the Telegraph and the Nineteenth Century's On-line Pioneers*, New York: Walker Publishing Company.
Thompson, R.L. (1947) *Wiring a Continent: The History of the Telegraph Industry in the United States 1832–1866*, Princeton, NJ: Princeton University Press.

DCL

MUMFORD, Lewis (1895–1990)

Lewis Mumford was born in Flushing, New York on 29 October 1895, the son of Lewis Mack and Elvina Mumford; he was born out of wedlock and his father's identity was concealed from him for almost fifty years. He died at his home near New York on 26 January 1990. He married Sophia Wittenberg in 1921, and they had two children. Mumford graduated from Stuyvesant High School in 1912, and went on to study at both New York University and Columbia University, but never graduated. After serving in the US Navy from 1918 to 1919, Mumford became a journalist and also spent some time in Britain, studying with one of his heroes, the biologist and urban planner Patrick Geddes; he was also briefly editor of the *Sociological Review*. In the 1920s he settled down to make a living from his writing and devoted himself to this for the rest of his career, although he occasionally served as a visiting professor at universities including Dartmouth, Stanford, Berkeley, the University of Pennsylvania and Massachusetts Institute of Technology. He became known as a leading writer on the history of technology, architecture and urbanization, and his books received many awards.

In the 1920s and 1930s Mumford's views were strongly influenced by his socialist beliefs and displayed a strong leaning towards utopianism. The book that made his international reputation, *Technics and Civilization* (1934), classifies the history of technology into three periods, the eotechnic, the paleotechnic and the neotechnic. The eotechnic age was the period before the Industrial Revolution – most of human history, in fact – when technology was based on 'natural' and renewable power sources such as wind, water and muscle. Then came the paleotechnic phase of industrialization founded on the exploitation of fossil fuels, and, says Mumford, a consequent exploitation of the working classes by those who had control of technology and so could concentrate power into their own hands. The third phase, the neotechnic, was that into which he felt civilization was about to enter: new scientific developments and above all common access to electrical power would democratize power and allow the masses to participate in its use and distribution.

Although the neotechnic utopia he predicted never came about, Mumford continued to believe in its possibility. In his later, darker and more pessimistic work, Mumford laid the blame for the failure of his vision on the capitalist system. Notably in *The Myth of the Machine* (1967), Mumford describes instead a dystopian nightmare, a 'megatechnic wasteland' in which society is dominated by bureaucracy, and control of technology remains centred in the hands of a few. At the centre of the wasteland, he says, is 'Organization Man – he who stands at once as the creator and creature, the originator and the ultimate victim, of the megamachine' (Mumford 1967, vol 1: 276). The ideal 'organization man', by which Mumford means administrators and managers, is in fact a machine, a robot creature whose only function is to achieve efficiency and productivity; all human feeling, all sensibilities, all love of art and of one's fellow creatures, have been stamped out. Organization man, says Mumford, gave us the gas chamber and atrocities in Vietnam; he cites Adolf Eichmann as an exemplar of the type.

This sort of society, says Mumford, has only two possible ends. On the one hand, organization man may triumph and the world may indeed become the kind of place that George Orwell described in *1984*. But organization man faces a threat, one of his own creation: the rapid rise of mass communications, allowing the instantaneous transmission of large volumes of information and knowledge from one place to another. Mumford does not believe that the iron hierarchies built by organization man will be able to cope with this onslaught of information; he believes they will lapse into a kind of 'electronic entropy', and will crumble and fall, leaving society with little or no structure of any kind. He sharply attacks Marshall McLuhan's concept of the global village, dubbing this 'audio-visual tribalism' (Mumford 1967, vol. 1: 297), and sees the onset of the information revolution as leading not to utopia but to the breakdown of all sense of location and belonging, of cultural nihilism.

This is a bleak work, and reading it serves as a useful antidote to the madly optimistic works on the future of information technology which appeared from many quarters in the 1990s. Mumford's brutal choice, between iron bureaucracy on the one hand and information overload followed by cultural obliteration on the other, has serious implications, ones that modern writers on organization and management need to address. The social and, indeed, political dangers in an age of globalization are well recognized; less so, it seems, are the implications of the free flow of information brought about by the Internet and wireless communication. Finding a balance between these two alternatives, between excessive rationalism and information-based chaos, may be the single greatest management challenge of the coming century.

BIBLIOGRAPHY
Miller, D.L. (1982) *Lewis Mumford: A Life*, Pittsburgh, PA: University of Pittsburgh Press.

Mumford, L. (1934) *Technics and Civilization*, London: George Routledge and Sons.
—— (1967) *The Myth of the Machine*, 2 vols, London: Secker and Warburg.

MLW

MURDOCH, Keith Rupert (1931–)

Rupert Murdoch was born in Melbourne, Australia on 11 March 1931. His father, Sir Richard Murdoch, was a renowned war correspondent who became an important newspaper publisher. After schooling at Geelong Grammar School and working part-time at the *Melbourne Herald*, Murdoch attended Worcester College, Oxford in 1950. He took an MA in economics in 1953 and spent two years as a sub-editor on the *Daily Express*. When his father died in 1954 Murdoch returned to Australia to take over the afternoon daily *Adelaide News*. He met and married Anna Troy – a trainee on the *Sydney Daily* – in 1967. In 1974 he moved to New York, and he became an American citizen in 1985. Divorced in 1998, Murdoch married Wendy Deng, an employee of Star TV in Hong Kong.

Turning minor profits into huge success at the *Adelaide News*, Murdoch established a pattern for all his newspapers: expanded sports coverage, eye-catching headlines and sex-and-scandal stories. He also acquired troubled newspapers cheaply in Perth (1956) and Sydney (1960), and in 1964 set up *The Australian*, the first national newspaper in Australia, and Murdoch's first broadsheet. Expanding into Britain in 1969, he cut aggressive deals to take control of the unashamedly populist *News of the World* and a struggling liberal daily, the *Sun*. Under Murdoch, the *Sun* became the best-selling British newspaper

(claiming over 10 million readers daily in 1997). In the early 1970s Murdoch entered the US market, buying the *San Antonio News*, the *New York Post* and numerous magazines, and establishing the tabloid *National Star*. He bought his first British broadsheet, *The Times*, in 1981. In 1986, eager to exploit new cost-efficient printing technology, Murdoch moved his entire printing operation to a purpose-built site in Wapping in London. There he sacked more than 5,000 striking employees and used lorry deliveries to avoid picket lines until the dismissed workers finally accepted a £60 million settlement in February 1987.

Since his acquisition of Twentieth-Century Fox in 1985, Murdoch had also been building a television network to rival the biggest in the United States. The global success of programmes such as *The Simpsons* and *The X-Files* funded aggressive bids for key sporting events, gaining Murdoch's media channels a growing audience share. Meanwhile, in 1990 Murdoch's British satellite broadcaster Sky TV swallowed its major rival, British Satellite Broadcasting, to form BSkyB. Murdoch had been quick to see the cost advantages of DTH (direct-to-home) satellite television broadcasts, which had no need of costly cable networks, and by the end of 1995 BSkyB had some 3.6 million British subscribers (only 1.3 million homes had cable). In addition, the purchase of Star TV in 1993 from LI Ka-sheng enabled News International to broadcast from Hong Kong to nearly forty Asian countries (including China, India and Japan), while 1997 saw the launch of satellite television in Brazil and Mexico.

By 1990 Murdoch's News International corporation had debts of $7 billion, but controlled newspapers, publishing companies, television and radio stations, a film studio, Internet services and a baseball team. By 2000 its net worth was quoted at $5.3 billion, with nearly 800 businesses across more than fifty countries. Although critics accuse Murdoch of having undue influence in sport and public affairs, he argues that 'capitalists are always trying to stab each other in the back, [so] free markets do not lead to monopolies' (Crainer 1998: 19). He was one of the first to appreciate the practical implications of globalization and to turn these to business advantage. He has been a pioneer of global business, using new technology to build a media empire with operations around the world.

BIBLIOGRAPHY
Crainer, S. (1998) *Business the Rupert Murdoch Way*, Oxford: Capstone.
Jeremy, D.J. (1998) *A Business History of Britain, 1900–1990s*, Oxford and New York: Oxford University Press.
Murdoch, R. (1989) 'Freedom in Broadcasting', MacTaggart Lecture at the Edinburgh International Film Festival, 25 August.
Rodnitzky, L. (1998) 'Murdoch, Rupert', *Britannica: Year in Review 1998*, http://www.britannica.com, 31 January 2001.

SC

N

NADER, Ralph (1934–)

Ralph Nader was born in Winsted, Connecticut on 27 February 1934, the son of Lebanese-born entrepreneurs Nathra and Rose Nader. His outlook was very much shaped by his parents' ideals. While working in the family restaurant, Ralph took part in constant intense discussions of social issues conducted by his father. The Naders took the American dream and obligations of education and citizenship very seriously (Buckhorn 1972; Carry 1972). For them, success included what one did to help others.

Graduating from high school in 1951, Nader entered Princeton University the same year. He graduated in 1955 and then entered Harvard Law School, graduating in 1958. He began to practice law in Hartford; his early cases involved accident, divorce and estate cases.

Early in his career Nader was drawn to the issue of car safety, after seeing what had happened to a small child in an accident. By 1964 he was working as a consultant for the US Department of Labor. It was then that he began to write *Unsafe at Any Speed*, a book which criticized General Motors (GM) for building an unsafe compact car, the Chevrolet Corvair. After the book was published in late 1965, Nader was investigated by private detectives hired by the company. The company itself was investigated by Congress, and Nader later sued GM and won.

Nader used the winnings from his lawsuit to fund the Center for the Study of Responsive Law, which he organized in Washington in 1968. Hiring student activists, whom he trained to set up public interest lobbies elsewhere across the nation, Nader in the late 1960s and late 1970s launched detailed investigations of both government and business. He saw himself as the direct heir of the 1890s American populists and progressive 'muckrakers' such as Upton Sinclair.

'Nader's Raiders', as his volunteers became known, investigated not only the car industry but the Food and Drug Administration, the Interstate Commerce Commission, the chemical industry, airlines, the medical profession, and a number of other workplace and environmental concerns. His efforts resulted in the passage by the administration of Lyndon Johnson of the National Traffic and Motor Vehicle Safety Act, the Highway Safety Act, the Wholesome Meat Act, and the Natural Gas Pipeline Safety Act. The normally pro-business Nixon administration approved the creation of the Occupational Health and Safety Administration in 1970 and created the Environmental Protection Agency in 1972, largely on account of Nader's constant efforts. Car makers recalled thousands of defective cars and equipped cars with seatbelts and airbags. Businesses were forced to take environmental concerns into account in both public relations and deeds.

By 1974 Nader presided over a whole public industry of his own, equivalent in size to the conglomerates he sought to challenge. Almost 150 public interest research groups operated on campuses in over twenty states and in Ontario, Canada. Public Citizen alone was worth over $400 million, and Nader directed over a score of other groups. Critics such as his former associate David Sanford accused him of creating his own monopoly to battle other monopolies.

Nader evolved in the 1970s from consumerism to populism. A Nader study on corporate power written by Morton Mintz and Jerry Cohen, *America, Inc.* (1971), alleged that unsafe vehicles, adulterated foods, pollution and other corporate abuses cost American consumers $200 billion a year. Limited liability and role in job creation enabled corporate executives to damage the public interest with impunity. Zoning, urban renewal, taxation and other laws could be bent to serve private interests.

For Nader, the 'invisible hand' had its place, as did the counterweight of organized labour and activist government. All, however, were to be managed by 'the daily vigilance of advocacy' of citizen lobbies strong enough to control them (Mintz and Cohen 1970: xv). He recommended federal chartering of corporations, criminal liability for executives accountable for destruction of life and property, campaign finance reform and the promotion of alternative technologies. In his ideal system, described by Sanford, big corporations would not be nationalized but broken up into small, environmentally friendly ones accountable to bodies of citizen activists.

Nader's work caused many to begin to regard corporate power with suspicion. Although he greatly strengthened the lobbies seeking to balance business power, his influence declined after recession struck in 1975 and Ronald Reagan was elected in 1980. He became more radical in the 1980s and 1990s as he saw both major parties embracing an agenda dictated by globalization, prompting him to run for president as the candidate of the Green Party in 1996 and again in 2000.

BIBLIOGRAPHY

Buckhorn, R.F. (1972) *Nader, The People's Lawyer*, Englewood Cliffs, NJ: Prentice-Hall.

Carry, C. (1972) *Citizen Nader*, New York: Saturday Review Press.
Mintz, M. and Cohen, J.S. (1971) *America, Inc., Who Owns and Operates the United States*, New York Dial Press.
Sanford, D. (1976) *Me & Ralph: Is Ralph Nader Unsafe for America?*, Washington, DC: The New Republic Book Company.

DCL

NELSON, Richard R. (1930–)

Richard Nelson was born in New York City in 1930. He received his BA from Oberlin College in 1952, and his Ph.D. in economics at Yale in 1956. From its inception his career has involved 'real world' economic issues. A formative influence on Nelson's study of the interaction between government technology policy, industrial innovation and economic growth was his employment with the RAND Corporation. After teaching at Oberlin in the year following graduation from Yale, Nelson joined RAND in Santa Monica, California as an economist. A non-profit corporation, RAND derives its name from the contraction of the phrase 'research and development', and derived its initial funding from the US Air Force. RAND was established shortly after the end of the Second World War within the organization of the US aircraft manufacturer, Douglas Aircraft. In 1948 it was incorporated as an independent private corporation to provide research and consulting services to government officials and agencies working on national defence issues. By 1957, when Nelson joined RAND, the corporation had expanded its research scope well beyond national security policy into US domestic policy, especially economic policy.

After two years at RAND and a year teaching at Carnegie Institute of Technology, Nelson served for two years as senior staff economist on the Council of Economic Advisers to the President of the United States. During Nelson's service the council was influential in recommending policies that were intended to implement President John F. Kennedy's goal of 'getting America moving again' following the 1958–9 recession. Following two years at the council Nelson returned to RAND. While there he co-authored studies on technology, economic growth and public policy (Nelson *et al.* 1967) and on structural change in a developing economy (Nelson *et al.* 1971).

According to Hodgson (1999), Nelson passed from being a neoclassical growth theorist to 'almost a full blown evolutionary theorist' in the period 1964–8, his second stay at RAND. During this period he was reunited with Sidney WINTER, with whom he had worked both at the council and during his earlier employment at RAND. Portions of their evolutionary analysis were first presented in a series of articles, but publication of *An Evolutionary Theory of Economic Change* in 1982 marked the first full exposition.

The straightforward objective of *An Evolutionary Theory* is to develop an evolutionary theory of the capabilities and behaviour of business firms in a market environment and to develop models consistent with the theory. 'Evolutionary' is used in the broad sense as involving processes of long-term and progressive change. The authors take care to point out where they share agreement on some points with what they call 'orthodox' (neoclassical) economic theory, but, at the same time, they clearly delineate their differences. These differences are with the orthodox economic model centred on equilibrium analysis, and in which firms are governed exclusively by profit maximization as a consequence of the orthodox assumption of rational, that is profit-maximizing, behaviour by economic actors, with choices both precisely known and given. For the authors, orthodoxy's commitment to maximization and equilibrium analysis leaves orthodox economic theory unable to deal with economic change or technological innovation.

Nelson and Winter acknowledge that their theory borrows ideas from biology. The key borrowings are the ideas of 'organizational genetics' and 'economic natural selection'. These ideas are the foundation for the three principal concepts in their formulation of a theory of evolutionary economic change; the concepts of organizational routine, organizational search and selection environment.

An Evolutionary Theory uses the word 'routine' to describe regular and predictable behaviour patterns of firms. The authors use 'routine' in the same sense that 'program' or 'routine' is used in computer programming. A routine can refer to a repetitive pattern of activity within a firm, to an individual skill, or to the regular functioning of individual or organizational performance. These routines play the role that genes play in biological evolutionary theory. They are embedded in the firm much as genes are within an organism, and can, but need not necessarily, determine its actual behaviour, since the environment also plays a part. These routines are 'organizational memory'; an important means of storing operational knowledge. To say that firm behaviour is governed by routine is not, say the authors, the same as saying that it is unchanging. However it is important to recognize 'that the flexibility of routinized behaviour is of limited scope and that a changing environment can force firms to risk their very survival on attempts to modify their routines' (Nelson and Winter 1982: 400).

But by what means do firms change routines? The authors use the term 'search' to encompass all firm activities that involve evaluating current routines and consideration of modification, change or replacement. Unlike the orthodox economic model of clearly defined choices with a decision rule of profit maximization, search involves uncertainty, and perceived alternatives may give way to alternatives discovered during the search itself (Nelson and Winter 1982: 171). While search is partly routinized, the element of uncertainty makes search a stochastic process. If routines are the genes in this evolutionary theory, then search routines stochastically generate mutations.

Finally, evolutionary theory considers the dynamics of 'selection'. Firms in evolutionary theory seek profits, but profit maximization is not their single decision rule. Evolutionary theory incorporates the concept that profitable firms expand and unprofitable ones contract. Firms that possess superior routines will grow faster than those that do not. Differential growth plays the same role in Nelson and Winter's evolutionary theory as it does in biological theory.

The 'selection environment' of the firm encompasses all of the considerations that affect its well-being and growth. The selection environment is made up of circumstances external to the firms in the industry being studied, as well as by the characteristics and behaviour of the other firms in the industry. Nelson and Winter return to SCHUMPETER's evolutionary system to describe the role of market competition within a sector as a form of evolutionary selection, involving innovation. Firms are motivated to introduce better products and processes; 'better' processes mean lower production costs and 'better' products mean those that consumers will buy at a cost above price. Either way, the reward is higher monetary profits for the innovator. Profitable firms grow and take market share from less innovative competitors, forcing them to contract, and to try to imitate the profitable firms' innovative actions.

Reading *An Evolutionary Theory*, one is struck by the common sense it contains and how the ideas presented strike familiar notes of basic business experience. Perhaps, as the authors declare, after one gets used to the viewpoint of evolutionary theory, much of what one sees is familiar. They are also forthright in acknowledging Schumpeter's 'pervasive' influence in their work, and contributions to evolutionary theory by CYERT and MARCH, SIMON, WILLIAMSON and Knight, among others, are also acknowledged (Nelson and Winter 1982: 33–45).

The use of analogies from biology in economics has been subject to challenge, and the authors cite PENROSE's 1952 article as raising the issue whether there was in economics a counterpart to genetic inheritance. The authors assert that, while pleased to exploit ideas from biology that offer help in understanding economic problems, they disclaim any intention to pursue biological analogies for their own sake or in order to progress towards what they call 'an abstract, higher-level evolutionary theory that would incorporate a range of existing theories' (Nelson and Winter 1982: 11). Making exact analogies between the two disciplines may or may not be possible. Yet the business landscape depicted in *An Evolutionary Theory* rings more true as a depiction of contemporary business than the landscape painted by orthodox economic theory. Business history in the past thirty years provides ample support for the evolutionary thesis that simply being able capably to produce a given set of products with a given technology will not assure a firm's long-term survival. Rather, to be successful for any length of time, a firm must be able to innovate (Nelson 1991: 68).

Nelson presented his theory of the reasons for differential firm performance based on evolutionary economics in his 1991 article, 'Why Do Firms Differ, and How Does it Matter?'. Here he contrasted the perspective of neoclassical (orthodox) economics in studying how industries work with the perspective of management scholars, who are interested in the behaviour and performance of individual firms.

In his presentation of the theory of dynamic firm capabilities, Nelson first reviewed the theory of the firm presented in *An Evolutionary Theory*, as well as the works of CHANDLER, Teece and Prahalad and HAMEL, among others. Nelson presented his own views by focusing on three interrelated features of a firm: its strategy, its structure and what he termed its 'core capabilities' (Nelson 1991: 67).

Nelson's concept of strategy is strategy as understood by business historians and management scholars, a set of broad commitments made by a firm that define and rationalize its objectives and how it intends to pursue them. In contrast to neoclassical theory, these commitments may be matters of faith or tradition on the part of top management rather than a result of calculation. Further, strategies do not determine the details of firm action, only what Nelson calls its 'broad contours'.

Nelson's concept of firm structure follows Chandler. For Nelson, however, firm strategy defines structure in a general way, rather than providing a specific structure. A firm's structure is the way it is set up to follow its strategy and, in Nelson's words, 'work out the details' (Nelson 1994: 244). According to Nelson, 'strategy and structure call forth and mold organizational capabilities', but what an organization can do and do well involves consideration of its core capabilities (Nelson 1991: 68). Core capabilities are founded on the 'routines' described in *An Evolutionary Theory*. Routines are a hierarchy of higher-order decision procedures for determining what things should be done, and lower-level organizational skills that determine how those things should be done.

Core capabilities are different from the concept of the core competences of the corporation, discussed by Prahalad and Hamel (1990). Core capabilities need not be 'hard technology', but include competence in functions such as marketing, distribution and logistics. In addition, core capabilities have significant organizational components (Dosi *et al.* 2000: 5–6). Firm diversity is to be expected, given the premise of evolutionary theory that it is not possible for a firm to 'know' with certainty what strategy or strategies will guarantee success. Firms will therefore choose different strategies, and these will lead to different structures, and development of different core capabilities. From a public policy point of view firm diversity is crucial to economic progress, because diversity means

that firms will explore different ways of doing things in order to find better ways of doing things (Nelson 1991: 69, 72).

Nelson revisited his earlier studies of economic growth theory when he examined differing explanations for the 'Asian Miracle' (Nelson and Pack 1999). One set of explanations are subsumed under the 'assimilation' rubric; this theory stresses public policy in newly industrializing countries (NICs) that encouraged entrepreneurship, innovation and learning, all of which facilitated the adoption of technologies from more advanced nations. In contrast, the 'accumulation' theory, often associated with Krugman (1994), proposes that the massive investment in physical and human capital made by Asian NICs is sufficient in itself to explain the 'Asian Miracle'. Nelson and Pack come down on the side of the 'assimilationists', asserting that learning, technology absorption and forceful entrepreneurship, when coupled with large investments in physical and human capital, complement each other and result in economic growth. In support, the authors return to the theory of the firm articulated in Nelson's earlier works.

The article argues that when firms choose to do things new to them and to their community, this involves risk taking, which, to be successful, requires learning. Learning proceeds at different levels – at the level of individuals and teams, at the firm level and at the industry level. According to the authors, explanations of the 'Asian Miracle' that focus only on increased levels of investment miss this dynamic process.

In a biographical note on Nelson, Hodgson (1994) observes that Nelson's aim has been to help develop economics as an operational and empirically enriched science which can engage with real-world problems. Nelson's works offer ample testimony to the accuracy of the observation, and to the achievement of that aim. He is at present George Blumenthal Professor of International and Public Affairs, Business and Law at Columbia University.

BIBLIOGRAPHY

Dosi, G., Nelson, R.R. and Winter, S.G. (eds) (2000) *The Nature and Dynamics of Organizational Capabilities*, New York: Oxford University Press.

Hodgson, G. (1994) 'Richard R. Nelson', in *The Elgar Companion to Institutional and Evolutionary Economics, L–Z*, Aldershot, and Brookfield, VT: Edward Elgar, 126–8.

—— (1999) *Evolution and Economics: On Evolutionary Economics and the Evolution of Economics*, Cheltenham and Northampton, MA: Edward Elgar, 157–8.

Krugman, P. (1994) 'The Myth of Asia's Miracle', *Foreign Affairs* (December): 62–78.

Nelson, R.R. (1991) 'Why Do Firms Differ, and How Does it Matter?', *Strategic Management Journal* 12: 61–74.

—— (ed.) (1993) *National Innovation Systems: A Comparative Analysis*, New York: Oxford University Press.

—— (1994) 'Theory of the Firm (II)', in P.J. Boettke (ed.), *The Elgar Companion to Institutional and Evolutionary Economics, A–K*, Aldershot and Brookfield, VT: Edward Elgar, 241–6.

—— (1996) *The Sources of Economic Growth*, Cambridge, MA: Harvard University Press.

Nelson, R.R. and Mowery, D. (eds) (1999) *Sources of Industrial Leadership: Studies of Seven Industries*, Cambridge: Cambridge University Press.

Nelson, R.R. and Pack, H. (1999) 'The Asian Miracle and Modern Growth Theory', *The Economic Journal*, 109(July): 416–36.

Nelson, R.R. and Winter, S. (1982) *An Evolutionary Theory of Economic Change*, Cambridge, MA: Harvard University Press.

Nelson, R.R., Peck, M.J. and Kalachek, E.D. (1967) *Technology, Economic Growth and Public Policy*, Washington, DC: The Brookings Institution.

Nelson, R.R., Schultz, T.P. and Slighton, R.L. (1971) *Structural Change in a Developing Economy: Colombia's Problems and Prospects*, Princeton, NJ: Princeton University Press.

Penrose, E. (1952) 'Biological Analogies in the Theory of the Firm', *American Economic Review* 42: 804–19.

Prahalad, C.K. and Hamel, G. (1990) 'The Core Competence of the Corporation', *Harvard Business Review* (May): 79–91.

SR

NOYCE, Robert (1927–90)

Robert Noyce was born in Burlington, Iowa on 12 December 1927, the son of Ralph and Harriet Noyce, and died in Austin, Texas on 3 June 1990. His father was a Congregationalist minister. After a BA at Grinnell College in 1949, Noyce took his Ph.D. in electrical engineering from Massachusetts Institute of Technology in 1953. He worked first as a research engineer with Philco in Philadelphia, and then with the Shockley Semiconductor Laboratory in California. In 1957 he left Shockley to set up Fairchild Semiconductors in Mountain View, California. He was director of research of Fairchild from 1957 to 1959, then vice-president and general manager from 1959 to 1968. While at Fairchild, Noyce became the first to discover a reliable process for making semiconductors from silicon chips, and it was this that made the company's name.

Despite Fairchild's success, Noyce felt the company had become too big. Feeling that he could work best in a small company environment, in 1968 he and a partner, Gordon Moore, left Fairchild to establish Intel in Santa Clara, California. Among the employees who followed them from Fairchild to Intel was the Hungarian-American engineer Andrew GROVE. Intel prospered, but in 1979 Noyce handed over the reins of the company to Grove and set off to found another new business, Sematech, a consortium between the US government, academia and the semiconductor industry. He was named to the National Inventors Hall of Fame in 1983, and the National Business Hall of Fame in 1989.

Noyce was driven by a passion for innovation, which he believed to be essential for both business and national success. The great motivation for innovation, he believed, is the need for change. Successful innovation requires risk taking, but also confidence in the outcome. Innovative workers need to be challenged, but they also need to feel needed; their work must mean something, to themselves and others. He always believed that the best organizations are small; when Fairchild grew to be too big, he left to try to replicate the small company 'feel' at Intel, and then again at Sematech. Andrew Grove ultimately proved to be more able to pull together large organizations and maintain control without losing motivation.

Noyce had a strongly egalitarian approach to business: Krass (1998) says that even car parking was on a first-come first-served basis, with no reserved spots for executives. Noyce's companies were democratic and decentralized, with decisions made at a low level through group consultation and no tight controls. The only thing Noyce demanded from his teams was results: so long as teams hit or exceeded their targets, he was satisfied. He remains a classic example of the techno-entrepreneur, motivated by a desire for innovation at all costs, a core vision of what innovation will achieve, and a belief that innovation should mean prosperity for all of society, not just the innovator's own firm. These common beliefs can be found among many of the leading managers of the information revolution, from EDISON down to present-day figures such as Mitch KAPOR and Jim CLARK.

BIBLIOGRAPHY

Jackson, T. (1997) *Inside Intel: How Andy Grove Built the World's Most Successful Chip Company*, London: HarperCollins.

Krass, P. (1998) *The Book of Leadership Wisdom*, New York: John Wiley, 140–49.

MLW

NOYES, Pierrepont Burt (1870–1959)

Pierrepont Burt Noyes was born in Oneida, New York on 18 August 1870, and died there on 15 April 1959. He was the son of John Humphrey Noyes, the founder of the Oneida community, and Harriet Worden. He studied at Colgate University before returning to Oneida in 1894. He married Corinna Kinsley in 1894, and they had three children.

Noyes's father, John Humphrey Noyes, was the originator of the quasi-religious doctrine on which the Oneida community had been founded in 1848. This doctrine, like many utopian socialist movements of the nineteenth century, was based on communal living and property held in common. A perfectibilist, Noyes believed that human perfection was possible in this life, and saw tolerance, equality and sharing of goods as essential to reaching that goal. He was also a freethinker, and the community practised group marriage and sexual liberation. Unusually, however, the Oneida community was also self-sufficient and highly successful in commercial terms, developing businesses in areas such as silk production, fruit canning and the making of silver-plate tableware.

Internal dissent eventually brought about the community's end. John Humphrey Noyes left Oneida in 1880, dying in 1886, and the new leaders decided to dissolve the community. Rather than physically sharing out property, however, they took the somewhat unusual step of converting the commune to a joint stock company, giving shares to all adult members of the former community. Thus in 1880 the Oneida community became Oneida Community Ltd. However, none of the leaders had much commercial experience or acumen, and the business remained static into the 1890s.

In 1894 Pierrepont Noyes, resolving to lift the fortunes of the business, returned to Oneida with the aim of modernizing the firm. Most of the directors were against him, but Noyes persuaded the individual shareholders to support him at a general meeting. As a result of this palace coup he took virtual control of the company, becoming general manager from 1899 to 1926, president from 1910 to 1950, and honorary president from 1950 until his death.

Noyes decided to focus the business on one product line, tableware; the other businesses were gradually sold off to raise capital. The silverplate business was dominated by the firm of Rogers in Connecticut, and most competitors tried to undercut it on price. Noyes decided to attack on quality instead, and launched the Community Plate range as a premium premium brand, priced slightly higher but of significantly better quality and design. At the same time he created a selling organization to market the product. The first pattern, Avalon was marketed in 1902. Take-off was slow at first, with some resistance from retailers, but Noyes responded with strong advertising and promotional campaigns aimed directly at the consumer to stimulate demand. In 1910 Oneida launched a groundbreaking series of advertisements built around illustrations of young, pretty stylish girls by the artist Coles Phillips, which associated the product with smart, attractive young people. Oneida also got endorsements by leading socialites which further enhanced the brand's appeal.

With no formal business education or training, Noyes had proved to be an adept commercial manager. He was equally adroit at labour relations. Determined not to sacrifice the original ideals of equality and democracy which had motivated the Oneida community, he saw how these could be turned to the advantage of both the workers and the business as a whole. He saw employee welfare not in terms of philanthropy but as a duty. He once remarked that employers should 'make no welfare moves from fear, but always and only because you believe that company success should add to the comfort and happiness of every member of the working group', and that, 'when your employees really believe that you take a practical interest in their welfare and that you mean what you say, you will have acquired an asset money alone could never buy' (Edwards 1948: 8). He believed that the best form of welfare came through paying good wages.

For all his emphasis on equality, Noyes could be authoritarian when he needed to be: in 1899 he broke a strike at the company's Niagara Falls plant, not because he was opposed to unions – quite the contrary – but because he did not believe the Oneida ethic could work in a unionized shop. Fiercely loyal to his own workers, he asked for and usually got their strong loyalty in turn. Lowenthal (1927) reports that during the recession of 1921 Noyes called a meeting at the plant and asked the workers if they would take a pay cut in exchange for a greater share of profits should any be made; the proposal 'received the greatest handclap in the history of the company' (1927: 117).

During the First World War Noyes served as an adviser to the US government, and then was a member of the Interallied Rhineland Commission in Coblenz from 1919 to 1920, where he argued against some of the more punitive measures taken against defeated Germany. He was the author of several books on Oneida, on the political situation in Europe, and also a novel. His last public act was to serve as president of the Saratoga Springs Authority, overseeing the $5 million development which made Saratoga Springs into North America's leading spa.

BIBLIOGRAPHY

Edmonds, W.D. (1948) *The First Hundred Years, 1848–1948*, Oneida, NY: Oneida Ltd.

Lowenthal, E. (1927) 'The Labor Policy of the Oneida Community Ltd.', *Journal of Political Economy* 35(February): 114–26.

Noyes, P. (1937) *My Father's House: An Oneida Boyhood*, London: John Murray.

ML

O

Olds was born in Geneva, Ohio on 3 June 1864, the son of a blacksmith-machinist. He died at home in Lansing, Michigan on 26 August 1950. In 1880 the family moved to Lansing where his father opened a machine shop. Olds attended the local school before dropping out at sixteen to work full-time in the family firm. Five years later he bought out his brother's interest and took over the running of the firm. He met and married Metta Woodward in 1889.

Olds turned the firm's fortunes around by developing an improved steam engine that used a gasoline burner. Sales of the steam engine rose steadily and in 1896, ten years after its introduction, sales were six times those of 1885. The engines became the core business of the firm, and he began to experiment putting them to other uses, and developed crude prototype three-wheeled steam-powered vehicles. By 1892 the steamer had been described favourably in the press, leading the Francis Times Company of London to purchase the Olds steamer.

Olds soon switched to the internal combustion engine, having decided that steam engines had too many problems to be practical for road vehicles. In 1893 he began working on his version of an internal combustion engine, which was patented in 1896. The engine was an instant success, and necessitated another (the third) factory expansion. He gave his first public demonstration of a single-cylinder engined carriage in August 1896. The demand for the Olds engine was such that it was deemed too risky to divert resources away from the traditional business. He then established the Olds Motor Vehicle Company in 1897 to make gasoline-powered cars, but lacked the capital to engage in serious production. Subsequently he formed a new concern, merging the two original firms to form the Olds Motor Works, with financial backing from a Detroit businessman, and moved the works to a new factory in Detroit. After experimenting with numerous models including electric cars, he concentrated in 1900 on the first Oldsmobile, propelled by a single-cylinder engine mounted under the seat. It was designed to be an inexpensive car, and it became popular with New Yorkers, competing directly with the popular Locomobile steamer. Olds had no difficulty in finding dealers to sell his cars, as demand for the inexpensive vehicle grew very rapidly.

Olds expanded production facilities, setting up a new factory in Lansing, and continuing to increase production and sales, reaching a US record figure of 2,500 cars in 1902, and a world record of 3,000 in 1903. In 1904 Olds Motor Works was by far the world's leading producer.

The Olds factory assembled parts made by other firms all over the United States. The physical separation of component manufacture from assembly made it possible for a high degree of specialization of labour and equipment, providing the firm with the opportunity to capitalize on economies of scale. To keep up with the unprecedented demand, Olds was forced to focus on and improve the efficiency of his assembly operations. He employed production methods that were later developed more fully by Henry FORD. The organization of the Olds factory in Detroit was laid out according to the flow-of-materials principle. Vehicles were moved around the factory on wooden trolleys (prior to this each car was made in one location with the workers and parts coming to each), the work force was assigned to specific tasks along the route, and components were placed in convenient locations.

Olds had had to relinquish considerable control of the company in order to raise the finance he needed, and when other managers wanted to change production procedures, he lost the battle: the directors replaced him in 1904 with a new general manager. Undaunted, he immediately set up the REO company in Lansing, which produced its first car in 1905. He developed a stronger, more powerful car in addition to the runabout model, and it was this that accounted for REO's success; by 1907 it was one of the top five firms in the United States. The Olds Motor Works company, meanwhile, was taken over in 1908 when General Motors was founded to take control of Olds, Cadillac and other firms.

Olds began to leave more of the company business to his staff, and the early success of REO faded. He did lead the firm into producing trucks in 1911, which it continued to produce for forty years after car manufacture ceased in 1936. He stepped down as president of the firm in 1923 to become chairman, all the while dabbling with other inventions, developing one of the first powered mowers, working on diesel engines and indulging his hobbies of boating and travelling. The Great Depression led him to take a more active role in the firm, but he finally left the company in 1936, when the directors rejected his ideas for revitalizing the company.

Olds was a talented inventor, and often produced innovative responses to problems.

His inventions and designs such as the powered mower and the electric car showed considerable far-sightedness. He seemed to be able to capture the mood of his markets in his products, first with the inexpensive Oldsmobile, then with the powerful REO models, and later on with the introduction of his trucks. As an early and talented pioneer of the automobile industry, Olds was remarkable both for developing initial product concepts and for establishing original mass-production facilities.

BIBLIOGRAPHY
Bardou, J.P., Chanaron, J.-J., Fridenson, P. and Laux, J.M. (1982) *The Automobile Revolution: The Impact of an Industry*, Durham, NC: University of North Carolina Press.

AJ

OLSEN, Kenneth Harry (1926–)

Kenneth Harry Olsen was born in Bridgeport, Connecticut on 20 February 1926, the son of Oswald and Svea Olsen. He married Eeva-liisa Aulikki Valve in 1950. After service in the US Navy from 1944 to 1946, Olsen took a BS in electrical engineering at the Massachusetts Institute of Technology (MIT) in 1950, followed by an MS in 1952. He worked at MIT's Lincoln Laboratory until 1957, then left to start Digital Equipment Corporation (DEC) in Maynard, Massachusetts. He founded DEC with five partners and $70,000 borrowed from venture capitalists, setting up operations in part of a former flour mill. Olsen was DEC's president until 1991. He was also a director of Polaroid for a number of years, and was among the board members who voted to remove the company's founder Edwin LAND from the board in 1975; in 1991 he himself suffered the same fate at the hands of his own board. He remains president emeritus of DEC.

Olsen had an early love of electronics, and was experimenting with radios while still a boy. His work at MIT in the immediate postwar period, and exposure to the work of MIT faculty and alumni such as Jay Wright FORRESTER and WANG An showed him the possibilities of computers. Olsen's initial vision was to develop smaller computers which would have the same processing power as large mainframes, providing desktop computer processing for scientists and engineers. The launch of the mini-computer heralded a new age in computer development, leading ultimately to the development of the personal computer and the laptop. In the 1960s and 1970s DEC led the way in personal computers, outstripping larger rivals such as IBM.

In establishing DEC, Olsen set up what may have been the first matrix organization. He himself referred to it as a 'product line system'. In DEC, employees' and managers' roles were defined not so much by what department they were working in, but what product they were working on. Each product line was assigned to a cross-disciplinary team which worked solely on that product. The system was deliberately designed to produce rivalry and even conflict between teams; by building conflict into the system, Olsen felt he could use the resulting tension in a creative way, impelling the teams to greater efforts. This system worked well when the company was small and growing rapidly. Its weaknesses became apparent, however, once DEC became larger. The entire matrix organization depended on Olsen himself, at the centre of the matrix, to hold it all together. By many accounts he could be an inconsistent and difficult employer to work for, with a strong temper when results did not go his way.

In 1982–3 the cracks in the system began to show and DEC's profits slumped as share of the personal computer market was taken away by aggressive rivals such as Steve JOBS at Apple Computers. Olsen responded by restructuring what had been an open, entrepreneurial company, instituting better controls and more centralized management systems. Even though the organization became more conventional, however, much of the old culture remained. Managers in DEC continued to have considerable freedom, and DEC remained an informal place with no dress code and with Olsen on first-name terms with his employees. A balance between freedom and discipline seemed to have been struck, and DEC bounced back in the mid-1980s with new product lines in network computers, where it became the market leader.

BIBLIOGRAPHY
Rifkin, G. and Harrar, G. (1988) *The Ultimate Entrepreneur: The Story of Ken Olsen and Digital Equipment Corporation*, Chicago: Contemporary Books.

MLW

P

PACKARD, David (1912–66)

David Packard was born in Pueblo, Colorado on 7 September 1912 and died in Stanford, California on 26 March 1996. The son of a lawyer, Sperry Sidney Packard, and his wife Ella, a high-school teacher, the young Packard was an avid reader of books on science and electricity while in elementary school, and built his first vacuum-tube radio receiver at the age of twelve. He became a proficient ham radio operator while in high school, and went on to enrol as an electrical engineering student at Stanford University in California. There he met William HEWLETT, a fellow student who shared his passion for electronics.

Packard was awarded his bachelor of arts degree at Stanford in 1934. After some months of graduate study at the University of Colorado he moved to Schenectady, New York, to work in the vacuum-tube engineering department of General Electric. After solving a production failure problem with the vacuum tubes by spending time on the factory floor and working closely with the employees there, Packard learned that what he would later call 'management by walking around' could be a simple yet effective way for supervisors to get to know their employees and understand the work they were doing.

In 1938 Packard returned to Stanford on fellowship to study the theory of the vacuum tube. He renewed his friendship with Hewlett, and they formed a business partnership aimed at using their combined training in circuit technology and manufacturing processes to design and manufacture electronic products. They called themselves Hewlett-Packard Company after flipping a coin to decide whose name should appear first on the company masthead. The garage of the house they were renting in Palo Alto, California became their workshop. The garage was later designated by the state of California as an official historical landmark and the birthplace of that high-tech region of California now called Silicon Valley.

Packard and Hewlett began their business with $538 in working capital and soon were taking custom orders for apparatus ranging from air-conditioning control units to foul-line indicators for bowling alleys. In 1939 they switched their focus from custom orders to mass-produced instruments, with particular emphasis on low-cost audio oscillators that could generate controlled signals at predetermined frequencies. These units were used to check the performance of amplifiers and broadcast transmitters. The Walt Disney Studios bought eight of them, at $71.50 a piece, to use as part of the sound equipment for the movie *Fantasia*. By the end of that year the partnership had grossed $5,369 with a net profit of $1,563. They would show a profit every year thereafter.

During the Second World War, Hewlett-Packard expanded rapidly to meet the electronic needs of the US defence industry, building instruments to measure and test electronic equipment. They moved from the garage to a rented building, and hired staff to do their sheet-metal work, cabinet-making and machinery designs. Packard looked after the business and administrative matters, and was seen as the 'dynamic manager' of the firm. Hewlett, responsible for product design and manufacture, was the 'engineering brains'. He spent part of the war as an officer in the US Army Signal Corps while Packard ran the company alone.

Business declined rapidly after the war. Staff who had been hired for defence-related assembly line work had to be laid off. Key technical staff were retained, however, and gradually the business rebounded. During the 1950s Hewlett-Packard's product line grew to include hundreds of electronic measuring devices for a wide range of frequencies. In 1951 the company had 215 employees and reported sales of $5.5 million. In 1958 the company had 1,778 employees and sales of $30 million. In 1959 the company established an overseas marketing division in Geneva, and a manufacturing plant in Böblingen, West Germany.

By the end of the 1960s Hewlett-Packard was the world's largest producer of electronic measuring devices, with seventeen manufacturing divisions and 160 sales offices in the USA, Europe, South America and Asia. Packard served as chairman of the board and chief executive officer of the company – with Hewlett as president – until 1969, when he left the company to become Deputy Secretary of Defense in the first Nixon administration. Packard served in that capacity for two years, and found that government bureaucracy ran counter to the principles of efficiency that Hewlett-Packard held dear. It was, he said, 'like pushing on one end of a forty-foot rope, and trying to get the other end to do what you want' (Packard 1995: 184).

Packard was re-elected chairman of Hewlett-Packard after he resigned his government post in 1971. A year later, Hewlett-Packard introduced a hand-held calculator that became an instant success and made the slide rule obsolete. The year after that, the company began to make inroads into the general consumer market with its minicomputers, scanners and desktop printers.

In 1995 Hewlett-Packard had more than 100,000 employees on its payroll, and produced revenues of $31 billion. The same year, Packard published a book about the company's approach to business (Packard 1995). He wrote that he had tried to retain a small company atmosphere at Hewlett-Packard even as the company expanded around the world, and that his emphasis on high employee morale and fringe benefits had resulted in a low personnel turnover rate. His management philosophy, which he called the 'HP Way', involved encouraging employees to work towards a common goal in an atmosphere of shared purpose and individual freedom. He characterized this as 'management by objective', and said it was vastly superior to the system – once common in American business – in which organizations operated under 'military-type corporate directives and tight controls' (Packard 1995: 152).

Packard was generous with his money. In 1964 he and his wife founded the David and Lucile Packard Foundation in Los Altos, California, to support universities, community groups, youth agencies, family planning centres and hospitals dependent on private funding and volunteer leadership. When he died his entire $6.6 billion fortune went to the David and Lucile Packard Foundation, making it America's third-largest charity.

BIBLIOGRAPHY
Packard, D. (1995) *The HP Way: How Bill Hewlett and I Built Our Company*, New York: HarperCollins.

BB

PARKER, Cornelia Stratton (b. 1885)

Little is known of Parker's life; the only clues come from her biography of her husband, the economist Carleton Parker (1879–1918). Born Cornelia Stratton in 1885, she met and married Parker in 1903 and accompanied him to Harvard and later to Heidelberg, where he studied. Parker was a left-leaning intellectual and economist of labour, and his wife became interested in the subject as well. The Parkers moved to Seattle, where Carleton Parker taught economics until his sudden death late in 1918. Cornelia went on to become a minor novelist.

Cornelia Parker's interest in the labour movement led her to write one book of significance to management, *Working With the Working Woman* (1922). The book is a series of chapters based on interviews with individual women workers, mostly factory workers. It builds up a full portrait of each, based on both the interviews and Parker's own observations of the women at work and during rest breaks. This was a novel practice, as Parker herself was well aware: in her introduction, she argues that the study of labour ought to be dynamic, as it is intimately linked to human nature. She believed that most academic studies of the problems of labour were too theoretical, and not grounded in observation:

> Suppose that for the moment your main intellectual interest was to ascertain what the average worker ... thought about his [sic] jobs and things in general. To what books could you turn? Indeed I have come to feel that in the pages of O. Henry there is more to be gleaned on the psychology of the working class than books to be found on economics shelves.
>
> (Parker 1922: viii)

In taking this view, Parker was well in advance of her time; large-scale academic studies of the behaviour of individual workers in the workplace did not begin until the following decade. Her purpose in undertaking the study, she says, is to advance industrial welfare; information gained through direct contact with individual workers can be used to improve the lot of the workers more generally. She calls for more and

better understanding between workers and employers, and argues that improving the lot of the worker will result in more energetic and enthusiastic employees, and thus better productivity and efficiency.

Parker also deserves recognition as one of the first to focus specifically on the roles and behaviours of women in the workplace. By the early 1920s, female employment in manufacturing was widespread in both the United States and Europe, but little or no attention had been previously paid to the socialization of women in the workplace or the impact of factory work on their lives; virtually all studies focused exclusively on male workers. Some companies such as Cadbury did set up separate personnel departments for female employees, but in most cases the prime purpose was to ensure that the morals of female factory workers were properly looked after. Parker's work gave women in the workplace a voice.

BIBLIOGRAPHY
Parker, C.S. (1919) *American Idyll: The Life of Carleton H. Parker*, Boston: Atlantic Monthly Press.
——— (1922) *Working With the Working Woman*, New York: Harper and Bros.

MLW

PATTERSON, John Henry (1844–1922)

John Henry Patterson was born in Dayton, Ohio on 13 December 1844, the son of Jefferson and Julia Patterson. He died on board a train while travelling to Atlantic City, New Jersey on 7 May 1922. He married Katharine Beck in 1888; they had two children. His family were well-to-do Ohio landowners, and Patterson received a good education and went on to attend Dartmouth College, taking a degree in 1867. He served in the Union Army during the American Civil War, but to his disappointment his regiment never saw action. After completing his degree he returned to Ohio and went into business with his brother, Frank Patterson, dealing in coal and mining equipment. The business struggled, and eventually failed in 1883. However, the experience had one important impact on Patterson; struggling to manage cash flow, he chanced across a recent invention, the cash register, which had been patented by James Ritty. Cash registers were being made on a small scale by the National Manufacturing Company in Dayton, and Patterson purchased two machines. So impressed was he by their potential that he purchased the company, even though it was then making a loss, changing the name to National Cash Register (NCR) and throwing himself into this new business. The company's first factory was established in 1888, and growth was rapid thereafter; although he continued to manufacture his cash registers from a single factory in Dayton, by 1900 he was selling across the country and around the world.

Patterson faced the problem faced by many high-tech businesses, namely that of creating a market for innovative technologies. Few people outside of Dayton had ever heard of cash registers, and even fewer recognized their potential in terms of controlling costs and revenue, and cutting down on theft and loss. Yet Patterson knew the market was there; the problem was how to stimulate demand. His response was what he called 'constructive selling', or proactive marketing of his products through a campaign that was at least as much about providing information to customers as it was about urging them to buy the product. In doing so, Patterson revolutionized American sales management.

At the core of his sales programme was the creation of a dedicated sales force which worked as a coordinated team according to a centrally determined strategy. Rather than being simply turned loose to sell according to their own methods, each salesman was set a defined territory and was issued with a precise set of instructions on selling techniques. This latter included a period of staff training for each salesman before they were sent into the field. Patterson told his salesmen not to emphasize the product's technical capabilities – most customers would have little interest in knowing how a cash register actually worked – but instead to analyse the customer's business, work out how a cash register could help that business, and impart this information to the customer. Relationship building and information were thus at the heart of Patterson's sales strategy. Like John North WILLYS at Overland, who adopted a similar approach, Patterson managed his sales personnel closely, encouraging them and motivating them, providing training and organizing sales conventions.

Patterson was also an innovator in labour management. NCR was one of the first firms in the United States to set up a labour department to focus specifically on human resource issues. According to one story, while touring the Dayton factory Patterson observed a female employee heating her lunch on a radiator. Appalled at the lack of facilities, he set up a canteen and offered workers free lunches; when the workers refused to accept what they saw as charity, Patterson priced the lunches at five cents. Honour was satisfied on both sides, and workers flocked to use the canteen. Following on from this, Patterson began offering other benefits such as health care, gymnasiums and exercise facilities, and later paid vacation excursions to resorts and attractions such as the St Louis World's Fair. His attitude to labour management was strongly paternalistic, and occasionally cranky – the wives of all male employees were required to attend compulsory cooking classes, organized and paid for by the company – but were always well intentioned. Accused by other business leaders of being excessively 'soft' in his treatment of employees, Patterson replied that the cost of employee benefits was repaid to the firm in terms of higher productivity and lower rates of sickness and absenteeism:

One of the most profitable investments that can he made in a manufacturing plant is to give the largest possible advantages in the way of conveniences and sanitary arrangements. Every kind of legitimate comfort and convenience that may be provided for operatives is a source of profit to the employer, although apart from the moral obligation to care for the health and comfort of the employee.

(Becker 1906: 552)

Patterson came to be regarded as the model of an enlightened employer. In 1899 he was visited by the former socialist leader Herbert CASSON, then in the process of recovering from his disillusion with his former cause and looking for a new one. An interview with Patterson and a tour of the NCR factory convinced him that capitalism had many good features, and launched him on his later career as a journalist, writer and efficiency expert.

Patterson's technological advantage in his field could not be long maintained, and by 1900 rival cash register makers were springing up across the country. His response was energetic and, some said, unprincipled: he bought out as many competitors as he could, and drove most of the rest out of the market. In this Patterson was aided by the hard-nosed manager of the Rochester branch office, Thomas J. WATSON, whom Patterson brought to head office and eventually promoted to be his deputy. In 1912, however, the US government stepped in and charged thirty NCR managers, Patterson and Watson included, with violations of anti-trust legislation. Convicted, Patterson and Watson were fined $5,000 and sentenced to a year in prison. Shortly thereafter, Dayton was badly affected by tornadoes and flooding, and thousands of people were made homeless. Patterson stopped all work at the factory, sent his employees into the affected areas to distribute food and relief supplies, his medical department provided doctors and nurses to tend the sick, and Watson went to New York to organize the despatch of further supplies by train. In the aftermath of the disaster, thousands petitioned President Wilson to grant Patterson a pardon; in fact, the conviction was overturned by an appeal court in 1915.

Patterson was badly affected by the death of his wife in 1894, and became more eccentric as he grew older; a hypochondriac, he affected a variety of unusual diets, and insisted that his long-suffering senior executives should share these with him. He grew solitary and increasingly difficult to deal with, leading to a quarrel with and the departure of Watson, his most talented executive. On the credit side, he became a strong proponent of world peace; although during the First World War his company made munitions for the US Army, he took the lead in returning to do business in Germany and was a strong supporter of the League of Nations. He died while going to seek a health cure in Atlantic City. He left behind him a legacy as a pioneer in both human resources management and marketing.

BIBLIOGRAPHY

Becker, O.M. (1906) 'The Square Deal in Works Management', *Engineering Magazine* (January): 536–54.

Casson, H.N. (1931) *The Story of My Life*, London: Efficiency Magazine.

Crowther, S. (1923) *John H. Patterson: Pioneer in Industrial Welfare*, London: William Heinemann.

Johnson, R. and Lynch, R. (1932) *The Sales Strategy of John H. Patterson*, Chicago: Dartnell.

MLW

PEMBERTON, John (1831–88)

John Pemberton was born in Knoxville, Georgia and died in Atlanta, Georgia on 16

August 1888. He married Anna Lewis in 1853; they had one child. He was educated at Southern Botanico Medical College in Georgia, where he learned the practice of herbal medicine. Graduating in 1850, he went to Philadelphia where he trained as a pharmacist, and then set up a pharmacy business in the small town of Oglethorp, Georgia. In 1855 he relocated to Columbus, Georgia, where he built up a successful practice. During the US Civil War Pemberton served as an officer of cavalry. In the closing stages of the war he organized a 'home guard' unit known as Pemberton's Cavalry to defend the area around Columbus from the approaching Union Army, and on 18 April 1865 in one of the last battles of the war, he led his troopers into action. He was badly wounded in the battle, and remained in pain for the rest of his life; Pendergast (1993) relates that as a result, Pemberton was for a long period addicted to morphine, the only reliable painkiller then available.

Following the war Pemberton resumed his practice and for the first time began experimenting with patent medicines, developing a few moderately successful products. Encouraged by the response in the market, he relocated his business to Atlanta in 1869, hoping to reach a larger audience. He devoted much of his time to research, building up a vast library on botany and chemistry, and experimenting with new products, mostly elixirs for rheumatism or the treatment of chronic pain generally, or tonics to promote general health. The prohibitionist movement was beginning to be active in the southern United States at this time, and alternatives to beer and spirits were growing in popularity; soda fountains were beginning to become a feature of American towns, and new drinks such as Dr Pepper (invented in Texas by Charles Alderton in 1885) were becoming popular. Pemberton also began developing recipes for soda fountain drinks. In 1886 he began experimenting with the use of the coca leaf as a tonic (the leaf was then of course best known for its energizing qualities, primarily among the inhabitants of the high Andes), partly in response to an article praising its powers by Sigmund Freud.

Pemberton's first drink recipe was in fact an alcoholic one, called Wine-Coca; as the name suggests, it was wine infused with a small amount of coca, and was a direct imitation of a recipe devised by a Frenchman, Angelo Mariani. His Vin Mariani had been very popular (the pope and Queen Victoria were among his customers), and Pemberton's drink was one of many imitations. Pemberton, however, saw that non-alcoholic drinks were where the market was going and by the end of 1885 was experimenting with the cola nut, grown in West Africa and widely used there as a source of energy. In 1886 he launched the soft drink that would go on to become the world's most famous brand: Coca-Cola.

Although the new drink was an immediate success, Pemberton's final two years of life were not easy ones. Not a good businessman, he took in partners who cheated him and he was engaged in numerous lawsuits. He himself spent most of his time working on perfecting his recipe, adding the various essences and flavours that go to make up the modern drink (the use of the coca leaf was phased out not long after Pemberton's death, once the drug's properties became more fully known). Pemberton's career was one of patient and tireless experimentation: with a clear vision of the product he wanted, he refused to be satisfied with anything less than total success. Although he is not responsible for the branding of Coca-Cola, he gave his successors the product to make that brand possible.

BIBLIOGRAPHY
Pendergast, M. (1993) *For God, Country and Coca-Cola*, London: Phoenix.

MLW

PENNEY, James Cash, Jr (1875–1971)

James Cash Penney, Jr was born on a farm in Caldwell County near Hamilton, Missouri on 16 September 1875. He died of a heart attack in New York on 12 February 1971. His father, James Cash Penney, Sr, was a Baptist preacher and civic leader who, with his wife Mary Frances Paxton, raised twelve children. The strong religious beliefs and strict moral values of the household moulded Penney's character, and later gave his business dealings a distinctive cast. He was encouraged to tip his hat to trees as a rehearsal for how he should greet ladies, and from the age of eight he had to work to pay for his own shoes and clothes. His first entrepreneurial venture was raising pigs, which drew the ire of neighbours. After graduating from high school in 1893, Penney went to work on the family farm rather than pursuing his dream of attending college, a luxury his family could not afford. Poorly suited for life on the farm, Penney took a job arranged by his father at the Hamilton dry goods store of J. M. Hale and Bros. It was a good fit: so energetic was the young clerk that within a few years his pay was boosted from just over $27 a year to $300.

On the advice of his doctor, who feared Penney would succumb to tuberculosis, he moved to Denver, Colorado in 1897. He secured a job at the Joslin dry goods store, but quit because he disliked haggling with customers about prices. The practice of marking goods with 'one price' had yet to become commonplace in America. Penney then bought a meat market in Longmont, Colorado, but that venture failed when Penney lost the biggest account – a local hotel – because he refused to continue the custom of supplying the hotel's cook with a free bottle of whisky each week.

At the aptly named Golden Rule clothing store, Penney found a working environment suitable to his moral code. Golden Rule then operated eighteen stores in the Midwest and Rocky Mountain states, owned by Thomas M. Callahan, who often shared ownership in individual stores with friends, relatives and former clerks. Seeing promise in Penney, Callahan and his Wyoming partner offered him a position in their store in Evanston, Illinois. Penney thrived, and on 14 April 1902 became a partner in a new Golden Rule store in Kemmerer, Wyoming. His initial investment of $2,000 – $1,500 of it borrowed from a bank – returned $29,000 in sales and $8,000 in profits the first year.

Penney dreamed of expansion. After buying Callahan's and Johnson's shares in three Wyoming stores, Penney opened new Golden Rule stores in Idaho and Utah. The stores were known for their low prices, 'one-price' policy, cash-only sales and fair dealings. In 1899 Penney married Berta Alva Hess and the couple had two sons, one of whom often slept in a drawer by the cash register.

Although prospering, Penney earned a reputation as being extraordinarily frugal with a dollar. When his managers travelled out of town, they were required to walk in order to save the five-cent trolley fare, and sleep two or three to a bed in their hotel. Penny-pinching contributed to the death of his wife, who contracted a fatal dose of pneumonia in 1910 after walking home in a snowstorm following a tonsillectomy. Penney, then aged thirty-five, was shattered by the loss, and took a long tour through Europe and the Middle East.

During his travels, Penney fashioned a plan to take his 22-store chain national. In early 1913 he incorporated the firm as J.C. Penney Company, although the stores continued to use the Golden Rule name for another six years. The company's unusual ownership structure – each store had its own class of stock and paid profits (or incurred loses) separate from the larger company – attracted an ambitious class of managers. Eastern bankers remained wary of investing in the firm until it began issuing company-wide stock and dividends in the 1920s.

Penney stepped down as company president in 1917, by which time the chain had 177 stores and annual sales of some $14 million. He became chairman of the board, leaving operational responsibility in the hands of the new president, Earl Corder Sams, an eleven-year veteran of the firm. Penney thereafter focused on recruiting new 'associates' to the company. His standards were exacting: only 100 out of every 5,000 applicants was offered a position, and then only those deemed to have potential as future owners.

In 1919 Penney married Mary Hortense Kimball, who gave birth to a son the following year. The couple built a lavish estate in Miami, where the thrifty merchant began to enjoy the fruits of his labours. Mary Penney died in 1923. Penney turned increasingly to civic causes and religious philanthropy. These included a 125,000-acre cooperative farm for homesteaders, a retirement home for ministers and sponsorship of *Christian Herald Magazine*. In 1926 Penney married Caroline Autenrieth, twenty years his junior, and the couple had two daughters. As the decade came to a close, Penney's wealth was said to exceed $40 million. The company went public on 23 October 1929, six days before the Great Crash. As the major shareholder in the 1,400-store company, Penney watched the price of the firm's stock plummet from $120 to $13 per share.

Once again, he rebounded. After selling his Miami home and checking into a sanatorium, Penney experienced a religious epiphany that gave him renewed hope and determination. With the help of friends and associates, he slowly rebuilt his financial holdings, although for several years in the 1930s and 1940s he had to draw a salary, the first time he had done so since 1909. He stepped down as chairman of the board in 1946, but completed another term from 1950 to 1958. During his second term, Penney was the lone voice among top managers in opposing the company's introduction of credit cards. He still believed that debt would undermine the character of his customers and encourage them to overspend. In his twilight years, Penney enjoyed recounting for the media tales from his early career in business.

DBS

PENROSE, Edith Elura Tilton (1914–96)

Edith Penrose was born on Sunset Boulevard in Los Angeles on 15 November 1914. She died at Waterbeach, Cambridgeshire in October 1996. She attended the University of California at Berkeley, where she was granted a scholarship after her first semester, and graduated with a BA in economics in 1936. She attended summer extension classes taught by E.F. ('Pen') Penrose, a British-born economist, and also acted as his assistant. In 1939 Pen joined the International Labour Organzation (ILO) in Geneva, and Edith followed, taking a place there as a researcher. Her first work *Food Control in Great Britain*, published by the ILO in 1940, analysed the problems of production, distribution and consumption of food in wartime Britain. When Pen took a job in London as economic adviser to John Winant, the US ambassador to Britain, who had previously worked at the ILO, Edith joined Winant's staff as a researcher. As Pen was at the time involved in a network of economists working on postwar planning, she had many opportunities for interaction with prominent economists, such as SCHUMPETER, by whom she was greatly influenced, and also Keynes, Meade, D.H. Robinson, Austin Robinson, H.D. Henderson, Robbins, Jewkes and others.

Edith married Pen in 1945. After the war the Penroses joined the US delegation to the United Nations. In 1947 Pen accepted a chair in human geography in Baltimore; Edith then started her master's degree and moved on to doctoral studies at Johns Hopkins University under the supervision of Fritz Machlup, receiving her Ph.D. in 1951. She then took a position as lecturer and research associate at Johns Hopkins, where she remained until 1959. She then taught at the London School of Economics and the School of Oriental and African Studies, where she had a joint readership in economics until 1978. On her retirement in 1978 she held a professorship of political economy at INSEAD, where she was also associate dean for research and development. She taught at other institutions including the universities of Baghdad, Cairo and Khartoum, and the American University of Beirut, and consulted for governments including those of India, Tanzania and Indonesia. When Pen passed away in 1984, she moved to Waterbeach, near Cambridge, to be close to her two sons, continuing to lead a full personal, academic and consulting life until her death. She participated in several governing bodies and committees including the Council of the Overseas Development Institute, the board of the Commonwealth Development Corporation and the Pharmaceuticals Committee, and continued to offer consulting services to governments.

Penrose's interest in the growth of firms started to grow when she undertook fieldwork at the Hercules Powder Company, under Fritz Machlup's supervision. She realized that traditional economic theory was not dealing with the growth of firms. Her work at Hercules Powder gave birth to her ideas about the growth of the firm, which she first shaped in an article for *American Economic Review* in 1955, and then in her book *The Theory of the Growth of the Firm* (1959) and an article for *Business History Review* about The Hercules Powder Company (1960; see also Penrose 1956a, 1956b).

Her stay in the Arab world in the 1960s also spurred her interest in the oil industry, and multinationals in general, especially in reference to the impact that multinational firms may have as investors in developing countries (see Penrose 1956a, 1964, 1968, 1973a, 1973b, 1989, 1990). While her main theme revolved around the growth of firms, her interest in multinationals, developing countries and policy followed as a direct offshoot of the former. At INSEAD she elaborated on the way firms grow and die, and more generally on the ways in which firms change. In the years after her retirement, Penrose focused more on the issues of cooperation and networking of firms, being interested in whether alliances, clusters and business networks could be accommodated within her theory, and also with the idea of a theory of the change ('metamorphosis') of firms.

Her work gained widespread recognition at the time, but the major interest came in the 1980s, especially in terms of the context of the resource-based (or competence-based or knowledge-based) theory of the firm. In contrast to traditional economic theory that offered little understanding of the processes taking place *inside* the firm, Penrose offered insights to understanding the firm as a 'real life', 'flesh and blood' organization of the real business world, emphasizing the generation of knowledge that takes place within it. She defines the firm as a collection of (tangible and intangible) resources, bound together under an administrative coordination and authoritative communication. Firms differ from markets exactly because activities within the firm take place under authoritative coordination, while in the market they do not. In her theory, the product, market and technology are *not* givens over time, and demand may be found elsewhere than in the 'traditional' line of products of the firm, or created by the firm. Management is not a fixed factor either. The availability and quality of (managerial, entrepreneurial and other) services rendered by resources to the firm very much depend on the firm's internal workings. The firm grows by making profitable use of its 'excess' (generated via knowledge creation) productive resources in order to exploit *perceived* opportunities.

Penrose defines a firm's 'productive opportunity' as the entrepreneurs' *perception* of both the environment and the internal abilities of the firm to exploit it profitably. The productive opportunity of the firm is not fixed: it may change with a change in external conditions, and/or with a change in a firm's knowledge and, consequently, with a change in the internal supply of productive services (rendered by its resources). A firm's growth rate is therefore determined by both its perception of profitable opportunities in the environment and (relatedly) its resources. Individual firms grow with different rates since they do not possess the same resources and they are not subject to the same constraints by their environment.

It follows that the existence of *unused* productive services within the firm is of great significance for the inducement of the process of growth. During the ordinary activity of the firm, some resources are normally not fully utilized (mainly due to indivisibility of resources). Furthermore, as the firm as a working group gains experience (which may change both acquired knowledge and the ability to use it), *new* productive services may be created, which furthermore are unique to the firm's configuration of resources and cannot be found in the market or easily copied by other firms. Therefore, as resources are freed and new services become available, a firm has an *endogenous* incentive to expand, that is to use the services of its resources more profitably and/or make fuller use of its existing resources. As a result of indivisibilities, expansion may lead to further resources which are not fully used, sustaining the internal stimuli to growth.

The *rate* of growth of the firm is thus different for different firms, and may decline for the very same reasons that it may increase. That is, the capacities of the existing managerial personnel (and the existing size of the firm) both limit the amount of activity that can be physically planned, and, consequently, the amount of new personnel and other productive resources that can be profitably absorbed in the firm. Further, the environment may no longer allow for an increasing rate of growth and profitable expansion: competition may become keener, and entry into new, even 'neighbouring' areas (where one only of the following is *not* new: technology, market, product) may be costly or legally impossible. Although a firm may infinitely generate new, unused productive services as well as face opportunities for expansion, its internal structure and capabilities may not

allow it profitably to exploit them. It follows that the accumulation of knowledge through experience determines the growth trajectory of the firm and the latter determines the path (as a combination of opportunities and internal capabilities for their exploitation) for further growth.

Therefore, there may exist limits to the rate of growth, but not to size. Firms may grow infinitely, but larger firms may experience slower growth rates and (as) they may also face keener competition. Further, it is likely that large firms cannot take advantage of all the opportunities available to them; therefore, in a growing economy there will always exist profitable opportunities ('interstices' of activity within an economy) available to small firms. It is, therefore, expected that concentration will tend to be restricted, albeit not the absolute size of firms. However, the basic dilemma is that competition, 'at once the god and the devil' (Penrose 1959: 265), induces innovation but may also lead to industry structures that hinder growth (see also Penrose 1956b).

The new knowledge and services available in the firm might also be useful for the production of products other than the existing ones (Penrose 1959: 114). It is thus likely that when a firm produces for a market of which the rate of growth is not sufficient to accommodate its growth potential (its idle resources and accumulated knowledge), then it may exploit opportunities for expansion through diversification into new products or markets. In fact, Penrose maintains that, since firms are defined in reference to their (unique) resources, 'diversification' is the normal course of events for a growing firm.

It is also possible that (external) expansion through merger and/or acquisition may be a profitable opportunity for a firm, or a less costly way to obtain the productive services (notably managerial) and knowledge necessary for diversification in a new field. External expansion may bear the same limitations as internal expansion: the existing resources of the firm determine the extent to which new resources might be absorbed and organically integrated into the firm.

Profits are significant as a motivating power, as a *condition* of successful growth of the firm, which in turn results in long-term profits. In this sense, profit would be desired for the 'sake of the firm itself and in order to make more profit through expansion (Penrose 1959: 29). It is maintained that it is indirectly, through the growth of firms, that individuals gain satisfaction and increase their personal utility, not directly through the realization of profit itself. According to Penrose, 'growth and profits become equivalent as the criteria for the selection of investment programmes' (1959: 30) if the firm seeks profit to reinvest it in the firm and not to pay out to the capital owners more than needed to maintain a supporting capital structure for the firm.

To summarize, Penrose explained the growth of firms, based on their continuously generating 'excess' productive services, which can be profitably redeployed to 'neighbouring' activities and markets. The centrepiece of her analysis is the *accumulation of knowledge*, in firms and individuals, as well as the concept that the firm is more than a collection of individuals' capabilities and skills. A firm's knowledge, capabilities and skill determine both the 'perceived' profitable opportunities as well as the ability to exploit and enhance them. Penrose applied this insight to firms' integration, including the multinational firm, industry organization and the wider sphere (see Penrose 1956a, 1956b, 1987, 1989).

Penrose's work is widely viewed as the basis of what is commonly called competence-based, resource-based or knowledge-based perspective. However, her contribution is far broader than that, and it is safe to suggest that she had gained a place alongside the twentieth century's leading economists including Ronald COASE, Friedrich von HAYEK and Joseph Schumpeter.

Acknowledgements

I am deeply grateful to Christos Pitelis and Perran Penrose for invaluable help, and for providing me with all relevant material and support.

BIBLIOGRAPHY

Penrose, E.T. (1940) *Food Control in Great Britain*, Geneva: ILO.

—— (1955) 'Research on the Business Firms: Limits to Growth and Size of Firms', *American Economic Review* 45(2).

—— (1956a) 'Foreign Investment and the Growth of the Firm', *Economic Journal* 46(June).

—— (1956b) 'Towards a Theory of Industrial Concentration', *Economic Record* (May).

—— (1959) *The Theory of the Growth of the Firm*, Oxford: Basil Blackwell; 3rd edn, Oxford: Oxford University Press, 1995.

—— (1960) 'The Growth of the Firm – A Case Study: The Hercules Powder Company', *Business History Review* 34(1): 1–23.

—— (1964) 'Monopoly and Competition in the International Petroleum Industry', *The Yearbook of World Affairs*, London: Stevens, vol. 18.

—— (1968) 'Problems Associated with the Growth of International Firms', in *Tijdschrift voor Vennootschappen, Vereiningingen en Stichtingen 9*.

—— (1971) *The Growth of Firms, Middle East and Other Essays*, London: Cass.

—— (1973a) 'International Patenting and the Less Developed Countries', *Economic Journal* 83(September): 768–86.

—— (1973b) 'The Changing Role of Multinational Corporations in Developing Countries', paper submitted to the United Nations Groups of Eminent Persons to Study the Impact of Multinational Corporations on Development and on International Relations, Geneva.

Penrose, E.T. (1987) 'Multinational

Corporations', in *The New Palgrave: A Dictionary of Economics*, London: Macmillan, 562–4.

Penrose, E.T. (1989) 'History, the Social Sciences and Economic Theory with Special Reference to Multinational Enterprise', in A. Teichova, M. Levy-Leboyer and H. Nussbaum (eds), *Multinational Enterprise in Historical Perspective*, Cambridge: Cambridge University Press.

—— (1990) '"Dumping2", "Unfair" Competition and Multinational Corporations', *Japan and the World Economy* 1(May).

—— (1996) 'Growth of the Firm and Networking', in M. Warner (ed.), *International Encyclopedia of Business and Management*, London: Routledge, vol. 2, 1716–24.

Penrose, E.T. and Penrose, E.F. (1978) *Iraq: International Relations and National Development*, Westview, CT: Benn.

Penrose, P. and Pitelis, C. (1999) 'Edith Elura Tilton Penrose: Life, Contribution and Influence', *Contributions to Political Economy*, special issue on Edith Penrose, 18.

—— (2001) 'Edith Penrose', *Reader's Guide to Social Sciences*, London: Fitzroy Dearborn.

Pitelis, C. and Pseiridis, A. (1999) 'Transaction Costs versus Resource Value?', *Journal of Economic Studies* 26(3): 221–40.

—— (2001) 'Resource-based Economics', *Reader's Guide to Social Sciences*, London: Fitzroy Dearborn.

Pitelis, C. (2001) *The Theory of the Growth of the Firm: The Penrosean Legacy*, Oxford: Oxford University Press.

AP

PETER, Laurence Johnston (1919–90)

Laurence Johnston Peter was born in Vancouver, British Columbia on 16 September 1919 and died in Los Angeles on 12 January 1990. He attended the University of British Columbia, where he trained as a teacher, graduating in 1941; he went on to work as a teacher and school psychologist, specializing in work with emotionally disturbed or damaged children. He took a doctorate in education from Washington State University in 1963, and taught at the University of British Columbia from 1963 to 1964 before moving to the University of Southern California where he became associate professor of education and coordinator of programmes for emotionally disturbed children. He achieved fame with the publication in 1969 of *The Peter Principle*, which, for a short time at least, was one of America's most talked-about books on organization and motivation.

The Peter Principle is that 'in a hierarchy, every employee tends to rise to the level of his own incompetence'. According to Peter, organizations promote employees to senior positions on the basis of merit; but they tend to do so on the basis of how well the employee is carrying out his or her present job, not how well he or she will be able to carry out the job into which he or she is being promoted. In other words, promotion is a reward for previous achievements, and bears little or no relation to the future needs of either the organization or the employee. This becomes a problem when, as is often the case, employees and managers are promoted into positions for which they are not suited. At this point the 'level of incompetence' has been reached; further promotion will not be forthcoming, and dissatisfaction on the part of both employee and employer is the result.

The Peter Principle is now a very well-recognized phenomenon, although there is little evidence that many organizations do much to counteract it. Peters went on to produce several more caustic commentaries on bureaucracy and organizations, and has achieved posthumous fame as an aphorist with scores of Web sites featuring his better-known sayings such as, 'Bureaucracy defends the status quo long after the quo has lost its status', and the evergreen 'An economist is an expert who will know tomorrow why the things he predicted yesterday did not happen today'.

BIBLIOGRAPHY
Peters, L.J. (1969) *The Peter Principle*, London: Pan.

PETERS, Thomas J. (1942–)

Thomas J. Peters was born in Baltimore, Maryland on 7 November 1942. After taking a bachelor's degree from Cornell University, he served in the US Navy from 1966 to 1970, seeing action in the Vietnam War. On discharge from the navy he became a consultant with Peate Marwick Mitchell, from 1970 to 1973, taking an MBA from Stanford University in 1972 (he later received a Ph.D. from Stanford in 1977). In 1973 Peters joined the US Government Office of Management and Budget, first as director of a cabinet committee on international narcotics control and then as assistant to the director for federal drug abuse policy. In 1974 Peters moved to San Francisco and joined management consultants McKinsey and Company.

While with McKinsey, Peters became interested in the concepts of organizational effectiveness and excellence. His service in the navy and with the US government had shown him what excessive bureaucratization and rationalism could lead to, and he began searching for a freer, more effective form of organization. As his ideas developed he became the firm's principal practice leader on organizational effectiveness, and developed a reputation as a speaker and writer. Working with his colleague

Robert Waterman, Peters distilled his ideas over the previous decade into a book, *In Search of Excellence* (1982), which went on to sell more than a million copies worldwide and became one of the most popular management books of all time.

Peters, now world-famous as a pundit, left McKinsey to set up his own consulting firm, the Tom Peters Group in Palo Alto, California. As well as running seminars and doing consulting work, he wrote for many years a weekly column which was syndicated in many US newspapers, and presented a television series on the Public Broadcasting System. He also produced several more highly popular books, notably *A Passion for Excellence* (1985), *Thriving on Chaos* (1987) and *Liberation Management* (1992).

In *In Search of Excellence*, Peters began with a basic assumption that there are 'excellent' companies, ones whose achievements can be measured in terms of profitability, growth, record of innovation, share price and so on. Based on their experience as consultants, Peters and Waterman develop what they call the '7-S' model, of seven organizational variables: structure, strategy, systems, skills, staff, style and shared values. The latter is at the centre of the model, and is obviously most important. In Peters' view, excellence is a cultural factor, with companies needing to make sure employees buy into that culture. Another feature of excellent companies, he says, is their ability to manage ambiguity and paradox. He gives a list of eight factors which he says define the successful company: (1) a bias for action; (2) being close to the customer; (3) autonomy and entrepreneurship; (4) productivity through people; (5) hands-on, value-driven leadership; (6) 'sticking to the knitting' (staying close to the business you know); (7) simple organizational form; and (8) a combination of central core values with decentralized organization, or 'tight-loose' properties (Peters and Waterman 1982: 13–16).

The achievement of quality in products and services and an orientation towards customers are part of excellence, but Peters puts the greatest emphasis on 'organizational excellence', which in his view means streamlining and simplifying organizations. In *In Search of Excellence*, Peters calls for organizations to employ fewer specialists and more generalists, to scrap complicated systems of command and control for systems which are simpler and more flexible, and to reduce the number of layers of management, insisting that 'middle management is dead' (Peters and Waterman 1982: 758). However, companies will only be successful in becoming more flexible if they can change their basic mindsets and the attitudes to their managers. His foremost target is the scientific-technical-rational approach to management that evolved out of scientific management and Taylorism in the early twentieth century:

Professionalism in management is regularly equated with hard-headed rationality... The numerative, rationalist approach to management dominates the business schools. It teaches us that well-trained professional managers can manage anything. It seeks detached, analytical justification for all decisions. It is right enough to be dangerously wrong, and it has arguably led us seriously astray.

(Peters and Waterman 1982: 29)

Peters goes on to attack concepts such as economies of scale and low-cost production, which according to orthodox management thinking are the only ways to achieve profitability and success: 'The numerative, analytical component has an in-built conservative bias. Cost reduction becomes priority number one and revenue enhancement takes a back seat' (Peters and Waterman 1982: 44). It is almost impossible, he believes, to spend too much money on focusing on customers; without new products and new customers, no company can survive for long, but these cannot be achieved through rigid bureaucracy or strict cost control.

The huge success of *In Search of Excellence* was followed by *A Passion for Excellence*, which dwelt on many of the same themes. In his later work, however, especially *Thriving on Chaos* and *Liberation Management*, Peters takes his philosophy of management to further lengths. He continues his assault on bureaucracy, at times taking this to extremes and urging organizations to scrap all hierarchy; control is the enemy of entrepreneurship, and the latter must be promoted at all costs. In a world of globalization and rapid technological change, Peters sees change moving at such a rate that it amounts almost to chaos. Instead of trying to defend against change, however, organizations should embrace and even create change. He is in favour of 'stirring the pot', shaking up organizations and people so as to stimulate them and encourage new ideas. He attacks any notion that successful systems should be left well enough alone, as exemplified in the old American saying, 'if it ain't broke, don't fix it'; Peters' response is, 'if it's not broke, it's because you haven't looked hard enough. Fix it anyway.' Organizations should never be allowed to settle, never be given time enough to build up defensive routines. Only through this constant process of change and regeneration can businesses survive.

Apart from bearing an astonishing resemblance to Mao Zedong's theory of permanent revolution, Peters' theories of management chaos, though revolutionary, have attracted much criticism. The idea of management chaos conflicts with a basic human need for stability, which is shared by most workers and most managers in most organizations; the bitter hostility to the wave of corporate downsizings in the United States, which was inspired in part by Peters' ideas, showed graphically how few companies could actually live up to Peters' revolutionary ideas in practice. His early recipes for success have also been criticized, with critics pointing gleefully to the fact that many of the 'excellent' companies profiled in 1982 did not manage to survive into the 1990s.

His ideas have their admitted weaknesses, but Peters did achieve a revolution of sorts: he

PETERS

startled American management into life. By 1980, depressed by two oil price shocks and wavering in the face of aggressive foreign competition, American management had become almost bankrupt of new ideas. Peters made it clear that change was not only possible but also desirable, and in doing so opened the door for later gurus such as Rosabeth Moss KANTER and Warren BENNIS. Thanks to his immense popularity and easy writing style, his works became highly popular; he still has an immense following, at times approaching cult status. Ironically, given his views on middle managers, his greatest audience is among middle managers. Baffled, he wrote in 1992: 'Am I a middle management basher? Yes. Are most of the people who come to my seminars middle managers? Yes. Why do they come? Beats me' (Peters 1992: 715).

BIBLIOGRAPHY

Peters, T.J. (1987) *Thriving on Chaos: Handbook for a Management Revolution*, New York: Knopf.
—— (1991) *Beyond Hierarchy: Organizations in the 1990s*, New York: Knopf.
—— (1992) *Liberation Management: Necessary Disorganization for the Nanosecond Nineties*, New York: Knopf.
—— (1994) *The Pursuit of Wow! Every Person's Guide to Topsy-turvy Times*, New York: Vintage.
Peters, T.J. and Austin, N. (1985) *A Passion for Excellence: The Leadership Difference*, New York: Random House.
Peters, T.J. and Waterman, R.H. (1982) *In Search of Excellence: Lessons from America's Best-run Companies*, New York: Harper and Row.
Witzel, M. (1998) 'Peters, Thomas J.', in M. Warner (ed.), *IEBM Handbook of Management Thinking*, London: International Thomson Business Press, 526–30.

MLW

POLANYI, Karl (1886–1964)

Karl Polanyi was born in Vienna on 25 October 1886 and died near Toronto on 23 April 1964; he is buried in Dumbarton, Ontario. Polanyi grew up in Hungary. His father was an entrepreneur. Polanyi attended the University of Budapest and then went on to receive a law degree from Kolozsvár in July 1909. In 1912 he became a barrister in Budapest, where he associated with other socialist thinkers. Polanyi's socialism, however, was Catholic rather than Marxist.

Even before the First World War, he had been arrested for socialist activities. Serving as a cavalry officer in the Austro-Hungarian army during the war, he was captured by the Russians. Following the armistice and the dissolution of the Habsburg state, Polanyi returned to Vienna, where he married Ilona Duczynka in 1923. From 1924 to 1933 he worked as a foreign affairs journalist.

Polanyi's career paralleled and overlapped that of his chief intellectual rival, the Austrian Ludwig von Mises. Like Mises, Polanyi grew up in the Austrian monarchy, served in the First World War and returned to Vienna in the 1920s, only to leave Austria in the 1930s in fear of fascism. He first went to Britain, where he lectured for the Workers Educational Association, and the extramural departments of Oxford University and the University of London. In 1935 he contributed a chapter on fascism to a book called *Christianity and the Social Revolution*.

Polanyi moved on to the United States in 1940, where he lectured at Bennington College until 1943. His final destination was Toronto, Canada. His wife Ilona, a revolutionary Marxist, was deemed too radical to be allowed to enter the United States. The socialist Polanyi, like the libertarian Mises, was ostracized in American academia. He could only find employment as a visiting professor at Columbia University from 1947 to 1953, and commuted between New York and Toronto until his retirement in 1953.

Polanyi and Mises carried on a long intellectual battle with one another, which spanned several decades and both sides of the Atlantic. The debate between them was sharp and irreconcilable. Mises was a radical free market purist who spent his entire adult life crusading for a doctrine of absolute *laissez-faire* capitalism. For Mises, the market was the natural order of society, and any efforts to meddle with its workings was a violation of that order. Unlike Mises, a deist, Polanyi was motivated by a Catholic faith which saw human society as more than a collection of individuals. The community, not the market, formed the natural order of society. Polanyi's interpretation of history even went so far as to deny the existence of markets in remote antiquity. At the core of Polanyi's thought and vision of history was the prevalence of planning, regulation, social welfare and other forms of economic cooperation and interventionism from Mesopotamia, through Greece, Rome, the Middle Ages to early modern times. In 1944 he set forth these ideas in his best-known work, *The Great Transformation*.

The Great Transformation surveyed the history of industrialization in nineteenth-century Britain, and argued that the relatively *laissez-faire* system of the mid-Victorians did not arise naturally but was imposed by governmental fiat. Quoting from this work, Keith Rankin cites Polanyi's argument that:

> There was nothing natural about laissez-faire; free markets could never have come into being merely by allowing things to take their course ... Laissez-faire itself was enforced by the state. The [1830s and 1840s] saw not only an outburst of legislation repealing restrictive regulations, but also an enormous increase in the administrational bureaucracy able to fulfil the tasks set by the adherents of liberalism ... laissez-faire was not a method to achieve a thing, it was the thing to be achieved.
>
> (Rankin 1998: 2)

Government regulation of this market system was introduced not by socialists but by businessmen and conservatives, themselves concerned at the destructive impact of an unfettered market upon the physical as well as the social health of their subjects. Aristocrats and peasants in many European states joined hands to regulate factories and impose tariffs to protect domestic agriculture.

In a February 1947 article in *Commentary*, Polanyi further developed his critique of the market system. In his view, the *laissez-faire* system of the nineteenth century was both a reaction to industrialization and a violent break with all that had preceded it. The market system operated on the basis of incentives: the threat of hunger for the worker, profit for the employer: '"Economic motives" reigned supreme in a world of their own, and the individual was made to act on them under pain of being trodden under foot by the juggernaut market. Such a forced conversion to a utilitarian outlook fatefully warped Western man's understanding of himself' (Polanyi 1971: 63).

Polanyi looked at the economies of aboriginal tribes in which, while people were very poor by modern standards, individuals were never left to starve on their own. He also insisted that the profit motive of individual gain was largely absent. Even as markets developed in antiquity, medieval times and the sixteenth century, or in the regulated systems of the eighteenth century, the economic system was merged in the social. Societies before 1825 were regulated by tradition, custom, religion, rank and status. Markets existed, but they did not link up to dominate society as a whole:

> The motive of gain was specific to merchants, as was valor to the knight, piety to the priest, and pride to the craftsman. The notion of making the motive of gain universal never entered the heads of our ancestors. At no time prior to the second quarter of the nineteenth century were markets more than a subordinate feature in society.
>
> (Polanyi 1971: 67)

The rise of the market to become the dominant institution in society was sudden. The revolution in society was one of kind, not just of degree. Everything was now bought and sold instead of being produced domestically. Farming became a business instead of a way of life. Labour as well became a commodity on the free market. The Poor Law Reform of 1834 created the workhouse on the premise that poverty was to be punished so that the indigent would be left with the alternative of work or starvation. The Bank Act of 1844 erected the gold standard, and the 1846 repeal of the Corn Laws made peasants everywhere subject to market forces. By the end of the 1840s, argued Polanyi, the market society was fully erected, being based upon (1) a flexible labour market, in which the value of a worker was decided by the price his labour earned; (2) a self-regulating gold standard which subjected money to global market forces; and (3) a system of free trade, in which commodities flowed from country to country regardless of the social consequences.

Polanyi also questioned the concept that people's motives ought to be purely economic. If they appeared to be so, as libertarian economists seemed to imply, it was because society was now organized around economic motives. Opinions on human nature, he insisted, would tend to mirror the business ideology if the countervailing values of honour, citizenship, moral duty and common decency were deemed irrelevant. Human relationships were now embedded in the market economy instead of the other way around. His later works, *Trade and Market in the Early Empires* (1957) and *Dahomey and the Slave Trade*, published posthumously in 1966, sought to provide historical evidence for his market critique.

As with the free market Austrian economists with whom he battled, Polanyi's influence was slight until the 1990s, when some scholars began to take notice of his writings. Polanyi's ideas have not been without their strong critics, notably Professor R.J.H. Latham of the University College of Swansea. Looking at Dahomey, Latham rebutted Polanyi's attempt to minimize the role of markets even in primitive societies. Even in a tribal culture, copper rods served as different denominations of currency and prices fluctuated, contrary to what Polanyi had said. Latham, a firm believer in the role of markets in antiquity, considered Polanyi and his followers to have been motivated by a socialist agenda. Because they disliked markets, he reasoned, they wanted to prove they were not essential. Most scholars of antiquity now agree with Latham instead of Polanyi. Prices, the essential agreement of market exchange, were quoted in ancient Sumer. Polanyi's thesis of an ancient world in which capitalism played a minimal role has been largely demolished.

In spite of its shortcomings, Polanyi's thought remains important. His contention that a mixed economy has always existed and had to exist remains a strong one. Capitalism, prices and market forces were certainly a strong part of the natural order from the beginning, but Polanyi was correct in arguing that the mitigating forces of government, church and community were equally part of that order. It is because of this that critics of *laissez-faire* such as Rankin, continued to see Polanyi's thought as relevant to a 1990s global economy which has conjured forth an economic order not unlike that which Polanyi himself questioned.

BIBLIOGRAPHY

'Karl Polanyi' (n.d.) The School of Cooperative Individualism, http://www.geocities.com/Athens/Acropolis/5148/polanyibio.html, 10 October 2000.

'Karl Polanyi' (1999) *The McGraw-Hill Encyclopedia of World Biography*, Detroit, MI: Gale Research, Inc., vol. 12, 372.

Latham, R.J.H. (n.d). 'Karl Polanyi: Some Observations', *Electronic Seminars in History*, http://ihr.sas.ac.uk/ihr/esh/arch-polanyi.html, 31 October 2000.

Polanyi, K. (1957) *The Great*

Transformation, 2nd edn, New York: Rinehart and Co.

Polanyi, K. (1971) 'Our Obsolete Market Mentality', *Commentary* 3(February): 109–17, in K. Polanyi, *Primitive, Archaic, and Modern Economies, Essays of Karl Polanyi*, ed. G. Dalton, Boston: Beacon Press, 59–77.

Rankin, K. (1998) 'Karl Polanyi on the Utopia of the "Self-regulating Market"', in K. Rankin, 'Compulsory Freedom', *New Zealand Political Review* 7(4): 12–15, http://www.geocities.com/Athens/Academy/1223/nzpr1998_4Polanyi.html, 2 October 2000.

DCL

POOR, Henry Varnum (1812–1905)

Henry Varnum Poor was born in Andover, Maine on 8 December 1812, the son of Silvanus and Mary Poor. He died in Brookline, Massachusetts on 4 January 1905. He married Mary Pierce in 1841. The first of his family to attend college, Poor graduated from Bowdoin with an AB in 1835, and joined his uncle's law firm, being called to the bar in 1838. Poor and his brother, John Poor, set up their own law practice in Bangor, which they managed until 1848, and the brothers also made money by investing money in the growing timber industry in Maine. John Poor became a minor railway magnate, being heavily involved in the building of the Maine railway network in the 1840s, and it was here that Henry Poor first began to learn about the railway industry.

In 1849 John Poor purchased the *American Railroad Journal* and asked Henry Poor to take over as manager and editor. Poor served in this capacity from 1848 to 1861, also publishing the landmark *History of the Railroads and Canals of the United States of America* in

1860, one of the first comprehensive industry directories to be published. In 1861 Poor left the journal to become an editorial writer for the *New York Times*. Here he wrote an influential series of columns on economics, money and banking, some of which formed the basis of his later books. He was also an important member of the American and Geographical Statistical Society, serving for a time as editor of its journal and, as a skilled cartographer, often producing maps for the society himself.

Poor retained his interest in the transportation industries, especially the railroads. He was secretary of Union Pacific from 1862 to 1864, and then in 1867 set up a business in partnership with his son, H.V. and H.W. Poor, to import machinery and rails, especially from Germany, where Alfred Krupp had become one of the American railway industry's major suppliers. The business also branched out into publishing, and Poor returned to one of his most important ideas, the provision of industry-wide information to managers in investors. In 1868 he launched the annual *Manual of Railroads of the United States*, a full summary of statistics concerning existing railroads and those being built. Later known as *Poor's Manual of Railroads*, it also branched out to cover related industries in the transportation sector. *Poor's Directory of Railway Officials* followed in 1886 and *Poor's Handbook of Investment Securities* in 1890, although both these publications had limited lives.

The idea of business information barely existed in Poor's day, although news sheets providing financial and other data were in circulation, and in Europe, Paul Julius Reuter had established the first wire service in the 1850s, and was providing financial and political news to the major markets and the larger daily newspapers. Poor, however, was less concerned with the ephemera of the daily news than with building up a picture of individual companies and of the industry as a whole over time. His great-grandson Alfred CHANDLER, who has written the definitive work on Poor, suggested that initially Poor saw himself as the friend of the companies: publishing more information about their work and financial progress ought to lead to better relationships with the financial community on which they depended. When the railroad barons failed to see that openness was the best policy, however, Poor realized that the interests of investors were not being well served. Companies were not disclosing vital information, and in only a few states of the union was there any duty on them to do so; even in these cases the law was being poorly enforced, if at all. Here, then, was the problem:

It is not uncommon for leading companies to publish no reports whatever. Some make them unwillingly, with no design to convey information upon the subjects to which they relate. Reports that are full and explicit are accessible only to a small number of parties interested. Fewer still have the means of comparing results for consecutive years, without which it is impossible to form a correct opinion as to the manner in which a work has been conducted, or of its present or prospective value. A single statement, as experience has shown, is a very unsafe ground on which to base an opinion. A high degree of apparent prosperity that one report may show, has not unfrequently been followed by bankruptcy before the annual occasion for another.

(Poor 1860: v)

He goes on to state his own purpose:

What is wanted, consequently, is a work which shall embody within convenient compass a statement of the organization and condition of all our companies, and at the same time present a history of their occupations from year to year, which would necessarily reflect the character of their management, the extent and value of their traffic, and supply abundant illustrations, with which to compare similar enterprises

that might be made the subject of investigation and inquiry.

(Poor 1860: v)

As well as providing information, Poor also wrote accompanying commentaries, especially in the later *Poor's Manuals*. He was a constant critic of practices such as stock watering and the keeping of dual sets of accounts. He never failed to urge both government and industry to adopt measures for greater transparency.

Poor was concerned with the problem of management, especially following the economic downturn of 1857, and discussed this problem repeatedly in his editorials in *American Railroad Journal*. Influenced by a visit to Britain in 1858, he argued that US railway operators needed 'systematic organization, communication, and information' (Chandler 1956: 155). Important was the balance between control – essential if the railways were to run safely and to time – and freedom, equally essential if the company was not to become bogged down in bureaucracy (a trait which he claimed was characteristic of British industry and government). The key requirement, then, was for leadership which could provide both control and dynamism. Such leadership, Poor felt, was all too often lacking. Most railway managers were

unacquainted with [the duties] of every important department under them; there is, consequently, no connecting link between the different departments of service, and no intelligence to guide them to a common end. In such a case it will not be long before the *morale* necessary to a high state of discipline is completely broken. Instead of a unit, the different departments of service will often be arranged in hostile attitudes towards each other. Parties in influential positions, being left to themselves, soon come to regard their own interests as the chief objects of concern.

(Poor, quoted in Chandler 1956: 157)

Failure in leadership and top management were, Poor believed, due to lack of knowledge and training on the part of those in positions of management. He complained that too many railroad presidents were financiers with little or no knowledge of the railway industry. He discusses the problems of ownership and control and, according to Chandler, argues for the separation of the two, but he is also aware of the problems such separation can bring: shareholders of joint-stock companies are usually very much divorced from the realities of running a corporation and can exercise little supervision over the salaried executives to whom such duties are entrusted, while the latter in turn may lack motivation as their simple salaries provide much less incentive than a share in the profits might. The important link here is the board of directors, which existed to provide knowledgeable supervision, to represent the interests of the company to the shareholders and vice versa.

Poor continued to press these concerns throughout his career. He wrote on other fields as well, notably economics: *The Money Question* (1898) includes an interesting discussion of the differences between 'metallic money' and 'symbolic money', or moneys of exchange and moneys of account, showing how the latter were coming to be of more importance in the United States as the economy continued to grow. It is his work on information and management, however, that stands out from other writings on business of the time. Chandler has often referred to Poor as the first philosopher of management, and in the US context that is undoubtedly true: no other American writer of the nineteenth century wrote so comprehensively on the problems of management or was so clear about the solutions required.

BIBLIOGRAPHY
Chandler, A.D. (1956) *Henry Varnum Poor*, Cambridge, MA: Harvard University Press.

Poor, H.V. (1860) *History of the Railroads and Canals of the United States of America*, New York: John W. Schultz and Co.
—— (1898) *The Money Question*, New York: H.V. and H.W. Poor.

MLW

PORTER, Michael E. (1947–)

Michael Porter was born in Ann Arbor, Michigan on 23 May 1947 to Howard Eugene and Stana Porter. As the son of a career army officer, he lived and travelled throughout the world. In high school, he was an all-state football and baseball player. He received a BSE with high honours in aerospace and mechanical engineering from Princeton University in 1969, where he also played intercollegiate golf and made the 1968 National Collegiate Athletic Association Golf All-American Team. After graduating, Porter served in the US Army Reserve with the rank of captain. In 1971 he received an MBA with high distinction from Harvard Business School, and was a George F. Baker Scholar; in 1973 he took a Ph.D. in business economics at Harvard and won the David A. Wells Prize in Economics for outstanding doctoral research. He joined the Harvard Business School faculty in 1973 as an assistant professor, was made associate professor in 1977, professor in 1982, and C. Roland Christesen Professor of Business Administration in 1990. His theories now form the foundation for one of the required courses at the school.

Porter has served as an adviser on competitive strategy to many leading US and international companies, among them AT&T, Credit Suisse First Boston, DuPont, Edward Jones, Procter and Gamble, and Royal Dutch/Shell. He also serves on the boards of directors of

Parametric Technology Corporation, R&B Falcon Corporation and ThermoQuest Corporation. He has acted as strategy adviser for community organizations including Brigham and Women's Hospital, the Institute of Contemporary Art and WGBH (Boston) public television. Porter also serves as a counsellor to the federal government. He was appointed by President Ronald Reagan in 1983 to the President's Commission on Industrial Competitiveness, and chaired its strategy committee. He continues to play an active role in US economic policy with Congress, the Executive Branch, and other groups. He is a member of the Executive Committee of the Council on Competitiveness, a private sector organization made up of chief executive officers of major corporations, unions and universities, and has contributed intellectual leadership to the Council's Competitiveness Index, Clusters of Innovation and other projects. He currently works with the heads of state of Central American countries to develop an economic strategy for that region. He is also the co-founder of the Centre for Middle East Competitive Strategy, an effort that brings together business and government leaders from Egypt, Israel, Jordan and Palestine to advance the competitive potential of the Middle East. He has maintained a long-time interest in the aesthetics and business of music and art, having worked on problems of strategy with arts organizations and aspiring musicians.

Porter has written sixteen books and over sixty articles. His book *Competitive Strategy: Techniques for Analyzing Industries and Competitors*, published in 1980, is in its thirty-second printing and has been translated into seventeen languages. In this book Porter developed a framework for analysing competitive forces in an industry's environment in order to identify the opportunities and threats confronting a company. His framework, known as the *five forces model*, focuses on five factors that shape competition within an industry: (1) the risk of new entry by potential competitors;

(2) the degree of rivalry among established companies within an industry; (3) the bargaining power of buyers; (4) the bargaining power of suppliers; and (5) the threat of substitute products. Porter argues that the stronger each of these forces is, the more limited is the ability of established companies to raise prices and earn greater profits.

He also introduced the concept of the value chain that sums up the activities undertaken by the firm that add value to the product. He has also argued that low cost and differentiation are two basic strategies for creating value and attaining a competitive advantage in an industry. This concept views a firm as a chain or network of basic activities that add value to its products and services, and thus add a margin of value to the firm. In the value chain conceptual framework, some business activities are primary processes; others are support processes. This five forces framework can highlight where competitive strategies can best be applied in a business.

Porter's 1990 book, *The Competitive Advantage of Nations*, develops a new theory of how nations, states and regions compete, and their sources of economic prosperity. He identifies four attributes that significantly affect the global competitiveness of companies: (1) factor endowments; (2) demand conditions; (3) related and supporting industries; and (4) strategy, structure and rivalry. Porter speaks of these four attributes as constituting the 'diamond'. He argues that firms are most likely to succeed in industries or industry segments in which conditions with regard to the four attributes are favourable. He also argues that the diamond's attributes form a mutually reinforcing system whereby changes to one attribute will affect the other three attributes. The ideas in this book have guided economic policy throughout the world. He has published follow-up books about national competitiveness in New Zealand, Canada, Sweden and Switzerland.

Interestingly, Porter wrote *The Competitive Advantage of Nations* at a time when business wisdom held that globalization was becoming more important. He argued that the opposite was true. In his view, national (or regional) circumstances have always played a central role in the success of firms. *The Competitive Advantage of Nations* also has some sharp theories on 'managerial universalism., the idea that one set of rules for good management can be applied to companies across the world, regardless of local circumstances. Just-in-time and other inventory management techniques make sense in Japan, where space is at a premium, but are out of place in America's Midwest. Performance-related pay works well in America, with its tradition of individualism and competition, but fails hopelessly in Japan, with its emphasis on collectivism. Thus he suggests that countries should cultivate their idiosyncrasies, rather than trying to force themselves into some universal model.

His book *On Competition* (1998) includes eleven articles previously published in the *Harvard Business Review* and two entirely new articles, 'Clusters and Competition' and 'Competition Across Locations'. His article 'What is Strategy?' focuses on company strategy. Here, Porter articulates a distinction crucial to his new work, namely that operational effectiveness simply means performing the same activities better than your competitors. Practices such as benchmarking, total quality management and lean manufacturing are all necessary and valuable routes to improving operational effectiveness. But while superior operational effectiveness can be a source of short-run competitive advantage, in the long run it is not sufficient. The 'rapid diffusion of best practices' means that industries become more efficient without individual companies becoming more profitable. Even more dangerously, benchmarking means that companies become more alike.

Instead, Porter suggests, companies need to position themselves so as to be different from their competitors. They achieve this not by discovering their core competency but rather by identifying opportunities in the industry.

The furniture retailer Ikea, for instance, tries to be all things to a particular group of people who are being targeted, namely 'young furniture buyers who want style at low cost'. Jiffy Lube, on the other hand, tries to be one thing to all people. In both cases, the companies have a clear sense of how their strategies differ from those of their competitors. In *On Competition*, Porter argues that operational effectiveness means running the same race faster; but strategy means running a different race, the one you have set yourself up to win.

As noted above, Porter is involved in assisting many states and local governments in enhancing competitiveness. For example, his *pro bono* work on an economic strategy for Massachusetts, beginning with the report *The Competitive Advantage of Massachusetts* (1991), has resulted in new legislation and numerous other state initiatives. He inspired and later chaired Governor William F. Weld's Council on Economic Growth and Technology in the state of Connecticut, and helped author the 1998 Cluster Bill which was passed unanimously by the Connecticut legislature. His presentation on the economy of New Zealand at Wellington Town Hall in November 1998 concluded that New Zealand had managed to reduce government's role in the economy in areas where this was inappropriate. On the corporate side, New Zealand has restructured, downsized and put its house in order. He suggested that the country's challenge in the future would be to build and invest, which would require a combination of public and private effort. He emphasized that this challenge would require not only a technocrat's list of economic policies, but also a vision and a sense of purpose that could be disseminated widely in society.

Porter's paper *The Determinants of National Innovative Capacity* (2000), with Scott Stern and Jeffrey L. Ferman, found an important role for research and development manpower and spending, policy choices such as the extent of IP protection and openness to international trade, the share of research performed by the academic sector and funded by the private sector, and the degree of techno-logical specialization. International patenting productivity also depends on each individual country's knowledge 'stock'. Further, national innovative capacity influences downstream commercialization, such as achieving a high market share of high-technology export markets. Finally, there has been convergence among Organization for Economic Cooperation and Development (OECD) coun-tries in terms of the estimated level of innova-tive capacity over the past quarter-century.

Porter has won many prestigious awards including Harvard's David A. Wells Prize in Economics for his research in industrial orga-nization, three Mckinsey Awards for the best *Harvard Business Review* article of the year, and the 1980 Graham and Dodd Award of the Financial Analyst Federation. He received the George R. Terry Book Award of the Academy of Management in 1985 for *On Competitive Advantage*. He was elected a fellow of the Academy of Management in 1988, and a fellow of the Royal Swedish Academy of Engineering Sciences in 1991. In 1991 he was the recipient of the Charles Coolidge Pralin Award for important contribution to the fields of marketing and strategy given by the American Marketing Association. The Massachusetts State Legislature also honoured Porter for his work on Massachusetts com-petitiveness in 1991. In 1993 he was named the Richard D. Irwin Outstanding Educator in Business Policy and Strategy by the Academy of Management. In 1997 he received the Adam Smith Award of the National Association of Business Economists.

In 1998 the Academy of Management awarded Porter with the group's first ever Distinguished Award for his contribution to the field of management. The Strategic Management Society recently voted Porter the most influential living strategiest, while McKinsey and Company have referred to him as the single most important strategist working today, and possibly in all time (Surowiecki 1999). His impact on both corporate and national strategic thinking, and approaches to competitiveness marks him out as one of the outstanding thinkers on management.

BIBLIOGRAPHY

Hill, C.W.L. and Jones, G.R. (1998) *Strategic Management Theory*, 4th edn, Boston: Houghton Mifflin.

Porter, M. (1976) *Interbrand Choice, Strategy and Bilateral Market Power*, Cambridge, MA: Harvard Economic Studies, Harvard University Press.

—— (1980) *Competitive Strategy: Techniques for Analyzing Industries and Competitors*, New York: The Free Press.

—— (1982) *Cases in Competitive Strategy*, New York: The Free Press.

—— (1985) *Competitive Advantage: Creating and Sustaining Superior Performance*, New York: The Free Press.

—— (ed.) (1986) *Competition in Global Industries*, Boston: Harvard Business School Press.

—— (1990) *The Competitive Advantage of Nations*, New York: The Free Press.

—— (1991) *Strategy: Seeking and Securing Competitive Advantage*, Boston: Harvard Business School Press.

—— (1998) *On Competition*, Boston: Harvard Business School Press.

Porter, M. and Monitor Company (1992) *Canada at the Crossroads: The Reality of a New Competitive Environment*, Ottawa: Business Council on National Issues and Minister of Supply and Services.

Porter, M., Caves, R.E. and Spence, A.M. (1980) *Competition in the Open Economy*, Cambridge, MA: Harvard Economic Studies, Harvard University Press.

Porter, M., Crocombe, G.T. and Enright, M.J. (1991) *Upgrading New Zealand's Competitive Advantage*. Auckland: Oxford University Press.

Porter, M., Sölvell, O. and Zander, I. (1991) *Advantage Sweden*, Stockholm, Sweden: Norstedts Förlag AB; 2nd edn, 1993.

Porter, M., Stern, S. and Ferman, J.L (2000)

The Determinants of National Innovative Capacity, New York: National Bureau of Economic Research.

Porter, M., Takeuchi, H. and Sakakibara, M. (2000) *Can Japan Compete?*, Tokyo: Diamond; Basingstoke: Macmillan; New York: Basic Books.

Porter, M., Borner, S., Weder, R. and Enright, M.J. (1991) *Internationale Wettbewerbsvorteile: Ein Strategisches Konzept fur die Schweiz* (International Competitive Advantage: A New Strategic Concept for Switzerland), Frankfurt: Campus Verlag.

Porter, M., Spence, A.M., Scott, J.T. and Caves, R.E. (1977) *Studies in Canadian Industrial Organization*, Ottawa: Canadian Royal Commission on Corporate Concentration.

Porter, M., Christensen, C.R., Andrews, K., Bower, J. and Hamermesh, R. (1986) *Business Policy: Text and Cases*, 6th edn, Homewood, IL: Richard D. Irwin.

Surowiecki, J. (1999) 'The Return of Michael Porter', *Fortune* 139(2).

Witzel, M. (1998) 'Porter, Michael E.', in M. Warner (ed.), *The IEBM Handbook of Management Thinking*, London: International Thomson Business Press, 544–8.

KR

PROCTER, William Cooper (1862–1934)

William Cooper Procter was born in Glendale, Ohio on 25 August 1862, the son of William Procter, a soap-maker, and his wife Charlotte. He died of pneumonia in Cincinnati on 2 May 1934. He married Jane Johnston in 1889; they had no children. After schooling in Cincinnati, Procter was educated at Princeton University, where he took a bachelor of science degree in 1883. He then returned to Cincinnati to work for the family business, Procter & Gamble, founded in 1837 by his father and his uncle, James Gamble. Procter began by working on the factory floor, learning about the technical aspects of the business, and also learning more about the nature and character of the workers. In 1890 he became general manager of the company, and succeeded his father as president in 1907, stepping down from the latter position in 1930 to become chairman of the board.

Under Procter's leadership, Procter & Gamble grew from being a large regional company specializing in soap to a multinational business diversified into many areas of food production. Procter oversaw diversification into such areas as cooking oils, and developed the successful brand Crisco, the first all-vegetable shortening. New product development continued in soaps and detergents, and continued its reputation for successful marketing and advertising following the company's original Ivory brand soap. During the period 1900–20 Procter & Gamble was one of the USA's leading advertisers in terms of dollars spent, but unlike other food producers such as Heinz, the company branded its leading products individually rather than creating a corporate brand.

Procter was also notably in advance of his time in terms of labour relations and employee welfare. His was one of the first companies in the United States to introduce profit sharing (1887) and later, after the company's incorporation in 1890, stock sharing; employees were given stock at intervals and were encouraged to buy more. Comprehensive health insurance was introduced in 1915. In 1923 Procter restructured his relationship with his chief customers, the food wholesalers, to allow for more consistent production, which offered the company considerable efficiencies and also enabled Procter to offer his workers 'guaranteed employment'; eliminating cycles in demand meant that he could guarantee continuous work. A radical and far-sighted manager, Procter laid the foundations of the modern consumer goods giant that is Procter & Gamble.

PULITZER, Joseph (1847–1911)

Joseph Pulitzer was born in Mako, Hungary on 10 April 1847, the son of Philip and Louise Pulitzer. He died on board his yacht *Liberty* in harbour at Charleston, South Carolina on 29 October 1911. He married Kate Davis in 1878, and they had seven children. His father was a prosperous merchant, and Pulitzer was well educated by private tutors. He left home at seventeen, after his father's death and his mother's remarriage, with a view to joining the army; poor eyesight disqualified him from most European armies, but he was accepted for service in the American Civil War, then ongoing, and in 1864 arrived in New York and enlisted. He did not find military life to his taste, however, and at the war's end returned to civilian life and worked as a casual labourer, first in New York and later in St Louis, Missouri, which had a large German-speaking population.

Chance and personal connections got him a job on *Westliche Post*, the city's German-language newspaper, as a reporter. Well-educated, intelligent and inquisitive, he had the chief talents of a good journalist and developed a particular reputation for exposing government and corporate corruption. Finally mastering English after a long study, he became prominent in Missouri society, serving briefly as a state legislator and also for a term as police commissioner in St Louis. In 1870 he shot and wounded a rival who had accused him of writing a false story; when he was arrested, supporters rallied around Pulitzer and paid his court costs and resulting fine. By 1871 he was part owner of the *Post*, already well-to-do, and

planning to leave journalism and study law before entering politics.

Chance again intervened when one of the city's leading newspapers, the *St. Louis Evening Dispatch*, went bankrupt and Pulitzer was offered the chance to buy it cheaply. Acquiring the business for $2,500 in 1878, Pulitzer was then offered a merger by another struggling paper, the *Evening Post*. In 1879 he bought out his partners' interests and formally combined the two titles as the *St. Louis Post-Dispatch*, with himself as owner and editor. Within a few years his paper dominated journalism in Missouri and indeed the Midwest, combining crime reporting, gossip, political coverage, satire and exposés of corruption in high places, always a Pulitzer speciality.

In 1883 Pulitzer was offered the chance to buy the *New York World* by its owner, Jay GOULD. He paid $346,000 for the paper, and in two years had increased its circulation from 15,000 to 150,000. The *World* dominated New York journalism and was widely imitated. Although Pulitzer is widely regarded as the first purveyor of mass popular journalism, his initial recipe was not much different from that of James Gordon BENNETT beginning in the 1940s: a mixture of scandal and sensation on the one hand and hard news and quality reportage on the other. The same recipe was being employed to great effect by William Randolph HEARST, who in 1895 purchased the *New York Journal* and entered a vigorous, often bitter competition with Pulitzer. This competition reached its height during the Spanish–American War in 1898, when both papers tried to outdo each other in hysterical jingoism.

By this point both newspapers were losing money. Correctly judging that Hearst had the deeper pockets and could afford the losses for longer, Pulitzer changed strategy. Abandoning the downmarket end of journalism to Hearst, he rid the paper of much of its sensationalist image and began concentrating on hard news and issues of the day. The paper had a strongly Democratic focus, reflecting its owner's own view, and campaigned on a number of political issues, most notably the use of public funds to purchase rights to build the Panama Canal. In 1904 Pulitzer appointed Frank J. Cobb as editor of the *World*, and working together the two made the newspaper the most respected in the United States; it held much the same position as the *New York Times* or the *Washington Post* at the end of the century.

As a manager, Pulitzer was characterized by a close attention to detail, and an almost instinctive understanding of his product – what was newsworthy and what was not – and of what his readers wanted. As noted, his approach to the marketing of journalism resembled that of Bennett, but he brought more of his personal idealism into his managerial style. Personally, he was a difficult man to work for, particularly as his health declined. A workaholic, he suffered constantly from health problems brought on by stress. He was always directly involved in the day-to-day management of his newspapers, and although his capacity for work was phenomenal, he could not cope with the strain forever: his eyesight began to fail and by 1892 he was virtually blind. By 1905 he was delegating more work to Cobb and his other executives, and began to travel, seeking cures for his various ailments. He made a number of endowments in his will, including $2 million to found a school of journalism at Columbia University and, most famously, endowing the annual Pulitzer Prizes for journalism, writing and the arts. The *World* declined after the retirement of Cobb in 1923, but the *St. Louis Post-Despatch*, under the editorship of Pulitzer's son Joseph, Jr, went on to become one of the USA's best and most respected newspapers.

BIBLIOGRAPHY
Juergens, G. (1966) *Joseph Pulitzer and the New York World*, Princeton, NJ: Princeton University Press.
Seitz, D.C. (1924) *Joseph Pulitzer: His Life and Letters*, New York: Simon and Schuster.

MLW

PULLMAN, George Mortimer (1831–97)

George Mortimer Pullman was born in Brockton, New York on 3 March 1831 and died of a heart attack in Chicago on 19 October 1897. The third of ten children, Pullman was forced to quit school at the age of fourteen and went to work as a clerk in a country store. By the time he was twenty-six he had accumulated a significant amount of capital, and decided to move west to Chicago. There his fortune grew as he emerged as an important general building contractor for the new, fast-growing metropolis. He was then involved in a number of enterprises, including banking and a shirt factory, as well as a year in the Colorado goldfields.

Returning to Chicago, Pullman decided to focus all his energies on the railroad sleeping car business. In the mid-1860s he began building luxury cars for rail lines operating out of Chicago, by then the railroad centre of the United States. In 1867 he organized the Pullman Palace Car Company, capitalized at $1 million. Allied with department store magnate Marshall Field and other leading Chicago business figures, his business continued to grow rapidly. With the support of Andrew CARNEGIE, his company took over the powerful and much larger Woodruff's Central Transportation Company to dominate the industry in America. Expanding beyond national boundaries, Pullman marketed his cars in England, Ireland, Italy, Canada, Mexico and India. However, the heart of his business remained in the United States, where by 1890 Pullman operated over 2,000 cars on 200,000 kilometres (120,000 miles) of railroad. His operations had grown to include the manufacture of sleeping, dining, parlour, and other cars for the railroad industry.

As Pullman came to hold a near monopoly, he determined to build an enormous car shop and model company town south of Chicago to build ordinary coaches, freight, baggage and other cars. He purchased 1,500 hectares (3,700 acres) of land and hired architects to design what he believed would be a scientifically planned city that would serve as a model for the new urban industrial order emerging in America. Completed in 1881, the new town of Pullman was widely heralded in the press and by informed observers; it also gained added notoriety in connection with the 1893 Columbian Exposition in Chicago.

Pullman's reputation as an industrial statesman was undermined the following year. When the devastating Panic of 1893 erupted and economic hard times began, Pullman began laying off workers and slashed wages by 25 per cent. But the rents charged to his employees remained high, as did the dividends paid to company stockholders. When his workers, who had joined the new American Railway Union (ARU) led by Eugene V. Debs, protested and called a strike he adamantly refused to negotiate. The resulting sympathy strike by the ARU spread to all but one of the nation's transcontinental railroads and resulted in the largest strike of the nineteenth century. The ARU was destroyed after federal troops were called out from Chicago to the Pacific, but Pullman's reputation was permanently damaged. Few celebrated his central role in the creation and operation of passenger traffic on the American railroad system. Pullman never recovered from the criticisms, and died a tormented man three years later.

BIBLIOGRAPHY

Buder, S. (1967) *Pullman: An Experiment in Industrial Order and Community Planning, 1880–1930*, New York: Oxford University Press.

Leyendecker, L.E. (1992) *Palace Car Prince: A Biography of George Mortimer Pullman*, Niwot, CO: University Press of Colorado.

Lindsey, A. (1942) *The Pullman Strike: The Story of a Unique Experiment and of a Great Labor Upheaval*, Chicago: University of Chicago Press.

Schneirov, R., Stromquist, S. and Salvatore, N. (eds) (1999) *The Pullman Strike and the Crisis of the 1890s*, Urbana, IL: University of Illinois Press.

Smith, C. (1995) *Urban Disorder and the Shape of Belief: The Great Chicago Fire, the Haymarket Bomb, and the Model Town of Pullman*, Chicago: University of Chicago Press.

WTW

R

RAND, Ayn (1905–82)

Ayn Rand was born in St Petersburg, Russia on 2 February 1905 as Alissa Rosenbaum, and died in New York on 6 March 1982. She became a leading advocate for capitalism as a moral as well as an economic system. A bright and highly individualistic child with dreams of being a romantic novelist, she rejected both the religion and collectivism that so strongly marked Russian culture. Her hatred of Russian life and admiration for the United States was heightened by the experiences of the Bolshevik Revolution which later inspired her 1936 novel *We the Living*. After studying history at the University of Petrograd from 1921–4, she secured an exit visa in 1925 to allow her to visit her relatives in the United States. She never returned to Russia.

Settling in Hollywood in 1926, she was hired by Cecil B. DeMille as a screenwriter. She changed her name to Ayn Rand, the last name being inspired by the Remington Rand typewriter. Three years later she met and married Frank O'Connor. She became an American citizen in 1931. In spite of America being for them the land of opportunity, Frank and Ayn Rand O'Connor had to struggle throughout the 1930s. Anti-communist writers were not popular in a decade in which some Hollywood actors flirted with Marxism. Rand sold screenplays to support both herself and her husband. Her first major success, the novel *The Fountainhead*, was published in 1943 after being rejected by a dozen publishers. It even-tually became a best-seller and made Rand a visible literary figure.

Rand began work in 1946 upon *Atlas Shrugged*, which was published in 1957; it is the most comprehensive statement of her objectivist philosophy. It was one of the most popular and influential books of the twentieth century, having sold over five million copies. This powerful novel centres around two families of businesspeople, the Taggarts and the D'Anconias. James Taggart, president of Taggart Transcontinental Railroads, caricatures the socially responsible capitalist who has compromised with the mixed economy and notions of social responsibility. His daughter, Dagney, a Rand heroine, just wants to make money.

Rand then introduces her entrepreneurial superman, John Galt, who, like all of her characters, is an idealized black and white figure. Galt, an executive at the Twentieth Century Motor Company, speaks out against the new socialist management philosophy of his company. Meanwhile, all the producers in society – businesspeople, doctors, scientists and others – are disappearing. As they disappear, society begins to collapse and bureaucrats, represented by the repulsive Wesley Mouch, issue new regulations to hamper the productive and reward the shiftless. Another Rand hero, the pirate Ragnar Dannarskjöld, raids the American welfare state, sending handouts to socialist dictatorships.

The world continues to fall apart, in the manner of Bolshevik Russia, until John Galt broadcasts to the world that the cause of civilization's collapse is government's looting of the productive capitalists, technicians and artists. The cause of this looting is the morality of altruism, according to which people try to live their lives for the benefit of others instead of making decisions on the basis of rational self-interest. At the end of the novel, the producers have fled to a secret community in a valley in Colorado where they plan the reconstruction of Rand's ideal society.

Rand elaborated on her philosophy in her works of the 1960s. *For the New Intellectual* (1961) offered a version of history in which capitalists were persecuted by the 'Attila' of state plunder and the force of religion, which Rand, a dogmatic atheist, described as the 'Witch Doctor'. *The Virtue of Selfishness* (1964) laid out her view of morality, which some critics have decried as Nietzschean. Denying the existence of God, Rand still insisted absolute truth existed: A was A. While rejecting violence and fraud, she required people to make moral choices based upon rational self-interest.

Rand's extreme individualism led her to *laissez-faire* capitalism as the only rational system allowing free moral choices. Her total free market vision, expressed in *Capitalism: The Unknown Ideal* (1967), drew much from that of Ludwig von MISES. Like Mises, Rand advocated a return to the gold standard, the abolition of welfare, an end to anti-trust actions, and total non-intervention by the government in the market-place. Business was America's true persecuted minority, monopolies were created by government in the first place, and a true *laissez-faire* system would generate so much prosperity that redistributionist programmes would not be needed. For Rand, it was not enough that capitalism was efficient. It was moral of and by itself, because it was a logical extension of her concept of rational selfishness.

Rand's influence upon American culture was much greater than has been commonly realized. An organized objectivist movement led by Leonard Peikoff is headquartered in southern California. One of her disciples, Federal Reserve Chairman Alan Greenspan, is arguably the most powerful economic figure in the world. Hundreds of thousands have read her novels and have been converted to libertarian ideas. The best-selling books of real-estate salesman Robert Ringer, especially *Looking Out for Number One* (1977), presenting Randian ideas in folksy, popular form, have also influenced millions.

Largely as a result of her work, *laissez-faire* ideas became far more respectable in the last quarter of the twentieth century. Critics, and these have included conservatives as well as leftists, have decried her philosophy as helping to inspire what Christopher Lasch called a 'culture of narcissism', which has undermined community and citizenship.

BIBLIOGRAPHY

Branden, B. (1986) *The Passion of Ayn Rand*, Garden City, NY: Doubleday.

Den Uyl, D.J. and Rasmussen, D.B. (1984) *The Philosophic Thought of Ayn Rand*, Chicago: University of Illinois Press.

O'Neill, W.F. (1977) *With Charity Toward None: An Analysis of Ayn Rand's Philosophy*, Totowa, NJ: Littlefield, Adams and Co.

Rand, A. (1936) *We the Living*, New York: New American Library, 1959.

—— (1943) *The Fountainhead*, New York: New American Library, 1971.

—— (1957) *Atlas Shrugged*, New York: New American Library.

—— (1961) *For the New Intellectual*, New York: New American Library.

—— (ed.) (1967) *Capitalism: The Unknown Ideal*, New York: New American Library.

Ringer, R.J. (1977) *Looking Out for Number One*, New York: Funk and Wagnalls.

—— (1979) *Restoring the American Dream*, New York: Harper and Row.

Sciabarra, C.M. (1995) *Ayn Rand: The*

Russian Radical, University Park, PA: Pennsylvania University Press.

DCL

REICH, Robert (1946–)

Robert Reich was born in Scranton, Pennsylvania on 24 June 1946. He graduated from Dartmouth College with a BA in economics in 1968 and was awarded a Rhodes Scholarship to Oxford, where he gained an MA in 1970. He studied law at Yale Law School and received his doctorate in 1973. He served as assistant to the solicitor-general in the US Justice Department from 1974 to 1976, but finding law too abstracted from real life, sought some way of combining law and economics, and accepted a job as director of policy planning for the Federal Trade Commission from 1976 to 1981. He joined the faculty of Harvard's J.F. Kennedy School of Government in 1981, teaching business and politics, where his classes were so popular that students entered a lottery to attend his course. He is married and has two sons.

His first book, *Minding America's Business* (1982) looked at the USA's falling share of world trade, and recommended that the United States adopt a formal industrial policy. His ideas received much attention from critics and supporters alike. His ideas were widely accepted by Democrat politicians in the late 1980s, influencing Michael Dukakis, US presidential candidate in 1988, and later President Bill Clinton. As secretary of labor (from 1993) in Clinton's administration, he backed the North American Free Trade Agreement and called for higher minimum wages and tax incentives to discourage corporate layoffs. He became an advocate for the unemployed and underemployed.

Reich is best known for his book *The Work of Nations* (1991), in which he explores the social consequences of the transformation of an emerging global economy, making an important contribution to the current thinking on globalization. Throughout his writing he displays the characteristics of a synthesist, overcoming traditional boundaries between business and government, right and left, East and West, and competition and cooperation. He combines the perspectives of a number of disciplines in addressing the problems of the changing economy and the political challenges it generates. This is particularly evident in *The Next American Frontier* (1983), where he used history and anthropology alongside economics to describe the challenge then facing the United States, such as building a strong economic future, securing jobs and prosperity for its citizens. This book hit the political mood of the time and became influential in mainstream politics.

Underpinning Reich's analysis of the American economy was his belief that it was the re-enactment of the cultural stories and myths of a society that guide a society's behaviour. He explored and labelled these beliefs, for example 'The Rot at the Top', 'The Triumphant Individual' and the 'Scientific Manager'. Often, he noted, these beliefs were outdated, and together combined to create blind spots and distortions in economies. He also asserted that there had been a fundamental split between business values and civic/political values. He declared that social, human and civic issues were at the heart of the US economic malaise, an inseparable part of creating wealth in a knowledge economy, as opposed to an unresolved residue or by-product. Reich asserted that organizations are going to have to adapt to confront these economic realities, requiring the participation of government in business and a re-evaluation of prevailing myths.

Reich has been a constant critic of conventional wisdom. His criticism of scientific management rests on his analysis that the very values (efficiency, specialization and the separation of planning from action) that contributed to the hegemony of the United States from the 1920s to the 1960s are now contributing to its failures. Reich notes that the principles of scientific management have continued in the mergers and acquisitions of companies, most of which have failed to perform, as they represent only the rearrangement of industrial assets. Reich stresses that this has serious consequences in the form of higher employee turnover and, in turn, reduced capability for innovation. This tendency has been exacerbated by the trend for American new product ideas to be commercially developed and manufactured in Japan. These activities are resulting in the loss of experience and learning, constituting high-value skills. Reich asserts that this stance is driven by the American passion for the individual over the community. Reich views individualism not as ending in triumph but as leading to 'traffic jams'. He condemns this belief in the 'triumphant individual', and he himself takes the side of the public, the society, rather than the individual, asserting that innovation is a complex, collective process, not an individual skill. He attributes to this individualism the cause of the proliferation of regulations and lawyers, and claims that it will lead to eventual deadlock.

Reich's analysis of the declining performance of US business (and UK business) reveals a number of causes. Among these is the lack of training of business leaders in the process of innovation; a requirement for radical reorganization of corporate hierarchy to achieve collaborative and power-sharing arrangements with workers and unions; the lack of organizational capability to upgrade human skills quickly; and scientific management's tendency to focus on quantities and to miss qualities. He recommends that a model of 'the Benevolent Community' should be fostered in which a social system is based on reciprocal obligation, so that government should provide incentives to business to develop human resource. In this way market

forces can be assisted rather than opposed. He stresses that the market is not an 'it' but a 'we', and that we must choose how we develop and adjust to the demands of the international market. Reich asks us to acknowledge that economic development and complex creation are cooperative enterprises, and that it is a 'triumphant team' that will be best able to handle knowledge overload and create complexity.

Reich's writing has been described as more like that of a popular social anthropologist and political essayist than that of someone trained in economics and law. This approach has made his analysis of economic situations rich in breadth, although, some claim, unspecific in his recommended solutions. Reich's analysis has synthesized ideas and cultures traditionally split by dichotomies, and is acknowledged as having produced insightful and useful thinking on the outlook for traditional Western economies.

BIBLIOGRAPHY

Hampden-Turner, C. (1998) 'Reich, Robert', in M. Warner (ed.), *IEBM Handbook of Management Thinking*, London: International Thomson Business Press, 549–54.

Reich, R.B. (1982) *Minding America's Business*, New York: Times Books.

—— (1983) *The Next American Frontier*, New York: Times Books.

—— (1991) *The Work of Nations: Preparing Ourselves for 21st Century Capitalism*, New York: Knopf.

AJ

REYNOLDS, Richard Joshua (1850–1918)

Richard Joshua Reynolds was born in Patrick County, Virginia on 20 July 1850, the son of

Hardin and Nancy Reynolds. He died of pancreatic cancer at his home near Winston-Salem, North Carolina on 29 July 1918. He married Mary Smith in 1905, and they had four children. His family were one of the most prominent in Virginia, with large holdings of land and slaves; his father, a farmer and tobacco merchant, had also diversified into banking and the production of chewing tobacco. Reynolds himself worked on his father's farm and later in the tobacco factory during school holidays. Following the American Civil War he attended Emory and Henry College, but dropped out before completing his degree and went to work for his father on a full-time basis; he later attended a business college in Baltimore. In 1873 he entered a formal partnership with his father, but soon found that the business was badly located, far from the nearest railway, and unlikely to grow much further. In 1874 he moved to Winston-Salem and set up his own factory producing chewing tobacco, in a location that had better access to railways and was closer to the prime tobacco-growing regions of North Carolina. The firm, later incorporated as R.J. Reynolds Tobacco Company, grew rapidly. Reynolds used the distribution opportunities offered by the railway to put him in touch with the large urban markets of the eastern United States, and backed these up with advertising campaigns.

However, Reynolds lacked the capital to undertake further expansion, and in the 1890s came under pressure from the tobacco trust, American Tobacco Company, which was driving other competitors out of the market. Reynolds, much against his will, finally joined the trust in 1899, managing to keep a measure of independence and control. He chafed at the restrictions imposed by the trust, particularly those that prevented him from entering the growing smoking tobacco market; in 1907, when the US government launched an antitrust suit against American Tobacco, Reynolds began making and selling first smoking tobacco and then cigarettes in defiance of the trust. By 1911 he was free of the trust and the R.J. Reynolds Tobacco Company began an aggressive marketing campaign centred around one of the most famous cigarette brand names of all time: Camel. By 1918 the company was selling $100 million worth of cigarettes worldwide.

Reynolds saw Camel through its early years but, becoming increasingly ill, he handed over control of the firm and retired. As a manager, he is chiefly notable for his marketing strategy, which combined the development of new products with effective branding and advertising, but also emphasized distribution systems and quality products. The present-day condemnation of tobacco producers should not be allowed to obscure his abilities and achievements. •

BIBLIOGRAPHY
Lach, E.J., Jr (1999) 'Reynolds, Richard Joshua', in J.A. Garraty and M.C. Carnes (eds), *American National Biography*, Oxford: Oxford University Press, vol. 30, 384–5.
Tilley, N.M. (1985) *The R.J. Reynolds Tobacco Company*, Chapel Hill, NC: University of North Carolina Press.

MLW

RICKENBACKER, Edward Vernon
(1890–1973)

Edward Vernon Rickenbacker was born in Columbus, Ohio on 8 October 1890 and died in Zurich, Switzerland on 23 July 1973. Rickenbacker came from a poor German-Swiss immigrant family, and was a self-taught mechanical genius. As a young man he became a successful automobile racer, and in 1918 was the USA's leading fighter pilot in the First

World War, shooting down twenty-two German aircraft and four observation balloons over the Western Front.

An ambitious and highly energetic man, Rickenbacker used his status as a war hero and his personal connections gained as a racer to engage in several business enterprises, including an ill-conceived automobile manufacturing firm that produced vehicles bearing his name. Eventually, after failing as a manufacturer, Rickenbacker in the 1930s became associated with General Motors (GM), then the world's largest industrial corporation. GM had interests in aviation, and Ernest R. Breech, a GM executive placed in charge of one of those interests, assigned Rickenbacker managerial responsibility for the firm that became Eastern Air Lines. Rickenbacker assumed responsibility in 1935, and became head of Eastern in 1938. Laurance Rockefeller was among the investors.

Rickenbacker soon built Eastern into the nation's second largest and most profitable air carrier. He practiced a hands-on, personal and paternalistic style of management. He emphasized achieving low costs and reliable, safe service. During the Second World War, the airline's fleet operated under military control. Rickenbacker also served during the war, and in 1942 a B-17 bomber on which he was travelling, carrying secret instructions, crashed in the South Pacific. Rickenbacker and the crew floated in a raft for three weeks, during which time one crewman died, before they were rescued. This episode made Rickenbacker a hero once again. During the war a feature film, *Captain Eddie*, was produced to help rally American morale.

After the war and back at his desk in New York, Rickenbacker expanded Eastern's routes and enlarged its fleet as four-engined aircraft entered civilian service. During the 1940s Eastern's earnings sometimes surpassed those of the rest of the industry. These profits hid, for a time, problems that eventually proved Rickenbacker's and Eastern's undoing. The American airline industry at the time was closely regulated by the Civil Aeronautics Board (CAB), which awarded routes and offered airmail subsidies to struggling carriers. Rickenbacker was inept in this environment. His outspoken criticism of government regulation, and of the men who issued the regulations, earned Eastern powerful enemies. The CAB awarded subsidized rivals routes in Eastern's most lucrative markets while at the same time preventing Eastern from gaining transcontinental markets. Airline competition then involved service, not price, and Rickenbacker, with his emphasis on low costs and efficiency, alienated many passengers. This situation, combined with poor decisions on aircraft purchases, including a failure to invest quickly in jets, meant that Eastern began to suffer severely. In 1963 its board of directors, led by Rockefeller, forced Rickenbacker to retire.

BIBLIOGRAPHY

Farr, F. (1979) *Rickenbacker's Luck: An American Life*, Boston: Houghton Mifflin.

Lewis, W.D. (2000) 'A Man Born out of Season: Edward V. Rickenbacker, Eastern Air Lines, and the Civil Aeronautics Board', in W.D. Lewis (ed.), *Airline Executives and Federal Regulation: Case Studies in American Enterprise from the Airmail Era to the Dawn of the Jet Age*, Columbus, OH: Ohio State University Press.

Rickenbacker, E.V. (1967) *Rickenbacker: An Autobiography*, Englewood Cliffs, NJ: Prentice-Hall.

KAK

ROCKEFELLER, John Davison, Sr
(1839–1937)

John Davison Rockefeller was born in Richford, New York on 8 July 1839, the son of William Avery Rockefeller and Eliza

Davison Rockefeller, and died in Florida on 23 May 1937. His family was of French Huguenot descent, allegedly from the Rocquefeuilles, a noble family of Languedoc. His father, a farmer, had a lifestyle that contrasted sharply with that of his devout Baptist wife; Big Bill, as his father was called, was very liberal in his moral values, somewhat unstable, and regarded as a charming huckster and confidence man by those who knew him. The Rockefellers moved from place to place in upstate New York as Big Bill, or 'Devil Bill', as he was sometimes called, peddled various medicines and supposed cures for cancer.

By the time the family settled in Cleveland, Ohio in 1853, the young Rockefeller could no longer endure his father's lifestyle. His outlook had been very much moulded by his mother. Rockefeller, now fourteen or fifteen, was a deeply religious young Baptist; he would retain this faith all his life, and it would shape his entire outlook. By the time he entered high school in 1854, Rockefeller was already forming the philosophy that would govern his career. This was the pure embodiment of the Protestant work ethic as described by the German sociologist Max Weber. Unlike his father, he saw business as God's calling for himself, not an end in itself. One had to work hard, not to acquire luxuries but to demonstrate one's calling before God. Being a Baptist, Rockefeller rejected the notion of predestination; one's salvation was a matter of free will. He abhorred slavery and supported the abolitionist cause, believing that people should rise or fall by their own efforts.

Belief in hard work, the discipline of tithing, thrift, self-denial, punctuality and rejection of frivolous luxuries were very much a part of the boy's value system by the time he was sixteen. Rockefeller was already entrepreneur in his outlook. He disdained hereditary privilege and priestly hierarchies in favour of an ethic of total personal responsibility before God and human. He did, however, have a strong admiration for large successful businesses and was determined to work for one. Anxious to escape

from the misery of his family life and be self-supporting, Rockefeller walked the streets of Cleveland looking for someone who would hire him as a bookkeeper. However, no wanted to hire him as he was too young. Undaunted despite constant rejection, Rockefeller was finally hired by the shipping firm Hewitt and Tuttle in September 1855.

Even though he had to work his first three months without pay, Rockefeller soon impressed his bosses with his meticulous approach to auditing. He loved working with numbers, and saw the importance of strict accounting, which saved his firm much in wasted cash. He worked for Hewitt and Tuttle for the next four years, his apprenticeship in business. In 1859, taking his savings, Rockefeller formed a shipping partnership with a British immigrant, William Clark. Clark and Rockefeller had a shaky start, so shaky that Rockefeller had to go to his father for a loan – for which his father charged him 10 per cent interest and could foreclose at any time. Clark and Rockefeller nonetheless did well enough in its first year of shipping and trading business to earn $450,000 in receipts.

Two developments catapulted Rockefeller from obscurity to becoming a power rivalled only by Andrew CARNEGIE, John Pierpont MORGAN and the White House. The first was the discovery of oil in Pennsylvania in 1859; the second was the coming of the American Civil War.

While Rockefeller deeply sympathized with the Union cause, his obligation to take care of his family and his business helped persuade him to hire a replacement to join the army. In the meantime the war made him very rich. The Union factories turned to kerosene to lubricate their machines, and the cities of the North and Europe used kerosene to light their streets. Rockefeller turned to refining as the most stable aspect of the new high-growth business. Soon the partnership added several other members. Rockefeller himself managed the accounts scrupulously, making the firm account for every nickel. The firm thrived during the war and eventually Rockefeller bought out Clark, the company becoming known as Rockefeller and Andrews. Meanwhile in 1864 he married Laura Spelman. Laura bore him three surviving daughters and a son, John D. Rockefeller, Jr (1874–1960).

The period following the Civil War well deserves the name given it by Mark Twain: the Gilded Age. It was an age of self-made men and worship of entrepreneurs. Books on self-help, typified by the Horatio Alger stories, became best-sellers. William Dean Howells's *The Rise of Silas Lapham* satirized the demise of the old gentry elites in favour of upstarts such as Rockefeller. In 1866 Rockefeller started a new oil firm, Standard Oil, with offices in New York headed by his brother William. Rockefeller now saw his future in oil, but, given the libertine nature of life in the oil patch and the undue risks of drilling, he continued to concentrate on the refining of kerosene.

Rockefeller recognized 'petroleum as the basis of an enduring economic revolution' (Chernow 1999: 102). He believed sincerely that God had called him to the refining business. This business, however, was highly competitive, and such competition endangered not only his own business but the industry as a whole. Rockefeller, allegedly the embodiment of entrepreneurial capitalism, believed, like many of the large industrialists of his age, that too many refiners chasing too few markets was ruinous for the economy and the country, not to mention for John D. Rockefeller.

Chartering the Standard Oil Company of Ohio in 1870, Rockefeller launched an all-out effort to corner the market in refining. Already worth $1 million and in control of one-tenth of the industry, Standard resorted to a number of tactics to undercut and eventually buy out its competitors. One of these tactics was to secure first discounts and then rebates of shipping charges from the railroads. This cut Rockefeller's transportation costs. Small shippers could not compete.

In 1872 Rockefeller organized a cartel called the South Improvement Company. This was, according to Collier and Horowitz (1976), one of the pioneer holding companies. It could hold stock both inside and outside Pennsylvania, where it was chartered. Railroads would pool their operations with refiners such as South Improvement, and raise freight rates while rebating the refiners within the pool. Riots broke out in Pennsylvania, and the arrangement was banned by the Pennsylvania legislature.

Rockefeller's next tactic was to force his rivals into selling their companies to him. Between 1872 and 1879 Standard bought out its rivals by giving them fair prices. Rockefeller perfected his own refining process, squeezing out inefficiencies at every step. He scanned accounts for waste, but still delegated a great deal of power. During the 1870s Rockefeller continued to pay and treat his employees well, even making them shareholders, permitting Standard to enjoy labour peace at a time of depression when railroads like the Pennsylvania were torn with violent strikes.

Standard faced a challenge in 1877 from Pennsylvania Railroad president Tom Scott, who wanted to branch into refining. Rockefeller then ordered 600 new tank cars to be put on the New York Central and Erie lines and shut down his refineries in Pittsburgh. He slashed kerosene prices in all of Scott's markets. Faced with both Rockefeller and the rail strike of 1877, which had to be crushed by federal troops, Scott gave up on refining. A consortium of other Pennsylvania producers attempted to build an independent pipeline from the oilfields to Williamsport on the Susquehanna. Rockefeller responded by laying a pipeline of his own and increasing his advantage over the railroads.

By 1883 Standard Oil controlled 90 per cent of American refining and the pipeline industry. The company was, however, becoming more and more unpopular. State legislators began investigations of its monopoly, and lawsuits followed, forcing Rockefeller to discontinue receiving rebates from the railroads. In the meantime, Rockefeller created yet another new form of business organization destined to dominate the American business world from the 1880s until the First World War: the trust.

In 1882, Rockefeller organized the Standard Oil Trust. He took the legal concept whereby a parent could hold property in trust for a minor, and applied it to oil companies. All of the shares held by the thirty-seven stockholders of the forty Standard companies in several states were transferred to a new group of nine trustees, led by Rockefeller himself. Stockholders were issued trust certificates, shares in the new umbrella corporation, of which the nine trustees owned two-thirds of the shares and thus of the original companies. Legally, the forty firms were independent, but in practice they were a $70 million monopoly in which all profits went to the Standard Oil Company of Ohio.

Standard Oil began to drill for its own crude oil, investing in new fields in Ohio and exploiting them through a new process which allowed the sulphuric oil of Ohio to be refined. In addition, Rockefeller began operations in Europe, Asia and Latin America, turning Standard into a multinational corporation. Following Standard's lead, other industries such as the whisky and sugar industries began to thwart state anti-monopoly laws by setting up trusts, so that by 1890 the trust was the dominant form of American corporate organization. In that year Congress passed the Sherman Anti-trust Act, which had little power and was used more against labour than against business.

Standard was investigated for unfair trading practices by the US Congress in 1888, and its trust was dissolved in 1892 by the Ohio Supreme Court. By this time Rockefeller held $23 million in vast investments outside the oil industry as well as within it. These included sixteen railroads, nineteen mining companies and several banks. By 1893 Rockefeller also had acquired the richest iron ore deposits in the world in the Mesabi range of Minnesota,

which would ultimately provide 60 per cent of American iron ore; he leased these to the Carnegie Steel Company in 1896. A million tons a year of iron ore was now shipped from Rockefeller mines in Rockefeller ships to Rockefeller freight cars to steel mills owned by Carnegie and Morgan.

Rockefeller founded a new trust in New Jersey in 1899. Standard Oil of New Jersey was a holding company permitted by that state's law to hold stock in other companies. It was run by Rockefeller and fourteen other directors, who controlled an empire of $205 million in 1900, and $360 million by 1906. It was the most powerful company in the nation, rivalled only by US Steel, although the rise of Shell and new independent Texas oilmen would cut its worldwide share of petroleum production to around 60 per cent.

The enormous size of Standard Oil and its holdings continued to attract public criticism. A new US president, Theodore Roosevelt, took office in 1901. Roosevelt was less tolerant of monopoly than his predecessors. Rockefeller's reputation was further tarnished by the publication in 1904 of *The History of the Standard Oil Company* by journalist Ida M. TARBELL. Written by the daughter of an oilman whom Rockefeller had decades ago put out of business, *The History of the Standard Oil Company* presented a detailed indictment of decade after decade of Rockefeller practices. To Tarbell, Standard Oil was the embodiment of a trust phenomenon that threatened to undermine not only free competition but democracy itself:

The Standard Oil Trust ... was the first in the field, and it has furnished the methods, the charter, and the traditions for its followers. It is the most perfectly developed trust in existence; that is, it satisfies most nearly the trust ideal of entire control of the commodity in which it deals. Its vast profits have led its officers into various allied interests, such as railroads, shipping, gas, copper, iron, steel, as well as into banks and trust companies, and to the acquiring and solidifying of these interests it has applied the methods used in building up the Oil Trust. It has led in the struggle against legislation directed against combinations. Its power in state and Federal government, in the press, in the college, in the pulpit, is generally recognised. The perfection of the organisation of the Standard, the ability and daring with which it has carried out its projects, make it the pre-eminent trust of the world – the one whose story is best fitted to illuminate the subject of combinations of capital.

(Tarbell 1904: vii)

Rockefeller sold his Minnesota iron holdings to US Steel and began to withdraw from active management of the Standard Oil concerns. His strong conviction that God had given him his fortune (almost $1 billion) and held him accountable for its use, plus the growing public resentment of that fortune, led him to giving on massive scale. Rockefeller chose to direct his charitable efforts, managed by the Rockefeller Foundation, into activities such as education and medical research. In his lifetime he gave away an estimated half a billion dollars. The Standard Oil trust, following a prolonged antitrust suit initiated by the Roosevelt administration in 1906, was dissolved in 1911, creating Esso (later Exxon), Mobil, Chevron, Atlantic and several other oil giants.

Rockefeller's legacy was enormous. He had created the American petroleum industry, the trust form of organization and a huge philanthropic foundation. His great-grandchildren would ultimately distinguish themselves in public service. David Rockefeller (1915–) became director of the Chase Manhattan Bank; Nelson Rockefeller (1908–79) was governor of New York for almost four terms and vice-president of the United States in 1975–6. Winthrop Rockefeller (1912–73) became governor of Arkansas. A great-great-grandson, John D. Rockefeller IV (1937–) became a US Senator from West Virginia.

Rockefeller is the best known and arguably the most successful figure in American business history. Much was written about him both during and after his lifetime, but until Ron Chernow's epic 1999 biography, *Titan: The Life of John D. Rockefeller, Sr.*, little was known about the personality and inner thoughts of one of the great leaders of world business. The story of Rockefeller is much more than just the history of Standard Oil.

BIBLIOGRAPHY

Chernow, R. (1999) *Titan: The Life of John D. Rockefeller, Sr.*, New York: Random House.

Collier, P. and Horowitz, D. (1976) *The Rockefellers: An American Dynasty*, New York: New American Library.

'John Davison Rockefeller' (1999) *The McGraw-Hill Encyclopedia of World Biography*, Detroit, MI: Gale Research, Inc., vol. 13, 226–8.

Tarbell, I.M. (1904) *The History of the Standard Oil Company*, New York: McClure, Phillips and Co.; http://www.history.rochester.edu/fuels/tarbell/preface.htm, 31 January 2001.

Yergin, D. (1991) *The Prize: The Epic Quest for Oil, Money, and Power*, New York: Simon and Schuster.

DCL

ROETHLISBERGER, Fritz Jules
(1898–1974)

Fritz Jules Roethlisberger was born in New York City on 29 October 1898, the son of Friedrich and Lina Roethlisberger. He died in Cambridge, Massachusetts on 17 May 1974. He married Margaret Dixon in 1925; they had one daughter. After taking an AB at Columbia University Roethlisberger moved to Boston, where he received a BS in chemical engineering from Massachusetts Institute of Technology in 1922 and then worked in the chemical industry until 1924; he then attended Harvard University, taking an MA in 1925 (he later received an honorary doctorate from the University of St Gall, Switzerland). From 1927 to 1930 he was instructor in industrial research at Harvard, being made assistant professor in 1930 and associate professor in 1938; he became professor of human relations in 1946, retiring in 1967 as professor emeritus.

Over the course of his long career Roethlisberger produced a number of books and articles, most focusing on issues concerning personnel management or human resources management. In his approach he was strongly influenced by the human relations school, especially Elton MAYO, with whom he worked on several occasions, and Mary Parker FOLLETT. It was through Mayo that he became involved in the research project that would make his name, the research programme at the Hawthorne plant, near Chicago.

Hawthorne was owned by Western Electric, a subsidiary of AT&T, which employed around 10,000 people in the business of making telephone equipment, including receivers and switches. In 1924 the company began a fairly simple study on the relationship between the level of illumination in the workplace and employee productivity, with a view to testing a hypothesis that changing lighting levels could increase productivity. Contrary to expectations, the study initially appeared to show an inverse correlation between lighting and productivity (i.e., the more the light was reduced, the more productivity increased). But the workers, when interviewed, commented that they found the brighter light more pleasant and stimulating. From 1924 to 1928 Western Electric and the National Research Council (NRC) of the National Academy of Sciences conducted several further studies on the effects of productivity on environmental factors, all of which provided unexpected results. In early 1928 the NRC withdrew from the research, and the company turned instead to Elton Mayo at Harvard.

Mayo and the Western Electric researchers noticed that one of the findings of the research appeared to be a correlation between employee productivity and the nature and duration of breaks for rest. Discarding the illumination, theory, the researchers turned instead to the study of fatigue and its impacts. The researchers concentrated on a small work unit, the Relay Assembly Test Room, with five workers who were working in isolation from the shop floor; thus both environmental factors and work times could be readily controlled. The research team found that productivity declined as fatigue rose (i.e., with longer working days and/or fewer rest breaks), and management instituted longer rest breaks throughout the company. But as a result of this measure, productivity rose only slightly.

After studying the findings again, the research team concluded that the changes in productivity noted in the Relay Assembly Test Room were a result, not of increased or reduced fatigue, but of the more stimulating working environment provided by the researchers themselves and the company supervisors who worked with them. Attention from their superiors and interest in the programme itself had, even if only subconsciously, stimulated the workers in the team and caused output to rise. Ironically, the researchers had been attempting to create a controlled environment:

but trying to do so in itself produced the biggest change of all; in other words, the investigators had not been studying an ordinary shop situation but a socially contrived situation of their own making. *The experiment they had planned to conduct was quite different from the experiment they had actually performed.* They had not studied the relationship between output and fatigue, monotony, etc., so much as they had performed a most interesting psychological and sociological experiment. In the process of setting the conditions for the test, they had altered completely the social situation of the operators and their customary

attitudes and interpersonal relations.
(Roethlisberger and Dickson 1939: 138,
italics added)

At this point, the investigation changed its focus:

No longer were the investigators interested in testing for the effects of single variables. In the place of a controlled experiment, they substituted the notion of a social situation which needed to be described and understood as a system of interdependent elements. This situation included not only the external events but the meanings which individuals assigned to them: their attitudes toward them and their preoccupations about them. Rather than trying to keep these 'psychological' factors constant, the investigators had to regard them as important variables in the situation. As much attention had to be given to these psychological factors as to output in assessing the external changes which took place.
(Roethlisberger and Dickson 1939:
138–9)

The result was to broaden the investigation to take in a wider and wider range of concepts, looking at worker motivation and attitudes in the workplace, and also covering the entire company. Mayo and his colleagues designed an interviewing programme designed to elicit more information about worker attitudes, and by 1933 this had extended to cover the entire company, 10,000 employees in all, the largest social science study of its type undertaken up until that time.

Input came both from Western Electric itself, and from several departments and schools at Harvard University, and the results were extensively analysed and discussed. Thomas North WHITEHEAD and Lyndall Urwick, as well as Mayo himself, went on to produce important analyses of the work done at Hawthorne. The official report on the experiments, however, was entrusted to Roethlisberger and to W.J.

Dickson, a Western Electric executive who had been closely involved with the project. Their 600-page report, *Management and the Worker*, appeared in 1939 and became a foundational text in the studies of human relations and organization behaviour.

Roethlisberger and Dickson, after describing the experiments and their results in great and conclusive detail, reached one overwhelming conclusion: organizations are not machine-like constructs, they are social systems. They argued that business organizations have two functions: 'that of producing a product and that of creating and distributing satisfactions among the individual members of the organization' (Roethlisberger and Dickson 1939: 552). As a result:

The industrial concern is continually confronted, therefore, with two sets of major problems: (1) problems of external balance, and (2) problems of internal equilibrium. The problems of external balance are generally assumed to be economic; that is, problems of competition, adjusting the organization to meet changing price levels, etc. The problems of internal equilibrium are chiefly concerned with the maintenance of a kind of social organization in which individuals and groups through working together can satisfy their own desires.
(Roethlisberger and Dickson 1939: 552)

Thus, they say, every industrial concern has two parallel yet interdependent types of organization: the technical organization, which includes the physical environment, plant, tools, machinery, raw materials and so on, and the human organization, which consists of the people who work there and their social structure. Each depends on the other: the people need the plant to carry out their work, the plant without people is simply so much inert metal. Within the human organization, there are again two interdependent concepts: that of the individual, with his or her own needs and motivations, and the social organization, consisting of not only the formal hierarchy but also the informal relationships which develop between members of the group. Relationships can be graded by 'degrees of intimacy' according to greater or lesser social distance. Every member of the business, say the authors, from the directors to the lowest shop-floor workers, is part of these relationships and is motivated to at least some degree by non-economic concerns. This is a fact of organizational life.

The conclusion is that personnel management, or what today would be known as human resource management, needs to be reoriented. Although factors such as fatigue and the physical environment can be important, much more important is the social environment within which work is conducted. Mental stimuli are at least as important, if not more so, than physical ones. Nor are these mental stimuli always necessarily rational and economic in nature; the 'logic of sentiment' can be as important as the logic of efficiency.

This necessarily brief summary shows some ways in which Roethlisberger and Dickson reconceptualized the business organization. The ideas themselves are not entirely new; the notion of interdependence had been raised by KIMBALL and more especially by KNOEPPEL and others who developed the biological metaphor of organization, and are even hinted at in the early nineteenth century by Andrew Ure. Never before, however, had such ideas had such strong and rigorous scientific backing. Although Roethlisberger and Dickson's work has subsequently been much improved upon, especially in the field of motivation by writers such as MASLOW and HERZBERG, many of their basic concepts remain sound, and it is hard to avoid the notion that much later work in this field has been so much reinvention of the wheel.

Roethlisberger went on to a long career at Harvard, producing several more notable works on human relations in the workplace, and collaborating with Dickson on *Counseling in an Organization: A Sequel to the Hawthorne Researches* (1966). Although never as high profile in his field as, for example, Mayo or Herzberg, he nevertheless helped to produce a highly detailed analysis of and thoughtful conclusions to one of the most important workplace studies ever undertaken.

BIBLIOGRAPHY

Dickson, W.J. and Roethlisberger, F.J. (1966) *Counseling in an Organization: A Sequel to the Hawthorne Researches*, Boston, MA: Harvard Business School Press.

Roethlisberger, F.J. (1941) *Management and Morale*, Cambridge, MA: Harvard University Pres.

—— (1954) *Training for Human Relations*, Cambridge, MA: Harvard University Press.

Roethlisberger, F.J. and Dickson, W.J. (1939) *Management and the Worker*, Cambridge, MA: Harvard University Press.

Smith, R.M. (1986) *The American Business System and the Theory and Practice of Social Science: The Case of Harvard Business School, 1925–1945*, New York: Garland.

Zaleznick, A., Christensen, C.R. and Roethlisberger, F.J. (1958) *The Motivation, Productivity and Satisfaction of Workers*, Boston, MA: Harvard Business School Press.

MLW

S

SAMUELSON, Paul Anthony (1915–)

Paul Anthony Samuelson was born in Gary, Indiana on 15 May 1915. He was an undergraduate student at the University of Chicago from 1932 to 1935, after which he went to Harvard University as a graduate student and then a junior fellow. In 1940 he moved to the Massachusetts Institute of Technology (MIT) as an assistant professor. There has been speculation about Harvard's failure to match MIT's offer; anti-Semitism, Samuelson's brashness and the unwillingness of existing professors to appoint someone so much smarter than them have all been suggested. At MIT, he became a full professor in 1947 and institute professor in 1966. While there, he was responsible for helping turn his department into one of the world's leading economics departments. His introductory textbook (Samuelson 1948) became one of the most influential ever written. He contributed regularly to *Newsweek* and was an adviser to President John F. Kennedy. In 1970 he was awarded the Nobel Memorial Prize for Economics.

Perhaps more than any other economist, Samuelson established the style in which economics was undertaken in the postwar period. As an undergraduate, he saw that the use of mathematics would transform economics, and in his graduate work he applied mathematical analysis to a wide range of problems, ranging from consumers' behaviour to the business cycle and the theory of international trade. Many of the articles he published during this period had a profound influence on the subject. His Ph.D. thesis (Samuelson 1947), based on work done whilst a research fellow at Harvard, exhibited three features that came to characterize postwar mathematical economics: the use of constrained optimiZation to model behaviour; explicit analysis of dynamics; and the derivation of predictions about how variables would change when conditions changed.

Samuelson's theory of revealed preference illustrates the way Samuelson used mathematical analysis to cut through problems. He sought to base the theory of consumer behaviour on a set of simple axioms, the most important of which was the axiom of revealed preference. This stated that if a consumer chooses bundle of goods A when he or she could have chosen B, then A is revealed preferred to B, and B will never be chosen if A is available. Using this, Samuelson was able to derive virtually all the results that had previously been derived using more elaborate theories. Consumer theory was presented as the theory of rational choice.

His move to Harvard in 1935 meant that Samuelson was at the centre of the Keynesian revolution in US economics. His textbook was not the first to cover Keynesian economics but it was by far the most influential. The so-called 45°-line diagram in which aggregate expenditure determined the equilibrium level of national income, without any reference to aggregate supply, became the standard way to present Keynesian economics. In the 1950s Samuelson introduced the idea of the 'neoclassical synthesis' in which this Keynesian theory of income determination was combined with the use of supply and demand theory to analyse individual markets and problems of resource allocation. This remained the dominant approach to economics until the profession distanced itself from Keynesianism in the 1970s.

An important aspect of the application of mathematics to economics during the 1940s and 1950s was the use of linear models. Samuelson's main contribution to this literature was a book written with Robert Dorfman and Robert Solow (Dorfman *et al*. 1958). This book showed how problems that had traditionally been tackled using differential calculus could instead be handled using methods such as linear programming.

Samuelson's work is almost impossible to summarize adequately in a short entry, for he has contributed to most areas of economics. In addition to those mentioned so far (and he continued to work on consumer theory, international trade and economic dynamics), he made important contributions to the theory of finance, capital theory, intertemporal equilibrium, and the analysis of inflation and unemployment. Even this list is not exhaustive. With a characteristic, if justifiable, lack of modesty, Samuelson has said that 'in talking about modern economics I am talking about me' (Samuelson 1990: 63). He describes himself as a generalist, with a finger in every pie. This is why the best way to sum up his work is to say that his main contribution has been to transform the way economists have set about doing their work.

BIBLIOGRAPHY
Backhouse, R.E. (1998) 'Samuelson, Paul Anthony', in M. Warner (ed.), *IEBM Handbook of Management Thinking*, London: International Thomson Business Press, 560–65.
Dorfman, R., Samuelson, P.A. and Solow, R.M. (1958) *Linear Programming and Economic Analysis*, New York: McGraw-Hill.
Feiwel, G.R. (ed.) (1982) *Samuelson and Neoclassical Economics*, Boston: Kluwer Nijhoff.
Fischer, S. (1987) 'Samuelson, Paul Anthony', in J. Eatwell, M. Milgate and P. Newman (eds), *The New Palgrave Dictionary of Economics*, London: Macmillan.
Samuelson, P.A. (1947) *Foundations of Economic Analysis*, Cambridge, MA: Harvard University Press.
—— (1948) *Economics: An Introductory Analysis*, New York: McGraw Hill.
—— (1966–86) *The Collected Scientific Papers of Paul A. Samuelson*, Cambridge, MA and London: MIT Press, 5 vols.
—— (1990) 'Paul A. Samuelson', in W. Breit and R.W. Spencer (eds), *Lives of the Laureates: Ten Nobel Economists*, 2nd edn, Cambridge, MA, and London: MIT Press.

REB

SANDERS, Harlan (1890–1980)

Harlan Sanders was born in Henryville, Indiana on 9 September 1890. He died of leukaemia in Louisville, Kentucky on 16 December 1980. Sanders learned to cook as a small boy when, following the death of his father, his mother went out to work. He took his first job as a farmhand at the age of ten, became a streetcar conductor at the age of fifteen, and at sixteen joined the US Army and served in Cuba. He went on to hold a variety of jobs, including selling insurance and running a river ferry; he studied law by correspondence and appears to have undertaken legal work at some point, though it is uncertain if he was ever called to the bar. In 1930 Sanders established a roadside service station and restaurant in Corbin, Kentucky, which, thanks to his cooking skills, rapidly became famous; by the end of the decade he had expanded to a 140-seat restaurant that was mentioned in national cuisine guides, and had been made an honorary colonel of militia by the governor of Kentucky in reward for his services to tourism.

In 1955 a new interstate highway was completed which bypassed the town. Sanders, who had previously refused offers to purchase his restaurant, now found himself almost bankrupt. Aged sixty-five, he set out to reinvent his business. His most famous recipe, for fried chicken, was his sole remaining asset. Sanders began travelling the country, often sleeping in his car, visiting restaurants, cooking his food and persuading the owners to buy his products. The deal Sanders made was something between a licensing agreement and an in-store franchise; for each meal cooked and sold according to his recipes, the owners paid Sanders a percentage of the profits. By 1964 Sanders had signed up more than 600 restaurants; as his recipe became more popular, many of the restaurants began to offer this as their main menu item. These arrangements were characterized by a high degree of trust: Sanders seldom signed contracts and relied on his partners to keep their bargain. In later years he encouraged restaurants in the chain to feel part of a family, and helped establish the highly active Association of Kentucky Fried Chicken franchisees.

Sanders sold his business in 1974 for $2 million. Now in his mid-seventies, he remained active as a spokesman for the firm and his image became a key part of the developing Kentucky Fried Chicken brand. Animated cartoon images of the Colonel have continued to feature in Kentucky Fried Chicken advertisements long after his death. Not an outstanding all-round manager, Sanders was a good marketer and is an interesting example of how to 'live a brand'; his career surely refutes an idea that management ability and age are in any way connected.

SARNOFF, David (1891–1971)

David Sarnoff was born on 27 February 1891 in Uzlian, Russia to Abraham, a house painter, and Leah Privin Sarnoff. He died in New York City on 12 December 1971. Sarnoff married Lizette Hermant; the couple had three sons.

Sarnoff emigrated to the United States in 1900. Because his father died prematurely, he ended his formal education with the eighth grade. He initially worked as a newspaper peddler, then, due to a fortuitous wrong turning, went to work for the Commercial Cable Company instead of his original choice, the *New York Herald*. This job introduced him to the world of electronics. He continued reading and studying, and taught himself Morse code and telegraphy. Shortly thereafter he joined the Marconi Wireless Telegraph Company of America as an office boy. From there he rose rapidly to become commercial manager in 1917. During this period, he achieved his first public notoriety as a telegraph operator receiving the names of survivors from the *Titanic*. While he may have embellished his role in this incident, he certainly understood the value of publicity and self-promotion.

Sarnoff claims to have broached the idea of a 'radio music box', putting radios in homes for commercial broadcasting of music and news, to Marconi executives prior to the First World War, but they felt that his idea was impractical. When RCA acquired Marconi Wireless, its chairman, Owen YOUNG, invited Sarnoff to write a prospectus on the company. This time, Sarnoff's radio music box proposal found more interested listeners. He rose rapidly in RCA's hierarchy, and helped launch the National Broadcasting Company (NBC) in 1926. He pushed RCA to acquire Victor Company, a producer of records and victrolas, in order to integrate vertically in the music business. He hoped that the radio would purvey high-quality programming; to that end, he hired Italian conductor Arturo Toscanini to conduct the NBC Orchestra. Still, he was pragmatic and realized that much of the programming would have to appeal to less cultured tastes. By 1930 he was the president of RCA. He was highly successful in navigating the company through anti-trust negotiations; he was known as a tough negotiator who thwarted the Justice Department's anti-trust action, which failed to strip RCA of any of its patents. He gained a reputation for ruthlessness in patent fights, although Philo Farnsworth prevailed in a bitter court fight over the image dissector, and RCA had to license Farnsworth's invention.

Sarnoff served in the US Army Signal Corps during the Second World War as General Dwight Eisenhower's communications consultant, and eventually became a brigadier general. He was proud of his service record, and usually insisted on employees and family referring to him as 'General'.

Perhaps Sarnoff's two most memorable later achievements were his early recognition of the potential of television and then of colour television. As visionary as he was, television surprised him: 'I honestly didn't think TV would catch on as fast as it did ... Hell, I'd bet it would be a neighborhood movie house in the home' (*New York Times* 1971: 43). Conversely, he lost the television ratings war to CBS by 1950, as William Paley raided NBC of its comedic talent, including Jack Benny.

Sarnoff retired as CEO of RCA in 1966 but continued as chairman of the board until his death. A commentator for the *New York Times* wrote: 'Mr. Sarnoff's gift was to recognize at an early stage the promise of an innovation in communications and then apply the economic muscle to convert the promise into performance' (Gould 1971: 43).

BIBLIOGRAPHY

Dreher, C. (1977) *Sarnoff: An American Success*, New York: Quadrangle/The New York Times Book Co.
Gould, J. (1971) 'Sarnoff: Mr. Do-It of Broadcasting', *New York Times* 121(41, 596), sect. 1: 43.
Lewis, T. (1991) *Empire of the Air: The Men Who Made Radio*, New York: Edward Burlingame Books.
New York Times (1971) 'David Sarnoff of RCA Is Dead; Visionary Broadcast Pioneer', *New York Times* 121(41, 596), sect. 1: 1, 43.

DS

SCHEIN, Edgar H. (1928–)

Edgar H. Schein was born in Zurich, Switzerland on 5 March 1928 and spent his childhood in Czechoslovakia and Russia before his father moved the family to Chicago, where he lectured in physics at the University of Chicago. Schein himself was educated at the University of Chicago, at Stanford University, where he received a master's degree in psychology in 1949, and at Harvard University, where he received his Ph.D. in social psychology in 1952. He was chief of the Social Psychology Section of the Walter Reed Army Institute of Research while serving in the US Army as a captain from 1952 to 1956. He then joined the Sloan School of Management at the Massachusetts Institute of Technology (MIT) in 1956 and was made a professor of organizational psychology and management in 1964. From 1968 to 1971 Schein was the undergraduate planning professor at MIT, and in 1972 he became chairman of the organization studies group, a position he held until 1982. In 1978 he was named the Sloan Fellows Professor of Management, a chair he held until 1990. At present he is Sloan Fellows Professor Management Emeritus, and continues at the Sloan School half-time as a senior lecturer. He is also the founding editor of *Reflections*, the journal of the Society for Organization Learning devoted to connecting academics, consultants, and practitioners around the issues of knowledge creation, dissemination and utilization.

449

Schein has been a prolific researcher, writer, teacher and consultant. Besides his numerous articles in professional journals he has authored fourteen books including *Organisational Psychology* (1980), *Organizational Culture and Leadership* (1992) and *The Corporation Culture Survival Guide* (1999). He was co-editor, with the late Richard Beckhard, of the Addison Wesley Series on Organization Development, which has published more than thirty titles since its inception in 1969.

Schein takes the view that organizational psychology is slowly moving from an individualistic point of view towards a more integrated view based on social psychology, sociology and anthropology. Schein goes on to point out that culture as a 'a pattern which shares basic assumptions' as well as 'a shared definition of primary task, mission and strategy as well as shared goals', is a central dimension in this evolution. Our failure to take culture seriously may stem from our methods of enquiry, which emphasize abstractions that can be measured. More ethnographic or clinical observations are needed.

Schein notes that organizational psychology was introduced in the early 1960s by LEVITT and Bass, as well as himself. At that time, much of the emphasis was on the individual and only lip-service was paid to the organizational sociologists. Business schools called it organizational behaviour, a term with which Schein has always been uncomfortable, calling it an 'oxymoron'. The newly formed subject group at MIT was instead called organizational studies. According to Schein, psychology has not paid enough attention to sociologists and anthropologists, whose traditions have been to go out into the field and observe a phenomenon at length before trying to understand it. Schein goes on to stress that the field will only progress when we have a set of concepts that are 'anchored in and derived from concrete observations of real behaviour in real organisation'.

Another issue in this area of research is the connection between social needs and empirical research. This link became very apparent in Schein's study of the behaviour of prisoners of war in the Korean conflict. The conflicts of psychology at that time were not capable of explaining the observed behaviour there. The phenomenon of 'coercive persuasion', subsequently development in detail by Schein, can be used to explain why so many of the programmes of organization development and organization learning that are launched with great enthusiasm do not seem to succeed.

Perhaps Schein's most important contribution involves the three cultures of management. In a typical organization, the *operators* are the line managers and the workers who make and deliver the products and services that fulfil the organization's basic needs. The *engineers* involve the core technology that underlines what the organization does. This group includes the technocrats and core designers in any function group. Finally, there are the executives who share a common set of assumptions based on the daily realities of their status and role. Their daily reality is often financial, and the essence of this role is accountability to the owner-shareholders, which usually involves share prices and financial results. Organization studies will not be mature, says Schein, until we begin to study, observe and absorb these three cultures.

Schein's consulting work focuses on organizational culture, organization development, process consultation and career dynamics, and among his past and current clients are major corporations both in the United States and overseas, such as Digital Equipment Corporation, Ciba-Geigy, Apple, Citibank, General Foods, Procter & Gamble, ICI, Motorola, Hewlett-Packard, Exxon, Shell and the Economic Development Board of Singapore. He has received many honours and awards for his writing including the Social Science Research Council Auxiliary Research Award (1968), the Gordon Hardwick Award of the Middle Atlantic Placement Association (1967), and most recently the Lifetime Achievement Award in Workplace Learning and Performance of the American Society of

Training Directors and the Everett Cherington Hughes Award for Career Scholarship from the Careers Division of the Academy of Management, both in 2000. He is a Fellow of the American Psychological Association and the Academy of Management. Schein and his wife Mary have three children and seven grandchildren; they live in Cambridge, Massachusetts.

BIBLIOGRAPHY
Joynt, P. (1998) 'Schein, Edgar', in M. Warner (ed.), *IEBM Handbook of Management Thinking*, London: International Thomson Business Press, 566–70.
Schein, E.H. (1978) *Career Dynamics*, Reading, MA: Addison-Wesley.
——— (1980) *Organizational Psychology*, 3rd edn, Englewood Cliffs, NJ: Prentice-Hall.
——— (1985) *Organizational Culture and Leadership*, San Francisco: Jossey-Bass, 1985; 2nd edn, 1992.
——— (1987–8) *Process Consultation*, revised edn, 2 vols, Reading, MA: Addison Wesley-Longmans.
——— (1999a) *Process Consultation Revisited: Building the Helping Relationship*, Reading, MA: Addison Wesley-Longmans.
——— (1999b) *The Corporation Culture Survival Guide: Sense and Nonsense about Corporate Culture*, San Francisco: Jossey-Bass.

PJ

SCHÖN, Donald Alan (1930–97)

Donald Alan Schön was born in Boston on 30 September 1930, the son of Marcus and Anne Schön. He died there on 13 September 1997.

He married Nancy Quint in 1952, and they had four children. After taking a BA from Yale University in 1947, Schön spent a year in graduate studies at the Sorbonne from 1949 to 1950, returning to the United States to take an MA at Harvard University in 1952, followed by a Ph.D. in 1955. He was then assistant professor of philosophy at the University of Kansas City before joining the consulting firm Arthur D. Little, where he served as head of the research and development division from 1957. From there he went on to hold several government posts, finally returning to academia as a professor in the department of urban studies and planning at Massachusetts Institute of Technology.

Schön is perhaps best known for his development of the concept of 'action science' and its application to management and organization studies. The term 'action science' is an attempt to set Schön's philosophy of thinking apart from 'normal science', itself a term first used by T.S. KUHN to describe the dominant set of scientific assumptions and praxis that go to make up a particular paradigm. Schön sees in much of normal science an inherent danger: organizations tend to use science in a detached and reductionist way that often ignores or overlooks the dynamic nature of both the environment in which organizations exist and the constantly evolving and changing organizations themselves. Organizations have a tendency to learn, if not exactly by rote, then at least according to preset patterns of what learning is. The result can be that errors are not only created through learning but are also built into the learning process.

Action science, says Schön, breaks free from the confines of normal science by putting the researcher into direct contact with the manager. In action science, researchers and managers work together both to define problems and to come up with solutions. In his work with Chris ARGYRIS, Schön developed the concept of action science more fully, in particular its capability to produce double-loop feedback, which can actually change the way organizations think and approach problems. The ability to learn from prior action is also discussed in detail in one of Schön's best-known books, *The Reflective Practitioner* (1983).

Schön's approach to organizational learning is on the one hand philosophical, yet on the other hand very strongly linked to his views on technology. In his early work Schön pondered on the relationship between the evolution of invention – that is, of mechanical devices and physical instruments – and the evolution of ideas and concepts: how far do these influence each other, and how do the currents of influence flow? The influence of Kuhn is strongest in these early works, but it continues to stand out in his later thinking as well; the need for reflective learning that uses analysis of past actions to construct a solid basis for future action is an underlying if not dominant theme in nearly all his writing.

BIBLIOGRAPHY

Argyris, C. and Schön, D. (1974) *Theory in Practice: Increasing Professional Effectiveness*, San Fransicso: Jossey-Bass.
—— (1978) *Organizational Learning: A Theory of Action Perspective*, Reading, MA: Addison-Wesley.
Schön, D. (1967a) *Invention and the Evolution of Ideas*, London: Tavistock.
—— (1967b) *Technology and Change*, New York: Delacorte.
—— (1983) *The Reflective Practitioner*, New York: Basic Books.

MLW

SCHUMPETER, Joseph Alois (1883–1950)

Joseph Alois Schumpeter was born in Triesch, Moravia, in the Austro-Hungarian empire (today called Trest, part of the Czech Republic) on 8 February 1883. He died in Taconic, Connecticut on 8 January 1950. He was born into a middle-class family with a long-standing entrepreneurial tradition in textile manufacturing, and he would have probably followed the footsteps of his ancestors but for the death of his father in 1887, which provoked a major change in the course of his life. In 1893 his mother, the daughter of a physician, married a retired army general, an aristocrat with access to the high society of Vienna, the centre of the Austro-Hungarian empire. Hence Schumpeter grew up in aristocratic circles, attending the Theresianum Gymnasium, an elitist school for the sons of the aristocracy. From 1901 onwards he studied law, economics and political science at the University of Vienna and obtained a doctorate in law in 1906.

Schumpeter devoted most of his attention to the study of economics, and during his formative years, Vienna offered a most stimulating environment for such an endeavour. On the one hand, there were the founders of the 'Austrian school', Menger, von Wieser and Böhm-Bawerk, who pioneered a version of marginalist economics that emphasized the subjective aspect of utility. Although they rejected the emphasis on economic history in favour of abstract theorizing derived from individual behaviour, they also (von Wieser in particular) appreciated and engaged in historical and sociological research, and Schumpeter maintained this ambivalent approach throughout his future work. Marxist thought also exercised an influence on the Viennese academic circles, and it certainly played a role in Schumpeter's inclination to think in terms of grand socioeconomic processes. Finally, many of Schumpeter's fellow students were of outstanding potential; some of them would later become important economists (for example, Ludwig von MISES, another crucial figure in the Austrian school) and political leaders. In this environment, Schumpeter early demonstrated his brilliance and critical spirit. Hence it is not surprising that the emergence of many of Schumpeter's ideas can be traced back to his studies in Vienna.

After graduation, Schumpeter spent an enjoyable and productive year in England. He was a research student at the London School of Economics, but he also took an active part in social life in London. He occasionally visited Cambridge (where he met Alfred Marshall and Francis Edgeworth), Oxford and other universities. In 1907 he married Gladys Ricarde Seaver, a daughter of a dignitary of the Church of England, and moved to Cairo to practice law. In the following year he published his first book, *Das Wesen und der Haupthalt der Theoretischer Nationalokonomie* (The Nature and Essence of Theoretical Economics). This study of economic methodology secured him a lectureship in political economy at the University of Vienna (1909) and an associate professorship at the University of Czernowitz (now Chervotsy, Ukraine), a post that he occupied between 1909 and 1911. During these years, Schumpeter wrote his masterpiece in economic theory, *Theorie der wirtschaftlichen Entwicklung* (The Theory of Economic Development) (1912). In 1911 he was appointed full professor of political economy at the University of Graz. In Graz he completed his first work in economic history, *Epochen and Dogmen- und Methodengeschichte* (Economic Doctrine and Method: A Historical Sketch) (1914). When he accepted an offer to spend the year 1913–14 as an exchange professor at Columbia University, his already estranged wife decided to stay in England. In 1914 she refused to return with him to Austria, especially when the First World War broke out. That effectively meant the end to their marriage, although the formal dissolution took place at Schumpeter's request in 1920.

Schumpeter's research output after graduation until about 1916 was enormous. In less than a decade he produced numerous articles and three books, tackling the foundations of economics and its history. His work made him a rising star in academic circles. However, that did not satisfy his professional ambitions, and he entered the political arena. After several attempts, he finally became the minister of finance of Austria in 1919. His uncompromising character and proneness to intrigue, combined with a limited talent for practical politics and a disastrous situation of public finance after the war, made his political career short-lived and unsuccessful. After dismissal from the government, he briefly returned to teaching in Graz, but left academia in 1921 to become president of the Biedermann Bank. Although the post carried few responsibilities, it brought Schumpeter considerable financial rewards that enabled him to resume a lavish lifestyle. He also used a credit line to invest in various businesses, a strategy which paid off until the economic crisis of 1924. The bank had to be restructured, and Schumpeter was not only dismissed, but also ended up in debt that burdened him throughout the next decade of his life.

Schumpeter returned to academia in 1925, becoming professor of economics and public finance at the University of Bonn. He also married Anna Reisinger, a young woman from a working-class Viennese family. In 1926, however, events took a disastrous turn. The death of his mother, who was arguably the most influential person in his life, was almost immediately followed by the death of his wife in childbirth, at which time he also lost his newborn son. These personal tragedies had profound consequences. Schumpeter became even more pessimistic and depressed, and his devotion to his wife and mother evolved into a cult in which they were treated as his private saints. Moreover, his ability to concentrate on work was diminished for years. He sought diversion in travelling and lecturing, and he rarely engaged in serious research. Instead he wrote for trade journals in order to pay off his debts. In 1927–8 Schumpeter visited Harvard University as a visiting professor. When he failed to secure a chair at the University of Berlin, he accepted an offer to move permanently to Harvard, where he was professor of economics from 1932 until his death in 1950. This radical change helped him devote himself almost exclusively to work. This orientation was further strengthened by his marriage to a fellow economist Elisabeth Boody Firuski in 1937. During the last period of his life, Schumpeter completed an ambitious book on *Business Cycles* (1939), today often neglected, and his most famous work, *Capitalism, Socialism and Democracy* (1942). He was co-founder and president of the Econometric Society (1939–41). He also presided over the American Economic Association (1948–9) and the International Economic Association (1949–50). His last work, *History of Economic Analysis* (1954), was still unfinished when he died. It was edited, completed and arranged for publication by his wife.

Entrepreneurship and innovation assume the central role in Schumpeter's theory of economic development. His analysis of capitalist development begins with a stationary state of economy, where there is no space for profit, because competition among employers forces them to pay workers the total value of their contribution. This also applies to the owners of other resources used in production (such as land). Even under these circumstances the economy may grow, for example due to population growth or altered consumer preferences. However, Schumpeter did not regard such growth as economic development, because it was caused by external, non-economic factors. In his view, economic development occurs and profits are created only when the equilibrium is disturbed through innovations in production. The profits that are created in the process are the result of the intelligence and courage of the entrepreneur, and thus rightfully belong to him or her. In other words, Schumpeterian entrepreneurs create innovative combinations of factors of production, bear the risks, and capture the resulting profits. The emphasis is not on mere technological inventions, because they may not have economic consequences at all, but on the creative combining of pre-existing factors of production. These 'new combinations' of factors can have various forms, including the introduction of new technologies, the creation of new products,

the opening of new markets, finding new sources of raw materials (or components) and creating a new position with an industry. According to Schumpeter, entrepreneurship requires not only intellect, but also courage to challenge established ways of doing business, strength to break the resistance to change and willingness to bear the associated risks. Consequently, only few individuals possess these necessary qualities, but that turns them into the main agents of economic and social change.

Entrepreneurship is not restricted to modern capitalism. Schumpeter finds its rudimentary forms even in ancient societies. However, since Schumpeter's entrepreneurs, by definition, lack the necessary capital, entrepreneurship could reach its full potential only when sufficient amount of credit provided by the banking system became available. Schumpeter even defined modern capitalism as a system in which entrepreneurial innovations are financed by borrowed money, i.e. in which the creation of credit becomes a routine commercial activity and in which owners of capital share the risk associated with entrepreneurial activity. In his later writings Schumpeter redefined his theory of the entrepreneur in less individualistic terms, accepting that the entrepreneurial function in society is often carried out cooperatively by groups of individuals, organizations and even by the state. Israel Kirzner (1986), a prominent representative of the Austrian school of economic theory, underlined the complementary aspect of entrepreneurial activity to the one presented by Schumpeter. Since market can be viewed as a process of creative discovery, where uncertainty and different perceptions are inevitable, at any moment there are entrepreneurial opportunities that do not require any innovative activity in the strict sense; that is, these opportunities already exist, but are not noticed by others. Kirzner's view of entrepreneurship emphasizes alertness to information and fast response to noticed possibilities, rather than innovation in the strict sense of the word.

Entrepreneurship and innovation are not continuous processes. They appear in groups and waves, whereby the appearance of a few entrepreneurs facilitates the entrepreneurial activity of others. Schumpeter used this insight to explain the cyclical nature of economic activity, including both shorter and longer business cycles. The logic of innovative activity brings about cyclical movements whose length depends upon the character and the period of implementation of the innovation. Whenever a new wave of innovations occurs, the entrepreneurs are eventually followed by many imitators. At a certain point, investment and credit expansion reach excessive levels. Initial competitive advantages enjoyed by the innovators are gradually eroded because the diffusion of innovations reduces the profit margins. The final result is the downturn of the economy. Schumpeter views the recessions of economic activity as both inescapable and beneficial, because they bring about a healthy process of restructuring that enlarges opportunities for the next wave of innovations. And that facilitates further changes in the structure of the economy and another wave of (to use Schumpeter's famous phrase) 'creative destruction' and economic development.

In his most widely read book, *Capitalism, Socialism and Democracy*, Schumpeter engaged in multidisciplinary analysis and speculations about the future of capitalism, the possibilities of socialism, and the compatibility of socialism with democracy. According to Schumpeter, individual initiative, innovation, risk taking and 'creative destruction' are inherent characteristics of capitalism and their preservation is necessary for the sustainability of the capitalist system. From a purely economic point of view, capitalism is unlikely to reach a crisis that may put its survival in jeopardy, because technological development, investment opportunities, population growth and other relevant factors conducive to prosperity still offer considerable opportunities for evolution and growth. This is especially the case for large corporations in a monopoly position. Large monopolies can

devote more resources to research and development. They may be more attractive to qualified employees and more successful in preventing imitation. On the other hand, the dynamic nature of capitalism and the threat of possible 'creative destruction' preserve them from complacency. However, when the wider social context is taken into account, the capitalist mode of production displays major shortcomings. Developed capitalism has become so economically successful that it has undermined the entrepreneurial behaviour and the social institutions that enabled its ascent. In their quest for efficiency, the big corporations have mechanized the process of invention, by organizing it within bureaucratic research and development departments. In a world of business accustomed to constant change, little space is left for individualist entrepreneurs. They have been replaced by teams of trained specialists and managers, who have turned the technological progress and the running of business into routine activities.

Moreover, Schumpeter (1942: 125) claimed that 'capitalism – and not merely economic activity in general – has after all been the propelling force of the rationalization of human behaviour'. Rationalization of human behaviour and ideas has pushed aside metaphysical, mystical and romantic ideas. By bringing about a critical mentality, capitalism has undermined the moral authority of social institutions (such as the family) and bourgeois values necessary for its prosperity. By emphasizing the hostility towards capitalism, espoused by much of the media, as well as by many intellectuals, Schumpeter foresaw a possibility that this critical mentality could eventually turn against capitalism itself – against private property and the whole corpus of bourgeois values. In such a world, the mentality of which would hinder bold and heroic entrepreneurs, capitalism would be prone to atrophy. Profits and interest rates would converge to zero, whereas the bourgeois class dependent upon them would tend to disappear. Managers of business corporations would resemble bureaucracy. Such developments could lead society towards social-ism, as a system defined by collective control over the means of production and over pro-duction itself. Contrary to most non-Marxist economists, Schumpeter argues that socialism is possible, that it is compatible with human nature, and even that it can, under certain con-ditions, be more efficient than capitalism. Moreover, Schumpeter believed in the possible compatibility of socialism and democracy. Whilst presenting the latter issue, he offered an innovative theory of democracy, somewhat similar to Max WEBER's views on the subject. Schumpeter's theory regards democracy as a competition of politicians for the votes of the electors rather than as a process of attainment of the common good through elected repre-sentatives. By drawing the analogy between economic and political processes, he provides inspiration for the application of rational choice theory in political science. In the end, it should be stressed that Schumpeter's speculations about the possibilities of socialism are not deter-ministic. As the inventor of the term 'method-ological individualism' (an explanation of all social phenomena in terms of the individuals involved), he believed in individual choice, and preferred to speak in terms of 'observable ten-dencies' without committing himself to any definite vision of the future.

As a young economist, Schumpeter was invited by Weber to join the group of theoret-ical economists, economic historians and soci-ologists that worked on the *Handbook of Socioeconomics*, a project that attempted to facilitate the dialogue between various approaches to social and economic realities. Although Weber's death prevented the suc-cessful completion of the project, it encouraged Schumpeter's aspirations towards a broader definition of economics. From the beginning of his career, he was aware that social processes form an indivisible whole despite the variety of scientific disciplines used in the study of social reality. Although much of Schumpeter's work belongs to theoretical economics, he also produced historical and sociological studies, and remained an advocate of the 'socioeco-nomic' approach. In his view, expressed in *History of Economic Analysis*, socioeconom-ics consists of four complementary fields. These are economic theory, economic history, economic sociology and statistics. In other words, purely theoretical approaches to eco-nomics should be balanced with insights into concrete historical developments, providing recognition of the differences in the economic systems of different societies. Moreover, research should also include the social institu-tions relevant for economic action, such as property and contract, as well as understand-ing and command of statistical methods. Schumpeter argued that the education of econ-omists should encompass all of these areas. In spite of acknowledging the social context of economic processes, he insisted on the separa-tion of economics from politics, because he feared that political considerations might be incompatible with its scientific character. Although he advanced a rather broad and comprehensive definition of socioeconomics, his own work did not fulfil all of its aspira-tions, but rather provided some important pieces of the socioeconomic puzzle that is still being tackled by social scientists. Towards the end of his life, Schumpeter's preferences shifted towards historical research, and his last book, *History of Economic Analysis*, actually pre-sented a history of socioeconomics (Swedberg 1991). Despite occasional statements that have not endured the test of time, this monumental book continues to be one of the main refer-ences for the historians of economic thought.

Schumpeter remains a giant figure in the development of economics, because of the sig-nificance and insightfulness of his ideas, and despite some simplifications and exaggerations. Although he left no school of thought behind him, renewed interest in his work has been fuelled by the recent changes in the economic landscape. Schumpeter's fears of the total bureaucratization of business have not been realized. On the contrary, the social, techno-logical and cultural changes have reinforced the dynamic nature of modern capitalism, resulting in the erosion of bureaucratic structures in business, as well as in the resurgence of market individualism and innovative entrepreneurship throughout the last two decades. Reinforcement of market-based and entrepreneurial principles has even led to their application in other social domains ranging from government to education and health care. However, the excesses of market individualism, and the accompanying erosion of bourgeois values and social institutions that have traditionally sustained capitalism, have also provoked a renewed interest in the social and political context of business. The need for sociological understandings of economic processes, as well as the need to balance the dynamics of the market with wider societal concerns have contributed to the development of economic sociology. Despite the significant differences displayed by various current researchers of these phenomena, many of the pertinent concerns can be traced back to Schumpeter. He did not always provide the right answers or predictions, but many of the questions he raised are of lasting significance. Schumpeter's writings on innovation, entrepreneurship and business cycles have inspired empirical and theoretical discussions on the nature of technological change, the diffusion of innovations, and the links between market structure and innovative activity.

Schumpeter will be remembered as one of the last economic visionaries, who attempted to develop a grand theory of socioeconomic processes. Meanwhile, economics has become a predominantly technical field, which leaves little space for non-mathematical approaches. Although Schumpeter welcomed the advance of mathematical economics he did not leave a significant legacy in that area. His work is nowadays often more interesting to economic sociologists than to 'pure' economists, who may be inspired by his concerns, but who will often research them in a different manner. The notion of creative destruction, and the importance of entrepreneurship, innovation and risk have become commonplace in thinking about the economic reality and are built into contemporary ideas on corporate strategy and the management of the process of innovation. The search for sustainable competitive advantages, and their inevitable erosion due to competition, are Schumpeterian themes recognizable to every theorist and practitioner of management. The profound nature and pace of technological, social and economic change has turned entrepreneurial behaviour into an expected mode of action, which is actively sought and promoted in various organizations. Despite Schumpeter's view of incompatibility of entrepreneurship and management, nowadays it is widely accepted that organizations of all sizes should simultaneously adopt both practices. The need for innovation and the need for the rational use of resources are not only viewed as potentially compatible, but also as mutually reinforcing.

BIBLIOGRAPHY
Heertje, A. (1994) 'Schumpeter, Joseph Alois', in J. Eatwell, M. Millgate and P. Newman (eds), *The New Palgrave: A Dictionary of Economics*, London: Macmillan, vol. 4, 263–7.
Heilbroner, R. (1991) *The Worldly Philosophers*, rev. edn, London: Penguin.
Kirzner, I.M. (1986) *Discovery and the Capitalist Process*, Chicago: University of Chicago Press.
Marz, E. (1991) *Joseph Schumpeter: Scholar, Teacher and Politician*, New Haven, CT: Yale University Press.
Schumpeter, J.A. (1908) *Das Wesen und der Haupthalt der Theoretischer Nationalokonomie* (The Nature and Essence of Theoretical Economics), Leipzig: Duncker and Humblot.
——— (1912) *Theorie der wirtschaftlichen Entwicklung*, Leipzig: Duncker and Humblot; trans. R. Opie, *The Theory of Economic Development*, Cambridge, MA: Harvard University Press, 1934.
Schumpeter, J.A. (1914) *Epochen and Dogmen- und Methodengeschichte*,

Tubingen: J.C.B. Mohr; trans. R. Aris, *Economic Doctrine and Method: A Historical Sketch*, London: Allen and Unwin, 1954.

Schumpeter, J.A. (1939) *Business Cycles: A Theoretical, Historical and Statistical Analysis of the Capitalist Process*, 2 vols, New York: McGraw-Hill.

—— (1942) *Capitalism, Socialism and Democracy*, London: Unwin Paperbacks, 1987.

—— (1954) *History of Economic Analysis*, ed. E. Boody Schumpeter. New York: Oxford University Press.

Swedberg, R. (1991) *Joseph A. Schumpeter: His Life and Work*, Cambridge: Polity Press.

DR

SCHWAB, Charles Michael (1862–1939)

Charles Michael Schwab was born in Williamsburg, Pennsylvania on 18 February 1862 and died in New York City on 18 September 1939. The son of a woollen mill worker who later ran a livery stable, Schwab was raised from the age of twelve in the farming community of Loretto, Pennsylvania. Educated by Roman Catholic nuns and Franciscan priests, he left high school before graduation and took a job as a bookkeeper and clerk at a grocery store located near the entrance to Andrew CARNEGIE's Edgar Thomson Steel Works in the industrial town of Braddock, Pennsylvania. The grocery job did not challenge him. Within two months, aged seventeen, he was working as an unskilled engineer's helper at the Thomson mill, which produced the steel from which rails and bridges were made.

Although he lacked formal training, Schwab advanced quickly to the job of acting chief engineer. By parlaying a little knowledge and a lot of bluff, he was able to create the impression that he knew what he was doing. This was typical of a pattern revealed by Schwab throughout his life. Whenever he felt sufficiently motivated, either by intellectual curiosity or by the hope of a promotion, he would plunge into a subject, however unfamiliar, and master it. He taught himself chemistry and metallurgy better to understand the intricacies of steelmaking, and taught himself drafting so that he could design and build blast furnaces and railway bridges. His gift for handling people and his receptiveness to new industrial methods elevated him rapidly in the business. By the age of nineteen, he was assistant manager of the Thomson plant.

Schwab benefited directly from Carnegie's strategy of promoting those employees in his mills who displayed ambition and initiative, and who shared his passion for technological innovation. During the 1870s, the Scottish-born industrialist had become a leader in the American steel industry by embracing any new manufacturing processes that could reduce the cost of making steel, and by constantly spending money to improve the productive efficiency of his enterprises.

In 1886, at the age of twenty-four, Schwab became general superintendent of Carnegie's Homestead works in Pittsburgh. Three years later, the plant superintendent at the Thomson works was killed in a furnace explosion and Schwab returned to Braddock to take over his position. Aged twenty-seven, only a decade after he had started work at the Thomson plant as a dollar-a-day labourer, Schwab became general superintendent of the largest steel works in the United States and cemented his reputation as the foremost production expert in the industry.

Schwab adopted Carnegie's strategy of motivating his workers by rewarding them for maximum effort. He recruited capable subordinates and gave them positive incentives, bonuses and promotions rather than threatening to fine or fire them if their efforts fell short.

'I treat men as I want to be treated myself,' he said. 'Every man, no matter how high his position, is susceptible to encouragement' (Hessen 1975: 124). By using such incentives, Schwab was able to maintain a high level of production and general harmony at the Thomson plant.

Other Carnegie plants did not enjoy the same measure of peace and goodwill that Schwab brought to the Thomson works. In 1892 one of the most violent strikes in American industrial history erupted at the Homestead plant following a move by the management to cut wages by 15 per cent. Schwab had to go back to the plant to restore peace. He settled the strike, got the men back to work and did his utmost to soften the blow of labour's defeat by keeping to a minimum recriminations and accusations. Schwab's success at improving labour relations at Homestead while simultaneously increasing production efficiency guaranteed his future with the Carnegie Steel Company. In 1897, at the age of thirty-five, Schwab became president of the company with a salary combined with a partnership share arrangement that brought him annual compensation of more than $1 million.

Schwab was president of Carnegie Steel for four years. During that time the company became America's largest source of primary steel for firms that fabricated the steel into finished products such as tubes, hoops, wires and structural beams. However, as the demand for fabricated steel products declined so did the demand for primary steel. Schwab looked for other ways to preserve Carnegie's dominant position in the market. He met with Wall Street financier J.P. MORGAN and broached the idea of creating a huge steel combine from several competing companies. The sale of the Carnegie company to Morgan became the main step in organizing this conglomerate, which was named the United States Steel Corporation. The 39-year-old Schwab – at Morgan's insistence – became its first president. During his two years at the helm of the new corporation – America's

first billion-dollar industrial enterprise – he earned more than $2 million annually.

Schwab did not adjust well to his new position. He resented having to share authority with US Steel's directors, whom he despised because they were lawyers and bankers, not 'practical steelmen' like himself. He bought a small company, Bethlehem Steel, as a personal investment and when the Morgan faction at US Steel held him responsible for a merger that went sour, he resigned from the giant conglomerate and turned his attention to Bethlehem. Within a few years he transformed it into the foremost rival of the steel giant that he had earlier helped to create.

When Schwab took over Bethlehem, he discarded almost all the policies of former manager Frederick W. TAYLOR, the pioneer of scientific management (Hessen 1975: 166). Taylor had in fact been dismissed by the owners in April 1901, six weeks before Schwab bought the controlling interest in the company. Bethlehem's owners had been particularly displeased by a Taylor proposal to cut the work force from 400 to 140. Famously, Taylor had introduced a system of paying premiums to Bethlehem employees who worked faster than their colleagues, and had applied time study and motion study methods to streamline various aspects of the company's operations. Schwab replaced 'scientific management' with a so-called 'drive system' which gave Bethlehem department heads the freedom to use whatever management methods worked best for them.

Bethlehem was a profitable small company that produced steel forgings for guns and marine engines. Schwab vowed to make it 'the greatest armour plate and gun factory in the world'. With expanding orders for guns, munitions and submarines both before and during the First World War, Schwab saw production rise to levels that made Bethlehem a prime arsenal for the Allied powers. He also spurred American shipbuilding to new heights. In 1918 he was appointed director-general of the US Shipping Board's Emergency Fleet Corporation, with a mandate to build a 'bridge of ships' between America and Europe. He served in the administration of President Woodrow Wilson at his own expense, without any salary except for a symbolic one dollar per year.

After the war, Schwab entered into semi-retirement. He built a huge mansion for himself and his wife Rana in the hills above Loretto, Virginia, and distanced himself from the day-to-day operations of Bethlehem Steel as it expanded with acquisition of iron ore mines and operating subsidiaries. However, as the single largest owner of Bethlehem, with shares once valued at $54 million, Schwab did maintain a close watch over the company's operations. In Eugene Grace he had a president whose business goals mirrored his own. Both believed in an aggressive expansionist strategy for Bethlehem, both believed in compensating workers according to their individual performances, and both vehemently opposed labour unions because a union system of standardized wages ran counter to the Bethlehem system of rewarding individual initiative.

During the 1920s, a United States House Committee accused Bethlehem of billing the government for personal expenses incurred by Schwab during his wartime service with the Emergency Fleet Corporation. Schwab was cleared of that charge, but then faced another accusation of wrongdoing relating to $11 million of 'excess profits' made by Bethlehem on its wartime shipping contracts. That case was not resolved until 1942, more than two years after Schwab's death, when once again he was exonerated.

Schwab entered the last decade of his life with enormous wealth and prestige. At its height, his personal fortune was conservatively estimated at more than $25 million. However, unsound investments outside the steel industry and a lavish lifestyle that included regular high-stakes gambling in Monte Carlo and the upkeep on his mansions in New York and Virginia severely depleted his resources. He died insolvent, with assets appraised at $1.39 million and liabilities estimated at $1.73 million, for a net deficit of approximately $338,000.

BIBLIOGRAPHY
Hessen, R. (1975) *Steel Titan: The Life of Charles M. Schwab*, New York: Oxford University Press.

BB

SCOTT, Walter Dill (1869–1955)

Walter Dill Scott was born near Cooksville, Illinois on 1 May 1869, the son of James Sterling Scott, a farmer, and his wife Henrietta. He died in Evanston, Illinois on 24 September 1955. He married Marcy Miller in 1898; they had two children. After taking an AB at Northwestern University in 1895, he studied at McCormick Theological Seminary and then attended the University of Leipzig, receiving a Ph.D. in psychology in 1900. He joined the faculty of Northwestern in 1900, becoming assistant professor of psychology in 1901 and professor in 1908. From 1909 he served jointly as professor of advertising at Northwestern's business school. He served as director of the university's psychology laboratory from 1901 to 1920, when he resigned the post upon becoming president of the university; he served in this role until his retirement as professor emeritus in 1939.

From 1916 to 1917 Scott served as director of the bureau of salesmanship research at the Carnegie Institute of Technology. From 1917 to 1919 he worked with the US Army, setting up the Committee on the Classification of Personnel, and was rewarded with the rank of colonel and the Distinguished Service Medal in 1919. He was active in a number of professional bodies, including the Psychology Association (of which he was elected president in 1919), the Taylor Society and the Industrial Relations Association. He was made a chevalier of the Legion of Honour in 1938.

Scott's work extended in many directions, including industrial psychology and educational administration, but it his application of psychology to advertising, most notably in *The Psychology of Advertising* (1913, revised and expanded in 1921) that has had the greatest lasting impact. He begins from a premise that, as a form of communication, 'advertising is a case of mind meeting mind' and that 'no advertisement that defies the established laws of advertising can hope to be successful' (Scott 1921: 2). To demonstrate how advertising works, he develops a model of 'attention-comprehension-understanding'. The message must first get the customer's *attention*, and it must do so by appealing to his or her perceptive senses. He describes attention as the 'gateway' to the customer's mind. Once the message is through the gateway, however, it must still be *comprehended*; that is, the customer must know what the message is about and to what product it refers. Finally, the customer must *understand* what relevance the message has to himself or herself; that is, will the product being advertised satisfy some personal need or desire? This is an early form of the model known as AIDA (awareness, interest, desire, action), still used by advertisers today.

Scott also devotes a great deal of attention to the practicalities of implementing his theory, looking at the optical and psychological impacts of various types of illustration, typeface and copy. He devotes several chapters to the senses and nature of cognition, and shows how advertising appeals to the senses in various ways; he also discusses the role of memory and retention. Using scores of practical examples, he shows how advertisers can construct a 'story' that will appeal to the audience. At the same time, he warns against overshooting the audience and thus gaining attention at the cost of comprehension; overly complex advertising is worse than no advertising at all. Of advertising copy, he says: 'Copy *in itself* should not be interesting. The copy should make the article advertised more interesting' (Scott 1921: 39).

More than any other individual, Scott showed how scientific principle and practice could be applied to advertising and marketing.

Although advertising theory has become more sophisticated in the last several years, much of Scott's basic work remains sound: to the contemporary reader, his insights still seem as fresh as when they were first written.

BIBLIOGRAPHY

Cattell, J.M., Cattell, J. and Ross, E.E. (1941) *Leaders in Education*, 2nd edn, Lancaster, PA: The Science Press.

Scott, W.D. (1921) *The Psychology of Advertising*, Chicago: Dodd, Mead and Co., revised version of 1913 edn.

'The Walter Dill Scott Website', http://uts.cc.utexas.edu/~wdscott, 2 April 2001.

MLW

SEARS, Richard Warren (1863–1914)

Richard Warren Sears was born in Stewartville, Minnesota on 7 December 1863, the son of James Sears, a wagon-maker and later a farmer, and his wife Eliza. He died in Waukesha, Wisconsin on 28 September 1914. In 1895 he married Anna Meckstroth; they had four children. Sears' father died when he was sixteen and he left school to take a job and help support the family. At seventeen he was a telegraph operator for the St Paul and Duluth Railroad, and later became a station manager in North Redwood, Minnesota. Here he set up a trading business on the side. In 1886 he purchased cheaply a consignment of watches that had been refused by a local jeweller, and sold them through mail order at considerable profit. Continuing in this line, in 1886 he moved to Minneapolis and set up a mail-order watch business, R.W. Sears Watch Company, recruiting watchmaker A.C. Roebuck to carry out repairs on defective products. In 1889 he sold the business and retired to a farm in Iowa;

however, apparently unable to settle down (he was still under forty), he teamed up again with Roebuck to establish Sears, Roebuck and Company, selling jewellery and watches by mail order. In 1893 Roebuck sold his interests and, with new partners, Sears moved his head office to Chicago and began rapidly to expand the company's range of products; by 1908 it was marketing over 100,000 products by mail order. Sales grew from $500,000 in 1895 to over $11 million just five years later.

Sears was a born marketing man: he wrote all his own advertising copy and used a variety of promotional methods to attract customers to his goods. The most famous of all these was the Sears Roebuck catalogue which was sent out to prospective buyers. Like his rival Aaron Montgomery WARD a decade or so earlier, Sears realized the potential of using the catalogue not only to sell products but also to sell a lifestyle. The handsomely produced catalogues inspired customers on lonely Midwestern farms by teaching them about the outside world, stimulating demand both for new products and new ways of living. Through the period 1890–1910 Sears Roebuck and Montgomery Ward engaged in fierce competition, but their joint efforts grew the market at such an astounding rate that both were able to prosper.

However, Sears was a poor organizer and never mastered financial management. Disputes over the latter led to his break with Roebuck and later several other partners. From 1893 to 1909 responsibility for organization and finance rested with Julius Rosenwald, who spent much of his time reining in Sears' ever more grandiose plans for expansion. In 1909, during an economic downturn, Rosenwald lost patience and forced Sears' resignation as president. He cut all ties with the company shortly thereafter and retired once more to his farm. A promotional genius and inveterate risk-taker, in the end he failed to manage the problems of growth and consolidation.

BIBLIOGRAPHY

Weil, G.A. (1977) *Sears Roebuck,U.S.A.: The Great American Catalog Store and How it Grew*, New York: Stein and Day.

SENGE, Peter M. (1947–)

Senge took a bachelor's degree in engineering from Stanford University and a master's degree in social systems modelling, followed by a Ph.D. in system dynamics from the Massachusetts Institute of Technology (MIT) in 1978. He joined the faculty of MIT, and is currently director of the Systems Thinking and Organizational Learning Program at MIT's Sloan School of Management. He is also co-founder of the consulting firm Innovation Associates, established in 1982. He became prominent following the publication of *The Fifth Discipline* in 1990, which became one of the most popular and talked about management books of the early 1990s. Married with two children, he lives in Massachusetts.

Despite his engineering background, Senge became convinced during his early years at MIT that the most important systems embedded in business organizations were mental rather than physical. His approach to systems dynamics was strongly influenced by Jay Wright FORRESTER, the pioneer of the field and then on faculty at MIT, and in the 1980s Senge began applying Forrester's concepts to mental systems. As he notes in the introduction to *The Fifth Discipline*, he was also very strongly influenced by work carried out in the mid- and late 1980s at Royal Dutch/Shell, by a team which included Arie De Geus, which concluded that continuous learning was possibly a company's only sustainable form of competitive advantage. These two themes, mental systems and the importance of knowledge, came together in *The Fifth Discipline*.

At the core of *The Fifth Discipline* is the development of the theory of the 'learning organization'. This idea had originally been developed by the Shell team and De Geus, and had been described in outline by the latter in an article in *Harvard Business Review* a couple of years previously (De Geus 1988). However, Senge deserves full credit for expanding on this idea and showing how it can work in practice. He defines learning organizations as:

> organizations where people continually expand their capacity to create the results they truly desire, where new and expansive patterns of thinking are nurtured, where collective aspiration is set free, and where people are continually learning how to learn together.
>
> (Senge 1990: 3)

This definition is of course extremely fuzzy, and lack of clarity about concepts and practices is one criticism which has been levelled against Senge. This criticism may be unfair: learning *is* a fuzzy process, and not one for which any hard and fast prescriptive rules can be established. Throughout the book, Senge is concerned not with explaining *how* organizations and people learn, but in creating a climate *in which* they can learn. His goal is to create an organizational culture and architecture where thinking and learning are done not just by top management but by everyone. In this way, a climate of organizational creativity and innovation can be developed, and knowledge, the competitive advantage of the future, can be generated and circulated freely. He draws here on earlier work on interdependence and on the social nature of organizations, and argues that knowledge generation and circulation are contingent on the establishment and management of such interdependences, across the organization and at a variety of levels.

At the heart of the organization, says Senge, is the organizational learning cycle. This has three components. We begin by learning new skills and capabilities. As we do so, we become more capable and more confident; our awareness changes, we view our jobs, our tools, our colleagues, our customers and so on in different ways. New awareness and knowledge lead to deeper changes in our attitudes and beliefs; we become aware of new ways of looking at the world. This change in beliefs in turn necessitates the need to learn new skills so as to explore our new beliefs more fully, and so on the cycle goes. It is not just individual people who learn in this way, Senge believes; organizations do so as well. His view of the learning cycle is an interesting complement to Max BOISOT's idea of a 'communications space' within which learning is conducted, and also to the slightly later views on organizational knowledge generation of Nonaka Ikujiro.

In order to master organizational learning, organizations need to harmonize within their members and themselves five key 'component technologies': (1) personal mastery; (2) mental models; (3) building shared vision; (4) team learning; and (5) systems thinking, the 'fifth discipline' of the title. Personal mastery does not mean power over others but mastery of oneself, as in the sense of mastering a skill or a craft; it is allied to assets such as confidence and capability. Mental models are the fundamental assumptions or generalizations that we make about our work and ourselves; everyone has these, but the important thing is to ensure that these models are supporting or enabling creativity and learning, rather than hindering it or preventing it (as in the case of ARGYRIS's defensive routines). Following on from this, building shared vision means the creation of a mental model which represents the whole organization, a common set of assumptions and beliefs that all members can buy into; creating shared vision of this type is, says Senge, one of the key functions of a leader. Team learning is perhaps the most difficult to master. Senge argues that teams learn better than individuals, citing the examples of sports teams or symphony orchestras where the learning and knowledge of the whole is more powerful than the learning of any one individual. The key to team learning, says Senge, is dialogue, 'the capacity of a member of a team to suspend assumptions and enter into a genuine "thinking together"' (Senge 1990: 10). Ensuring the free flow of thoughts and ideas is the key to team learning, which in turn is the key to broader organizational learning.

Systems thinking is defined as 'a discipline for seeing wholes', for seeing interrelationships and interdependences rather than cause and effect, and seeing cycles or 'circles of causality' rather than snapshots; in other words, an approach which sees the organization holistically and dynamically rather than mechanistically. It is to this complex concept that much of the book is devoted. Senge argues that as individuals we already perform systems thinking in some everyday tasks, such as driving a car or playing a piano; the individual routines and actions required to perform these tasks are embedded in our thinking, and our conscious processes are left free to focus on the overall task. The problem, then, is how to transfer this kind of thinking to organizations.

The Fifth Discipline, which sold over 750,000 copies, should be seen not in isolation but as the culmination of a long chain of ideas, writing and experiments concerning how organizations function and how they generate and use knowledge. The problem has been perplexing writers for at least a century, but most prior to Senge had done no more than approach some aspect of the problem, for example focusing on the need for teamwork or on the need for shared vision. Senge's achievement is to link a wide variety of ideas together under the umbrella of 'systems thinking'. The idea of a holistic view of the organization, which can be traced back at least as far as the pioneers of organization thinking, Dexter KIMBALL and Charles KNOEPPEL, is expressed not as a desired goal but as an absolute necessity. Organizations *are* systems, says Senge; it is up to us to begin to think of them as such.

The role of the leader in initiating systems thinking and development of the learning cycle is only touched on in *The Fifth Discipline*, and

Senge and his colleagues later addressed this issue in *The Fifth Discipline Workbook* (1994), a practical guide to the concepts in the original. Here Senge develops an architecture for the learning organization, which is symbolized by an extremely old-fashioned pyramid. At the top of the learning organization, says Senge, there must be guiding ideas, which set core philosophy and articulate vision and purpose; it is the task of the organization's leaders to provide these. Further down come two other classes of ideas, what Senge calls 'theory, method and tools', the 'process concepts' by which learning is done, and 'innovations in infrastructure' which help facilitate learning and the diffusion of ideas. In Senge's learning organization, then, the leaders set the tone but the actual production work of learning is carried out at lower levels within the organization.

There are problems with Senge's view of organizations, not the least of which is how to ensure motivation within the learning organization. Although he uses the term 'learning organization', a more apt description might well be 'thinking organization'. In Senge's organizations, people do not just learn by rote, they use their learning to create new ideas. But where is the motivation to do this to come from? The answer is that providing such motivation is the role of the leader, through the guiding values mentioned above; but Senge is less than specific about how such values are to be created and transmitted.

This quibble aside, *The Fifth Discipline* made a major contribution to modern understandings of the role of knowledge in organization. At the time of writing, with the growth of knowledge management as a discipline, Senge's work is taking on renewed value.

BIBLIOGRAPHY
De Geus, A. (1988) 'Planning as Learning', *Harvard Business Review* (March–April): 70–74.
Senge, P.M. (1990) *The Fifth Discipline: The Art and Practice of the Learning*

Organization, New York: Doubleday.

Senge, P.M., Roberts, C., Ross, R.B., Smith, B.J. and Kleiner, A. (1994) *The Fifth Discipline Workbook: Strategies and Notes for Building a Learning Organization*, London: Nicholas Brealey.

MLW

SHAW, Arch Wilkinson (1876–1962)

Arch Wilkinson Shaw was born in Jackson, Michigan on 4 August 1876, the son of James and Estelle Shaw. He died in Chicago on 9 March 1962. He married Eulah Paddock some time before 1900; they had two sons. After taking a BA from Harvard University (he later took an AM degree from Olivet College), Shaw returned to Michigan to go into business and in 1903 set up the publishing company A.W. Shaw and Company, publishers of professional textbooks. The business did well, as the universities of Michigan, Illinois and the Midwest more generally were growing and attracting more students and professors. Shaw began to build up a network of professional contacts among American universities which both ensured him a flow of books to publish and built up a steady clientele. By 1910 he was increasingly focusing on books concerning business and management.

Apart from publishing, Shaw's other venture was into breakfast cereals. A long-time friend of William K. KELLOGG, he supported the latter's efforts to break away from his brother, Dr John Harvey Kellogg, and set up an independent business producing corn flakes, which the Kelloggs had invented a few years earlier. He helped manage advertising and promotion for the original Sanitas Food Company, and when Kellogg separated his business from that of his brother and launched the Battle Creek Toasted Corn Flake Company (later Kellogg

Company) in 1906, Shaw was a partner. To Shaw must go much of the credit for the early marketing and packaging used by Kellogg in developing the corn flakes brand, and Shaw also helped Kellogg develop his early advertising campaigns.

Shaw had long been aware of the need for more and better management education, and was an early supporter of the establishment of the Harvard Business School in 1908. He was one of Dean Edwin GAY's most loyal supporters in the difficult early years of the school, and used his network of personal and professional contacts to help recruit lecturers. He himself taught at Harvard Business School from 1911 to 1917, and served on the school's board of overseers from 1911 to 1929. He and Gay agreed on many of the fundamental principles behind the school, including the need to have more historical analysis and teach business history to students, a tradition that remains strong at Harvard (Cuff 1996). Shaw was also one of the pioneers of the case study method of teaching, and developed many of the original business cases used at Harvard; innovatively, he also developed 'live' case studies which gave students a chance to study 'live action' problems. Shaw was also one of the motivating forces behind the establishment of the Bureau of Business Research, one of the initial functions of which was to supply case study material, and backed Paul CHERINGTON's early research work. He continued to be a strong supporter of the school, and when in 1922 *Harvard Business Review* was founded, Shaw undertook to publish it on the school's behalf. Shaw also served as director of the National Bureau of Economic Research from 1920 to 1937, and was chairman of the President's Commission on Recent Economic Changes from 1927 to 1940, working well with the Roosevelt administration despite his own Republican political leanings.

It was as an editor and publisher that Shaw made his mark. The company published scores of business and management books by leading academics and practitioners, ranging from

practical textbooks and manuals to highly theoretical works. From 1910 to 1930, if not
longer, A.W. Shaw was the USA's leading
business book publisher. It also published two
of the most important business journals of all
time: *Harvard Business Review*, mentioned
above, and *System*, which later evolved into
Industrial Management. *System*, vied with the
Engineering Magazine for the title of leading
management journal in the United States; both
were strongly oriented towards scientific management, though of the two *System* tended to
be more eclectic and bring in more high-profile
writers. Businessmen and writers as diverse as
the manufacturers John North WILLYS and
Thomas J. WATSON, the consultant Herbert
CASSON, the journalist Ida TARBELL and the
psychologist Donald Laird contributed articles
at various times. Shaw, who edited the journal
for most of its life, deliberately went out of his
way to seek to include provocative and challenging points of view, including ones with
which he did not agree. Marketing, organization, new technology, personnel relations and
every other aspect of business were covered.
Shaw had the vision to commission Ida Tarbell's
path-breaking series of articles on the new role
of women in the workplace, despite the fact
that her name was anathema to many of his
readers; in the end, Tarbell's articles were considered and highly thoughtful, and were very
well received. When Henry Ford opened his
new car assembly line at River Rouge, Michigan
in 1927, *System* devoted several pages to the
plant and its technical innovations.

Shaw himself wrote little, contributing only
the occasional article to his own journal and to
others. He did produce two standard textbooks while teaching at Harvard Business
School, *Some Problems in Market Distribution*
(1912) and *An Approach to Business Problems*
(1916). The former is sometimes hailed as the
foundational text of American marketing
thought, but in fact it is little more than its title
suggests, a consideration of issues surrounding
distribution; a full description of the elements
of marketing does not appear until the work of

Paul Cherington, Fred CLARK and Melvin
COPELAND a few years later, although it can be
argued that Shaw knew all three men and his
thinking may have influenced theirs. *An
Approach to Business Problems* is another
teaching text which is of interest largely in
that it shows how scientific analysis can be
used to assess business problems and develop
solutions.

Few people did more to search out and dis-
seminate new ideas in management thought in
the early twentieth century than Shaw.
Through his publishing, through his unstinting
support for Harvard and other business
schools, and most of all through the pages of
System, Shaw opened the eyes and minds of
two generations of American managers to new
and better ways of performing their tasks. A full
appreciation of the contribution of this outstanding figure in US management history
remains to be written.

BIBLIOGRAPHY
Cuff, R.D. (1996) 'Edwin F. Gay, Arch W.
Shaw, and the Uses of History in Graduate
Education for Managers', *Journal of
Management History* 2(3): 9–25.
Shaw, A.W. (1912) *Some Problems in
Market Distribution*, Cambridge, MA:
Harvard University Press.
——— (1916) *An Approach to Business
Problems*, Cambridge, MA: Harvard
University Press.

MLW

SIMON, Herbert Alexander (1916–2001)

Herbert Alexander Simon was born in
Milwaukee, Wisconsin on 15 June 1916. He
died in Pittsburgh, Pennsylvania on 8 February
2001. He married Dorothea Pye in 1937, and
they had three children. Simon's central goal

throughout his career was to construct a unified, usable science of human behaviour, one that could define and protect the role of rational choice (and thus conscious planning or design) in human affairs. Simon began his pursuit of this goal in the 1930s by taking a new approach to the study of administration, one that focused on the psychology of decision making in organizations. In doing so, he was strongly influenced by his training (both under-graduate and graduate) in political science at the University of Chicago and by his experience working at the Bureau of Public Administration (BPA) in Berkeley, California.

At Chicago, Simon came to embrace the pos-itivism of the philosopher Rudolf Carnap, the psychological approach to politics of Charles Merriam and Harold Lasswell, the empiricism of political scientists Harold Gosnell and Leonard White, and the mathematical orienta-tion of the biologist Nicholas Rashevsky and the economist Henry Schultz. At the BPA (from 1939 to 1942) Simon applied what he had learned in Chicago in a series of studies that broke new ground in the measurement of gov-ernment services. The first of these studies, one on *Determining Work Loads for Professional Staff in a Public Welfare Agency*, was particu-larly notable as one of the largest early field experiments in social science, comparable in scale (though not in fame) to the Hawthorne Experiments conducted earlier in the decade by Elton MAYO and Fritz ROETHLISBERGER.

Simon also worked on his dissertation during his three years at the BPA, completing it in the spring of 1942 and publishing it in 1947 as *Administrative Behavior*. This work, now in its fourth edition, is the most important single work in Simon's *oeuvre*, and it has been an important – and often controversial – part of management education since its publication.

After completing his thesis, Simon returned to Chicago to teach political science at the Illinois Institute of Technology (IIT), where he remained until 1949. While at IIT, he became a member of the Cowles Commission for Research in Economics, the world's leading centre for econometric analysis. (No fewer than ten of the regular attendees of the Cowles Commission's seminars during this period later won Nobel prizes in economics.) Through his association with the Cowles Commission, Simon became interested in the new theories of rational choice advanced by John von Neumann, Oskar Morgenstern and other game theorists. Although Simon approved of the mathematical rigour of game theory and neo-classical utility theory, he soon came to believe that they rested upon faulty assumptions about how individuals make choices. In particular, he argued that these theories overlooked the 'boundedness' of human rationality: individu-als, in Simon's view, never could know enough or process information fast enough to make objectively rational decisions.

This 'principle of bounded rationality' was the foundation of all of Simon's work, whether in political science, economics, psychology, phi-losophy or computer science. Although a seem-ingly simple concept, it had revolutionary impli-cations in every one of these fields. In eco-nomics, for instance, the idea of bounded ratio-nality undercut the reigning assumption of profit-maximizing rationality embodied in the neoclassical economist's *homo economicus*. Similarly, the concept of bounded rationality played an important role in the 'cognitive rev-olution' against strict behaviourism in experi-mental psychology, for the idea of bounded rationality presumed that the mind was an active agent in constructing our perceptions of the world. In the field of administration, this concept recast the role of the organization, treating it as an information-processing machine designed to maximize the rationality of its members' decisions by dividing large-scale information-processing problems into a hierarchy of tasks and sub-tasks. Significantly, in Simon's work the firm, the mind and the computer are all hierarchically organized infor-mation-processing machines, making the computer a model bureaucracy.

In 1949 Simon left IIT for a position at the new Graduate School of Industrial

Administration (GSIA) at Carnegie Tech (now Carnegie-Mellon University). Simon and his colleagues G.L. (Lee) Bach, James MARCH, Allen Newell, Richard CYERT, Harold Guetzkow and Franco Modigliani (among others) soon made the GSIA one of the leaders of a new movement in management education emphasizing quantitative methods and economic and behavioural research. While GSIA graduates were often criticized for lacking human relations training (and many felt the lack of it themselves), the concepts and methods advocated by Simon and his colleagues soon found their way into almost every business school, thanks in part to their aggressive promotion by the Ford Foundation in the 1960s.

In the mid-1950s Simon's interests began to shift away from the social environment of decision making and towards the internal organization of problem solving within the individual's mind. This shift was spurred by Simon's exposure to digital computers (and to Allen Newell) at the RAND Corporation in the early 1950s. In the computer Simon found a revolutionary new tool for psychological experimentation. In Newell Simon found a kindred spirit and a keen mind.

Newell joined Simon at Carnegie Tech in the autumn of 1954, ostensibly as Simon's graduate student but in truth as his colleague. From then on, the two worked closely together, so much so that it is almost impossible to distinguish their separate contributions, at least in computer science and psychology. The first fruits of their collaboration were the computer programs The Logic Theorist (first run on a computer in 1956) and The General Problem Solver (1958), which were designed to simulate the processes by which humans solved certain kinds of problems, especially mathematical proofs. The results of these simulations then served as the basis for their new theories of human problem solving, first in their landmark article 'Elements of a Theory of Human Problem Solving', and later in their magnum opus, Human Problem Solving (1972). The details of these theories take us beyond the

scope of this essay; suffice it to say that Simon and Newell's theory of human problem solving is an attempt to specify the basic processes and parameters of the human information-processing machine.

By 1965 Simon had moved far enough from his roots in organization theory to leave the GSIA and take up a new position at Carnegie-Mellon University as R.K. Mellon Professor of Computer Science and Psychology. Simon did retain his interest in economics, rational choice theory and administration after the move, writing some influential pieces on the potential impact of computers upon business organizations, but the bulk of the 500-plus books and articles he has published since the early 1960s have dealt with issues only indirectly related to management theory.

In Administrative Behavior Simon delivered a stinging critique of existing administrative theory, arguing that the central 'principles' of administration of Luther GULICK and Lyndal Urwick were mere 'proverbs', not statements appropriate to a true science. The rest of existing administrative science fared little better under Simon's assault, with Simon arguing that it almost universally lacked both empirical support and theoretical rigour. As a result, administrative science typically dealt with symptoms rather than with the underlying causes of bureaucratic disease.

Despite this harsh judgement, Simon believed that it was possible to salvage many elements from existing administrative theory. The key to this rescue operation would be the conceptual reorganization of the field. If a new theoretical framework could be constructed, then concepts such as specialization, hierarchy, authority and efficiency could be given precise definition and so be preserved. Existing data and hard-won practical experience likewise could be saved by being reinterpreted in terms of this new framework.

The key to this conceptual reorganization, to Simon, was to focus on the psychology of decision making in organizations. Drawing on Wittgenstein (and using chess as a recurrent example), Simon described a decision as being like a move in a game, where a specific action is taken (one out of a vast set of possible moves is chosen) in order to bring about a new configuration of the game board that is the world. To Simon, it was the task of knowledge to help us select the best move from the vast array of possible actions.

The number of possible options at any given moment are enormous, however, making it impossible for anyone to make a complete evaluation of the consequences of every move. There must exist, therefore, some means by which we limit the alternatives we consider and the depth to which we consider them. The key factor in this process, according to Simon, is organizational membership. (Later, in *Models of Man* (1957) and *Organizations* (1958), Simon would add a second key factor, the tendency for humans to 'satisfice' rather than to 'optimize' in their decision making.) Here is where Simon's theory of decision making intersects with the problems of administration and organization, and here is where Simon lays the groundwork for turning upside down the traditional understanding of organizations.

Previous analysts of organizations generally had viewed them as obstacles to rational thought because of the blinkered perspectives they often imposed upon their members. Simon turned this argument on its head, arguing that organizations were *essential* to rational thought *because* they limited the range of choices available to their members. To Simon, choice was not possible without limits, and freedom was not feasible without bounds. In his view, organizations enable their members to make decisions by virtue of the fact that they limit the sets of alternatives their members consider. Indeed, in Simon's view this enabling of decision by limiting the scope of choice is the ultimate purpose of all organization, and organizations are themselves decision-making machines. To him, organizations and individual decisions were structured in the same way, with the administrative hierarchy of superiors and subordinates corresponding to a hierarchy of goals

and sub-goals, from the CEO who decides broad policy down to the operative worker who implements it.

Drawing upon the work of Chester BARNARD, Simon argued that organizational membership produces two phenomena which limit the alternatives we consider and so enable us to make choices: authority and organizational identification. Authority, in its simplest sense, is the power to make decisions which guide the actions of another. As a member of an organization, the individual sets himself a general rule which permits the communicated decision of another to guide his own choices without deliberations on his own part. This general rule only applies to decisions within a certain area, the employee's 'zone of indifference', but it does enable the centralization of the function of decision making, so that a general plan of operations can govern the activities of all members of the organization.

Significantly, this understanding of authority makes it dependent upon the actions of the subordinate, not the status of the superior, helping Simon reconcile the hierarchical nature of authority relationships with his democratic ideals. When a subordinate does not permit his decisions to be guided by those of his superior, 'there is no authority, whatever may be the "paper" theory of organization' (Simon 1961: 125). Why, then, does the individual sacrifice the power to choose, even within a limited area, if he or she is not forced to do so?

First, Simon explained, there is in existence outside any particular organization a set of widely accepted premises as to the nature of the roles of superior and subordinate in any given organization. These institutionalized roles help individuals to form reliable expectations about the behaviours of others, and they teach the individual to suspend independent judgement within certain bounds.

Second, the individual chooses to accept the authority of the organization (and of his or her superiors within it) because he or she *identifies* with the organization, agreeing with its basic goals and the broad structure of authority it has created as a means towards achieving those goals. The individual who so identifies with the organization looks at things from the perspective of the organization, accepting the policies and goals of his or her superiors as premises for his or her own decisions. The individual does so for several reasons, of which probably the most important is that identification allows the myriad decisions of daily life to be integrated into a coherent plan, thus enabling both organizations and their members to make rational decisions.

Organizational identification thus provides a crucial link between the needs of the organization and the needs of the individual. It is a powerful, pervasive phenomenon, and without it all the benefits of rationally coordinated action would be unattainable. Its effects are not always benign, however, for, as Simon points out, people tend to identify with the sub-goals that guide their immediate decisions and with the sub-units of the organizations with which they have the most frequent contact.

Simon argued that this tendency to identify with sub-goals and sub-units can be seen in every area of life, from the behaviour of tax payers who identify with Oakland rather than the Bay area, to that of the fire chief who identifies with his department rather than the needs of the city as a whole, to that of the expert who identifies with his profession instead of the public interest. This tendency was dangerous – in fact, it lay at the root of all bigotry and parochialism – but it could be mitigated by education and intelligent organizational design.

Later, in *Organizations* and in *Models of Man*, Simon added a third explanation (beyond authority and organizational identification) for how individuals cope with the complexity of the world: the adoption of an extremely simple pay-off function. Instead of creating a vast, precise ordering of all possible outcomes, listing each one as marginally better or worse than the next, individuals tend to judge outcomes as either satisfactory or unsatisfactory. In short, people 'satisfice'; they do not optimize. This

simplification drastically reduces the computation necessary for the individual, making it possible for him or her to conduct simple tests of possible actions and to choose the first acceptable option.

Simon's later emphasis upon satisficing reflected his growing interest in and use of biological concepts, received primarily by way of W. Ross Ashby's cybernetic theories. For example, in the book *Organizations*, Simon reinterpreted the organization as being an organism itself and problem solving as being the method by which organisms adapted to their environment. (Solving a problem satisfactorily thus paralleled evolutionary survival.) By the late 1950s Simon had come to see these parallels as more than metaphors: to him, bureaucratic organizations, evolving organisms and adaptive machines were functionally equivalent.

Simon's sharp-edged behaviouralism, functionalism and positivism won him strong allies and fierce opponents. From the beginning, critics such as Dwight Waldo and Chris ARGYRIS have found fault with Simon's analysis of the distinction between facts and values, with his assumption that organizations are necessarily hierarchical, with his presumption that humans are virtually blank slates upon which organizations write their preferences, and with his seeming valorization of centralized authority. They (and others) also have criticized Simon's definitions of rationality as being either circular or empty. Similarly, Simon's later work in artificial intelligence and cognitive psychology has been criticized for trying to explain all things, from the deepest passions to the highest flights of creative expression, in terms of information processing. Hubert Dreyfus and Joseph Weizenbaum, for example, took aim at Simon and Newell's work in particular in their strident critiques of artificial intelligence, *What Computers Can't Do* (1979) and *Computer Power and Human Reason* (1972).

Despite such critiques, Simon has left a powerful legacy to modern management theory: it is now second nature to think of both humans and organizations as information processors, and few would deny that human rationality is bounded in significant ways by the limits of our ability to process information. If Simon himself did not optimize, he certainly satisficed at an extraordinarily high level.

Simon has had a varied and fascinating career, one that has spanned many years and multiple disciplines. He marched in the van of a series of revolutions that transformed how both scholars and laymen understood politics, economics and their own mental lives: the behavioural revolution in political science, the econometric revolution in economics and the cognitive revolution in psychology. He has been awarded the highest honours for lifetime achievement in each of these fields, including the 1978 Nobel Prize in Economics. In addition, Simon was also a pioneer in computer science, developing (with Allen Newell and J.C. Shaw) one of the first working artificial intelligence programs (the *Logic Theorist*) as well as the first list-processing languages. Simon and Newell received the Association for Computing Machinery's highest honour, the Turing Award, for their work in 1975. Simon has been a fixture in the world of science policy, playing major roles in the Social Sciences Research Council (of which he was chairman of the board from 1962 to 1965), the National Academy of Sciences (where he was instrumental in expanding the presence of the social sciences) and the President's Science Advisory Committee (1969–72).

In the field of management Simon is chiefly known for his work on organizational decision making and for his leading role in Carnegie-Tech's trend-setting Graduate School of Industrial Administration, which pioneered the introduction of concepts and methods from the behavioural sciences (especially quantitative methods) into management education in the 1950s and 1960s. Simon's ideas about decision making in organizations were expressed in hundreds of books and articles, the most notable of which were *Administrative Behavior, Public Administration* (with Donald Smithburg and Victor Thompson, 1950), *Models of Man, Organizations* (with James March and Harold Guetzkow) and *Human Problem Solving* (with Allen Newell, 1972).

BIBLIOGRAPHY

Ashby, W.R. (1952) *Design for a Brain*, New York: Wiley.

Barnard, C.A. (1938) *The Functions of the Executive*, Cambridge, MA: Harvard University Press, 1968.

Crowther-Heyck, H. (2000) 'Herbert Simon, Organization Man', Ph.D. thesis, Johns Hopkins University.

Dreyfus, H. (1979) *What Computers Can't Do: The Limits of Artificial Intelligence*, revised edn, New York: Harper and Row.

Gillespie, R. (1991) *Manufacturing Knowledge: A History of the Hawthorne Experiments*, Cambridge and New York: Cambridge University Press.

Gulick, L. and Urwick, L. (eds) (1937) *Papers on the Science of Administration*, New York: Columbia University, Institute of Public Administration.

March, J.G., Simon, H. and Guetzkow, H. (1958) *Organizations*, New York: Wiley.

Newell, A. and Simon, H. (1956) 'The Logic Theory Machine,' *IRE Transactions on Information Theory*, IT-2, vol. 3: 61–79.

—— (1972) *Human Problem Solving*, Englewood Cliffs, NJ: Prentice-Hall.

Ridley, C. and Simon, H. (1936) *Measuring Municipal Activities: A Survey of Suggested Criteria for Appraising Administration*, Chicago: International City Managers' Association; 2nd edn 1943.

Simon, H. (1941) 'The Planning Approach in Political Economy: Further Comment', *Quarterly Journal of Economics* 55(2): 325–30.

—— (1943) *Fiscal Aspects of Metropolitan Consolidation*, Berkeley, CA: Bureau of Public Administration.

Simon, H. (1946) 'The Proverbs of

Administration', *Public Administration Review* 6: 53–67.

—— (1947) *Administrative Behavior*, New York: Macmillan.

—— (1953) 'Birth of an Organization: The Economic Cooperation Administration', *Public Administration Review* 13: 227–36.

—— (1957) *Models of Man: Social and Rational Mathematical Essays on Rational Behavior in a Social Setting*, New York: John Wiley and Sons.

—— (1960) *The New Science of Management Decision*, Evanston, IL: Harper and Row.

—— (1977) *Models of Discovery, and Other Topics in the Methods of Science*, Boston: D. Reidel.

—— (1982) *Models of Bounded Rationality*, 2 vols, Cambridge, MA: MIT Press.

—— (1991a) *Models of My Life*, New York: Basic Books.

Simon, H. (1991b) 'Organizations and Markets,' *Journal of Economic Perspectives* 5(2): 25–44.

—— (1997) *An Empirically Based Microeconomics*, New York: Cambridge University Press.

Simon, H., Smithburg, D. and Thompson, V. (1950) *Public Administration*, New York: Knopf.

Simon, H., Divine, W., Cooper, E. and Chernin, M. (1941) *Determining Work Loads for Professional Staff in a Public Welfare Agency*, Berkeley, CA: Bureau of Public Administration.

Simon, H., Egidi, M., Marris, R. and Viale, R. (1992) *Economics, Bounded Rationality and the Cognitive Revolution*, Brookfield, VT: Edward Elgar.

Waring, S. (1991) *Taylorism Transformed: Scientific Management Theory since 1945*, Chapel Hill, NC: University of North Carolina Press.

Weizenbaum, J. (1972) *Computer Power and Human Reason: From Judgment to Calculation*, San Francisco: W.H. Freeman.

HC-H

SINGER, Isaac Merritt (1811–75)

Isaac Singer was born in Pittstown, New York on 27 October 1811 and died near Torquay, Devonshire on 23 July 1875. Singer was the youngest son of Adam Singer, a cooper, and Ruth Benson. Singer's father emigrated from Germany in the late 1760s, and shortened the family name from Reisinger after arriving in the United States. Singer left home at the age of twelve to live with his brother in Rochester, New York, where he worked at a variety of jobs and displayed a natural ability to understand how machines operated. Aged nineteen, however, he became enamoured with the theatre and for the next nineteen years he travelled the country as an actor. Singer did not achieve the fame he yearned for as a thespian, and in the mid-1840s he instead focused on developing his innate talents as a mechanic and inventor.

Singer first became involved in the sewing machine business in 1850 when he examined a machine being repaired in the Boston shop of Orson C. Phelps. The sewing machine was first invented in 1846 by Elias Howe, Jr, and over the years others similar machines appeared on the market. Singer quickly found several defects in the design of these machines, and came up with a new design that corrected them. Within a matter of days he completed a working model, and in 1851 he received a patent for his invention. A year later Singer, Phelps and a third partner formed I.M. Singer and Company to manufacture and market the product.

While one of Singer's main accomplishments was inventing a technically superior sewing machine, the firm he organized was also important in the overall development of modern business management techniques. The primary responsibility for this, however, was not Singer's but rather that of Edward CLARK. Singer brought Clark, a lawyer, into the firm as a partner in 1851 to end his patent infringement suits with Howe. Five years later, Clark formed a patent pool that settled these disputes and left Singer the dominant firm in the sewing machine industry. In 1863, when Singer formally retired from active participation in I.M. Singer and Company, Clark assumed control of the firm and helped to make it a truly innovative business. He changed the way the company assembled sewing machines by replacing workers with machines, a move that increased manufacturing efficiency and led to significant economies of scale. Clark also expanded production overseas to exploit the market for sewing machines in Europe. Finally, he vertically integrated the company by opening branch outlets that sold and serviced only Singer products, and introduced instalment credit to finance the sales of these expensive machines.

As a businessman, Singer gained a reputation as ruthless and sometimes unscrupulous person. He patented the sewing machine in his name only, and eventually pushed his two original partners out of business in order to increase his own profits. However, he lacked the skills necessary to manage the firm's day-to-day operations, and as the company prospered under Clark, Singer spent more time enjoying his growing personal fame and fortune. Singer's personal life was also very complex. He was a notorious lecher and profligate, and fathered twenty-four children by five women, but only married two of them. Public scandals surrounding these affairs led Singer to retire to his estate in England, where he lived until his death in 1875.

BIBLIOGRAPHY

Brandon, R. (1996) *Singer and the Sewing Machine: A Capitalist Romance*, New York: Kodansha International.

Hounshell, D. (1984), *From the American System to Mass Production, 1800–1932: The Development of Manufacturing Technology in the United States*, Baltimore: Johns Hopkins University Press.

DM

SLOAN, Alfred Pritchard, Jr (1875–1966)

Alfred Pritchard Sloan, Jr was born in New Haven, Connecticut on 23 May 1875, to Alfred P. and Katherine Sloan and died on 17 February 1966 in New York. Sloan grew up in a comfortable home. Moving to Brooklyn, New York in 1885, he studied at the Brooklyn Polytechnic Institute in 1886 and at the Massachusetts Institute of Technology from 1892 to 1895. In 1897 he married Irene Jackson.

After completing his education, Sloan began working for the Hyatt Roller Bearing Company of Newark, New Jersey. When Hyatt ran into difficulties, Sloan's wealthy father saved the company, but on condition that Sloan be made Hyatt's manager. Sloan lived very much for his work, allowing himself little or nothing in the way of leisure pursuits or diversions, and soon proved to be a good manager.

By 1900 Sloan had discovered a healthy new market for his firm's bearings in the burgeoning automobile industry: 'Our profits got up to about $60,000 a year, and the prospects improved as the young automobile industry opened up a new market' (Sloan 1964: 19). Here he made the acquaintance of pioneers of the industry such as Henry FORD, Walter CHRYSLER and, above all, William Crapo DURANT at the new firm of General Motors. By 1916 Sloan was running a $20 million business. He was already anticipating his special approach to management, dividing Hyatt into multiple divisions. The headquarters were in

Newark, the factories were in Harrison, New Jersey, the auto sales office was in Detroit and the tractor division was in Chicago.

William C. Durant had created GM in 1908, the same year that Henry Ford brought out his Model T. He had been a buggy manufacturer until he took over the fledgling Buick Motor Company, turning it into a profitable auto maker. The Buick became the model for high quality and reliability in other GM cars. GM was organized on the holding company model first pioneered by Standard Oil. By 1910, however, GM had run up serious debts and Durant lost control of his company. In partnership with Louis Chevrolet, he went on to create the greatest threat yet to Henry Ford; the low-cost Chevrolet quickly began to cut into Ford's sales. Durant's success with Chevrolet allowed him to put pressure on the banks and he recovered GM in 1916. The new GM, incorporated in Delaware, was now worth $ 100 million.

In 1916, in the process of reorganizing GM, Durant bought out Sloan's bearing company for $13,500,000. Sloan went with Durant to become the president of United Motors: 'For the first time my business horizon widened beyond a single component of the automobile' (Sloan 1964: 24). Sloan had been so dependent upon Henry Ford to buy his bearings that he thought that supplying GM would provide Hyatt with an alternative market, so it would not have to deal with Ford alone. He also knew that his bearings would soon become outmoded. Durant offered him far more money than he could make by holding onto Hyatt.

Sloan and Hyatt become partners in the GM enterprise. He owned half the shares in the new United Motors, which became GM's parts supplier. Sloan restructured the management at United Motors, creating a centralized and uniform system of accounting. By 1918 the firm had been fully integrated into GM; Sloan himself was now a GM vice-president and director.

Sloan admired the genius and integrity of Durant, but nonetheless observed that he tried to do too much, trying to make too many decisions while running GM on his own. When the recession of 1920 struck, Durant had to pay his debts with his GM stock, and Pierre S. DU PONT inherited the GM presidency. Du Pont knew much about chemistry but not much about cars. Sloan, on the other hand, knew a great deal about cars as well as management, and quickly became Du Pont's most valued adviser. From this position he was well situated to succeed to the presidency of GM in 1923.

Being in the right place at the right time helped Sloan to rise, but his own ideas of management played an equally important role. According to Brands (1999), Sloan saw two challenges facing GM: that of creating an efficient management structure, and that of challenging Henry Ford. GM, unlike Ford, was a trust-like federation of companies linked together through the holding firm of General Motors of Delaware. Sloan set out to perfect a management structure that was to be the opposite of Ford's. Ford was a highly centralized family business run by the whims of its founder. Within Ford at the time there was basically one division – Ford – making one model. Within General Motors there were five major divisions – Chevrolet, Pontiac, Oldsmobile, Buick and Cadillac, plus the suppliers. Each was still a firm unto itself, with different standards and practices, a system which lent itself to all kinds of wasteful inefficiencies. Ford, meanwhile, was at the pinnacle of his triumph, with the sturdy, reliable and affordable Model T becoming a true people's car. Hundreds of thousands of clerks, factory workers, farmers, tradesmen and small entrepreneurs could buy a used Model T for half the price of a new one, and a good Ford would last for years. Such was the challenge. What Sloan could see was the opportunity. When the owner, now used to having a car, wanted to trade in his Ford, he might have the appetite for a better, more stylish, more comfortable car. Henry Ford could scarcely offer him one in the early 1930s. Ford had one model which never changed. One could buy a Model T in any colour, Ford famously remarked, so long as it was black.

In contrast, Sloan could offer the consumer a variety of models and colours. He won his victory over Ford because he understood that the car industry and the economy as a whole were, by the 1920s, entering into a new era of mass marketing and consumerism. Sloan's idea was to market the cars produced by each of GM's divisions in such a way that they would capture market share from Ford and other competitors, instead of each other. To do so, he targeted each of his divisions to a different consumer market. If they were relatively poor, they could still afford an 800-dollar Chevrolet; if they did not want to appear poor, they could buy a Pontiac. Those who were of middle-income status could graduate to an Oldsmobile. The aspiring entrepreneur on the make would feel good in a Buick, while the executive who had made it would certainly want the comfort and prestige of a 6,000-dollar Cadillac. Equally important, both a clerk and a CEO could have a red, blue or green Chevrolet or Cadillac, if they so desired.

Sloan set about making the various GM companies work together, and in the process created a model that would dominate American business for seventy years. This model was decentralized but efficient. Every division knew exactly what was expected of it and its relationship to GM as a whole. All the direction of GM was vested in the chief executive officer. Power was delegated so that only a limited number of executives had access to Sloan, who was then able to focus on the larger picture. Every executive in Chevrolet, Buick, Cadillac or any of the truck or other divisions was able to provide information to any of the other divisions.

The structure of GM as it was developed under Sloan was later described by Peter DRUCKER in his famous 1946 *Concept of the Corporation*. GM was divided into a line organization and a staff organization. The line organization comprised the thirty manufacturing divisions: the five auto divisions, the truck division, the Fisher Body plants which were attached to the auto and truck divisions, the accessory supplier divisions, including Frigidaire, and the Diesel and aircraft divisions. The line organization was to be supervised by the president. The staff organization, headed by the chairman of the board, who was also the chief executive officer, handled the service aspects not only of manufacturing, but also engineering, sales, research, personnel, finance, advertising and litigation. Each of these staff offices was led by a vice-president. The staff organizations coordinated the policies of the divisions. At the very centre of the structure, the president, his two executive vice-presidents (line), the chairman of the board, and his vice-chairman (staff) oversaw the entire operation and all major decisions.

In peace time, GM employed 250,000 people, led by 500 senior managers. Sloan recognized that everything could in no way be run from the top down. On the other hand, GM existed to make autos, meaning that its divisions had to work together as well as independently. The GM Corporation was more than just a holding company; Sloan and his top managers had to know everything that was going on, whether it was in a Chevrolet plant or a small ball bearing plant. The managers, especially of Chevrolet, Buick or Fisher, had to be allowed to manage and have their own authority. All divisions were entitled to have their own staff, production managers, sales managers, comptrollers and chief engineers, as if they were independent firms. According to Drucker, 'each division is organized as an autonomous unit' (Drucker 1972: 42). Most of the divisions other than Chevrolet, Buick, and Fisher were organized in related groups under a GM vice-president who represented them in central management.

The Sloan model was revolutionary and innovative for the 1920s. It was, says Drucker, 'an essay in federalism' able to 'combine the greatest corporate unity with the greatest divisional autonomy and responsibility' (Drucker 1972: 46). Conceived in 1923, it was put into practice at a time when GM was still mired in the postwar recession of the Harding years. Company sales were down 30 per cent in 1924 from 1923. Rapid recovery soon changed this picture, allowing Sloan's new strategies of management and marketing to overtake Ford by the end of the 1920s.

In his years as president of GM (1923–37), Sloan developed his vision of decentralization into a complete social philosophy. He hoped that it would increase speed, accountability, corporate unity and fairness, and that it would help democratize the company while leaving no doubt as to who was in charge. Divisions and managers which were not productive would have to stand on their own and turn a profit. Those managers, however, would know exactly what the company and their division were doing and why they were doing it.

Central management set the total production goals not only for GM but for each division, rewarded good managers and fired bad ones, and set the price ranges within which the various divisions would operate. According to Drucker, the chief function of the central management was the 'responsibility to think ahead ... as it more than anything else makes General Motors a unified institution with but one purpose' (Drucker 1972: 51, emphasis in the original). Beyond this, the divisional manager was free to organize the particulars of production, purchasing and marketing on his own initiative, with the help of the staff bodies.

According to Langworth and Norbye (1986), Sloan regarded the low-priced Chevrolet as his major tool in capturing the economy end of the market. In 1924, however, it was no match for the Model T. Sloan priced his Chevrolets slightly above the Ford, pitching to consumers that, for a little more money, they could get a car that was an improvement upon the Model T. Throughout 1925 and 1926 Chevrolet gained on Ford; when Ford shut down his plants to retool for the Model A, Chevrolet captured the market.

The roaring 1920s were the age of marketing, and few were better at it than Sloan.

Through the General Motors Acceptance Corporation, Sloan encouraged his customers to buy GM cars on monthly credit, creating a huge new market as consumers were able to lay down monthly payments for their Chevrolets and Pontiacs rather than paying the entire cash price for the car at once. By 1925 and 1926 most Americans buying cars were doing so on the instalment plan. By the late 1920s a large number of people were also using their old cars as down-payment on their new ones.

Sloan will also be remembered for inaugurating planned obsolescence. Henry Ford's Model Ts were the same in 1925 as in 1910; people drove them for years. For Sloan, style changes were made every year. GM cars were designed to last only for a few years, until a customer was ready to buy a newer model.

The Great Depression hit the auto industry severely. The shake-out in the market eliminated most independents and small makers, leaving GM, Ford and Chrysler to dominate the market. Despite massive layoffs and plant closings, people continued to buy cars even during the 1930s. GM was better able to weather the storm than its rivals, largely due to Sloan's cautious business strategy. Sloan estimated 'the highest return consistent with attainable volume', as well as the 'standard volume' he thought the firm could average over the business cycle. Based upon this, Sloan's planners figured the 'standard price' they would need to charge to get the return they wanted from the number of cars they had estimated. GM would then consistently stick with its price as the business cycle waxed and waned. The standard-volume costing concept, according to Sloan, 'permitted us to appraise and analyze our costs from one year to the next on a basis unaffected by changes in volume at a given plant capacity' (Sloan 1964: 146). At the same time it 'served as a gauge of the efficiency of our performance from one month to the next as well as from one year to the next' (Sloan 1964: 146).

Although the volume of GM sales fell by two-thirds during the Great Depression, Sloan's systematic forecasting allowed GM not only to show a profit and pay a dividend during every year of the depression, but to cement its domination over the auto market. By 1937 GM accounted for 80 per cent of auto industry profits and 45 per cent of the auto market (Brands 1999). Sloan did not want a larger share of the market lest this provoke the Department of Justice to initiate an anti-trust suit and accuse the corporation of monopoly. Between 1926 and 1938 GM achieved a return of 18 per cent on its investment despite the worst economic slump in history.

As the economy began to recover, employees began to assert their own rights. GM survived and profited during the Depression at the cost of many of its workers, half of whom were laid off during 1930–32. With the coming of the New Deal and a partial recovery, the United Auto Workers (UAW), feeling they had a sympathetic president in the White House, sought to organize GM plants in Michigan and elsewhere. During 1937 the Fisher Body and other works were shut down by union workers. Unlike public officials in the past, President Franklin D. Roosevelt and Governor Frank Murphy did not send troops to crush the workers, but rather pressured Sloan to negotiate, while Ford and Chrysler were recapturing segments of GM's market. Sloan recognized the UAW, which then went on to unionize Chrysler and, ultimately, Ford, although the latter held out until the Second World War. Sloan's concession to the rights of labour, although made reluctantly, signified the recognition by American management of labour as an equal partner.

By the eve of the Second World War, Alfred P. Sloan presided over the biggest corporation in America. Sloan compared GM's structure to that of the military; Peter DRUCKER compared it to that of the Roman Catholic Church. Despite this, Sloan was in reality neither a general nor a pontiff. His personal style of management was radically different from that of his rival, Henry Ford, whom Sloan viewed as inflexible, autocratic and unresponsive to consumer demand: 'Dictatorship is the most effective form of administration, provided the dictator knows the complete answer to all questions. But he never does and never will' (Brands 1999: 118). One business writer has observed that Sloan was:

> as different from Mr. Ford as a man could be. He makes suggestions. He does not give commands. If he cannot persuade his subordinates that a certain policy is wise, that policy does not go through. The same principle applies to them in turn. They must persuade their own associates.
>
> (Brands 1999: 118)

Fortune saw GM reproducing the federal structure of the United States itself:

> In essence, it is the democratic method applied to management, with the committee taking the place of the deliberative assembly. Each division head is a boss who can be overruled by no individual, is rarely overruled by a group. To put it another way, what Mr. Sloan has done is to set up a federal system, in which each state or division has a large degree of autonomy, only certain powers being reserved to the central government.
>
> (Brands 1999: 117)

As the depression gave way to war, Sloan, now chairman of the board and CEO, having retired as president, retooled his gargantuan firm from making cars to military trucks, shells, aircraft engines and tanks. He retired as chief executive in 1946 and as chairman in 1956. When he died Alfred Sloan left behind him a corporation that was the world's unchallenged leader in motor vehicles and which defined the very paradigm of 1950s corporate management.

BIBLIOGRAPHY

Brands, H.W. (1999) *Masters of Enterprise: Giants of American Business from John Jacob Astor and J.P. Morgan to Bill Gates and Oprah Winfrey*, New York: The Free Press.

Chandler, A.D., Jr (1964) *Giant Enterprise: Ford, General Motors and the Automobile Industry*, New York: Harcourt, Brace and World.

Crabb, R. (1969) *Birth of a Giant: The Men and Incidents that Gave America the Motorcar*, Philadelphia: Chilton Book Company.

Drucker, P.F. (1972) *Concept of the Corporation*, 2nd edn, New York: The John Day Company.

Langworth, R.M. and Norbye, J.P. (1986) *The Complete History of General Motors: 1908–1986*, New York: Beekman House.

Mooney, J.D. and Reilly, A.C. (1931) *Onward Industry! The Principles of Organization and Their Significance to Modern Industry*, New York: Harper and Bros.

'SLOAN, Alfred Pritchard' (1999) in J.A. Garraty and M. Carnes (eds), *American National Biography,* New York: Oxford University Press, vol. 20, 91–2.

Sloan, A.P., Jr (1964) *My Years with General Motors*, ed. J.D. McDonald, intro. by P. Drucker, New York: Currency Doubleday, 1990.

Sloan, A.P., Jr and Sparkes, B. (1941) *Adventures of a White Collar Man*, New York: Books for Libraries.

DCL

SNOW, Charles C. (1945–)

Charles Snow was born in San Diego, California. He took his BSc in business management from San Diego University in 1967, and went on to receive a Ph.D. from the University of California, Berkeley in 1972, where he met and formed a working partnership with Raymond MILES. Long interested in the problems of strategy and organization, he collaborated with Miles on a seminal book, *Organizational Strategy, Structure and Process* (1978). His later work has continued to focus on themes of strategy and organization.

Miles and Snow are best known for exploring the linkage between organization strategy, structure and process, and their conclusion that structure and process need to be aligned as closely as possible with strategy, a concept known as 'organizational fitness for purpose'. The choice of strategy and the resulting decisions concerning structure and process are made by the senior executives and powerholders within the organization, what Miles and Snow term the 'dominant coalition' that governs it, and it is the nature of their perception and reaction that determines organizational and strategic response. They summarize the problem as follows:

the strategic choice approach essentially argues that the effectiveness of organizational adaptation hinges on the dominant coalition's perception of environmental conditions and the decisions it makes concerning how the organization will cope with these conditions ... this complex and dynamic process can be broken apart into three major problems: entrepreneurial, administrative and engineering.

(Miles and Snow 1978: 21)

These three problems together form the 'adaptive cycle', with entrepreneurial/strategic choice problems influencing engineering and process decisions; these in turn impact on the organizational structure required for effectiveness; and, closing the circle, the administrative structure's ability to anticipate and understand change affects the quality of entrepreneurial response. Depending on how organizations manage their adaptive cycle, Miles and Snow say, they can be classified into one of four types: (1) defenders, who concentrate on existing markets and stress the need to engineer cost-effective responses to current market problems; (2) prospectors, who emphasize the entrepreneurial portion of the cycle and concentrate on new markets; (3) analysers, who look for a balance between all three elements; and (4) reactors, who fail to adopt a market strategy at all. Reactors, they argue, are created when the balance between strategy, structure and process breaks down and organizations lose their fitness for purpose. In his later work, notably Snow (1989), Snow has gone on to examine the human resource management implications of this theory of fitness.

BIBLIOGRAPHY

Miles, R.E. and Snow, C.C. (1978) *Organizational Strategy, Structure and Process*, New York: McGraw-Hill.

—— (1984) 'Fit, Failure and the Hall of Fame', *California Management Review* 26(3): 10–28.

Pitts, R.A. and Snow, C.C. (1986) *Strategies for Corporate Success*, New York: Wiley.

Snow, C.C. (ed.) (1989) *Strategy, Organization Design and Human Resource Management*, New York: JAI Press.

Witzel, M. (1998) 'Miles, Raymond E. and Snow, Charles C.', in M. Warner (ed.), *IEBM Handbook of Management Thinking*, London: International Thomson Business Press, 455–60.

MLW

SORENSON, Charles (1881–1968)

Charles Sorenson was born in Copenhagen, Denmark, the son of Soren and Eva Sorenson. He died in Bethesda, Maryland on 13 August 1968. He married twice, to Helen Mitchell in 1904 and, after her death, to Edith Montgomery in 1960; there was one son from the first marriage. The family emigrated to the United States in 1888 and Sorenson apprenticed as a pattern-maker working with his father. The family, having settled first in Pennsylvania, later moved to Milwaukee and then Detroit. In the latter city Sorenson made the acquaintance of Tom Cooper, a former bicycle racing champion who was then engaged in building racing cars with Henry FORD. Sorenson's talents as a draughtsman and designer played an important role in the design of the successful 999 racing car, and in 1905 Sorenson joined Ford's company as a pattern-maker. Here he gained Ford's trust and was promoted rapidly, first to take charge of the foundry, then to assistant production manager and later production manager of the Model T Ford. With James COUZENS and William KNUDSEN, Sorenson became part of the highly talented management team at Highland Park that made Ford supreme in the motor industry for nearly two decades.

Sorenson's later career at Ford is controversial. While Couzens, Knudsen and other senior managers quarrelled with the increasingly autocratic Ford and left the company, Sorenson remained loyal. Content to remain in the background and always apparently willing to obey Ford's will, he became one of the few men on whom Ford felt he could rely. He seems to have made at least some attempt to mitigate Ford's worst excesses, particularly his treatment of his son Edsel FORD, for whom Sorenson had both respect and sympathy, and also played a key role in persuading Ford to abandon the ageing Model T. Sorenson's greatest triumphs were the design and construction of the state-of-the-art manufacturing and assembly plant at River Rouge, which opened in 1927, and the launch of the Model A that same year.

During the late 1930s Sorenson became involved in a power struggle with Harry Bennett, the thuggish chief of Ford's internal security service, who was gradually acquiring a hold over the ageing Ford. In 1940 Sorenson and Edsel Ford, with difficulty, persuaded Ford to join the government's aircraft production programme, and from 1941 to 1942 Sorenson was engaged in designing and building a production plant for four-engined B-24 Liberator bombers at Willow Run, Michigan. The project was initially plagued with problems, but by 1943 Willow Run was turning out bombers at an astonishing rate of one aircraft per hour. Away from headquarters in Detroit, however, Sorenson could no longer defend himself against Bennett's plots, and in March 1944 he resigned from Ford. In June that year he took on the presidency of Willys Overland, and helped the company make the transition from wartime to peacetime production, stepping down in 1946 and retiring altogether in 1950.

As a manger, Sorenson remains a controversial figure. At Ford he earned the nickname 'Cast Iron Charlie', partly for his preference for using low-cost cast metal parts rather than ones made from forged metal, but also in reference to his own personality. Though vehemently anti-union, his tough, populist approach and blunt manner endeared him to (at least some) Ford employees, who respected him for his honesty. In 1920, touring a truck assembly plant in the Soviet Union, he was astonished to be greeted with shouts of 'Hi, Charlie!' from the men on the assembly line; it transpired that some of the men had formerly worked at Highland Park, and their stories had made him an almost legendary figure in Russian automotive circles. (Asked during the same visit how he would modernize an ageing steel foundry, he replied bluntly, 'Blow it up.')

To some modern observers he is the epitome of the old style of driving, anti-union manager. Tough and conservative he undoubtedly was, but he also had a genius for organizing and getting results. By the time he retired, he reckoned, he had participated in the building of thirty million automobiles.

BIBLIOGRAPHY
Sorenson, C.E. and Williamson, S.T. (1957) *Forty Years with Ford*, London: Jonathan Cape.

MLW

SPALDING, Albert Goodwill (1850–1915)

Albert Goodwill Spalding was born on 2 September 1850 in Byron, Illinois to James and Harriet Spalding. He died on 9 September 1915 at Point Loma, California. After the death of his father, a prosperous farmer, Spalding's mother moved the family to Rockford, Illinois. Here Spalding attended the Rockford Commercial College. He married twice, to Josie Keith in 1875 and, following her death, to Elizabeth Mayer Churchill in 1901. They had one son.

Spalding claimed to have begun playing baseball by accident, but he became a teenage pitching sensation. He became a professional player in 1871. His triumph over Harry Wright's Cincinnati Red Stockings led to a professional contract with the Boston Red Stockings of the newly formed National Association. Spalding quickly became a dominant pitcher in the league.

Spalding's association with Wright was fruitful in that Wright, an early proponent of professional baseball, possessed much business acumen. By the 1875 season, however, Spalding and some team-mates were negotiating to leave the Boston team and join William Hulbert's new Chicago White Stockings team. In his later years, Spalding claimed to have given Hulbert the idea of forming their own league, the National League. The latter represented a shift from a player-dominated league to one dominated by capitalists and management. As Spalding wrote in his *America's National Game*, 'means ought to be adopted to separate the control of the executive management from the players and the playing of the game' (Spalding 1911: 193). He played briefly for Chicago before switching to managing the team, and eventually became its president. He contributed to the growing control of the sport by business interests, and he fought any increase in player control of the professional game, especially by crushing the Players' League of 1890. Conversely, Spalding sought to attract more genteel patrons, attempting to ban gambling, drinking and general rowdiness. He also attempted to widen baseball's fan base by touring and promoting baseball games around the world.

Spalding recognized the profit potential in selling sporting goods. In 1876 he and his brother opened a sporting goods store in Chicago with $800 supplied by their mother (Levine 1985: 73). He understood the importance of promotion, and after winning a contract to publish the official league book, published his own 'official' baseball guide, *Spalding's Official Baseball Guide*. He also won a contract to supply the league with its official baseballs. The league imprimatur boosted Spalding's ability to sell his baseballs and other sporting equipment to consumers. He leveraged the advantages inherent in supplying official baseballs and publishing the guide by manufacturing his own goods and by diversifying into other sports. He eventually dominated the sporting goods market: 'In the space of sixteen years, a modest $800 speculation had become a multimillion dollar business and made its namesake a millionaire' (Levine 1985: 81). Spalding was conscious of the public antipathy towards monopolies, so he sometimes resorted to subterfuges to defuse any such antipathy. After acquiring the A.J. Reach company, he continued to use the Reach label on some baseballs, creating the fiction of two completely separate companies.

Spalding was elected to the Baseball Hall of Fame in 1939. Some dubbed him 'The Father of Baseball'. Certainly Spalding's approach to professional sports, with its emphasis on management's control of the game, players and publicity, has been much emulated.

BIBLIOGRAPHY
Levine, P. (1985) *A.G. Spalding and the Rise of Baseball*, New York: Oxford University Press.
Spalding, A. (1911) *America's National Game: Historic Facts Concerning the Beginning, Evolution, Development and Popularity of Base Ball*, Lincoln, NB: University of Nebraska Press, 1992.

DS

STARBUCK, William Haynes (1934–)

William Haynes Starbuck was born in Portland, Indiana on 20 September 1934. He took a bachelor's degree in physics from Harvard University in 1956 and then entered postgraduate studies at the Carnegie Institute of Technology. Originally intending to study mathematics, he was persuaded by Richard CYERT to focus instead on behavioural sciences and business administration. Starbuck went on to complete his MSc at Carnegie in 1959 and his Ph.D. in 1964. He has taught at Purdue, Cornell and Wisconsin-Milwaukee, as well as taking a number of visiting lectureships and professorships in Europe, and is currently ITT Professor of Creative Management at New York University. Starbuck was also president of the Academy of Management in 1997–8, and has served as editor of *Administrative Science Quarterly*.

Starbuck's work over the past four decades has ranged across many fields, but he is best known for his research and writings on management and organizational behaviour. His approach is grounded in part in behaviour psychology, but other disciplines are referred to as well. Starbuck argues that the assumption that managerial behaviour and decision making are grounded in rational motives and practices in unfounded, and that managers do not always engage in rational analysis by analysing problems, seeking solutions and taking appropriate actions; rather, in many cases they will take actions and then invent problems which justify those actions. Organizational ideologies are often built on the backs of such 'action-generating' activity. But rather than trying to strip away such behaviours and develop a wholly technical-rational form of management, Starbuck argues that to some extent such apparently non-rational behaviour must be accepted. In his later work he has questioned whether true objectivity is even possible, and has challenged the epistemological assumptions on which management and management science are both based. His work has important implications for both the nature of organizational knowledge and for the nature and structure of organizations themselves.

BIBLIOGRAPHY
Starbuck, W.H. (1983) 'Organizations as Action Generators', *American Sociological Review* 48: 91–102.
Starbuck, W.H. and Milliken, F. (1988) 'Executives Perceptual Filtres: What They Notice and How It Makes Sense', in D.C. Hambrick (ed.), *The Executive Effect: Concepts and Methods for Studying Top Managers*, New York: JAI Press.

STRASSMAN, W. Paul (1926–)

W. Paul Strassman was born in Berlin on 26 July 1926, the son of Irwin and Otto Strassman. He married Elizabeth Franck in 1952; they have three children. After serving in the US Navy from 1944 to 1946, Strassman earned a BA *magna cum laude* from the University of Texas, Austin in 1949, followed by an MA from Columbia University in 1950 and a Ph.D. from the University of Maryland in 1956. He worked as an economics analyst for the US Department of Commerce from 1951 to 1952. In 1956 he joined the faculty of Michigan State University, becoming associate professor of economics in 1959 and professor in 1963. He is consultant to a number of businesses and organizations including the World Bank.

Strassman has been an important writer on technology issues for many years, and his *Technological Change and Economic Development* (1968) is a valuable study of the linkage between the two. In a recent work, *The Business Value of Computers* (1990), Strassman has sought to apply principles of economics to the management of information. He sees information, decision making and management as inextricably bound together, and proposes the calculation of a 'return on management' (ROM) which will quantify in monetary terms the amount of added value that management brings to the operations of a business. The amount of management value added will depend, he says, on management's ability to manage information, since the latter commodity is central to management's ability to function.

Strassman cautions against over-reliance on technology; a computer's value on its own, he says, is only what it will fetch at auction. It is up to managers to use the computer as a tool to add value to the businesses they manage. It is the information that a computer can process, not the artefact itself, that renders it useful. Strassman's concept of management as an information-based activity had by the end of the 1990s become widely accepted in both thinking and, increasingly, in practice.

BIBLIOGRAPHY
Kennedy, C. (1996) *Managing With the Gurus*, London: Century.
Strassman, P. (1968) *Technological Change and Economic Development*, Ithaca, NY: Cornell University Press.
—— (1990) *The Business Value of Computers*, New Canaan, CT: Information Economics Press.

STRAUSS, Levi (1829–1902)

Levi Strauss was born in Butterheim, Bavaria on 26 February 1829, the son of Hirsch and Rebecca Strauss. He died in San Francisco, California on 26 September 1902. After the death of his father in 1845, the family emigrated to New York, where Strauss worked in a dry goods store owned and managed by his elder brothers. In 1853 he moved to San Francisco, then a boom town following the discovery of gold near Sacramento in 1849. Here, reasoning that those who get rich in gold rushes are not the miners themselves but those who sell supplies to the miners, he established a dry goods business. Strauss prospered through the 1850s and 1860s, and built up one of San Francisco's leading retail businesses in partnership with his brother-in-law David Stern; he became an important benefactor and pillar of the community.

In 1872 Strauss was contacted by Jacob Davis, a tailor in Reno, Nevada. Davis had developed a new method of making trousers by inserting metal rivets at the points where seams were most likely to wear (such as around the waist and at the bottoms of pockets). He wanted to patent the process but lacked money, and asked if Strauss would come in as his partner. In 1873 Davis and Strauss were jointly granted the patent for 'riveted waist overalls', and set up a manufacturing facility in San Francisco making trousers out of blue denim. The original system involved putting out work to seamstresses, but the demand grew rapidly and in the 1870s Strauss began building factories. In 1890 the '501' trademark first appeared, but long before this the name of Levi Strauss itself had become synonymous with the blue denim trousers or 'jeans' that he had designed and marketed so successfully (blue jeans are still known in parts of the United States as 'Levis').

In 1890 Strauss retired and handed over the business to his nephews. He continued to be active in San Francisco society until his death. The business was virtually destroyed by the San Francisco fire of 1906, but so strong was its market that Strauss's successors were able quickly to rebuild and return the firm to profitability. Strauss remains known as the creator of one of the most enduring brand names in history.

SWIFT, Louis Franklin (1861–1937)

Louis Franklin Swift was born in Sagamore, Massachusetts on 27 September 1861, the eldest son of Gustavus and Annie Maria Swift. He died of heart disease in Chicago on 12 May 1937. He married Ida Butler in 1880, and they had six children. The Swifts came from an old-established New England family, and claimed descent from the original seventeenth-century colonists on the *Mayflower*. In 1875 the family moved to Chicago, where Gustavus Swift founded a successful meat-packing business, buying cattle and other livestock reared in the American Midwest and West, slaughtering and processing the animals and shipping the meat to the rapidly growing urban centres of the East. After leaving high school Swift joined the family firm and worked in the stockyards as a buyer and later in charge of a department; his five brothers all joined the firm at various stages and served in management positions as well. In 1885 Swift and Company incorporated, and Louis Swift served as treasurer and later as vice-president. On the death of his father in 1903 Swift took over as president, remaining in that post until his retirement in 1931.

If Gustavus Swift was the entrepreneurial founder of the business, Louis Swift was the second-generation consolidator who gave the business a sound management structure and launched it into spectacular growth. Sales rose from $200 million in 1903 to $700 million by the time Swift retired. By 1931 he presided over a vast and diverse business that included 55,000 employees and more than 150 plants.

His management style was highly personal, and although he delegated much management to his brothers and the other managers in the firm's hierarchy, he made frequent inspection visits to outlying facilities and insisted on a system of weekly reports from all senior managers which would give him full and timely information. He preferred talking to people one-on-one to chairing meetings, and once described all meetings as a waste of time; he was seemingly at his happiest on the stockyard floor chatting to employees. His inspection visits were intended to survey not only the efficiency of each operation but also its cleanliness and hygiene, and the conditions in which employees had to work; Swift had a strong interest in worker welfare, and provided notably better pay and conditions than his rivals at Armour and Company.

In 1902 Gustavus Swift had joined forces with Armour and several other meat packers to form the National Packing Company, but a suit under anti-trust legislation soon followed and the trust was dissolved. Unfortunately for Swift, government investigators continued to suspect the meat-packing industry of monopolistic practices. Swift was a strong believer in 'integrated marketing', by which the firm controlled most of its own distribution network, a practice he felt necessary to ensuring that the distribution chain worked efficiently; however, in 1917 anti-trust investigators forced Swift, Armour and other firms to dispose of many of their distribution functions. Swift protested vigorously. Partly in response to this move by the government, he established one of the first corporate bureaux of business research in the United States, and hired academics such as L.D.H. WELD and A.T. KEARNEY to staff it. One of the tasks of the bureau was to investigate the best and most efficient methods of marketing. The 'integrated marketing' debate continued to rumble on into the 1920s, with a notable debate on the subject taking place between Weld and Lewis HANEY in 1920–21.

An innovative and successful company, Swift owed much of its establishment and rise to the solid leadership and sound management principles of Louis Swift. In an age when the separation of ownership and control was fast taking hold, Swift showed that professionalism in management and the ownership of capital were not incompatible.

BIBLIOGRAPHY
Swift, L.F. and Van Vlissingen, A. (1970) *The Yankee of the Yards*, New York: AMS Press.

MLW

T

TARBELL, Ida Minerva (1857–1944)

Ida Minerva Tarbell was born in Erie County, Pennsylvania, the daughter of Franklin and Esther Tarbell. She died in Bethel, Connecticut on 6 January 1944. After graduating from Allegheny College in 1880, one of only five women students there, she taught in a seminary in Ohio and then was associate editor of *The Chautauquan* (1883–91). She then spent three years in Paris, which city she says she fell in love with at first sight, studying at the Collège de France and the Sorbonne, and supporting herself by writing for *McClure's* magazine. The quality of her writing gained attention, and in 1894 she was invited to New York to become assistant editor of *McClure's*. She made an early name for herself as a biographer, with works on Napoleon, Madame Roland and Abraham Lincoln all published by 1900; she remains one of Lincoln's most perceptive and accomplished biographers. While at *McLure's* she also researched and wrote her two-volume *The History of the Standard Oil Company* (1904), which caused considerable uproar when it was published. She was one of the group of investigative journalists who were dubbed 'the muck-rakers' by Theodore Roosevelt, campaigning against business corruption.

From 1906 to 1915 Tarbell was co-owner and associate editor of *American Magazine*. She left the magazine in 1915 to work as an independent writer and lecturer. She was a member of President Woodrow Wilson's Industrial Conference in 1919, and later also of President Warren Harding's Unemployment Conference. Throughout the 1920s she was regarded as an influential commentator.

As she describes in her autobiography, the decision to write a book about Standard Oil, the giant oil trust created by John D. ROCKEFELLER, grew out of a concern felt by her and her colleagues that the trusts were stifling competition and were engaging in unethical practices largely hidden from the public. Standard was chosen as a target because it was the largest and most successful of the trusts. She did not regard herself as a crusader; instead she and her colleagues 'were undertaking what we regarded as a legitimate piece of historical work. We were neither apologists nor critics, only journalists intent on discovering what had gone into the making of this the most perfect of all monopolies' (Tarbell 1939: 206). Friends and family warned her that she would never succeed, and Standard would take measures to prevent her. Instead, Standard decided to cooperate. Through a mutual acquaintance, Mark Twain, Tarbell heard that a senior Standard executive, Henry Rogers, was anxious to meet her. The two met and, somewhat to their mutual surprise, became friends. Rogers struck a deal; he would make information available to Tarbell if she would offer her criticisms for rebuttal before publishing. From 1902 to 1904 the two engaged in a series of clandestine meetings and argued out the various points Tarbell had raised; true to her word, she published Standard's defences along with her own points in the final work. Through Rogers she was able to meet Henry FLAGLER, a former associate and now bitter critic of Rockefeller, who gave her further information. Her requests to meet Rockefeller himself were politely refused.

The final publication is a highly detailed account of how the Standard Oil trust was established and run, and it stands as a landmark piece of business history. Tarbell was scrupulously fair to her subjects, and commented that there was much that was admirable about both Standard and Rockefeller: the company was well managed and efficient, and Rockefeller was undoubtedly a great man. The sting comes in the book's tail, at the end of volume 2 when she sums up her criticisms:

> The Standard men have nothing to do with public affairs, except as it is necessary to manipulate them 'for the good of the oil business'. The notion that the business man must not appear in politics and religion save as a 'stand-patter' – not even as a thinking, aggressive force – is demoralizing, intellectually and morally.
>
> (Tarbell 1904, vol. 2: 290)

She goes on:

> There is something alarming to those who believe that commerce should be a peaceful pursuit, and who believe that moral law holds good throughout the entire range of human relations, in knowing that so large a body of young men in this country are consciously or unconsciously growing up with the idea that business is war and that morals have nothing to do with its practice.
>
> And what are we going to do about it? For it is *our* business. We, the people of the United States, and nobody else, must cure whatever is wrong in the industrial situation, typified by this narrative of the growth of the Standard Oil Company.
>
> (Tarbell 1904, vol. 2: 291–2)

The book received very wide publicity, and aroused considerable antagonism against the trusts. In 1906 the Roosevelt administration prosecuted Standard Oil for violation of the Sherman Anti-trust Act; in 1911 the company was found guilty and fined $29 million, and in 1911 it was finally broken up.

Despite her muckraker image, Tarbell was not anti-business; rather, she called for business to be conducted in a fair and ethical manner. The opposite side of the coin to Standard Oil can be found in her portrayal of Owen D. YOUNG, a business leader whom she saw as being responsive to change in social and economic conditions and who was doing his best to promote change and best practice; she particularly approved of his views on education (Tarbell 1932).

In *New Ideals in Business* (1916) Tarbell called for business leaders to take a deeper interest in their human material. She approved of the scientific management movement, which she saw as being able to offer work for all, with different jobs available to those with different levels of skill and knowledge, even the infirm. She argued that the primary task of management is to find the potential in every worker and bring this out to the fullest, for the benefit of the company and the worker alike: 'The first need of the employer is to awaken interest and faith in his particular effort' (Tarbell 1916: 323). The best facilities and the best equipment will all be wasted, she said, if the workers are unwilling or unable to support the goals of management.

A curious blend of reformer and conservative, Tarbell did not support female emancipation and even argued in 1912 that the woman's place is in the home: the first duty of a woman, she said, is to 'prepare the citizen of the future' and to 'socialize the home' (it should be noted that Tarbell herself did not conform to this role in any way; she never married). Yet in 1921 she wrote a landmark series of articles for Arch Shaw's journal *Industrial Management*, the successor to

System, in which she defined the role of women in business, and in the final article notes the important role women have to play in the 'new industrial professions' such as labour management, welfare work and health and safety. She cites the example of Nesta B. Edwards, a Chicago-based work-place safety consultant who set up her own consulting agency in 1913 and was one of the world's first female management consultants. Tarbell herself remains one of the most remarkable women ever to have appeared on the management scene.

BIBLIOGRAPHY

Tarbell, I.M. (1904) *The History of the Standard Oil Company*, 2 vols, New York: McClure, Phillips and Co.

—— (1912) *The Business of Being a Woman*, New York: Macmillan.

—— (1916) *New Ideals in Business*, New York: Macmillan.

—— (1932) *Owen D. Young: A New Type of Industrial Leader*, New York: Macmillan.

—— (1939) *All in the Day's Work: An Autobiography*, New York: Macmillan.

Uglow, J. (1989) *The Macmillan Dictionary of Women's Biography*, 2nd edn, London: Macmillan.

MLW

TAYLOR, Frederick Winslow (1856–1915)

Frederick Winslow Taylor was born in Germantown, Pennsylvania on 20 March 1856, the second of three children of Franklin Taylor and Emily Winslow. He died of pneumonia in Philadelphia on 21 March 1915. He married Louise Spooner in 1884, and they adopted three children. Taylor's father hailed from an old Pennsylvania Quaker family and was a Princeton-educated lawyer who was able, thanks to inherited wealth, to retire early and pursue a life of intellectual and cultural enrichment. His mother was a former teacher from an old New England family in the whaling business. In his youth, he attended the Germantown Academy. When he was twelve, Taylor and his family went to Europe where they travelled for three years. Upon returning, Taylor spent two years at a prep school, Phillips Exeter Academy in New Hampshire. Subsequently he passed the Harvard admissions examination with honours.

Taylor was an avid athlete, and in 1881 he and his brother-in-law won the first US Lawn Tennis Association doubles championship. He was active in many other sports, and invented several kinds of improved sporting equipment including tennis rackets and nets, and golf putters. Yet despite his athleticism, Taylor suffered from chronic ill health. While at Exeter, Taylor developed headaches and vision problems which prevented his attending Harvard. Poor vision, insomnia and nightmares plagued him for the rest of his life, driving him in the end to experiment with sleeping harness and 'nightmare fighting machines' (Sicilia 1993: vi).

Unable to take up formal studies in engineering, Taylor secured an apprenticeship in 1874 as a pattern-maker and machinist at Enterprise Hydraulic Works in Philadelphia, completing his apprenticeship in 1878. Family connections enabled him to get a job with Midvale Steel Company of Philadelphia, headed by the leading machine tool-maker William Sellers. He began as a machinist, rising to the positions of foreman, master mechanic and chief engineer over the next twelve years. He also enrolled in the Stevens Institute of Technology, where he was awarded a degree in mechanical engineering in 1883, a year before Henry GANTT and three years before TAKEO Toshisuke. Midvale was a period of observation, experimentation and learning for Taylor, during which he gradually began to formulate and test his basic ideas about scientific management. In the 1880s he began studying tool-cutting operations and developed a number of improvements including a new type of high-speed steel for cutting tools (a prolific inventor, Taylor would ultimately register over 100 patents). He also began experimenting with ways of controlling worker output.

By 1886, however, it had become clear that Taylor's prospects at Midvale were limited: the company had been sold to new owners who were more actively involved in management, and he could no longer look forward to becoming head of the business. In 1890 he left Midvale and took a post as general manager of the newly-established Manufacturing Investment Company in Madison, Maine, a pulp and paper business set up by a group of wealthy investors led by J.P. MORGAN. He found the job disappointing, to say the least; the backers constantly interfered in the management of the firm, and when he tried to introduce the methods he had developed at Midvale there was considerable resistance. He quit after three years and returned to Philadelphia, where he set up an engineering consultancy practice. He also began refining and developing further the ideas with which he had experimented at Midvale, and in 1895 presented his paper *A Piece Rate System* to the American Society of Mechanical Engineers. This paper may fairly be said to mark the formal beginning of scientific management.

Taylor's work in this respect must be considered in context. From the beginning of the American factory system, the New England textile mills' factory managers 'had struggled to match the relentless pace of spinning and weaving with the irregular work patterns common among workers' (Sicilia 1993: viii). Few factories achieved optimum efficiency; indeed, in most cases there were no systems of measurement for determining what optimum efficiency might be, let alone whether it was being achieved. Although a few notably efficient mass-production operations had been established, notably by firearms-makers such as Samuel COLT and Oliver WINCHESTER, at the government-owned Springfield arsenal, and also by the combine-harvester manufacturer Cyrus Hall MCCORMICK, most factory owners only noticed inefficiencies when their profits began to decline; and their usual response in such cases was simply to cut wages rather than to investigate the underlying causes of the problem. Such practices, especially in the boom-and-bust economy of the late nineteenth century in America, provoked a number of violent and bloody strikes such as that at the works of the railway sleeping car builder George PULLMAN.

Wiser heads felt that there had to be a solution to the problems of industrial efficiency and labour unrest, and sought it in new methods of management. In 1886 the engineer Henry TOWNE had presented a paper to the American Society of Mechanical Engineers calling for new approaches to engineering shop management, and in particular to new ways of managing workers. Three years later, when president of the Society, Towne presented his paper on gain sharing as motivational plan for increasing worker output; this was followed in 1891 by Frederick HALSEY's premium plan. Both these systems attracted much attention, and the Halsey system was implemented with some success. However, as Drury (1915) notes, both plans had their problems. Taylor's response, based on his work at Midvale, was an amended piece-rate system or 'differential rate system', a bonus system which offered higher wages to workers who exceeded quotas for work completed within a given time. Taylor explains the system thus:

The differential rate system of piece-work consists briefly in offering two different rates for the same job: a high price per piece, in case the work is finished in the shortest time possible and in perfect condition, and a low price, if it takes a longer time to do the job, or if there are any imperfections in the work. (The high rate should be such that the workman can earn more per day than is usually paid in similar establishments.) This is directly the opposite of the ordinary plan of piece-work, in which the wages of the workmen are reduced when they increase their productivity.

(Taylor 1895: 35)

The differential rate plan would, Taylor believed, improve productivity by giving workers an incentive to increase output. It would also eliminate 'soldiering', 'gold-bricking' and other practices whereby workers deliberately slowed their pace of work to a level that suited themselves; if given a choice of idleness and an average wage or working hard and a good wage, he believed, most good workers would choose the latter. Taylor developed something of an obsession with soldiering, which he had first encountered at Midvale, and which he saw as a sin besetting many industrial enterprises and which needed to be eliminated. Under questioning following the presentation of the paper, however, he accepted that to be effective, a differential piece-rate system such as he proposed would require workers to be highly skilled, trained and motivated; it was probably beyond the ability of the average untrained worker to reach the productivity levels he considered satisfactory. Perhaps the most perceptive comment from the audience was that made by Henry Gantt, who said that for the system to work, the man setting the piece rate would have to be a manager of exceptional skill and judgement (Taylor 1895).

In 1898 Taylor was called in as a consultant by the Bethlehem Iron Company (later Bethlehem Steel Company), where he remained for the next three years. At Bethlehem he gathered around him a team of colleagues including Henry Gantt and Carl BARTH, and this group began to tackle the problem that Gantt had identified, that of assessing the nature of the work for which the workers were to be rewarded. To make the system work, it was necessary first to analyse each task performed during each process, and divide each task as far as possible into sub-tasks. By constant measurements using stop-watches, an optimum time for each task could be arrived at. Payment systems then used these times as a benchmark. But the Taylor system of management meant far more. In order to achieve ultimate efficiency, labour was divided to the utmost possible degree. Workers were to be intensively trained in only a minute variety of tasks, which they would carry out in a machine-like process. As Sicilia (1993: ix) says, 'the task was re-engineered for maximum efficiency, with the smallest details accounted for, including the number, interval and duration of rest periods'.

By 1901 the climate at Bethlehem was deteriorating. Although Taylor claimed with some justice that productivity figures had greatly improved, his methods had aroused resentment among both workers and managers. Taylor himself was dismissed shortly before the plant was sold to Charles M. SCHWAB; Gantt remained until the end of the year, then resigned as well. The Bethlehem experiment was over, but it had made Taylor famous. It formed the basis of his book *Shop Management*, published in 1903, in which he expands more fully on his philosophy of management. He refers to the current state of management as 'uneven', and says it is necessary to iron out irregularities and make uniform systems. Clearly stung by earlier criticisms from both within and without the labour movement that his system acted against the workers, he argues that the best systems of management are those in which the interests of employee and employer are so mutually intertwined that they cannot be separated (Taylor 1903: 20).

Over the next decade, Taylor built up his consulting practice and became a world-famous figure. *Shop Management* and his final major work *The Principles of Scientific Management* (1911) were read all across the United States and inspired men such as Morris Cooke,

Sanford THOMPSON and Horace HATHAWAY to become 'Taylorists'. The consulting firms of Taylor and his associates implemented his system in some 180 factories in the United States and more in Europe. Japanese engineers such as Takeo Toshisuke and Araki Toichiro took elements of the system back to Japan. In France, Henri Le Chatelier read *Shop Management* and became a convert, as later did Charles de Freminville; during the First World War his ideas came to the attention of Lyndall Urwick, who worked to introduce a modified version of Taylorism to Britain. The term 'scientific management' to describe the entire system of analysis, control and re-engineering which Taylor had developed was coined at a meeting of some of the leading members of the circle at Henry Gantt's New York apartment in 1911; Taylor himself was not present, but he clearly had no objection as he used the term for the title of his book later that year.

Yet not all was roses in the world of scientific management. Harrington EMERSON, who had independently developed his own school of management, the efficiency movement, met Taylor on one occasion in 1903 and seems to have taken a dislike to him; they rarely met or corresponded after that. Frank GILBRETH, who independently had developed a form of task re-engineering known as motion study, was enthusiastic about Taylor's methods and worked with him happily until he learned that some of Taylor's more zealous disciples were claiming the credit for developing motion study for Taylor himself; his wife, the brilliant psychologist Lillian GILBRETH whose work prefigures that antithesis of Taylorism, the human relations movement, took a violent dislike to Taylor. Never an easy man to work for or with, Taylor eventually alienated even his most loyal lieutenant, Henry Gantt. In fairness, it should be said that by 1911 the health of both Taylor and his wife had deteriorated badly. He spent the last three years of his life caring devotedly for Louise, and himself died in 1915.

In its entirety, Taylor's system of improving factory efficiency was comprehensive, from new methods of inventory control and accounting to new forms of logistics and personnel management. But it was Taylor's labour control systems that attracted the most attention – and generated the most controversy. More than any other aspect of Taylor's 'scientific management' system, his name came to be associated with his unusual and highly mechanized method of controlling work and workers.

According to Taylor, factory work was riddled with inefficiencies for two key reasons: workers were poorly trained and poorly motivated. The first problem, he argued, stemmed from the fact that industrial workers learned on the job. Methods were passed down from one generation of worker to the next informally. Standard practice was determined, not by any kind of rigorous analysis and training, but rather through what Taylor referred to as 'rule of thumb'. In this way, inefficient techniques were handed down, unquestioned, from experienced to novice workers. Along with this, Taylor said, workers often deliberately worked at below optimal rates by 'soldiering' and 'gold-bricking'. Because they were paid the same no matter how much they produced, workers had little motivation to work hard and much to stall and produce at a leisurely pace.

Scientific management was designed to address both of these perceived problems. Taylor or one of his 'disciples' would begin by observing a worker performing a task. The Taylorite would break the task down into minute parts, taking into account the exact times and distances travelled in the worker's motions, his output, rest periods, equipment, posture, and so on. A task might be dissected into hundreds of discrete components. The scientific manager then would go about redesigning the task in order to minimize wasted motion and other inefficiencies. This might involve the use of new equipment as well as complete retraining of the worker. Finally, the worker was timed performing the job the new way, and this output was used to establish a new 'par' rate. Other workers were then retrained, and expected to produce at the new par rate. If they did, they typically earned a higher wage than before. But if they fell below the par rate on a given day, their pay would be docked.

With these methods, Taylor and his followers achieved some dramatic results. Output in some test cases rose severalfold. Along with this, worker pay typically was increased between 30 and 100 percent. This entirely eliminated the impulse to 'soldier', Taylor argued. Everyone would win: plant managers and owners, as they saw their output per worker soar, and workers, because of the significant raises.

In practice, scientific management was plagued with difficulties, and attracted the opposition and scorn of workers. Taylor's most famous case – a worker that he featured in the pages of *The Principles of Scientific Management* – demonstrates the point. 'Schmidt' (actually an immigrant worker named Henry Knoll), carried 12.5 tons of pig iron a day before his job was 'Taylorized', and 47 tons afterwards. For this 376 percent increase in output, Schmidt was given a 60 percent pay raise. So management benefited proportionately much more than workers from Taylorism (in spite of Taylor's utopian claims to be bringing managers and workers together in common cause). Moreover, could Schmidt sustain the new pace? Could his fellow workers? How would he cope with his complete loss of autonomy and discretion on the job? The modern reader of this anecdote is irresistibly reminded of the case of the Russian coal miner Andrei Stakhanov, who, with proper training and equipment, was able to achieve fantastic feats of production; as a result, the Stalinist authorities set similar targets for *all* miners regardless of training and capability (later, of course, it emerged that the Stakhanov production figures were a hoax). Taylor's mindset with regard to Schmidt evinces a similar attitude; if Schmidt could be trained in this manner, anyone could. He had

a fundamentally condescending attitude towards industrial workers, whom he saw as simplistic brutes who were motivated solely by money and who could not be trusted to made decisions on the job. For these and other reasons, unions complained about 'speed-ups' and staunchly resisted managers' attempts to institute scientific management labour control systems.

And yet Taylor was not the callous advocate of machine bureaucracy that he is often portrayed as being. His Quaker background had given him a strong sense of humanity, and he genuinely believed, as is clear from his later works, that his system would better the lot of the workers. By working harder, said Taylor, they would earn more money and be able to improve their lives. His system offered every worker the incentive to earn a decent wage; he never accepted in principle what actually happened in fact, which is that as soon as productivity levels reached a certain peak, unscrupulous employers cut the rates (this problem was recognized by Gantt, who devoted some effort to trying to resolve it).

Scientific management was instituted only in about 180 factories, and only about two-thirds of those cases were reported to be successful. Still, Taylorism was enormously influential in the industrialized – and industrializing – world. *The Principles of Scientific Management* was translated into French, German, Italian, Swedish, Spanish, Dutch and Japanese. Between the world wars, the Soviets and the Germans, among others, embraced Taylorism (and Fordism) to speed economic recovery and bolster their respective economic systems. Much of the first Soviet Five-year Plan of 1928 was inspired by Taylorism. In the United States factories that assembled complicated machinery (such as cars) relied on Taylorist methods. Over time, the mind-numbing aspects of Taylorism were somewhat ameliorated as managers began to understand the complex motivations of workers. Yet modern-day corporations, from

fast-food restaurants to automobile manufacturers to express mail delivery services,
rely heavily on the methods of scientific management.

Taylor's approach was an engineer's
approach to work taken to its logical conclusion. In effect, he attempted to make
human work into a completely controlled
and mechanized function – one more component of machine production. In that sense,
his approach was a culmination of long-
standing efforts by factory owners to bring
work into conformity with the machine,
which began in America with the regimented
daily work schedules of the mill girls in early
nineteenth-century Lowell, Massachusetts.
No system subordinated the worker to the
machine more effectively than scientific management – or demonstrated more clearly the
drawbacks of doing so.

Taylor left an indelible imprint on management thought. In his own time, scientific
management was widely adopted around the
world. In the modern world, Taylor's influence is equally pervasive:

Today it is only a modest overstatement
to say that we are all Taylorized, that from
assembly-line task timed to a fraction of a
second, to lawyers recording their time by
fractions of an hour, to standardized
McDonald's hamburgers, to information
operators constrained to grant only so
many seconds per call, modern life itself
has become Taylorized.

(Kanigel 1997: 14)

Kanigel and other critics, notably political
economists such as WALLERSTEIN and cultural
critics such as MUMFORD, have damned Taylor
and his system as dehumanizing and deskilling
(although these elements were already present
in the factory system). The fact that his work
was admired by Lenin and Trotsky and
became a core feature of Soviet and later
Communist Chinese management systems is
often offered as further evidence against him.

But in fairness, it should be pointed out that
Taylor neither expected nor approved of the
subsequent abuses of his system. The following passage, from *Scientific Management*
shows both the strength of his convictions
and the ultimate fatal weaknesses of the
powerful management system he created:

Perhaps the most prominent single element in
modern scientific management is the task
idea. The work of every workman is fully
planned out by the management at least one
day in advance, and each man receives in
most cases complete written instructions,
describing in detail the task which he is to
accomplish, as well as the means to be used
in doing the work. And the work planned in
advance in this way constitutes a task which
is to be solved, as explained above, not by the
workman alone, but in almost all cases by the
joint effort of the workman and the management. This task specifies not only what is
to be done but how it is to be done and the
exact time allowed for doing it. And
whenever the workman succeeds in doing
his task right, and within the time limit specified, he receives an addition of from 30 per
cent. to 100 per cent. to his ordinary wages.
These tasks are carefully planned, so that
both good and careful work are called for in
their performance, but it is distinctly to be
understood that no workman is to be called
upon to work at a pace which would be inju-
rious to his health. The task is always so regulated that the man who is well suited to his
job will thrive while working at this rate
during a long term of years and will grow
happier and more prosperous, instead of
being overworked. Scientific management
consists very largely in preparing for and
carrying out these tasks.

(Taylor 1911: 39)

On the one hand, there is an emphasis on
teamwork, planning, coordination and efficiency; on the other hand, there is domination,
'control freakery' and an open door to abuse

and dehumanization. In the end, Frederick Winslow Taylor not only gave the world a new management system but he himself came to personify the dilemma of modern management: how to manage efficiently and humanely at the same time.

BIBLIOGRAPHY

Drury, H.B. (1915) *Scientific Management*, New York: Longmans Green.

Hoxie, R.F. (1915) *Scientific Management and Labor*, New York: D. Appleton and Co.

Kanigel, R. (1997) *The One Best Way*, New York: Viking.

Sicilia, D.B. (1993) 'Foreword', *The Principles of Scientific Management*, Norwalk, CT: The Easton Press.

Taylor, F.W. (1895) *A Piece Rate System*, New York: American Society of Mechanical Engineers; repr. Bristol: Thoemmes Press, 2000.

—— (1903) *Shop Management*, New York: Harper and Row.

—— (1911) *The Principles of Scientific Management*, New York: Harper and Row; repr. Norwalk, CT: The Easton Press, 1993.

Wrege, C.D. and Greenwood, R. (1991) *Frederick W. Taylor, the Father of Scientific Management: Myth and Reality*, Homewood, IL: Business One Irwin.

EK
DBS
MLW

TEAD, Ordway (1891–1973)

Ordway Tead was born in Somerville, Massachusetts on 10 September 1891, the son of Edward and Louise Tead. He died in Westport, Connecticut sometime in November 1973. He took his AB from Amherst College but did not go on to any higher education (although he later received ten honorary doctorates). After serving as a fellow of Amherst College from 1912–14 he co-founded the industrial consulting firm Valentine, Tead and Gregg in 1915. From 1917 to 1919 he held a position with the Bureau of Industrial Research in New York, and in 1917–18 organized and taught war emergency employment management courses at Columbia University; he went on to lecture at Columbia on a part-time basis until 1950, and was also a member of the department of industry at the New York School of Social Work from 1920 to 1929.

In 1920 Tead joined the publisher McGraw-Hill and served as their director of business publications from 1920 to 1925. He then moved to Harper and Bros, where he was editor, social and economics books, from 1925 until his retirement in 1961. He also served as chairman of the New York City Board of Education from 1938 to 1953.

Over his long career – his first books was published in 1918 and he continued to write until the early 1960s – Tead was a prolific writer and produced a number of books on industry, management, economics and politics. He is best known, however, as an early and influential writer on personnel management. *Personnel Administration: Its Principles and Practices* (1920), written with Henry C. Metcalf, became a standard text in the field and was referred to by later writers for several decades. Written immediately after the First World War, when the need for higher standards in personnel management and labour relations was becoming widely recognized, Tead and Metcalf set out, first, to explain the need for personnel management and its foundational values, and second, to show how a personnel department should be organized and managed. They define personnel management as a specific discipline:

Personnel administration is the direction and coordination of the human relations of

493

any organization with a view to getting the maximum necessary production with a minimum of effort and friction, and with a proper regard for the genuine well-being of the workers.

(Tead and Metcalf 1920: 2)

They see personnel management as a staff function, and believe the personnel department should report directly to the company president or chief executive officer. Those engaged in the field should be properly trained in the principles of psychology as well as the principles of management, and they call for the introduction of professional standards. A chapter, 'Human Values in Industry', is devoted to studying the motivations of workers in business organizations, and Tead and Metcalf enumerate a number of social values – love of family, the creative impulse, the desire to possess, the desire for approval, the desire for justice and so on – which motivate workers as individuals and which need to be understood when considering workplace relations. By treating workers as individual social beings in a non-formal rational way, Tead and Metcalf lay the grounds for what later became known as the human relations school.

BIBLIOGRAPHY
Cattell, J.M., Cattell, J. and Ross, E.E. (1941) *Leaders in Education*, 2nd edn, Lancaster, PA: The Science Press.
Tead, O. (1918) *Instincts in Industry*, New York: McGraw-Hill.
—— (1935a) *The Art of Leadership*, New York: Harper and Bros.
—— (1935b) *Creative Management*, New York: Harper and Bros.
Tead, O. and Metcalf, H. (1920) *Personnel Administration: Its Principles and Practice*, New York: McGraw-Hill.

MLW

TEAGLE, Walter Clark (1878–1962)

Walter Clark Teagle was born in Cleveland, Ohio on 1 May 1878, the son of John and Amelie Teagle. He died on 9 January 1962. He married twice, to Edith Murray in 1903 and, after her death, to Rowena Lee in 1910; there was one son from the second marriage. Teagle took a degree in chemical engineering from Cornell University in 1899 and then joined his father's oil refining company, Scofield, Shurmer and Teagle, where he worked as a chemist and later as a salesman, taking over the latter role from his father. In 1901 Teagle helped the company take a major stake in new oilfields in Texas, pushing them into the front rank of major oil producers.

Teagle's enterprise quickly attracted the attention of John D. ROCKEFELLER, whose younger brother William was married to the daughter of William Scofield, a partner of John Teagle. The Rockefellers believed that by acquiring Scofield, Shurmer and Teagle, they could acquire two assets at once: the latter company's oil fields, and the emerging management talent of the younger Teagle. Later in 1901 a buyout was agreed, with Teagle handling the latter stages himself after his father fell ill. After the sale Teagle was offered and accepted the post of head of marketing at Republic Oil, a subsidiary of Rockefeller's Standard Oil. In 1903 he was promoted to the head of Standard Oil's export division, and in 1909 joined the board of directors.

In 1911, following the prosecution of an anti-trust suit against Standard Oil by the US government, the trust was broken up into thirty-four separate companies. Teagle joined one of the larger of these, Standard Oil Company (New Jersey), commonly known as Jersey Standard. In 1914 he became president of Jersey Standard's Canadian affiliates, and in 1917 was called back to become president and chief executive officer of Jersey Standard itself. He remained in this post until 1937, then becoming chairman of the board; he retired in 1942.

As president of Standard Oil, Teagle pushed aggressively for overseas business, opening up new oil fields in Venezuela, Indonesia and Persia, and turning the former subsidiary into a major worldwide oil producer in its own right. Internally, he achieved two important reforms. First, he moved quickly to dispel the extremely hostile relations that had developed between workers and management at Jersey Standard, raising wages and setting up works consultation committees which would allows workers to both air grievances and make suggestions for improvements. Although this measure of worker participation was limited in scope, it was almost unprecedented for the US oil industry at that time, and gave Jersey Standard a measure of labour peace throughout Teagle's twenty years at the top. Second, Teagle moved to restructure the management of Jersey Standard. As described by Chandler (1962), the company Teagle inherited had a traditional management structure tightly controlled from the centre by a group of executives who still managed directly most day-to-day production and operations tasks. Teagle believed that the task of top management should be to set policy and direct strategy, and that responsibility for day-to-day operations should be devolved downwards. Aware of the reforms of Pierre DU PONT at Du Pont, Teagle set up a similar structure at Jersey Standard, setting up the various affiliates as semi-independent companies and turning Jersey Standard into a holding company, thus creating one of the first multidivisional firms in the United States. As Chandler relates, Teagle met with some opposition to these changes from within his own management and had to proceed slowly and with considerable diplomacy and tact; it was not until 1927 that the reforms were complete. A further major reorganization of the holding company itself followed in 1933.

Teagle, freed from operational responsibilities, now began to concentrate on global strategy. In 1928 he negotiated the Achnacarry Agreements with John Cadman of Anglo-Persian Oil (later British Petroleum) and Henri Deterding of Royal Dutch/Shell, effectively setting up a cartel to control a large portion of the world oil market. He also developed links with the German chemical combine I.G. Farben for the conducting of joint research, which led to some important patents and new product development for Jersey Standard. This move rebounded on Teagle after the United States entered the Second World War late in 1941, when Jersey Standard's links with the German firm were investigated by the US Justice Department, and newspapers called for Teagle to be charged with treason. He resigned as chairman of the board and retired from business altogether, devoting himself to his favourite hobby, fishing, for the remainder of his life.

Teagle made his managerial mark as a salesman, and he remained a skilled bargainer and negotiator, but his greatest asset as a manager was his ability to understand clearly how power and control flowed through organizations. He was never fully satisfied with any of his efforts at reorganization, and engaged in fairly continuous improvement of everything from the company's petroleum distribution chain to reporting and control within head office. He was also a strong team manager, and gathered around him a highly competent group of executives. The Achnacarry cartel and the agreements with I.G. Farben have tarnished his reputation; setting these aside, he was a talented organizer and highly able manager who gave his company a worldwide reputation.

BIBLIOGRAPHY

Chandler, A.D. (1962) *Strategy and Structure: Chapters in the History of the American Industrial Enterprise*, Cambridge, MA: MIT Press.

Wall, B.H. and Gibb, G.S. (1974) *Teagle of Jersey Standard*, New Orleans, LA: Tulane University Press.

MLW

THOMPSON, James David (1920–73)

James David Thompson was born in Indianapolis, Indiana on 11 January 1920, and died in Nashville, Tennessee in September 1973. He married Mary Mettenbrink in 1946. After taking his doctorate at the University of North Carolina in 1953 he held several academic posts, and was the founder-editor of the journal *Administrative Science Quarterly* in 1955. He was teaching at Vanderbilt University in Nashville at the time of his death.

Although his academic career was all too brief, Thompson's work on organization theory, particularly on interdependence, was of great importance, and continues to be widely cited. He begins from a position which suggests that all corporations operate to some degree in conditions of uncertainty:

> the central problem for complex organizations is one of coping with uncertainty ... we suggest that organizations cope with uncertainty by creating certain parts specifically to deal with it, specializing other parts in operating under conditions of certainty or near-certainty. In this case, articulation of these specialized parts becomes significant. We also suggest that technologies and environments are major sources of uncertainty for organizations, and that differences in these dimensions will result in differences in organizations.
>
> (Thompson 1967: 13)

Managers must strive to reduce uncertainty and yet simultaneously be accepting of it. Thompson was an advocate of organizations based on open systems, which he saw as being able to incorporate uncertainty by focusing on survival, rather than on goals, as is the case in closed systems. He follows CYERT and MARCH's view of organizations as coalitions of mutual interests, and says that the management of these coalitions is thus a key part of the manager's role. One of the organization survival responses in open systems is the creation of linkages, or interdependence.

According to Mackenzie and Hollensbe (1998), Thompson developed five different types of linkage. Technology/interdependence linkages are those where technology enables relationships to be developed between staff members or between staff and customers, often through long chains of complex sub-linkages. Power and authority/interdependence linkages are those whereby individuals create linkages in order to increase their own power, and reduce uncertainty and perceived risk. Task environment/interdependence linkages are those where individuals create linkages across organizational boundaries in order to make task functions easier and/or more efficient. Decision strategies/interdependence linkages are those cases where linkages are created to allow input from others to be fed into decision-making processes. Finally, goal-setting strategies/interdependence linkages are those whereby goals are discussed and agreed in a cooperative manner.

Thompson sees these interdependences as a powerful tool for reducing uncertainty within organizations. Although interdependence at some levels happens naturally, he believes organizations should do more to foster and encourage cooperation and interdependence.

BIBLIOGRAPHY
Mackenzie, K.D. and Hollensbe, E.C. (1998) 'Thompson, James David', in M. Warner (ed.), *IEBM Handbook of Management Thinking*, London: International Thomson Business Press, 661–6.
Thompson, James David (1967) *Organizations in Action: Social Science Bases of Administrative Theory*, New York: McGraw-Hill.

MLW

THOMPSON, Sanford Eleazer
(1867–1949)

Sanford Eleazer Thompson was born in Ogdensburg, New York on 13 February 1867 and died in Phoenix, Arizona on 25 February 1949. After taking a degree in engineering from the Massachusetts Institute of Technology in 1889, he held a series of posts as an engineer and draughtsman with companies in Maine and Massachusetts. In 1896 he established a private practice as a consulting engineer in Newton Highlands, Massachusetts, and in the same year began his long association with Frederick W. TAYLOR. He worked as a consultant primarily to the building and construction industry until 1917; after a period of military service in the First World War, he established Thompson and Lichtner Company, an engineering and management consultancy based in Brookline, Massachusetts, with himself as senior partner and, later, president. He served on the Hoover Commission on the Elimination of Waste in Industry in 1921, and on a number of other advisory boards and bodies through the 1920s and 1930s; during the Second World War he served as a consultant to the secretary of war.

Thompson did not work closely with Taylor in the way that Carl BARTH or Horace HATHAWAY did, but the two men were in frequent contact and had considerable influence on each other's work. Urwick (1956) suggests that Taylor had a great respect for Thompson, and frequently praised his knowledge and abilities. Thompson's main contribution to scientific management was the development of the time study. His practice was to divide jobs into the smallest possible elements and then time each element using a stopwatch. Once the times of all the elements had been recorded, Thompson would then work out systems for reducing the times of each as far as possible, to make the workflow faster and more efficient. This system, first tried out in the building industry, was later adopted by Taylor and his colleagues as an important element of

scientific management. To opponents of scientific management, however, the time study was particularly associated with the sweating of labour, and Thompson was vilified by labour union leaders in particular. Time study also caused widespread resentment in Britain on its introduction to factories there.

BIBLIOGRAPHY
Drury, H.B. (1915) *Scientific Management*, New York: Columbia University Press.
Urwick, L.F. (ed.) (1956) *The Golden Book of Management*, London: Newman Neame.

THOMSON, John Edgar (1808–74)

J. Edgar Thomson was born in Springfield Township, Delaware County, Pennsylvania on 10 February 1808 and died in Philadelphia after a series of heart attacks on 27 May 1874. Born into a middle-class family in rural Pennsylvania, Thomson did not do well academically and had little formal education. Through his surveyor father's connections, he began his work life as a rodman. He soon rose quickly within the railroad industry, becoming chief engineer on several construction projects. In 1834 he became chief engineer of the Georgia railroad and embarked upon an ambitious construction programme. That experience served as an important educational experience for Thomson, who honed his managerial and investment skills.

Thirteen years later, Thomson agreed to become chief engineer on the project to construct the Pennsylvania railroad from Philadelphia to Pittsburgh. By 1852 Thomson was president of the line, in which post he served until 1874. As president, he introduced a wide variety of innovations that served as important models for other railroads, and for other industries. By the time of the American

Civil War, he had converted much of his railroad from wood to coal; he was also the first to adopt the Westinghouse air brake system (1869). Thomson also devised and implemented new forms of corporate organization, accounting systems and many other important reforms. Simultaneously, he embarked upon an aggressive construction programme, growing the line until it incorporated some 8 per cent of the nation's railroad mileage by the time of his death.

To implement his programmes, Thomson assembled a brilliant array of managerial talent at the Pennsylvania railroad, while allying himself with a new generation of bold industrial figures outside the line. That cast included Tom Scott, Andrew CARNEGIE, Herman Haupt, George Washington Cass, Donald Cameron, John Scott, William Palmer, George PULLMAN, Jay Cooke, and the investment banking firm of Drexel, Morgan including J.P. MORGAN. His rail empire grew to include lines spanning the area from Duluth, Minnesota to Mexico. Since his earlier experience in the South, Thomson had always been attracted by cutting-edge industries in economically undeveloped or under-developed regions. Consequently, he and his allies invested heavily in Western transcontinental and related rail lines. He was an important supporter of Philadelphia investment banker Jay Cooke, whose firm controlled the Northern Pacific. Thomson's greatest, albeit short-lived, triumph was in 1871, when he became president of the Union Pacific, marking the high point of the rail empire that he and his allies controlled. His investment group at one point also controlled the Northern Pacific, Texas and Pacific, Atlantic and Pacific, Kansas Pacific and Denver and Rio Grande railroads, making him a pioneer in the rise of big business, as well as in the railroad industry, in the industrializing United States. The Pennsylvania was at the time the largest corporation in the world.

The Panic of 1873 quickly devastated that accomplishment, and Thomson. He scrambled hard to shore up the Pennsylvania, which was burdened by the heavy debt incurred by its expansion, as well as his personal fortune, which declined between 75 and 85 per cent to an estate of $1,300,000. Exhausted by his business reverses, he suffered a series of heart attacks and died in 1874. Aside from funds to support his widow and niece, he left the remainder of his estate to establish the J. Edgar Thomson Foundation to care for female orphans of railway men.

BIBLIOGRAPHY
Burgess, George H., and Kennedy, Miles C. (1949) *Centennial History of the Pennsylvania Railroad Company, 1846–1946*, Philadelphia: Pennsylvania Railroad Company.
Ward, James A. (1980) *J. Edgar Thomson: Master of the Pennsylvania*, Westport, CT: Greenwood Press.

WTW

THUROW, Lester Carl (1938–)

Lester Thurow was born in Livingston, Montana on 7 May 1938, the son of a Methodist pastor. After working in the copper mines of Montana, he studied economics at Williams College, Massachusetts and Oxford University, and finally took his Ph.D. at Harvard in 1964. From 1965 to 1968 Thurow was an assistant professor of economics at Harvard, later transferring to the Massachusetts Institute of Technology (MIT), where he taught from 1968 onward.

According to Goldsworthy (1995), Thurow chose economics as his life vocation as a means of changing society for the better. He was a strong supporter of the US Democratic Party, and served briefly as a staff economist on President Lyndon B. Johnson's Council of Economic Advisors. In 1972 he became an adviser to Democratic presidential candidate

George McGovern, when he co-authored a plan to replace the welfare system with a negative income tax. McGovern's defeat failed to discourage Thurow in his concern over an economic inequality which he saw as worsening as the affluence of the 1960s gave way to the inflation, unemployment and declining productivity of the 1970s.

By the late 1970s Thurow was resisting the neo-conservative trend in economic policy that would help elect Ronald Reagan in 1980. In that same year Thurow published *The Zero-sum Society*, his first mass-circulation book. *The Zero-sum Society* expanded his discussion of inequality to address the new issue of American industrial decline, to which it was now linked. In the late 1970s and early 1980s the American trade deficit ballooned, and imports of Japanese automobiles devastated the motor industry in Detroit. Thurow viewed the US economy like a card game in which one person's gain was another's loss. The growing disparity between rich and poor was now being aggravated by a decline in productivity. To remedy both of these, Thurow advocated deregulation of energy, affirmative action hiring of minorities, corporate income tax cuts, and government investment in new industries. *The Zero-sum Society* sold well, but its more interventionist prescriptions were clearly out of vogue in the Reagan era.

Thurow cited European and Japanese models for solutions to America's evident economic decline. He called for an industrial strategy of investment in education and job training in which government, business and labour were partners, not adversaries. These themes were restated in *Head to Head* (1992). The major struggle of the future would be an economic one between American, Japanese and European models of capitalism. He predicted that Europe, led by Germany, would have the advantage due to its population and education.

In *The Future of Capitalism* (1996) Thurow's concern with American inequalities and competitiveness expanded to include a concern with globalization and the information age. The world was shifting from an economy based on industrial capital to one based upon intellectual capital, creating a radical new form of capitalism. In spite of the evident American comeback, Thurow still distrusted reliance upon market forces and preferred to put his faith in public investment in education and research as much as he had in the 1980s.

Building Wealth, Thurow's most recent book, was published in 1999. The currents of the 1990s had made him somewhat less statist and more optimistic about American competitiveness than he had been in the previous decade. *Building Wealth* represented a continuation of the theme elaborated upon in *The Future of Capitalism*: how can egalitarian economics be adapted to the global information age? The book was written at a time when the American model of shareholder capitalism appeared invincible *vis-à-vis* its rivals. During the 1990s the American economy added $2 trillion to its gross domestic product, growing at 4 per cent a year with virtually full employment and no inflation. In contrast, the much-touted Japanese, Korean and other Asian models were undergoing a virtual meltdown. Germany and the rest of Europe, with their rigid labour policies and high-tax welfare states, were not only stagnant and having to downsize, but led the world in no major industry.

The strong criticisms of economic individualism that have always marked Thurow's thinking nevertheless remained even in 1999. The United States might enjoy full employment, but the wealth created by its bubble economy was likely to be short term. The bottom fifth of the population was heavily in debt, and real wages for most Americans were lower than in 1973.

Thurow's solution derived from his axiom that the wealth of a society was like a pyramid, which rested not upon futures speculation but upon the solid productivity of its citizens. Real wealth was now found in knowledge and the control of knowledge. The richest people in the world no longer owned factories or farms so much as the knowledge keys to vital technologies such as computers and biotechnology. The key to competitiveness, Thurow argued in *Building Wealth*, was investment in research and in training human capital.

Still teaching management and economics at MIT, Lester Thurow is an abiding and articulate defender of socially conscious capitalism aided by activist government policies, seeking to adapt both to the postindustrial age of the twenty-first century.

BIBLIOGRAPHY

Goldsworthy, J. (1995) 'Thurow, Lester C(arl) 1938–', *Contemporary Authors, New Revision Series*, New York: Gale Research, Inc., vol. 45, 441–4.

Thurow, L.C. (1980) *The Zero-sum Society: Distribution and the Possibilities for Economic Change*, New York: Basic Books.

—— (1983) *Dangerous Currents: The State of Economics*, New York: Random House.

—— (1985) *The Zero-sum Solution: Building a World-Class American Economy*, New York: Simon and Schuster.

—— (1992) *Head to Head : The Coming Economic Battle among Japan, Europe, and America*, New York: William Morrow.

—— (1996) *The Future of Capitalism: How Today's Economic Forces Shape Tomorrow's World*, New York: William Morrow.

—— (1999) *Building Wealth: The New Rules for Individuals, Companies, and Nations in a Knowledge-Based Economy*, New York: HarperCollins.

—— (2000) 'Biography', http://www.lthurow.com/bio.htm, 12 October.

—— (2003) 3) *Fortune Favours the Bold: What We Must Do to Build a New and Lasting Global Prosperity*, New York: HarpberBusiness.

DCL

TOFFLER, Alvin (1928–)

Alvin Toffler was born in New York on 28 October 1928 and grew up in Brooklyn. He had decided to be a writer by the time he was seven years old, stimulated by current affairs quiz games he played daily with his father. He worked on the school newspaper while at high school, and later enrolled at New York University to study English, where he received his BA in 1949. It was there that he met and later married Adelaide (Heidi) Farrell, with whom he shared similar political views. Heidi later became his writing partner and co-authored his books. They have a daughter, Karen.

After graduation the Tofflers moved to Cleveland, taking up factory jobs, and started an organizing campaign for a labour union. Heidi worked as union shop steward on the floor of an aluminium foundry, while Alvin worked as an assembly-line welder and millwright at a steel-making plant. They describe these experiences as an extremely important influence on their later work, and a useful antidote to highly abstract thinking. Alvin Toffler returned to writing by taking up an associate editorship at a trade magazine for the welding supply industry, and then talking his way into a job as Washington correspondent for a small Philadelphia paper. Subsequently he became Washington correspondent for various newspapers and magazines from 1957 to 1959. Toffler describes this period as 'a fantastic education, where political figures emerged from the stereotypes and appeared as human beings' (Kehoe 1997). He was made associate editor of *Fortune* magazine in New

York in 1959, but retired in 1961 to become a freelance writer, which he has remained since that time. An article he wrote in 1965 describing the condition of 'future shock' became the seed of his famous book of the same title. Toffler became a member of faculty at the New School for Social Research from 1965 to 1967, visiting professor at Cornell University in 1969, and a visiting scholar of the Russell Sage Foundation from 1969 to 1970.

Future Shock (1970) was an international bestseller within weeks of its publication. The 'future shock' of the title refers to the 'sense of shattering stress and disorientation' (Toffler in Kehoe 1997) of those subjected to too much change in too short a time. Capturing the widespread unease felt about rapid technological change in the late 1960s, it was described as a book that shaped people's perceptions of their times. Toffler argued that not only was accelerating change hard to adapt to, but that acceleration itself has effects on the system. The speed of change requires faster decision making, and all decision systems have limits to how fast they can make complex decisions. Thus the difficulty presented by the increased pace of change is, in Toffler's view, more to do with decision overload than information overload.

Toffler's study of the effects of rapid technological and social change was widely credited with astute observation and synthesis. *Future Shock* is now seen as having been an important catalyst to getting people to pay attention to what lay ahead. Toffler was awarded the McKinsey Foundation Book Award in 1970, and the Prix du Meilleur Livre Étranger (France) in 1972, both for *Future Shock*, as well as the National Council for the Advancement of Educational writing award in 1969 for *Schoolhouse in the City*.

The Tofflers characterized the 1960s as facing not so much the crisis of communism or the crisis of capitalism, but the general crisis of industrialism. They described the situation as 'beyond the age of mass production' (Toffler in Kehoe 1997) and showing signs of a 'demassification of the entire industrial process', where mass production and distribution give way to more individual and greater diversity. Their follow-up book, *The Third Wave* (1981), painted a portrait of a world being reconstructed by information. The 'third wave' denotes the technology-driven information age, emerging after the industrial age (the 'second wave'), and represents the third wave of major evolution for civilization. This book too was well received and became a bestseller. Amongst the foresight they displayed in the book were discussions of likely developments such as the Internet and teleworking. The Tofflers also described the changing role of consumers and producers, and the emergence of a combined role as 'prosumer'.

The success of their analysis has been ascribed to not having attempted to 'predict the future ... but by interpreting the present in a new way, a way that makes more sense the further into the future one goes' (Schwartz 1993) by Peter SCHWARTZ. Their ability to describe the changes they saw through the eyes of ordinary working people contributed greatly to the popularity of the books. However, critics sometimes describe their ideas as too vague and simplistic.   .

The Tofflers' wide-ranging social writings struck a chord with the young US Republican politician Newt Gingrich, and they developed a lasting friendship. Through this relationship their work has influenced Republican political thinking, although the Tofflers describe themselves as neither Republican or Democrat. The third wave they describe has yet to be acknowledged by conventional political parties, and thus expresses itself outside the party system. A principal policy recommendation of the Tofflers has been to clear the way for third-wave information-age citizens and entrepreneurs by dismantling second-wave institutions. Toffler has however acted as spokesman for Gingrich's Progress and Freedom Foundation. The Tofflers advocate devolution of power and called for 'decision division', in which decisions are divided up and allocated to the appropriate level – international, regional or local – as an important principle for governance in the information age of the twenty-first century. Toffler described this as 'the peaceful push of power and decision-making downward'.

The Tofflers' political profile and the success of their writings has put them in great demand as public speakers. Best known as they are for being popular futurists, they prefer to describe themselves as social critics. Their reflection on the nature of change facing societies has led to a renewed analysis of current social structures and institutions, and has raised awareness, on a large scale, of the need for contemplating change.

BIBLIOGRAPHY

Impoco, J. (1995) 'Speaker Gingrich's Intellectual Gurus', *US News & World Report*, 13 February.

Kehoe, J. (1997) 'More Sneak Previews from the Future Shock Gurus', *Biography Magazine*.

Schwartz, P. (1993) 'Shock Wave (Anti) Warrior', *Wired* (November).

Toffler, A. (1970) *Future Shock*, London: The Bodley Head.

Toffler, A. and Toffler, H. (1981) *The Third Wave*, London: William Collins Sons.

AJ

TOWNE, Henry Robinson (1844–1924)

Henry Robinson Towne was born in Philadelphia on 28 August 1844, into an old and respected family of the city. He died in Philadelphia on 15 October 1924. He was educated at private schools and then at the University of Pennsylvania, and Urwick (1956) says he also studied at the Sorbonne. He trained as an engineer and draughtsman at the Port Richmond Iron Works in the United States, and also studied engineering in Europe.

In 1868, while working as an engineer in Philadelphia, Towne met Linus Yale, Jr, and the two men decided to go into business on their own, founding the Yale Lock Company in Stamford, Connecticut (in 1883 this became the Yale and Towne Manufacturing Company). Yale died in 1868 shortly after the company was set up, and Towne was left in sole control as president; he held this post until 1916, stepping back then to become chairman of the board.

Early on in his career Towne had developed an appreciation of the problems of running a manufacturing business that went beyond the simple demands of engineering. He joined the American Society of Mechanical Engineers in 1882, two years after its foundation, and in 1886 presented a paper in which he called for the society to look at the problems connected with engineering shop management. He decried the present situation: 'The management of works is unorganized, is almost without literature, has no organ or medium for the interchange of experience, and is without association or organization of any kind' (quoted in Urwick 1956: 26). Although this call met with some resistance within the society, many of whose members believed that management issues were a distraction from the problems of engineering, a number of those who heard or read Towne's paper began devoting their energies to the search for scientific principles which could be applied to management; among them were Frederick HALSEY and Frederick Winslow TAYLOR.

Towne himself went on to become president of the society in 1889, in which year he led a delegation of American engineers to the Paris Exhibition, where he met, among others, Gustave Eiffel. In that year too he presented another paper to the society, this one on the subject of wages for engineering shop workers. The most common system then in use was profit sharing, which had its origins in Europe but had been widely taken up in the United States. Towne felt that the profit-sharing system was fundamentally unfair to workers for several reasons, and was thus not likely to provide sufficient motivation for more efficient working or increased output. The chief problem, he felt, was that a company's profits could be affected by many factors beyond the workers' control, such as fluctuations in raw materials prices or customer demand, or the efficiency of the managerial and sales staff in getting the goods delivered to and sold in the market.

Towne proposed a revised version of profit sharing which he called 'gain sharing'. As Drury (1915: 39) says, 'His plan was to isolate in the bookkeeping those components of cost which the laborer has it in his power to influence, and base the division of profits upon the amount in reduction of these costs.' Unlike most profit-sharing plans, Towne did not see gain sharing as being the primary means of reward for the worker; indeed, he believed that once the maximum realistic efficiency gains had been achieved, there would be no point in trying to continue the system. The system, then, was a short-term method of achieving efficiency and was never intended to be permanent.

Drury comments that the plan probably left too much power in the hands of the employer, who determined the levels of efficiency to be achieved and the level of the bonus in a somewhat arbitrary fashion. Nevertheless, Towne's idea did spark considerable interest in the subject of using bonus systems to achieve greater efficiency and output; within a decade, the much more successful systems developed by Halsey and Taylor had also been proposed in papers to the society. In 1905 Towne himself invited the Taylor team led by Carl BARTH to install the Taylor system at Yale and Towne.

BIBLIOGRAPHY

Drury, H.B. (1915) *Scientific Management*, New York: Columbia University Press.
Urwick, L.F. (1956) *The Golden Book of Management*, London: Newman Neame.

MLW

TRIPPE, Juan Terry (1899–1981)

Juan Terry Trippe was born in Sea Bright, New Jersey on 27 June 1899 and died at his apartment in New York City on 3 April 1981. He was named in memory of his mother's Venezuelan great-aunt, Juanita Terry. His father, Charles White Trippe, who was descended from a seventeenth-century English immigrant, was a New York investment banker. As a child, Trippe attended the exclusive Bovée School in New York and then was sent away at age fourteen to the Hill School in Pottstown, Pennsylvania.

When he was ten, Trippe's 'father took him to an air race over lower New York Bay. The Statue of Liberty was one of the turning pylons ... From then on young Trippe yearned to be an aviator' (Daley 1980: 6). His father made it possible in a number a ways for Trippe to pursue his dream, sending him at the age of seventeen first to the Marconi School to learn Morse code and radio, then to the Curtiss Flying School in Miami. In 1917 Trippe enrolled in Yale University but left in December to join the Marine Corps as a flying cadet, his father having pulled political strings to get him in after Trippe had failed the vision examination (Bender and Altschul 1982: 43). He may have learned a lesson, because throughout his business career Trippe appreciated the importance of, and frequently used, political connections. He subsequently was transferred to the navy, where he trained and qualified for night flying. The Armistice was signed before Trippe was sent overseas, and he returned to Yale, where he played football and golf and rowed for the crew team. However, a football injury that necessitated a risky operation to fuse the lower vertebrae of his spine ended his days as an athlete. Shortly after Trippe turned twenty-one, his father died suddenly, and within a year the bank his father had founded failed. Even with the diminished resources of the family, however, Trippe was able to finish his studies at Yale, where he remained very active, becoming editor of the

Graphic, an illustrated literary magazine, and secretary of the Yale Aeronautical Society, a flying club that purchased several war-surplus planes and engaged in intercollegiate flying competitions. Trippe graduated from Yale in 1922.

Trippe then took a job with the prominent New York investment banking house of Lee, Higginson and Company, but yearned to get into the aviation business. In 1923, with several thousand dollars of his own money and help from several relatives and friends, he incorporated Long Island Airways (capitalized at $5,000) and operated it essentially as a sightseeing and taxi service for the wealthy. When fierce competition caused the company to falter, he called on his college friends and other connections to form a new company to bid on an air-mail contract between New York and Boston. Trippe clearly never liked competition for contracts: in 1926, with help from Cornelius Vanderbilt (Sonny) Whitney, William H. Vanderbilt and William Rockefeller, he formed Eastern Air Transport, which quickly merged with its rival bidder for the contract, Colonial Airways. From that point on, as is the case in many start-up industries, the manoeuvring was fast and furious. Trippe was a visionary and began plans for immediate expansion. He created several subsidiary companies intended to serve the Midwest and Canada, which scared some of his New England associates (but not his old friends, who stuck with him) and, battling the board and feeling constrained, he left Colonial (which was later merged into American Airlines). He then looked south and linked up with the Dutch aircraft designer and manufacturer Anthony Fokker, who had his eyes on Latin America. On 2 June 1927 Trippe and his allies formed the Aviation Corporation of America (capitalized at $300,000) to bid against two rivals for the first international air-mail contract between Key West, Florida and Havana, Cuba. While one of the rivals (J.K. Montgomery's Pan American Airways) won the contract, Trippe had flown to Cuba

and obtained exclusive landing rights for his own airline from Cuba's President Machado. As had happened before and would happen many times in the future, a deal was struck among the competitors and on 23 June 1927 the Aviation Corporation of the Americas (capitalized at $500,000) was formed. Sonny Whitney was named chairman of the board and Trippe became the president and general manager. The operating subsidiary was to be known as Pan American Airways, which in 1931 became the name of the parent company (Davies 1987: 4).

An important personal effect of the successful launching of Pan Am was that his long-time love's family now felt that he was sufficiently successful to be allowed to marry into the family. In 1928 Trippe married Elizabeth Stettinius, daughter of J.P. Morgan partner Edward R. Stettinius and brother of future Secretary of State Edward R. Stettinius Jr. They went on to have four children.

After obtaining the important Key West–Havana air-mail contract, the company soon offered a passenger service on the route, expanding from there by bidding on air-mail contracts in the Caribbean, Mexico and eventually all of Latin America. It bought out or merged with foreign competitors when deemed necessary. By the end of 1929 its routes covered 18,000 kilometres (11,000 miles). On 31 July 1933, on the first occasion that Trippe appeared on the cover of *Time* magazine (he featured again in 1949), the magazine wrote of the 34-year-old Trippe:

Besides seeing his system grow to be the world's largest, President Trippe last year had the pleasant experience of seeing it make a little money. A $510,000 deficit was wiped out, with $188,000 left over. Of the company's $8,387,000 income, about $6,500,000 came from fat U.S. airmail contracts – a fact of which much is made by critics of the Post Office's airmail policy. In defense President Trippe points out that his company must develop and build all its own navigation facilities, such as the U.S. provides for domestic operators; and that it competes not against other privately-owned lines but against foreign government subsidies.

(*Time* 1933: 39)

Trippe never hesitated to call on the help of the US government, which frequently was responsive. Pan American became the 'chosen instrument' of US policy in commercially penetrating Latin America (Newton 1978).

In another important move, the company hired Charles A. Lindbergh as a technical adviser. By the early 1930s Trippe and his company, with Lindbergh's help, were exploring the possibility of opening both Pacific and Atlantic routes. A deal to wait for the British to become capable of flying the Atlantic led him to focus first on the Pacific. At the time, no aeroplane was capable of crossing such a large expanse, but Lindbergh had mapped out potential routes. In a move that was to become characteristic, Trippe chose to work closely with aircraft manufacturers to develop a flying boat (so-called because they landed on water) larger than any existing aircraft. In 1931 he accepted bids from both Sikorsky Aero Engineering and the Glenn L. Martin Company for three planes each. The Martin M-130, to be used over the Pacific, was the larger of the two. It was a four-engine monoplane capable of carrying forty-one passengers with a range of 5,000 kilometres (3,000 miles). Trippe called these aeroplanes 'Clipper Ships'. Pan American inaugurated trans-Pacific airline service in November 1935. The route of the *China Clipper* took it from San Francisco through Honolulu, Midway Island, Wake Island, Guam and finally to Manila in a mere seven days (Davies 1987: 28–39). But in order to tackle the Atlantic, Trippe needed a larger aeroplane and in 1936 ordered a design competition. Over the objections of Lindbergh, who thought the design mediocre, Trippe awarded a contract for six aeroplanes to Boeing Air Transport for its B-314, a seventy-four seat, 290-kph (180-mph) Clipper Ship with a range of 5,600 kilometres (3,500 miles) (Bender and Altschul 1982: 264).

Delivery of the plane was late and the board was not happy with Trippe's continuously expansionary policies or his failure to delegate responsibilities. The Pacific route was losing money. For ten months in 1939 Sonny Whitney took control of the company, although Trippe remained active. But it quickly became apparent that Trippe was the only executive who could master (or knew, for Trippe was known to hold information very closely) the detailed operations of the company. Control was given back to Trippe at the beginning of 1940. In the midst of this organizational turmoil, the first Transatlantic mail and passenger service, from New York to Marseilles, was launched in May and June. Service from New York to Lisbon was inaugurated soon after, but the outbreak of war disrupted air travel.

Pan American's bases and facilities, especially in Latin America, became a major military asset during the war. The airline became a full-time contract carrier for the government for its duration. For his service to the nation, Trippe was awarded the Medal of Merit from the Secretary of War. But by the end of the war, the political environment in which Pan American operated had changed drastically. The airline had to deal not only with individual governments, but also with complex governmental and intergovernmental regulatory structures. In the United States the Civil Aeronautics Board (CAB), created in 1938, was responsible for awarding international routes. The foundation for the economic regulation of international aviation in the postwar period was the Bermuda Agreement of 1946, a bilateral agreement between Britain and the United States that became a model for many similar agreements. The machinery of regulation was to be implemented by the International Air Transportation Association (IATA), re-established in 1945, and its Traffic Conferences

(Chuang 1972: 28–29). Trippe would have severe conflicts with this organization.

Any hopes that Trippe had for Pan American remaining the 'chosen instrument' of the government after the war were dashed as the CAB sought to foster competition (on service, not price) between carriers. In 1947 his attempt to merge with a major rival, Howard Hughes's Trans World Airlines, failed, but in 1950 Trippe did manage to buy out another rival, American Overseas Airlines (a subsidiary of American Airlines), leaving two major American international carriers: the newly named Pan American World Airways and TWA. With large passenger aeroplanes no longer limited to landing on water, the Clipper Ships entered history. Trippe continued to order up-to-date planes from Curtiss, Boeing and Douglas. One of Trippe's greatest innovations in postwar international air travel was to introduce, over the strenuous objections of the IATA and the carriers of other nations at first, tourist-class fares to Europe. As *Time* magazine noted on 28 March 1949:

It was the old luxury approach which limited travel by air. Trippe proclaims in his high and earnest voice: 'The average man has been the prisoner of two keepers, time and money.' Having conquered time, Trippe hopes to cut fares so that anybody with a two-week vacation – the Detroit auto mechanic and the Oak Park schoolmarm – can spend it abroad.
(*Time* 1949: 84)

He successfully introduced tourist class in 1952; and became President of IATA in 1955.

In October 1955 Trippe made another bold move, this time on equipment: Pan American was the first company to order commercial jet airliners. In order to cut fares Trippe had to expand capacity, so he ordered forty-five aircraft, twenty-five Douglas DC-8s and twenty Boeing 707s, each with twice the capacity and twice the speed of the biggest of their piston-driven predecessors. This move stunned the industry. Over the course of the next fifteen years, Pan American acquired 120 Boeing 707s. The company was growing, and Trippe contracted with a developer to construct a building that could house its corporate headquarters. The Pan American Building, designed by Walter Gropius and Pietro Bellushci and located in the heart of New York, was dedicated in 1963 (Gandt 1995: 39–43). But Trippe wanted still more unit capacity (and hence lower seat-mile costs). In April 1966 Pan American launched the era of the jumbo jet by placing an order for twenty Boeing 747s, an aeroplane twice as big (but no faster) than the 707. Trippe retired from the presidency (but remained active on the board) in 1968 before the inaugural international flight of the 747, which occurred in January 1970. But on this occasion Trippe may have extended the company too far. The recession of the early 1970s and energy crisis of the mid-1970s hurt the airlines badly, especially Pan American. Although Pan American gained domestic routes in 1980 through a merger with National Airlines, this did not save the company. Juan Trippe died in 1981, mercifully before the collapse of the airline he created.

Although he may not have had the best managerial skills, Juan Trippe was a skilled negotiator and a visionary businessman. He played consummately both within the system and against the system (or received wisdom) when necessary, and helped to bring affordable international air travel to millions who otherwise would not have had the opportunity. In 1998 he was named by *Time* as one of the twenty most influential business geniuses of the twentieth century. As James M. Landis, former chairman of the CAB, once said of him, 'Juan Trippe is thinking about the next decade ... If anybody ever flies to the moon, the very next day Trippe will ask CAB to authorize regular service' (*Time* 1949: 89).

BIBLIOGRAPHY
Bender, M. and Altschul, S. (1982) *The Chosen Instrument*, New York: Simon

and Schuster.

Chuang, R.Y. (1972) *The International Air Transport Association*, Leiden: A.W. Sijthoff.

Daley, R. (1980) *An American Saga*, New York: Random House.

Davies, R.E.G. (1987) *Pan Am: An Airline and its Aircraft*, New York: Orion Books.

Gandt, R. (1995) *Skygods: The Fall of Pan Am*, New York: William Morrow.

Kauffman, S.B. (1995) *Pan Am Pioneer*, Lubbock, TX: Texas Tech University Press.

Newton, W.P. (1978) *The Perilous Sky: U.S. Aviation Diplomacy and Latin America, 1919–1931*, Coral Gables, FL: University of Miami Press.

Time (1933), 31 July.

Time (1949), 28 March.

WJH

TRIST, Eric Lansdown (1909–93)

Eric Lansdown Trist was born in Dover, Kent on 11 September 1909 and died in Carmel, California on 4 June 1993. He was the only child of a Cornish mariner, Frederick James Lansdown Trist and Alexina Middleton, a Scot. The family lived in Dover, where Trist's father worked for the maritime defence forces. Trist attended St Martin's elementary school in Dover, and later the Dover County Boys' High School, where in his final years he was encouraged to study for a university scholarship. He won a scholarship to Pembroke College, Cambridge, where, friendless but hard working, he studied English under Ivor A. Richards and psychology under Frederick Bartlett. Trist was an outstanding scholar, and in his finals won the Distinction Star, an award which had not been given at Cambridge for many years. He acted in plays and joined the Labour Club, making a few friends but not becoming as well known as his contemporaries Anthony Blunt, Alistair Cook, Michael Redgrave and Guy Burgess.

Trist was interested in psychoanalysis. He became enthralled by the work of Kurt LEWIN and, with a first-class degree in English and the Moral Sciences Tripos, won a two-year Commonwealth Fund Fellowship to begin studies under Edward Sapir at Yale University in September 1933. While in the United States he attended seminars by Clark Hull, Sapir and Lewin, and became acquainted personally with Frederick B. Skinner. As a Commonwealth Fellow he toured the United States in summer and reported to the Fund on his impressions. After the tour he noted the deleterious impact of the business depression, and served voluntary organizations to help ameliorate the distress among the unemployed and poverty-stricken. In this work he was joined by Virginia Traylor, a woman with ideas similar to his, whom he had met shortly after arriving in America. They married shortly before he left for England in the summer of 1935.

In England Trist was saddened and surprised to find that there was no employment for him at Cambridge; he applied to be a university lecturer in New Zealand, and also to be a teacher at his old school. He then met the social psychologist Oscar Oeser, who was familiar with Kurt Lewin's work in the United States and had Pilgrim Trust research funds to study the impact of youth unemployment in Dundee, Scotland. The Trists worked for three years on that project, and in the last year Trist was acting head of the department of psychology at St Andrews University while Oeser was on leave.

At the outbreak of the Second World War Trist was employed at the Maudsley Psychiatric Hospital and housed in Mill Hill School, London. He studied mental casualties who had suffered at Dunkirk and in the 1940 London Blitz. He attracted the attention of medical men from London's Tavistock Clinic, and was able to quit Maudsley Hospital and join them by volunteering to enter the army. Trist and his wife were then sent to Edinburgh, where they helped devise the War Office Selection Boards (WOSBs), an innovative method for selecting men to be army officers (Murray 1990). Towards the end of the war Trist was a chief psychologist to the Civil Resettlement Units for repatriated soldiers who had spent the war in prison camps and were unfit for civilian life in England (Wilson *et al.* 1947).

Demobilized in September 1946, Trist and some of the Tavistock group who had worked on wartime problems helped establish a group to prepare for the reconstruction of British industry. They attracted funds from the Rockefeller Foundation, and used these to establish the Tavistock Institute of Human Relations, an entity separated from the Tavistock Clinic in order to meet the requirements of Britain's national health programme. Members of the institute were to enter psychoanalytic training and, under supervision, to apply what they knew to human and social problems in industrial organizations. Trist worked on a coal mining project which revealed the value of past practices for the modern organization of coal mining (Trist *et al.* 1963). The work attracted great interest outside Britain, but little from those in the coal industry for whom it was originally carried out. From the study, Trist developed the socio-technical system theory for organizations that would give rise to much of the work he and Fred EMERY would carry out during the 1960s in Europe and North America.

When the early research grants came to an end, the Tavistock researchers turned to consulting for industry, especially Unilever, whose executive selection procedures were much helped by the experience of the Tavistock workers in devising the WOSB techniques and group methods of training. Because there were few places where their work could be published, a journal was established, *Human Relations*, which under Trist's editorship soon acquired a notable reputation. During the 1950s Trist worked long hours in the rapidly growing Tavistock Institute, and at the same time his wife became seriously ill and eventually died. He remarried in 1959. He had had a son by his first marriage; he and his second wife Beulah, who had worked for seventeen years at the Tavistock Institute, had one daughter.

Trist retired from the Tavistock Institute in 1966. In Britain he thought his work had gone through four stages: the first centred on the social psychological studies of unemployment in Dundee; the second concerned his group dynamics work in the army and later in a psychoanalytic context; the third involved the completion of his socio-technical research in the coal industry; and finally, his work on socio-organizational ecology which began with the paper, 'The Causal Texture of Organizational Environments' (Emery and Trist 1965).

In July 1966 Trist became a professor of organizational behaviour and social ecology at the Graduate School of Business Administration at the University of California, Los Angeles. Unfortunately, he was put with a group of scholars who researched and taught management theory, a subject to which he was not attuned, and three years later Russell ACKOFF asked Trist to join him at the Management and Behavioural Science Centre at the Wharton School, University of Pennsylvania. On the east coast of the United States Trist worked on a large action research project at Rushton coal mine (Trist and Murray 1993: 417–50). The project was a mixture of failure and success. Then Trist carried out his Jamestown Study, in a manufacturing town in northwestern New York state. This was a study in industrial anthropology, in which Trist established the value of a point of stability, a 'continuant' as he would call it, in a change-making organization (Trist 1993: 209–10). This was the first time he had used the socio-technical approach at a community level in the United States. Later, in Canada, he worked on a project involved with the policy of reducing government expenditure on a community. In the early 1970s he examined the uses to which an international engineering company had put socio-technical studies, and when many of them failed, undertook the task of establishing why.

In 1974 Trist retired from the Wharton School and went to the faculty of environmental studies at York University in Toronto, where he was a professor of organizational behaviour and social ecology. He recalled this as the happiest period of his working life (Trist 1993: 211). For ten years he worked on quality of life projects, conducted search conferences and acted as a consultant to many organizations. After a short period in the department of management at the University of Minnesota, Trist retired to Gainesville, Florida, and later went to Carmel, California, where he and Beulah could be closer to their children.

While Trist's theoretical interests developed from those of a social psychologist to those of a social ecologist, his approach to social research methods moved from action research to the search conference and to action learning. His experience was both theoretical and practical, and he believed that changes in methodology would lead to new insights, and that in the social sciences more could be discovered when one used unconventional methods of enquiry. A few years before he died, Trist was asked to write an autobiography. It appeared under the title 'Guilty of Enthusiasm', the reason he believed he had not attracted sufficient interest from his British mentors to be given a chance for an academic career at Cambridge. This publication includes a full bibliography of Trist's work (Trist 1993).

Trist's final project began in the late 1980s after he had undergone heart surgery and several other major illnesses. He wanted to leave behind a comprehensive account of the Tavistock Institute's influence. He wrote to many colleagues, asking them to present their early work in a form that could be put into a three-volume anthology. This work was compiled and edited largely by Trist and his wife Beulah, Hugh Murray and Trist's lifelong colleague, Fred Emery, to whom he frequently acknowledged a deep and lasting intellectual debt (Trist and Murray 1990, 1993; Trist *et al.* 1997).

BIBLIOGRAPHY

Emery, F.E., and Trist, E.L. (1965) 'The Causal Texture of Organizational Environments', *Human Relations* 13: 21–32.

Murray, H. (1990) 'The Transformation of Selection Procedures: The War Office Selection Boards', in E.L. Trist and H. Murray (eds), *The Social Engagement of Social Science: A Tavistock Anthology: Volume I: The Socio-psychological Perspective*, Philadelphia: University of Pennsylvania Press, 45–67.

Trist, E.L. (1993) 'Guilty of Enthusiasm', in A.G. Bedeian (ed.), *Management Laureates: A Collection of Biographical Essays*. Greenwich, CT and London: JAI Press, 191–221.

Trist, E.L. and Emery, F.E. (1960) 'Socio-technical Systems', in C.W. Churchman and M. Verhurst (eds), *Management Science, Models and Techniques*, London: Pergamon Press, 83–97.

Trist, E.L. and Murray, H. (eds) (1990) *The Social Engagement of Social Science: A Tavistock Anthology: Volume I: The Socio-psychological Perspective*, Philadelphia: University of Pennsylvania Press.

—— (eds.) (1993) *The Social Engagement of Social Science: A Tavistock Anthology: Volume II: The Socio-technical Perspective*, Philadelphia: University of Pennsylvania Press.

Trist, E.L., Emery, F.E. and Murray, H. (eds) (1997) *The Social Engagement of Social Science: A Tavistock Anthology: Volume III The Socio-ecological Perspective*, Philadelphia: University of Pennsylvania.

Trist, E.L., Higgin, G., Murray, H. and Pollock, A. (1963) *Organizational Choice: Capabilities of Groups at the Coal Face under Changing Technologies: The Loss, Rediscovery and Transformation of a Work Tradition*, New York: Garland and London: Tavistock Publications.

Weisbord, M.R. (1992) *Discovering Common Ground*, San Francisco: Berrett-Koehler Publishers.

Wilson, A.T.M., Trist, E.L. and Curle, A. (1947) 'Transitional Communities and Social Reconnection: A Study of the Civil Resettlement of British Prisoners of War', *Human Relations* 1(1): 42–68 and 1(2): 240–90.

RT

TURNBO-MALONE, Annie Minerva (1869–1957)

Annie Minerva Turnbo was born in Metropolis, Illinois on 9 August 1869, the ninth child of Robert and Isabella Turnbo. She died in Chicago on 10 May 1957. Her parents, who may have been former slaves, lived in Kentucky, where Robert Turnbo served in the Union army during the American Civil War. After the war they relocated to Illinois, where Annie Turnbo was educated, although illness forced her to leave high school before graduation. While still in her teens she had developed an interest in hairdressing and hair care, and later studied chemistry in order to learn more about the subject. In 1900 she began marketing a hair-growth preparation which she made herself. Encouraged by the response, she moved to St Louis, Missouri, where she could have access to a larger market, and began making and selling her products door to door.

The St Louis World's Fair of 1904 brought her considerable publicity and she rapidly expanded her operations, touring the country to give personal demonstrations. and launching advertising campaigns in black newspapers and magazines. The product line also diversified to include hair-growth preparations, hair straighteners, pomades and beauty products. A franchising system was set up to handle sales across the country. The Poro brand was established and trademarked in 1906 in an effort to discourage counterfeit versions of her products, and in 1910 the first purpose-built factory was established; this was expanded in 1917 into the first Poro College, a combination factory, workshop and black community centre. Turnbo, who had married Aaron Malone in 1914, also became involved in philanthropy and in Republican politics. By 1924 she was the world's first female self-made millionaire; by the 1930s she was worth as much as $14 million.

An innovative and creative businesswoman in many ways, Turnbo-Malone used franchising effectively to expand her sales network. Direct employees, at the production centres and Poro Colleges that sprang up across the country, were primarily women and were recruited with the promise that work with Poro would make them self-sufficient and financially independent. Training programmes gave each recruit a set of skills that could be used outside the company as well as within it (one of Turnbo-Malone's fiercest competitors, Sarah Breedlove Walker, was trained at a Poro College). However, an incentive scheme coupled with a strong sense of community engendered strong loyalties in most employees.

Nevertheless, as a manager she had her blind spots, and one of these was financial management; Ingham and Feldman (1994) note that she was regularly swindled by both dishonest managers and outsiders who took advantage of her generosity. Among these was her husband, whom she divorced in 1927 and who then attempted to claim half of her business. She was also repeatedly sued for non-payment of federal taxes, and in 1951 her business was seized by bailiffs in lieu of unpaid taxes. Ingham and Feldman (1994) believe she suffered through not having competent professional advice. But if the final two decades of her career could serve as a case study in business decline, the first three show a remarkable grasp of the fundamentals of marketing and sales. To have come so far as she did against a twofold racial and social barrier bespeaks a considerable talent, and today Annie Turnbo-Malone still serves as a role model for managers from minority group backgrounds.

BIBLIOGRAPHY
Ingham, J.N. and Feldman, L.B. (1994) *African-American Business Leaders: A Biographical Dictionary*, Westport, CT: Greenwood Press.

MLW

TURNER, Robert Edward, III (1938–)

Ted Turner was born in Cincinnati, Ohio on 19 November 1938. He had a difficult childhood: his father was a violent alcoholic, and his sister died of lupus cerebritis when she was fifteen. When Turner was nine, his family moved to Georgia, where his father set up a billboard advertising company which made him a millionaire. Turner attended the Georgia Military Academy and McCallie School, principally distinguishing himself as a troublemaker, before majoring (to his father's disgust) in classics at Brown University. A series of escapades there culminated in 1959 with his expulsion for having a woman in his dormitory. In 1960 Turner married Judy Nye (the marriage lasted only two years) and began working long hours as manager of the Macon branch of the family firm. Within two years he had doubled sales and, when his father shot himself in 1963, Turner took control of the company. In 1964 he married Jane Shirley Smith. Turner purchased the Atlanta Braves baseball team (1976) and the Atlanta Hawks

basketball team (1977), captained the *Courageous* to victory in the 1977 America's Cup (he was drunk when he collected the winners' trophy) and was named 'Yachtsman of the Year' four times, and was voted 'Man of the Year' in 1991 by *Time* magazine. After a highly publicized romance, Turner married the actress Jane Fonda, from whom he separated in 2000. He has also established the Turner Foundation to support environmental causes, and donated $1 billion to the United Nations.

In 1970 Turner purchased Channel 17, an independent television station in Atlanta, Georgia, which was then in grave financial straits. It became the WTBS 'superstation', and by 1976 was using new satellite-to-cable delivery technology to broadcast cheap sport and entertainment to some two million viewers. Turner was ultimately broadcasting to 160 million households in some 200 countries. In 1980 he set up Cable News Network (CNN), the first television channel to broadcast news twenty-four hours a day. Through its coverage of the assassination attempt on President Reagan (1981), the *Challenger* space shuttle disaster (1986) and especially the Gulf War (1990–91), CNN's policy of getting reports back to their viewers first, and from the thick of the action, brought it awards and huge audiences. Turner went on to create Turner Network Television (1988) and the Cartoon Network (1992), before merging with Time Warner for $7.5 billion in 1995. The deal made Time Warner the largest entertainment corporation in the world; with a 10 per cent holding (more than $2.5 billion worth of stock), Turner was its largest shareholder, as well as vice-chairman and head of broadcasting.

While he has always been bold, Turner was not always successful. He is thought to have lost $20 million in failing to win a hostile bid for the CBS network, and spent $300–$500 million more than he needed in the 1986 acquisition of Metro-Goldwyn-Mayer/United Artists (MGM/UA). He courted controversy with the 'colorization' of many of the black-and-white films held in the MGM archive, and the debts incurred by the acquisition forced him to resell MGM/UA, as well as a large part of the Turner Broadcasting System (TBS), although he retained both a controlling interest in TBS and the 4,000-strong MGM film archive. Despite these occasional setbacks, however, Turner has proved remarkably adept at reading market potential and exploiting new technologies to meet and create demand.

BIBLIOGRAPHY

Bibb, P. (1994) *Ted Turner: It Ain't As Easy As It Looks*, London: Virgin.

Lowe, J. (ed.) (1999) *Ted Turner Speaks: Insights from the World's Greatest Maverick*, New York: John Wiley and Sons.

Turner, T. and Jobson, G. (1979) *The Racing Edge*, New York: Simon and Schuster.

SC

U

UEBERROTH, Peter (1937–)

Peter Ueberroth was born in Evanston, Illinois to Victor and Laura (Larson) Ueberroth on 2 September 1937. He graduated with a bachelor's degree in business administration from San Jose State University in 1959. While attending San Jose State, he played varsity water polo. He married Virginia Mae Nicolaus in September 1959. They have four children.

Ueberroth became a manager and then vice-president of Trans International. He then started an air shuttle service between Los Angeles and the 1962 Spokane World's Fair, but this business failed. Undaunted, he started a second business, Transportation Consultants, a centralized reservation service for small airlines, hotels and passenger ships. He built this company under the umbrella of a holding company, First Travel Corporation, which became the 'largest travel enterprise in North America next to American Express' (Romano 1984: D4). For this success, he was selected as president of the Los Angeles Olympic Organizing Committee (LAOOC) on 26 March 1979.

Since the Los Angeles city government refused to help finance the 1984 Olympic games, Ueberroth was forced to depend entirely upon private funding. He auctioned off the television rights and exceeded expectations by getting $225 million from ABC and $75 million from foreign broadcasters (Morrow 1985: 23). He decided to use existing facilities for as many events as possible, but when new construction was necessary, he acquired corporate sponsorships for underwriting the costs. He organized publicity events, such as the 82-day relay of the Olympic torch across the United States. The LAOOC recruited 50,000 volunteer workers. Ueberroth even waived his annual salary. Critics claimed that he commercialized the games, but the Olympics ended with a surplus of over $200 million. For his efforts, *Time* and *The Sporting News* voted him their 1984 Man of the Year.

With his Olympic success, Ueberroth's popularity soared. Major league baseball offered him a job as commissioner of baseball upon completion of his Olympic duties. Ueberroth insisted that the owners give him full control and that he would not merely serve their interests. Cowed by his public standing, the baseball owners gave him powers that they denied his predecessor, Bowie Kuhn (Lindsay 1984).

Ueberroth took over as commissioner when baseball was in turmoil, both on the field and fiscally. He cracked down on drug use, tried to reduce gambling influences in baseball, attempted to get more blacks and minorities into front-office positions, and improved the profitability of baseball's major league. One of his first successes as commissioner was in resolving the 'superstations' problem in major league baseball, whereby teams with broadcasting contracts with television stations that reached a national audience agreed to share their broadcasting revenue with other teams. Ueberroth also helped defuse a potentially lengthy strike in 1985.

In these successes, Ueberroth's forceful management style inevitably created friction with some associates and employees. During his tenure as LAOOC president, some critics considered him dictatorial. Ueberroth admitted that he was frequently forceful, but claimed that he was a decisive person with a flair for solving problems. Certainly his record reveals his managerial abilities. He demonstrates what an imaginative, strong-willed manager can do, even under seemingly unpropitious circumstances such as with the LAOOC.

Since resigning as commissioner, Ueberroth has attempted to resurrect various airlines, has headed the Rebuild Los Angeles Commission, and has taken over the Doubletree hotel chain with mixed success.

BIBLIOGRAPHY

Lindsey, R. (1984) 'Baseball Hires Strong-willed Businessman', *New York Times*, 11 March, sect. 5: 1.

Morrow, L. (1985) 'Feeling Proud Again: Olympic Organizer Peter Ueberroth Masterminds an Extraordinary Spectacle, and Shows what America's Entrepreneurial Spirit Can Do', *Time* 125(1): 20–31.

Nightingale, D. (1984) 'Peter V. Ueberroth: Baseball's Commissioner-to-be Says he Thrives on Solving Problems, Making Decisions', *The Sporting News* 199: 40.

Romano, L. (1984) 'Grand Master of the Games: Peter Ueberroth, Taking Olympic Hurdles in Stride', *Washington Post*, 11 August: D1 and D4.

Ueberroth, P. with Levin, R. and Quinn, A. (1985) *Made in America: His Own Story*, New York: William Morrow and Co.

DS

V

VAIL, Theodore Newton (1845–1920)

Theodore Newton Vail was born near Minerva, Ohio on 16 July 1845, the son of Davis and Phoebe Vail. He died in Baltimore, Maryland on 16 April 1920. He married twice, first to Emma Righter in 1869 and, after her death, to Mabel Sanderson in 1907; there was one child from the first marriage. After finishing high school Vail went to New York City, where he found work as a telegraph operator with Western Union. Returning home, from 1866 to 1868 he then became a telegraph operator with Union Pacific Railway in Wyoming Territory. Following his marriage the following year he relocated to Omaha, Nebraska and took up a post as a clerk in the railway mail service. Here he made a number of improvements to the service, including the development of a more efficient scheme for sorting the mail, achievements that came to the notice of the organization's head office in Washington. Vail was posted to Washington in 1873, becoming assistant general superintendent of railway mail in 1874 and general superintendent in 1876.

In the latter year, Vail met Gardiner Greene Alexander, an associate of Alexander Graham BELL and a shareholder in the venture which had been set up to commercialize the latter's invention of the telephone. In 1878 Vail accepted an offer to become general manager of the company, which from 1880 was known as American Bell. At the time Bell telephone was installing local exchanges in major cities, but long-distance telephone communication between cities was not yet possible. Vail, a true visionary in this respect, saw that long-distance telephone communications was an area where there was both real need and real growth; what is more, he had his experience of working with the railway mail service to know how to organize such a service, provided the technological barriers could be overcome. Staving off an attempt by his former employers, Western Union, to enter the telephone market, Vail maintained Bell's near monopoly and moved first to develop inter-city telephone communications, and second to merge and harmonize the operations of the various local networks to permit the use of standard equipment and signals. In 1885 he set up a Bell subsidiary, American Telephone & Telegraph (AT&T) to manage and integrate the various networks.

Vail had long been in conflict with his shareholders, who believed the integrated approach required too costly an investment and preferred instead to concentrate on growing local networks. As this directly conflicted with Vail's own approach, he resigned in 1997. For the next twenty years he busied himself with a variety of speculative ventures. He returned to the presidency of AT&T (which had by now bought out and owned its former parent, American Bell) at the request of J.P. MORGAN, who had acquired AT&T and was busily taking over and amalgamating other competing telephone companies under its leadership. Vail thoroughly approved of Morgan's strategy; he was not in favour of competition generally, and in infrastructure industries such as telephones he regarded it as actively harmful. With Morgan's backing, Vail continued to buy up smaller rivals and also purchased Western Union, securing a virtual monopoly of all telecommunications. Profits were ploughed into research, with constant improvement in telephone networks leading to a fully intergrated transcontinental network by 1915. The network was briefly nationalized in 1917, but was transferred back to private ownership following the end of the First World War. He died a few years later, leaving the organization he had built poised to become still more powerful later in the century under the leadership of Harold GENEEN.

Vail's philosophy of business, or at least of the telephone industry, is interesting and is worth summarizing briefly here. In a series of essays written during the war, he spelled out his vision of 'universality', with telephone exchanges across America and indeed across the world being connected into a single global communications network. He regarded the service AT&T provided as being of the utmost importance to society, and that importance transcended not only the customer's right to choose in the market but also the shareholders' right to control and profit maximization. Were competition to be unchained in the industry, he argued, the result would be competing standards and systems – what the modern computer industry refers to as 'protocols' – and the benefits of interconnectivity and universality would not be achieved. So strong were his views that he even accepted the need for a certain amount of government control, to prevent the firm from abusing its power, and also to protect this vital service from the vagaries of the market. His views foreshadow some more recent comments, especially by the Internet's creator Tim BERNERS-LEE, who has consistently argued that the management of the Internet itself should be kept out of the commercial domain and that it should be treated as a public good. His views on the need for global standards and technical protocols continue to echo around the global software and computer industries.

BIBLIOGRAPHY

Paine, A.B. (1929) *Theodore N. Vail: A Biography*, New York: Harper and Bros.
Vail, T.N. (1917) *Views on Public Questions*, New York.
────── (1918) *Wire Systems: Discussion of Electrical Intelligence*, Washington, DC.

MLW

VANDERBILT, Cornelius (1794–1877)

According to the biography by Arthur T. Vanderbilt II (1989), Cornelius Vanderbilt was born on Staten Island, New York on 27 May 1794, to Cornelius and Phoebe Vanderbilt and died in New York on 4 January 1877. The elder Cornelius, of Dutch descent, farmed and traded on his barge in New York harbour. Cornelius the younger learned to sail even as a boy, and at a very early age developed both a talent for hard work and making money. By 1810 he was able to persuade his family to help him fit out his own barge, and the 16-year-old Vanderbilt quickly established a reputation for himself as a trader. Young, brash and crude, the 'Commodore', as the older traders called him, was also fair and reliable. Even if it was stormy or raining, Vanderbilt would deliver both passengers and goods.

His business began to grow during the war of 1812 as his barge delivered food from upstate to New York City, which was besieged by the British blockade. Cornelius married his cousin Sophia in 1813. An entrepreneur, Vanderbilt was always looking for fresh opportunities to expand. He fitted out an old war-surplus schooner and began harvesting the oysters of Chesapeake Bay. Acquiring more boats, he concentrated on the East Coast trade.

Vanderbilt was never timid in terms of taking major risks in diversifying his business. No matter how much he had invested in a given business technology, he was prepared to cut his losses and start anew if he saw that a new technology was destined to replace the old. He abandoned sail for steamboats, and later steamboats for railways. This allowed him to survive and prosper long after most of his contemporaries were gone.

Seeing his sailing ships outrun by the new steamers, Vanderbilt determined to gain steamboat experience by working as a pilot and captain for one Thomas Gibbons. Here Vanderbilt made his first mark on history. His trading voyages for Gibbons intruded upon a monopoly granted by the State of New York to Robert Fulton and Robert Livingston. Vanderbilt undercut them, charging his customers one dollar as opposed to the four charged by the Fulton monopoly. The latter's attorney, Aaron Ogden, went first to the New York and then to the United States Supreme Court. The famous landmark case of *Gibbons vs Ogden* (1824), of which Vanderbilt had been the cause, established the freedom of entrepreneurs from state monopolies and helped create a unified American market.

Vanderbilt rose in the ranks of Gibbons's firm to manage four steamboats and accumulate $30,000. He then went into business for himself in 1829. By this time Vanderbilt's business strategy had fully emerged. It was a combination of undercutting his competitors and 'winning through intimidation'. Vanderbilt would slash his rates and drive his competition out of business, or threaten to. Then, when he had a monopoly, he would raise his rates. Vanderbilt was no match for the steamboat companies running from New York to Philadelphia, but he bluffed them into thinking Gibbons would support him in a rate war. They paid Vanderbilt not to compete. Vanderbilt then took on the Hudson River Steamboat Association, cutting his fares from three dollars to one dollar to ten cents – and then to nothing. Vanderbilt could sustain the losses more easily than the others, who paid him $150,000 simply to go away.

By the 1840s 'Commodore' Vanderbilt was already a millionaire operating steamships on the waterways of New York, New England and as far south as Charleston and Havana. His empire expanded still more when gold was discovered in California in 1848. Prospectors sailed from New York to cross the narrow stretch of Panama to meet ships on the other side. Vanderbilt chartered his Accessory Transit Company and built a network of ports, roads and steamship lines crossing Nicaragua by 1851. Carrying 2,000 passengers a month, he made, between 1851 and 1860, an annual profit of $1 million. As before, Vanderbilt undercut and destroyed his competition. Officials in his own Panama company tried to defraud him, so he built his own Panama line and forced the other Panama transit lines to pay him not to compete with them. Vanderbilt took the money, and then bought his rivals out.

By 1862 the 'Commodore' was worth, according to Arthur T. Vanderbilt (1989), $40 million. He was now convinced, however, that the age of the steamboat was passing and that the railroad, which he had come to despise following his own serious injury in an accident in 1833, was the industry of the future. He was sixty-eight years old, but his passion for making money was unabated. Vanderbilt was no CARNEGIE, MORGAN or ROCKEFELLER, whose business philosophies recognized making money as a means to more social ends. Vanderbilt wanted to make money for the sheer joy and prestige of doing so; it was the source of his self-esteem. This endeared him to many reared on the self-help literature of the 1870s, but it caused others like Mark Twain to castigate him severely. John D. Rockefeller made sure that his oil products were the best on the market; Vanderbilt, according to his detractors, cut corners everywhere he could. The food and conditions on his steamboats and later on his rail lines were fine for those who paid more, but the poorer passengers had to accept substandard service. There were few life preservers on his ships, and his rail cars smelled and leaked in the rain.

Vanderbilt's greatest accomplishment would be his last: the expansion of the New York Central Railway into the largest corporation in 1870s America. To his credit, he did improve rail service on the routes he bought and consolidated. He began in 1862 by purchasing the New York and Harlem Railroad. He then proceeded to acquisition of the Hudson River Railroad, which ran up to Albany. Here he met opposition from his old friend Daniel DREW, who was one of the Hudson's directors and who persuaded the New York legislature to sell the railway's shares short on the stock market. When many lawmakers had mortgaged their homes, Vanderbilt bought up the shares and kept driving the stock higher until Drew surrendered.

Vanderbilt now fought to acquire the 800-kilometre (500-mile) New York Central between Albany and Buffalo, which connected with Drew's steamboat line at Albany. In January of 1867 the Hudson froze, and only Vanderbilt's Hudson railway could move the Central's goods. Vanderbilt refused, forcing the Central to make him its president on 11 December 1867. Still not satisfied, he moved in 1868 to buy the maverick Erie Railway operated by Jay GOULD, Drew, and James Fisk, all three of whom were just as clever as and even more ruthless than Vanderbilt, bribing legislatures and embezzling from the Erie. The Erie directors issued 100,000 shares of worthless stock to deter Vanderbilt, but when he sought their arrest they fled New York State.

Vanderbilt was now master of a railroad empire stretching from New York to the Midwest. He tore up the seventeen different gauges then existing and replaced them with new British steel rails. He built bigger freight cars, added sleeping cars, terminals (including Grand Central Station) and grain elevators. The almost 1,200 kilometres (750 miles) of track included both a freight and a passenger line. The Central had 408 engines, 445 passenger cars and 9,076 freight cars. Vanderbilt dealt with the huge fixed costs by severe economies and a very small administrative staff.

By the time of his death Cornelius Vanderbilt was the last survivor of the old Jacksonian business culture. He had shown that firms could survive and prosper by constant adaptation to new economic realities. He had become the richest man in America: his estate was valued at $95 million, more than the entire United States Treasury. Not well liked in business circles due to his lack of social manner and sense of *noblesse oblige*, he nevertheless died believing himself a hero. His bequest, the Central, linked New York and Chicago and made possible the vast economies of scale that allowed other American corporations to grow and prosper.

BIBLIOGRAPHY

Brands, H.W. (1999) *Masters of Enterprise: Giants of American Business from John Jacob Astor and J.P. Morgan to Bill Gates and Oprah Winfrey*, New York: The Free Press.

Klein, M. (1986) *The Life and Legend of Jay Gould*, Baltimore, MD: Johns Hopkins University Press.

Martin, A. (1992) *Railroads Triumphant, the Growth, Rejection, and Rebirth of a Vital American Force*, New York: Oxford University Press.

Vanderbilt, A.T., II (1989) *Fortune's Children: The Fall of the House of Vanderbilt*, New York: William Morrow.

DCL

VANDERBILT, William Henry (1821–85)

William Henry Vanderbilt, the eldest son of steamboat and railway magnate Cornelius VANDERBILT, was born on Staten Island, New York on 8 May 1821. He died in New York on

8 December 1885. His upbringing and much of his youth were very harsh. In spite of his family's great wealth, 'Billy' Vanderbilt was cruelly treated by his father, who spoke to him roughly, accused him of stupidity, told him he would amount to little, and regarded him as unworthy to take part in the father's steamboat business. He attended Columbia Grammar School, which he left in 1839. He was then sent to work under Daniel DREW, where he studied accounting. In 1842 Drew offered the younger Vanderbilt a partnership in his brokerage house, but Vanderbilt declined.

Vanderbilt was then given a farm on Staten Island by his father, who felt his son lacked the ability to be a successful businessman. Working to expand the farm, he soon proved his father wrong, yet his father continued to belittle him and refused to help when Vanderbilt mortgaged the farm in the hope of expanding it. When William successfully swindled his father, however, Cornelius developed a new respect for him and paid off the mortgage (Vanderbilt 1989). In fact, it seems that Vanderbilt had inherited many of his father's entrepreneurial virtues and fewer of his vices. He made his farm the most successful on Staten Island, and raised four children from his wife, Maria Louisa Kissam. He was relatively honest and fair in his dealings with others, and more sociable than his father, whom the New York business establishment considered quite ill-mannered.

Vanderbilt became involved in railways slowly, from about 1864 on. He acquired the bankrupt Staten Island railroad, and turned it into a profit-making operation. He managed the line so meticulously and carefully that even his father was impressed enough to make him vice-president of the New York Central, and then his heir. As president of the New York Central and owner of seven-eighths of its stock, William Vanderbilt was now the richest person in America and, as ruler of its largest corporation, arguably among the most powerful; he held life-and-death power over entire businesses and cities such as Albany and Buffalo, which were utterly dependent upon the Central.

In spite of his power, William Vanderbilt was far more modest and cautious than his father. This was evident almost from the moment he inherited the Central. The mid-1870s was a trying time for American railways, which had been greatly overbuilt when the Panic of 1873 struck. By July 1877 the Pennsylvania, Erie and other lines were forced into a renewed round of wage reductions. In the first major labour war in American history, workers and the unemployed in Pennsylvania destroyed tracks, depots and freight cars. The unrest was so severe that President Rutherford B. Hayes had to send federal troops into Pennsylvania.

There was, however, no violence in New York, thanks to Vanderbilt. The Central earned almost $30 million in profits but its workers were paid only around a dollar per day. When the other lines slashed wages by 10 per cent in 1877, Vanderbilt followed suit; were he not to have done so, the Central's stock would have fallen even more than it did. But what William did, and what his father would never have done, was to attempt a conciliatory approach with his workers. He offered to divide $100,000 among those employees that refrained from striking and promised that when profits permitted he would restore their wages to the original rate. This offer was enough to maintain industrial peace: almost 9,000 of the 11,000 Central employees accepted the offer, and the Central kept running. Vanderbilt kept his word and full wages were restored by October 1877.

In spite of this triumph, which represented the first halting step towards a new philosophy of labour–management relations, Vanderbilt remained haunted by his father's reputation. During 1878–9 some of his brothers and sisters contested Cornelius's will, which had promised virtually everything to William. The resulting trial exposed much of the father's wrongdoing to the public eye. Vanderbilt was made the scapegoat for every accident on the Central, was caricatured in the press and subjected to increasing scrutiny by the New York legislature.

Cornelius Vanderbilt would have resorted to any means necessary to defeat any threat to his holdings. William Vanderbilt decided instead to reduce his interests in the business, and formed a close alliance with John Pierpont MORGAN, who sold 300,000 Central shares to British investors in return for a seat on the Central's board. Vanderbilt's conservatism limited the future growth of the Central and prevented it from becoming a truly transcontinental road. Even his remaining holdings had to be defended when Central was forced into a rate war with the Pennsylvania railroad by Jay GOULD. Gould, who had been a major rival of Cornelius Vanderbilt, now underwrote the construction of a West Shore line which went up the west bank of the Hudson and the opposite bank of the Mohawk from the Central. When the West Shore line began running in July 1883, Vanderbilt slashed his own rates, bankrupting the upstart within a year. The line was then bought by the Pennsylvania, which had far more power to hurt the Central. Both the West Shore and the Central continued to slash rates. The effect on the Central was devastating: its earnings fell from $33.7 million in 1883 to $24.4 million in 1885. Vanderbilt retaliated against the Penn by enlisting the aid of Andrew CARNEGIE and John D. ROCKEFELLER to build a line across southern Pennsylvania. At this point, both the British investors and Morgan began to panic. Vanderbilt accepted a settlement brokered by Morgan with Chauncy Depew of the Central and George Roberts of the Penn on Morgan's yacht, the *Corsair*. The Central obtained the West Shore line, the Penn got the South Pennsylvania line, and the rate war ended.

Vanderbilt's image as a conciliator was further enhanced. His style was now seen in almost every way to contrast with that of his father. He delegated power, listened to others, cultivated an open managerial style, and considered the quality of service to be as important as the bottom line. Nevertheless, William Vanderbilt was running a business and a business had to make money. When he cancelled an unprofitable mail service,

a *Chicago Tribune* reporter in October of 1882 accused him of putting the interests of his stockholders above the public. Vanderbilt's comment, 'The public be d-d', taken out of context, adorned newspapers all over the country, and was quickly adopted by journalists and politicians. What Vanderbilt actually had said was that he desired to do what he could for humanity in genera, but had to make sure he ran his railway on business principles and benefit the railway and its stockholders first. If the public needed the mail route, they needed to make it pay.

The sad result was that one of the more progressive managers of the 'Gilded Age', who protected his railway and improved labour relations, became labelled as one of the 'Robber Barons' when he was far less deserving of the title than others. At his death Vanderbilt left the Central, then worth almost $200 million, as one of the two largest and best-managed railways in the country.

BIBLIOGRAPHY
Klein, M. (1986) *The Life and Legend of Jay Gould*, Baltimore, MD: Johns Hopkins University Press.
Martin, A. (1992) *Railroads Triumphant: the Growth, Rejection, and Rebirth of a Vital American Force*, New York: Oxford University Press.
Vanderbilt, A.T., II (1989) *Fortune's Children: The Fall of the House of Vanderbilt*, New York: William Morrow and Co.

DCL

VEBLEN, Thorstein Bunde (1857–1929)

Thorstein Bunde Veblen was born in Valders, Wisconsin on 30 July 1857, the sixth of the twelve children of Thomas and Kari Veblen,

Norwegian immigrant farmers on what was then the American frontier. He died of heart disease near Menlo Park, California on 3 August 1929. When he was eight the family moved to a larger farm in Minnesota, where his father became prosperous and a pillar of the local Norwegian immigrant community. Veblen himself grew up in this community speaking little English and with little contact with or knowledge of the outside world. Even as a boy, he developed a reputation for argumentativeness and combativeness.

Veblen's father was a strong believer in the virtues of higher education, and when Veblen was seventeen he was sent to Carleton College, a strict institution with a strong focus on moral philosophy and theology. Students and faculty alike lived to a stern rule of discipline, against which Veblen rebelled frequently (he once delivered a lecture to his scandalized classmates on the virtues of cannibalism). He graduated in 1880 with a BA and a pronounced dislike of discipline and systems. After a brief spell as a teacher, he moved to the East, where he studied philosophy at Johns Hopkins University in Baltimore; among his teachers here was Charles Sanders Peirce. Failing to receive a scholarship, he then moved to Yale University, where he completed a Ph.D. on Kant and his followers. Here the dominant influence on Veblen was the sociologist William Graham Sumner, who introduced Veblen to the evolutionary theories of Charles Darwin and Herbert Spencer.

After completing his Ph.D., Veblen was unable to find teaching work and finally returned home. In 1888 he married Ellen Rolfe, the daughter of a Midwest industrialist, and the two lived together on one her father's Iowa farms, reading and studying. Veblen became strongly attracted to utopian brands of socialism, and resolved to return to university, this time to study economics. At Cornell University, tutored by the economist J. Laurence Loughlin, Veblen attempted to reconcile socialism with Spencerian evolutionary theory. When Loughlin left to found the economics department at the

University of Chicago in 1892, Veblen went with him to take up a post in the department. Chicago at the time had a very distinguished faculty, including scholars such as Loughlin, Jacques Loeb, Franz Boas and John Dewey, and here Veblen finally found a role for himself, teaching and writing in an intellectually stimulating environment. He took over the editorship of the *Journal of Political Economy*, which post he held for some seventeen years, and made the journal into one of the most stimulating and radical publications in its field. His most brilliant work, including *The Theory of the Leisure Class* (1899), was produced during this period. Despite his sarcastic, abrasive manner, Veblen attracted a circle of gifted students including Robert HOXIE and Wesley Clair MITCHELL. However, his personal relationships remained as difficult as ever – a string of affairs with female students led to the breakdown of his marriage (the Veblens finally divorced in 1911) – and the combination of private immorality and his unorthodox approach to economics meant that Veblen found little favour with the university authorities. He was promoted to assistant professor in 1900, but never reached any higher rank.

In fact, it was Veblen's private life that ultimately did him the most harm. Although the university might frown, *The Theory of the Leisure Class* and *The Theory of Business Enterprise* (1904) won widespread acclaim. However, his sexual conduct grew increasingly scandalous. Finally forced to leave Chicago in 1906, he took up an associate professorship at Stanford University, but was fired for sexual misconduct in 1909. Eventually he found a teaching post at the University of Missouri, and after his divorce remarried to Anne Bradley in 1914, but by now his health was breaking down and he was unable to take a full teaching load. The Veblen household, which now included Anne Veblen's two daughters by her first marriage, seems to have been an unusual one to say the least. Veblen believed that time spent doing household chores was time wasted; for example, he forbade the washing of dishes until every dish in the house had been used, whereupon the dirty dishes were stacked in the sink, a hose was turned on them, and they were left to dry (this, it may be supposed, allowed Veblen to view at first hand the evolution of biological organisms).

In 1918 Veblen left Missouri to take a short-lived government appointment in Washington, DC; when this ended he moved to New York, where he became editor of *The Dial*, a magazine covering political and social affairs founded by Ralph Waldo Emerson. His anti-establishment writings created a considerable stir, but this post too ended after a year (during this period his second wife became mentally ill, was declared insane in 1919, and died in 1920). Veblen then was offered a post at the School of Social Research in New York, which he held until 1927. Tired and ill, he retired to a cabin on a hillside near Menlo Park, California, where he died in 1929.

Clark (1999: 1223) describes Veblen as 'the last man in America who knew everything'. Although his subject of study was economic institutions, his approach to that subject transcended disciplines. His study of evolutionary theory, particularly the writings of Spencer, led him to believe that the principles of evolution underpinned not only growth and development in the natural world but also human behaviour. The inevitability of progress postulated by Marxist and liberal theories, and the belief in equilibrium found in neoclassical economics he regarded alike as illusions: the world of economic institutions is dynamic, evolving, and full of flux and change. Any individual discipline, such as economics, allows the study of only one aspect of institutions; to view them in the round, it is necessary to take a cross-disciplinary approach involving economics, sociology, philosophy and the natural sciences.

Veblen's evolutionary view of organizations, which draws heavily on the biological sciences, is perhaps his most famous contribution. Like the natural world, he says, the world of economic institutions is full of waste; also as in the natural world, some forms of economic behaviour are 'parasitic', living off the efforts of others (Veblen includes advertising and selling in this category, 1904: 64). Yet despite these factors, the forces of evolution and natural selection are constantly at work. He believes that the business enterprise as an institution will decay and decline naturally; there is no permanence in the world of business. This is particularly so, he says, as businesses as institutions are unstable hybrids based on freedom and liberty on the one hand (entrepreneurship), and restriction and control on the other (management). These contradictions will eventually tear them apart.

The evolutionary theory of organizations and society is described in detail in *The Theory of the Leisure Class*. In *The Theory of Business Enterprise*, Veblen applies the theory more specifically to businesses, and it is this book which is probably the most significant of his works for the study of management. Here his cross-disciplinary approach embraces not only both the technology and the machines around which modern businesses are built, but also the scientists, engineers and other technical staff who design and use the technology. This combination of technology design and use Veblen calls the 'machine process'; it is this process, he says, which is at the heart of modern industry. Without the technology, the work of the labour force is limited; without the labour force, the technology sits idle and useless. The modern business enterprise, then, has produced a symbiosis between human and machine, a whole which is greater than the sum of its parts. Therefore, rather than studying only technology or only people, we needed to study the enterprise as a combination of all the factors of production and consumption associated with it.

The urgency of this study is clear. We live, says Veblen, in an era dominated by business organizations: 'no single factor in the cultural situation has an importance equal to that of the business man and his work' (Veblen 1904: 3). Business shapes society: but the reverse is also true, and the relationship between them can be likened once again to a biological symbiosis, with the two concepts evolving in parallel. The institution has an effect on its environment, but also responds and evolves in response to environmental stimuli. Veblen, with John COMMONS, is usually described as one of the founders of institutional economics, the study of collective economic behaviour which in turn had a strong impact on the study of organization behaviour from a managerial perspective. But whereas Commons was more concerned with the internal dynamics and functioning of institutions, Veblen attempts to explain the external forces that create change and flux.

Like WALLERSTEIN, who was much influenced by him, Veblen does not believe in determinism or in any concept of an 'end' to economic development; there is no 'final form' that economic institutions will take, and he believes that developments along multiple lines are possible. Yet there is a paradox here, one which runs throughout most of his work. On the one hand, he believes economic institutions evolve through para-natural processes; but this does not stop him from roundly criticizing them on moral grounds. For example, he felt that one of the shortcomings of the business enterprise in its modern form was that its managers tended to have too much of a short-term focus on profits; he argued that the present state of the industrial arts was sufficient to provide for all human needs, and enterprise should be directed to this end rather than purely for profit. In another, sharper passage from *The Theory of Business Enterprise*, he criticizes managers for condoning wastefulness on the one hand, and 'sweating' their workers on the other:

While it is in the nature of things unavoidable that the management of industry by modern business methods should involve a large misdirection of effort and a very large waste of goods and services, it is also true that the aims and ideals to which this manner of economic life gives effect act

forcibly to offset all this incidental futility ... It makes up for its wastefulness by the added strain which it throws upon those engaged in the productive work.

(Veblen 1904: 65)

While this criticism may well have had, and still have, much validity – very similar comments can be found in the work of the leading writers of the efficiency movement, such as Harrington EMERSON and Herbert CASSON – this and similar views seem to sit uneasily with the natural science approach. This quibble aside, however, Veblen's theory of the evolution of economic institutions remains a powerful tool for the understanding of organizations, their nature and their behaviour.

BIBLIOGRAPHY
Clark, C.M.A. (1999) 'Veblen, Thorstein Bunde', in P.A. O'Hara (ed.), *Encyclopedia of Political Economy*, London: Routledge, vol. 2, 1223–6.
Daugert, S.M. (1950) *The Philosophy of Thorstein Veblen*, New York: King's Crown Press, Columbia University.
Dorfman, J. (1934) *Thorstein Veblen and His America*, New York: Viking.
Veblen, T.B. (1899) *The Theory of the Leisure Class: An Economic Study in the Evolution of Institutions*, New York: Macmillan.
—— (1904) *The Theory of Business Enterprise*, New York: Charles Scribner's Sons.
—— (1914) *The Instinct of Workmanship, and the State of the Industrial Arts*, New Brunswick, NJ: Transaction Books, 1990.
—— (1919) *The Place of Science in Modern Civilization, and Other Essays*, New Brunswick, NJ: Transaction Books, 1990.

MLW

W

WALLERSTEIN, Immanuel (1930–)

Immanuel Wallerstein was born in New York on 28 September 1930, the son of Lazar and Sally Wallerstein. He attended Columbia University, where he took his BA in 1951; after service in the US Army from 1951 to 1953, he returned to Columbia and took his MA in 1954, and his Ph.D. in 1959. He was assistant professor at Columbia from 1949 to 1963, and associate professor of sociology from 1963 to 1971. He then moved to McGill University in Montreal, where he was professor of sociology from 1971 to 1976. In the latter year he was appointed distinguished professor of sociology at Binghamton University, and was also appointed director of the Fernand Braudel Centre for the Study of Economies, Historical Systems and Civilizations. He married Beatrice Friedman in 1964; they have one daughter.

Wallerstein is the leading exponent of world system theory, and is often credited with originating the theory. This concept argues that the capitalist economic and social system has spread beyond national boundaries. Whereas traditional economics and political science linked economic and political systems to states, Wallerstein argued that capitalism had become a supra-national force, and was in the process of harmonizing all the world's varied political and economic systems into one world order. The roots of this theory go far back: Wallerstein acknowledges the influence of Marx and SCHUMPETER, while from the other end of the political spectrum BURNHAM's *The Managerial Revolution* (1941) voices many of the same views regarding the objectives of managerial capitalism. His three-volume master work, *The Modern World-system*, published over the course of the period 1974–89, spells out both the underlying theory and Wallerstein's own views of the nature of the capitalist world system.

However, Wallerstein does not view the growth and expansion of capitalism as the end of history. Indeed, in two essays, *Historical Capitalism* and *Capitalist Civilization* (1983), he argues that capitalism is itself the product of historical forces. He links the historical growth of capitalism to the accumulation of profits, surplus capital which was then re-invested in the economy. Capitalism has always been, he says, a self-expanding system; continued expansion is essential to its survival. In the eighteenth and nineteenth centuries, capitalist expansion became linked to the liberal ideal of progress, and so it was argued that progress and the accumulation and expansion of capital were inseparable. (Marxism, by contrast, argued that continuous progress was possible *without* the accumulation of capital; this, says Wallerstein, was one of several traps into which it fell.)

Wallerstein does not believe that capitalism will remain dominant, nor does he believe that progress is inevitable. Quite the contrary:

Progress is not inevitable. We are struggling for it. And the form the struggle is taking is not that of socialism versus capitalism, but that of a transition to a relatively classless society versus a transition to some new class-based mode of production. (Wallerstein 1983: 107)

With a nod towards Fernand Braudel's concept of the *longue durée*, Wallerstein says that capitalism is a historical trend, one with many strong features, but also one which has inherent weakness. Like all historical systems, it has a limited life and will ultimately give way to a new model. He suggests three possibilities: neo-feudalism, with local technologically based hierarchies (presumably engaged in rivalry); democratic fascism (in effect a form of technocracy); or a more utopian decentralized and egalitarian global society. He believes the third system to be the most desirable, but concedes too that it is the least likely (Wallerstein 1983: 162–3).

Wallerstein's work in the 1970s and 1980s both prefigured and heavily influenced globalization theory in the 1980s and 1990s. In his own writing on globalization (1991), he comments on the role of culture in globalization, describing it as the primary battleground where the struggle between globalizing and localizing forces is being fought. Culture, he says, is used by the strong to dominate the weak; here he is alluding to the spread of American culture around the world through media and advertising. Yet, he says, cultural values can also be a weapon in the hands of the weak, a core of ideas around which resistance can be built. Here he points to the growing trend towards nationalism in many countries and regions around the world (trends that have been greatly strengthened in the 1990s). Paradoxically, then, globalization is leading to both a homogeneous global culture *and* stronger and more distinctive national cultures at one and the same time.

Wallerstein is no friend of the capitalist system, but he is also a realist. His writings on globalization and the evolution of historical capitalism both have strong consequences for management. Of particular importance is his suggestion that the capitalist paradigm will end, and be succeeded by another. This will not happen in a moment; instead, just as capitalism grew and evolved over centuries, so the new dominant order will also grow and evolve. If we accept Wallerstein's view that the decline of capitalism is inevitable, then we are left to speculate, first, what this new order will be and how we will recognize it, and second, how management will have to evolve and adapt to meet the demands of the new paradigm. At all events, Wallerstein offers us a useful reminder of the need for management thinking to recognize the dynamic nature of its subject.

BIBLIOGRAPHY
Wallerstein, I. (1974–89) *The Modern World-system*, San Diego, CA: Academic Press, 3 vols.
—— (1979) *The Capitalist World-Economy*, New York: Cambridge University Press.
—— (1983) *Historical Capitalism, with Capitalist Civilization*, New York: Verso.
—— (1991) *Geopolitics and Geoculture: Essays on the Changing World-system*, Cambridge: Cambridge University Press.

MLW

WALTON, Sam (1918–92)

Sam Walton was born in Kingfisher, Oklahoma on 29 March 1918 and died in Little Rock, Arkansas on 5 April 1992. A child of the Depression, he grew up in Columbia, Missouri and worked his way through school to earn a degree in economics from the University of Missouri in 1940. He entered the US Army Reserves as a second lieutenant, then enrolled in a management training programme at the J.C. Penney department store in Des Moines, Iowa for $85 a month.

After serving in the US Army during the Second World War, Walton opened a franchised Ben Franklin five-and-ten-cent variety store in Newport, Arkansas in 1945. Over the next five years he ran a succession of Ben Franklin stores in various rural communities in the state of Arkansas. These were traditional small-town stores with relatively high price mark-ups on the merchandise. Walton suggested to Ben Franklin company executives that they introduce the stores into the urban market as a discount chain. When they rejected his proposal, Walton decided to start a chain on his own. He opened the first Wal-Mart store in Rogers, Arkansas in 1962, selling a wide variety of brand-name merchandise at low prices.

At that time, American manufacturers disliked discount retailing because it threatened their control of the market-place, and traditional retailers hated the practice because it meant having to sell more goods for the same return. However, Walton could see where retailing was going. In the same year that he opened his first Wal-Mart, S.S. Kresge launched its discount K-Mart chain in the United States, F.W. WOOLWORTH started Woolco, and Dayton Hudson launched its Target chain. Discounting had come to America on a large scale.

The big American chains located their discount stores in or near large cities, but Walton set out to prove that discounting could also work in small towns. Once committed to the concept, he resolved not just to imitate the other franchised chains but to become a leader in the discount retail field. Volume buying directly from manufacturers and a cheap and efficient delivery system enabled Wal-Mart to sell high-quality, low-cost merchandise in locations where there was little competition from other retail chains. 'Low prices every day', became Walton's slogan.

Walton strategically situated his stores in rural locations where they could simultaneously serve two or three small communities. He built large warehouses within one day's driving distance from these out-of-the-way locations to keep the stores constantly supplied with merchandise, using Wal-Mart's own trucking service. This decentralized distribution system, combined with Walton's management policy of rewarding low-paid employees with profit-sharing incentives, helped spur growth. The Wal-Mart chain rapidly expanded across rural America, with 190 stores by 1977 and 750 stores by 1984.

To grow at the pace he desired, Walton poured money into information technology, installing a sophisticated computer system to control inventory, and building a satellite network to aid in communications and tracking between stores. During the mid-1980s, Sears Roebuck and K-Mart both had more stores in operation and led Wal-Mart in total sales volume. However, Wal-Mart had a faster growth rate and eventually surpassed both of its competitors in profits earned.

In 1985 *Forbes* magazine declared Walton the richest man in America, with a personal fortune estimated at more than $9 billion. This came as a surprise to many because – operating far away from the eyes of Wall Street – Walton had spent much of his career unnoticed by the public or the press. Also, his frugal lifestyle offered no hint of his great wealth. The populist retail magnate preferred to drive a half-ton pickup truck rather than ride in a limousine. He got five-dollar haircuts at unpretentious barber shops, and stayed at budget motels on his frequent visits to his stores.

Walton stepped down as Wal-Mart's chief executive officer in 1988, but remained active as company chairman until his death. In 1991 Wal-Mart became America's largest retailer, with 1,700 stores. Total annual sales from Wal-Mart and its merchandising associates, Sam's Club, Supercenter and Hypermart, were estimated at close to $50 billion.

Walton kept wages low along with his prices. But he inspired company loyalty in employees who were motivated to believe in what Wal-Mart could accomplish, and who could retire with comfortable pensions thanks to his profit-sharing plan. By the time of his death in 1992, Walton had made his own family the wealthiest in the United States, with a net worth of more than $20 billion. After Walton's death, Wal-Mart expanded internationally, taking over discount chains in Canada, Britain and Germany to become one of the world's largest retailers.

BIBLIOGRAPHY

Huey, J. and Walton, S. (1992) *Sam Walton, Made In America: My Story*, New York: Doubleday.

Trimble, V.H. (1990) *Sam Walton: The Inside Story of America's Richest Man*, New York: Dutton.

BB

WANAMAKER, John (1838–1922)

John Wanamaker was born in Philadelphia on 11 July 1838 and died there on 12 December 1922. In the late 1850s Wanamaker and his brother-in-law, Nathan Brown, set up a small men's clothing store in Philadelphia, called Oak Hall. The business did well through the US Civil War, and Wanamaker, who became sole owner following Brown's death, expanded the store considerably. In 1876 he purchased a former depot of the Pennsylvania Railroad, apparently intending to sell or lease space to other merchants. When little interest was forthcoming, however, Wanamaker decided to convert the space instead into a department store, selling a broad range of items under a single retail brand name. Wanamaker's subsequent development of this store and a second outlet in New York, which opened in 1896, were strongly influenced by the earlier department stores of Aristide Boucicaut in Paris and William Whiteley in London. However, in bringing the department store concept to America, Wanamaker also added some American touches, possibly taken from catalogue retailing, including money-back guarantees and large-scale advertising.

Wanamaker's two stores became famous across the United States, and inspired many emulators. He himself branched out into other business activities: he was an early supporter of Henry FORD, and for a time was the distributor of Ford automobiles for the whole of the eastern seaboard, an activity that likely made him at least as much money as the department stores. President Benjamin Harrison appointed him postmaster general in 1889, and he served in this role until 1893. A well-known philanthropist, he became a much loved figure in Philadelphia society, and his funeral in 1922 was a major public occasion. Thomas EDISON was among his pallbearers.

Like the Boucicauts but unlike Whiteley, Wanamaker was a paternalist who cared deeply about his employees' physical and spiritual welfare. He was one of the first retailers to introduce company pensions funds and paid vacations. He also believed strongly that a business has duties and responsibilities to the society it serves, claiming that 'society is not constituted for the benefit of any one particular class of the population' and 'neither can any business rise or thrive except at the will of the people who are served by it' (Wanamaker 1900: 129). He goes on to argue that modern retailing has served to assist the consumer by driving prices down. In a startling passage, Wanamaker urges consumers to be vigilant and to demand the best in service and prices from retailers, for should they begin to take the service they are offered for granted, it will begin to deteriorate; only if consumers are proactive in expressing their needs, in both business and politics, will they get the service they desire:

It rests with the people to commend and command what serves them best. It is only when the fuel ceases that the fires of good government or good business methods burn out. If the public chooses to permit unwarranted taxation or restrictions upon private business enterprise, large or small, that cheapens whatever enters into the daily wants of every home, it only adds to the expense of living. Whatever the fixed charges of business are, whether they come from wastefulness or ignorance of merchant or legislator, it is the consumer who in the last analysis foots the bill. The keys of every public question are in the hands of the people, and it is the people alone who, by neglect and discouragement, slow up and stop the wheels of progress.

(Wanamaker 1900: 135)

BIBLIOGRAPHY

Wanamaker, J. (1900) 'The Evolution of Mercantile Business', *Annals of the American Academy of Political and Social Science* 15(suppl.): 123–35.

MLW

WANG An (1920–90)

Wang An was born in Shanghai on 7 February 1920, the son of an English teacher. He died in Lincoln, Massachusetts on 24 March 1990. After taking a BS degrees from Jiaotong University in 1940, he taught at the university from 1940 to 1941, then worked as an engineer with Central China Radio Works from 1941 to 1945. His parents and elder sister all perished during the Second World War. Wang left China shortly after peace was restored, having secured a studentship to Harvard University. He took an MS from Harvard in 1946, and a Ph.D. in applied physics in 1948. He married Lorraine Chiu in 1949; they had three children.

On graduating, Wang was a research fellow at Harvard from 1948 to 1951, working with one of the pioneers of the American computer industry, Howard Aiken. His work at Harvard led to a revolution in the use of magnetic core memory for information storage, increasing the speed and processing ability of computers and opening up wider possibilities for the application of computers in industrial use. In 1951 Wang left Harvard to set up Wang Laboratories, a business venture for the exploitation of his scientific work. In the commercial world, he was a pioneer in the field of computer numerical control (CNC), developing applications for lathes and milling machines and photo-typesetting equipment. He also began research into integrated circuit technology, and by the late 1950s he had developed a system for using integrated circuits as 'building blocks' for programmable computers.

In the 1960s, with the market for CNC technology moving ahead, Wang diversified into desktop calculators, launching his famous 300 series, built around integrated circuits he himself had designed. As before, when competition in the calculator market began to heat up, he diversified again, this time developing the first word processors and selling them into the mass market in the 1970s. This was followed by a move into personal computers in the 1980s. In every case, Wang was either the first mover or among the first wave, and in every case his marketing effort successfully reached new technology adopters and created a strong brand image of high technology combined with utility. In the 1980s Wang Laboratories was one of the most admired companies in the United States.

Despite the emphasis on very high technology, Wang's own management style was traditional and strongly founded on Confucian culture (see Confucius). He believed in close personal contact between managers and employees, and stressed the responsibilities of the former to the latter. He had a very strong sense of his own obligations to employees, customers and shareholders; he believed that without them, his business would not be a success, and he owed each of these groups something in return. In China, before and during the Second World War, Wang had seen and felt the consequence of the exercise of power without responsibility by the Chinese warlords and the invading Japanese army. His strong Confucian ethics were in part a consequence of that experience.

Outside authority cannot enforce ethical behaviour, said Wang; ethics must come from within the person, and from within the organization. Merely complying with law and regulation is not enough; a manager should always strive to be more ethical than he or she is required to be. He was against corruption, and refused to give bribes to get business in the Third World; he was one of the first American business leaders to shut down his operation in South Africa during apartheid. Unethical behaviour, he said, caused harm that would negate any good the company had done in the world through its products. He identified his business very strongly with himself, and demanded of the organization the same ethical standards that he aspired to personally. Quoting an ancient Chinese saying that a person's worth is judged by their reputation, Wang argued that anything that damaged the company's reputation damaged his own reputation as well.

BIBLIOGRAPHY
Krass, P. (1998) *The Book of Leadership Wisdom*, New York: John Wiley and Sons, 258–63.
Wang, A. and Linden, E. (1986) *Lessons: An Autobiography*, Reading, MA: Addison-Wesley.

MLW

WARD, Aaron Montgomery (1844–1913)

Aaron Montgomery Ward was born in Chatham, New Jersey on 17 February 1844 (there is some uncertainty about the precise date), the son of Sylvester and Julia Ward. He died in Pasadena, California on 7 December 1913. He married Elizabeth Cobb in 1872; they had one daughter. The family moved to Michigan when Ward was a boy, and his father kept a general store; Ward himself left school at fourteen and worked as a boy labourer in a brickyard. In 1861 he moved to St Joseph, Michigan and found a job in another general store; within three years he had risen to the post of store manager. In 1865 he moved to Chicago, where he worked first as a clerk in a dry goods store and then as a travelling salesman there and in St Louis, Missouri.

Ward first hit on the idea of mail-order retailing while travelling through the small towns of the Midwest in the 1860s. The quality of retail goods on offer was poor and prices were high. At the same time, the coming of the railways was putting these towns within easy reach of the large manufacturing centres of the West. He began by taking orders for goods as he travelled, buying directly from manufacturers, and selling on a cash, low-margin basis in the towns through which he travelled. As the business grew more sophisticated he began taking orders and despatching goods through the post. By cutting out a number of middlemen, Ward could bring down the retail prices of the goods he sold and still make a profit.

The Chicago Fire of 1871 wiped out his stock, but by the next year Ward was back in business with a partner, his brother-in-law George Thorne. Through his wife's family connections he developed a relationship with a Midwest farmers' cooperative, the National Grange, giving him access to the Grange's members and giving him a target market for mail-order advertising. The same formula was repeated with other groups across the country. In marketing, Ward was at pains to build up a personal relationship with his clients, many of whom were farmers and their wives in isolated communities, and who appreciated the perception of human contact; customers were always addressed by name, and letters responding to enquiries were often handwritten. Ward's famous catalogues became known as 'dream books', putting images of the manufactured consumer goods of the wealthy east before the eyes of the often poor farmers of the West, and encouraging the latter to aspire to higher things. Meanwhile behind the scenes the firm developed systems for managing stock and inventory, taking orders and despatching goods. Among his innovations here was a guarantee that customers could return their goods by post within ten days if not satisfied. Ward was and remains a model of efficient catalogue retailing, and even with often wafer-thin margins, profits grew rapidly.

Ward's story is of interest today in that the marketing and distribution problems he had to solve were very similar to those experienced by e-commerce firms from the late 1990s onward. His success can be largely attributed to his balanced approach to marketing; not only did he design a product mix and manage a promotion strategy which targeted consumers appropriately, but he also established a highly effective distribution system (this last being the Achilles heel of many 'dotcom' retailers). In his own time, Ward was far ahead of other retailers in his marketing approach, and marketing textbooks as late as the 1930s were still using Montgomery Ward as a case example for mail-order retailing.

The company was incorporated in 1889 as Montgomery Ward and Company, with Ward as president, but four years later he sold his share and retired to raise horses on his farm in Wisconsin and to spend the winters in California. The firm continued to grow rapidly under the management of George Thorne and his sons. Both Ward and his wife left sums totalling over $8 million to Northwestern University after their deaths.

BIBLIOGRAPHY

'Pursuit of a Dream: The Story of Aaron Montgomery Ward' (2000), http://www.wads.com/HTML/AaronHistory.html, 14 February 2001.

Raucher, A.R. (1999) 'Ward, Aaron Montgomery', in J.A. Garraty and M. Carnes (eds), *American National Biography*, New York: Oxford University Press, vol. 10, 619–20.

MLW

WASHINGTON, Booker Taliaferro (1856–1915)

Booker Taliaferro Washington was born in Franklin County, Virginia on 5 April 1856, the son of Jane, a slave woman, and an unidentified white man. He died of heart disease in Tuskegee, Alabama on 14 November 1915. He adopted the name Washington possibly in honour of his stepfather, Washington Ferguson, a slave who married his mother a few years later. The family were freed at the end of the American Civil War when Washington was nine, and they moved to Malden, Virginia, where his father found work in a salt refinery. Washington's life changed when, around the age of eleven or twelve, he was given a job as a houseboy at the home of General Lewis Ruffner and his wife Viola. Mrs Ruffner, a former schoolteacher, taught Washington to read and write, and arranged for his further education. He studied at the Hampton Normal and Agricultural Institute in Virginia and at the Wayland Seminary in Washington, DC, then found a job as a teacher at the Hampton Institute, where he impressed his superiors with his knowledge and ability.

In 1881 Washington was recommended for the post of principal at the Tuskegee Normal and Industrial Institute in Alabama, a new training school for black Americans. Taking over the institute from its founding, he built it up to the point where, by 1915, it had 200 staff and 2,000 students. Although Tuskegee provided mostly vocational education, it gave many black Americans valuable first experience in the world of business.

In 1900, with funding provided by Andrew CARNEGIE, Washington founded the National Negro Business League (NNBL). The NNBL sought to provide support and assistance for black-owned businesses; Washington himself took a close interest in the founding of new businesses by black owner-managers, and was personally involved with some of these. Between them, Tuskegee and the NNBL served, as Ingham and Feldman (1994: 703) put it, 'the cradle of the black middle class'. After the first generation of owner-managers following the American Civil War, there developed a gradual sense of professionalism in business management. Not a manager himself, Washington probably did more than any other individual in the United States to make the concepts of business management available to the country's black citizens.

Washington's concern was to integrate the black and white communities peacefully and through economic means, and he saw the provision of trade and management skills as the main route to this goal. Accordingly, he persistently refused to become involved in confrontationalist race politics, which earned him the admiration of many white Americans but condemnation from other leaders of the black community.

BIBLIOGRAPHY
Harlan, L.R. (1983) Booker T.
  Washington: The Wizard of Tuskegee,
  New York: Oxford University Press.
Ingham, J.N. and Feldman, L.B. (1994)
  African-American Business Leaders: A
  Biographical Dictionary, Westport, CT:
  Greenwood Press.

MLW

WATSON, Thomas John (1874–1956)

Thomas John Watson was born in East Campbell, New York on 17 February 1874, the son of Thomas Watson, a farmer, and his wife Jane. He died in New York City on 8 May 1956. He married Jeanette Kittredge in 1913, and they had three children. After finishing school Watson took a bookkeeping course at the Miller School of Commerce in Elmira, New York and in 1892 took his first job as a bookkeeper. Finding accountancy not to his taste, he became instead a travelling salesman, a career to which he was temperamentally suited and which he enjoyed; he sold various goods, including sewing machines and musical instruments and became quite successful. Retiring from the road, he and a partner set up a small chain of butcher's shops, but this ended in disaster when his partner defrauded him and then disappeared. Disposing of the company's assets, Watson returned a newly acquired cash register to the Buffalo office of the manufacturers, National Cash Register (NCR). While he was in the office, he asked for a job and was told there was a vacancy as a salesman.

Legend has it that Watson did not sell a single cash register during his first week at NCR, and his initial performance was so poor that he came close to losing his job. If true, this would not be surprising. NCR's sales policy as defined by the company's founder and owner, John PATTERSON, was very strict; salesmen were required to learn about the client's business and then explain how a cash register could help that business, an approach requiring patience and tact, and quite unlike the huckstering approach Watson had learned during his years on the road. However, he mastered the new technique and became a star salesman for NCR, rising to head the Rochester office in 1899. During the first decade of the twentieth century, NCR was threatened with increasing levels of competition as new cash register makers sprang up following the expiry of NCR's original patent. With market share declining, Patterson looked around his business for an executive who could reinvigorate the firm's sales force. He chose Watson.

Watson arrived at the head office in Daytona in 1908 and took up the post of general sales manager; by 1910 he was Patterson's deputy. Together they made an able if unscrupulous management team, buying up competitors when they could and driving them out of the market through tactics such as price discounting when they could not. In 1912 the US Department of Justice stepped in and charged Watson, Patterson and a number of other NCR executives with violation of anti-trust laws. They were convicted in 1913. The stresses of the trial and an increasingly poor relationship between Patterson and Watson, each of whom seems to have been jealous of the other, led Watson to leave NCR late in 1913.

On his departure from Dayton, Watson was promptly recruited by the New York financier Charles Flint to take over a firm he had just established, the Computing-Tabulating-Recording Company (CTR). The core of this new business was the Tabulating Machine Company founded in 1896 by Hermann Hollerith to develop tabulating machines for the US Census, amalgamated with several other similar businesses. Watson initially served as general manager, but when his anti-trust conviction was overturned on appeal in 1914, he was named president. He realized that the punched card technology developed by Hollerith was a considerable technological breakthrough, and focused the business on calculating machines. Contracts with the government and a growing number of private firms gave the business a basis for almost continuous growth, interrupted only briefly by the Great Depression. In 1924 the name was changed to International Business Machines (IBM).

Watson's initial approach to this market was much the same as it had been with NCR:

to control the market as tightly as possible. Initially, he leased his machines, rather than selling them, and one of the conditions of contract was that customers had to use IBM's own punch cards. This resulted in several anti-trust suits, the first of which compelled IBM to allow other firms to supply punch cards, and the second of which forced the company to offer its machines for sale as well as lease. Unsurprisingly, Watson developed an almost pathological hatred of government interference in business, which, given that government was one of his biggest customers, made at the time for difficult relationships. But by the 1930s he had learned a different strategy. Given its size and its large and sophisticated sales organization, IBM could always keep abreast of the market provided it could innovate and bring in new products faster than its customers.

Until the end of the 1930s Watson refused to consider abandoning punch card technology. By the 1940s, he was changing his mind, spurred on to some extent by his son, Thomas WATSON, Jr. An increasing amount of the company's resources began to be devoted to the new technology of electronic and electromechanical computers. IBM financed the design and construction of the Mark I automatic calculator by researchers at Harvard and, from 1945 onward, began development work in computers in its own laboratories. The SSEC (Selective Sequence Electronic Calculator) which was completed in 1948 was not, as has often been claimed, the world's first electromechanical computer – that honour properly belongs to Colossus, built to support the code-breaking teams at Bletchley Park in Britain during the war. But Colossus was broken up at war's end and its designs destroyed; whereas IBM was able to advance and improve on its design, and, in the 1950s, launch the first computers on the commercial market, the 700 series.

This was almost Watson's last major project as president. Increasingly ill with ulcers which had been exacerbated by heavy smoking, he retired as chairman in May 1956 and handed over to his son, dying a month later. He left behind a company that, despite various attempts by the government to restrict it, had grown in power and reach until it dominated the world computer market, a market which it had created almost single-handedly. To Watson, too, IBM owed its corporate culture, its legendary dark-suited, highly motivated sales force, and its equally famous motto, 'Think!'. He created a strong corporate culture through vehicles such as the company magazine, *Business Machines*, founded in the 1920s. A tough employer, Watson punished failure but he also liked to reward success. He stressed equal opportunities, and promoted on merit, always encouraging employees to better themselves; he rewarded those who came forward with suggestions, and at times consulted with the work force before making major decisions (Watson 1926). In an article in the magazine *System*, Watson declared:

> When a man comes into this business, no matter what his capacity, the job of being president is as accessible to him as the next one above him. And that man in this business who is not looking for and does not recognize outstanding ability on the part of a man under him, and who fails to give that ability an opportunity to express itself in greater responsibility and better work, is of no further use to us.
>
> (Watson 1926: 154)

BIBLIOGRAPHY
Rodgers, W. (1969) *Think: A Biography of the Watsons and IBM*, London: Weidenfeld and Nicolson.
Watson, T.W. (1926) 'To Make a Business Grow – Begin Growing Men!', *System* (August): 151–4.

MLW

WATSON, Thomas John, Jr (1914–93)

Thomas John Watson, Jr was born in Summit, New Jersey on 8 January 1914, the son of Thomas J. WATSON and his wife Jeannette. He died in Greenwich, Connecticut on 31 December 1993. He married Olive Cawley in 1941, and they went on to have five children. After taking a BA from Brown University in 1937, he became a salesman with his father's company, International Business Machines (IBM) in downtown New York. Upon the USA's entry into the Second World War, Watson joined the US Army Air Force and trained as a pilot, serving for a time on the air supply routes between Alaska and the Soviet Union. Returning to IBM after demobilization, he became vice-president and a director in 1946, and executive vice-president in 1949; he was made president in 1952, and succeeded his father as chairman in 1956 shortly before the latter's death.

Over the next fifteen years, Watson led IBM and America into the computer age. IBM had already been experimenting with computers in the 1940s, largely at the insistence of the younger Watson, and early in the 1950s under his presidency IBM marketed the 700 series, the world's first commercially available computers. In the 1960s he oversaw the $5 billion research programme that led to the development of the highly successful 360 series, the first computers to use integrated circuits rather than transistors. Throughout this period, IBM was not only the world's largest computer firm, it was also the most technologically advanced. The 360 series was so far ahead of anything else being produced that many of IBM's larger rivals simply exited the market; not until the 1970s would new young companies begin to challenge IBM's hegemony.

In terms of management style, Watson differed greatly from his father. He saw his own job as dealing with policy and strategy, and delegated many responsibilities, decentralizing the company to some extent. He improved pay and benefits for employees, but did not abandon the traditional corporate culture, seeing this was one of the company's great strengths. His other major change was vastly to increase the company's research and development budget, to the point where this budget alone exceeded the gross revenues of many of its rivals. IBM's research facilities became among the best in the world; it remains the only corporation to have ever won a Nobel prize for physics.

Watson suffered a heart attack in 1970, in part brought about by the strain of yet another anti-trust lawsuit. He had resigned as president in 1961 and now stepped down as chairman as well, remaining a director until 1979; but thanks to his father's aggressive stock buying in the 1920s and 1930s he was still a major shareholder and took a close interest in running the company. A Democrat and friend of President Jimmy Carter, he served from 1977 to 1979 as chairman of the General Advisory Committee on Arms Control and Disarmament, and in 1979 was named US ambassador to the Soviet Union, serving through the difficult period of the Russian invasion of Afghanistan in 1980. He resigned following the election of the Republican Ronald Reagan in 1980. During the 1980s Watson watched with some anxiety as IBM began to struggle in the face of aggressive competition. He was quietly critical of the chairman, Paul Akers, and lived to see the replacement of Akers with Lou Gerstner in 1993, but not the competitive fightback that followed.

BIBLIOGRAPHY
Rodgers, W. (1969) *Think: A Biography of the Watsons and IBM*, London: Weidenfeld and Nicolson.
Watson, T.J. and Petre, P. (1990) *Father, Son & Co.: My Life at IBM and Beyond*, New York: Bantam.

MLW

WEINBERG, Sidney James (1891–1969)

Sidney James Weinberg was born in Brooklyn, New York, the third of eleven children of Pincus Weinberg, a liquor dealer. He died in New York on 23 July 1969. He married Helen Livingston in 1920; they had two sons. Leaving school at fifteen, he found a job as an assistant porter at the banking house of Goldman Sachs; he was later promoted to office boy. 'For many years Henry Goldman and Sam Sachs [the founding partners] did not know his name and addresses him simply as "boy" (Endlich 1999: 71). He later became friendly with Paul Sachs, a junior partner and Sam Sachs's son, who was impressed with Weinberg's intelligence and initiative, and put him in charge of the mail room. He served in the US Navy during the First World War and then rejoined Goldman Sachs as a salesman for commercial paper accounts. So successful was he that by 1927 he had been made partner and in 1929 was named senior partner. He worked well with Walter Sachs, who had succeeded his father; the latter acted as managing partner, looking after the day-to-day running of the business, while Weinberg concentrated on developing the business.

The years after the Wall Street Crash of 1929 were hard ones and the bank lost money for five years in a row, but it survived where others failed. In 1932 Weinberg saw an opportunity and bought several competing commercial paper houses that were then on the brink of bankruptcy; this daring move gave Goldman Sachs dominance of the market once the economy had recovered. During the 1930s and 1940s Weinberg slowly built up a network of contacts with the largest and most powerful companies in the United States, and also with its political leaders. He became a non-executive director of a number of firms and always took his duties seriously, attending meetings and making effective, if sometimes blunt, contributions to debates on strategy and policy. During the Second World War he served as vice-chairman of the War Production Board, recruiting captains of industry to fill important posts, in which role he became known as 'the body-snatcher'. In 1947 Weinberg met Henry FORD II, who had recently taken over as chairman of the Ford Motor Company. The two men immediately became friends, despite the difference in their ages. Weinberg became a director of Ford, and played a pivotal role in the reconstruction of the firm that followed, which helped set Ford on the road to recovery after years of decline.

Weinberg 'shaped Goldman Sachs in his image', and the ways of doing business that he developed remained in place long after his death. Like his rival André MEYER at Lazards, Weinberg was an autocrat who dominated the management of the bank and was responsible for virtually all its new business. He personally controlled the vast network of relationships on which the bank depended. In an era of increasing impersonalization and technocracy in management, examples such as Weinberg and Meyer show how powerful the impact of a dominant personality can still be.

BIBLIOGRAPHY
Endlich, L. (1999) *Goldman Sachs*, New York: Alfred A. Knopf.

MLW

WELCH, John Francis, Jr (1935–)

Jack Welch was born into a middle-class family in Salem, Massachusetts, the only child of a train conductor/union leader. Welch's father worked gruelling hours to support the family, often leaving the house at 5:30 a.m. and not returning home until 7:30 p.m. His mother, Grace, and young Jack used to wait for hours at the station for the elder Welch's shift to end. Years later, Welch recalled that the talks he had with Grace at the station served as his earliest education. His mother also instilled in him a fierce will to be successful

through playing games of blackjack and gin rummy as they waited. 'I had a pal in my mom', Welch later said. 'We had a great relationship. It was a powerful, unique, wonderful, reinforcing experience' (Byrne 1998). Welch's competitive fires were evident in his teenage years when he played hockey, basketball and baseball. In high school, Welch was co-captain of the golf team, lettered in hockey and served as treasurer of the senior class. Classmates recall the five-foot eight-inch Welch as a feisty competitor who had a limitless desire to win.

Welch combined popularity and intelligence with a quick wit. He was the class jokester, but did not let his sense of humour get in the way of his education. As soon as he could read, his father brought home newspapers from the train, and young Jack devoured them, reading everything he could find. Although neither of his parents finished high school, with his mother's encouragement Welch went on to study chemical engineering at the University of Massachusetts, the first person in his family to go to college. Several professors acted as Welch's mentors and persuaded him to attend graduate school. He then went on to earn a doctorate in 1960 from the University of Illinois. When he received this degree, his mother was so proud that she called the Salem newspaper to report that 'Dr Welch' had received his Ph.D.

Welch joined General Electric (GE) as a junior engineer in Pittsfield, Massachusetts, after graduate school, GE being one of the three companies that had offered him a job. Frustrated by the company's bureaucracy, Welch quit a year later. He saw little room for advancement at GE. His boss, Reuben Gutoff, recognized Welch's talent, and talked him into staying. Gutoff promised Welch that he would provide him a more entrepreneurial work environment, but one backed with all the resources of a corporate giant. Welch stayed, and began his climb up the corporate ladder. By 1967 he was among the rising young stars in the GE plastics division. He kept a small-company mentality and entrepreneurial work ethic, fighting against the bureaucratic malaise that could stifle ideas and action. He was also willing to be combative to get what he wanted. In his early years, he helped GE Plastics grow from a $28-million afterthought into a billion-dollar business. Under Welch's leadership, the division enjoyed a 50 per cent sales increase each year from 1968 to 1977. The success of the plastics division proved that Welch deserved a spot on the fast track at GE.

Welch moved through several different divisions as he progressed. At the age of forty-two, he was named one of the corporation's three vice-chairmen and moved to corporate headquarters in Fairfield, Connecticut. After a fierce competition for the top spot, Welch was named chairman in 1981, the youngest chief executive ever appointed at GE. 'I think I'm the most happy man in America today', Welch said at the time, 'and I'm certainly the most fortunate'.

Welch attracted controversy almost immediately. He was much different than his predecessor, the British gentleman Reginald H. Jones. Welch was brash, and told managers that if they did not move fast enough, he would 'kick ass'. The new leader was obsessed with turning GE into a flexible, lean enterprise. He adopted a creed, which has since become famous in business history, that GE had to rank first or second in every market in which it did business or get out of the segment.

An early spotlight was thrust on Welch when GE purchased RCA, the parent company of NBC, in late 1985 for $6.3 billion. At the time this was the largest corporate acquisition in history, and it also brought RCA back into the family; GE had founded RCA in 1919, but had to sell the subsidiary in 1933 because of anti-trust threats. After the initial euphoria surrounding the deal wore off, however, Welch realized that NBC was losing $150 million a year, despite dominating prime-time television and news rating. After cutting costs at NBC and replacing unhappy network executives, Welch set high financial goals and turned the business around. By 1997, after more than a decade of Welch's cajoling, NBC had become the undisputed leader of network television. GE transformed NBC into a profitable company that still delivered quality programming.

Welch and GE found economic success across the board, but over his first seven years he cast off nearly 25 per cent of GE's work force, a total of more than 100,000 workers. The mass layoffs earned Welch the derogatory nickname 'Neutron Jack', after the type of nuclear weapon that kills people but leaves buildings standing. Critics equated his name with corporate greed, arrogance and contempt for workers. GE also sold off many of its traditional businesses, such as housewares and televisions, and moved into high-tech manufacturing, broadcasting and investment banking. Welch took risks that changed the company's ingrained corporate culture to fit his strategic vision.

Welch's supporters countered by noting GE's amazing return on equity. In Welch's first six years, GE's total return to shareholders reached 273 percent versus 126 percent for the S&P 500 index. Welch's goal was simple but bold: he wanted GE to become the most competitive business enterprise in the world. Despite picking up other nicknames, such as 'Trader Jack' (from his love of acquisitions), Welch transformed his image as GE's fortunes improved. Soon critics and supporters alike began regarding Welch as the best CEO in the world. Business analysts had always watched the company for the latest management trends, but under Welch's tenure, GE came to define successful business management.

Part of Welch's improving image was his emphasis on GE's Management Development Institute corporate training programme. The Crotonville training centre in Croton-on-Hudson, New York is known within GE as 'The Pit'. The company spends approximately $500 million a year on education and training at Crotonville. Welch appeared personally at the centre more than 250 times over seventeen years, and worked with 15,000 GE managers and executives. 'The students see all of Jack here, the management theorist, strategic thinker, business teacher, and corporate icon who made it to the top despite his working-class background' (Byrne 1998).

In recent years, Welch has turned his attention to 'people' issues and has worked to create a sense of informality at the company. This push has allowed communications to open across layers and fostered a sense of entrepreneurship at the world's largest corporation. Throughout the year, Welch meets with managers across several levels of leadership. The meetings also allow Welch to assess his management team, and to get his own opinions and agenda disseminated to the larger group. Each manager then takes the initiative to implement Welch's policies within the division.

When Welch needs information, he often slips into factories and plants unexpectedly. A Welch trademark has been the handwritten letters he dashes off to employees. Welch writes them out and then faxes them all over the company. He sees this extra effort as another way of breaking through the bureaucracy that initially hindered his progress at GE. In his own words, 'The idea flow from the human spirit is absolutely unlimited. All you have to do is tap into that well. I don't like to use the word efficiency. It's creativity. It's a belief that every person counts' (Byrne 1998).

Since taking over in 1981, Welch has used the company's economic diversity as a tool to move into other industries with fast-growing profits. He has reshaped GE with more than 500 acquisitions worth $53.2 billion. Welch was also instrumental in the mid- to late 1980s movement among American companies to become leaner, tougher and more globally competitive. GE's non-US sales grew to 45 per cent in 1994, up from 22 per cent in 1986.

Welch instituted a strategy called 'Six Sigma', a quality improvement programme that generates fewer than 3.4 defects per million operations in a manufacturing or service process. Despite the programme's huge investment in training thousands of employees, Welch believes Six Sigma will save GE billions of dollars. In 1995 Welch launched the programme with 200 projects, but the next year the total reached 3,000 and then 6,000 in 1997. The productivity gains and profit of $320 million exceeded Welch's expectations. As a result of Six Sigma's early success, Welch expected $750 million in net benefits in 1998.

General Electric is at the opposite end of the spectrum from online startups and Internet ventures, but after initial hesitation, Welch caught e-commerce fever with a vengeance. In early 1999 he demanded the company become an e-business and directed the company's top 500 executives to execute on that goal within several months. Welch predicted that GE could reduce its annual administrative expenses by 30 to 50 per cent within eighteen months using the Internet, trimming an estimated $10 billion from its annual budget by the time the programme is fully functional. Welch announced that e-commerce would 'change the DNA of GE forever by energizing and revitalizing every corner of this company' (Burke 2000: 55).

Beginning its own direct e-commerce programmes, GE set up a business unit called Global eXchange Services (GXS) to build online exchanges and auctions. Welch personally fuelled the growth of GXS by investing several hundred million dollars in the unit, which provides software, infrastructure systems and consulting services to companies that want to build online exchanges. Early clients included Daimler Chrysler, J.C. Penney, and Procter and Gamble. Building its own online market-places allows GE to squeeze profits from its enormous supplier base, and to use operating efficiencies to improve revenues. In 2000, GE claimed to sell over $7 billion of goods and services over the Internet and conducted over $6 billion in online auctions.

Like many great leaders, Welch is both revered and feared within GE. While there is not exactly a cult of personality, Welch realizes what his leadership symbolizes within the company and to the outside world. To many observers, Welch is as synonymous with GE as Thomas EDISON himself. Welch routinely ranks as the world's top CEO, and GE is consistently one of the most admired companies around the globe. Welch's rise at GE coincided with the media's fascination with corporate executives, and thus Welch has also been viewed as a celebrity throughout his tenure at GE, with coverage ranging from profiles on various television news programmes to stories discussing his latest golf exploits. Critics, however, claim Welch leads by fear and that GE workers have only to look back to the 'Neutron Jack' days to see to what lengths he will go to meet profit and efficiency figures.

Welch announced his retirement in November 1999. For years, the consideration of who would serve after Welch had played out like a Shakespearean drama, but speculation finally ended in November 2000 when Welch named long-time protégé Jeffrey R. Immelt president of the company. However, Welch delayed his retirement until the end of 2001 to shepherd the merger of industrial giant Honeywell, acquired in October 2000 for $45 billion, by far GE's largest purchase.

Welch's last great work at GE has been to manage this acquisition, which will leave GE with 460,000 employees and revenues of $176 billion. The deal was vintage Welch. He learned of discussions between Honeywell and GE's rival United Technologies. and quickly moved in to snatch the company away. Questions surfaced almost immediately. How would Honeywell, under-performing since its own merger with AlliedSignal less than a year earlier, fit into the high-growth culture of GE? Welch counters by pointing out the complementary areas between the two, including strengths in aircraft avionics and engines, industrial systems, power generation and plastics. The challenges will be in integrating Honeywell into GE's Six Sigma programme and achieving the efficiencies Welch demands, considering that many of Honeywell's divisions are not performing well.

GE now employs nearly half a million people in more than 100 countries. A $100 investment in GE the day Welch took over in 1981 would have been worth over $2,000 in 1998. He also achieved his goal of making GE the company with the highest market value in the world. In 1997 GE's stock value eclipsed $200 billion. In the twenty years Welch has been at the top of GE, sales have increased 360 per cent (from $28 billion to $130 billion), while profits have risen 650 per cent (from $1.7 billion to $12.7 billion). Few executives could lead an enterprise of this magnitude; Welch has been successful by almost any estimation.

It is impossible to pin down exactly how Welch has achieved the lofty goals he has set continually at GE. His competitive nature, goal-driven management style and willingness to innovate certainly play a role in his success. Perhaps, however, it is simply that Welch may be the hardest working CEO ever. While leading a company worth more than $200 billion, he also finds the time to know by sight the names and responsibilities of the top 1,000 leaders at GE. Welch meets and interacts directly with several thousand employees each year. Few business leaders of Welch's stature manage to have this kind of face-to-face time with employees.

Critics of Welch and GE have insinuated that the company manipulates its financial figures to sustain its record growth figures, and that Welch is little more than a Napoleonic figure driven by his own ego. In the mid-1980s, Welch himself labelled his management style 'constructive conflict', a willingness to argue with subordinates, a mixture of aggressiveness and arrogance. Welch also tightly controls the career moves of GE's managers. Others simply overlook Welch's tenacity and abrasive style in light of the amazing financial figures he delivers.

Much of Welch's success can be attributed to his ability to manage the complexity that GE represents, while at the same time inspiring his employees with a 'gee-whiz' attitude that exudes confidence and success. Characteristically upbeat, Welch summed up his thoughts on his career: 'I have the greatest job in the world. We go from broadcasting, engines, plastics, the power system – anything you want, we've got a game going. So from an intellectual standpoint, you're learning every day' (Huey 1999: 163). In the near future the world will learn more about Welch's success from his own perspective when Time Warner Books publishes his memoirs, for which it paid a $7-million advance. He is donating the money to charity.

In his final letter to shareholders in the GE 2000 Annual Report, Welch outlined his vision for the future of GE and provided a glimpse into the company's past successes. GE stands 'more agile than others a fraction of our size, a high-spirited company where people are free to dream and encouraged to act and to take risks.' These ideals, combined with the GE tradition of execution, encompass the 'Welch Culture' that has made General Electric a truly revolutionary corporation and Welch himself one of history's greatest business executives. Jack Welch's own story transcends business. In many respects, his life is the embodiment of the American success story, the idea that anyone can reach the top through the combination of a good upbringing, education and hard work.

BIBLIOGRAPHY

Burke, J. (2000) 'The Last Internet Company', *Red Herring* (December): 53–7.

Byrne, J. (1998) 'Jack: A Close-up Look at How America's #1 Manager Runs GE', *Business Week* (June): 90–110.

Gyon, J. (1988) 'Combative Chief: GE Chairman Welch Though Much Praised, Starts to Draw Critics', *Wall Street Journal*, 4 August.

Huey, J. (1999) 'The Jack and Herb Show', *Fortune* (January): 163.

Lowe, J. (1998) *Jack Welch Speaks: Wisdom from the World's Greatest Business Leader*, New York: John Wiley and Sons.

O'Boyle, T.F. (1998) *At Any Cost: Jack Welch, General Electric, and the Pursuit of Profit*, New York: Knopf.

Slater, R. (1999) *Jack Welch and the GE Way: Management Insights and Leadership Secrets of the Legendary CEO*, New York: McGraw-Hill.

——— (1993) *The New GE: How Jack Welch Revived an American Institution*, Homewood, IL: Business One Irwin.

Tichy, N.M. and Sherman, S. (1993) *Control Your Destiny or Someone Else Will: How Jack Welch is Making General Electric the World's Most Competitive Company*, New York: Doubleday.

BPB

WELD, Louis Dwight Harvell (b. 1882)

Louis Dwight Harvell Weld was born in Hyde Park, Massachusetts on 18 April 1882, the son of Stuart and Anna Weld. His date of death is not known. He took his AB at Bowdoin College in 1905, followed by an MA from the University of Illinois in 1907 and a Ph.D. from Columbia University in 1908. He taught economics at the University of Washington (1908–1909) and the University of Pennsylvania (1909–10), and worked with the US Census Bureau (1910–12). He was assistant professor of economics and chief of the division of agricultural economics at University of Minnesota from 1912 to 1915, and was professor of business administration at Sheffield Scientific School, Yale University, from 1915 to 1917. He joined the meat-packing firm of Swift in 1917 as manager of the commercial research department, handing over the post in 1926 to A.T. KEARNEY before returning to academia. He married Barbara Applegate in 1909, and they had two children.

Like contemporary writers on marketing, such as CHERINGTON and COPELAND, Weld saw distribution as the most important element in marketing. His own area of focus, the marketing of agricultural produce, tended to reinforce this tendency; in the United States in the early twentieth century, the major challenge facing large food producers such as Swift was how to get the product from the farm to the (primarily urban) consumer while it was still fresh. But while most of his contemporaries argued for marketing systems which used a variety of middlemen to facilitate distribution, Weld believed that middlemen were ultimately inefficient. In *The Marketing of Farm Products* (1916), he noted that the cost of marketing agricultural produce – which cost he defined as the difference between the final retail price and the proportion of that price received by farmer – could vary from 25 to 70 per cent, depending on the commodity. The period after 1910 saw rapid rises in the retail price of food, especially in urban centres, and Weld believed these rises were due to the inefficient actions of the middlemen. The problems of inefficiency were compounded by problems such as fraud, dishonesty and misrepresentation of goods, all of which worked against the interests of the consumer.

Weld argued that greater control needed to be extended over the distribution system. Although he saw a role for government in this regard, he believed the main onus lay with producing firms. He was an early proponent of what came to be known as 'integrated marketing', whereby producers established their own transport and wholesale operations. One of the first industries to take up this model was meat-packing, where large firms such as Swift and Armour found that by managing their own distribution they could move their products from the cattle ranches of the Midwest to the cities of the east more quickly and more efficiently. Weld himself played a key role in the development of this system at Swift.

However, integrated marketing had its opponents, notably the economist Lewis HANEY, who argued that the practice gave the producers excessive power over retailers and consumers, and, far from being efficient, itself generated waste in the form of excessive advertising and other marketing costs. Weld disputed Haney's views in a debate conducted in the pages of *American Economic Review* over the course of 1920–21 and was able to rebut most of the latter's arguments, and his integrated marketing model spread from meat-packing and agricultural produce into many other sectors over the course of the 1920s and 1930s.

BIBLIOGRAPHY
Assael, H. (ed.) (1979) *A Pioneer in Marketing: L.D.H. Weld, An Original Anthology*, New York: Ayer.
Weld, L.D.H. (1916) *The Marketing of Farm Products*, New York: Macmillan.
—— (1921) 'Integration in Marketing: A Reply to L.H. Haney', *American Economic Review* 11: 93–7.
Weld, L.D.H., Haney, L.H. and Gray, L.C. (1921) 'Is Large-scale Centralized Organization of Marketing in the Interest of the Public? Roundtable Discussion', *American Economic Review* 10(supp.): 215–24.

MLW

WESTINGHOUSE, George (1846–1914)

George Westinghouse was born in Central Bridge, New York on 6 October 1846 and died in New York City on 12 March 1914. At an early age, Westinghouse went to work in his father's agricultural manufacturing firm, where he developed skills in mechanical drawing, design, equipment operations, personnel management and marketing. After serving in both the army and navy during the American Civil

War, Westinghouse entered Union College to study engineering. With a mind geared more towards inventiveness than scholarly pursuits, he left Union after three months and returned to his father's shop.

While on a business trip for his father's firm, Westinghouse was delayed when two cars from the preceding train jumped the track. Noting how cumbersome and time-consuming was the task to return the cars to the rail, Westinghouse invented a device that would make this easier. Thus began a life-long association with railroads. Within three years, Westinghouse had patented one of the most important safety features of modern rail: the air brake. Using compressed air, the brake allowed an engineer to bring a train to a stop within a short space of time and distance without having to signal brakemen who would move from car to car setting mechanical brakes. The new brake averted many accidents, injuries and time-consuming delays. In 1869 the Westinghouse Air Brake Company was formed to manufacture the new invention.

In 1881 Westinghouse diversified into railway signalling, founding the Union Signal and Switch Company. Although the first signals depended on the compressed air systems familiar to his braking systems, Westinghouse soon turned to the idea of electric control. After obtaining and perfecting patents for the Gaulard and Gibbs transformer, Westinghouse once again diversified his interests, and in 1886 the Westinghouse Electric Company was born. In contrast to Thomas EDISON's emphasis on direct current systems, Westinghouse focused on alternating current, which allowed for the transmission of power over greater distances. Years of public debate concerning the safety of alternating current followed. However, by 1893 Westinghouse had won the battle, and he provided the lighting system for the 1893 Chicago World's Fair. Subsequently, Westinghouse won contracts to convert the energy of Niagara Falls into electric power, and provided equipment to power elevated trains and subway systems in several major cities. Westinghouse's initial success with alternating current was partially a result of the acquisition and refinement of Tesla's polyphase motor. As the demand for power grew, more efficient and compact generation of power was made possible by Westinghouse's acquisition and modification of the Parsons steam turbine.

Westinghouse was known as a caring employer. Indeed, Samuel Gompers, founder and first president of the American Federation of Labor, said that if all employers treated their employees with the same consideration as Westinghouse, there would be no need for unions (American Society of Mechanical Engineers 1936). In 1881 Westinghouse shortened the working week by introducing the Saturday afternoon holiday. He kept all of his men employed through the Panic of the early 1890s, and provided modern housing as well as educational and recreational facilities for employees of the Air Brake Company.

Over the course of his career Westinghouse organized sixty companies (American Society of Mechanical Engineers 1936), had significant administrative and/or financial influence over forty-three other firms (Prout 1922), and amassed 360 patents (see list in Prout 1922). He directed his inventive mind towards problems whose solutions were valuable to society. However, it was his ability to transfer his inventions, and those of others, to the manufacturing floor and ultimately to the market that led to the creation of a business empire worth more the $50 million at his death.

BIBLIOGRAPHY

American Society of Mechanical Engineers (1936) *George Westinghouse Commemoration: A Forum Presenting the Career and Achievements of George Westinghouse on the 90th Anniversary of his Birth*, New York: American Society of Mechanical Engineers.

Prout, H.G. (1922) *A Life of George*

Westinghouse, New York: Charles
Scribner's Sons.

JH

WHITEHEAD, Thomas North
(1891–1969)

Thomas North Whitehead was born in
Cambridge, UK on 31 December 1891 and
died in Cambridge, Massachusetts on 22
November 1969. He was the son of the distinguished philosopher Alfred North
Whitehead (with whom he is occasionally
confused in management literature) and his
wife Evelyn. He married Margaret Schuster in
1920, and they had three children. After
schooling at Bedales, Whitehead took his BA
from Trinity College, Cambridge in 1913. He
had completed one year of an engineering programme at University College London when
the First World War broke out; he served from
1914 to 1918 as an officer in the British Army,
with service in France and East Africa.
Returning to University College London,
Whitehead completed his engineering studies
in 1920, and from 1921 to 1931 served as a
scientific officer with the Admiralty.

In 1931 Whitehead moved to the United
States, where he was assistant professor, and
later associate professor, at Harvard Business
School until the outbreak of the Second
World War in 1939. During this period he
worked with Fritz ROETHLISBERGER, Elton
MAYO, Lyndall URWICK and others on the
famous Hawthorne Experiments at Western
Electric. In 1940 Whitehead returned to
London, where he served as adviser on
American affairs to the British Foreign Office,
and also enlisted as a private in the Home
Guard. In 1943 he returned to the United
States and resumed his post at Harvard
Business School, serving also as director of the

management training programme at Radcliff
College from 1944 to 1955. He retired in
1958, dividing his time between Britain and
the United States thereafter.

Over the course of his career, Whitehead
played a not insignificant role in the development of the human relations school and on
thinking and practice in the fields of organization behaviour and human resource management. As well as his work at Hawthorne, he
also wrote several books, the best known of
which is *Leadership in a Free Society* (1936).
Although this book shows strongly the influence of Mayo's *The Human Problems of
Industrial Civilization*, Whitehead nonetheless
has a number of significant ideas.

Whitehead believes that structure and organization are natural parts of all human activity:

> Structure arises as soon as people begin to
> do something together ... Some part of such
> a structure is logically compelled by the
> technical requirements of the group's
> activity, but other parts are not so necessi-
> tated and arise from the tendency of the
> group to enrich its social experience by a
> complication and regulation of human rela-
> tions.
>
> (Whitehead 1936: 3)

He makes a distinction between primary
groups, whose members are all in close prox-
imity and are usually known to each other,
such as villages, and secondary groups, whose
members are dispersed and not know each
other, such as large, geographically dispersed
companies. In factories members do not know
each other, but he sees them as exhibiting
primary group characteristics nonetheless; here
it is not the individual that is the unit of
analysis, but the work group or team.

It is these groups, Whitehead argues, and the
relations between them which are at the heart
of the human problems of industry. All organizations are composed of social relationships,
social action and social sentiment; even a
simple matter like exchanging tools in the

workplace is a social act. Businesses are supremely important social organizations: 'It is the economic motive *within a social setting* that is of importance to human beings, for these two together constitute social living, from which most human satisfactions are ultimately derived' (Whitehead 1936: 21). He goes on to state that:

Business is the universal pattern of stable social organization everywhere and always. Men seek the society of their fellow creatures, but they need something more than mere physical propinquity. To be satisfying, social contacts must provide for activities performed in common which lead to an immediate pleasure in the exercise of social skills and sentiments, and which are also logically ordered in terms of an ulterior purpose; by these means, stable relationships between persons become established. The ulterior purpose is to contribute to the future social situation.
(Whitehead 1936: 30, italics original)

Later he notes that businesses are now so prominent that they have to some extent usurped the functions of other organizations, and should be aware of their social responsibilities accordingly.

All successful and stable organizations, says Whitehead, have the following characteristics: (1) they yield immediate social satisfactions; (2) they are purposeful in the sense of being concerned in ordering the future; (3) they are organized around material objects or commodities for which society has a regard; and (4) they involve a high regard for certain codes of behaviour, customary ways, or ethical and moral standards and ideals (Whitehead 1936: 30).

From this standpoint Whitehead goes on to consider the nature and role of leadership. He says that 'a leader is in some sense chosen by the rest of the group as one who is both able and willing to assist them in doing that which they already wish to do' (Whitehead

1936: 69), and argues that executives are social beings – whether or not they know or accept this – and their attitudes are conditioned by society. It follows that 'social ineptitude' is the greatest problem of management, managers must manage with the consent of the managed, and failure leads to social disintegration.

BIBLIOGRAPHY
Whitehead, T.N. (1936) *Leadership in a Free Society: A Study in Human Relations Based on an Analysis of Present-day Industrial Civilization*, London: Oxford University Press.

MLW

WIENER, Norbert (1894–1964)

Norbert Wiener was born in Columbia, Missouri on 26 November 1894 and died of heart failure in Stockholm, Sweden on 18 March 1964. His father Leo was a Russian Jew who came to America at the age of nineteen to found a vegetarian socialist community. After abandoning his initial intentions and taking up a variety of manual jobs, Leo Wiener became a teacher in Kansas City. In 1896 the family moved to Boston, where Norbert Wiener's father was appointed instructor of Slavic languages and literature at Harvard University. Recognized early as a prodigy, Norbert was subjected to rigorous education imposed by his father, and their complex and ambivalent relationship marked his future intellectual and personal development. He studied mathematics and philosophy at Tufts College and Harvard University, and completed a doctorate in philosophy at the age of eighteen. He spent the following two years as a postdoctoral student and scholar, mainly in Cambridge, UK and Göttingen, Germany.

After a few years of shifting interests between philosophy, mathematics and engineering, in 1919 Wiener joined the department of mathematics at the Massachusetts Institute of Technology (MIT), where he was professor of mathematics. He spent most of his academic career at MIT. In 1935–6, while on leave from MIT, Wiener served as research professor at the Tsing Hua University in Peking. He was a member of the National Academy of Sciences from 1934 until his resignation in protest seven years later. He received three honorary doctorates and several prizes, including the Bocher Prize of the American Mathematical Society in 1933 and the US National Medal of Science in 1964. During the Second World War he developed mathematical methods in radar and navy projectiles, useful for the military, which subsequently led to great improvements in communication engineering. After the war he devoted much attention to the social and ethical aspects of the development and use of technology, and publicly refused to take part in any work for the army. Moreover, his position as an independent intellectual was characterized by an extremely sceptical view about the political, military and business elites. Wiener viewed them as 'unwilling to examine their value premises, as not educable on deeper issues' (Heims 1980: 328).

Although formally a mathematician working in highly abstract areas such as integral equations and harmonic analysis, Wiener never gave up the ambition to use mathematics as a tool of wider philosophical understanding. Even in mathematics, he never actually specialized. His numerous (over 200) scientific papers cover areas from potential theory and statistical mechanics to relativity theory and quantum mechanics. In Wiener's view, mathematical theories could be used for the formulation of general principles that govern both human and non-human systems; an intuition that would eventually lead to the new, interdisciplinary science of cybernetics. The breadth of his interests proved to be both

a blessing and a curse. In his research papers he covered a vast range of innovative topics in mathematics and theoretical physics, but he was also occasionally criticized for an alleged lack of order. He was also a rather poor lecturer, a feature related to his absent-minded personality, but perhaps also to his relentless need to search for connections between seemingly disparate issues.

However, it was precisely the complexity and holistic nature of his views which made him a driving force in formulating and popularizing the principles of cybernetics. And his perhaps paradoxical ability to reach the general reading audience – which was demonstrated both in the popularizing of various scientific and social issues, and in his autobiographical prose (*Ex-prodigy*, 1952; *I am a Mathematician*, 1956) – further cemented his central role in the new scientific discipline. Wiener discussed his initial insights with the Mexican physiologist Arturo Rosenblueth, and in a series of scientific conferences, held between 1946 and 1953, with an interdisciplinary group of scholars including the anthropologist Gregory Bateson and the founders of game theory, John von Neumann and Oskar Morgenstern.

Wiener presented the foundations of cybernetics in his book *Cybernetics: Or Control and Communication in the Animal and the Machine* (1948). This rather short book was a report on recent developments in science and technology. It started with a discussion of the nature of time and the development of statistical mechanics, but the main focus was on information and communication theory. Consequently, it also dealt with models of the brain and computers. Although the concepts in use originated from physics and electrical engineering, Wiener also applied them in areas such as psychopathology, politics and society. This breadth of topic becomes understandable when we consider one of the central postulates of the book. Wiener (1948: 187) wrote 'that any organism is held together ... by possession of means for the acquisition, use, retention, and transmission of information'. By drawing parallels and demonstrating links between biological systems and the systems produced by human beings (including both the machines and the systems of communication and interaction in society), Wiener tackled the main issue of 'control and communication' (or, using a modern term, self-regulation) of all systems.

Analysis of the common features of self-regulation of complex and probabilistic systems (whose behaviour does not follow a fixed pattern of events) required an adequate conceptual framework. An important role in it was given to the ideas of feedback and homeostasis. Feedback loops describe the link between the information fed into a system and the information coming out of the system; since the process is cyclical, the output influences the subsequent input and vice versa. The feedback mechanism continuously measures the difference between the actual and the desired situation, and either reduces this difference (so-called negative feedback) or increases it (positive feedback). Homeostasis involves a process of control of the system in which the certain variables are held between desired limits. That gives systems an important degree of stability, and hence preserves their vital functions, which is, for instance, crucial for living organisms. In spite of its partly mathematical and technical content, *Cybernetics* became a notable success. In his next book on the subject, *The Human Use of Human Beings: Cybernetics and Society* (1950), Wiener eliminated the technical jargon and concentrated on the human and social implications of his thinking. His final work, *God and Golem, Inc.* (1964) was a further exploration of cybernetics in the context of society, ethics and religion. He remains known as the 'father of cybernetics'.

The concepts and principles of cybernetics can be applied to various complex systems: the brain, the machine, the company and the whole economy alike. Consequently, these concepts have been found useful in an extremely wide range of disciplines, including biology, medicine, anthropology, ecology, economics and management. When it comes to management, an important application of Wiener's ideas can be found in the work of Stafford Beer. In *Cybernetics and Management* (1959), Beer demonstrated some ways of using cybernetics in the analysis of management issues, whereas in his later writings he developed the 'viable system model', a tool for analysis and design of complex business and non-business organizations (*Brain of the Firm*, 1981; *Diagnosing the System for Organisations*, 1985). Moreover, in its more colloquial use, the term 'feedback' has pervaded the modern approach to thinking, problem solving and communication. In management, flattening organizational hierarchies and the need for employees to play an active role at various hierarchical levels of the organization have contributed to the wide use of the idea of feedback in management literature.

BIBLIOGRAPHY

Beer, S. (1959) *Cybernetics and Management*, London: The English University Press.

—— (1981) *Brain of the Firm*, 2nd edn, Chichester: Wiley.

—— (1985) *Diagnosing Systems for Organisations*, Chichester: Wiley.

Bullock, A. and Woodings, R.B. (eds) (1983) *The Fontana Dictionary of Modern Thinkers*, London: Fontana Press.

Espejo, R. and Reyes, A. (1996) 'Wiener, Norbert', in M. Warner (ed.), *International Encyclopedia of Business and Management*, London: International Thomson Business Press/Routledge, vol. 6, 5038–43.

Heims, S. (1980) *John von Neumann and Norbert Wiener: From Mathematics to the Technologies of Life and Death*, Cambridge, MA: MIT Press.

Wiener, N. (1948) *Cybernetics: Or Control*

and Communication in the Animal and the Machine, New York: Wiley.

Wiener, N. (1950) *The Human Use of Human Beings: Cybernetics and Society*, Boston: Houghton Mifflin.

—— (1952) *Ex-prodigy*, Cambridge, MA: MIT Press.

—— (1956) *I am a Mathematician*, London: Victor Gollancz.

—— (1964) *God and Golem, Inc.*, Cambridge, MA: MIT Press.

DR

WILLIAMSON, Oliver Eaton (1932–)

Oliver Eaton Williamson was born in Superior, Wisconsin on 27 September 1932. Several years after obtaining a bachelor's degree at the Massachusetts Institute of Technology in 1955, he enrolled in the MBA programme at Stanford University. There he encountered a major figure in economic thought, who influenced his future professional development, the future Nobel laureate Kenneth ARROW – he taught him 'about the importance of information and not to shoe-horn difficult problems into orthodox boxes' (Williamson in Blaug 1999: 1175). He received his MBA in 1960 and subsequently moved to Carnegie-Mellon University in Pittsburgh, where he developed an affinity with interdisciplinary research, and obtained his Ph.D. in 1963.

In Pittsburgh, Williamson met another innovative researcher and future recipient of the Nobel Prize for Economics, Herbert SIMON, who influenced him even more strongly than had Arrow. Simon's idea of 'bounded rationality', expressed in his book *Models of Man* (1957), became one of the behavioural assumptions built into Williamson's understanding of human economic action. Simon argued that humans cannot perform complete rational calculations, which are assumed in mainstream (neoclassical) economics. Human rationality is bounded because gathering all the relevant information is impossible, and human power of computation is limited. Therefore, economic agents 'satisfice' rather than maximize in the strict sense; they do not seek the absolutely best solutions, but the satisfactory ones. In addition to bounded rationality, Williamson portrays economic agents as prone to 'opportunism' or, as he puts it 'self-interest seeking with guile'. He does not claim that all economic agents are opportunists. However, since some of them are, it may be costly to distinguish between them, and that, for Williamson, provides a justification for the assumption of opportunism.

Williamson's recognition within the academic community was rapid. He achieved prominence through the article 'Managerial Discretion and Business Behaviour', published in the *American Economic Review* in 1963, in which he argued that managers maximize their own utility, rather than profits or sales. Economic research at the time allowed the possibility of a conflict of interest between shareholders and managers. Consequently, several authors offered theories of economic behaviour that modified the classic assumption of profit maximization. Baumol (1959) suggested that companies maximize sales, whereas Marris (1964) argued in favour of maximization of a balanced rate of growth of the company. Williamson's article and subsequent book *The Economics of Discretionary Behavior* (1964) suggested another innovative alternative.

This gave an important impetus to Williamson's academic career. His first teaching post was at the University of California at Berkeley, where he spent two years as assistant professor of economics. He was appointed associate professor of economics at the University of Pennsylvania in 1965; he became professor of economics in 1968, and held the post for fifteen years. He also did consultancy work for the US Department of

Justice, devoting much of his attention to anti-trust issues (1966–9). In 1983 Williamson became a fellow of the American Academy of Arts and Sciences and moved to Yale University, becoming Gordon B. Tweedy Professor of Economics of Law and Organization. In 1988 he returned to the University of California at Berkeley, where he is Edgar F. Kaiser Professor of Business Administration, professor of economics and professor of law. He became a member of the National Academy of Sciences in 1994. He has presided over several academic associations, including the American Law and Economics Association (1997–8) and the Western Economic Association, USA (1999–2000). Following Ronald COASE and Douglas North, he is currently president of the International Society for New Institutional Economics (1999–2001).

Williamson's reputation is predominantly based on the development and application of 'transaction cost economics' through numerous publications. The most important of these are two significant books, *Markets and Hierarchies* (1975) and *The Economic Institutions of Capitalism* (1985). Since every economic transaction can either be carried out through the market or within the boundaries of the firm, one requires an explanation for the existence of firms. Coase suggested that the explanation is to be found in lower relative costs of organizing certain transactions within the firm. Following Coase, Williamson argued that the firm is predominantly a mechanism for economizing on transaction costs related to negotiation, enforcement and adaptation of economic transactions. Since the human agents are viewed as boundedly rational and prone to opportunism, the transactions have to be embodied in contracts, which define the obligations of the agents and put them under the protection of the law. It is argued that certain conditions contribute to the carrying out of a transaction within the firm. That is the case when the rights and obligations of the contracting parties in all future stages of the transaction cannot be exactly specified (uncertainty), or when one or both parties make substantial investments in assets that cannot be easily used for transactions with other partners (asset specificity). Williamson pursued the implications of the transaction cost argument through analysing various economic issues, including the internal organization of the firm, the emergence of multi-divisional organizational structures, the analysis of vertical integration of companies and anti-trust policy. Other adherents of transaction cost economics have applied it even more widely. Williamson's influence has also spread to business and legal studies. Moreover, the transaction cost approach influenced not just academia but also general business audiences, being treated 'not just as positive theory of business practices but also as a normative theory of organizational choice and design' (Masten 1993: 120).

Williamson's work provided important contributions to the analysis of economic institutions. It was instrumental in providing a more comprehensive view of the firm. Even in economic analysis, firms cannot be viewed simply as production functions, mechanisms of transformation of factors of production such as labour or capital into finished products. The firm should also be analysed as a governance structure with specific internal organization. By accepting most of the assumptions of mainstream economics – individuals are perceived as utility maximizers with stable preferences and so on – Williamson was able to introduce some insights from other disciplines, such as law and organizational theory, into the discourse of economics. However, that also meant that he had to distinguish himself from the theorists that previously analysed economic institutions, such as VEBLEN, COMMONS, GALBRAITH and others, because they assumed that social institutions shape and transform individual preferences, values and conceptions. Williamson hence coined the term 'new institutional economics' to describe his approach and to distinguish it from earlier institutionalist approaches, and the term has now achieved widespread use. It is associated with a wide range of theorists, the most important of whom are North and Coase.

The method used by Williamson amounts to analysing the relative efficiency of particular organizational arrangements. The organizations with lower transaction costs are thus viewed as more efficient, and more likely to survive and prevail over other such arrangements. Critics, such as Hodgson (1998), claim that this approach is inherently static and cannot encompass the dynamic aspects of economic life such as technological change or human learning. Ghoshal and Moran (1996) suggest that the advantage of organizations over markets is not in controlling human opportunism, but in leveraging human ability for cooperation, initiative and learning, arguing that the normative implications of transaction cost economics make it 'bad for practice' in management.

Despite important academic and policy results (especially in the area of anti-trust regulations), it remains questionable whether Williamson's theory has resulted in a viable approach to strategic management. Its strategic implications seem to be rather simple. For instance, Williamson (1991) argued that economizing is more fundamental than strategizing. However, it seems reasonable to note that relatively low transaction costs may be necessary, but that they are not sufficient for the prosperity of a firm. To survive and thrive, firms also need a good strategic position within their industry or strategic group (see PORTER); and, perhaps even more importantly, they need valuable resources and capabilities (see PENROSE, TEECE.)

BIBLIOGRAPHY

Baumol, W.J. (1959) *Business Behavior, Value and Growth*, New York: Macmillan.

Blaug, M. (ed.) (1999) *Who's Who in Economics*, 3rd edn, Aldershot: Edward Elgar.

Ghoshal, S. and Moran, P. (1996), 'Bad For Practice: A Critique of the Transaction Cost Theory', *The Academy of Management Review* 21(1): 13–47.

Hodgson, G.M. (1996) 'Williamson, Oliver E.', in M. Warner (ed.), *International Encyclopedia of Business and Management*, London: International Thomson Business Press/Routledge, vol. 6, 5044–7.

—— (1998) 'Evolutionary and Competence-Based Theories of the Firm', *Journal of Economic Studies* 25(1): 25–56.

Marris, R. (1964) *The Economic Theory of Managerial Capitalism*, Glencoe: Free Press.

Masten, S.E. (1993) 'Transaction Costs, Mistakes, and Performance: Assessing the Importance of Governance', *Managerial and Decision Economics* 14: 119–29.

Simon, H.A. (1957) *Models of Man: Social and Rational: Mathematical Essays on Rational Human Behavior in a Social Setting*, New York: Garland.

Williamson, O.E. (1963) 'Managerial Discretion and Business Behaviour', *American Economic Review* 53(5): 1032–57.

—— (1964) *The Economics of Discretionary Behavior: Managerial Objectives in a Theory of The Firm*, Englewood Cliffs, NJ: Prentice Hall.

—— (1975) *Markets and Hierarchies: Analysis and Antitrust Applications*, New York: Free Press.

—— (1985) *The Economic Institutions of Capitalism: Firms, Markets, Relational Contracting*, New York: Free Press.

—— (1991) 'Strategizing, Economizing and Economic Organization', *Strategic Management Journal* 12(Special Winter): 75–94.

DR

WILLYS, John North (1873–1935)

John North Willys was born in Canandaigua, New York on 25 October 1873, the son of David and Lydia Willys. He died in Riverdale, New York on 6 August 1935. He married Isabel Van Wie in 1897, and they had one daughter; after their divorce in 1934 he married Florence Dolan. Willys's first business venture was at the age of fifteen, when he bought a share in a laundry (he sold this a year later for a profit). At eighteen he opened a bicycle retail business, and proved a good salesman but a poor financial manager. In 1899 he realized that the automobile would shortly supplant the bicycle and set up an agency for selling Pierce-Arrow and Rambler cars. In 1906 he established the American Motor Car Sales Company in New York and became sole distributor for the Overland company in Indianapolis. When Overland went bankrupt in 1907, Willys took over the company, staved off its creditors and instituted a sales programme that brought the company back to profitability within a year.

In 1909, having purchased several other small manufacturers and parts makers, Willys reorganized the firm as Willys-Overland, based in Toledo, Ohio. The company entered into fierce competition with Ford, producing cars that were both better designed and more reliable than the Model T; and Willys was easily Henry Ford's superior in marketing management. Between 1912 and 1918 Willys was the second largest car-maker in the country and threatened on several occasions to overhaul Ford. But Willys pushed his expansion too hard, and the firm was plagued by debt. He lost control of the company in 1920 when his bankers brought in Walter CHRYSLER to reorganize the company. Under Chrysler, Willys-Overland went into receivership in 1922, but Willys was able to regain control following Chrysler's departure the following year and rebuilt the firm. By 1928 Willys-Overland again ranked third in national sales, following Ford and Chrysler. Willys sold his stock in the firm in 1929, intending to retire, and from 1930 to 1932 served as US ambassador to Poland.

During the Depression, Willys-Overland ran into trouble again and went into receivership in 1933. Willys returned home to reorganize and rebuild the firm once again. His genius for salesmanship and marketing came to the fore, and by 1934 the firm was making a profit once more. Worn out by work and his recent divorce, Willys suffered a heart attack in May 1935 but continued working until his death later that year.

As a manager, Willys suffered from two handicaps: first, he was a poor financial manager and, in boom times, tended to expand too rapidly and overextend; and second, he chose his own subordinate managers poorly and was unable to delegate. This was best (or worst) illustrated by the bloody strike at the firm's Toledo plant in 1919. While Willys had been directly in charge at Toledo he had enjoyed excellent relations with his workers, but these deteriorated almost immediately after his departure to set up a new plant in New York. These problems meant that Willys spent a good part of his career involved in crisis management.

Against this must be set his skills as a sales manager. He had an almost instinctive understanding of his market; what is more, he knew how to apply his understanding of psychology to his sales force. He established one of the first large-scale car dealership networks in the United States, backing up his dealers with promotions, advertising and credit plans which helped them attract customers and made it easier for them to sell cars. In an article in *System* in 1917, Willys describes how he developed a 'family spirit' among dealers, engendering loyalty through devices such as newsletters and dealership conventions. In the first of these, in 1916, 9,000 dealers and family members came to the plant in Toledo, travelling on Pullman railway cars paid for by the company, to tour the plant, meet Willys, be entertained and generally be made to feel part of the team. Willys's lasting legacy to marketing is his understanding of motivation and how, by motivating salesmen and customers alike, sales success could be achieved.

BIBLIOGRAPHY

Furlong, P.J. (1999) 'Willys, John North', in J.A. Garraty and M. Carnes (eds), *American National Biography*, New York: Oxford University Press, vol. 10, 550–51.

Willys, J.N. (1917) 'Are We Selling as Much as We Should?', *System* 32: 711–13.

MLW

WINCHESTER, Oliver Fisher (1810–80)

Oliver Fisher Winchester was born in Boston, Massachusetts on 30 November 1810, the son of Samuel and Hannah Winchester. He died in New Haven, Connecticut on 11 December 1880. He married Jane Hope in 1834; they had two children. Winchester's father died when he was seven, and as a boy he went to work on a farm; he later apprenticed as a carpenter, and worked for a time as a builder in Baltimore. Having accumulated a little capital, he founded a men's clothing store and shirt manufacturing business; in 1847 he sold the retail side of the business and relocated the manufacturing operation to New York, moving on to New Haven in 1850. The business prospered, and Winchester invested some of his capital in a new company, Volcanic Repeating Arms, which held a number of patents including one for a lever-action breech-loading rifle. Winchester became a director of the firm in 1855.

Volcanic was a highly innovative firm whose weapons designs and production techniques were far in advance of their time, and the firm had difficulty finding a market, the more so as the US Army harboured a strong prejudice against repeating rifles and refused to buy them. Volcanic went into receivership in 1858, but Winchester was able to acquire the assets and reorganized the firm as the New Haven Repeating Arms Company, with himself as president. He began a process which he would continue throughout his career, buying patents for new firearms designs and hiring the most able gunsmiths in the business, such as David Wesson and Benjamin Henry, to build them. He also took advantage of the factory production techniques which had been developed in nearby Hartford by Samuel COLT. In the 1860s the firm produced the Henry rifle, an extremely effective repeater which, though banned by the army, was often purchased privately by Union cavalry regiments; of this weapon's firepower, a Confederate general once remarked that 'the Yankees can load on Sunday and fire all week'. The New Haven Repeating Arms Company became the Henry Repeating Arms Company and then, in 1866, the Winchester Repeating Arms Company.

Winchester himself was an adept designer and personally patented several improvements to his weapons, but he tended on the whole to rely on recruiting talented engineers and designers to handle the production side of the business. He devoted his efforts to marketing, and succeeded in making the Winchester name a household word in the United States; what Colt was to handguns, Winchester was to rifles (Madis 1961). His simple, well-designed and highly effective weapons were greatly in demand among both the frontiersmen and the Indian tribes of the American West. Eschewing the flashy, personal promotions favoured by Colt and his representatives, Winchester concentrated on emphasizing quality and effectiveness. By the twentieth century Winchester, like Colt, had become part of American folklore. Winchester himself became a pillar of the New England establishment, serving as lieutenant-governor of Connecticut and donating money to Yale University.

BIBLIOGRAPHY
Madis, G. (1961) *The Winchester Book*,
Dallas, TX: Taylor Publishing Co.

MLW

WINTER, Sidney G., Jr (1935–)

Sidney G. Winter was born in Iowa City, Iowa. He was educated at Swarthmore College in Swarthmore, Pennsylvania, from where he graduated with a BA in economics in 1956, and at Yale University, where he earned an MA in 1957. After serving as a research economist at the RAND Corporation and a staff member on the Council of Economic Advisers, in both cases working alongside Richard NELSON, Winter returned to Yale for a Ph.D., which was awarded in 1964. Subsequently he taught economics at the University of California at Berkeley from 1963 to 1966, and again held a position at the RAND Corporation from 1967 to 1968. He then served as professor of economics at the University of Michigan until 1976, and from 1976 to 1989 held a professorship at Yale University, again crossing paths with Richard Nelson. In 1989 he joined the US General Accounting Office as chief economist, leaving that post in 1993 to become Deloitte and Touche Professor of Management at the Wharton School, University of Pennsylvania. Since 1999 he has also been co-director of the Reginald H. Jones Center for Management Policy, Strategy and Organization at Wharton.

Winter is one of the key contributors to evolutionary economics. He has laid the foundation for the application of evolutionary theory to economics and management. At the same time, he has demonstrated that this does not necessarily drive the analysis towards *laissez-faire* conclusions. His book *An Evolutionary Theory of Economic Change* (1982), written with Richard Nelson, presents 'the most extensive and rigorous application of the evolutionary metaphor from biology in economics to date' and has led to 'a revolution in our way of thinking about economic change in general and the firm in particular' (Hodgson 1999: 166), for example by proposing an alternative framework for the analysis of the firm to the profit-maximizing framework. The modelling approach contained in the book has had the important effect of demonstrating 'that it is not impossible to treat evolutionary-economic processes in a systematic way' (Andersen 1994: 133). The growing use of the term 'evolutionary economics' in the last two decades can to a large part be attributed to this book. Throughout his career, Winter has contributed significantly to elaborating the theoretical framework of evolutionary economics and has continually applied it to economic and business phenomena.

In his Ph.D. thesis, Winter (1964) delivered the first extended critique of Milton FRIEDMAN's (1953) natural selection argument. His argument is that it does not matter whether the behaviour of economic actors is determined by utility maximization or follows other rules. If the firm is not exhibiting a behaviour that in effect is like that of utility maximizers, then the firm will perform less well than its competitors. Because of this, it will in principle have to go out of business. For Friedman, this constitutes a process of 'natural selection': only those firms which are acting as if they are maximizing utility will survive. He thus draws on what he claims to be an evolutionary argument for defending the utility maximization hypothesis.

Winter critized this position. His main argument is as follows. The 'evolutionary' argument as made by Friedman is incomplete: even if there would be something like a selection of firms, it has to be explained why and how the firms that have behaved as if they would have maximized in one period, and have been 'selected' through competition in that period, are continuing to behave in this mode over time. In other words, an explanation of the mechanism of inheritance (of the behaviour that is as if maximizing) is lacking from Friedman's account. In Winter's own words:

> A theory of natural selection must characterize the basic sources of continuity in the evolutionary process. In the biological case, this basic source is the genetic transmission of characteristics. If there were no causal link between the characteristics of the n-th generation and the characteristics of the n+1st, there could be no natural selection and no evolution.
>
> (Winter 1975: 96)

However, contrary to Friedman's claims, even if that mechanism could be provided, it would not establish an argument for the utility-maximization hypothesis. For example, the fact that certain firms are selected for their behaviour and others are ceasing to exist leads to a change in the competition and thus in the selection environment, so that it is not clear why, in this altered environment, the same firms should continue to have the good fortune to be closer to maximizing behavior than their competitors (Winter 1964: 240).

Working on this missing link in the evolutionary explanation of economic behaviour (but without the objective of showing that this is led by utility maximization), Winter was then led to identify a crucial characteristic that the mechanism of inheritance has to have if such an explanation is supposed to work. In order for selection to operate effectively, there has to be a certain degree of stability. In other words, the unit of selection has to be such that it is restricted from changing randomly. In his further works, Winter went on to identify some possible candidates for such units of selection and inheritance, and of the mechanisms that explain their change and their stability. He contemplates 'routine application of established rules, procedures, and policies' (Winter 1971: 240–41), and states that 'the

decision rules themselves are the economic counterpart of generic inheritance' (Winter 1971: 245). In an early joint paper with Nelson, he acknowledges that 'these decision rules may be quite complex patterns of routinized behaviour, keyed to market prices or other environmental signals' (Nelson and Winter 1973: 441). In a 1975 paper, he introduces an important distinction between rules and the action evoked by them. This adds another argument to his critique of the Friedman argument:

> Let us suppose, tentatively, that what corresponds to a genotype in the theory of the firm is a *rule of action* or *strategy*. What the environment operates on, and rewards and punishes, is not the rule but the actions evoked from the rule by variables in the environment itself. This is a major objection to any claim that economic natural selection tends to produce situations in which the surviving *rules* are optimizing ones.
>
> (Winter 1975: 97)

In this paper Winter also presents the notion of routines as the missing link and the equivalent to genes in biological theory (Winter 1975: 101). Thus, drawing the analogy with biological evolution had become viable because Winter had identified an analytical unit in economics which had gene-like stability and the capacity to 'mutate'. At the same time, Winter (1987b) has been cautious to emphasize that the evolutionary mode of explanation is a general one, of which evolutionary economics is just one of many possible applications.

This idea of routines as the equivalent to genes is applied and elaborated in *An Evolutionary Theory of Economic Change*:

> Our general term for all regular and predictable behavioral patterns of firms is 'routine' ... In our evolutionary theory, these routines play the role that genes play in biological evolutionary theory. They are

a persistent feature of the organism and determine its possible behavior (though actual behavior is determined also by the environment); they are heritable in the sense that tomorrow's organisms generated from today's have much of the same characteristics, and they are selectable in the sense that organisms with certain routines may do better than others, and, if so, their relative importance in the population (industry) is augmented over time.

(Nelson and Winter 1982: 14)

This book, in particular, has led to a wide diffusion of the idea of routines as the equivalent of genes in the economic realm. More generally, the resurgence of evolutionary economics is largely due to this work. In particular, the link made by Nelson and Winter between routines, organizational and individual skills, and tacit knowledge has been important for management research. It has provided a major input into strategic management theory, resource-based theory, the organizational learning debate and knowledge management.

A second important effect of the book is based on the evolutionary models it presents. Emphasizing – in the Schumpeterian tradition – that disequilibria and change rather than equilibria are of interest in economics, Nelson and Winter present a model of evolutionary processes in economics. They present a highly general modelling scheme, out of which they then develop a number of generic and specific types of models. The one that has been documented best and that has become most widely used is a model of the evolution of production techniques and other behavioural rules of an industry producing a homogeneous product (Nelson and Winter 1982, chaps 9 and 12). The model revolves around decision rules, search and selection. The importance of the model they propose is to have developed a computer-implementable concept of an evolutionary economic processes (Andersen 1994: 131), demonstrating that 'it is not impossible to treat evolutionary-economic processes in a

systematic way' (Andersen 1994: 133). It is also interesting to note that their model encompasses the neoclassical case, that is equilibrium-based economic theorizing, as a special case of their theory.

However, the most important contribution of the book is the sketching out of an evolutionary economic research programme that encompasses 'explicit attention to phenomena such as entry, exit, "learning curves", vintage effects in productive capital, merger and strategy change' as well as 'strategic interdependence and product differentiation' (Nelson and Winter 1982: 408). This research programme has met with a vivid response. Starting in 1984 Winter himself has continued to deliver key contributions to both these broad avenues: a string of papers have developed further the conceptual analysis of the firm, of routines, and of selection and replication mechanisms (see, for example, Winter 1986, 1987a, 1991, 1994, 1995). Since 1995 he has increasingly been engaged in collaboration with European researchers (see Malerba et al. 1999).

Winter's importance is as a key contributor and pioneer of evolutionary theory in economics, and management and business theory. He has been largely responsible for evolutionary theorizing as we know it today. He has been a leading critic of Friedman's argument and thus also of Friedman's interpretation of 'evolutionary theorizing'. Without Winter's early and forceful objection, 'evolutionary' theorizing in economics might have become no more than just a variation on the utility-maximizing paradigm. This means that Winter has been crucial for enabling us to have a body of evolutionary theorizing which can provide alternative explanations for such economic phenomena that standard theory cannot adequately explain. Those are, first of all, phenomena of change, such as technological or institutional change on the macro level, or organizational change, organizational learning and growth on the micro level. Second, he has identified crucial gaps in the evolutionary theory in economics and has set them on the evolutionary research agenda: the mechanism of inheritance, the unit of selection and inheritance and the selection mechanism, to name just a few. Over the last three decades, he has continuously developed ideas on each of these, thus building up our understanding of them and improving the explanatory power and the conceptual tools of evolutionary theory in economics and business. Third, he has contributed significantly to a new kind of modelling in economics, models that are 'closer to reality'. This has been achieved by means of behavioural assumptions which are derived from empirical observation (in contrast to those of utility maximization) by modelling specific cases (an industry, for example) instead of building general models, and by basing model assumptions on historical studies of these cases (see, for example, Malerba *et al.* 1999). This also shows a fourth important contribution: his work is driven by a desire to address the concern for greater behavioural reality.

Thus, much of his work – although at the same time of a highly conceptual and abstract kind – is attempting to understand firms, change of firms and industries, learning in organizations, technological change and the nature of competitive advantage. His work is a rare blend of interest in understanding the phenomena of economic and business life and in further developing the conceptual frameworks of economic theory. Winter has had great influence in both areas. His thinking about different elements of the evolutionary framework in economics has led to a new impetus for evolutionary theorizing in economics and management. His thinking on routines has (at least implicitly) been used by many contributors to debates in the area of business and management, for example in the theory of the firm, organizational learning, knowledge management and strategic management.

BIBLIOGRAPHY
Andersen, E.S. (1994) *Evolutionary Economics: Post-Schumpeterian Contributions*, London: Pinter.
Friedman, M. (1953) *Essays in Positive Economics*, Chicago: University of Chicago Press.
Hodgson, G.M. (1999) *Evolution and Institutions: On Evolutionary Economics and the Evolution of Economics*, Cheltenham: Edward Elgar.
Malerba, F., Nelson, R., Orsenigo, L. and Winter, S. (1999) '"History-Friendly" Models of Industry Evolution: The Computer Industry', *Industrial and Corporate Change* 8(1): 3–40.
Nelson, R. and Winter, S. (1973) 'Toward an Evolutionary Theory of Economic Capabilities', *American Economic Review (Papers and Proceedings)* 68(2): 440–49.
——— (1982) *An Evolutionary Theory of Economic Change*, Cambridge, MA: Belknap Press of Harvard University Press.
Winter, S.G. (1964) 'Economic "Natural Selection" and the Theory of the Firm', *Yale Economic Essays* 4: 225–72; repr. in G.M. Hodgson (ed.), *The Foundations of Evolutionary Economics: 1890–1973*, vol. 2, *International Library of Critical Writings in Economics*, Cheltenham: Edward Elgar, 1998.
——— (1971) 'Satisficing, Selection, and the Innovating Remnant', *Quarterly Journal of Economics* 85: 237–61.
——— (1975) 'Optimization and Evolution in the Theory of the Firm', in R. Day and T. Groves (eds), *Adaptive Economic Models*, New York: Academic Press, 73–118.
——— (1984) 'Schumpeterian Competition in Alternative Technological Regimes', *Journal of Economic Behavior and Organization* 5: 287–320.
——— (1986) 'The Research Program of the Behavioral Theory of the Firm: Orthodox Critique and Evolutionary Perspective', in B. Gilad and S. Kaish (eds), *Handbook of Behavioral Economics*, Greenwich, CT: JAI Press, vol. A, 151–88.
——— (1987a) 'Knowledge and Competence

as Strategic Assets', in D. Teece (ed.), *The Competitive Challenge: Strategies for Industrial Innovation and Renewal*, Cambridge, MA: Ballinger, 157–84.

Winter, S.G. (1987b) 'Natural Selection and Evolution', in J. Eatwell, M. Milgate and P. Newman (eds), *The New Palgrave: A Dictionary of Economics*, London and Basingstoke: Macmillan, vol. 3, 614–17.

—— (1991) 'On Coase, Competence and the Corporation', in O.E. Williamson and S.G. Winter (eds), *The Nature of the Firm: Origins, Evolution and Development*, Oxford: Oxford University Press, 179–95.

—— (1994) 'Organizing for Continuous Improvement: Evolutionary Theory Meets the Quality Revolution', in J. Baum and J. Singh (eds), *Evolutionary Dynamics of Organisations*, Oxford: Oxford University Press, 90–108.

—— (1995) 'Four Rs of Profitability: Rents, Resources, Routines, and Replication', in C. Montgomery (ed.), *Resource-based and Evolutionary Theories of the Firm: Towards a Synthesis*, Dordrecht: Kluwer, 147–78.

MB

WOOD, Robert Elkington (1879–1969)

Robert Elkington Wood was born in Kansas City, Missouri on 13 June 1879, the eldest of the five children of a merchant, Robert Whitney Wood, and his schoolteacher wife, Lillie Collins. He died in Lake Forest, Illinois on 6 November 1969. A bright and ambitious student, Wood aspired to attend Yale, but that was beyond his family's means, so he instead attended the US Military Academy at West Point, New York. Graduating in 1900, Wood fought against rebels in the Philippines for two years, then returned to the United States. While teaching French at West Point he met Mary Butler Hardwick, whom he married in 1908. The couple went on to have five children.

In 1905 Wood was transferred to the Panama Canal Zone, where he became special aide to General George W. Goethals, who was directing the massive construction project. As chief procurement officer responsible for supplying the work crews with food and housing, Wood demonstrated the brilliant logistical skills that would define much of his professional career. Such skills were in great demand in the private sector, and after leaving the army Wood was recruited by the Du Pont Company of Delaware to provision its factory workers. He then moved to the General Asphalt Company as assistant to the president in charge of production. With the outbreak of the First World War, Wood volunteered for service, and was put in charge of managing the supply lines between the United States and France. He rose quickly to the rank of brigadier general and acting quartermaster general, and thereafter – in military service and private life alike – was known as 'General Wood'. For his great contributions in reorganizing and streamlining army logistics, Wood was awarded the Distinguished Service Medal in 1919.

Wood returned to the private sector, becoming general merchandise manager, then vice-president, at the giant mail order house Montgomery Ward. But his strategic vision of the firm clashed with that of president Theodore Merseles and others. A student of demographic data, Wood had observed a marked decline in farm income, and was convinced that the proliferation of the automobile was going to transform the American retail market. He therefore advocated that Ward shift its focus from the rural mail order business to large urban stores. Frustrated that Ward did not heed his advice, he quit in 1924 to take a position at competitor Sears, Roebuck that had been created especially for him: vice-president of factories and retail stores.

Wood's power and influence at Sears grew rapidly. He became president in 1928, and chairman in 1939, retiring as president only because of the firm's mandatory retirement age policy; he effectively continued to manage the firm after 1939. In 1925 Sears opened seven retail stores; by 1939 there were 500, and the firm was grossing $575 million. Wood was able to engineer this rapid growth in part thanks to his decentralized management approach, which he deemed 'cooperative democracy'. Whereas in the 1920s more than 80 per cent of Sears stores had been managed from the Chicago headquarters, by the 1940s only 20 per cent of the much larger network of outlets was Chicago-controlled. Wood also moved Sears into the insurance business in 1931 by establishing the Allstate Insurance Company, which expanded from car insurance to becoming a full service provider.

Wood's Sears was in many ways a male culture. He recruited ambitious young men to cultivate and promote through the ranks, and admonished his mostly male sales force to become involved in the civic life of their communities. He increasingly emphasized 'hard' items (as opposed to clothing, linens and other 'soft' dry goods) such as tools and large, big-ticket appliances. Wood opposed attempts to unionize Sears, but he also put in place a generous pension plan that grew to become the company's largest shareholder.

After the Second World War, while many US businesspeople remained fearful that economic depression might return, Wood pushed Sears to expand into Latin America and Canada. When he retired in 1954, Sears had annual sales of $3 billion. He stepped down from the board to become honorary chairman in 1968. During Wood's tenure, the number of Sears employees had grown nearly tenfold, from 23,000 to 200,000. An Episcopalian Republican who nevertheless supported the New Deal, Wood served on numerous corporate boards and as Chairman of the Federal Reserve Bank of Chicago.

DBS

WOOLWORTH, Frank Winfield
(1852–1919)

Frank Winfield Woolworth was born on a farm in Rodman, New York on 13 April 1852, the son of John Hubbell Woolworth and Fanny McBrier. He died at his Glen Cove, New York, country estate on 8 August 1919. The family moved to nearby Great Bend, where Woolworth attended common schools. At the age of sixteen he spent a few months studying commerce at a commercial college in Watertown, New York. Woolworth returned to work on the family farm, but also put in stints as an unpaid assistant in a South Bend general store. Spurning a career on the farm, he took a job at Augsbury & Moore's dry goods store in Watertown, New York, where he rose from an unpaid trainee to clerk in six months. During the next few years, Woolworth changed jobs twice, returned to the family farm for a rest cure, and married Jennie Creighton, a seamstress from Picton, Ontario. In 1877 he returned to his former employer in Watertown, now renamed Moore & Smith after a change in ownership.

There Woolworth introduced the key innovation that would define his approach to retailing. Woolworth borrowed an idea from a former salesman at A. Bushnell and Company – the 'five cent' counter, in which all goods sold for the same low price – and modified it by building large self-service counters. Because customers selected the items themselves, the store could replace skilled male clerks with lower paid young women. With a loan guarantee from W.H. Moore, Woolworth opened a store of his own in Utica, New York. In spite of its grandiose name – the Great Five-Cent Store – the venture failed, as did two of the next four stores he opened by 1882. Building on the success of the other two stores, however, Woolworth began to take on partners, including Moore, and gained a firm foothold in the market.

In 1886, with seven stores in his burgeoning chain, Woolworth set up an administrative and purchasing office in New York City, and moved the company's home office to Brooklyn four years later. While expanding in the 1890s, he introduced a number of employee benefits, including a weekly minimum wage of $2.50 and paid vacations. Woolworth also tapped into important new sources of supply in Europe by importing massive quantities of toys from Germany, vases from Bohemia, and laces, china and other goods from other sources.

The chain expanded rapidly in the early 1900s, in part through merger with other retailers. In 1904 Woolworth bought more than forty rival stores in the Midwest and Middle Atlantic, followed by another wave of acquisitions in 1912. Incorporated as F.W. Woolworth and Company in 1905, the chain adopted a distinctive, uniform look for its stores: bright red storefronts with large display windows emblazoned with a gold 'W' logo. As the capstone of his retailing empire, Woolworth commissioned the construction of a New York City skyscraper in 1910. Designed by architect Cass Gilbert and dedicated by President Woodrow Wilson three years later, the Woolworth building, at 240 metres (787 feet), was the tallest building in the world until surpassed by the Chrysler Building in 1930. Woolworth had financed the $13 million project himself.

Woolworth had been plagued by various health problems throughout his life, and in 1919 he developed a case of septic poisoning in his gums that took his life. By that time his chain of five-and-ten stores had grown to 1,081, and his personal fortune to $27 million. Woolworth stores dotted the town centres across America and overseas, their vast bins of inexpensive imported goods a draw for millions of bargain hunters.

DBS

WRIGLEY, William (1861–1932)

Wrigley was born in Philadelphia on 30 April 1861, the son of William Wrigley, a soapmaker, and his wife Mary. He died in Phoenix, Arizona on 26 January 1932. He married Ada Foote in 1885; they had two children. At eleven he went to work in his father's soap factory, and at thirteen he became a travelling salesman. In 1891 he set up his own business making and selling a variety of products but eventually specialized in chewing gum, then increasing in popularity. At first Wrigley simply ran a marketing organization, buying his chewing gum from a manufacturer and devoting his attention to running his sales organization. After trying out various brands, Wrigley introduced 'Spearmint' in 1899. The brand had little impact at first, but Wrigley experimented with various promotional strategies and finally, in 1907, launched a large-scale advertising campaign that broke through to public consciousness and made the brand a national success.

Wrigley later bought out his main supplier and incorporated the William J. Wrigley Corporation in 1911; thereafter his products spread rapidly through the whole world, and for a time the Wrigley name was probably the second most visible American brand after Coca-Cola. By the end of the 1920s Wrigley had factories in six countries and world-wide sales figures in excess of $75 million. Wrigley, always a keen baseball fan, spent some of his money buying baseball teams in Chicago and Los Angeles; the home stadium of the Chicago Cubs is still known as Wrigley Field. Wrigley also bought and developed the resort island of Santa Catalina in California.

As a manger, Wrigley is most notable for his skill in marketing. He was a 'trial and error' marketer who always experimented with a number of promotional strategies until he found one that worked; persistence and a good judgement of market needs were his strengths.

Y

YOUNG, Owen D. (1874–1962)

Owen D. Young was born in Van Hornesville, New York on 27 October 1874 to Jacob, a farmer, and Ida Brandlow Young, and died in St Augustine, Florida on 11 July 1962. He graduated from St Lawrence University in 1894 and from the Boston University Law School in 1896. He married Josephine Sheldon Edmonds, with whom he had five children. Upon her death, he married Louise Powis Clark. Later in life, when he was considered a potential candidate for president of the United States, a commentator noted that, 'His career is in the best American tradition: farm boy, homespun college student, law clerk, junior partner, man of large affairs' (Merz 1931: 276).

Upon graduation from law school (which he completed in two years instead of the normal three in order to save money), Young practised law in Boston, becoming a partner in the Charles H. Tyler law firm. He handled a case against General Electric (GE), and his performance so impressed GE's president, Charles Coffin, that he became general counsel for GE. In 1922 he became chairman of the board, a position he held until 1929; he continued as chairman of the company's executive committee until 1933. During his tenure, Young displayed an interest in the welfare of workers and implemented employee stock ownership plans and unemployment insurance.

President Woodrow Wilson twice enlisted Young's assistance: in 1919 he appointed Young to the Second Industrial Conference to formulate a plan to prevent industrial strife, and later the president, concerned that key electronics patents would fall into foreign hands, also asked Young to organize a company (Radio Corporation of America) to maintain American control of the patents. The result was an unwieldy consortium of firms, including General Electric, AT&T, United Fruit, Westinghouse and General Motors. Today, such a consortium might be deemed contrary to United States anti-trust laws, and indeed the Justice Department broke up the organization in the 1930s. RCA survived the anti-trust turmoil in large part due to Young's protégé, David SARNOFF.

Young's most prominent achievements came from his work with Charles Dawes. The two were instrumental in creating the Dawes Plan for German reparations after the First World War, although Dawes later remarked that, '[Young] told me what to do, I told the others they must do it, and they did' (Merz 1931: 278). His work was widely lauded for its 'fairness, broadness of vision, energy and ability' (New York Times 1962: 25), and he was later enlisted in drawing up what became known as the 'Young Plan' for rehabilitating Germany's fiscal system. This plan included a call for the creation of a world bank. His own banking experience came from serving as deputy chairman and later chairman of the New York Federal Reserve Bank. Young believed that 'the improvement of the world financial structure was of fundamental importance to the continued economic expansion of the United States, the payment of German reparations, and the very survival of capitalism' (Costigliola 1972: 605). He disdained the plaudits for his efforts and stated, in response to a proposed ticker-tape parade in New York City, 'Please let me come home quietly' (Merz 1931: 276).

Young's activities marked him as an attractive political candidate, and he was mentioned as a possible nominee for the Democratic presidential candidacy in 1932, especially in light of his extensive experience in international affairs. Franklin Roosevelt got the nomination, and Young never served in elected office. Although he was also mentioned as a possible candidate for other offices, he was content to retire to the family farm, having often declared that older people should step aside for younger people.

BIBLIOGRAPHY

Costigliola, F. (1972) 'The Other Side of Isolationism: The Establishment of the First World Bank, 1929–1930', *Journal of American History* 59(3): 602–20.

Merz, C. (1931) 'If Owen D. Young Were Nominated', *Harper's Magazine* 163(August): 275–83.

New York Times (1962) 'Owen D. Young, 87, Industrialist, Dies', *New York Times* 111(38, 155), sect. 1: 1, 25.

DS

INDEX OF NAMES

561